SO-AXU-398

The Editor

MICHAEL A. PETERMAN is Professor of English at Trent University. He is the author of *Robertson Davies*, *Susanna Moodie: A Life*, and *"This Great Epoch of Our Lives": Susanna Moodie's "Roughing It in the Bush."* He is the editor of *The Backwoods of Canada* by Catharine Parr Traill, and is co-editor of *Susanna Moodie: Letters of a Lifetime* with Carl Ballstadt and Elizabeth Hopkins, *Letters of Love and Duty: The Correspondence of John and Susanna Moodie* with Carl Ballstadt and Elizabeth Hopkins, *Forest and Other Gleanings: The Fugitive Writings of Catharine Parr Traill* with Carl Ballstadt, and *"I Bless You in My Heart": Selected Correspondence of Catharine Parr Traill* with Carl Ballstadt and Elizabeth Hopkins. He is a past editor of the *Journal of Canadian Studies*.

W. W. NORTON & COMPANY, INC.
Also Publishes

THE NORTON ANTHOLOGY OF AFRICAN AMERICAN LITERATURE
edited by Henry Louis Gates Jr. and Nellie Y. McKay et al.

THE NORTON ANTHOLOGY OF AMERICAN LITERATURE
edited by Nina Baym et al.

THE NORTON ANTHOLOGY OF CHILDREN'S LITERATURE
edited by Jack Zipes et al.

THE NORTON ANTHOLOGY OF CONTEMPORARY FICTION
edited by R. V. Cassill and Joyce Carol Oates

THE NORTON ANTHOLOGY OF ENGLISH LITERATURE
edited by M. H. Abrams and Stephen Greenblatt et al.

THE NORTON ANTHOLOGY OF LITERATURE BY WOMEN
edited by Sandra M. Gilbert and Susan Gubar

THE NORTON ANTHOLOGY OF MODERN AND CONTEMPORARY POETRY
edited by Jahan Ramazani, Richard Ellmann, and Robert O'Clair

THE NORTON ANTHOLOGY OF POETRY
edited by Margaret Ferguson, Mary Jo Salter, and Jon Stallworthy

THE NORTON ANTHOLOGY OF SHORT FICTION
edited by R. V. Cassill and Richard Bausch

THE NORTON ANTHOLOGY OF THEORY AND CRITICISM
edited by Vincent B. Leitch et al.

THE NORTON ANTHOLOGY OF WORLD LITERATURE
edited by Sarah Lawall et al.

THE NORTON FACSIMILE OF THE FIRST FOLIO OF SHAKESPEARE
prepared by Charlton Hinman

THE NORTON INTRODUCTION TO LITERATURE
edited by Alison Booth, J. Paul Hunter, and Kelly J. Mays

THE NORTON INTRODUCTION TO THE SHORT NOVEL
edited by Jerome Beaty

THE NORTON READER
edited by Linda H. Peterson and John C. Brereton

THE NORTON SAMPLER
edited by Thomas Cooley

THE NORTON SHAKESPEARE, BASED ON THE OXFORD EDITION
edited by Stephen Greenblatt et al.

For a complete list of Norton Critical Editions, visit
www.wwnorton.com/college/english/nce_home.htm

A NORTON CRITICAL EDITION

Susanna Moodie

ROUGHING IT IN THE BUSH

AUTHORITATIVE TEXT
BACKGROUNDS
CRITICISM

Edited by

MICHAEL A. PETERMAN

TRENT UNIVERSITY

W. W. NORTON & COMPANY

New York • *London*

W. W. Norton & Company has been independent since its founding in 1923, when William Warder Norton and Mary D. Herter Norton first published lectures delivered at the People's Institute, the adult education division of New York City's Cooper Union. The Nortons soon expanded their program beyond the Institute, publishing books by celebrated academics from America and abroad. By midcentury, the two major pillars of Norton's publishing program—trade books and college texts—were firmly established. In the 1950s, the Norton family transferred control of the company to its employees, and today—with a staff of four hundred and a comparable number of trade, college, and professional titles published each year—W. W. Norton & Company stands as the largest and oldest publishing house owned wholly by its employees.

To my editorial colleagues, Carl Ballstadt and Elizabeth Hopkins

Cheers,
Michael

Copyright © 2007 by W. W. Norton & Company, Inc.

All rights reserved
Printed in the United States of America
First Edition

The text of this book is composed in Fairfield Medium
with the display set in Bernhard Modern.

Composition by PennSet, Inc.
Manufacturing by the Courier Companies—Westford division.
Book design by Antonina Krass.
Production manager: Benjamin Reynolds.

Library of Congress Cataloging-in-Publication Data

Moodie, Susanna, 1803–1885.
    Roughing it in the bush: authoritative text, backgrounds, criticism / Susanna Moodie; edited by Michael A. Peterman.
        p. cm. — (A Norton critical edition)
    Includes bibliographical references.

    ISBN-13: 978-0-393-92667-5 (pbk.)
    ISBN-10: 0-393-92667-2 (pbk.)

    1. Ontario—Description and travel. 2. Frontier and pioneer life—Ontario. 3. Moodie, Susanna, 1803–1885. 4. Pioneers—Ontario—Biography. 5. Women pioneers—Ontario—Biography. 6. Moodie, Susanna, 1803–1885—Criticism and interpretation. 7. Canadian literature—Women authors—History and criticism. 8. Frontier and pioneer life in literature. 9. Authors, Canadian—19th century—Biography. 10. Women authors, Canadian—Biography. I. Peterman, Michael A., 1942– II. Title.
    F1057.M82 2006
    917.13—dc22

                                                                    2006046848

W. W. Norton & Company, Inc., 500 Fifth Avenue, New York, NY 10110
www.wwnorton.com

W. W. Norton & Company Ltd., Castle House,
75/76 Wells Street, London W1T 3QT

1 2 3 4 5 6 7 8 9 0

Contents

Introduction

Roughing It in the Bush tells the story of the seven and a half years (1832–39) that Susanna and John Moodie, recently married emigrants from Britain, spent pioneering in two locations in the Upper Canadian backwoods. In that regard the book speaks for itself, though the commentary Susanna provides throughout the text sometimes seems fragmentary and puzzling to contemporary readers. First published in London in February 1852, the book has enjoyed a growing prominence in Canada over its 150-year history, drawing both high praise and some resentment and hostility from succeeding generations of readers who have felt its influence and power. Indeed, in the first decade of the twenty-first century, *Roughing It in the Bush* is widely recognized as one of the most important nineteenth-century books written in and about Canada.

Given its many editions, steady sales, and cultural resilience, *Roughing It in the Bush* is comparable only to Thomas Haliburton's sketches of the talkative Yankee clockmaker Sam Slick, peddling his goods to and criticizing the gullible Bluenosers of Nova Scotia. Though it was not published as a book in Canada until 1871, *Roughing It in the Bush* was a best seller in Britain and the United States immediately upon its first appearances in 1852. Since 1871 its many Canadian editions have been steady sellers, and much more so since 1962, when McClelland and Stewart made the book available as an inexpensive and abridged paperback aimed at schools and universities.[1] Since that time it has become a cultural marker and interpretive challenge for many scholars, creative writers and students. This Norton Critical Edition reintroduces the book to audiences beyond Canada, particularly in the United States; in the process it calls attention to its publishing history; the outlook, sensibility and reliability of its author; and the diverse historical, cultural and literary responses it has evoked over time.

Roughing It in the Bush has gone through several textual alterations in its history, but one thing is certain: It has held the attention of Canadian readers generation by generation. As a journalistic commentator noted in 1885, one could no more leave Hamlet out of Shakespeare's play than omit Susanna Moodie and *Roughing It in the Bush* from a discussion of letters in Canada.[2] In 1952 Percy Ghent, a knowledgeable antiquarian, used the occasion of the book's centenary

---

1. Sales figures from the McClelland and Stewart archives indicate that the edition sold over 17,000 copies between 1962 and 1968.
2. Peterborough *Daily Examiner*, July 25, 1885.

to deem it a classic for both its "historical value" and "its literary craftsmanship and charm."[3] While there are today many more points of departure for such a "discussion" of English-Canadian letters, few early books loom larger than this one in its content and multiple messages; it cast a long and lingering shadow over the colony in which it was written, and continues to elicit attention from literary critics, creative writers and cultural commentators. Margaret Atwood's *The Journals of Susanna Moodie* (1970) is the most vivid and powerful example of a fascination that endures. Atwood noted a double voice at work in Moodie's writing and saw in that doubleness a cultural identity uneasily shared by many Canadians.

Susanna and her sisters

Susanna Strickland was born in Bungay, Suffolk in December 1803, the sixth daughter of Thomas and Elizabeth Strickland. The family had recently left London, where Thomas had been the manager of the Greenland Docks. In rural Suffolk he sought a retreat suitable to his delicate health, the needs of his family, and his genteel aspirations. In 1808 while overseeing his business interests in the nearby city of Norwich, he bought Reydon Hall, an Elizabethan manor house a mile from the coastal town of Southwold. His intention was to retire there and educate his children, who now numbered eight, including two long-awaited sons.

Over the next decade the Strickland family sought to become part of the local East Anglian gentry. Forced by reversals to address his ongoing business interests more often than he had hoped, Thomas kept a home and office in Norwich and was often absent from Reydon. The girls were educated at home, either in Norwich or at Reydon Hall. As much as possible the parents oversaw the process and encouraged the development of their mathematical abilities, domestic and gardening skills, and literary interests. Thomas's library was the seat of much of the latter activity. Hence in 1818, when Thomas suddenly died, writing was already a preoccupation of and a potential vocation for his daughters.

In fact, five of the six Strickland girls became published writers by the early 1820s, drawing on family connections to gain access to Suffolk and London literary markets and opportunities. Only Sarah (1798–1890), known as the beauty of the family, chose not to engage in the challenges of authorship. For the others, writing became an important component of their genteel lives; it allowed them to earn some income or "pin money" for their personal and familial needs, and it provided a socially acceptable opportunity to put their names before the public. As Susanna's sister Catharine nostalgically observed in the 1850s, the Strickland girls at Reydon Hall reminded her a great deal of the Brontë family; writing was in their blood and an atmosphere of support and muted competition prevailed among them.[4]

---

3. "*Roughing It in the Bush*: Centenary of a Classic," Toronto *Telegram*, April 8, 1952.
4. "*I Bless You in My Heart*": *Selected Correspondence of Catharine Parr Traill* (1996), p. 264.

Susanna Strickland was the most impulsive and romantic of the sisters. By the time of her first known publication, a juvenile novel entitled *Spartacus: A Roman Story*, published by Newman in London in 1822, her oldest sisters, Elizabeth (1794–1875) and Agnes (1796–1874), were already in the process of establishing literary careers based in London. Typically, when the older sisters were home at Reydon, they functioned as teachers and mentors, imposing a testy control on the younger trio, Jane Margaret (1800–1888), Catharine (1802–1899), and Susanna (1803–1885). For her part, Susanna could not bear to be simply the youngest writer among the sisters. As a poet she aspired to vie with the already-prominent Agnes. With an air of defiance and an inclination for hero worship (Napoleon and William Wallace and the aforementioned Spartacus were among her favorites), she set out to make a name for herself, despite her relative inexperience. She was soon sending out poems to magazines and newspapers, submitting her writing to popular London annuals, and penning other book-length cautionary tales for the burgeoning children's book market in London. Several gentlemanly writers and editors befriended her and encouraged her progress, among them James Bird, a Suffolk poet and historian who with his wife Emma ran a bookstore and pharmacy in nearby Yoxford; Thomas Harral, a family friend who edited a popular London ladies' magazine, *La Belle Assemblée*, to which Susanna often contributed; and Thomas Pringle, a busy Scottish writer, editor, and antislavery advocate then living in London with his wife Margaret.

Even as Susanna aspired to new levels of literary recognition, she underwent a religious awakening that strongly affected her outlook and focused the direction of her spirituality. Under the influence of a minister named James Ritchie of nearby Wrentham, she converted from the Anglican faith, so valued by her family, to Congregationalism, thus briefly alienating herself from several of her sisters. While seeking a less ritualistic and more personal relationship with her God through non-conformist thinking, she also received lessons in the art of still-life painting from Ritchie's wife. She was now in her mid-twenties and, despite the Suffolk quiet of her daily activities, it was an exciting time for her.

Through the kindly Pringles, with whom she often stayed in London, Susanna met John Wedderburn Dunbar Moodie, the former Scottish officer she would soon marry. An Orcadian of good family and a pensioned veteran who had served with the Twenty-first Northern Fusiliers during the Napoleonic Wars, John Moodie (1797–1869) had emigrated to the Cape Town settlement in South Africa in the early 1820s to join a Scottish group that included the Pringles. Farming there with his brother Donald for nearly a decade, he maintained his connection with Thomas Pringle, even though Pringle was forced in 1826 to return to London; his outspoken antislavery journalism precipitated his expulsion from the colony.

In 1830, John Moodie arrived in London with two aspirations—to complete a book about his African adventures and to find a wife. Thirty-three years old, he was already an author, having published an account of his military service in the Netherlands during the Peninsular Wars. Susanna and John met socially at the Pringles' home and soon established a strong mutual passion that would sustain them through their various misadventures, successes and failures as immigrants to Upper Canada, and as writers, parents and prominent citizens in the colony.

While the courtship seems to have vied briefly with Susanna's recent religious conversion for her attention, the main problem facing their romance was money, the need somehow to establish for themselves a sufficient income on which to live comfortably in Britain. The fatherless Susanna had no dowry and only modest hopes of a small family inheritance. John was born into the Orcadian gentry, but the encumbered Moodie family estate, Melsetter, on the island of Hoy, offered nothing for a younger son. Months of uncertainty followed as John tested other family possibilities and tried to persuade Susanna to consider a life together on his South African farm. Recognizing that there was no immediate financial help in sight other than John's military pension, they agreed to marry solely on the basis of their love for each other. Their interim strategy was to leave London and settle temporarily in Southwold, the better to preserve their limited resources while Susanna enjoyed proximity to her mother, sisters and friends. However, with Susanna pregnant through the winter of 1831–32, the die was cast. Emigration, which had loomed as a strong possibility, now became a necessity.

The challenge of emigration

Still owning his South African farm, John Moodie kept up his hope of returning there to develop his property. However, Susanna was not attracted to life in so remote and dangerous a place, especially as John had described it in his manuscript. Moreover, by that time she had, through Thomas Pringle, grown acutely aware of the practice of slavery that was a fact of life in the Cape Colony. John Moodie was also sympathetic to the antislavery agenda that the Pringles advocated.

Alternatively, Canada called. The key was a family connection on Susanna's side. As an energetic seventeen-year-old, her brother Samuel (1805–1867) had gone to Upper Canada in 1825 to seek his fortune. After several years of hard work, he had made a promising life for himself and his young family through employment with the Canada Company and by trading astutely in available lands. In 1831 he had settled on Lake Katchewanook in the northern part of Douro Township. Douro was one of the "back" townships, the newly opened lands north of the townships along Lake Ontario or "the front." Sam's property was about ten miles north of the fledgling town of Peterborough and some fifty miles above Lake Ontario.

His letters home enthused about the great economic promise that lay in the development of the waterway that flowed southward from northern lakes like Stony and Clear through the Otonabee River, Rice Lake and the Trent River before emptying into Lake Ontario. Sam's property was well placed along that undeveloped natural system. The Moodies were further enticed by Robert Reid, Sam's father-in-law and a substantial Douro settler, who visited Southwold as part of a business trip home to Ireland in 1831. He provided detailed information and encouragement to the couple. After additional consultation with William Cattermole, an emigration official who visited Suffolk in 1831, John decided, with Susanna's concurrence, to follow Sam Strickland's example. He made plans for them and their daughter Katie to sail to Canada, via Edinburgh, in the late spring of 1832. The story of *Roughing It in the Bush* is the product of this life-changing decision. Clearly, Susanna did not want to leave England and would never have ventured across the ocean had there been a satisfactory alternative for her family's future. She had her mother and sisters in Southwold and, as her early poems and sketches make clear, she was strongly attracted to the Suffolk countryside of her childhood. Moreover, her writing career was progressing notably. In 1830 she had co-authored with her sister Agnes a collection of sheet music entitled *Patriotic Songs*. A year later, her first major book, *Enthusiasm, and Other Poems*, was published by subscription to positive reviews by the London firm of Smith, Elder. She continued to write for the popular literary and religious annuals and to produce cautionary tales for the children's book market. Moreover, through Thomas Pringle and others, she had been welcomed into a set of interesting writers, painters, and caricaturists in London. She was at best a hesitant emigrant; in *Roughing It in the Bush* she made her reluctance a major theme.

Mary Prince and Ashton Warner: awakening to slavery

Perhaps the most exhilarating of Susanna's early literary ventures occurred during an extended visit to the Pringle household. A convert to Congregationalism, she enjoyed the company of the open-minded and kindly Pringles. Indeed, she found in "Papa" Pringle a literary father figure and mentor. Pringle had been deeply affected by his South African experiences and what he saw as the curse of slavery in that colony. Returning to London, he wrote fondly about Africa even as he became an antislavery activist; by the early 1830s he was the secretary of the Anti-Slavery Society. Consistent with his views, he occasionally provided temporary shelter and employment for Caribbean slaves seeking their freedom in London. In his house on Clarington Square Susanna met both Mary Prince and Ashton Warner, and she was drawn to the poignancy and horror of their "simple and affecting narrative[s]."[5]

Heretofore she had been inattentive to the "criminality" of the system of slavery. Now having experienced the personal influence of the two visitors and having heard their stories, "the voice of truth and nature prevailed over my former prejudices."[6] Under Pringle's direction

---

5. *Negro Slavery Described by a Negro: Being the Narrative of Ashton Warner, a Native of St. Vincent's* (London, 1831), p. 6.
6. Ibid., p. 6.

and editorship, she served as amanuensis to both Mary Prince and Ashton Warner, recording their stories in autobiographical pamphlets that quickly became controversial publications in Britain upon their appearance in 1831. *The History of Mary Prince* proved so popular that it went through three printings that year; a fourth was in the planning stages when Thomas Pringle died suddenly in 1834. In recent years *The History of Mary Prince* has achieved a new level of recognition and prominence as "a groundbreaking oral narrative" and "the first known recorded autobiography by a freed West Indian slave."[7] As such it is studied in universities across the English-speaking world.

During this same period Susanna Strickland became Susanna Moodie. In ways she could not have anticipated, her views were broadening and becoming more liberal as her life changed. She had embraced a more personal religious outlook and had become a sharp critic of legalized slavery. It was a mark of her interest in and affection for "Black Mary" that Mary Prince was among the guests at her wedding to John Moodie on April 4, 1831, in London; "Papa" Pringle gave Susanna away and hosted the wedding dinner.

By the time their daughter Katie was born in Southwold on February 14, 1832, John and Susanna were well advanced in their plans to emigrate. Upper Canada had become their chosen destination. There lay, they convinced themselves, "independence and comfort," though they knew that they would have to devote years of effort and make many personal sacrifices to reach that goal. It was both a surprise and a support to them when they learned that Susanna's sister, Catharine Parr, had rather suddenly chosen to marry the widowed Thomas Traill, a Scottish friend of John Moodie; the newlyweds hurriedly made their own plans to follow the Moodies to Canada.

The Upper Canadian bush

Resistant as she was to any significant change, Susanna Moodie saw herself by 1832 as the loyal wife of an adventurous Scot; she deemed it her solemn duty to follow the challenging path they had mapped out together. However, the writer in her, ever alert to fresh subject matter, knew that there would be stories to tell and scenes to describe should they survive the ocean crossing and the transition to life in Canada's unsettled wilderness.

Once in Upper Canada she found little opportunity to write, though she, like John, occasionally jotted down poems in response to various events and feelings she experienced. With John serving as her 'agent,' they both sought out available newspaper and magazine outlets for their work. In their first three years in Canada, the Moodies placed pieces of their writing with the *Cobourg Star*, *The (New York) Albion* and its subsidiary *The Emigrant and Old Countryman*, a couple of short-lived Toronto magazines, Lincoln Sumner Fairfield's *The North*

---

7. *Nine Black Women, An Anthology of Nineteenth-Century Writers from the United States, Canada, Bermuda, and the Caribbean*, ed. Moira Ferguson (London: Routledge, 1998), pp. 53, 48.

American (Quarterly) Magazine, and various London magazines and annuals, notably *The Lady's Magazine*, then edited by Susanna's eldest sister, Elizabeth.

Roughing It in the Bush took more than a decade to develop in Susanna's mind. John Moodie first pitched the concept in 1835 to Richard Bentley, the London publisher of his two-volume *Ten Years in South Africa* (1835). Initially, however, Bentley was not encouraging. Hence the idea lay fallow while Susanna's sister and bush neighbor, Catharine, put together a manuscript of her emigration experiences from 1832 to 1835. It appeared in London as *The Backwoods of Canada* (1836), a volume in the "Entertaining Knowledge" library of the Society for the Diffusion of Useful Knowledge. No doubt Susanna took note both of its considerable success as an emigration account written specifically for women and of the several misconceptions that Catharine's book contained.[8] For her part, Susanna began writing poems for pay for John Lovell's *The Literary Garland*, a Montreal magazine, before she was able to leave the bush, but until she moved to Belleville she had insufficient time to work on longer prose pieces or to begin an account of her personal experiences in the bush. Distance in time and space would prove important in her later writing. Moreover, her final year in the bush proved a harrowing experience.[9]

Living comfortably in the town of Belleville in the mid-1840s and having established herself as a writer of serialized fiction for *The Literary Garland*, she was ready to begin writing the sketches that became *Roughing It in the Bush*. Her goal was to offer a more personal, probing, humorous, and accurate record of bush experience than her sister's optimistic and pragmatic account. She would write from an unabashedly female perspective and would not avoid the painful admission that emigrants of genteel outlook and background, like themselves, were ill-equipped to be workaday laborers in a struggling backwoods economy. Such people were doomed to failure if they chose to commit their limited capital and efforts to the pursuit of success in the bush. Indeed, by March 1839 the Traills had confirmed that verdict in their own case by finally selling their bush farm and moving to the nearby town of Peterborough.

Shaping the book

Susanna's organizing strategy was to use the then-popular sketch form to present her travels and the places she had visited, particular characters she had met along the way, and local customs and events she had observed or experienced. The sketch form allowed her a casual, leisurely, personalized, and anecdotal approach. She kept to chronology as much as possible, even as she realized that it was in the very nature of the sketch form to introduce temporal disjunctions to the

8. The Patrick Hamilton Ewing Collection (PHEC) at the National Library of Canada contains a copy of Catharine's presentation copy to Susanna; it is dated 1837.
9. See excerpts from Susanna Moodie's letters to her husband during 1839 in the "Backgrounds" section.

narrative flow. She also organized her story into two sections or volumes, one for each distinct experiment in settlement the Moodies undertook. The chapter headings and content suggest that she made some effort to parallel events and experiences from Volume I to II, from their first settlement near the Lake Ontario "front" to their years of "roughing it" in Douro Township.

The first volume accounts for a change in the Moodies' original plans based on advice received during their stay in the town of Cobourg. After weighing the pros and cons of going directly to their land grant in the backwoods where, they were warned, the unbroken forest prevailed and resources for settlers were limited, they chose to buy a partially cleared farm in Hamilton Township, about eight miles west of Cobourg and four miles east of Port Hope. There they stayed until February 1834. Beyond their struggles to adapt to new conditions, the most persistent problems they encountered were social. They found themselves plagued by the rude antics and anti-British hostility of their "Yankee" neighbors. Even lower-class English settlers like the O——s (see "The Charivari" chapter, beginning on p. 128) took advantage of their genteel British assumptions and goodwill. At the same time they found few residents of their own class and background who were willing to socialize. As such, they came to regret the distance between themselves and Susanna's siblings, Sam Strickland and Catharine Parr Traill, who lived so many miles to the north.

Volume II recounts the Moodies' relocation to their land grant in the Douro backwoods, a move they later came to see as their most foolish decision as emigrants. By then, John had bought more land adjacent to his original grant and had contracted for the construction of a log house on a low ridge above Lake Katchewanook, about a mile north of the Traills' homestead. Here in the spring of 1834, during what Susanna called their "halcyon days of the bush," they cleared land as their financial resources allowed and awaited further news about the promised development of the Otonabee River waterway, on which they had positioned themselves. However, unanticipated and nearly overwhelming problems loomed. With the persistent threat of cholera affecting ports in Britain and Canada, immigration to Upper Canada slowed noticeably. Moreover, as a result of the pervasive Depression of 1835–36, real-estate values and markets for farm produce stagnated, leaving the Moodies up a proverbial backwoods stump. John's decision in 1834 to sell his military pension for money to improve their backwoods property proved a grievous loss under these worsening conditions. There was little cash in the backwoods and the economy had slowed to a crawl.

Thus by the fall of 1837 the Moodies found themselves embarrassingly impoverished, tied to a large piece of property that awakened little market interest. They now had four young children—two daughters and two sons—to feed and clothe, and immediate prospects seemed grim. As such, they had to revise their genteel assumptions and rely increasingly on their personal resourcefulness. John Moodie's two military appointments (in 1838 to the Niagara district, and in 1839 to

Belleville and the Victoria District) came like blessings from above, providing a new source of income to a family plagued by debts and the daily struggle merely to survive. Despite its dangers and the immediate fears it aroused, the Rebellion of 1837 in the Canadas raised Susanna's hopes that her family might manage to find its way out of its trying situation. It also gave new direction to her flagging literary prospects.

The winter of 1839 proved a decisive time for Susanna in her lonely struggles. Another winter like it, she wrote to John, "will pile the turf over my head."[1] *Roughing It in the Bush* is a book of many moods, but its underlying feeling, as alive for her when she wrote her sketches as when she experienced them, is the sense of helplessness and entrapment that overtook her during that last long winter. Alone on the farm with only a female servant (Jenny Buchanan), Susanna and her children fell victim to several life-threatening illnesses, mastitis in her case and typhus and scarlet fever in theirs. While the book skirts these specific problems by means of two descriptive paragraphs,[2] the discovery of Susanna's monthly letters to John from January through July 1839 provides the reader with a much more detailed and harrowing sense of that dark period in her life. Available in full in *Letters of Love and Duty: The Correspondence of Susanna and John Moodie*, several of these letters are excerpted in the "Backgrounds" section of this edition to provide readers with a fuller sense of that final winter. Only when John Moodie received his appointment as the sheriff of Hastings County late in 1839 was he able to move his family to the town of Belleville.

Notable aspects of Roughing It in the Bush

A number of the sketches comprising *Roughing It in the Bush* first appeared in *The Literary Garland*, the most durable of Canada's pre-Confederation magazines. Susanna Moodie had eagerly begun to contribute to it while still in the bush; once in Belleville she became one of its most prolific writers, producing serialized fiction on a yearly basis, along with occasional poems. In 1847, Susanna submitted six "Canadian Sketches," which eventually became nine chapters of *Roughing It in the Bush*, Volume I. As well, for *The Victoria Magazine*, which she and John edited in Belleville for a year (1847–48), she wrote "A Visit to Grosse Isle" and "Quebec." In their original form, these magazine sketches show variants in phrasing, word choice, and selection of incident that suggest Susanna's sensitivity to differences in the taste and expectations of her Canadian and English readers.

Roughing It in the Bush is a work of several hands. It contains four sketches and several poems by John, suggesting that the Moodies saw the project as a family affair in which John's role was to offer helpful context for his wife's personalized sketches, contribute some serious and lighthearted poems, and provide audiences with information suit-

---

1. The letter is dated July 16, 1839. See *Letters of Love and Duty*, p. 159.
2. See the last paragraph of "The Whirlwind" and the first paragraph of "A Change in Our Prospects."

able to a male emigrant's interests and needs. A third contributor was Sam Strickland, who provided Susanna with a few anecdotes about Canadian "hurricanes" and with a wider range of backwoods experience than the Moodies could claim. It was Susanna's book to be sure, but it was bolstered by contributions that she felt would give it greater reach and authority.

Roughing It in the Bush is in fact the middle book in a trilogy of the Moodies' emigration experience. Two years after *Roughing It* appeared, Richard Bentley published *Flora Lyndsay*, a novel by Susanna. In a letter to her publisher, she described it as a thinly veiled work of fiction based upon their marriage and difficult decision to emigrate, their careful preparations, their trip to Edinburgh, and their long voyage across the Atlantic. She told Bentley, "I took a freak of cutting it out of the MS. and beginning the work at Grosse Isle."[3] In another letter she assured him that Flora's story is "no fiction."[4]

The marketing success of *Roughing It in the Bush* made Richard Bentley eager to have a post-bush sequel. He asked Susanna to provide readers with an informed look at life in settled Canadian towns as opposed to the bush. Working quickly while recuperating from a dangerous illness, Susanna cobbled together *Life in the Clearings versus the Bush* (1853), a collection of sketches about her Belleville experiences and recent travels to Toronto and Niagara Falls. Among them she included a few pieces that she had originally intended for *Roughing It in the Bush*, including "Michael McBride," which she had pulled from the *Roughing It* manuscript in response to Catholic criticism it received in a Montreal newspaper. The others were sketches—"Jeanie Burns" and "Lost Children"—which had been requested by Bentley in London, but had arrived too late for inclusion. For all its variety and despite Susanna's enthusiasm for it, *Life in the Clearings* proved a disappointment in London; however, sales of the American edition, published by DeWitt and Davenport in New York, were more encouraging.

Since its publication, *Roughing It in the Bush* has elicited both positive and antagonistic responses, generation by generation. Initially it sold so well that in 1853 the Moodies received reports that its American sales rivalled those of Harriet Beecher Stowe's *Uncle Tom's Cabin*.[5] Lydia Sigourney, one of the most popular American writers of the day, sent Susanna an affectionate fan letter, asserting that *Roughing It* was able to create more interest than a work of fiction could. In Canada, however, there was much criticism; the book seemed to warn darkly against emigration and to complain too much about everyday colonial conditions. One prominent Toronto reviewer deemed its author "An ape of the aristocracy" in her hauteur and preciousness.[6] Three years later Susanna summarized her frustration with Canadian readers in a letter to Richard Bentley:

---

3. Letter to Richard Bentley, dated late spring, 1853. See *Letters of a Lifetime*, p. 130.
4. Letter to Bentley, September 3, 1853. See *Letters of a Lifetime*, p. 131. Susanna toyed with two fictional names for herself, first Flora MacGregor and then Flora Lyndsay.
5. Letter to Richard Bentley dated late autumn, 1853. See *Letters of a Lifetime*, p. 136.
6. Charles Lindsay, *Toronto Examiner*, June 16, 1852. See below, pp. 405–07.

. . . You don't know the touchy nature of the people. . . . Will they ever forgive me for writing *Roughing It?* They know that it was the truth, but have I not been a mark for every vulgar editor of a village journal, throughout the length and breadth of the land to hurl a stone at, and point out as the enemy to Canada. Had I gained a fortune by that book, it would have been dearly earned by the constant annoyance I have experienced since its publication. . . .[7]

While the book went through several English and American editions, it was not published in Canada until 1871.[8] Since then it has seldom been out of print. Its record of emigration and pioneering experience, its personalized drama, its apparent contradictions of purpose and mood, and its persistently humorous responses have held readers' interest over the decades. Numerous Canadian writers, such as Robertson Davies, Margaret Atwood, Carol Shields, Tom King, Julie Johnston, Elizabeth Hopkins and Timothy Findley, have included Susanna in their novels, plays and poems, and two recent films have celebrated her life and legacy.[9] For many, *Roughing It in the Bush* suggests, if not defines, something of the nature of the Canadian imagination and the struggle to adapt to life in a northern environment. For others, it has given rise to a preoccupation with the author herself. Was Susanna Moodie, as Northrop Frye observed, "a one-woman British army of occupation"? Was she a too-shrill and persistent complainer? Was she an English snob who could not and would not adjust to frontier conditions? Or was she an astute observer of backwoods manners and morals? Was she a heroic pioneer and an extraordinary woman in her own right? Was she a writer of limited talent who somehow, through the intimacies of memoir and autobiography, unlocked the best of her talent?

No single view encompasses what Susanna Moodie has to say and what she represents. Rather, she stands as a persistent and challenging enigma for readers old and new.

---

7. Letter to Richard Bentley, August 19, 1856. See *Letters of a Lifetime,* pp. 169–70.
8. The Centre for the Editing of Canadian Texts (CEECT) volume of *Roughing It in the Bush,* ed. Carl Ballstadt (Carleton UP, 1987) offers a full account of the history of the various editions of the book in London, the United States and Canada. There were several re-issues published in the United States prior to 1900. The first Canadian edition appeared in Toronto in 1871 under the imprint of Hunter, Rose.
9. See Patrick Crowe's *The Enduring Enigma of Susanna Moodie* (1997) and the CBC film of *Sisters in the Wilderness: The Lives of Susanna Moodie and Catharine Parr Traill* (2004), based on Charlotte Gray's biography of the sisters.

The Text of
ROUGHING IT IN THE BUSH
or Life in Canada

I sketch from Nature, and the picture's true;
Whate'er the subject, whether grave or gay,
Painful experience in a distant land
Made it mine own.

to

Agnes Strickland,
Author of the "Lives of the Queens of England"

this simple tribute of affection
is dedicated,
by her sister,

Susanna Moodie

ROUGHING IT IN THE BUSH;

OR,

LIFE IN CANADA.

BY SUSANNA MOODIE.

I sketch from Nature, and the picture's true;
Whate'er the subject, whether grave or gay,
Painful experience in a distant land
Made it mine own.

IN TWO VOLUMES.

VOL. I.

LONDON:

RICHARD BENTLEY, 8, NEW BURLINGTON STREET,

Publisher in Ordinary to Her Majesty.

1852.

Fascimile title page of the first edition.

Contents

Advertisement

In justice to Mrs. Moodie, it is right to state that being still resident in the far-west of Canada, she has not been able to superintend this work whilst passing through the press. From this circumstance some verbal mistakes and oversights may have occurred, but the greatest care has been taken to avoid them.

Although well known as an authoress in Canada, and a member of a family which has enriched English literature with works of very high popularity, Mrs. Moodie is chiefly remembered in this country by a volume of Poems published in 1831, under her maiden name of Susanna Strickland.[1] During the rebellion in Canada,[2] her loyal lyrics, prompted by strong affection for her native country, were circulated and sung throughout the colony, and produced a great effect in rousing an enthusiastic feeling in favour of law and order. Another of her lyrical compositions, the charming Sleigh Song, printed in the present work, vol. i.,[3] has been extremely popular in Canada. The warmth of feeling which beams through every line, and the touching truthfulness of its details, won for it a reception there as universal as it was favourable.

The glowing narrative of personal incident and suffering which she gives in the present work, will no doubt attract general attention. It would be difficult to point out delineations of fortitude under privation, more interesting or more pathetic than those contained in her second volume.

London,
January 22, 1852.

1. Susanna Strickland, *Enthusiasm, and Other Poems* (London: Smith, Elder, 1831).
2. The Rebellion of 1837–38.
3. See "The Sleigh-Bells" in "Uncle Joe and His Family," pp. 95–96.

Introduction

In most instances, emigration is a matter of necessity, not of choice; and this is more especially true of the emigration of persons of respectable connections, or of any station or position in the world. Few educated persons, accustomed to the refinements and luxuries of European society, ever willingly relinquish those advantages, and place themselves beyond the protective influence of the wise and revered institutions of their native land, without the pressure of some urgent cause. Emigration may, indeed, generally be regarded as an act of severe duty, performed at the expense of personal enjoyment, and accompanied by the sacrifice of those local attachments which stamp the scenes amid which our childhood grew, in imperishable characters upon the heart. Nor is it until adversity has pressed sorely upon the proud and wounded spirit of the well-educated sons and daughters of old but impoverished families, that they gird up the loins of the mind, and arm themselves with fortitude to meet and dare the heartbreaking conflict.

The ordinary motives for the emigration of such persons may be summed up in a few brief words;—the emigrant's hope of bettering his condition, and of escaping from the vulgar sarcasms too often hurled at the less wealthy by the purse-proud, common-place people of the world. But there is a higher motive still, which has its origin in that love of independence which springs up spontaneously in the breasts of the high-souled children of a glorious land. They cannot labour in a menial capacity in the country where they were born and educated to command. They can trace no difference between themselves and the more fortunate individuals of a race whose blood warms their veins, and whose name they bear. The want of wealth alone places an impassable barrier between them and the more favoured offspring of the same parent stock; and they go forth to make for themselves a new name and to find another country, to forget the past and to live in the future, to exult in the prospect of their children being free and the land of their adoption great.

The choice of the country to which they devote their talents and energies depends less upon their pecuniary means than upon the fancy of the emigrant or the popularity of a name. From the year 1826 to 1829, Australia and the Swan River[1] were all the rage. No other portions of the habitable globe were deemed worthy of notice. These were the *El Dorados* and lands of Goshen to which all respectable emigrants eagerly flocked. Disappointment, as a matter of course, followed their high-raised expectations. Many of the most sanguine of these adventurers returned to their shores in a worse condition than when they left them. In 1830, the great tide of emigration flowed westward. Canada became the great land-mark for the rich in hope

1. The area of the first permanent British settlements in western Australia near present-day Perth.

and poor in purse. Public newspapers and private letters teemed with the unheard-of advantages to be derived from a settlement in this highly-favoured region.

Its salubrious climate, its fertile soil, commercial advantages, great water privileges, its proximity to the mother country, and last, not least, its almost total exemption from taxation—that bugbear which keeps honest John Bull[2] in a state of constant ferment—were the theme of every tongue, and lauded beyond all praise. The general interest, once excited, was industriously kept alive by pamphlets, published by interested parties, which prominently set forth all the *good* to be derived from a settlement in the Backwoods of Canada;[3] while they carefully concealed the toil and hardship to be endured in order to secure these advantages. They told of lands yielding forty bushels to the acre, but they said nothing of the years when these lands, with the most careful cultivation, would barely return fifteen; when rust and smut, engendered by the vicinity of damp over-hanging woods, would blast the fruits of the poor emigrant's labour, and almost deprive him of bread. They talked of log houses to be raised in a single day, by the generous exertions of friends and neighbours, but they never ventured upon a picture of the disgusting scenes of riot and low debauchery exhibited during the raising, or upon a description of the dwellings when raised—dens of dirt and misery, which would, in many instances, be shamed by an English pig-sty. The necessaries of life were described as inestimably cheap; but they forgot to add that in remote bush settlements, often twenty miles from a market town, and some of them even that distance from the nearest dwelling, the necessaries of life, which would be deemed indispensable to the European, could not be procured at all, or, if obtained, could only be so by sending a man and team through a blazed forest road,—a process far too expensive for frequent repetition.

Oh, ye dealers in wild lands—ye speculators in the folly and credulity of your fellow men—what a mass of misery, and of misrepresentation productive of that misery, have ye not to answer for! You had your acres to sell, and what to you were the worn-down frames and broken hearts of the infatuated purchasers? The public believed the plausible statements you made with such earnestness, and men of all grades rushed to hear your hired orators declaim upon the blessings to be obtained by the clearers of the wilderness.

Men who had been hopeless of supporting their families in comfort and independence at home, thought that they had only to come out to Canada to make their fortunes; almost even to realise the story told in the nursery, of the sheep and oxen that ran about the streets, ready roasted, and with knives and forks upon their backs. They were made to believe that if it did not actually rain gold, that precious metal could

---

2. The representative figure of England; Brother Jonathan was his contemporary American image, preceding Uncle Sam.
3. A general phrase for the back townships of Upper Canada, but one of particular resonance to Susanna as *The Backwoods of Canada* was the title of her sister Catharine's optimistic and popular book (London: Charles Knight, 1836) about her own settlement experience.

be obtained, as is now stated of California and Australia, by stooping to pick it up.

The infection became general. A Canada mania pervaded the middle ranks of British society; thousands and tens of thousands, for the space of three or four years landed upon these shores. A large majority of the higher class were officers of the army and navy, with their families—a class perfectly unfitted by their previous habits and education for contending with the stern realities of emigrant life. The hand that has long held the sword, and been accustomed to receive implicit obedience from those under its control, is seldom adapted to wield the spade and guide the plough, or try its strength against the stubborn trees of the forest. Nor will such persons submit cheerfully to the saucy familiarity of servants, who, republicans in spirit,[4] think themselves as good as their employers. Too many of these brave and honourable men were easy dupes to the designing land-speculators. Not having counted the cost, but only looked upon the bright side of the picture held up to their admiring gaze, they fell easily into the snares of their artful seducers.

To prove their zeal as colonists, they were induced to purchase large tracts of wild land in remote and unfavourable situations. This, while it impoverished and often proved the ruin of the unfortunate immigrant, possessed a double advantage to the seller. He obtained an exorbitant price for the land which he actually sold, while the residence of a respectable settler upon the spot greatly enhanced the value and price of all other lands in the neighbourhood.

It is not by such instruments as those I have just mentioned, that Providence works when it would reclaim the waste places of the earth, and make them subservient to the wants and happiness of its creatures. The Great Father of the souls and bodies of men knows the arm which wholesome labour from infancy has made strong, the nerves which have become iron by patient endurance, by exposure to weather, coarse fare, and rude shelter; and he chooses such, to send forth into the forest to hew out the rough paths for the advance of civilisation. These men become wealthy and prosperous, and form the bones and sinews of a great and rising country. Their labour is wealth, not exhaustion; it produces independence and content, not home-sickness and despair. What the Backwoods of Canada are to the industrious and ever-to-be-honoured sons of honest poverty, and what they are to the refined and accomplished gentleman, these simple sketches will endeavour to portray. They are drawn principally from my own experience, during a sojourn of nineteen years in the colony.

In order to diversify my subject, and make it as amusing as possible, I have between the sketches introduced a few small poems, all written during my residence in Canada, and descriptive of the country.

4. The phrase reflects the pro-British and anti-American bias the Moodies shared with many British emigrants.

In this pleasing task, I have been assisted by my husband, J. W.
Dunbar Moodie, author of "Ten Years in South Africa."[5]

Belleville, Upper Canada.

Canada

Canada, the blest—the free!
With prophetic glance, I see
Visions of thy future glory,
Giving to the world's great story
A page, with mighty meaning fraught,
That asks a wider range of thought.
Borne onward on the wings of Time,
I trace thy future course sublime;
And feel my anxious lot grow bright,
While musing on the glorious sight;—
Yea, my heart leaps up with glee
To hail thy noble destiny!

Even now thy sons inherit
All thy British mother's spirit.
Ah! no child of bondage thou;
With her blessing on thy brow,
And her deathless, old renown
Circling thee with freedom's crown,
And her love within thy heart,
Well may'st thou perform thy part,
And to coming years proclaim
Thou art worthy of her name.
Home of the homeless!—friend to all
Who suffer on this earthly ball!
On thy bosom sickly care
Quite forgets her squalid lair;
Gaunt famine, ghastly poverty
Before thy gracious aspect fly,
And hopes long crush'd, grow bright again.
And, smiling, point to hill and plain.

By thy winter's stainless snow,
Starry heavens of purer glow,
Glorious summers, fervid, bright,
Basking in one blaze of light;
By thy fair, salubrious clime;
By thy scenery sublime;
By thy mountains, streams, and woods;
By thy everlasting floods;

5. John Moodie's two-volume memoir, *Ten Years in South Africa: Including a Particular Description of the Wild Sports of That Country*, was published in London by Richard Bentley in 1835.

If greatness dwells beneath the skies,
Thou to greatness shall arise!

Nations old, and empires vast,
From the earth had darkly pass'd
Ere rose the fair auspicious morn
When thou, the last, not least, was born.
Through the desert solitude
Of trackless waters, forests rude,
Thy guardian angel sent a cry
All jubilant of victory!
"Joy," she cried, "to th' untill'd earth,
Let her joy in a mighty nation's birth,—
Night from the land has pass'd away,
The desert basks in noon of day.
Joy, to the sullen wilderness,
I come, her gloomy shades to bless,
To bid the bear and wild-cat yield
Their savage haunts to town and field.
Joy, to stout hearts and willing hands,
That win a right to these broad lands,
And reap the fruit of honest toil,
Lords of the rich, abundant soil.

"Joy, to the sons of want, who groan
In lands that cannot feed their own;
And seek, in stern, determined mood,
Homes in the land of lake and wood,
And leave their hearts' young hopes behind,
Friends in this distant world to find;
Led by that God, who from His throne
Regards the poor man's stifled moan.
Like one awaken'd from the dead,
The peasant lifts his drooping head,
Nerves his strong heart and sun-burnt hand,
To win a portion of the land,
That glooms before him far and wide
In frowning woods and surging tide
No more oppress'd, no more a slave,
Here freedom dwells beyond the wave.

"Joy, to those hardy sires who bore
The day's first heat—their toils are o'er;
Rude fathers of this rising land,
Theirs was a mission truly grand.
Brave peasants whom the Father, God,
Sent to reclaim the stubborn sod;
Well they perform'd their task, and won
Altar and hearth for the woodman's son.
Joy, to Canada's unborn heirs,
A deathless heritage is theirs;

For, sway'd by wise and holy laws,
Its voice shall aid the world's great cause,
Shall plead the rights of man, and claim
For humble worth an honest name;
Shall show the peasant-born can be,
When call'd to action, great and free.
Like fire, within the flint conceal'd,
By stern necessity reveal'd,
Kindles to life the stupid sod,
Images of perfect man and God.

"Joy, to thy unborn sons, for they
Shall hail a brighter, purer day;
When peace and Christian brotherhood
Shall form a stronger tie than blood—
And commerce, freed from tax and chain,
Shall build a bridge o'er earth and main;
And man shall prize the wealth of mind,
The greatest blessing to mankind;
True Christians, both in word and deed,
Ready in virtue's cause to bleed,
Against a world combined to stand,
And guard the honour of the land.
Joy, to the earth, when this shall be,
Time verges on eternity."

One

A Visit to Grosse Isle

Alas! that man's stern spirit e'er should mar
A scene so pure—so exquisite as this.

The dreadful cholera was depopulating Quebec and Montreal, when
our ship cast anchor off Grosse Isle, on the 30th of August, 1832, and
we were boarded a few minutes after by the health-officers.[1] One of
these gentlemen—a little, shrivelled-up Frenchman—from his solemn
aspect and attenuated figure, would have made no bad representative
of him who sat upon the pale horse.[2] He was the only grave Frenchman I had ever seen, and I naturally enough regarded him as a
phenomenon. His companion—a fine-looking fair-haired Scotchman
—though a little consequential in his manners, looked like one who in
his own person could combat and vanquish all the evils which flesh is
heir to. Such was the contrast between these doctors, that they would

1. The "dreadful cholera" had been raging in English and European ports in 1831–32 and
   there was great concern about its spreading to the new world. Grosse Isle was the medical
   station set up below Quebec City to identify and treat those carrying the disease and to
   check its spread in the Canadian colonies.
2. The image of death (Revelation 6:8). The description is part of Susanna's caustic caricature
   of the French professional class.

have formed very good emblems—one, of vigorous health; the other, of hopeless decay.

Our captain,[3] a rude blunt north-country sailor possessing certainly not more politeness than might be expected in a bear, received his sprucely dressed visitors on the deck, and, with very little courtesy, abruptly bade them follow him down into the cabin.

The officials were no sooner seated, than glancing hastily round the place, they commenced the following dialogue:—

"From what port, captain?"

Now, the captain had a peculiar language of his own, from which he commonly expunged all the connecting links. Small words, such as "and" and "the," he contrived to dispense with altogether.

"Scotland—sailed from port o' Leith, bound for Quebec, Montreal —general cargo—seventy-two steerage, four cabin passengers—brig, ninety-two tons burden, crew eight hands." Here he produced his credentials, and handed them to the strangers. The Scotchman just glanced over the documents, and laid them on the table.

"Had you a good passage out?"

"Tedious, baffling winds, heavy fogs, detained three weeks on Banks—foul weather making Gulf—short of water, people out of provisions, steerage passengers starving."

"Any case of sickness or death on board?"

"All sound as crickets."

"Any births?" lisped the little Frenchman.

The captain screwed up his mouth, and after a moment's reflection he replied, "Births? Why, yes; now I think on't, gentlemen, we had one female on board, who produced three at a birth."

"That's uncommon," said the Scotch doctor, with an air of lively curiosity. "Are the children alive and well? I should like much to see them." He started up, and knocked his head, for he was very tall, against the ceiling. "Confound your low cribs! I have nearly dashed out my brains."

"A hard task, that," looked the captain to me. He did not speak, but I knew by his sarcastic grin what was uppermost in his thoughts. "The young ones all males—fine thriving fellows. Step upon the deck, Sam Frazer," turning to his steward; "bring them down for doctors to see." Sam vanished, with a knowing wink to his superior, and quickly returned, bearing in his arms three fat, chuckle-headed bull-terriers; the sagacious mother following close at his heels, and looking ready to give and take offence on the slightest provocation.

"Here, gentlemen, are the babies," said Frazer, depositing his burden on the floor. "They do credit to the nursing of the brindled slut."

The old tar laughed, chuckled, and rubbed his hands in an ecstasy of delight at the indignation and disappointment visible in the countenance of the Scotch Esculapius,[4] who, angry as he was, wisely held his tongue. Not so the Frenchman; his rage scarcely knew bounds,—he

---

3. George Rodger[s], as identified in the *Quebec Gazette*, August 31, 1832, p. 2.
4. A Greek divinity who was the personification of medicine or the healing acts.

danced in a state of most ludicrous excitement,—he shook his fist at our rough captain, and screamed at the top of his voice,

"Sacré, you bête! You tink us dog, ven you try to pass your puppies on us for babies?"

"Hout, man, don't be angry," said the Scotchman, stifling a laugh; "you see 'tis only a joke!"

"Joke! me no understand such joke. Bête!" returned the angry Frenchman, bestowing a savage kick on one of the unoffending pups which was frisking about his feet. The pup yelped; the slut barked and leaped furiously at the offender, and was only kept from biting him by Sam, who could scarcely hold her back for laughing; the captain was uproarious; the offended Frenchman alone maintained a severe and dignified aspect. The dogs were at length dismissed, and peace restored.

After some further questioning from the officials, a bible was required for the captain to take an oath. Mine was mislaid, and there was none at hand.

"Confound it!" muttered the old sailor, tossing over the papers in his desk; "that scoundrel, Sam, always stows my traps out of the way." Then taking up from the table a book which I had been reading, which happened to be *Voltaire's History of Charles XII.*, he presented it, with as grave an air as he could assume, to the Frenchman. Taking for granted that it was the volume required, the little doctor was too polite to open the book, the captain was duly sworn, and the party returned to the deck.[5]

Here a new difficulty occurred, which nearly ended in a serious quarrel. The gentlemen requested the old sailor to give them a few feet of old planking, to repair some damage which their boat had sustained the day before. This the captain could not do. They seemed to think his refusal intentional, and took it as a personal affront. In no very gentle tones, they ordered him instantly to prepare his boats, and put his passengers on shore.

"Stiff breeze—short sea," returned the bluff old seaman; "great risk in making land—boats heavily laden with women and children will be swamped. Not a soul goes on shore this night."

"If you refuse to comply with our orders, we will report you to the authorities."

"I know my duty—you stick to yours. When the wind falls off, I'll see to it. Not a life shall be risked to please you or your authorities."

He turned upon his heel, and the medical men left the vessel in great disdain. We had every reason to be thankful for the firmness displayed by our rough commander. That same evening we saw eleven persons drowned, from another vessel close beside us, while attempting to make the shore.

By daybreak all was hurry and confusion on board the *Anne*. I watched boat after boat depart for the island, full of people and goods,

---

5. The substitution of Voltaire's *History of Charles XII* (1731) for the Bible is another joke on the French doctor, as Voltaire was famous for his atheism.

and envied them the glorious privilege of once more standing firmly on the earth, after two long months of rocking and rolling at sea. How ardently we anticipate pleasure, which often ends in positive pain! Such was my case when at last indulged in the gratification so eagerly desired. As cabin passengers, we were not included in the general order of purification, but were only obliged to send our servant, with the clothes and bedding we had used during the voyage, on shore, to be washed.

The ship was soon emptied of all her live cargo. My husband went off with the boats, to reconnoitre the island, and I was left alone with my baby, in the otherwise empty vessel. Even Oscar, the Captain's Scotch terrier, who had formed a devoted attachment to me during the voyage, forgot his allegiance, became possessed of the land mania, and was away with the rest. With the most intense desire to go on shore, I was doomed to look and long and envy every boatful of emigrants that glided past. Nor was this all; the ship was out of provisions, and I was condemned to undergo a rigid fast until the return of the boat, when the captain had promised a supply of fresh butter and bread. The vessel had been nine weeks at sea; the poor steerage passengers for the two last weeks had been out of food, and the captain had been obliged to feed them from the ship's stores. The promised bread was to be obtained from a small steam-boat, which plied daily between Quebec and the island, transporting convalescent emigrants and their goods in her upward trip, and provisions for the sick on her return.

How I reckoned on once more tasting bread and butter! The very thought of the treat in store served to sharpen my appetite, and render the long fast more irksome. I could now fully realise all Mrs. Bowdich's longings for English bread and butter, after her three years' travel through the burning African deserts, with her talented husband.[6]

"When we arrived at the hotel at Plymouth," said she, "and were asked what refreshment we chose—'Tea, and home-made bread and butter,' was my instant reply. 'Brown bread, if you please, and plenty of it.' I never enjoyed any luxury like it. I was positively ashamed of asking the waiter to refill the plate. After the execrable messes, and the hard ship-biscuit, imagine the luxury of a good slice of English bread and butter!"

At home, I laughed heartily at the lively energy with which that charming woman of genius related this little incident in her eventful history,—but off Grosse Isle, I realised it all.

As the sun rose above the horizon, all these matter-of-fact circumstances were gradually forgotten, and merged in the surpassing grandeur of the scene that rose majestically before me. The previous day had been dark and stormy; and a heavy fog had concealed the mountain chain, which forms the stupendous background to this sub-

---

6. Sarah Wallis Bowdich had travelled in Africa with her first husband from 1815–18. Susanna read her pieces in various English annuals, met her (she was now Mrs. Lee) in London in 1830, and admired her writing. See *Stories of Strange Lands; And Fragments from the Notes of a Traveller* (London, 1835).

lime view, entirely from our sight. As the clouds rolled away from their grey, bald brows, and cast into denser shadow the vast forest belt that girdled them round, they loomed out like mighty giants—Titans of the earth, in all their rugged and awful beauty—a thrill of wonder and delight pervaded my mind. The spectacle floated dimly on my sight—my eyes were blinded with tears—blinded with the excess of beauty. I turned to the right and to the left, I looked up and down the glorious river; never had I beheld so many striking objects blended into one mighty whole! Nature had lavished all her noblest features in producing that enchanting scene.

The rocky isle in front, with its neat farm-houses at the eastern point, and its high bluff at the western extremity, crowned with the telegraph—the middle space occupied by tents and sheds for the cholera patients, and its wooded shores dotted over with motley groups—added greatly to the picturesque effect of the land scene. Then the broad, glittering river, covered with boats darting to and fro, conveying passengers from twenty-five vessels, of various size and tonnage, which rode at anchor, with their flag flying from the mast-head, gave an air of life and interest to the whole. Turning to the south side of the St. Lawrence, I was not less struck with its low fertile shores, white houses, and neat churches, whose slender spires and bright tin roofs shone like silver as they caught the first rays of the sun. As far as the eye could reach, a line of white buildings extended along the bank; their background formed by the purple hue of the dense, interminable forest. It was a scene unlike any I had ever beheld, and to which Britain contains no parallel. Mackenzie, an old Scotch dragoon, who was one of our passengers, when he rose in the morning, and saw the parish of St. Thomas for the first time, exclaimed—"Weel, it beats a'! Can thae white clouts be a' houses? They look like claes hung out to drie!" There was some truth in this odd comparison, and for some minutes, I could scarcely convince myself that the white patches scattered so thickly over the opposite shore could be the dwellings of a busy, lively population.

"What sublime views of the north side of the river those *habitans*[7] of St. Thomas must enjoy," thought I. Perhaps familiarity with the scene has rendered them indifferent to its astonishing beauty.

Eastward, the view down the St. Lawrence towards the Gulf, is the finest of all, scarcely surpassed by anything in the world. Your eye follows the long range of lofty mountains until their blue summits are blended and lost in the blue of the sky. Some of these, partially cleared round the base, are sprinkled over with neat cottages; and the green slopes that spread around them are covered with flocks and herds. The surface of the splendid river is diversified with islands of every size and shape, some in wood, others partially cleared, and adorned with orchards and white farm-houses. As the early sun streamed upon the most prominent of these, leaving the others in deep shade, the effect

---

7. The *habitans* or *habitants* were French-Canadian farmers who farmed long, narrow plots of land that fronted on the St. Lawrence River.

was strangely novel and imposing. In more remote regions, where the forest has never yet echoed to the woodman's axe, or received the impress of civilisation, the first approach to the shore inspires a melancholy awe, which becomes painful in its intensity.

> Land of vast hills and mighty streams,
> The lofty sun that o'er thee beams
> On fairer clime sheds not his ray,
> When basking in the noon of day
> Thy waters dance in silver light,
> And o'er them frowning, dark as night,
> Thy shadowy forests, soaring high,
> Stretch forth beyond the aching eye,
> And blend in distance with the sky.
>
> And silence—awful silence broods
> Profoundly o'er these solitudes;
> Nought but the lapsing of the floods
> Breaks the deep stillness of the woods;
> A sense of desolation reigns
> O'er these unpeopled forest plains,
> Where sounds of life ne'er wake a tone
> Of cheerful praise round Nature's throne,
> Man finds himself with God—alone.

My day-dreams were dispelled by the return of the boat, which brought my husband and the captain from the island.

"No bread," said the latter, shaking his head; "you must be content to starve a little longer. Provision-ship not in till four o'clock." My husband smiled at the look of blank disappointment with which I received these unwelcome tidings. "Never mind, I have news which will comfort you. The officer who commands the station sent a note to me by an orderly, inviting us to spend the afternoon with him. He promises to show us everything worthy of notice on the island. Captain——[8] claims acquaintance with me; but I have not the least recollection of him. Would you like to go?"

"Oh, by all means. I long to see the lovely island. It looks a perfect paradise at this distance."

The rough sailor-captain screwed his mouth on one side, and gave me one of his comical looks, but he said nothing until he assisted in placing me and the baby in the boat.

"Don't be too sanguine, Mrs. Moodie; many things look well at a distance which are bad enough when near."

I scarcely regarded the old sailor's warning. So eager was I to go on shore—to put my foot upon the soil of the new world for the first time—I was in no humour to listen to any depreciation of what seemed so beautiful.

It was four o'clock when we landed on the rocks, which the rays of

8. Likely Captain Henry Reid of the 32nd Regiment, who was in charge of the Grosse Isle station in 1832.

an intensely scorching sun had rendered so hot that I could scarcely
place my foot upon them. How the people without shoes bore it, I cannot imagine. Never shall I forget the extraordinary spectacle that met
our sight the moment we passed the low range of bushes which formed
a screen in front of the river. A crowd of many hundred Irish emigrants
had been landed during the present and former day; and all this motley
crew—men, women, and children, who were not confined by sickness
to the sheds (which greatly resembled cattle-pens)—were employed in
washing clothes, or spreading them out on the rocks and bushes to dry.

The men and boys were *in* the water, while the women, with their
scanty garments tucked above their knees, were trampling their bedding in tubs, or in holes in the rocks, which the retiring tide had left
half full of water. Those who did not possess washing-tubs, pails, or
iron pots, or could not obtain access to a hole in the rocks, were running to and fro, screaming and scolding in no measured terms. The
confusion of Babel was among them. All talkers and no hearers—each
shouting and yelling in his or her uncouth dialect, and all accompanying their vociferations with violent and extraordinary gestures, quite
incomprehensible to the uninitiated. We were literally stunned by the
strife of tongues. I shrank, with feelings almost akin to fear, from the
hard-featured, sun-burnt harpies, as they elbowed rudely past me.

I had heard and read much of savages, and have since seen, during
my long residence in the bush, somewhat of uncivilised life; but the
Indian is one of Nature's gentlemen—he never says or does a rude or
vulgar thing. The vicious, uneducated barbarians who form the surplus of over-populous European countries, are far behind the wild
man in delicacy of feeling or natural courtesy. The people who covered
the island appeared perfectly destitute of shame, or even of a sense of
common decency. Many were almost naked, still more but partially
clothed. We turned in disgust from the revolting scene, but were unable to leave the spot until the captain had satisfied a noisy group of
his own people, who were demanding a supply of stores.

And here I must observe that our passengers, who were chiefly honest Scotch labourers and mechanics from the vicinity of Edinburgh,
and who while on board ship had conducted themselves with the
greatest propriety, and appeared the most quiet, orderly set of people
in the world, no sooner set foot upon the island than they became infected by the same spirit of insubordination and misrule, and were just
as insolent and noisy as the rest.

While our captain was vainly endeavouring to satisfy the unreasonable demands of his rebellious people, Moodie had discovered a woodland path that led to the back of the island. Sheltered by some
hazel-bushes from the intense heat of the sun, we sat down by the
cool, gushing river, out of sight, but, alas! not out of hearing of the
noisy, riotous crowd. Could we have shut out the profane sounds
which came to us on every breeze, how deeply should we have enjoyed
an hour amid the tranquil beauties of that retired and lovely spot!

The rocky banks of the island were adorned with beautiful ever-
greens, which sprang up spontaneously in every nook and crevice. I re-

marked many of our favourite garden shrubs among these wildings of nature. The fillagree, with its narrow, dark glossy-green leaves; the privet, with its modest white blossoms and purple berries; the lignum-vitae, with its strong resinous odour; the burnet-rose, and a great variety of elegant unknowns.

Here, the shores of the island and mainland, receding from each other, formed a small cove, overhung with lofty trees, clothed from the base to the summit with wild vines, that hung in graceful festoons from the topmost branches to the water's edge. The dark shadows of the mountains, thrown upon the water, as they towered to the height of some thousand feet above us, gave to the surface of the river an ebon hue. The sunbeams, dancing through the thick, quivering foliage, fell in stars of gold, or long lines of dazzling brightness, upon the deep black waters, producing the most novel and beautiful effects. It was a scene over which the spirit of peace might brood in silent adoration; but how spoiled by the discordant yells of the filthy beings who were sullying the purity of the air and water with contaminating sights and sounds!

We were now joined by the sergeant, who very kindly brought us his capful of ripe plums and hazel-nuts, the growth of the island; a joyful present, but marred by a note from Captain [Reid], who had found that he had been mistaken in his supposed knowledge of us, and politely apologised for not being allowed by the health-officers to receive any emigrant beyond the bounds appointed for the performance of quarantine.

I was deeply disappointed, but my husband laughingly told me that I had seen enough of the island; and turning to the good-natured soldier, remarked, that "it could be no easy task to keep such wild savages in order."

"You may well say that, sir—but our night scenes far exceed those of the day. You would think they were incarnate devils; singing, drinking, dancing, shouting, and cutting antics that would surprise the leader of a circus. They have no shame—are under no restraint—nobody knows them here, and they think they can speak and act as they please; and they are such thieves that they rob one another of the little they possess. The healthy actually run the risk of taking the cholera by robbing the sick. If you have not hired one or two stout, honest fellows from among your fellow-passengers to guard your clothes while they are drying, you will never see half of them again. They are a sad set, sir, a sad set. We could, perhaps, manage the men; but the women, sir!—the women! Oh, sir!"

Anxious as we were to return to the ship, we were obliged to remain until sun-down in our retired nook. We were hungry, tired, and out of spirits; the mosquitoes swarmed in myriads around us, tormenting the poor baby, who, not at all pleased with her first visit to the new world, filled the air with cries; when the captain came to tell us that the boat was ready. It was a welcome sound. Forcing our way once more through the still squabbling crowd, we gained the landing-place. Here we encountered a boat, just landing a fresh cargo of lively savages from the Emerald Isle. One fellow, of gigantic proportions, whose long, tattered great-coat just reached below the middle of his bare red legs, and, like charity, hid the defects of his other garments, or perhaps concealed his want of them, leaped upon the rocks, and flourishing aloft his shilelagh, bounded and capered like a wild goat from his native mountains. "Whurrah! my boys!" he cried, "Shure we'll all be jontlemen!"

"Pull away, my lads!" said the captain. Then turning to me, "Well, Mrs. Moodie, I hope that you have had enough of Grosse Isle. But could you have witnessed the scenes that I did this morning—"

Here he was interrupted by the wife of the old Scotch Dragoon, Mackenzie, running down to the boat, and laying her hand familiarly upon his shoulder, "Captain, dinna forget."

"Forget what?"

She whispered something confidentially in his ear.

"Oh, ho! the brandy!" he responded aloud. "I should have thought, Mrs. Mackenzie, that you had had enough of *that same*, on yon island?"

"Aye, sic a place for *decent* folk," returned the drunken body, shaking her head. "One needs a drap o' comfort, captain, to keep up one's heart avá."

The captain set up one of his boisterous laughs, as he pushed the boat from the shore. "Hollo! Sam Frazer! steer in, we have forgotten the stores."

"I hope not, captain," said I; "I have been starving since daybreak."

"The bread, the butter, the beef, the onions and potatoes are here, sir," said honest Sam, particularising each article.

"All right; pull for the ship. Mrs. Moodie, we will have a glorious supper, and mind you don't dream of Grosse Isle."

In a few minutes we were again on board. Thus ended my first day's experience of the land of all our hopes.

OH! CAN YOU LEAVE YOUR NATIVE LAND?[9]
A Canadian Song.

Oh! can you leave your native land
An exile's bride to be;
Your mother's home, and cheerful hearth,
To tempt the main with me;
Across the wide and stormy sea
To trace our foaming track,
And know the wave that heaves us on
Will never bear us back?

And can you in Canadian woods
With me the harvest bind,
Nor feel one lingering, sad regret

9. This poem first appeared in the short-lived *Canadian Literary Magazine*, 1:1 (April 1833), p. 56, published in York (Toronto).

For all you leave behind?
Can those dear hands, unused to toil,
    The woodman's wants supply,
Nor shrink beneath the chilly blast
    When wintry storms are nigh?

Amid the shades of forests dark,
    Our loved isle will appear
An Eden, whose delicious bloom
    Will make the wild more drear.
And you in solitude will weep
    O'er scenes beloved in vain,
And pine away your life to view
    Once more your native plain.

Then pause, dear girl! ere those fond lips
    Your wanderer's fate decide;
My spirit spurns the selfish wish—
    You must not be my bride.
But oh, that smile—those tearful eyes,
    My firmer purpose move—
Our hearts are one, and we will dare
    All perils thus to love![1]

Two

Quebec

Queen of the West!—upon thy rocky throne,
    In solitary grandeur sternly placed;
In awful majesty thou sitt'st alone,
    By Nature's master-hand supremely graced.
The world has not thy counterpart—thy dower,
Eternal beauty, strength, and matchless power.

The clouds enfold thee in their misty vest,
    The lightning glances harmless round thy brow;
The loud-voiced thunder cannot shake thy nest,
    Or warring waves that idly chafe below;
The storm above—the waters at thy feet—
May rage and foam, they but secure thy seat.

The mighty river, as it onward rushes,
    To pour its floods in ocean's dread abyss,
Checks at thy feet its fierce impetuous gushes,
    And gently fawns thy rocky base to kiss.
Stern eagle of the crag! thy hold should be
The mountain home of heaven-born liberty!

1. This song has been set to a beautiful plaintive air, by my husband. [*Author's note.*]

>   True to themselves, thy children may defy
>   The power and malice of a world combined;
>   While Britain's flag, beneath thy deep blue sky,
>   Spreads its rich folds and wantons in the wind;
>   The offspring of her glorious race of old
>   May rest securely in their mountain hold.

On the 2nd of September, the anchor was weighed, and we bade a long farewell to Grosse Isle. As our vessel struck into mid-channel, I cast a last lingering look at the beautiful shores we were leaving. Cradled in the arms of the St. Lawrence, and basking in the bright rays of the morning sun, the island and its sister group looked like a second Eden just emerged from the waters of chaos. With what joy could I have spent the rest of the fall in exploring the romantic features of that enchanting scene! But our bark spread her white wings to the favouring breeze, and the fairy vision gradually receded from my sight, to remain for ever on the tablets of memory.

The day was warm, and the cloudless heavens of that peculiar azure tint which gives to the Canadian skies and waters a brilliancy unknown in more northern latitudes. The air was pure and elastic, the sun shone out with uncommon splendour, lighting up the changing woods with a rich mellow colouring, composed of a thousand brilliant and vivid dyes. The mighty river rolled flashing and sparkling onward, impelled by a strong breeze, that tipped its short rolling surges with a crest of snowy foam.

Had there been no other object of interest in the landscape than this majestic river, its vast magnitude, and the depth and clearness of its waters, and its great importance to the colony, would have been sufficient to have riveted the attention, and claimed the admiration of every thinking mind.

Never shall I forget that short voyage from Grosse Isle to Quebec. I love to recall, after the lapse of so many years, every object that awoke in my breast emotions of astonishment and delight. What wonderful combinations of beauty, and grandeur, and power, at every winding of that noble river! How the mind expands with the sublimity of the spectacle, and soars upward in gratitude and adoration to the Author of all being, to thank Him for having made this lower world so wondrously fair—a living temple, heaven-arched, and capable of receiving the homage of all worshippers.

Every perception of my mind became absorbed into the one sense of seeing, when, upon rounding Point Levi,[1] we cast anchor before Quebec. What a scene!—Can the world produce such another? Edinburgh had been the *beau idéal* to me of all that was beautiful in Nature[2]—a vision of the northern Highlands had haunted my dreams across the

---

1. Point Levi (now referred to as Levi) is the point of land and village on the south shore of the St. Lawrence River opposite Quebec City.
2. Susanna Moodie had not travelled a great deal in her youth and had not left England prior to her trip to Edinburgh, which was the first phase of her emigration. In rapid order Edinburgh and Quebec City became new aesthetic high points for her. See *Flora Lyndsay* for her perceptions of Edinburgh.

Atlantic; but all these past recollections faded before the *present* of Quebec.

Nature has lavished all her grandest elements to form this astonishing panorama. There frowns the cloud-capped mountain, and below, the cataract foams and thunders; wood, and rock, and river combine to lend their aid in making the picture perfect, and worthy of its Divine Originator.

The precipitous bank upon which the city lies piled, reflected in the still deep waters at its base, greatly enhances the romantic beauty of the situation. The mellow and serene glow of the autumnal day harmonised so perfectly with the solemn grandeur of the scene around me, and sank so silently and deeply into my soul, that my spirit fell prostrate before it, and I melted involuntarily into tears. Yes, regardless of the eager crowds around me, I leant upon the side of the vessel and cried like a child—not tears of sorrow, but a gush from the heart of pure and unalloyed delight. I heard not the many voices murmuring in my ears—I saw not the anxious beings that thronged our narrow deck—my soul at that moment was alone with God. The shadow of His glory rested visibly on the stupendous objects that composed that magnificent scene; words are perfectly inadequate to describe the impression it made upon my mind—the emotions it produced. The only homage I was capable of offering at such a shrine was tears—tears the most heartfelt and sincere that ever flowed from human eyes. I never before felt so overpoweringly my own insignificance, and the boundless might and majesty of the Eternal.

Canadians, rejoice in your beautiful city! Rejoice and be worthy of her—for few, very few, of the sons of men can point to such a spot as Quebec—and exclaim, "She is ours!—God gave her to us, in her beauty and strength!—We will live for her glory—we will die to defend her liberty and rights—to raise her majestic brow high above the nations!"

Look at the situation of Quebec!—the city founded on the rock that proudly holds the height of the hill. The queen sitting enthroned above the waters, that curb their swiftness and their strength to kiss and fawn around her lovely feet.

Canadians!—as long as you remain true to yourselves and her, what foreign invader could ever dare to plant a hostile flag upon that rock-defended height, or set his foot upon a fortress rendered impregnable by the hand of Nature? United in friendship, loyalty, and love, what wonders may you not achieve? to what an enormous altitude of wealth and importance may you not arrive? Look at the St. Lawrence, that king of streams, that great artery flowing from the heart of the world, through the length and breadth of the land, carrying wealth and fertility in its course, and transporting from town to town along its beautiful shores the riches and produce of a thousand distant climes. What elements of future greatness and prosperity encircle you on every side! Never yield up these solid advantages to become an humble dependent on the great republic—wait patiently, loyally, lovingly, upon the illustrious parent from whom you sprang, and by whom you have been fostered into life and political importance; in the fulness of time she will proclaim your childhood past, and bid you stand up in your own strength, a free Canadian people!

British mothers of Canadian sons!—learn to feel for their country the same enthusiasm which fills your hearts when thinking of the glory of your own. Teach them to love Canada—to look upon her as the first, the happiest, the most independent country in the world! Exhort them to be worthy of her—to have faith in her present prosperity, in her future greatness, and to devote all their talents, when they themselves are men, to accomplish this noble object. Make your children proud of the land of their birth, the land which has given them bread—the land in which you have found an altar and a home; do this, and you will soon cease to lament your separation from the mother country, and the loss of those luxuries which you could not, in honour to yourself, enjoy; you will soon learn to love Canada as I now love it, who once viewed it with a hatred so intense that I longed to die, that death might effectually separate us for ever.

But, oh! beware of drawing disparaging contrasts between the colony and its illustrious parent. All such comparisons are cruel and unjust;—you cannot exalt the one at the expense of the other without committing an act of treason against both.

But I have wandered away from my subject into the regions of thought, and must again descend to common work-a-day realities.

The pleasure we experienced upon our first glance at Quebec was greatly damped by the sad conviction that the cholera-plague raged within her walls, while the almost ceaseless tolling of bells proclaimed a mournful tale of woe and death. Scarcely a person visited the vessel who was not in black, or who spoke not in tones of subdued grief. They advised us not to go on shore if we valued our lives, as strangers most commonly fell the first victims to the fatal malady. This was to me a severe disappointment, who felt an intense desire to climb to the crown of the rock, and survey the noble landscape at my feet. I yielded at last to the wishes of my husband, who did not himself resist the temptation in his own person, and endeavoured to content myself with the means of enjoyment placed within my reach. My eyes were never tired of wandering over the scene before me.

It is curious to observe how differently the objects which call forth intense admiration in some minds will affect others. The Scotch dragoon, Mackenzie, seeing me look, long and intently at the distant Falls of Montmorency,[3] drily observed,

"It may be a' vera fine; but it looks na' better to my thinken than hanks o' white woo' hung out o'er the bushes."

"Weel," cried another, "thae fa's are just bonnie; 'tis a braw land, nae doubt; but no' just so braw as auld Scotland."

"Hout, man! hauld your clavers, we shall a' be lairds here," said a third; "and ye maun wait a muckle time before they wad think aucht of you at hame."

---

3. The Falls were and are spectacular sights just east of Quebec City. They are located on the north shore of the St. Lawrence, opposite the west end of the Isle d'Orleans.

I was not a little amused at the extravagant expectations entertained by some of our steerage passengers. The sight of the Canadian shores had changed them into persons of great consequence. The poorest and the worst-dressed, the least-deserving and the most repulsive in mind and morals, exhibited most disgusting traits of self-importance. Vanity and presumption seemed to possess them altogether. They talked loudly of the rank and wealth of their connexions at home, and lamented the great sacrifices they had made in order to join brothers and cousins who had foolishly settled in this beggarly wooden country.

Girls, who were scarcely able to wash a floor decently, talked of service with contempt, unless tempted to change their resolution by the offer of twelve dollars a month. To endeavour to undeceive them was a useless and ungracious task. After having tried it with several without success, I left it to time and bitter experience to restore them to their sober senses. In spite of the remonstrances of the captain, and the dread of the cholera, they all rushed on shore to inspect the land of Goshen, and to endeavour to realise their absurd anticipations.

We were favoured, a few minutes after our arrival, with another visit from the health-officers; but in this instance both the gentlemen were Canadians. Grave, melancholy-looking men, who talked much and ominously of the prevailing disorder, and the impossibility of strangers escaping from its fearful ravages. This was not very consoling, and served to depress the cheerful tone of mind which, after all, is one of the best antidotes against this awful scourge. The cabin seemed to lighten, and the air to circulate more freely, after the departure of these professional ravens. The captain, as if by instinct, took an additional glass of grog, to shake off the sepulchral gloom their presence had inspired.

The visit of the doctors was followed by that of two of the officials of the Customs;—vulgar, illiterate men, who seating themselves at the cabin table, with a familiar nod to the captain, and a blank stare at us, commenced the following dialogue:—

Custom-house officer (*after making inquiries as to the general cargo of the vessel*):—"Any good brandy on board, captain?"

Captain (*gruffly*): "Yes."

Officer: "Best remedy for the cholera known. The only one the doctors can depend upon."

Captain (*taking the hint*): "Gentlemen, I'll send you up a dozen bottles this afternoon."

Officer: "Oh, thank you. We are sure to get it *genuine* from you. Any Edinburgh ale in your freight?"

Captain (*with a slight shrug*): "A few hundreds in cases. I'll send you a dozen with the brandy."

Both: "Capital!"

First officer: "Any short, large-bowled, Scotch pipes, with metallic lids?"

Captain (*quite impatiently*): "Yes, yes; I'll send you some to smoke, with the brandy.—What else?"

Officer: "We will now proceed to business."

My readers would have laughed, as I did, could they have seen how doggedly the old man shook his fist after these worthies as they left the vessel. "Scoundrels!" he muttered to himself; and then turning to me, "They rob us in this barefaced manner, and we dare not resist or complain, for fear of the trouble they can put us to. If I had those villains at sea, I'd give them a taste of brandy and ale that they would not relish."

The day wore away, and the lengthened shadows of the mountains fell upon the water, when the *Horsley Hill*, a large three-masted vessel from Waterford,[4] that we had left at the quarantine station, cast anchor a little above us. She was quickly boarded by the health-officers, and ordered round to take up her station below the castle. To accomplish this object she had to heave her anchor; when lo! a great pine-tree, which had been sunk in the river, became entangled in the chains. Uproarious was the mirth to which the incident gave rise among the crowds that thronged the decks of the many vessels then at anchor in the river. Speaking-trumpets resounded on every side; and my readers may be assured that the sea-serpent was not forgotten in the multitude of jokes which followed.

Laughter resounded on all sides; and in the midst of the noise and confusion, the captain of the *Horsley Hill* hoisted his colours downwards, as if making signals of distress, a mistake which provoked renewed and long continued mirth.

I laughed until my sides ached; little thinking how the *Horsley Hill* would pay us off for our mistimed hilarity.

Towards night, most of the steerage passengers returned, greatly dissatisfied with their first visit to the city, which they declared to be a filthy hole, that looked a great deal better from the ship's side than it did on shore. This, I have often been told, is literally the case. Here, as elsewhere, man has marred the magnificent creation of his Maker.

A dark and starless night closed in, accompanied by cold winds and drizzling rain. We seemed to have made a sudden leap from the torrid to the frigid zone. Two hours before, my light summer clothing was almost insupportable, and now a heavy and well-lined plaid formed but an inefficient screen from the inclemency of the weather. After watching for some time the singular effect produced by the lights in the town reflected in the water, and weary with a long day of anticipation and excitement, I made up my mind to leave the deck and retire to rest. I had just settled down my baby in her berth, when the vessel struck, with a sudden crash that sent a shiver through her whole frame. Alarmed, but not aware of the real danger that hung over us, I groped my way to the cabin, and thence ascended to the deck.

Here a scene of confusion prevailed that baffles description. By some strange fatality, the *Horsley Hill* had changed her position and run foul of us in the dark. The *Anne* was a small brig, and her unlucky

4. The *Horsley Hill*, sailing out of Waterford, Ireland, had arrived at Quebec on August 31, 1832, carrying 141 passengers. It had been damaged in a gale at sea and repaired in Jamaica en route to Canada, prior to its collision with the *Anne*.

neighbour a heavy three-masted vessel, with three hundred Irish emigrants on board; and as her bowsprit was directly across the bows of the *Anne*, and she anchored, and unable to free herself from the deadly embrace, there was no small danger of the poor brig going down in the unequal struggle.

Unable to comprehend what was going on, I raised my head above the companion ladder, just at the critical moment when the vessels were grappled together. The shrieks of the women, the shouts and oaths of the men, and the barking of the dogs in either ship, aided the dense darkness of the night in producing a most awful and stunning effect.

"What is the matter?" I gasped out. "What is the reason of this dreadful confusion?"

The captain was raging like a chafed bull, in the grasp of several frantic women, who were clinging, shrieking, to his knees.

With great difficulty I persuaded the women to accompany me below. The mate hurried off with the cabin light upon the deck, and we were left in total darkness to await the result.

A deep, strange silence fell upon my heart. It was not exactly fear, but a sort of nerving of my spirit to meet the worst. The cowardly behaviour of my companions inspired me with courage. I was ashamed of their pusillanimity and want of faith in the Divine Providence. I sat down, and calmly begged them to follow my example.

An old woman, called Williamson, a sad reprobate, in attempting to do so, set her foot within the fender, which the captain had converted into a repository for empty glass bottles; the smash that ensued was echoed by a shriek from the whole party.

"God guide us," cried the ancient dame; "but we are going into eternity. I shall be lost; my sins are more in number than the hairs of my head." This confession was followed by oaths and imprecations too blasphemous to repeat.

Shocked and disgusted at her profanity, I bade her pray, and not waste the few moments that might be hers in using oaths and bad language.

"Did you not hear the crash?" said she.

"I did; it was of your own making. Sit down and be quiet."

Here followed another shock, that made the vessel heave and tremble; and the dragging of the anchor increased the uneasy motion which began to fill the boldest of us with alarm.

"Mrs. Moodie, we are lost," said Margaret Williamson, the youngest daughter of the old woman, a pretty girl, who had been the belle of the ship, flinging herself on her knees before me, and grasping both my hands in hers. "Oh, pray for me! pray for me! I cannot, I dare not pray for myself; I was never taught a prayer." Her voice was choked with convulsive sobs, and scalding tears fell in torrents from her eyes over my hands. I never witnessed such an agony of despair. Before I could say one word to comfort her, another shock seemed to lift the vessel upwards. I felt my own blood run cold, expecting instantly to go down;

and thoughts of death, and the unknown eternity at our feet, flitted vaguely through my mind.

"If we stay here, we shall perish," cried the girl, springing to her feet. "Let us go on deck, mother, and take our chance with the rest."

"Stay," I said; "you are safer here. British sailors never leave women to perish. You have fathers, husbands, brothers on board, who will not forget you. I beseech you to remain patiently here until the danger is past." I might as well have preached to the winds. The headstrong creatures would no longer be controlled. They rushed simultaneously upon deck, just as the *Horsley Hill* swung off, carrying with her part of the outer frame of our deck and the larger portion of our stern. When tranquillity was restored, fatigued both in mind and body, I sunk into a profound sleep, and did not awake until the sun had risen high above the wave-encircled fortress of Quebec.

The stormy clouds had all dispersed during the night; the air was clear and balmy; the giant hills were robed in a blue, soft mist, which rolled around them in fleecy volumes. As the beams of the sun penetrated their shadowy folds, they gradually drew up like a curtain, and dissolved like wreaths of smoke into the clear air.

The moment I came on deck, my old friend Oscar greeted me with his usual joyous bark, and with the sagacity peculiar to his species, proceeded to shew me all the damage done to the vessel during the night. It was laughable to watch the motions of the poor brute, as he ran from place to place, stopping before, or jumping upon, every fractured portion of the deck, and barking out his indignation at the ruinous condition in which he found his marine home. Oscar had made eleven voyages in the *Anne*, and had twice saved the life of the captain. He was an ugly specimen of the Scotch terrier, and greatly resembled a bundle of old rope-yarn; but a more faithful or attached creature I never saw. The captain was not a little jealous of Oscar's friendship for me. I was the only person the dog had ever deigned to notice, and his master regarded it as an act of treason on the part of his four-footed favourite. When my arms were tired with nursing, I had only to lay my baby on my cloak on deck, and tell Oscar to watch her, and the good dog would lie down by her, and suffer her to tangle his long curls in her little hands, and pull his tail and ears in the most approved baby fashion, without offering the least opposition; but if any one dared to approach his charge, he was alive on the instant, placing his paws over the child, and growling furiously. He would have been a bold man who had approached the child to do her an injury. Oscar was the best plaything, and as sure a protector as Katie had.

During the day, many of our passengers took their departure; tired of the close confinement of the ship, and the long voyage, they were too impatient to remain on board until we reached Montreal. The mechanics obtained instant employment, and the girls who were old enough to work, procured situations as servants in the city. Before night, our numbers were greatly reduced. The old dragoon and his family, two Scotch fiddlers of the name of Duncan, a Highlander called Tam Grant, and his wife and little son, and our own party, were all that remained of the seventy-two passengers that left the Port of Leith in the brig *Anne*.[5]

In spite of the earnest entreaties of his young wife, the said Tam Grant, who was the most mercurial fellow in the world, would insist upon going on shore to see all the lions of the place. "Ah, Tam! Tam! ye will die o' the cholera," cried the weeping Maggie. "My heart will brak if ye dinna bide wi' me an' the bairnie." Tam was deaf as Ailsa Craig.[6] Regardless of tears and entreaties, he jumped into the boat, like a wilful man as he was, and my husband went with him. Fortunately for me, the latter returned safe to the vessel, in time to proceed with her to Montreal, in tow of the noble steamer, *British America*; but Tam, the volatile Tam was missing. During the reign of the cholera, what at another time would have appeared but a trifling incident, was now invested with doubt and terror. The distress of the poor wife knew no bounds. I think I see her now, as I saw her then, sitting upon the floor of the deck, her head buried between her knees, rocking herself to and fro, and weeping in the utter abandonment of her grief. "He is dead! he is dead! My dear, dear Tam! The pestilence has seized upon him; and I and the puir bairn are left alone in the strange land." All attempts at consolation were useless; she obstinately refused to listen to probabilities, or to be comforted. All through the night I heard her deep and bitter sobs, and the oft-repeated name of him that she had lost.

The sun was sinking over the plague-stricken city, gilding the changing woods and mountain peaks with ruddy light; the river mirrored back the gorgeous sky, and moved in billows of liquid gold; the very air seemed lighted up with heavenly fires, and sparkled with myriads of luminous particles, as I gazed my last upon that beautiful scene.

The tow-line was now attached from our ship to the *British America*, and in company with two other vessels, we followed fast in her foaming wake. Day lingered on the horizon just long enough to enable me to examine, with deep interest, the rocky heights of Abraham, the scene of our immortal Wolfe's victory and death;[7] and when the twilight faded into night, the moon arose in solemn beauty, and cast mysterious gleams upon the strange stern landscape. The wide river, flowing rapidly between its rugged banks, rolled in inky blackness beneath the overshadowing crags; while the waves in mid-channel flashed along in dazzling light, rendered more intense by the surrounding darkness. In this luminous track the huge steamer glided majestically forward, flinging showers of red earth-stars from the funnel into the clear air, and looking like some fiery demon of the night enveloped in smoke and flame.

The lofty groves of pine frowned down in hearse-like gloom upon the mighty river, and the deep stillness of the night, broken alone by

5. Leith is Edinburgh's seaport on the Firth of Forth.
6. Ailsa Craig is a granite-based island in the Firth of Clyde.
7. The Plains of Abraham sit high above the rocky cliffs to the west of Quebec's old city. They were the site of Major-General James Wolfe's victory over the French forces led by Montcalm in September 1759. In this victory, which solidified a British presence in Lower Canada, Wolfe suffered fatal wounds and became a hero of the British cause in Canada.

its hoarse wailings, filled my mind with sad forebodings,—alas! too prophetic of the future. Keenly, for the first time, I felt that I was a stranger in a strange land; my heart yearned intensely for my absent home. Home! the word had ceased to belong to my *present*—it was doomed to live for ever in the *past*; for what emigrant ever regarded the country of his exile as his *home*? To the land he has left, that name belongs for ever, and in no instance does he bestow it upon another. "I have got a letter from home!" "I have seen a friend from home!" "I dreamt last night that I was at home!" are expressions of every-day occurrence, to prove that the heart acknowledges no other home than the land of its birth.

From these sad reveries I was roused by the hoarse notes of the bagpipe. That well-known sound brought every Scotchman upon deck, and set every limb in motion on the decks of the other vessels. Determined not to be outdone, our fiddlers took up the strain, and a lively contest ensued between the rival musicians, which continued during the greater part of the night. The shouts of noisy revelry were in no way congenial to my feelings. Nothing tends so much to increase our melancholy as merry music when the heart is sad; and I left the scene with eyes brimful of tears, and my mind painfully agitated by sorrowful recollections and vain regrets.

> The strains we hear in foreign lands,
>   No echo from the heart can claim;
> The chords are swept by strangers' hands,
>   And kindle in the breast no flame,
>   Sweet though they be.
> No fond remembrance wakes to fling
>   Its hallow'd influence o'er the chords;
> As if a spirit touch'd the string,
>   Breathing, in soft harmonious words,
>   Deep melody.
>
> The music of our native shore
>   A thousand lovely scenes endears;
> In magic tones it murmurs o'er
>   The visions of our early years;—
>   The hopes of youth;
> It wreathes again the flowers we wreathed
>   In childhood's bright, unclouded day;
> It breathes again the vows we breathed,
>   At beauty's shrine, when hearts were gay
>   And whisper'd truth;
>
> It calls before our mental sight
>   Dear forms whose tuneful lips are mute,
> Bright, sunny eyes long closed in night,
>   Warm hearts now silent as the lute
>   That charm'd our ears;
> It thrills the breast with feelings deep,
>   Too deep for language to impart;

And bids the spirit joy and weep,
In tones that sink into the heart,
And melt in tears.[8]

Three

Our Journey Up the Country

Fly this plague-stricken spot! The hot, foul air
Is rank with pestilence—the crowded marts
And public ways, once populous with life,
Are still and noisome as a churchyard vault;
Aghast and shuddering, Nature holds her breath
In abject fear, and feels at her strong heart
The deadly fangs of death.

Of Montreal I can say but little. The cholera was at its height, and the fear of infection, which increased the nearer we approached its shores, cast a gloom over the scene, and prevented us from exploring its infected streets. That the feelings of all on board very nearly resembled our own might be read in the anxious faces of both passengers and crew. Our captain, who had never before hinted that he entertained any apprehensions on the subject, now confided to us his conviction that he should never quit the city alive: "This cursed cholera! Left it in Russia—found it on my return to Leith—meets me again in Canada. No escape the third time." If the captain's prediction proved true in his case, it was not so in ours. We left the cholera in England, we met it again in Scotland, and, under the providence of God, we escaped its fatal visitation in Canada.

Yet the fear and the dread of it on that first day caused me to throw many an anxious glance on my husband and my child. I had been very ill during the three weeks that our vessel was becalmed upon the Banks of Newfoundland, and to this circumstance I attribute my deliverance from the pestilence. I was weak and nervous when the vessel arrived at Quebec, but the voyage up the St. Lawrence, the fresh air and beautiful scenery were rapidly restoring me to health.

Montreal from the river wears a pleasing aspect, but it lacks the grandeur, the stern sublimity of Quebec. The fine mountain that forms the background to the city, the Island of St. Helens in front, and the junction of the St. Lawrence and the Ottawa—which run side by side, their respective boundaries only marked by a long ripple of white foam, and the darker blue tint of the former river,—constitute the most remarkable features in the landscape.

The town itself was, at that period, dirty and ill-paved; and the opening of all the sewers, in order to purify the place and stop the rav-

---

8. This poem, "Song: The Strains We Hear in Foreign Lands," first published in the *New York Albion; or British, Colonial and Foreign Weekly Gazette*, NS 1:9 (March 2, 1833), p. 72, was quite popular, and was republished in at least five Upper Canadian newspapers that same year.

ages of the pestilence, rendered the public thoroughfares almost impassable, and loaded the air with intolerable effluvia, more likely to produce than stay the course of the plague, the violence of which had, in all probability, been increased by these long-neglected receptacles of uncleanliness.

The dismal stories told us by the excise-officer who came to inspect the unloading of the vessel, of the frightful ravages of the cholera, by no means increased our desire to go on shore.

"It will be a miracle if you escape," he said. "Hundreds of emigrants die daily; and if Stephen Ayres had not providentially come among us, not a soul would have been alive at this moment in Montreal."[1]

"And who is Stephen Ayres?" said I.

"God only knows," was the grave reply. "There was a man sent from heaven, and his name was John."[2]

"But I thought this man was called Stephen?"

"Ay, so he calls himself; but 'tis certain that he is not of the earth. Flesh and blood could never do what he has done,—the hand of God is in it. Besides, no one knows who he is, or whence he comes. When the cholera was at the worst, and the hearts of all men stood still with fear, and our doctors could do nothing to stop its progress, this man, or angel, or saint, suddenly made his appearance in our streets. He came in great humility, seated in an ox-cart, and drawn by two lean oxen and a rope harness. Only think of that! Such a man in an *old ox-cart*, drawn by *rope harness!* The thing itself was a miracle. He made no parade about what he could do, but only fixed up a plain pasteboard notice, informing the public that he possessed an infallible remedy for the cholera, and would engage to cure all who sent for him."

"And was he successful?"

"Successful! It beats all belief; and his remedy so simple! For some days we all took him for a quack, and would have no faith in him at all, although he performed some wonderful cures upon poor folks, who could not afford to send for the doctor. The Indian village[3] was attacked by the disease, and he went out to them, and restored upwards of a hundred of the Indians to perfect health. They took the old lean oxen out of the cart, and drew him back to Montreal in triumph. This 'stablished him at once, and in a few days' time he made a fortune. The very doctors sent for him to cure them; and it is to be hoped that in a few days he will banish the cholera from the city."

"Do you know his famous remedy?"

"Do I not?—Did he not cure me when I was at the last gasp? Why, he makes no secret of it. It is all drawn from the maple-tree. First he rubs the patient all over with an ointment, made of hog's lard and

---

1. Stephen Ayres, a licenced doctor from New Jersey, successfully used his maple tree recipe to cure many sufferers of the Asiatic Cholera in the Montreal area. In November 1832 he petitioned the British government for "a pecuniary reward" for services rendered in Montreal during the past dangerous summer (see National Archives, British Military and Naval Records, RG 8, C Series, Vol. 301, pp. 122–25). Various newspapers reported on his work; some thought him a charlatan.
2. The exact phrasing of the introduction by the evangelist of John the Baptist in John 1:6.
3. The Indian village was Caughnawaga, north of Montreal.

maple-sugar and ashes, from the maple-tree; and he gives him a hot draught of maple-sugar and ley, which throws him into a violent perspiration. In about an hour the cramps subside; he falls into a quiet sleep, and when he awakes he is perfectly restored to health." Such were our first tidings of Stephen Ayres, the cholera doctor, who is universally believed to have effected some wonderful cures. He obtained a wide celebrity throughout the colony.[4]

The day of our arrival in the port of Montreal was spent in packing and preparing for our long journey up the country. At sunset, I went upon deck to enjoy the refreshing breeze that swept from the river. The evening was delightful; the white tents of the soldiers on the Island of St. Helens glittered in the beams of the sun, and the bugle-call, wafted over the waters, sounded so cheery and inspiring, that it banished all fears of the cholera, and, with fear, the heavy gloom that had clouded my mind since we left Quebec. I could once more hold sweet converse with nature, and enjoy the soft loveliness of the rich and harmonious scene.

A loud cry from one of the crew startled me; I turned to the river, and beheld a man struggling in the water a short distance from our vessel. He was a young sailor, who had fallen from the bowsprit of a ship near us.

There is something terribly exciting in beholding a fellow-creature in imminent peril, without having the power to help him. To witness his death-struggles,—to feel in your own person all the dreadful alternations of hope and fear,—and, finally, to see him die, with scarcely an effort made for his preservation. This was our case.

At the moment he fell into the water, a boat with three men was within a few yards of the spot, and actually sailed over the spot where he sank. Cries of "Shame!" from the crowd collected upon the bank of the river, had no effect in rousing these people to attempt the rescue of a perishing fellow-creature. The boat passed on. The drowning man again rose to the surface, the convulsive motion of his hands and feet visible above the water, but it was evident that the struggle would be his last.

"Is it possible that they will let a human being perish, and so near the shore, when an oar held out would save his life?" was the agonising question at my heart, as I gazed, half-maddened by excitement, on the fearful spectacle. The eyes of a multitude were fixed upon the same object—but not a hand stirred. Every one seemed to expect from his fellow an effort which he was incapable of attempting himself.

At this moment—splash!—a sailor plunged into the water from the deck of a neighbouring vessel, and dived after the drowning man. A deep "Thank God!" burst from my heart. I drew a freer breath as the brave fellow's head appeared above the water. He called to the men in the boat to throw him an oar, or the drowning man would be the death

---

4. A friend of mine, in this town, has an original portrait of this notable empiric—this man sent from heaven. The face is rather handsome, but has a keen, designing expression, and is evidently that of an American, from its complexion and features. [*Author's note.*]

of them both. Slowly they put back the boat,—the oar was handed; but it came too late! The sailor, whose name was Cook, had been obliged to shake off the hold of the dying man to save his own life. He dived again to the bottom, and succeeded in bringing to shore the body of the unfortunate being he had vainly endeavoured to succour. Shortly after, he came on board our vessel, foaming with passion at the barbarous indifference manifested by the men in the boat.

"Had they given me the oar in time, I could have saved him. I knew him well—he was an excellent fellow, and a good seaman. He has left a wife and three children in Liverpool. Poor Jane!—how can I tell her that I could not save her husband?"

He wept bitterly, and it was impossible for any of us to witness his emotion without joining in his grief.

From the mate I learned that this same young man had saved the lives of three women and a child when the boat was swamped at Grosse Isle, in attempting to land the passengers from the *Horsley Hill.*

Such acts of heroism are common in the lower walks of life. Thus, the purest gems are often encased in the rudest crust; and the finest feelings of the human heart are fostered in the chilling atmosphere of poverty.

While this sad event occupied all our thoughts, and gave rise to many painful reflections, an exclamation of unqualified delight at once changed the current of our thoughts, and filled us with surprise and pleasure. Maggy Grant had fainted in the arms of her husband.

Yes, there was Tam,—her dear, reckless Tam, after all her tears and lamentations, pressing his young wife to his heart, and calling her by a thousand endearing pet names.

He had met with some countrymen at Quebec, had taken too much whiskey on the joyful occasion, and lost his passage in the *Anne,* but had followed, a few hours later, in another steam-boat; and he assured the now happy Maggie, as he kissed the infant Tam, whom she held up to his admiring gaze, that he never would be guilty of the like again. Perhaps he kept his word; but I much fear that the first temptation would make the lively laddie forget his promise.

Our luggage having been removed to the Custom-house, including our bedding, the captain collected all the ship's flags for our accommodation, of which we formed a tolerably comfortable bed; and if our dreams were of England, could it be otherwise, with her glorious flag wrapped around us, and our heads resting upon the Union Jack?

In the morning we were obliged to visit the city to make the necessary arrangements for our upward journey.

The day was intensely hot. A bank of thunderclouds lowered heavily above the mountain, and the close, dusty streets were silent, and nearly deserted. Here and there might be seen a group of anxious-looking, care-worn, sickly emigrants, seated against a wall among their packages, and sadly ruminating upon their future prospects.

The sullen toll of the death-bell, the exposure of ready-made coffins in the undertakers' windows, and the oft-recurring notice placarded on the walls, of funerals furnished at such and such a place, at cheapest rate and shortest notice, painfully reminded us, at every turning of the street, that death was everywhere—perhaps lurking in our very path; we felt no desire to examine the beauties of the place. With this ominous feeling pervading our minds, public buildings possessed few attractions, and we determined to make our stay as short as possible.

Compared with the infected city, our ship appeared an ark of safety, and we returned to it with joy and confidence, too soon to be destroyed. We had scarcely re-entered our cabin, when tidings were brought to us that the cholera had made its appearance: a brother of the captain had been attacked.

It was advisable that we should leave the vessel immediately, before the intelligence could reach the health-officers. A few minutes sufficed to make the necessary preparations; and in less than half-an-hour we found ourselves occupying comfortable apartments in Goodenough's hotel, and our passage taken in the stage for the following morning.

The transition was like a dream. The change from the close, rank ship, to large, airy, well-furnished rooms and clean attendants, was a luxury we should have enjoyed had not the dread of the cholera involved all things around us in gloom and apprehension. No one spoke upon the subject; and yet it was evident that it was uppermost in the thoughts of all. Several emigrants had died of the terrible disorder during the week, beneath the very roof that sheltered us, and its ravages, we were told, had extended up the country as far as Kingston; so that it was still to be the phantom of our coming journey, if we were fortunate enough to escape from its head-quarters.

At six o'clock the following morning, we took our places in the coach for Lachine,[5] and our fears of the plague greatly diminished as we left the spires of Montreal in the distance. The journey from Montreal westward has been so well described by many gifted pens, that I shall say little about it. The banks of the St. Lawrence are picturesque and beautiful, particularly in those spots where there is a good view of the American side. The neat farm-houses looked to me, whose eyes had been so long accustomed to the watery waste, homes of beauty and happiness; and the splendid orchards, the trees at that season of the year being loaded with ripening fruit of all hues, were refreshing and delicious.

My partiality for the apples was regarded by a fellow-traveller with a species of horror. "Touch them not, if you value your life." Every draught of fresh air and water inspired me with renewed health and spirits, and I disregarded the well-meant advice; the gentleman who gave it had just recovered from the terrible disease. He was a middle-aged man, a farmer from the Upper Province, Canadian born. He had visited Montreal on business for the first time. "Well, sir," he said, in

5. By boat and stagecoach, the Moodies advanced westward toward Cobourg, passing through Lachine, Cornwall, and Prescott before sailing on the *William IV* past Brockville, the Thousand Islands, and Kingston.

answer to some questions put to him by my husband respecting the disease, "I can tell you what it is; a man smitten with the cholera stares death right in the face; and the torment he is suffering is so great that he would gladly die to get rid of it."

"You were fortunate, C[ummins],[6] to escape," said a backwood settler, who occupied the opposite seat; "many a younger man has died of it."

"Ay; but I believe I never should have taken it had it not been for some things they gave me for supper at the hotel; oysters, they called them, oysters; they were alive! I was once persuaded by a friend to eat them, and I liked them well enough at the time. But I declare to you that I felt them crawling over one another in my stomach all night. The next morning I was seized with the cholera."

"Did you swallow them whole, C[ummins]?" said the former spokesman, who seemed highly tickled by the evil doings of the oysters.

"To be sure. I tell you, the creatures are alive. You put them on your tongue, and I'll be bound you'll be glad to let them slip down as fast as you can."

"No wonder you had the cholera," said the backwoodsman, "you deserved it for your barbarity. If I had a good plate of oysters here, I'd teach you the way to eat them."

Our journey during the first day was performed partly by coach, partly by steam. It was nine o'clock in the evening when we landed at Cornwall, and took coach for Prescott. The country through which we passed appeared beautiful in the clear light of the moon; but the air was cold, and slightly sharpened by frost. This seemed strange to me in the early part of September, but it is very common in Canada. Nine passengers were closely packed into our narrow vehicle, but the sides being of canvas, and the open space allowed for windows unglazed, I shivered with cold, which amounted to a state of suffering, when the day broke, and we approached the little village of Matilda. It was unanimously voted by all hands that we should stop and breakfast at a small inn by the road-side, and warm ourselves before proceeding to Prescott.

The people in the tavern were not stirring, and it was some time before an old white-headed man unclosed the door, and showed us into a room, redolent with fumes of tobacco, and darkened by paper blinds. I asked him if he would allow me to take my infant into a room with a fire.

"I guess it was a pretty considerable cold night for the like of her," said he. "Come, I'll show you to the kitchen; there's always a fire there." I cheerfully followed, accompanied by our servant.

6. Cummins, the stagecoach traveller who complains of oyster poisoning, died of drink in 1838. John Moodie learned of his fate when, during his military service in Belleville, he met Col. Robert Wilkins (of Carrying Place in nearby Prince Edward County). In a letter to Susanna dated December 25, 1838, he told her of the now successful Wilkins, who, though unidentified in the text, was one of the nine passengers in the stagecoach the Moodies took from Lachine to Prescott (see *Letters of Love and Duty*, p. 112).

Our entrance was unexpected, and by no means agreeable to the persons we found there. A half-clothed, red-haired Irish servant was upon her knees, kindling up the fire; and a long, thin woman, with a sharp face, and an eye like a black snake, was just emerging from a bed in the corner. We soon discovered this apparition to be the mistress of the house.

"The people can't come in here!" she screamed in a shrill voice, darting daggers at the poor old man.

"Sure there's a baby, and the two women critters are perished with cold," pleaded the good old man.

"What's that to me? They have no business in my kitchen."

"Now, Almira, do hold on. It's the coach has stopped to breakfast with us; and you know we don't often get the chance."

All this time the fair Almira was dressing as fast as she could, and eyeing her unwelcome female guests, as we stood shivering over the fire.

"Breakfast!" she muttered, "what can we give them to eat? They pass our door a thousand times without any one alighting; and now, when we are out of everything, they must stop and order breakfast at such an unreasonable hour. How many are there of you?" turning fiercely to me.

"Nine," I answered, laconically, continuing to chafe the cold hands and feet of the child.

"Nine! That bit of beef will be nothing, cut into steaks for nine. What's to be done, Joe?" (to the old man.)

"Eggs and ham, summat of that dried venison, and pumpkin pie," responded the *aide-de-camp*, thoughtfully. "I don't know of any other fixings."

"Bestir yourself, then, and lay out the table, for the coach can't stay long," cried the virago, seizing a frying-pan from the wall, and preparing it for the reception of the eggs and ham. "I must have the fire to myself. People can't come crowding here, when I have to fix breakfast for nine; particularly when there is a good room elsewhere provided for their accommodation." I took the hint, and retreated to the parlour, where I found the rest of the passengers walking to and fro, and impatiently awaiting the advent of the breakfast.

To do Almira justice, she prepared from her scanty materials a very substantial breakfast in an incredibly short time, for which she charged us a quarter of a dollar per head.

At Prescott we embarked on board a fine new steamboat, *William IV.*, crowded with Irish emigrants, proceeding to Cobourg and Toronto.

While pacing the deck, my husband was greatly struck by the appearance of a middle-aged man and his wife, who sat apart from the rest, and seemed struggling with intense grief, which, in spite of all their efforts at concealment, was strongly impressed upon their features. Some time after, I fell into conversation with the woman, from whom I learned their little history. The husband was factor to a Scotch gentleman, of large landed property, who had employed him to visit

Canada, and report the capabilities of the country, prior to his investing a large sum of money in wild lands. The expenses of their voyage
had been paid, and everything up to that morning had prospered with
them. They had been blessed with a speedy passage, and were greatly
pleased with the country and the people; but of what avail was all this?
Their only son, a fine lad of fourteen, had died that day of the cholera,
and all their hopes for the future were buried in his grave. For his sake
they had sought a home in this far land; and here, at the very onset of
their new career, the fell disease had taken him from them for ever,—
here, where, in such a crowd, the poor heartbroken mother could not
even indulge her natural grief!

"Ah, for a place where I might greet!" she said; "it would relieve the
burning weight at my heart. But with sae many strange eyes glowering
upon me, I tak' shame to mysel' to greet."

"Ah, Jeannie, my puir woman," said the husband, grasping her
hand, "ye maun bear up; 'tis God's will; an sinfu' creatures like us
mauna repine. But oh, madam," turning to me, "we have sair hearts
the day!"

Poor bereaved creatures, how deeply I commiserated their grief,—
how I respected the poor father, in the stern efforts he made to conceal from indifferent spectators the anguish that weighed upon his
mind! Tears are the best balm that can be applied to the anguish of
the heart. Religion teaches man to bear his sorrows with becoming
fortitude, but tears contribute largely both to soften and to heal the
wounds from whence they flow.

At Brockville we took in a party of ladies, which somewhat relieved
the monotony of the cabin, and I was amused by listening to their
lively prattle, and the little gossip with which they strove to wile away
the tedium of the voyage. The day was too stormy to go upon deck,—
thunder and lightning, accompanied with torrents of rain. Amid the
confusion of the elements, I tried to get a peep at the Lake of the
Thousand Isles; but the driving storm blended all objects into one, and
I returned wet and disappointed to my berth. We passed Kingston at
midnight, and lost all our lady passengers but two. The gale continued
until daybreak, and noise and confusion prevailed all night, which
were greatly increased by the uproarious conduct of a wild Irish emigrant, who thought fit to make his bed upon the mat before the cabin
door. He sang, he shouted, and harangued his countrymen on the political state of the Emerald Isle, in a style which was loud if not eloquent. Sleep was impossible, whilst his stentorian lungs continued to
pour forth torrents of unmeaning sound.

Our Dutch stewardess was highly enraged. His conduct, she said,
"was perfectly ondacent." She opened the door, and bestowing upon
him several kicks, bade him get away "out of that," or she would complain to the captain.

In answer to this remonstrance, he caught her by the foot, and
pulled her down. Then waving the tattered remains of his straw hat in
the air, he shouted with an air of triumph, "Git out wid you, you ould
witch! Shure the ladies, the purty darlints, never sent you wid that

'ugly message to Pat,' who loves them so intirely that he manes to kape watch over them through the blessed night." Then making us a ludicrous bow, he continued, "Ladies, I'm at yer sarvice; I only wish I could get a dispensation from the Pope, and I'd marry yeas all." The stewardess bolted the door, and the mad fellow kept up such a racket that we all wished him at the bottom of the Ontario.

The following day was wet and gloomy. The storm had protracted the length of our voyage for several hours, and it was midnight when we landed at Cobourg.

THERE'S REST.[7]

(written at midnight on the River St. Lawrence.)

There's rest when eve, with dewy fingers,
    Draws the curtains of repose
Round the west, where light still lingers,
    And the day's last glory glows;
There's rest in heaven's unclouded blue,
    When twinkling stars steal one by one,
So softly on the gazer's view,
    As if they sought his glance to shun.

There's rest when o'er the silent meads
    The deepening shades of night advance;
And sighing through their fringe of reeds,
    The mighty stream's clear waters glance.
There's rest when all above is bright,
    And gently o'er these summer isles
The full moon pours her mellow light,
    And heaven on earth serenely smiles.

There's rest when angry storms are o'er,
    And fear no longer vigil keeps;
When winds are heard to rave no more,
    And ocean's troubled spirit sleeps;
There's rest when to the pebbly strand,—
    The lapsing billows slowly glide;
And, pillow'd on the golden sand,
    Breathes soft and low the slumbering tide.

There's rest, deep rest, at this still hour—
    A holy calm,—a pause profound;
Whose soothing spell and dreamy power
    Lulls into slumber all around.
There's rest for labour's hardy child,
    For Nature's tribes of earth and air,
Whose sacred balm and influence mild,
    Save guilt and sorrow, all may share.

7. Susanna wrote "There's Rest" during her trip up the St. Lawrence. She sent it to the New York *Albion* where it appeared on May 25, 1833 (NS1:21, p. 161). It was reprinted in several Canadian newspapers and magazines in 1833, 1834, and 1835.

> There's rest beneath the quiet sod,
>   When life and all its sorrows cease,
> And in the bosom of his God
>   The Christian finds eternal peace,—
> That peace the world cannot bestow,
>   The rest a Saviour's death pangs bought,
> To bid the weary pilgrim know
>   A rest surpassing human thought.

Four

Tom Wilson's Emigration

"Of all odd fellows, this fellow was the oddest. I have seen many strange fish in my days, but I never met with his equal."

About a month previous to our emigration to Canada, my husband said to me, "You need not expect me home to dinner to-day; I am going with my friend Wilson to Y[oxford][1] to hear Mr. C[attermole] lecture upon emigration to Canada.[2] He has just returned from the North American provinces, and his lectures are attended by vast numbers of persons who are anxious to obtain information on the subject. I got a note from your friend B[ird] this morning, begging me to come over and listen to his palaver; and as Wilson thinks of emigrating in the spring, he will be my walking companion."[3]

"Tom Wilson going to Canada?" said I, as the door closed on my better-half. "What a backwoodsman he will make! What a loss to the single ladies of S[outhwold]! What will they do without him at their balls and picnics?"

One of my sisters, who was writing at a table near me, was highly amused at this unexpected announcement. She fell back in her chair and indulged in a long and hearty laugh. I am certain that most of my readers would have joined in her laugh had they known the object which provoked her mirth. "Poor Tom is such a dreamer," said my sister, "it would be an act of charity in Moodie to persuade him from undertaking such a wild-goose chase; only that I fancy my good brother is possessed with the same mania."

---

1. Yoxford, a village about ten miles from Reydon. The Suffolk poet and author James Bird and his wife Emma, who ran a book store and pharmacy there, were good friends to the Strickland sisters.
2. William Cattermole, a Suffolk native, had been hired by the Canada Company to supply useful and encouraging information to prospective emigrants. He gave lectures in Suffolk over the winter of 1831–32 and on such occasions sold copies of his pamphlet *Emigration. The Advantages of Emigration to Canada, Being the Substance of Two Lectures, Delivered at The Town-Hall, Colchester, and The Mechanics' Institute, Ipswich, by William Cattermole, May, 1831.* Cattermole returned to Canada in March 1832 and died in the town of Hamilton in 1841.
3. Tom Wilson was Tom Wales, one of six sons of a respected Southwold family that had fallen on hard times. Agnes Strickland's letters to Susanna in Canada often mentioned the doings of the Wales offspring, including the disturbing news of Tom's marriage in 1837 to a "very low person" who was in trade (see National Library of Canada, PHEC, Series 1, April 23, 1837).

"Nay, God forbid!" said I. "I hope this Mr. C[attermole], with the unpronounceable name, will disgust them with his eloquence; for B[ird] writes me word, in his droll way, that he is a coarse, vulgar fellow, and lacks the dignity of a bear. Oh! I am certain they will return quite sickened with the Canadian project." Thus I laid the flattering unction to my soul, little dreaming that I and mine should share in the strange adventures of this oddest of all odd creatures.

It might be made a subject of curious inquiry to those who delight in human absurdities, if ever there were a character drawn in works of fiction so extravagantly ridiculous as some which daily experience presents to our view. We have encountered people in the broad thoroughfares of life more eccentric than ever we read of in books; people who, if all their foolish sayings and doings were duly recorded, would vie with the drollest creations of Hood,[4] or George Colman,[5] and put to shame the flights of Baron Munchausen.[6] Not that Tom Wilson was a romancer; oh, no! He was the very prose of prose, a man in a mist, who seemed afraid of moving about for fear of knocking his head against a tree, and finding a halter suspended to its branches—a man as helpless and as indolent as a baby.

Mr. Thomas, or Tom Wilson, as he was familiarly called by all his friends and acquaintances, was the son of a gentleman, who once possessed a large landed property in the neighbourhood; but an extravagant and profligate expenditure of the income which he derived from a fine estate which had descended from father to son through many generations, had greatly reduced the circumstances of the elder Wilson. Still, his family held a certain rank and standing in their native county, of which his evil courses, bad as they were, could not wholly deprive them. The young people—and a very large family they made of sons and daughters, twelve in number—were objects of interest and commiseration to all who knew them, while the worthless father was justly held in contempt and detestation. Our hero was the youngest of the six sons; and from his childhood he was famous for his nothing-to-doishness. He was too indolent to engage heart and soul in the manly sports of his comrades; and he never thought it necessary to commence learning his lessons until the school had been in an hour. As he grew up to man's estate, he might be seen dawdling about in a black frockcoat, jean trousers, and white kid gloves, making lazy bows to the pretty girls of his acquaintance; or dressed in a green shooting-jacket, with a gun across his shoulder, sauntering down the wooded lanes, with a brown spaniel dodging at his heels, and looking as sleepy and indolent as his master.

The slowness of all Tom's movements was strangely contrasted with his slight, elegant, and symmetrical figure; that looked as if it only

4. Thomas Hood (1799–1845), one of the most popular English humorists of the day and a regular contributor to magazines and annuals.
5. George Colman (1762–1836), a leading playwright in the English theater; his *John Bull* (1803) was a popular five-act comedy.
6. Baron Karl Friedrich Hieronymus von Münchhausen (1720–1797) was the source of Rudolf Erich Raspe's *Baron Münchausen's Narrative of His Marvellous Travels and Campaigns in Russia* (1785), a set of tall tales that was a favorite of the Strickland girls.

awaited the will of the owner to be the most active piece of human machinery that ever responded to the impulses of youth and health. But then, his face! What pencil could faithfully delineate features at once so comical and lugubrious—features that one moment expressed the most solemn seriousness, and the next, the most grotesque and absurd abandonment to mirth? In him, all extremes appeared to meet; the man was a contradiction to himself. Tom was a person of few words, and so intensely lazy that it required a strong effort of will to enable him to answer the questions of inquiring friends; and when at length aroused to exercise his colloquial powers, he performed the task in so original a manner that it never failed to upset the gravity of the interrogator. When he raised his large, prominent, leaden-coloured eyes from the ground, and looked the inquirer steadily in the face, the effect was irresistible; the laugh would come,—do your best to resist it.

Poor Tom took this mistimed merriment in very good part, generally answering with a ghastly contortion which he meant for a smile, or, if he did trouble himself to find words, with, "Well, that's funny! What makes you laugh? At me, I suppose? I don't wonder at it; I often laugh at myself."

Tom would have been a treasure to an undertaker. He would have been celebrated as a mute; he looked as if he had been born in a shroud, and rocked in a coffin. The gravity with which he could answer a ridiculous or impertinent question completely disarmed and turned the shafts of malice back upon his opponent. If Tom was himself an object of ridicule to many, he had a way of quietly ridiculing others that bade defiance to all competition. He could quiz with a smile, and put down insolence with an incredulous stare. A grave wink from those dreamy eyes would destroy the veracity of a travelled dandy for ever.

Tom was not without use in his day and generation; queer and awkward as he was, he was the soul of truth and honour. You might suspect his sanity—a matter always doubtful—but his honesty of heart and purpose, never.

When you met Tom in the streets, he was dressed with such neatness and care (to be sure it took him half the day to make his toilet), that it led many persons to imagine that this very ugly young man considered himself an Adonis; and I must confess that I rather inclined to this opinion. He always paced the public streets with a slow, deliberate tread, and with his eyes fixed intently on the ground—like a man who had lost his ideas, and was diligently employed in searching for them. I chanced to meet him one day in this dreamy mood.

"How do you do, Mr. Wilson?" He stared at me for several minutes, as if doubtful of my presence or identity.

"What was that you said?"

I repeated the question; and he answered, with one of his incredulous smiles,

"Was it to me you spoke? Oh, I am quite well, or I should not be walking here. By the way, did you see my dog?"

"How should I know your dog?"

"They say he resembles me. He's a queer dog, too; but I never could find out the likeness. Good night!"

This was at noonday; but Tom had a habit of taking light for darkness, and darkness for light, in all he did or said. He must have had different eyes and ears, and a different way of seeing, hearing, and comprehending, than is possessed by the generality of his species; and to such a length did he carry this abstraction of soul and sense, that he would often leave you abruptly in the middle of a sentence; and if you chanced to meet him some weeks after, he would resume the conversation with the very word at which he had cut short the thread of your discourse.

A lady once told him in jest that her youngest brother, a lad of twelve years old, had called his donkey Braham, in honour of the great singer of that name. Tom made no answer, but started abruptly away. Three months after, she happened to encounter him on the same spot, when he accosted her, without any previous salutation.

"You were telling me about a donkey, Miss ——, a donkey of your brother's—Braham, I think you called him—yes, Braham; a strange name for an ass! I wonder what the great Mr. Braham would say to that. Ha, ha, ha!"[7]

"Your memory must be excellent, Mr. Wilson, to enable you to remember such a trifling circumstance all this time."

"Trifling, do you call it? Why, I have thought of nothing else ever since."

From traits such as these my readers will be tempted to imagine him brother to the animal who had dwelt so long in his thoughts; but there were times when he surmounted this strange absence of mind, and could talk and act as sensibly as other folks.

On the death of his father, he emigrated to New South Wales, where he contrived to doze away seven years of his valueless existence, suffering his convict servants to rob him of everything, and finally to burn his dwelling. He returned to his native village, dressed as an Italian mendicant, with a monkey perched upon his shoulder, and playing airs of his own composition upon a hurdy-gurdy. In this disguise he sought the dwelling of an old bachelor uncle, and solicited his charity. But who that had once seen our friend Tom could ever forget him? Nature had no counterpart of one who in mind and form was alike original. The good-natured old soldier, at a glance, discovered his hopeful nephew, received him into his house with kindness, and had afforded him an asylum ever since.

One little anecdote of him at this period will illustrate the quiet love of mischief with which he was imbued. Travelling from W[rentham] to London in the stage-coach (railways were not invented in those days), he entered into conversation with an intelligent farmer who sat next him; New South Wales, and his residence in that colony, forming the leading topic. A dissenting minister who happened to be his *vis-à-vis*,

---

7. John Braham (1774–1856), a tenor and composer of great fame in England.

and who had annoyed him by making several impertinent remarks, suddenly asked him, with a sneer, how many years he had been there.

"Seven," returned Tom, in a solemn tone, without deigning a glance at his companion.

"I thought so," responded the other, thrusting his hands into his breeches pockets. "And pray, sir, what were you sent there for?"

"Stealing pigs," returned the incorrigible Tom, with the gravity of a judge. The words were scarcely pronounced when the questioner called the coachman to stop, preferring a ride outside in the rain to a seat within with a thief. Tom greatly enjoyed the hoax, which he used to tell with the merriest of all grave faces.

Besides being a devoted admirer of the fair sex, and always imagining himself in love with some unattainable beauty, he had a passionate craze for music, and played upon the violin and flute with considerable taste and execution. The sound of a favourite melody operated upon the breathing automation like magic, his frozen faculties experienced a sudden thaw, and the stream of life leaped and gambolled for a while with uncontrollable vivacity. He laughed, danced, sang, and made love in a breath, committing a thousand mad vagaries to make you acquainted with his existence.

My husband had a remarkably sweet-toned flute, and this flute Tom regarded with a species of idolatry.

"I break the Tenth Commandment, Moodie, whenever I hear you play upon that flute. Take care of your black wife," (a name he had bestowed upon the coveted treasure), "or I shall certainly run off with her."

"I am half afraid of you, Tom. I am sure if I were to die, and leave you my black wife as a legacy, you would be too much overjoyed to lament my death."

Such was the strange, helpless, whimsical being who now contemplated an emigration to Canada. How he succeeded in the speculation the sequel will show.

It was late in the evening before my husband and his friend Tom Wilson returned from Y[oxford]. I had provided a hot supper and a cup of coffee after their long walk, and they did ample justice to my care.

Tom was in unusually high spirits, and appeared wholly bent upon his Canadian expedition.

"Mr. C[attermole] must have been very eloquent, Mr. Wilson," said I, "to engage your attention for so many hours."

"Perhaps he was," returned Tom, after a pause of some minutes, during which he seemed to be groping for words in the salt-cellar, having deliberately turned out its contents upon the table-cloth. "We were hungry after our long walk, and he gave us an excellent dinner."

"But that had nothing to do with the substance of his lecture."

"It was the substance, after all," said Moodie, laughing; "and his audience seemed to think so, by the attention they paid to it during the discussion. But, come, Wilson, give my wife some account of the intellectual part of the entertainment."

"What! I—I—I—I give an account of the lecture? Why, my dear fellow, I never listened to one word of it!"

"I thought you went to Y[oxford] on purpose to obtain information on the subject of emigration to Canada?"

"Well, and so I did; but when the fellow pulled out his pamphlet, and said that it contained the substance of his lecture, and would only cost a shilling, I thought that it was better to secure the substance than endeavour to catch the shadow—so I bought the book, and spared myself the pain of listening to the oratory of the writer. Mrs. Moodie! he had a shocking delivery, a drawling, vulgar voice; and he spoke with such a nasal twang that I could not bear to look at him, or listen to him. He made such grammatical blunders, that my sides ached with laughing at him. Oh, I wish you could have seen the wretch! But here is the document, written in the same style in which it was spoken. Read it; you have a rich treat in store."

I took the pamphlet, not a little amused at his description of Mr. C[attermole], for whom I felt an uncharitable dislike.

"And how did you contrive to entertain yourself, Mr. Wilson, during his long address?"

"By thinking how many fools were collected together, to listen to one greater than the rest. By the way, Moodie, did you notice farmer Flitch?"

"No; where did he sit?"

"At the foot of the table. You must have seen him, he was too big to be overlooked. What a delightful squint he had! What a ridiculous likeness there was between him and the roast pig he was carving! I was wondering all dinner-time how that man contrived to cut up that pig; for one eye was fixed upon the ceiling, and the other leering very affectionately at me. It was very droll; was it not?"

"And what do you intend doing with yourself when you arrive in Canada?" said I.

"Find out some large hollow tree, and live like Bruin in the winter by sucking my paws. In the summer there will be plenty of mast and acorns to satisfy the wants of an abstemious fellow."

"But, joking apart, my dear fellow," said my husband, anxious to induce him to abandon a scheme so hopeless, "do you think that you are at all qualified for a life of toil and hardship?"

"*Are you?*" returned Tom, raising his large, bushy, black eyebrows to the top of his forehead, and fixing his leaden eyes steadfastly upon his interrogator, with an air of such absurd gravity that we burst into a hearty laugh.

"Now what do you laugh for? I am sure I asked you a very serious question."

"But your method of putting it is so unusual that you must excuse us for laughing."

"I don't want you to weep," said Tom; "but as to our qualifications, Moodie, I think them pretty equal. I know you think otherwise, but I will explain. Let me see; what was I going to say?—ah, I have it! You go with the intention of clearing land, and working for yourself, and doing a great deal. I have tried that before in New South Wales, and I know that it won't answer. Gentlemen can't work like labourers, and if they could, they won't—it is not in them, and that you will find out. You expect, by going to Canada, to make your fortune, or at least secure a comfortable independence. I anticipate no such results; yet I mean to go, partly out of a whim, partly to satisfy my curiosity whether it is a better country than New South Wales; and lastly, in the hope of bettering my condition in a small way, which at present is so bad that it can scarcely be worse. I mean to purchase a farm with the three hundred pounds I received last week from the sale of my father's property; and if the Canadian soil yields only half what Mr. C[attermole] says it does, I need not starve. But the refined habits in which you have been brought up, and your unfortunate literary propensities—(I say unfortunate, because you will seldom meet people in a colony who can or will sympathise with you in these pursuits)—they will make you an object of mistrust and envy to those who cannot appreciate them, and will be a source of constant mortification and disappointment to yourself. Thank God! I have no literary propensities; but in spite of the latter advantage, in all probability I shall make no exertion at all; so that your energy, damped by disgust and disappointment, and my laziness, will end in the same thing, and we shall both return like bad pennies to our native shores. But, as I have neither wife nor child to involve in my failure, I think, without much self-flattery, that my prospects are better than yours."

This was the longest speech I ever heard Tom utter; and, evidently astonished at himself, he sprang abruptly from the table, overset a cup of coffee into my lap, and wishing us *good day* (it was eleven o'clock at night), he ran out of the house.

There was more truth in poor Tom's words than at that moment we were willing to allow; for youth and hope were on our side in those days, and we were most ready to believe the suggestions of the latter.

My husband finally determined to emigrate to Canada, and in the hurry and bustle of a sudden preparation to depart, Tom and his affairs for a while were forgotten.

How dark and heavily did that frightful anticipation weigh upon my heart! As the time for our departure drew near, the thought of leaving my friends and native land became so intensely painful that it haunted me even in sleep. I seldom awoke without finding my pillow wet with tears. The glory of May was upon the earth—of an English May. The woods were bursting into leaf, the meadows and hedge-rows were flushed with flowers, and every grove and copsewood echoed to the warblings of birds and the humming of bees. To leave England at all was dreadful—to leave her at such a season was doubly so. I went to take a last look at the old Hall,[8] the beloved home of my childhood and youth; to wander once more beneath the shade of its venerable oaks—

8. Reydon Hall, which Thomas Strickland purchased in 1808, was home to Susanna for most of her childhood and youth. An Elizabethan manor house near the village of Reydon, it had impressive lawns and was the center of a set of tenant farms. It remained in Susanna's mother's possession until 1865. Reydon was about a mile and a half from the coastal town of Southwold, where Susanna, John and their daughter Katie (born February 14, 1832) were renting accommodations while they made their future plans.

to rest once more upon the velvet sward that carpeted their roots. It was while reposing beneath those noble trees that I had first indulged in those delicious dreams which are a foretaste of the enjoyments of the spirit-land. In them the soul breathes forth its aspirations in a language unknown to common minds; and that language is *Poetry*. Here annually, from year to year, I had renewed my friendship with the first primroses and violets, and listened with the untiring ear of love to the spring roundelay of the blackbird, whistled from among his bower of May blossoms. Here, I had discoursed sweet words to the tinkling brook, and learned from the melody of waters the music of natural sounds. In these beloved solitudes all the holy emotions which stir the human heart in its depths had been freely poured forth, and found a response in the harmonious voice of Nature, bearing aloft the choral song of earth to the throne of the Creator.

How hard it was to tear myself from scenes endeared to me by the most beautiful and sorrowful recollections, let those who have loved and suffered as I did, say. However the world had frowned upon me, Nature, arrayed in her green loveliness, had ever smiled upon me like an indulgent mother, holding out her loving arms to enfold to her bosom her erring but devoted child.

Dear, dear England! why was I forced by a stern necessity to leave you? What heinous crime had I committed, that I, who adored you, should be torn from your sacred bosom, to pine out my joyless existence in a foreign clime? Oh, that I might be permitted to return and die upon your wave-encircled shores, and rest my weary head and heart beneath your daisy-covered sod at last! Ah, these are vain outbursts of feeling—melancholy relapses of the spring home-sickness! Canada! thou art a noble, free, and rising country—the great fostering mother of the orphans of civilisation. The offspring of Britain, thou must be great, and I will and do love thee, land of my adoption, and of my children's birth; and, oh, dearer still to a mother's heart—land of their graves![9]

Whilst talking over our coming separation with my sister C[atharine],[1] we observed Tom Wilson walking slowly up the path that led to the house. He was dressed in a new shooting-jacket, with his gun lying carelessly across his shoulder, and an ugly pointer dog following at a little distance.

"Well, Mrs. Moodie, I am off," said Tom, shaking hands with my sister instead of me. "I suppose I shall see Moodie in London. What do you think of my dog?" patting him affectionately.

"I think him an ugly beast," said C[atharine]. "Do you mean to take him with you?"

9. By the time Susanna wrote *Roughing It in the Bush*, she had buried two of her seven children. George Arthur died in 1840 in Belleville two weeks after his birth and, more tragically and painfully, John Strickland, whose first year is described in the book, drowned in the Moira River at Belleville in June 1844.
1. Catharine Parr Strickland (1802–1899) was two years older than Susanna and her closest friend amongst her siblings.

"An ugly beast!—Duchess a beast? Why, she is a perfect beauty!—Beauty and the beast! Ha, ha, ha! I gave two guineas for her last night." (I thought of the old adage.)[2] "Mrs. Moodie, your sister is no judge of a dog."

"Very likely," returned C[atharine], laughing. "And you go to town to-night, Mr. Wilson? I thought as you came up to the house that you were equipped for shooting."

"To be sure; there is capital shooting in Canada."

"So I have heard—plenty of bears and wolves; I suppose you take out your dog and gun in anticipation?"

"True," said Tom.

"But you surely are not going to take that dog with you?"

"Indeed I am. She is a most valuable brute. The very best venture I could take. My brother Charles[3] has engaged our passage in the same vessel."

"It would be a pity to part you," said I. "May you prove as lucky a pair as Whittington and his cat."[4]

"Whittington! Whittington!" said Tom, staring at my sister, and beginning to dream, which he invariably did in the company of women. "Who was the gentleman?"

"A very old friend of mine, one whom I have known since I was a very little girl," said my sister; "but I have not time to tell you more about him now. If you go to St. Paul's Churchyard, and inquire for Sir Richard Whittington and his cat, you will get his history for a mere trifle."

"Do not mind her, Mr. Wilson, she is quizzing you," quoth I; "I wish you a safe voyage across the Atlantic; I wish I could add a happy meeting with your friends. But where shall we find friends in a strange land?"

"All in good time," said Tom. "I hope to have the pleasure of meeting you in the backwoods of Canada before three months are over. What adventures we shall have to tell one another! It will be capital. Good-bye."

"Tom has sailed," said Captain Charles Wilson, stepping into my little parlour a few days after his eccentric brother's last visit. "I saw him and Duchess safe on board. Odd as he is, I parted with him with a full heart; I felt as if we never should meet again. Poor Tom! he is the only brother left me now that I can love. Robert and I never agreed very well, and there is little chance of our meeting in this world. He is married, and settled down for life in New South Wales; and the rest, John, Richard, George, are all gone—all!"

"Was Tom in good spirits when you parted?"

2. "A fool and his money are soon parted."
3. According to Agnes Strickland, Charles Wales committed suicide, likely in 1836 or 1837 (see NLC, PHEC, Series 1, Correspondence, No. 116, ALS, Agnes to Susanna, April 23, 1837).
4. The story of Dick Whittington's cat was a favorite among the Strickland girls. Legend has it that Richard Whittington (c. 1350–1423), a medieval merchant, became rich when his cat attracted the attention of the king, who purchased it to rid his palace of mice and rats.

"Yes. He is a perfect contradiction. He always laughs and cries in the wrong place. 'Charles,' he said, with a loud laugh, 'tell the girls to get some new music against I return: and, hark ye! if I never come back, I leave them my Kangaroo Waltz as a legacy.' "

"What a strange creature!"

"Strange, indeed; you don't know half his oddities. He has very little money to take out with him, but he actually paid for two berths in the ship, that he might not chance to have a person who snored sleep near him. Thirty pounds thrown away upon the mere chance of a snoring companion! 'Besides, Charles,' quoth he, 'I cannot endure to share my little cabin with others; they will use my towels, and combs, and brushes, like that confounded rascal who slept in the same berth with me coming from New South Wales, who had the impudence to clean his teeth with my tooth-brush. Here I shall be all alone, happy and comfortable as a prince, and Duchess shall sleep in the after-berth, and be my queen.' And so we parted," continued Captain Charles. "May God take care of him, for he never could take care of himself."

"That puts me in mind of the reason he gave for not going with us. He was afraid that my baby would keep him awake of a night. He hates children, and says that he never will marry on that account."

We left the British shores on the 1st of July, and cast anchor, as I have already shown, under the Castle of St. Lewis, at Quebec, on the 2nd of September, 1832. Tom Wilson sailed the 1st of May and had a speedy passage, and was, as we heard from his friends, comfortably settled in the bush, had bought a farm, and meant to commence operations in the fall. All this was good news, and as he was settled near my brother's location,[5] we congratulated ourselves that our eccentric friend had found a home in the wilderness at last, and that we should soon see him again.

On the 9th of September, the steam-boat *William IV.* landed us at the then small but rising town of [Cobourg], on the Ontario. The night was dark and rainy; the boat was crowded with emigrants; and when we arrived at the inn, we learnt that there was no room for us— not a bed to be had; nor was it likely, owing to the number of strangers that had arrived for several weeks, that we could obtain one by searching farther. Moodie requested the use of a sofa for me during the night; but even that produced a demur from the landlord. Whilst I awaited the result in a passage, crowded with strange faces, a pair of eyes glanced upon me through the throng. Was it possible?—could it be Tom Wilson? Did any other human being possess such eyes, or use them in such an eccentric manner? In another second he had pushed his way to my side, whispering in my ear, "We met, 'twas in a crowd."[6]

"Tom Wilson, is that you?"

---

5. Susanna's brother, Samuel Strickland, had settled in Douro Township (Lot 18, Concession 7) on the east side of Lake Katchewanook, near what is now the town of Lakefield. He encouraged his sisters, Susanna and Catharine, and their husbands, to join him there and helped them arrange land grants near his property.

6. The line is from a popular song, "We Met," by Thomas Haynes Bayly (1797–1839), whose

"Do you doubt it? I flatter myself that there is no likeness of such a handsome fellow to be found in the world. It is I, I swear!—although very little of me is left to swear by. The best part of me I have left to fatten the musquitoes and black flies in that infernal bush. But where is Moodie?"

"There he is—trying to induce Mr. S[trong],[7] for love or money, to let me have a bed for the night."

"You shall have mine," said Tom. "I can sleep upon the floor of the parlour in a blanket, Indian fashion. It's a bargain—I'll go and settle it with the Yankee directly; he's the best fellow in the world! In the meanwhile here is a little parlour, which is a joint-stock affair between some of us young hopefuls for the time being. Step in here, and I will go for Moodie; I long to tell him what I think of this confounded country. But you will find it out all in good time," and, rubbing his hands together with a most lively and mischievous expression, he shouldered his way through trunks, and boxes, and anxious faces, to communicate to my husband the arrangement he had so kindly made for us.

"Accept this gentleman's offer, sir, till to-morrow," said Mr. S[trong], "I can then make more comfortable arrangements for your family; but we are crowded—crowded to excess. My wife and daughters are obliged to sleep in a little chamber over the stable, to give our guests more room. Hard that, I guess, for decent people to locate over the horses."

These matters settled, Moodie returned with Tom Wilson to the little parlour, in which I had already made myself at home.

"Well, now, is it not funny that I should be the first to welcome you to Canada?" said Tom.

"But what are you doing here, my dear fellow?"

"Shaking every day with the ague.[8] But I could laugh in spite of my teeth to hear them make such a confounded rattling; you would think they were all quarrelling which should first get out of my mouth. This shaking mania forms one of the chief attractions of this new country."

"I fear," said I, remarking how thin and pale he had become, "that this climate cannot agree with you."

"Nor I with the climate. Well, we shall soon be quits, for, to let you into a secret, I am now on my way to England."

"Impossible!"

"It is true."

"And the farm; what have you done with it?"

"Sold it."

"And your outfit?"

lyrical poetry and songs appeared in English magazines and annuals and were often reprinted in Canadian newspapers. See *Songs of the Boudoir, The Melodies Selected and the Poetry Written by Thomas Haynes Bayly* (London, 1830). The Moodies shared Tom Wales's love of song and song lyrics.

7. An American by birth, Oren Strong was the owner of the Steamboat Hotel in Cobourg. John Moodie and Strong became good friends while the Moodies stayed at his hotel.

8. The ague or "shaking mania," spread by mosquitoes, is an intermittent malarial fever that had a devastating effect on many new emigrants to Canada.

"Sold that too."

"To whom?"

"To one who will take better care of both than I did. Ah! such a country!—such people!—such rogues! It beats Australia hollow; you know your customers there—but here you have to find them out. Such a take-in!—God forgive them! I never could take care of money; and, one way or other, they have cheated me out of all mine. I have scarcely enough left to pay my passage home. But, to provide against the worst, I have bought a young bear, a splendid fellow, to make my peace with my uncle. You must see him; he is close by in the stable."

"To-morrow we will pay a visit to Bruin; but to-night do tell us something about yourself, and your residence in the bush."

"You will know enough about the bush by-and-bye. I am a bad historian," he continued, stretching out his legs and yawning horribly, "a worse biographer. I never can find words to relate facts. But I will try what I can do; mind, don't laugh at my blunders."

We promised to be serious—no easy matter while looking at and listening to Tom Wilson, and he gave us, at detached intervals, the following account of himself:—

"My troubles began at sea. We had a fair voyage, and all that; but my poor dog, my beautiful Duchess!—that beauty in the beast—died. I wanted to read the funeral service over her, but the captain interfered—the brute!—and threatened to throw me into the sea along with the dead bitch, as the unmannerly ruffian persisted in calling my canine friend. I never spoke to him again during the rest of the voyage. Nothing happened worth relating until I got to this place, where I chanced to meet a friend who knew your brother, and I went up with him to the woods. Most of the wise men of Gotham[9] we met on the road were bound to the woods; so I felt happy that I was, at least, in the fashion. Mr. —— was very kind, and spoke in raptures of the woods, which formed the theme of conversation during our journey—their beauty, their vastness, the comfort and independence enjoyed by those who had settled in them; and he so inspired me with the subject that I did nothing all day but sing as we rode along—

"A life in the woods for me;"

until we came to the woods, and then I soon learned to sing that same, as the Irishman says, on the other side of my mouth."

Here succeeded a long pause, during which friend Tom seemed mightily tickled with his reminiscences, for he leaned back in his chair, and from time to time gave way to loud, hollow bursts of laughter.

"Tom, Tom! are you going mad?" said my husband, shaking him.

"I never was sane, that I know of," returned he. "You know that it runs in the family. But do let me have my laugh out. The woods! Ha! ha! When I used to be roaming through those woods, shooting—

9. In English fairy tales, the wise men of Gotham were simpletons. Gotham is a village in Nottingham, England.

though not a thing could I ever find to shoot, for birds and beasts are not such fools as our English emigrants—and I chanced to think of you coming to spend the rest of your lives in the woods—I used to stop, and hold my sides, and laugh until the woods rang again. It was the only consolation I had."

"Good Heavens!" said I, "let us never go to the woods."

"You will repent if you do," continued Tom. "But let me proceed on my journey. My bones were well-nigh dislocated before we got to D[ouro]. The roads for the last twelve miles were nothing but a succession of mud-holes, covered with the most ingenious invention ever thought of for racking the limbs, called corduroy bridges; not breeches, mind you,—for I thought, whilst jolting up and down over them, that I should arrive at my destination minus that indispensable covering. It was night when we got to Mr. —— 's place. I was tired and hungry, my face disfigured and blistered by the unremitting attentions of the black-flies that rose in swarms from the river.[1] I thought to get a private room to wash and dress in, but there is no such thing as privacy in this country. In the bush, all things are in common; you cannot even get a bed without having to share it with a companion. A bed on the floor in a public sleeping-room! Think of that; a public sleeping-room!—men, women, and children, only divided by a paltry curtain. Oh, ye gods! think of the snoring, squalling, grumbling, puffing; think of the kicking, elbowing, and crowding; the suffocating heat—the musquitoes, with their infernal buzzing—and you will form some idea of the misery I endured the first night of my arrival in the bush.

"But these are not half the evils with which you have to contend. You are pestered with nocturnal visitants far more disagreeable than even the musquitoes, and must put up with annoyances more disgusting than the crowded, close room. And then, to appease the cravings of hunger, fat pork is served to you three times a-day. No wonder that the Jews eschewed the vile animal; they were people of taste. Pork, morning, noon, and night, swimming in its own grease! The bishop who complained of partridges every day should have been condemned to three months' feeding upon pork in the bush; and he would have become an anchorite, to escape the horrid sight of swine's flesh for ever spread before him. No wonder I am thin; I have been starved—starved upon pritters and pork, and that disgusting specimen of unleavened bread, yclept cakes in the pan.

"I had such a horror of the pork diet, that whenever I saw the dinner in progress I fled to the canoe, in the hope of drowning upon the waters all reminiscences of the hateful banquet; but even here the very fowls of the air and the reptiles of the deep lifted up their voices, and shouted, 'Pork, pork, pork!' "

M[oodie] remonstrated with his friend for deserting the country for such minor evils as these, which, after all, he said, could easily be borne.

---

1. The Otonabee River.

"Easily borne!" exclaimed the indignant Wilson. "Go and try them; and then tell me that. I did try to bear them with a good grace, but it would not do. I offended everybody with my grumbling. I was constantly reminded by the ladies of the house that gentlemen should not come to this country without they were able to put up with a *little* inconvenience; that I should make as good a settler as a butterfly in a beehive; that it was impossible to be nice about food and *dress* in the *bush*; that people must learn to eat what they could get, and be content to be shabby and dirty, like their neighbours in the *bush*,—until that horrid word *bush* became synonymous with all that was hateful and revolting in my mind.

"It was impossible to keep anything to myself. The children pulled my books to pieces to look at the pictures; and an impudent, bare-legged Irish servant-girl took my towels to wipe the dishes with, and my clothes-brush to black the shoes—an operation which she performed with a mixture of soot and grease. I thought I should be better off in a place of my own, so I bought a wild farm that was recommended to me, and paid for it double what it was worth. When I came to examine my estate, I found there was no house upon it, and I should have to wait until the fall to get one put up, and a few acres cleared for cultivation. I was glad to return to my old quarters.

"Finding nothing to shoot in the woods, I determined to amuse myself with fishing; but Mr. —— could not always lend his canoe, and there was no other to be had. To pass away the time, I set about making one. I bought an axe, and went to the forest to select a tree. About a mile from the lake, I found the largest pine I ever saw. I did not much like to try my maiden hand upon it, for it was the first and the last tree I ever cut down. But to it I went; and I blessed God that it reached the ground without killing me in its way thither. When I was about it, I thought I might as well make the canoe big enough; but the bulk of the tree deceived me in the length of my vessel, and I forgot to measure the one that belonged to Mr. ——. It took me six weeks hollowing it out, and when it was finished, it was as long as a sloop-of-war, and too unwieldy for all the oxen in the township to draw it to the water. After all my labour, my combats with those wood-demons the black-flies, sand-flies, and musquitoes, my boat remains a useless monument of my industry. And worse than this, the fatigue I had endured while working at it late and early, brought on the ague; which so disgusted me with the country that I sold my farm and all my traps for an old song; purchased Bruin to bear me company on my voyage home; and the moment I am able to get rid of this tormenting fever, I am off."

Argument and remonstrance were alike in vain, he could not be dissuaded from his purpose. Tom was as obstinate as his bear.

The next morning he conducted us to the stable to see Bruin. The young denizen of the forest was tied to the manger, quietly masticating a cob of Indian corn, which he held in his paw, and looked half human as he sat upon his haunches, regarding us with a solemn, melancholy

air. There was an extraordinary likeness, quite ludicrous, between Tom
and the bear. We said nothing, but exchanged glances. Tom read our
thoughts.

"Yes," said he, "there is a strong resemblance; I saw it when I bought
him. Perhaps we are brothers;" and taking in his hand the chain that
held the bear, he bestowed upon him sundry fraternal caresses, which
the ungrateful Bruin returned with low and savage growls.

"He can't flatter. He's all truth and sincerity. A child of nature, and
worthy to be my friend; the only Canadian I ever mean to acknowledge as such."

About an hour after this, poor Tom was shaking with ague, which in
a few days reduced him so low that I began to think he never would
see his native shores again. He bore the affliction very philosophically,
and all his well days he spent with us.

One day my husband was absent, having accompanied Mr. S[trong]
to inspect a farm, which he afterwards purchased, and I had to get
through the long day at the inn in the best manner I could. The local
papers were soon exhausted. At that period, they possessed little or no
interest for me. I was astonished and disgusted at the abusive manner
in which they were written, the freedom of the press being enjoyed to
an extent in this province unknown in more civilised communities.

Men, in Canada, may call one another rogues and miscreants, in
the most approved Billingsgate, through the medium of the newspapers, which are a sort of safety-valve to let off all the bad feelings and
malignant passions floating through the country, without any dread of
the horsewhip. Hence it is the commonest thing in the world to hear
one editor abusing, like a pickpocket, an opposition brother; calling
him *a reptile—a crawling thing—a calumniator—a hired vendor of lies;
and his paper a smut-machine—a vile engine of corruption*, as *base* and
degraded as the *proprietor*, &c. Of this description was the paper I now
held in my hand, which had the impudence to style itself the *Reformer*[2]—not of morals or manners, certainly, if one might judge by the
vulgar abuse that defiled every page of the precious document. I soon
flung it from me, thinking it worthy of the fate of many a better production in the olden times, that of being burned by the common hangman; but, happily, the office of hangman has become obsolete in
Canada, and the editors of these refined journals may go on abusing
their betters with impunity.

Books I had none, and I wished that Tom would make his appearance, and amuse me with his oddities; but he had suffered so much
from the ague the day before that when he did enter the room to lead
me to dinner, he looked like a walking corpse—the dead among the
living! so dark, so livid, so melancholy, it was really painful to look
upon him.

"I hope the ladies who frequent the ordinary won't fall in love with

---

2. Cobourg had two highly politicized newspapers in 1832: the conservative Cobourg *Star*,
which began publication in 1830, and the newly created and antagonistic reform paper, the
Cobourg *Reformer*, edited by the Reverend James Radcliffe. Moodie found the *Reformer* reprehensible.

me," said he, grinning at himself in the miserable looking-glass that formed the case of the Yankee clock, and was ostentatiously displayed on a side-table; "I look quite killing to-day. What a comfort it is, Mrs. M[oodie], to be above all rivalry."

In the middle of dinner, the company was disturbed by the entrance of a person who had the appearance of a gentleman, but who was evidently much flustered with drinking. He thrust his chair in between two gentlemen who sat near the head of the table, and in a loud voice demanded fish.

"Fish, sir?" said the obsequious waiter, a great favourite with all persons who frequented the hotel; "there is no fish, sir. There was a fine salmon, sir, had you come sooner; but 'tis all eaten, sir."

"Then fetch me some."

"I'll see what I can do, sir," said the obliging Tim, hurrying out.

Tom Wilson was at the head of the table, carving a roast pig, and was in the act of helping a lady, when the rude fellow thrust his fork into the pig, calling out as he did so,

"Hold, sir! give me some of that pig! You have eaten among you all the fish, and now you are going to appropriate the best parts of the pig."

Tom raised his eyebrows, and stared at the stranger in his peculiar manner, then very coolly placed the whole of the pig on his plate. "I have heard," he said, "of dog eating dog, but I never before saw pig eating pig."

"Sir! do you mean to insult me?" cried the stranger, his face crimsoning with anger.

"Only to tell you, sir, that you are no gentleman. Here, Tim," turning to the waiter, "go to the stable and bring in my bear; we will place him at the table to teach this man how to behave himself in the presence of ladies."

A general uproar ensued; the women left the table, while the entrance of the bear threw the gentlemen present into convulsions of laughter. It was too much for the human biped; he was forced to leave the room, and succumb to the bear.

My husband concluded his purchase of the farm, and invited Wilson to go with us into the country and try if change of air would be beneficial to him; for in his then weak state it was impossible for him to return to England. His funds were getting very low, and Tom thankfully accepted the offer. Leaving Bruin in the charge of Tim (who delighted in the oddities of the strange English gentleman), Tom made one of our party to [Hamilton Township].

THE LAMENT OF A CANADIAN EMIGRANT.[3]

Though distant, in spirit still present to me,
My best thoughts, my country, still linger with thee;
My fond heart beats quick, and my dim eyes run o'er,

3. This poem first appeared as "Home Thoughts of an Emigrant," in Sumner Lincoln Fairfield's *North American Quarterly Magazine* 8:36 (November 1836), p. 366.

When I muse on the last glance I gave to thy shore.
The chill mists of night round thy white cliffs were curl'd,
But I felt there was no spot like thee in the world—
No home to which memory so fondly would turn,
No thought that within me so madly would burn.

But one stood beside me whose presence repress'd
The deep pang of sorrow that troubled my breast;
And the babe on my bosom so calmly reclining,
Check'd the tears as they rose, and all useless repining.
The stern voice of duty compell'd me to roam,
From country and friends—the enjoyments of home;
But faith in the future my anguish restrain'd
And my soul in that dark hour of parting sustain'd.

Bless'd Isle of the Free! I must view thee no more;
My fortunes are cast on this far distant shore;
In the depths of dark forests my soul droops her wings;
In tall boughs above me no merry bird sings;
The sigh of the wild winds—the rush of the floods—
Is the only sad music that wakens the woods.

In dreams, lovely England! my spirit still hails
Thy soft waving woodlands, thy green, daisied vales.
When my heart shall grow cold to the mother that bore me,
When my soul, dearest Nature! shall cease to adore thee,
And beauty and virtue no longer impart
Delight to my bosom, and warmth to my heart,
Then the love I have cherish'd, my country, for thee,
In the breast of thy daughter extinguish'd shall be.

Five

Our First Settlement, and the Borrowing System

To lend, or not to lend—is that the question?

"Those who go a-borrowing, go a-sorrowing," saith the old adage; and
a wiser saw never came out of the mouth of experience. I have tested
the truth of this proverb since my settlement in Canada, many, many
times, to my cost; and what emigrant has not? So averse have I ever
been to this practice, that I would at all times rather quietly submit to
a temporary inconvenience than obtain anything I wanted in this manner. I verily believe that a demon of mischief presides over borrowed
goods, and takes a wicked pleasure in playing off a thousand malicious
pranks upon you the moment he enters your dwelling. Plates and
dishes, that had been the pride and ornament of their own cupboard
for years, no sooner enter upon foreign service than they are broken;
wine-glasses and tumblers, that have been handled by a hundred careless wenches in safety, scarcely pass into the hands of your servants

when they are sure to tumble upon the floor, and the accident turns out a compound fracture. If you borrow a garment of any kind, be sure that you will tear it; a watch, that you will break it; a jewel, that you will lose it; a book, that it will be stolen from you. There is no end to the trouble and vexation arising out of this evil habit. If you borrow a horse, and he has the reputation of being the best-behaved animal in the district, you no sooner become responsible for his conduct than he loses his character. The moment that you attempt to drive him, he shows that he has a will of his own, by taking the reins into his own management, and running away in a contrary direction to the road that you wished him to travel. He never gives over his eccentric capers until he has broken his own knees, and the borrowed carriage and harness. So anxious are you about his safety, that you have not a moment to bestow upon your own. And why?—the beast is borrowed, and you are expected to return him in as good condition as he came to you.

But of all evils, to borrow money is perhaps the worst. If of a friend, he ceases to be one the moment you feel that you are bound to him by the heavy clog of obligation. If of a usurer, the interest, in this country, soon doubles the original sum, and you owe an increasing debt, which in time swallows up all you possess.

When we first came to the colony, nothing surprised me more than the extent to which this pernicious custom was carried, both by the native Canadians, the European settlers, and the lower order of Americans. Many of the latter had spied out the goodness of the land, and *borrowed* various portions of it, without so much as asking leave of the absentee owners. Unfortunately, our new home was surrounded by these odious squatters, whom we found as ignorant as savages, without their courtesy and kindness.

The place we first occupied was purchased of Mr. C[lark],[1] a merchant, who took it in payment of sundry large debts which the owner, a New England loyalist, had been unable to settle. Old Joe H[arris],[2] the present occupant, had promised to quit it with his family, at the commencement of sleighing; and as the bargain was concluded in the month of September, and we were anxious to plough for fall wheat, it was necessary to be upon the spot. No house was to be found in the immediate neighbourhood, save a small dilapidated log tenement, on an adjoining farm (which was scarcely reclaimed from the bush) that had been some months without an owner. The merchant assured us that this could be made very comfortable until such time as it suited

---

1. Charles Clark, who ran a general store in Cobourg and traded in local lands, sold the Moodies the farm near Gage's Creek. He is the subject of a detailed description by John Moodie in the sketch "The Land Jobber," in which, curiously, Moodie identifies him as Mr. Q——.

2. Joseph Harris (1794–1890) lived with his wife Hannah and several children on Lot 32, Concession 4 of Hamilton Township, the farm developed by his father, Boltus Harris, who had claimed the land in 1797 as a United Empire Loyalist from Duchess County, New York. Boltus's brother, Myndert, had been an active Loyalist, while Boltus and family seem to have remained strongly American in their sentiments and loyalties. By 1832 Joe Harris had become deeply indebted to Charles Clark and had agreed to sell the family land while maintaining a temporary "right of possession," which he used to its full advantage. His personal aim was to move north to Rice Lake, near the town of Gore's Landing. There the Harris clan became firmly established in later years. He was not "a New England loyalist" per se.

H[arris] to remove, and the owner was willing to let us have it for the *moderate* sum of four dollars a month.[3]

Trusting to Mr. C[lark]'s word, and being strangers in the land, we never took the precaution to examine this delightful summer residence before entering upon it, but thought ourselves very fortunate in obtaining a temporary home so near our own property, the distance not exceeding half-a-mile. The agreement was drawn up, and we were told that we could take possession whenever it suited us.

The few weeks that I had sojourned in the country had by no means prepossessed me in its favour. The home-sickness was sore upon me, and all my solitary hours were spent in tears. My whole soul yielded itself up to a strong and overpowering grief. One simple word dwelt for ever in my heart, and swelled it to bursting—"Home!" I repeated it waking a thousand times a day, and my last prayer before I sank to sleep was still "Home! Oh, that I could return, if only to die at home!" And nightly I did return; my feet again trod the daisied meadows of England; the song of her birds was in my ears; I wept with delight to find myself once more wandering beneath the fragrant shade of her green hedge-rows; and I awoke to weep in earnest when I found it but a dream. But this is all digression, and has nothing to do with our unseen dwelling. The reader must bear with me in my fits of melancholy, and take me as I am.

It was the 22nd September that we left the Steam-boat Hotel, to take possession of our new abode. During the three weeks we had sojourned at [Cobourg], I had not seen a drop of rain, and I began to think that the fine weather would last for ever; but this eventful day arose in clouds. Moodie had hired a covered carriage to convey the baby, the servant-maid, and myself to the farm, as our driver prognosticated a wet day; while he followed with Tom Wilson and the teams that conveyed our luggage.

The scenery through which we were passing was so new to me, so unlike anything that I had ever beheld before, that in spite of its monotonous character, it won me from my melancholy, and I began to look about me with considerable interest. Not so my English servant, who declared that the woods were frightful to look upon; that it was a country only fit for wild beasts; that she hated it with all her heart and soul, and would go back as soon as she was able.

About a mile from the place of our destination the rain began to fall in torrents, and the air, which had been balmy as a spring morning, turned as chilly as that of a November day. Hannah shivered; the baby cried, and I drew my summer shawl as closely round as possible, to protect her from the sudden change in our hitherto delightful temperature. Just then, the carriage turned into a narrow, steep path, overhung with lofty woods, and after labouring up it with considerable difficulty, and at the risk of breaking our necks, it brought us at length

---

3. The dilapidated . . . tenement was on the property claimed by either Roswell or Willard Seaton. Assessment records suggest that several farms in Concession 3 of Hamilton Township were owned at this time by the Seatons, but they may have claimed this particular property through squatters' rights.

to a rocky upland clearing, partially covered with a second growth of timber, and surrounded on all sides by the dark forest.

"I guess," quoth our Yankee driver, "that at the bottom of this 'ere swell, you'll find yourself *to hum;*" and plunging into a short path cut through the wood, he pointed to a miserable hut, at the bottom of a steep descent, and cracking his whip, exclaimed, " 'Tis a smart location that. I wish you Britishers may enjoy it."

I gazed upon the place in perfect dismay, for I had never seen such a shed called a house before. "You must be mistaken; this is not a house, but a cattle-shed, or pig-sty."

The man turned his knowing, keen eye upon me, and smiled, half-humorously, half-maliciously, as he said,

"You were raised in the old country, I guess; you have much to learn, and more, perhaps, than you'll like to know, before the winter is over."

I was perfectly bewildered—I could only stare at the place, with my eyes swimming in tears; but as the horses plunged down into the broken hollow, my attention was drawn from my new residence to the perils which endangered life and limb at every step. The driver, however, was well used to such roads, and, steering us dexterously between the black stumps, at length drove up, not to the door, for there was none to the house, but to the open space from which that absent but very necessary appendage had been removed. Three young steers and two heifers, which the driver proceeded to drive out, were quietly reposing upon the floor. A few strokes of his whip, and a loud burst of gratuitous curses, soon effected an ejectment; and I dismounted, and took possession of this untenable tenement. Moodie was not yet in sight with the teams. I begged the man to stay until he arrived, as I felt terrified at being left alone in this wild, strange-looking place. He laughed, as well he might, at our fears, and said that he had a long way to go, and must be off; then, cracking his whip, and nodding to the girl, who was crying aloud, he went his way, and Hannah and myself were left standing in the middle of the dirty floor.

The prospect was indeed dreary. Without, pouring rain; within, a fireless hearth; a room with but one window, and that containing only one whole pane of glass; not an article of furniture to be seen, save an old painted pine-wood cradle, which had been left there by some freak of fortune. This, turned upon its side, served us for a seat, and there we impatiently awaited the arrival of Moodie, Wilson, and a man whom the former had hired that morning to assist on the farm. Where they were all to be stowed might have puzzled a more sagacious brain than mine. It is true there was a loft, but I could see no way of reaching it, for ladder there was none, so we amused ourselves, while waiting for the coming of our party, by abusing the place, the country, and our own dear selves for our folly in coming to it.

Now, when not only reconciled to Canada, but loving it, and feeling a deep interest in its present welfare, and the fair prospect of its future greatness, I often look back and laugh at the feelings with which I then regarded this noble country.

When things come to the worst, they generally mend. The males of our party no sooner arrived than they set about making things more comfortable. James, our servant, pulled up some of the decayed stumps, with which the small clearing that surrounded the shanty was thickly covered, and made a fire, and Hannah roused herself from the stupor of despair, and seized the corn-broom from the top of the loaded wagon, and began to sweep the house, raising such an intolerable cloud of dust that I was glad to throw my cloak over my head, and run out of doors, to avoid suffocation. Then commenced the awful bustle of unloading the two heavily-loaded wagons. The small space within the house was soon entirely blocked up with trunks and packages of all descriptions. There was scarcely room to move, without stumbling over some article of household stuff.

The rain poured in at the open door, beat in at the shattered window, and dropped upon our heads from the holes in the roof. The wind blew keenly through a thousand apertures in the log walls; and nothing could exceed the uncomfortableness of our situation. For a long time the box which contained a hammer and nails was not to be found. At length Hannah discovered it, tied up with some bedding which she was opening out in order to dry. I fortunately spied the door lying among some old boards at the back of the house, and Moodie immediately commenced fitting it to its place. This, once accomplished, was a great addition to our comfort. We then nailed a piece of white cloth entirely over the broken window, which, without diminishing the light, kept out the rain. James constructed a ladder out of the old bits of boards, and Tom Wilson assisted him in stowing the luggage away in the loft.

But what has the picture of misery and discomfort to do with borrowing? Patience, my dear, good friends; I will tell you all about it by-and-by.

While we were all busily employed—even the poor baby, who was lying upon a pillow in the old cradle, trying the strength of her lungs, and not a little irritated that no one was at leisure to regard her laudable endeavours to make herself heard—the door was suddenly pushed open, and the apparition of a woman squeezed itself into the crowded room. I left off arranging the furniture of a bed, that had been just put up in a corner, to meet my unexpected, and at that moment, not very welcome guest. Her whole appearance was so extraordinary that I felt quite at a loss how to address her.

Imagine a girl of seventeen or eighteen years of age, with sharp, knowing-looking features, a forward, impudent carriage, and a pert, flippant voice, standing upon one of the trunks, and surveying all our proceedings in the most impertinent manner. The creature was dressed in a ragged, dirty purple stuff gown, cut very low in the neck, with an old red cotton handkerchief tied over her head; her uncombed, tangled locks falling over her thin, inquisitive face, in a state of perfect nature. Her legs and feet were bare, and, in her coarse, dirty red hands, she swung to and fro an empty glass decanter.

"What can she want?" I asked myself. "What a strange creature!"

And there she stood, staring at me in the most unceremonious manner, her keen black eyes glancing obliquely to every corner of the room, which she examined with critical exactness.

Before I could speak to her, she commenced the conversation by drawling through her nose,

"Well, I guess you are fixing here."

I thought she had come to offer her services; and I told her that I did not want a girl, for I had brought one out with me.

"How!" responded the creature, "I hope you don't take me for a help. I'd have you to know that I'm as good a lady as yourself. No; I just stepped over to see what was going on. I seed the teams pass our'n about noon, and I says to father, 'Them strangers are cum; I'll go and look arter them.' 'Yes,' says he, 'do—and take the decanter along. May be they'll want one to put their whiskey in.' 'I'm goin' to,' says I; so cum across with it, an' here it is. But, mind—don't break it—'tis the only one we have to hum; and father says 'tis so mean to drink out of green glass."

My surprise increased every minute. It seemed such an act of disinterested generosity thus to anticipate wants we had never thought of. I was regularly taken in.

"My good girl," I began, "this is really very kind—but—"

"Now, don't go to call me 'gal'—and pass off your English airs on us. We are *genuine* Yankees, and think ourselves as good—yes, a great deal better than you. I am a young lady."

"Indeed!" said I, striving to repress my astonishment. "I am a stranger in the country, and my acquaintance with Canadian ladies and gentlemen is very small. I did not mean to offend you by using the term girl; I was going to assure you that we had no need of the decanter. We have bottles of our own—and we don't drink whiskey."

"How! Not drink whiskey? Why, you don't say! How ignorant you must be! May be they have no whiskey in the old country?"

"Yes, we have; but it is not like the Canadian whiskey. But, pray take the decanter home again—I am afraid that it will get broken in this confusion."

"No, no; father told me to leave it—and there it is;" and she planted it resolutely down on the trunk. "You will find a use for it till you have unpacked your own."

Seeing that she was determined to leave the bottle, I said no more about it, but asked her to tell me where the well was to be found.

"The well!" she repeated after me, with a sneer. "Who thinks of digging wells when they can get plenty of water from the creek?[4] There is a fine water privilege not a stone's-throw from the door," and jumping off the box, she disappeared as abruptly as she had entered. We all looked at each other; Tom Wilson was highly amused, and laughed until he held his sides.

"What tempted her to bring this empty bottle here?" said Moodie. "It is all an excuse; the visit, Tom, was meant for you."

---

4. Gage's Creek, which empties into Lake Ontario, runs through the property that the Moodies bought from Joe Harris.

"You'll know more about it in a few days," said James, looking up from his work. "That bottle is not brought here for nought."

I could not unravel the mystery, and thought no more about it, until it was again brought to my recollection by the damsel herself.

Our united efforts had effected a complete transformation in our uncouth dwelling. Sleeping-berths had been partitioned off for the men; shelves had been put up for the accommodation of books and crockery, a carpet covered the floor, and the chairs and tables we had brought from [Cobourg] gave an air of comfort to the place, which, on the first view of it, I deemed impossible. My husband, Mr. Wilson, and James, had walked over to inspect the farm, and I was sitting at the table at work, the baby creeping upon the floor, and Hannah preparing dinner. The sun shone warm and bright, and the open door admitted a current of fresh air, which tempered the heat of the fire.

"Well, I guess you look smart," said the Yankee damsel, presenting herself once more before me. "You old country folks are so stiff, you must have every thing nice, or you fret. But, then, you can easily do it; you have *stacks* of money; and you can fix everything right off with money."

"Pray take a seat," and I offered her a chair, "and be kind enough to tell me your name. I suppose you must live in the neighbourhood, although I cannot perceive any dwelling near us."

"My name! So you want to know my name. I arn't ashamed of my name; 'tis Emily S[eaton].[5] I am eldest daughter to the *gentleman* who owns this house."

"What must the father be," thought I, "if he resembles the young *lady*, his daughter?"

Imagine a young lady, dressed in ragged petticoats, through whose yawning rents peeped forth, from time to time, her bare red knees, with uncombed elf-locks, and a face and hands that looked as if they had been unwashed for a month—who did not know A from B, and despised those who did. While these reflections, combined with a thousand ludicrous images, were flitting through my mind, my strange visitor suddenly exclaimed.

"Have you done with that 'ere decanter I brought across yesterday?"

"Oh, yes! I have no occasion for it." I rose, took it from the shelf, and placed it in her hand.

"I guess you won't return it empty; that would be mean, father says. He wants it filled with whiskey."

The mystery was solved, the riddle made clear. I could contain my gravity no longer, but burst into a hearty fit of laughter, in which I was joined by Hannah. Our young lady was mortally offended; she tossed the decanter from hand to hand, and glared at us with her tiger-like eyes.

"You think yourselves smart! Why do you laugh in that way?"

"Excuse me—but you have such an odd way of borrowing that I

---

5. Emily Seaton, the daughter of "Old Satan." Her father was either Roswell or Willard Seaton. Susanna clearly relished the demonic spin that local residents had applied to the Seaton family name.

cannot help it. This bottle, it seems, was brought over for your own convenience, not for mine. I am sorry to disappoint you, but I have no whiskey."

"I guess spirits will do as well; I know there is some in that keg, for I smells it."

"It contains rum for the workmen."

"Better still. I calculate when you've been here a few months, you'll be too knowing to give rum to your helps. But old country folks are all fools, and that's the reason they get so easily sucked in, and be so soon wound-up. Cum, fill the bottle, and don't be stingy. In this country we all live by borrowing. If you want anything, why just send and borrow from us."

Thinking that this might be the custom of the country, I hastened to fill the decanter, hoping that I might get a little new milk for the poor weanling child in return; but when I asked my liberal visitor if she kept cows, and would lend me a little new milk for the baby, she burst out into high disdain. "Milk! Lend milk? I guess milk in the fall is worth a York shilling a quart.[6] I cannot sell you a drop under."

This was a wicked piece of extortion, as the same article in the towns, where, of course, it was in greater request, only brought three-pence the quart.

"If you'll pay me for it, I'll bring you some to-morrow. But mind—cash down."

"And when do you mean to return the rum?" I said, with some asperity.

"When father goes to the creek." This was the name given by my neighbours to the village of P[ort Hope],[7] distant about four miles.

Day after day I was tormented by this importune creature; she borrowed of me tea, sugar, candles, starch, blueing, irons, pots, bowls—in short, every article in common domestic use—while it was with the utmost difficulty we could get them returned. Articles of food, such as tea and sugar, or of convenience, like candles, starch, and soap, she never dreamed of being required at her hands. This method of living upon their neighbours is a most convenient one to unprincipled people, as it does not involve the penalty of stealing; and they can keep the goods without the unpleasant necessity of returning them, or feeling the moral obligation of being grateful for their use. Living eight miles from C[obourg], I found these constant encroachments a heavy burden on our poor purse; and being ignorant of the country, and residing in such a lonely, out-of-the-way place, surrounded by these savages, I was really afraid of denying their requests.

6. British and American currencies were both in use in the 1830s. A York shilling, also known as a New York shilling or a Yorker, was worth about 12 and a half cents, a dollar being worth 8 shillings.

7. Located at the mouth of the Ganaraska River, the town of Port Hope was originally called Smith's Creek, then simply the Creek. It vied with Cobourg, ten miles to the east, as an important port on Lake Ontario, but it lacked Cobourg's natural waterfront advantages. The first Moodie property was four miles from Port Hope and eight from Cobourg. Nevertheless, the Moodies favored Cobourg, which they knew, while the Harrises did their business in Port Hope.

The very day our new plough came home, the father of this bright damsel, who went by the familiar and unenviable title of *Old Satan*, came over to borrow it (though we afterwards found out that he had a good one of his own). The land had never been broken up, and was full of rocks and stumps, and he was anxious to save his own from injury; the consequence was that the borrowed implement came home unfit for use, just at the very time that we wanted to plough for fall wheat. The same happened to a spade and trowel, bought in order to plaster the house. Satan asked the loan of them for *one* hour for the same purpose, and we never saw them again.

The daughter came one morning, as usual, on one of these swindling expeditions, and demanded of me the loan of some *fine slack*. Not knowing what she meant by *fine slack*, and weary of her importunities, I said I had none. She went away in a rage. Shortly after she came again for some pepper. I was at work, and my work-box was open upon the table, well stored with threads and spools of all descriptions. Miss Satan cast her hawk's eye into it, and burst out in her usual rude manner,

"I guess you told me a tarnation big lie the other day."

Unaccustomed to such language, I rose from my seat, and pointing to the door, told her to walk out, as I did not choose to be insulted in my own house.

"Your house! I'm sure it's father's," returned the incorrigible wretch. "You told me that you had no *fine slack*, and you have *stacks* of it."

"What is fine slack?" said I, very pettishly.

"The stuff that's wound upon these 'ere pieces of wood," pouncing as she spoke upon one of my most serviceable spools.

"I cannot give you that; I want it myself."

"I didn't ask you to give it. I only wants to borrow it till father goes to the creek."

"I wish he would make haste, then, as I want a number of things which you have borrowed of me and which I cannot longer do without."

She gave me a knowing look, and carried off my spool in triumph.

I happened to mention the manner in which I was constantly annoyed by these people, to a worthy English farmer who resided near us; and he fell a-laughing, and told me that I did not know the Canadian Yankees as well as he did, or I should not be troubled with them long.

"The best way," says he, "to get rid of them, is to ask them sharply what they want; and if they give you no satisfactory answer, order them to leave the house; but I believe I can put you in a better way still. Buy some small article of them, and pay them a trifle over the price, and tell them to bring the change. I will lay my life upon it that it will be long before they trouble you again."

I was impatient to test the efficacy of his scheme. That very afternoon Miss Satan brought me a plate of butter for sale. The price was three and ninepence; twice the sum, by-the-by, that it was worth.

"I have no change," giving her a dollar; "but you can bring it me to-morrow."

Oh, blessed experiment! for the value of one quarter dollar I got rid of this dishonest girl for ever; rather than pay me, she never entered the house again.

About a month after this, I was busy making an apple-pie in the kitchen. A cadaverous-looking woman, very long-faced and witch-like, popped her ill-looking visage into the door, and drawled through her nose,

"Do you want to buy a *rooster*?"

Now, the sucking-pigs with which we had been regaled every day for three weeks at the tavern, were called *roasters*; and not understanding the familiar phrases of the country, I thought she had a sucking-pig to sell.

"Is it a good one?"

"I guess 'tis."

"What do you ask for it?"

"Two Yorkers."

"That is very cheap, if it is any weight. I don't like them under ten or twelve pounds."

"Ten or twelve pounds! Why, woman, what do you mean? Would you expect a rooster to be bigger nor a turkey?"

We stared at each other. There was evidently some misconception on my part.

"Bring the roaster up; and if I like it, I will buy it, though I must confess that I am not very fond of roast pig."

"Do you call this a pig?" said my she-merchant, drawing a fine game-cock from under her cloak.

I laughed heartily at my mistake, as I paid her down the money for the bonny bird. This little matter settled, I thought she would take her departure; but that roaster proved the dearest fowl to me that ever was bought.

"Do you keep backy and snuff here?" says she, sidling close up to me.

"We make no use of those articles."

"How! Not use backy and snuff? That's oncommon."

She paused, then added in a mysterious, confidential tone,

"I want to ask you how your tea-caddy stands?"

"It stands in the cupboard," said I, wondering what all this might mean.

"I know that; but have you any tea to spare?"

I now began to suspect what sort of a customer the stranger was.

"Oh, you want to borrow some? I have none to spare."

"You don't say so. Well, now, that's stingy. I never asked anything of you before. I am poor, and you are rich; besides, I'm troubled so with the headache, and nothing does me any good but a cup of strong tea."

"The money I have just given you will buy a quarter of a pound of the best."

"I guess that isn't mine. The fowl belonged to my neighbour. She's sick; and I promised to sell it for her to buy some physic. Money!" she added, in a coaxing tone, "Where should I get money? Lord bless you!

people in this country have no money; and those who come out with
piles of it, soon lose it. But Emily S[eaton] told me that you are nation
rich, and draw your money from the old country. So I guess you can
well afford to lend a neighbour a spoonful of tea."

"Neighbour! Where do you live, and what is your name?"

"My name is Betty Fye—old Betty Fye;[8] I live in the log shanty over
the creek, at the back of your'n. The farm belongs to my eldest son.
I'm a widow with twelve sons; and 'tis—hard to scratch along."

"Do you swear?"

"Swear! What harm? It eases one's mind when one's vexed. Everybody swears in this country. My boys all swear like Sam Hill;[9] and I
used to swear mighty big oaths till about a month ago, when the
Methody parson told me that if I did not leave it off I should go to a
tarnation bad place; so I dropped some of the worst of them."

"You would do wisely to drop the rest; women never swear in my
country."

"Well, you don't say! I always heer'd they were very ignorant. Will
you lend me the tea?"

The woman was such an original that I gave her what she wanted.
As she was going off, she took up one of the apples I was peeling.

"I guess you have a fine orchard?"

"They say the best in the district."

"We have no orchard to hum, and I guess you'll want *sarce*."

"Sarce! What is sarce?"

"Not know what sarce is? You are clever! Sarce is apples cut up and
dried, to make into pies in the winter. Now do you comprehend?"

I nodded.

"Well, I was going to say that I have no apples, and that you have a
tarnation big few of them; and if you'll give me twenty bushels of your
best apples, and find me with half a pound of coarse thread to string
them upon, I will make you a barrel of sarce on shares—that is, give
you one, and keep one for myself."

I had plenty of apples, and I gladly accepted her offer, and Mrs.
Betty Fye departed, elated with the success of her expedition.

I found to my cost, that, once admitted into the house, there was no
keeping her away. She borrowed everything that she could think of,
without once dreaming of restitution. I tried all ways of affronting her,
but without success. Winter came, and she was still at her old pranks.
Whenever I saw her coming down the lane, I used involuntarily to exclaim, "Betty Fye! Betty Fye! Fye upon Betty Fye! The Lord deliver me
from Betty Fye!" The last time I was honoured with a visit from this
worthy, she meant to favour me with a very large order upon my goods
and chattels.

"Well, Mrs. Fye, what do you want *to-day*?"

"So many things that I scarce know where to begin. Ah, what a

---

8. Betty Fye is difficult to identify but may have been Betty Goheen, as several Goheen families are identified in the Assessment Records for Hamilton Township. Susanna delighted in
giving this persistent borrower a name denoting disapproval.

9. The use of "Sam Hill" as a euphemism for "Hell" or "damn" dates back to the 1830s.

thing 'tis to be poor! First, I want you to lend me ten pounds of flour to make some Johnnie cakes."

"I thought they were made of Indian meal?"

"Yes, yes, when you've got the meal. I'm out of it, and this is a new fixing of my own invention. Lend me the flour, woman, and I'll bring you one of the cakes to taste."

This was said very coaxingly.

"Oh, pray don't trouble yourself. What next?" I was anxious to see how far her impudence would go, and determined to affront her if possible.

"I want you to lend me a gown, and a pair of stockings. I have to go to Oswego[1] to see my husband's sister, and I'd like to look decent."

"Mrs. Fye, I never lend my clothes to any one. If I lent them to you, I should never wear them again."

"So much the better for me," (with a knowing grin). "I guess if you won't lend me the gown, you will let me have some black slack to quilt a stuff petticoat, a quarter of a pound of tea and some sugar; and I will bring them back as soon as I can."

"I wonder when that will be. You owe me so many things that it will cost you more than you imagine to repay me."

"Since you're not going to mention what's past, I can't owe you much. But I will let you off the tea and the sugar, if you will lend me a five-dollar bill." This was too much for my patience longer to endure, and I answered sharply,

"Mrs. Fye, it surprises me that such proud people as you Americans should condescend to the meanness of borrowing from those whom you affect to despise. Besides, as you never repay us for what you pretend to borrow, I look upon it as a system of robbery. If strangers unfortunately settle among you, their good-nature is taxed to supply your domestic wants, at a ruinous expense, besides the mortification of finding that they have been deceived and tricked out of their property. If you would come honestly to me and say 'I want these things, I am too poor to buy them myself, and would be obliged to you to give them to me,' I should then acknowledge you as a common beggar, and treat you accordingly; give or not give, as it suited my convenience. But in the way in which you obtain these articles from me, you are spared even a debt of gratitude; for you well know that the many things which you have borrowed from me will be a debt owing to the day of judgment."

"S'pose they are," quoth Betty, not in the least abashed at my lecture on honesty, "you know what the Scripture saith, 'It is more blessed to give than to receive.' "

"Ay, there is an answer to that in the same book, which doubtless you may have heard," said I, disgusted with her hypocrisy, " 'The wicked borroweth, and payeth not again.' "[2]

Never shall I forget the furious passion into which this too apt quotation threw my unprincipled applicant. She lifted up her voice and

1. A town in upstate New York.
2. Acts 20:35 and Psalm 37:21.

cursed me, using some of the big oaths temporarily discarded for *con-science* sake. And so she left me, and I never looked upon her face again.

When I removed to our own house, the history of which, and its former owner, I will give by-and-by, we had a bony, red-headed, ruffianly American squatter, who had "left his country for his country's good,"[3] for an opposite neighbour. I had scarcely time to put my house in order before his family commenced borrowing, or stealing from me. It is even worse than stealing, the things procured from you being obtained on false pretences—adding lying to theft. Not having either an oven or a cooking-stove, which at that period were not so cheap or so common as they are now, I had provided myself with a large bake-kettle as a substitute. In this kettle we always cooked hot cakes for breakfast, preferring that to the trouble of thawing the frozen bread. This man's wife was in the habit of sending over for my kettle whenever she wanted to bake, which, as she had a large family, happened nearly every day, and I found her importunity a great nuisance.

I told the impudent lad so, who was generally sent for it; and asked him what they did to bake their bread before I came.

"I guess we had to eat cakes in the pan; but now we can borrow this kettle of your'n, mother can fix bread."

I told him that he could have the kettle this time; but I must decline letting his mother have it in future, for I wanted it for the same purpose.

The next day passed over. The night was intensely cold, and I did not rise so early as usual in the morning. My servant was away at a quilting bee, and we were still in bed, when I heard the latch of the kitchen-door lifted up, and a step crossed the floor. I jumped out of bed, and began to dress as fast as I could, when Philander called out, in his well-known nasal twang,

"Missus! I'm come for the kettle."

I (*through the partition*): "You can't have it this morning. We cannot get our breakfast without it."

Philander: "Nor more can the old woman to hum," and, snatching up the kettle, which had been left to warm on the hearth, he rushed out of the house, singing, at the top of his voice,

"Hurrah for the Yankee Boys!"

When James came home for his breakfast, I sent him across to demand the kettle, and the dame very coolly told him that when she had done with it I *might* have it, but she defied him to take it out of her house with her bread in it.

One word more about this lad, Philander, before we part with him. Without the least intimation that his company would be agreeable, or even tolerated, he favoured us with it at all hours of the day, opening the door and walking in and out whenever he felt inclined. I had given

---

3. The phrase was used to describe convicts who had been relocated to Australia and was frequently attributed to one such convict, George Barrington, in 1801.

him many broad hints that his presence was not required, but he paid not the slightest attention to what I said. One morning he marched in with his hat on, and threw himself down in the rocking-chair, just as I was going to dress my baby.

"Philander, I want to attend to the child; I cannot do it with you here. Will you oblige me by going into the kitchen?"

No answer. He seldom spoke during these visits, but wandered about the room, turning over our books and papers, looking at and handling everything. Nay, I have even known him to take a lid off from the pot on the fire, to examine its contents.

I repeated my request.

Philander: "Well, I guess I sha'n't hurt the young 'un. You can dress her."

I: "But not with you here."

Philander: "Why not? We never do anything that we are ashamed of."

I: "So it seems. But I want to sweep the room—you had better get out of the dust."

I took the broom from the corner, and began to sweep; still my visitor did not stir. The dust rose in clouds; he rubbed his eyes, and moved a little nearer to the door. Another sweep, and, to escape its inflictions, he mounted the threshold. I had him now at a fair advantage, and fairly swept him out, and shut the door in his face.

Philander (*looking through the window*): "Well, I guess you did me then; but 'tis deuced hard to outwit a Yankee."

This freed me from his company, and he, too, never repeated his visit; so I found by experience, that once smartly rebuked, they did not like to try their strength with you a second time.

When a sufficient time had elapsed for the drying of my twenty bushels of apples, I sent a Cornish lad, in our employ, to Betty Fye's, to inquire if they were ready, and when I should send the cart for them.

Dan returned with a yellow, smoke-dried string of pieces, dangling from his arm. Thinking that these were a specimen of the whole, I inquired when we were to send the barrel for the rest.

"Lord, Ma'am, this is all there be."

"Impossible! All out of twenty bushels of apples?"

"Yes," said the boy, with a grin. "The old witch told me that this was all that was left of your share; that when they were fixed enough, she put them under her bed for safety, and the mice and the children had eaten them all up but this string."

This ended my dealings with Betty Fye.

I had another incorrigible borrower in the person of old Betty B——.[4] This Betty was unlike the rest of my Yankee borrowers; she was handsome in her person, and remarkably civil, and she asked for the loan of everything in such a frank, pleasant manner, that for some

---

4. Probably Eliza Bedford, who was listed in the Assessment Records as a local resident without an identified property holding.

time I hardly knew how to refuse her. After I had been a loser to a considerable extent, and declined lending her any more, she refrained from coming to the house herself, but sent in her name the most beautiful boy in the world; a perfect cherub, with regular features, blue, smiling eyes, rosy cheeks, and lovely curling auburn hair, who said, in the softest tones imaginable, that mammy had sent him, with her *compliments*, to the English lady to ask the loan of a little sugar or tea. I could easily have refused the mother, but I could not find it in my heart to say nay to her sweet boy.

There was something original about Betty B——, and I must give a slight sketch of her.

She lived in a lone shanty in the woods, which had been erected by lumberers some years before, and which was destitute of a single acre of clearing; yet Betty had plenty of potatoes, without the trouble of planting, or the expense of buying; she never kept a cow, yet she sold butter and milk; but she had a fashion, and it proved a convenient one to her, of making pets of the cattle of her neighbours. If our cows strayed from their pastures, they were always found near Betty's shanty, for she regularly supplied them with salt, which formed a sort of bond of union between them; and, in return for these little attentions, they suffered themselves to be milked before they returned to their respective owners. Her mode of obtaining eggs and fowls was on the same economical plan, and we all looked upon Betty as a sort of freebooter, living upon the property of others. She had had three husbands, and he with whom she now lived was not her husband, although the father of the splendid child whose beauty so won upon my woman's heart. Her first husband was still living (a thing by no means uncommon among persons of her class in Canada), and though they had quarrelled and parted years ago, he occasionally visited his wife to see her eldest daughter, Betty the younger, who was his child. She was now a fine girl of sixteen, as beautiful as her little brother. Betty's second husband had been killed in one of our fields by a tree falling upon him while ploughing under it. He was buried upon the spot, part of the blackened stump forming his monument. In truth, Betty's character was none of the best, and many of the respectable farmers' wives regarded her with a jealous-eye.

"I am so jealous of that nasty Betty B——," said the wife of an Irish captain in the army, and our near neighbour, to me, one day as we were sitting at work together. She was a West Indian, and a negro by the mother's side, but an uncommonly fine-looking mulatto, very passionate, and very watchful over the conduct of her husband. "Are you not afraid of letting Captain Moodie go near her shanty?"

"No, indeed; and if I were so foolish as to be jealous, it would not be of old Betty, but of the beautiful young Betty, her daughter." Perhaps this was rather mischievous on my part, for the poor dark lady went off in a frantic fit of jealousy, but this time it was not of old Betty.

Another American squatter was always sending over to borrow a small-tooth comb, which she called a *vermin destroyer*; and once the same person asked the loan of a towel, as a friend had come from the

States to visit her, and the only one she had, had been made into a best "pinny" for the child; she likewise begged a sight in the looking-glass, as she wanted to try on a new cap, to see if it were fixed to her mind. This woman must have been a mirror of neatness when compared with her dirty neighbours.

One night I was roused up from my bed for the loan of a pair of "steelyards."[5] For what purpose, think you, gentle reader? To weigh a new-born infant. The process was performed by tying the poor squalling thing up in a small shawl, and suspending it to one of the hooks. The child was a fine boy, and weighed ten pounds, greatly to the delight of the Yankee father.

One of the drollest instances of borrowing I have ever heard of was told me by a friend. A maid-servant asked her mistress to go out on a particular afternoon, as she was going to have a party of her friends, and wanted the loan of the drawing-room.

It would be endless to enumerate our losses in this way; but, fortunately for us, the arrival of an English family in our immediate vicinity drew off the attention of our neighbours in that direction, and left us time to recover a little from their persecutions.

This system of borrowing is not wholly confined to the poor and ignorant; it pervades every class of society. If a party is given in any of the small villages, a boy is sent round from house to house, to collect all the plates and dishes, knives and forks, teaspoons and candlesticks, that are presentable, for the use of the company.

During my stay at the hotel, I took a dress out of my trunk, and hung it up upon a peg in my chamber, in order to remove the creases it had received from close packing. Returning from a walk in the afternoon, I found a note upon my dressing-table, inviting us to spend the evening with a clergyman's family in the village; and as it was nearly time to dress, I went to the peg to take down my gown. Was it a dream?—the gown was gone. I re-opened the trunk, to see if I had replaced it; I searched every corner of the room, but all in vain; nowhere could I discover the thing I sought. What had become of it? The question was a delicate one, which I did not like to put to the young ladies of the truly respectable establishment; still, the loss was great, and at that moment very inconvenient. While I was deliberating on what course to pursue, Miss S[trong] entered the room.

"I guess you missed your dress," she said, with a smile.

"Do you know where it is?"

"Oh, sure. Miss L——, the dressmaker, came in just after you left. She is a very particular friend of mine, and I showed her your dress. She admired it above all things, and borrowed it, to get the pattern for Miss R——'s wedding dress. She promised to return it tomorrow."

"Provoking! I wanted it to-night. Who ever heard of borrowing a person's dress without the leave of the owner? Truly, this is a free-and-easy country!"

One very severe winter night, a neighbour borrowed of me a blan-

---

5. A portable balance device used to weigh produce and supplies.

ket—it was one of my best—for the use of a stranger who was passing the night at her house. I could not well refuse; but at that time, the world pressed me sore, and I could ill spare it. Two years elapsed, and I saw no more of my blanket; at length I sent a note to the lady, requesting it to be returned. I got a very short answer back, and the blanket, alas! worn threadbare; the borrower stating that she had sent the article, but really she did not know what to do without it, as she wanted it to cover the children's bed. She certainly forgot that I, too, had children, who wanted covering as well as her own. But I have said so much of the ill results of others' borrowing, that I will close this sketch by relating my own experience in this way.

After removing to the bush, many misfortunes befell us, which deprived us of our income, and reduced us to great poverty. In fact we were strangers, and the knowing ones took us in; and for many years we struggled with hardships which would have broken stouter hearts than ours, had not our trust been placed in the Almighty, who among all our troubles never wholly deserted us.

While my husband was absent on the frontier during the rebellions,[6] my youngest boy fell very sick,[7] and required my utmost care, both by night and day. To attend to him properly, a candle burning during the night was necessary. The last candle was burnt out; I had no money to buy another, and no fat from which I could make one. I hated borrowing; but, for the dear child's sake, I overcame my scruples, and succeeded in procuring a candle from a good neighbour, but with strict injunctions (for it was *her last*), that I must return it if I did not require it during the night.

I went home quite grateful with my prize. It was a clear moonlight night—the dear boy was better, so I told old Jenny, my Irish servant,[8] to go to bed, as I would lie down in my clothes by the child, and if he were worse I would get up and light the candle. It happened that a pane of glass was broken out of the window-frame, and I had supplied its place by fitting in a shingle; my friend Emilia S[hairp] had a large Tom-cat,[9] who, when his mistress was absent, often paid me a predatory or borrowing visit; and Tom had a practice of pushing in this wooden pane, in order to pursue his lawless depredations. I had forgotten all this, and never dreaming that Tom would appropriate such light food, I left the candle lying in the middle of the table, just under the window.

Between sleeping and waking, I heard the pane gently pushed in.

---

6. The "rebellions" of 1837 occurred in both Upper and Lower Canada. Here, seeking further examples of borrowing, Susanna shifts ahead to her time in the backwoods, which comprises Volume II of the book.

7. Susanna's third son, John Strickland Moodie, born October 16, 1838.

8. Jenny Buchanan, a loyal servant who worked for the Moodies in the backwoods and for a time in Belleville.

9. Charlotte Emilia Shairp was Susanna's closest friend during her time in the backwoods. The daughter of Major Alexander Morduant Shairp of the Royal Marines, Emilia had come to the Peterborough area in 1833 with her family and married Lieutenant Alexander Morduant Shairp who was likely her cousin. They had settled on a land grant in Douro (Lot 21, Concession 5) near the Moodies. Emilia accompanied Susanna on "The Walk to Dummer" (see p. 296).

The thought instantly struck me that it was Tom, and that, for lack of something better, he might steal my precious candle.

I sprang up from the bed, just in time to see him dart through the broken window, dragging the long white candle after him. I flew to the door, and pursued him *half* over the field, but all to no purpose. I can see him now, as I saw him then, scampering away for dear life, with his prize trailing behind him, gleaming like a silver tail in the bright light of the moon.

Ah! never did I feel more acutely the truth of the proverb, "Those that go a-borrowing go a-sorrowing," than I did that night. My poor boy awoke ill and feverish, and I had no light to assist him, or even to look into his sweet face, to see how far I dared hope that the light of day would find him better.

OH CANADA! THY GLOOMY WOODS.[1]
A Song.

Oh Canada! thy gloomy woods
  Will never cheer the heart;
The murmur of thy mighty floods
  But cause fresh tears to start
From those whose fondest wishes rest
  Beyond the distant main;
Who, 'mid the forests of the West,
  Sigh for their homes again.

I, too, have felt the chilling blight
  Their shadows cast on me,
My thought by day—my dream by night—
  Was of my own country.
But independent souls will brave
  All hardships to be free;
No more I weep to cross the wave,
  My native land to see.

But ever as a thought most bless'd,
  Her distant shores will rise,
In all their spring-tide beauty dress'd,
  To cheer my mental eyes.
And, treasured in my inmost heart,
  The friends I left behind;
But reason's voice, that bade us part,
  Now bids me be resign'd.

I see my children round me play,
  My husband's smiles approve;
I dash regretful tears away,

---

1. The poem first appeared in *The Emigrant: A Journal of Domestic News from England, Ireland, Scotland and Wales* 2:26 (July 2, 1834), p. 4. *The Emigrant*, like the *Albion*, was edited and published in New York City by Charles Sherren Bartlett.

> And lift my thoughts above:
> In humble gratitude to bless
> The Almighty hand that spread
> Our table in the wilderness,
> And gave my infants bread.

Six

Old Satan and Tom Wilson's Nose

> A nose, kind sir! Sure mother Nature,
> With all her freaks, ne'er formed this feature.
> If such were mine, I'd try and trade it,
> And swear the gods had never made it.

After reducing the log cabin into some sort of order, we contrived, with the aid of a few boards, to make a bed-closet for poor Tom Wilson, who continued to shake every day with the pitiless ague. There was no way of admitting light and air into this domicile, which opened into the general apartment, but through a square hole cut in one of the planks, just wide enough to admit a man's head through the aperture. Here we made Tom a comfortable bed on the floor, and did the best we could to nurse him through his sickness. His long, thin face, emaciated with disease, and surrounded by huge black whiskers, and a beard of a week's growth, looked perfectly unearthly. He had only to stare at the baby to frighten her almost out of her wits.

"How fond that young one is of me," he would say; "she cries for joy at the sight of me."

Among his curiosities, and he had many, he held in great esteem a huge nose, made hollow to fit his face, which his father, a being almost as eccentric as himself, had carved out of boxwood. When he slipped this nose over his own (which was no beautiful classical specimen of a nasal organ), it made a most perfect and hideous disguise. The mother who bore him never would have recognised her accomplished son.

Numberless were the tricks he played off with this nose. Once he walked through the streets of [Cobourg], with this proboscis attached to his face. "What a nose! Look at the man with the nose!" cried all the boys in the street. A party of Irish emigrants passed at the moment. The men, with the courtesy natural to their nation, forbore to laugh in the gentleman's face; but after they had passed, Tom looked back, and saw them bent half double in convulsions of mirth. Tom made the party a low bow, gravely took off his nose, and put it in his pocket.

The day after this frolic, he had a very severe fit of the ague, and looked so ill that I really entertained fears for his life. The hot fit had just left him, and he lay upon his bed bedewed with a cold perspiration, in a state of complete exhaustion.

"Poor Tom," said I, "he has passed a horrible day, but the worst is over, and I will make him a cup of coffee." While preparing it, Old Satan came in and began to talk to my husband. He happened to sit directly opposite the aperture which gave light and air to Tom's berth. This man was disgustingly ugly. He had lost one eye in a quarrel. It had been gouged out in the barbarous conflict, and the side of his face presented a succession of horrible scars inflicted by the teeth of his savage adversary. The nickname he had acquired through the country sufficiently testified to the respectability of his character, and dreadful tales were told of him in the neighbourhood, where he was alike feared and hated.

The rude fellow, with his accustomed insolence, began abusing the old country folks.

The English were great bullies, he said; they thought no one could fight but themselves; but the Yankees had whipped them, and would whip them again. He was not afear'd of them, he never was afear'd in his life.

Scarcely were the words out of his mouth, when a horrible apparition presented itself to his view. Slowly rising from his bed, and putting on the fictitious nose, while he drew his white night-cap over his ghastly and livid brow, Tom thrust his face through the aperture, and uttered a diabolical cry; then sank down upon his unseen couch as noiselessly as he had arisen. The cry was like nothing human, and it was echoed by an involuntary scream from the lips of our maid-servant and myself.

"Good God! what's that?" cried Satan, falling back in his chair, and pointing to the vacant aperture. "Did you hear it? did you see it? It beats the universe. I never saw a ghost or the devil before!"

Moodie, who had recognised the ghost, and greatly enjoyed the fun, pretended profound ignorance, and coolly insinuated that Old Satan had lost his senses. The man was bewildered; he stared at the vacant aperture, then at us in turn, as if he doubted the accuracy of his own vision. " 'Tis tarnation odd," he said; "but the women heard it too."

"I heard a sound," I said, "a dreadful sound, but I saw no ghost."

"Sure an' 't was himsel'," said my lowland Scotch girl, who now perceived the joke; "he was a seeken' to gie us puir bodies a wee fricht."

"How long have you been subject to these sort of fits?" said I. "You had better speak to the doctor about them. Such fancies, if they are not attended to, often end in madness."

"Mad!" (very indignantly) "I guess I'm not mad, but as wide awake as you are. Did I not see it with my own eyes? And then the noise—I could not make such a tarnation outcry to save my life. But be it man or devil, I don't care, I'm not afear'd," doubling his fist very undecidedly at the hole. Again the ghastly head was protruded—the dreadful eyes rolled wildly in their hollow sockets, and a yell more appalling than the former rang through the room. The man sprang from his chair, which he overturned in his fright, and stood for an instant with his one eyeball starting from his head, and glaring upon the spectre; his cheeks deadly pale; the cold perspiration streaming from his face; his lips dissevered, and his teeth chattering in his head.

"There—there—there. Look—look, it comes again!—the devil!—the
devil!"

Here Tom, who still kept his eyes fixed upon his victim, gave a
knowing wink, and thrust his tongue out of his mouth.

"He is coming!—he is coming!" cried the affrighted wretch; and
clearing the open doorway with one leap, he fled across the field at full
speed. The stream intercepted his path—he passed it at a bound,
plunged into the forest, and was out of sight.

"Ha, ha, ha!" chuckled poor Tom, sinking down exhausted on his
bed. "Oh that I had strength to follow up my advantage, I would lead
Old Satan such a chase that he should think his namesake was in
truth behind him."

During the six weeks that we inhabited that wretched cabin, we
never were troubled by Old Satan again.

As Tom slowly recovered, and began to regain his appetite, his soul
sickened over the salt beef and pork, which, owing to our distance
from [Cobourg], formed our principal fare. He positively refused to
touch the *sad* bread, as my Yankee neighbours very appropriately
termed the unleavened cakes in the pan; and it was no easy matter to
send a man on horseback eight miles to fetch a loaf of bread.

"Do, my dear Mrs. Moodie, like a good Christian as you are, give me
a morsel of the baby's biscuit, and try and make us some decent bread.
The stuff your servant gives us is uneatable," said Wilson to me, in
most imploring accents.

"Most willingly. But I have no yeast; and I never baked in one of
those strange kettles in my life."

"I'll go to old Joe's wife and borrow some," said he;[1] "they are always
borrowing of you." Away he went across the field, but soon returned. I
looked into his jug—it was empty. "No luck," said he; "those stingy
wretches had just baked a fine batch of bread, and they would neither
lend nor sell a loaf; but they told me how to make their milk-
emptyings."

"Well; discuss the same;" but I much doubted if he could remember
the recipe.

"You are to take an old tin pan," said he, sitting down on the stool,
and poking the fire with a stick.

"Must it be an old one?" said I, laughing.

"Of course; they said so."

"And what am I to put into it?"

"Patience; let me begin at the beginning. Some flour and some
milk—but, by George! I've forgot all about it. I was wondering as I
came across the field why they called the yeast *milk*-emptyings, and
that put the way to make it quite out of my head. But never mind; it is
only ten o'clock by my watch, I having nothing to do; I will go again."

He went. Would I had been there to hear the colloquy between him
and Mrs. Joe; he described it something to this effect:—

Mrs. Joe: "Well, stranger, what do you want now?"

1. Hannah Harris (1802–1883), the wife of "Uncle Joe."

Tom: "I have forgotten the way you told me how to make the bread."
Mrs. Joe: "I never told you how to make bread. I guess you are a
fool. People have to raise bread before they can bake it. Pray who sent
you to make game of me? I guess somebody as wise as yourself."
Tom: "The lady at whose house I am staying."
Mrs. Joe: "*Lady*! I can tell you that we have no *ladies* here. So the
old woman who lives in the old log shanty in the hollow don't know
how to make bread. A clever wife that! Are you her husband?" (*Tom
shakes his head.*)—"Her brother?"—(*Another shake.*)—"Her son? Do
you hear? or are you deaf?" (*Going quite close up to him.*)
Tom (*moving back*): "Mistress, I'm not deaf; and who or what I am
is nothing to you. Will you oblige me by telling me how to make the
mill-emptyings; and this time I'll put it down in my pocket-book."
Mrs. Joe (*with a strong sneer*): "Mill-emptyings! Milk, I told you. So
you expect me to answer your questions, and give back nothing in return. Get you gone; I'll tell you no more about it."
Tom (*bowing very low*): "Thank you for your *civility*. Is the old
woman who lives in the little shanty near the apple-trees more obliging?"
Mrs. Joe: "That's my husband's mother.[2] You may try. I guess she'll
give you an answer." (*Exit, slamming the door in his face.*)
"And what did you do then?" said I.
"Oh, went of course. The door was open, and I reconnoitred the
premises before I ventured in. I liked the phiz of the old woman a deal
better than that of her daughter-in-law, although it was cunning and
inquisitive, and as sharp as a needle. She was busy shelling cobs of Indian corn into a barrel. I rapped at the door. She told me to come in,
and in I stepped. She asked me if I wanted her. I told her my errand,
at which she laughed heartily."
Old woman: "You are from the old country, I guess, or you would
know how to make *milk*-emptyings. Now, I always prefer *bran*-
emptyings. They make the best bread. The milk, I opine, gives it a
sourish taste, and the bran is the least trouble."
Tom: "Then let us have the bran, by all means. How do you make
it?"
Old woman: "I put a double handful of bran into a small pot, or kettle, but a jug will do, and a teaspoonful of salt; but mind you don't kill
it with salt, for if you do, it won't rise. I then add as much warm water,
at blood-heat, as will mix it into a stiff batter. I then put the jug into a
pan of warm water, and set it on the hearth near the fire, and keep it
at the same heat until it rises, which it generally will do, if you attend
to it, in two or three hours' time. When the bran cracks at the top, and
you see white bubbles rising through it, you may strain it into your
flour, and lay your bread. It makes good bread."
Tom: "My good woman, I am greatly obliged to you. We have no
bran; can you give me a small quantity?"

---

2. Anna Noxon Harris, the estranged mother of Uncle Joe, who insisted on living by herself in
a small cabin across Gage's Creek from the main house. Joe was her only surviving child.

Old woman: "I never give anything. You Englishers, who come out with stacks of money, can afford to buy."

Tom: "Sell me a small quantity."

Old woman: "I guess I will." (*Edging quite close, and fixing her sharp eyes on him.*) "You must be very rich to buy bran."

Tom (*quizzically*): "Oh, very rich."

Old woman: "How do you get your money?"

Tom (*sarcastically*): "I don't steal it."

Old woman: "Pr'aps not. I guess you'll soon let others do that for you, if you don't take care. Are the people you live with related to you?"

Tom (*hardly able to keep his gravity*): "On Eve's side. They are my friends."

Old woman (*in surprise*): "And do they keep you for nothing, or do you work for your meat?"

Tom (*impatiently*): "Is that bran ready?" (*The old woman goes to the binn, and measures out a quart of bran.*) "What am I to pay you?"

Old woman: "A York shilling."

Tom (*wishing to test her honesty*): "Is there any difference between a York shilling and a shilling of British currency?"[3]

Old woman (*evasively*): "I guess not. Is there not a place in England called York?" (*Looking up and leering knowingly in his face.*)

Tom (*laughing*): "You are not going to come York over me in that way, or Yankee either. There is threepence for your pound of bran; you are enormously paid."

Old woman (*calling after him*): "But the recipe; do you allow nothing for the recipe?"

Tom: "It is included in the price of the bran."

"And so," said he, "I came laughing away, rejoicing in my sleeve that I had disappointed the avaricious old cheat."

The next thing to be done was to set the bran rising. By the help of Tom's recipe, it was duly mixed in the coffee-pot, and placed within a tin pan, full of hot water, by the side of the fire. I have often heard it said that a watched pot never boils; and there certainly was no lack of watchers in this case. Tom sat for hours regarding it with his large heavy eyes, the maid inspected it from time to time, and scarce ten minutes were suffered to elapse without my testing the heat of the water, and the state of the emptyings; but the day slipped slowly away, and night drew on, and yet the watched pot gave no signs of vitality. Tom sighed deeply when we sat down to tea with the old fare.

"Never mind," said he, "we shall get some good bread in the morning; it must get up by that time, I will wait till then. I could almost starve before I could touch these leaden cakes."

The tea-things were removed. Tom took up his flute, and commenced a series of the wildest voluntary airs that ever were breathed forth by human lungs. Mad jigs, to which the gravest of mankind might have cut eccentric capers. We were all convulsed with laughter.

3. See Chapter Five, note 6, p. 65.

In the midst of one of these droll movements, Tom suddenly hopped like a kangaroo (which feat he performed by raising himself upon tiptoes, then flinging himself forward with a stooping jerk), towards the hearth, and squinting down into the coffee-pot in the most quizzical manner, exclaimed, "Miserable chaff! If that does not make you rise nothing will."

I left the bran all night by the fire. Early in the morning I had the satisfaction of finding that it had risen high above the rim of the pot, and was surrounded by a fine crown of bubbles.

"Better late than never," thought I, as I emptied the emptyings into my flour. "Tom is not up yet. I will make him so happy with a loaf of new bread, nice home-baked bread, for his breakfast." It was my first Canadian loaf. I felt quite proud of it, and I placed it in the odd machine in which it was to be baked. I did not understand the method of baking in these ovens; or that my bread should have remained in the kettle for half an hour, until it had risen the second time, before I applied the fire to it, in order that the bread should be light. It not only required experience to know when it was in a fit state for baking, but the oven should have been brought to a proper temperature to receive the bread. Ignorant of all this, I put my unrisen loaf into a cold kettle, and heaped a large quantity of hot ashes above and below. The first intimation I had of the results of my experiment was the disagreeable odour of burning bread filling the house.

"What is this horrid smell?" cried Tom, issuing from his domicile, in his short sleeves. "Do open the door, Bell (*to the maid*); I feel quite sick."

"It is the bread," said I, taking off the lid of the oven with the tongs. "Dear me, it is all burnt!"

"And smells as sour as vinegar," says he. "The black bread of Sparta!"[4]

Alas! for my maiden loaf! With rueful face I placed it on the breakfast table. "I hoped to have given you a treat, but I fear you will find it worse than the cakes in the pan."

"You may be sure of that," said Tom, as he stuck his knife into the loaf, and drew it forth covered with raw dough. "Oh, Mrs. Moodie! I hope you make better books than bread."

We were all sadly disappointed. The others submitted to my failure good-naturedly, and made it the subject of many droll, but not unkindly, witticisms. For myself, I could have borne the severest infliction from the pen of the most formidable critic with more fortitude than I bore the cutting up of my first loaf of bread.

After breakfast, Moodie and Wilson rode into the town; and when they returned at night brought several long letters for me. Ah! those first kind letters from home! Never shall I forget the rapture with which I grasped them—the eager, trembling haste with which I tore them open, while the blinding tears which filled my eyes hindered me

4. Possibly a reference to Plutarch, who described in *The Ancient Customs of the Spartans* the black broth of the Spartans, a dietary component of Spartan training, which King Dionysus of Sicily spat out in disgust after it was prepared especially for him.

for some minutes from reading a word which they contained. Sixteen years have slowly passed away—it appears half a century—but never, never can home letters give me the intense joy those letters did. After seven years' exile,[5] the hope of return grows feeble, the means are still less in our power, and our friends give up all hope of our return; their letters grow fewer and colder, their expressions of attachment are less vivid; the heart has formed new ties, and the poor emigrant is nearly forgotten. Double those years, and it is as if the grave had closed over you, and the hearts that once knew and loved you know you no more.

Tom, too, had a large packet of letters, which he read with great glee. After re-perusing them, he declared his intention of setting off on his return home the next day.[6] We tried to persuade him to stay until the following spring, and make a fair trial of the country. Arguments were thrown away upon him; the next morning our eccentric friend was ready to start.

"Good-bye!" quoth he, shaking me by the hand as if he meant to sever it from the wrist. "When next we meet it will be in New South Wales, and I hope by that time you will know how to make better bread." And thus ended Tom Wilson's emigration to Canada. He brought out three hundred pounds, British currency; he remained in the country just four months, and returned to England with barely enough to pay his passage home.

THE BACKWOODSMAN.[7]

Son of the isles! rave not to me
Of the old world's pride and luxury;
Why did you cross the western deep,
Thus like a love-lorn maid to weep
O'er comforts gone and pleasures fled,
'Mid forests wild to earn your bread?

Did you expect that Art would vie
With Nature here, to please the eye;
That stately tower, and fancy cot,
Would grace each rude concession lot;
That, independent of your hearth,
Men would admit your claims to birth?

No tyrant's fetter binds the soul,
The mind of man's above control;
Necessity, that makes the slave,

5. Here Susanna Moodie places her experience and the writing of *Roughing It in the Bush* in perspective. Recalling the receipt of her first letters from home in October 1832, she thinks back on her seven-year sojourn in the bush (September 1832 to December 1839) and her entire stay in Canada. "Sixteen years" dates her drafting of the manuscript to 1848 in Belleville.

6. Having weighed the situation on the previous day, Tom Wales opted to return to England on one of the last ships leaving Cobourg before the onset of winter.

7. Originally published in *The Emigrant* (New York) 2:25 (June 25, 1834), p. 4, under the title "The Canadian Woodsman." The poem was popular among Canadian readers, reprinted at least ten times in Upper and Lower Canada between 1834 and 1843.

Has taught the free a course more brave.
With bold, determined heart to dare
The ills that all are born to share.

Believe me, youth, the truly great
Stoop not to mourn o'er fallen state;
They make their wants and wishes less,
And rise superior to distress;
The glebe they break—the sheaf they bind—
But elevates a noble mind.

Contented in my rugged cot,
Your lordly towers I envy not;
Though rude our clime and coarse our cheer,
True independence greets you here;
Amid these forests, dark and wild,
Dwells honest labour's hardy child.

His happy lot I gladly share,
And breathe a purer, freer air;
No more by wealthy upstarts spurn'd,
The bread is sweet by labour earn'd;
Indulgent heaven has bless'd the soil,
And plenty crowns the woodman's toil.

Beneath his axe, the forest yields
Its thorny maze to fertile fields;
This goodly breadth of well-till'd land,
Well purchased by his own right hand,
With conscience clear, he can bequeath
His children, when he sleeps in death.

Seven

Uncle Joe and His Family

Ay, your rogue is a laughing rogue, and not a whit the less dangerous
for the smile on his lip, which comes not from an honest heart, which
reflects the light of the soul through the eye. All is hollow and dark
within; and the contortion of the lip, like the phosphoric glow upon
decayed timber, only serves to point out the rottenness within.

Uncle Joe! I see him now before me, with his jolly red face, twinkling
black eyes, and rubicund nose. No thin, weasel-faced Yankee was he,
looking as if he lived upon 'cute ideas and speculations all his life; yet
Yankee he was by birth, ay, and in mind, too; for a more knowing fellow at a bargain never crossed the lakes to abuse British institutions
and locate himself comfortably among the despised Britishers. But,
then, he had such a good-natured, fat face, such a mischievous, mirth-
loving smile, and such a merry, roguish expression in those small, jet-

black, glittering eyes, that you suffered yourself to be taken in by him, without offering the least resistance to his impositions.

Uncle Joe's father had been a New England loyalist, and his doubtful attachment to the British government had been repaid by a grant of land in the township of H[amilton]. He was the first settler in that township, and chose his location in a remote spot, for the sake of a beautiful natural spring, which bubbled up in a small stone basin in the green bank at the back of the house.

"Father might have had the pick of the township," quoth Uncle Joe; "but the old coon preferred that sup of good water to the site of a town. Well, I guess it's seldom I trouble the spring; and whenever I step that way to water the horses, I think what a tarnation fool the old one was, to throw away such a chance of making his fortune, for such cold lap."

"Your father was a temperance man?"

"Temperance!—He had been fond enough of the whiskey bottle in his day. He drank up a good farm in the United States, and then he thought he could not do better than turn loyal, and get one here for nothing. He did not care a cent, not he, for the King of England. He thought himself as good, any how. But he found that he would have to work hard here to scratch along, and he was mightily plagued with the rheumatics, and some old woman told him that good spring water was the best cure for that; so he chose this poor, light, stony land on account of the spring, and took to hard work and drinking cold water in his old age."

"How did the change agree with him?"

"I guess better than could have been expected. He planted that fine orchard, and cleared his hundred acres, and we got along slick enough as long as the old fellow lived."

"And what happened after his death, that obliged you to part with your land?"

"Bad times—bad crops," said Uncle Joe, lifting his shoulders. "I had not my father's way of scraping money together. I made some deuced clever speculations, but they all failed. I married young, and got a large family; and the women critters ran up heavy bills at the stores, and the crops did not yield enough to pay them; and from bad we got to worse, and Mr. C[lark] put in an execution, and seized upon the whole concern. He sold it to your man for double what it cost him; and you got all that my father toiled for during the last twenty years of his life for less than half the cash he laid out upon clearing it."

"And had the whiskey nothing to do with this change?" said I, looking him in the face suspiciously.

"Not a bit! When a man gets into difficulties, it is the only thing to keep him from sinking outright. When your husband has had as many troubles as I have had, he will know how to value the whiskey bottle."

This conversation was interrupted by a queer-looking urchin of five years old, dressed in a long-tailed coat and trousers, popping his black shock head in at the door, and calling out,

"Uncle Joe!—You're wanted to hum."

"Is that your nephew?"

"No! I guess 'tis my woman's eldest son," said Uncle Joe, rising, "but they call me Uncle Joe. 'Tis a spry chap that—as cunning as a fox. I tell you what it is—he will make a smart man. Go home, Ammon, and tell your ma that I am coming."

"I won't," said the boy; "you may go hum and tell her yourself. She has wanted wood cut this hour, and you'll catch it!"

Away ran the dutiful son, but not before he had applied his forefinger significantly to the side of his nose, and, with a knowing wink, pointed in the direction of home.

Uncle Joe obeyed the signal, drily remarking that he could not leave the barn door without the old hen clucking him back.

At this period we were still living in Old Satan's log house, and anxiously looking out for the first snow to put us in possession of the good substantial log dwelling occupied by Uncle Joe and his family, which consisted of a brown brood of seven girls, and the highly-prized boy who rejoiced in the extraordinary name of Ammon.[1]

Strange names are to be found in this free country. What think you, gentle reader, of *Solomon Sly*, *Reynard Fox*, and *Hiram Dolittle*; all veritable names, and belonging to substantial yeomen? After Ammon and Ichabod, I should not be at all surprised to meet with Judas Iscariot, Pilate, and Herod. And then the female appellations!—But the subject is a delicate one, and I will forbear to touch upon it. I have enjoyed many a hearty laugh over the strange affectations which people designate here *very handsome names*. I prefer the old homely Jewish names, such as that which it pleased my godfather and godmothers to bestow upon me, to one of those high-sounding christianities, the Minervas, Cinderellas, and Almerias of Canada. The love of singular names is here carried to a marvellous extent. It was only yesterday that, in passing through one busy village, I stopped in astonishment before a tombstone headed thus:—"Sacred to the memory of *Silence* Sharman, the beloved wife of Asa Sharman." Was the woman deaf and dumb, or did her friends hope by bestowing upon her such an impossible name to still the voice of Nature, and check, by an admonitory appellative, the active spirit that lives in the tongue of woman? Truly, Asa Sharman, if thy wife was silent by name as well as by nature, thou wert a fortunate man!

But to return to Uncle Joe. He made many fair promises of leaving the residence we had bought, the moment he had sold his crops and could remove his family. We could see no interest which could be served by his deceiving us, and therefore we believed him, striving to make ourselves as comfortable as we could in the meantime in our present wretched abode. But matters are never so bad but that they may be worse. One day when we were at dinner, a waggon drove up to

---

1. A Harris family geneology lists four girls, including Pheobe (1819–1833), and Ammon, the only son, who was born in 1829. A second son named Joseph was born just before the Harrises moved to Rice Lake.

the door, and Mr. [Clark] alighted, accompanied by a fine-looking, middle-aged man, who proved to be Captain S[hea],[2] who had just arrived from Demerara with his wife and family. Mr. [Clark], who had purchased the farm of Old Satan, had brought Captain S[hea] over to inspect the land, as he wished to buy a farm, and settle in that neighbourhood. With some difficulty I contrived to accommodate the visitors with seats, and provide them with a tolerable dinner. Fortunately, Moodie had brought in a brace of fine fat partridges that morning; these the servant transferred to a pot of boiling water, in which she immersed them for the space of a minute—a novel but very expeditious way of removing the feathers, which then come off at the least touch. In less than ten minutes they were stuffed, trussed, and in the bake-kettle; and before the gentlemen returned from walking over the farm, the dinner was on the table.

To our utter consternation, Captain S[hea] agreed to purchase, and asked if we could give him possession in a week!

"Good heavens!" cried I, glancing reproachfully at Mr. [Clark], who was discussing his partridge with stoical indifference. "What will become of us? Where are we to go?"

"Oh, make yourself easy; I will force that old witch, Joe's mother, to clear out."

"But 'tis impossible to stow ourselves into that pig-sty."

"It will only be for a week or two, at farthest. This is October; Joe will be sure to be off by the first of sleighing."

"But if she refuses to give up the place?"

"Oh, leave her to me. I'll talk her over," said the knowing land speculator. "Let it come to the worst," he said, turning to my husband, "she will go out for the sake of a few dollars. By-the-by, she refused to bar the dower when I bought the place; we must cajole her out of that. It is a fine afternoon; suppose we walk over the hill, and try our luck with the old nigger?"

I felt so anxious about the result of the negotiation, that, throwing my cloak over my shoulders, and tying on my bonnet without the assistance of a glass, I took my husband's arm, and we walked forth.

It was a bright, clear afternoon, the first week in October, and the fading woods, not yet denuded of their gorgeous foliage, glowed in a mellow, golden light. A soft purple haze rested on the bold outline of the Haldemand hills, and in the rugged beauty of the wild landscape I soon forgot the purport of our visit to the old woman's log hut.

On reaching the ridge of the hill, the lovely valley in which our future home lay smiled peacefully upon us from amidst its fruitful orchards, still loaded with their rich, ripe fruit.

"What a pretty place it is!" thought I, for the first time feeling something like a local interest in the spot springing up in my heart. "How I wish those odious people would give us possession of the home which for some time has been our own!"

2. Captain Francis Shea of the 27th Regiment of Foot moved his family of twelve to Lot 30, Concession 4 of Hamilton Township in 1832. He appeared on the Hamilton Township Assessment Rolls for that property in 1833.

The log hut that we were approaching, and in which the old woman, H[arris], resided by herself—having quarrelled years ago with her son's wife—was of the smallest dimensions, only containing one room, which served the old dame for kitchen, and bed-room, and all. The open door, and a few glazed panes, supplied it with light and air; while a huge hearth, on which crackled two enormous logs—which are technically termed a front and a back stick—took up nearly half the domicile; and the old woman's bed, which was covered with an unexceptionably clean patched quilt, nearly the other half, leaving just room for a small home-made deal table, of the rudest workmanship, two basswood-bottomed chairs, stained red, one of which was a rocking-chair, appropriated solely to the old woman's use, and a spinning-wheel. Amidst this muddle of things—for small as was the quantum of furniture, it was all crowded into such a tiny space that you had to squeeze your way through it in the best manner you could—we found the old woman, with a red cotton handkerchief tied over her grey locks, hood-fashion, shelling white bush-beans into a wooden bowl. Without rising from her seat, she pointed to the only remaining chair. "I guess, miss, you can sit there; and if the others can't stand, they can make a seat of my bed."

The gentlemen assured her that they were not tired, and could dispense with seats. Mr. [Clark] then went up to the old woman, and proffering his hand, asked after her health in his blandest manner.

"I'm none the better for seeing you, or the like of you," was the ungracious reply. "You have cheated my poor boy out of his good farm; and I hope it may prove a bad bargain to you and yours."

"Mrs. H[arris]," returned the land speculator, nothing ruffled by her unceremonious greeting, "I could not help your son giving way to drink, and getting into my debt. If people will be so imprudent, they cannot be so stupid as to imagine that others can suffer for their folly."

"*Suffer!*" repeated the old woman, flashing her small, keen black eyes upon him with a glance of withering scorn. "You suffer! I wonder what the widows and orphans you have cheated would say to that? My son was a poor, weak, silly fool, to be sucked in by the like of you. For a debt of eight hundred dollars—the goods never cost you four hundred—you take from us our good farm; and these, I s'pose," pointing to my husband and me, "are the folk you sold it to. Pray, miss," turning quickly to me, "what might your man give for the place?"

"Three hundred pounds in cash."

"Poor sufferer!" again sneered the hag. "Four hundred dollars is a very *small* profit in as many weeks. Well, I guess, you beat the Yankees hollow. And pray, what brought you here to-day, scenting about you like a carrion-crow? We have no more land for you to seize from us."

Moodie now stepped forward, and briefly explained our situation, offering the old woman anything in reason to give up the cottage and reside with her son until he removed from the premises; which, he added, must be in a very short time.

The old dame regarded him with a sarcastic smile. "I guess Joe will take his own time. The house is not built which is to receive him; and he is not a man to turn his back upon a warm hearth to camp in the wilderness. You were *green* when you bought a farm of that man, without getting along with it the right of possession."

"But, Mrs. H[arris], your son promised to go out the first of sleighing."

"Wheugh!" said the old woman. "Would you have a man give away his hat and leave his own head bare? It's neither the first snow nor the last frost that will turn Joe out of his comfortable home. I tell you all that he will stay here, if it is only to plague you."

Threats and remonstrances were alike useless, the old woman remained inexorable; and we were just turning to leave the house, when the cunning old fox exclaimed, "And now, what will you give me to leave my place?"

"Twelve dollars, if you give us possession next Monday," said my husband.

"Twelve dollars! I guess you won't get me out for that."

"The rent would not be worth more than a dollar a month," said Mr. [Clark], pointing with his cane to the dilapidated walls. "Mr. Moodie has offered you a year's rent for the place."

"It may not be worth a cent," returned the woman; "for it will give everybody the rheumatism that stays a week in it—but it is worth that to me, and more nor double that just now to him. But I will not be hard with him," continued she, rocking herself to and fro. "Say twenty dollars, and I will turn out on Monday."

"I dare say you will," said Mr. [Clark], "and who do you think would be fool enough to give you such an exorbitant sum for a ruined old shed like this?"

"Mind your own business, and make your own bargains," returned the old woman, tartly. "The devil himself could not deal with you, for I guess he would have the worst of it. What do you say, sir?" and she fixed her keen eyes upon my husband, as if she would read his thoughts. "Will you agree to my price?"

"It is a very high one, Mrs. H[arris]; but as I cannot help myself, and you take advantage of that, I suppose I must give it."

" 'Tis a bargain," cried the old crone, holding out her hard, bony hard. "Come, cash down!"

"Not until you give me possession on Monday next; or you might serve me as your son has done."

"Ha!" said the old woman, laughing and rubbing her hands together; "you begin to see daylight, do you? In a few months, with the help of him," pointing to Mr. [Clark], "you will be able to go alone; but have a care of your teacher, for it's no good that you will learn from him. But will you *really* stand to your word, mister?" she added, in a coaxing tone, "if I go out on Monday?"

"To be sure I will; I never break my word."

"Well, I guess you are not so clever as our people, for they only keep it as long as it suits them. You have an honest look; I will trust you; but I will not trust him," nodding to Mr. [Clark], "he can buy and sell his word as fast as a horse can trot. So on Monday I will turn out my traps. I have lived here six-and-thirty years; 'tis a pretty place, and it vexes me to leave it," continued the poor creature, as a touch of natural feeling softened and agitated her world-hardened heart. "There is not an acre in cultivation but I helped to clear it, nor a tree in yonder orchard but I held it while my poor man, who is dead and gone, planted it; and I have watched the trees bud from year to year, until their boughs overshadowed the hut, where all my children, but Joe, were born. Yes, I came here young, and in my prime; and I must leave it in age and poverty. My children and husband are dead, and their bones rest beneath the turf in the burying-ground on the side of the hill. Of all that once gathered about my knees, Joe and his young ones alone remain. And it is hard, very hard, that I must leave their graves to be turned by the plough of a stranger."

I felt for the desolate old creature—the tears rushed to my eyes; but there was no moisture in hers. No rain from the heart could filter through that iron soil.

"Be assured, Mrs. H[arris]," said Moodie, "that the dead will be held sacred; the place will never be disturbed by me."

"Perhaps not; but it is not long that you will remain here. I have seen a good deal in my time; but I never saw a gentleman from the old country make a good Canadian farmer. The work is rough and hard, and they get out of humour with it, and leave it to their hired helps, and then all goes wrong. They are cheated on all sides, and in despair take to the whiskey bottle, and that fixes them. I tell you what it is, mister—I give you just three years to spend your money and ruin yourself; and then you will become a confirmed drunkard, like the rest."

The first part of her prophecy was only too true. Thank God! the last has never been fulfilled, and never can be.

Perceiving that the old woman was not a little elated with her bargain, Mr. [Clark] urged upon her the propriety of barring the dower.[3] At first, she was outrageous, and very abusive, and rejected all his proposals with contempt; vowing that she would meet him in a certain place below, before she would sign away her right to the property.

"Listen to reason, Mrs. H[arris]," said the land speculator. "If you will sign the papers before the proper authorities, the next time your son drives you to C[obourg], I will give you a silk gown."

"Pshaw! Buy a shroud for yourself; you will need it before I want a silk gown," was the ungracious reply.

"Consider, woman; a black silk of the best quality."

"To mourn in for my sins, or for the loss of the farm?"

"Twelve yards," continued Mr. [Clark], without noticing her rejoinder, "at a dollar a yard. Think what a nice church-going gown it will make."

"To the devil with you! I never go to church."

"I thought as much," said Mr. [Clark], winking to us. "Well, my dear madam, what will satisfy you?"

"I'll do it for twenty dollars," returned the old woman, rocking her-

---

3. Anna Harris had a legal right to a part of her husband's property. To bar the dower was to eliminate that right.

self to and fro in her chair; her eyes twinkling, and her hands moving convulsively, as if she already grasped the money so dear to her soul.

"Agreed," said the land speculator. "When will you be in town?"

"On Tuesday, if I be alive. But, remember, I'll not sign till I have my hand on the money."

"Never fear," said Mr. [Clark], as we quitted the house; then, turning to me, he added, with a peculiar smile, "That's a devilish smart woman. She would have made a clever lawyer."

Monday came, and with it all the bustle of moving, and, as is generally the case on such occasions, it turned out a very wet day. I left Old Satan's hut without regret, glad, at any rate, to be in a place of my own, however humble. Our new habitation, though small, had a decided advantage over the one we were leaving. It stood on a gentle slope; and a narrow but lovely stream, full of pretty speckled trout, ran murmuring under the little window; the house, also, was surrounded by fine fruit-trees.

I know not how it was, but the sound of that tinkling brook,[4] for ever rolling by, filled my heart with a strange melancholy, which for many nights deprived me of rest. I loved it, too. The voice of waters, in the stillness of night, always had an extraordinary effect upon my mind. Their ceaseless motion and perpetual sound convey to me the idea of life—eternal life; and looking upon them, glancing and flashing on, now in sunshine, now in shade, now hoarsely chiding with the opposing rock, now leaping triumphantly over it,—creates within me a feeling of mysterious awe of which I never could wholly divest myself.

A portion of my own spirit seemed to pass into that little stream. In its deep wailings and fretful sighs, I fancied myself lamenting for the land I had left for ever; and its restless and impetuous rushings against the stones which choked its passage, were mournful types of my own mental struggles against the strange destiny which hemmed me in. Through the day the stream still moaned and travelled on,—but, engaged in my novel and distasteful occupations, I heard it not; but whenever my winged thoughts flew homeward, then the voice of the brook spoke deeply and sadly to my heart, and my tears flowed unchecked to its plaintive and harmonious music.

In a few hours I had my new abode more comfortably arranged than the old one, although its dimensions were much smaller. The location was beautiful, and I was greatly consoled by this circumstance. The aspect of Nature ever did, and I hope ever will continue,

"To shoot marvellous strength into my heart."[5]

As long as we remain true to the Divine Mother, so long will she remain faithful to her suffering children.

4. Gage's Creek.
5. Susanna refers to a passage from the play *Wallenstein* by Friedrich Schiller (1759–1805), translated as *The Death of Wallenstein* in 1800 by Samuel Taylor Coleridge (1772–1834). In a mood of deep melancholy, Wallenstein muses on a lost friend:

   He is the star of my nativity,
   And often marvellously hath his aspect
   Shot strength into my heart.

At that period my love for Canada was a feeling very nearly allied to that which the condemned criminal entertains for his cell—his only hope of escape being through the portals of the grave.

The fall rains had commenced. In a few days the cold wintry showers swept all the gorgeous crimson from the trees; and a bleak and desolate waste presented itself to the shuddering spectator. But, in spite of wind and rain, my little tenement was never free from the intrusion of Uncle Joe's wife and children. Their house stood about a stone's throw from the hut we occupied, in the same meadow, and they seemed to look upon it still as their own, although we had literally paid for it twice over. Fine strapping girls they were, from five years old to fourteen, but rude and unnurtured as so many bears. They would come in without the least ceremony, and young as they were, ask me a thousand impertinent questions; and when I civilly requested them to leave the room, they would range themselves upon the doorstep, watching my motions, with their black eyes gleaming upon me through their tangled, uncombed locks. Their company was a great annoyance, for it obliged me to put a painful restraint upon the thoughtfulness in which it was so delightful to me to indulge. Their visits were not visits of love, but of mere idle curiosity, not unmingled with malicious hatred.

The simplicity, the fond, confiding faith of childhood, is unknown in Canada. There are no children here. The boy is a miniature man—knowing, keen, and wide awake; as able to drive a bargain and take an advantage of his juvenile companion as the grown-up, world-hardened man. The girl, a gossiping flirt, full of vanity and affectation, with a premature love of finery, and an acute perception of the advantages to be derived from wealth, and from keeping up a certain appearance in the world.

The flowers, the green grass, the glorious sunshine, the birds of the air, and the young lambs gambolling down the verdant slopes, which fill the heart of a British child with a fond ecstasy, bathing the young spirit in Elysium, would float unnoticed before the vision of a Canadian child; while the sight of a dollar, or a new dress, or a gay bonnet, would swell its proud bosom with self-importance and delight. The glorious blush of modest diffidence, the tear of gentle sympathy, are so rare on the cheek, or in the eye of the young, that their appearance creates a feeling of surprise. Such perfect self-reliance in beings so new to the world is painful to a thinking mind. It betrays a great want of sensibility and mental culture, and a melancholy knowledge of the arts of life.

For a week I was alone, my good Scotch girl having left me to visit her father. Some small baby-articles were needed to be washed, and after making a great preparation, I determined to try my unskilled hand upon the operation. The fact is, I knew nothing about the task I had imposed upon myself, and in a few minutes rubbed the skin off my wrists, without getting the clothes clean.

The door was open, as it generally was, even during the coldest winter days, in order to let in more light, and let out the smoke, which otherwise would have enveloped us like a cloud. I was so busy that I did not perceive that I was watched by the cold, heavy, dark eyes of Mrs. Joe, who, with a sneering laugh, exclaimed.

"Well, thank God! I am glad to see you brought to work at last. I hope you may have to work as hard as I have. I don't see, not I, why you, who are no better than me, should sit still all day, like a lady!"

"Mrs. H[arris]," said I, not a little annoyed at her presence, "what concern is it of yours whether I work or sit still? I never interfere with you. If you took it into your head to lie in bed all day, I should never trouble myself about it."

"Ah, I guess you don't look upon us as fellow-critters, you are so proud and grand. I s'pose you Britishers are not made of flesh and blood like us. You don't choose to sit down at meat with your helps. Now, I calculate, we think them a great deal better nor you."

"Of course," said I, "they are more suited to you than we are; they are uneducated, and so are you. This is no fault in either; but it might teach you to pay a little more respect to those who are possessed of superior advantages. But, Mrs. H[arris], my helps, as you call them, are civil and obliging, and never make unprovoked and malicious speeches. If they could so far forget themselves, I should order them to leave the house."

"Oh, I see what you are up to," replied the insolent dame; "you mean to say that if I were your help you would turn me out of your house; but I'm a free-born American, and I won't go at your bidding. Don't think I come here out of regard to you. No, I hate you all; and I rejoice to see you at the wash-tub, and I wish that you may be brought down upon your knees to scrub the floors."

This speech only caused a smile, and yet I felt hurt and astonished that a woman whom I had never done anything to offend should be so gratuitously spiteful.

In the evening she sent two of her brood over to borrow my "long iron," as she called an Italian iron. I was just getting my baby to sleep, sitting upon a low stool by the fire. I pointed to the iron upon the shelf, and told the girl to take it. She did so, but stood beside me, holding it carelessly in her hand, and staring at the baby, who had just sunk to sleep upon my lap.

The next moment the heavy iron fell from her relaxed grasp, giving me a severe blow upon my knee and foot; and glanced so near the child's head that it drew from me a cry of terror.

"I guess that was nigh braining the child," quoth Miss Amanda, with the greatest coolness, and without making the least apology. Master Ammon burst into a loud laugh. "If it had, Mandy, I guess we'd have cotched it." Provoked at their insolence, I told them to leave the house. The tears were in my eyes, for I felt certain that had they injured the child, it would not have caused them the least regret.

The next day, as we were standing at the door, my husband was greatly amused by seeing fat Uncle Joe chasing the rebellious Ammon over the meadow in front of the house. Joe was out of breath, panting and puffing like a small steam-engine, and his face flushed to deep red with excitement and passion. "You——young scoundrel!" he cried, half choked with fury, "if I catch up to you, I'll take the skin off you!"

"You——old scoundrel, you may have my skin if you can get at me," retorted the precocious child, as he jumped up upon the top of the high fence, and doubled his fist in a menacing manner at his father.

"That boy is growing too bad," said Uncle Joe, coming up to us out of breath, the perspiration streaming down his face. "It is time to break him in, or he'll get the master of us all."

"You should have begun that before," said Moodie. "He seems a hopeful pupil."

"Oh, as to that, a little swearing is manly," returned the father; "I swear myself, I know, and as the old cock crows, so crows the young one. It is not his swearing that I care a pin for, but he will not do a thing I tell him to."

"Swearing is a dreadful vice," said I, "and, wicked as it is in the mouth of a grown-up person, it is perfectly shocking in a child; it painfully tells he has been brought up without the fear of God."

"Pooh! pooh! that's all cant; there is no harm in a few oaths, and I cannot drive oxen and horses without swearing. I dare say that you can swear too when you are riled, but you are too cunning to let us hear you."

I could not help laughing outright at this supposition, but replied very quietly, "Those who practice such iniquities never take any pains to conceal them. The concealment would infer a feeling of shame; and when people are conscious of their guilt, they are in the road to improvement." The man walked whistling away, and the wicked child returned unpunished to his home.

The next minute the old woman came in. "I guess you can give me a piece of silk for a hood," said she, "the weather is growing considerable cold."

"Surely it cannot well be colder than it is at present," said I, giving her the rocking-chair by the fire.

"Wait a while; you know nothing of a Canadian winter. This is only November; after the Christmas thaw, you'll know something about cold. It is seven-and-thirty years ago since I and my man left the U-nited States. It was called the year of the great winter. I tell you, woman, that the snow lay so deep on the earth, that it blocked up all the roads, and we could drive a sleigh whither we pleased, right over the snake fences. All the cleared land was one wide white level plain; it was a year of scarcity, and we were half starved; but the severe cold was far worse nor the want of provisions. A long and bitter journey we had of it; but I was young then, and pretty well used to trouble and fatigue; my man stuck to the British government. More fool he! I was an American born, and my heart was with the true cause. But his father was English, and, says he, 'I'll live and die under their flag.' So he dragged me from my comfortable fireside to seek a home in the far Canadian wilderness. Trouble! I guess you think you have your troubles; but what are they to mine?" She paused, took a pinch of snuff, offered me the box, sighed painfully, pushed the red handkerchief from her high, narrow, wrinkled brow, and continued:—"Joe was a baby then, and I had another helpless critter in my lap—an adopted child. My sister had died from it, and I was nursing it at the same breast with my boy. Well, we had to perform a journey of four hundred miles in an ox-cart, which carried, besides me and the children, all our household stuff. Our way lay chiefly through the forest, and we made but slow progress. Oh! what a bitter cold night it was when we reached the swampy woods where the city of Rochester now stands. The oxen were covered with icicles, and their breath sent up clouds of steam. 'Nathan,'[6] says I to my man, 'you must stop and kindle a fire; I am dead with cold, and I fear the babes will be frozen.' We began looking about for a good spot to camp in, when I spied a light through the trees. It was a lone shanty, occupied by two French lumberers. The men were kind; they rubbed our frozen limbs with snow, and shared with us their supper and buffalo skins. On that very spot where we camped that night, where we heard nothing but the wind soughing amongst the trees, and the rushing of the river, now stands the great city of Rochester. I went there two years ago, to the funeral of a brother. It seemed to me like a dream. Where we foddered our beasts by the shanty fire now stands the largest hotel in the city; and my husband left this fine growing country to starve here."

I was so much interested in the old woman's narrative—for she was really possessed of no ordinary capacity, and, though rude and uneducated, might have been a very superior person under different circumstances—that I rummaged among my stores, and soon found a piece of black silk, which I gave her for the hood she required.

The old woman examined it carefully over, smiled to herself, but, like all her people, was too proud to return a word of thanks. One gift to the family always involved another.

"Have you any cotton-batting, or black sewing-silk, to give me, to quilt it with?"

"No."

"Humph!" returned the old dame, in a tone which seemed to contradict my assertion. She then settled herself in her chair, and, after shaking her foot awhile, and fixing her piercing eyes upon me for some minutes, she commenced the following list of interrogatories:—

"Is your father alive?"

"No; he died many years ago, when I was a young girl."

"Is your mother alive?"

"Yes."

"What is her name?" I satisfied her on this point.

"Did she ever marry again?"

"She might have done so, but she loved her husband too well, and preferred living single."

"Humph! We have no such notions here. What was your father?"

"A gentleman, who lived upon his own estate."

"Did he die rich?"

---

6. Presumably the familiar name of Boltus Harris.

"He lost the greater part of his property from being surety for another."

"That's a foolish business. My man burnt his fingers with that. And what brought you out to this poor country—you, who are no more fit for it than I am to be a fine lady?"

"The promise of a large grant of land, and the false statements we heard regarding it."

"Do you like the country?"

"No; and I fear I never shall."

"I thought not; for the drop is always on your cheek, the children tell me; and those young ones have keen eyes. Now, take my advice: return while your money lasts; the longer you remain in Canada the less you will like it; and when your money is all spent, you will be like a bird in a cage; you may beat your wings against the bars, but you can't get out." There was a long pause. I hoped that my guest had sufficiently gratified her curiosity, when she again commenced:—

"How do you get your money? Do you draw it from the old country, or have you it with you in cash?"

Provoked by her pertinacity, and seeing no end to her cross-questioning, I replied, very impatiently, "Mrs. H[arris], is it the custom in your country to catechise strangers whenever you meet with them?"

"What do you mean?" she said, colouring, I believe, for the first time in her life.

"I mean," quoth I, "an evil habit of asking impertinent questions."

The old woman got up, and left the house without speaking another word.

THE SLEIGH-BELLS.[7]

'Tis merry to hear, at evening time,
By the blazing hearth the sleigh-bells chime;
To know the bounding steeds bring near
The loved one to our bosoms dear.
Ah, lightly we spring the fire to raise,
Till the rafters glow with the ruddy blaze;
Those merry sleigh-bells, our hearts keep time
Responsive to their fairy chime.
Ding-dong, ding-dong o'er vale and hill,
Their welcome notes are trembling still.

'Tis he, and blithely the gay bells sound,
As glides his sleigh o'er the frozen ground;

7. Many versions have been given of this song, and it has been set to music in the States. I here give the original copy, written whilst leaning on the open door of my shanty, and watching for the return of my husband. [*Author's note.*]

The poem first appeared in *The Albion, or British, Colonial, and Foreign Weekly Gazette* (New York) 1:9 (March 2, 1833), p. 72. In writing to the editor (February 14, 1833), Susanna described it as "the first flight of my muse on Canadian shores" (see *Letters of a Lifetime*, p. 90). It was reprinted in at least ten Canadian newspapers and magazines. It also appeared in the London annual *Friendship's Offering*, edited by her friend Thomas Pringle (London: Smith and Elder, 1834), p. 96, and in a New York magazine, *The Knickerbocker*, edited by Charles Fenno Hoffman (January 1834), p. 73.

Hark! he has pass'd the dark pine wood,
He crosses now the ice-bound flood,
And hails the light at the open door
That tells his toilsome journey's o'er.
The merry sleigh-bells! My fond heart swells
And throbs to hear the welcome bells;
Ding-dong, ding-dong, o'er ice and snow,
A voice of gladness, on they go.

Our hut is small, and rude our cheer,
But love has spread the banquet here;
And childhood springs to be caress'd
By our beloved and welcome guest.
With a smiling brow his tale he tells,
The urchins ring the merry sleigh-bells;
The merry sleigh-bells, with shout and song
They drag the noisy string along;
Ding-dong, ding-dong, the father's come
The gay bells ring his welcome home.

From the cedar swamp the gaunt wolves howl,
From the oak loud whoops the felon owl;
The snow-storm sweeps in thunder past,
The forest creaks beneath the blast;
No more I list, with boding fear,
The sleigh-bells' distant chime to hear.
The merry-sleigh bells, with soothing power
Shed gladness on the evening hour.
Ding-dong, ding-dong, what rapture swells
The music of those joyous bells!

Eight

John Monaghan

Dear mother Nature! on thy ample breast
Hast thou not room for thy neglected son?
A stern necessity has driven him forth
Alone and friendless. He has naught but thee,
And the strong hand and stronger heart thou gavest,
To win with patient toil his daily bread.

A few days after the old woman's visit to the cottage, our servant James absented himself for a week,[1] without asking leave, or giving any intimation of his intention. He had under his care a fine pair of horses, a yoke of oxen, three cows, and a numerous family of pigs, besides having to chop all the fire wood required for our use. His unexpected departure caused no small trouble in the family; and when the

---

1. Likely James Noble—see "Canadian Sketches III: Our Borrowing," *The Literary Garland*, NS 5 (1847), p. 199.

truant at last made his appearance, Moodie discharged him altogether. The winter had now fairly set in—the iron winter of 1833. The snow was unusually deep, and it being our first winter in Canada, and passed in such a miserable dwelling, we felt it very severely. In spite of all my boasted fortitude—and I think my powers of endurance have been tried to the uttermost since my sojourn in this country—the rigour of the climate subdued my proud, independent English spirit, and I actually shamed my womanhood, and cried with the cold. Yes, I ought to blush at evincing such unpardonable weakness; but I was foolish and inexperienced, and unaccustomed to the yoke.

My husband did not much relish performing the menial duties of a servant in such weather, but he did not complain, and in the meantime commenced an active inquiry for a man to supply the place of the one we had lost; but at that season of the year no one was to be had.

It was a bitter, freezing night. A sharp wind howled without, and drove the fine snow through the chinks in the door, almost to the hearth-stone, on which two immense blocks of maple shed forth a cheering glow, brightening the narrow window-panes, and making the blackened rafters ruddy with the heart-invigorating blaze.

The toils of the day were over, the supper things cleared away, and the door closed for the night. Moodie had taken up his flute, the sweet companion of happier days, at the earnest request of our home-sick Scotch servant-girl, to cheer her drooping spirits by playing some of the touching national airs of the glorious mountain land, the land of chivalry and song, the heroic North. Before retiring to rest, Bell, who had an exquisite ear for music, kept time with foot and hand, while large tears gathered in her soft blue eyes.

"Ay, 'tis bonnie thae songs; but they mak' me greet, an' my puir heart is sair, sair when I think on the bonnie braes and the days o' lang syne."

Poor Bell! Her heart was among the hills, and mine had wandered far, far away to the green groves and meadows of my own fair land. The music and our reveries were alike abruptly banished by a sharp blow upon the door. Bell rose and opened it, when a strange, wild-looking lad, barefooted, and with no other covering to his head than the thick matted locks of raven blackness that hung like a cloud over his swarthy, sunburnt visage, burst into the room.

"Guidness defend us! Wha ha'e we here?" screamed Bell, retreating into a corner. "The puir callant's no cannie."[2]

My husband turned hastily round to meet the intruder, and I raised the candle from the table the better to distinguish his face; while Bell, from her hiding-place, regarded him with unequivocal glances of fear and mistrust, waving her hands to me, and pointing significantly to the open door, as if silently beseeching me to tell her master to turn him out.

"Shut the door, man," said Moodie, whose long scrutiny of the

2. A popular Scottish phrasing meaning the "poor lad" or "poor fellow" is not "gentle" or "tractable."

strange being before us seemed upon the whole satisfactory; "we shall be frozen."

"Thin, faith, sir, that's what I am," said the lad, in a rich brogue, which told, without asking, the country to which he belonged. Then stretching his bare hands to the fire, he continued, "By Jove, sir, I was never so near gone in my life!"

"Where do you come from, and what is your business here? You must be aware that this is a very late hour to take a house by storm in this way."

"Thrue for you, sir. But necessity knows no law; and the condition you see me in must plade for me. First, thin, sir, I came from the township of D[ummer], and want a masther; and next to that, bedad! I want something to ate. As I'm alive, and 'tis a thousand pities that I'm alive at all at all, for shure God Almighty never made sich a misfortunate crather afore nor since; I have had nothing to put in my head since I ran away from my ould masther, Mr. F——, yesterday at noon. Money I have none, sir; the divil a cent. I have neither a shoe to my foot nor a hat to my head, and if you refuse to shelter me the night, I must be contint to perish in the snow, for I have not a frind in the wide wurld."[3]

The lad covered his face with his hands, and sobbed aloud.

"Bell," I whispered; "go to the cupboard and get the poor fellow something to eat. The boy is starving."

"Dinna heed him, mistress, dinna credit his lees. He is ane o' those wicked Papists wha ha' just stepped in to rob and murder us."[4]

"Nonsense! Do as I bid you."

"I winna be fashed aboot him. An' if he bides here, I'll e'en flit by the first blink o' the morn."

"Isabel, for shame! Is this acting like a Christian, or doing as you would be done by?"

Bell was as obstinate as a rock, not only refusing to put down any food for the famished lad, but reiterating her threat of leaving the house if he were suffered to remain. My husband, no longer able to endure her selfish and absurd conduct, got angry in good earnest, and told her that she might please herself; that he did not mean to ask her leave as to whom he received into his house. I, for my part, had no idea that she would realise her threat. She was an excellent servant, clean, honest, and industrious, and loved the dear baby.

"You will think better of it in the morning," said I, as I rose and placed before the lad some cold beef and bread, and a bowl of milk, to which the runaway did ample justice.

---

3. John Monaghan came to Dummer Township with a family identified only as the F——s. Once he joined the Moodies in the winter of 1832–33, he stayed in their service, accompanying them to Douro in February 1834. The last sign of him is his enlistment as a private with a regiment formed in Douro Township in the wake of what was called the Mackenzie Rebellion (1837–38).

4. The tension between Protestants and Catholics was deeply antagonistic in Upper Canada, fuelled by hostilities brought over from Britain. It would remain so into the twentieth century. The Scottish servant Bell's fear of "Papists" reveals this powerful but irrational prejudice.

"Why did you quit your master, my lad?" said Moodie.

"Because I could live wid him no longer. You see, sir, I'm a poor foundling from the Belfast Asylum, shoved out by the mother that bore me, upon the wide wurld, long before I knew that I was in it. As I was too young to spake for myself intirely, she put me into a basket, wid a label round my neck, to tell the folks that my name was John Monaghan. This was all I ever got from my parents; and who or what they were, I never knew, not I, for they never claimed me; bad cess to them! But I've no doubt it's a fine illigant gintleman he was, and herself a handsome rich young lady, who dared not own me for fear of affronting the rich jintry, her father and mother. Poor folk, sir, are never ashamed of their children; 'tis all the threasure they have, sir; but my parents were ashamed of me, and they thrust me out to the stranger and the hard bread of depindence." The poor lad sighed deeply, and I began to feel a growing interest in his sad history.

"Have you been in the country long?"

"Four years, madam. You know my master, Mr. F——; he brought me out wid him as his apprentice, and during the voyage he trated me well. But the young men, his sons, are tyrants, and full of durty pride; and I could not agree wid them at all at all. Yesterday, I forgot to take the oxen out of the yoke, and Musther William tied me up to a stump, and bate me with the raw hide. Shure the marks are on my showlthers yet. I left the oxen and the yoke, and turned my back upon them all, for the hot blood was bilin' widin me; and I felt that if I stayed it would be him that would get the worst of it. No one had ever cared for me since I was born, so I thought it was high time to take care of myself. I had heard your name, sir, and I thought I would find you out; and if you want a lad, I will work for you for my kape, and a few dacent clothes."

A bargain was soon made. Moodie agreed to give Monaghan six dollars a month, which he thankfully accepted; and I told Bell to prepare his bed in a corner of the kitchen. But mistress Bell thought fit to rebel. Having been guilty of one act of insubordination, she determined to be consistent, and throw off the yoke altogether. She declared that she would do no such thing; that her life and that all our lives were in danger; and that she would never stay another night under the same roof with that Papist vagabond.

"Papist!" cried the indignant lad, his dark eyes flashing fire, "I'm no Papist, but a Protestant like yourself; and I hope a deuced dale better Christian. You take me for a thief; yet shure a thief would have waited till you were all in bed and asleep, and not stepped in forenint you all in this fashion."

There was both truth and nature in the lad's argument; but Bell like an obstinate woman as she was, chose to adhere to her own opinion. Nay, she even carried her absurd prejudices so far that she brought her mattress and laid it down on the floor in my room, for fear that the Irish vagabond should murder her during the night. By the break of day she was off; leaving me for the rest of the winter without a servant. Monaghan did all in his power to supply her place; he lighted the fires, swept the house, milked the cows, nursed the baby, and often cooked the dinner for me, and endeavoured by a thousand little attentions to show the gratitude he really felt for our kindness. To little Katie he attached himself in an extraordinary manner. All his spare time he spent in making little sleighs and toys for her, or in dragging her in the said sleighs up and down the steep hills in front of the house, wrapped up in a blanket. Of a night, he cooked her mess of bread and milk, as she sat by the fire, and his greatest delight was to feed her himself. After this operation was over, he would carry her round the floor on his back, and sing her songs in native Irish. Katie always greeted his return from the woods with a scream of joy, holding up her fair arms to clasp the neck of her dark favourite.

"Now the Lord love you for a darlint!" he would cry, as he caught her to his heart. "Shure you are the only one of the crathers he ever made who can love poor John Monaghan. Brothers and sisters I have none—I stand alone in the wurld, and your bonny wee face is the sweetest thing it contains for me. Och, jewil! I could lay down my life for you, and be proud to do that same."

Though careless and reckless about everything that concerned himself, John was honest and true. He loved us for the compassion we had shown him; and he would have resented any injury offered to our persons with his best blood.

But if we were pleased with our new servant, Uncle Joe and his family were not, and they commenced a series of petty persecutions that annoyed him greatly, and kindled into a flame all the fiery particles of his irritable nature.

Moodie had purchased several tons of hay of a neighbouring farmer, for the use of his cattle, and it had to be stowed into the same barn with some flax and straw that belonged to Uncle Joe. Going early one morning to fodder the cattle, John found Uncle Joe feeding his cows with his master's hay, and as it had diminished greatly in a very short time, he accused him in no measured terms of being the thief. The other very coolly replied that he had taken a little of the hay in order to repay himself for his flax, that Monaghan had stolen for the oxen. "Now by the powers!" quoth John, kindling into wrath, "that is adding a big lie to a dirthy petty larceny. I take your flax, you ould villain! Shure I know that flax is grown to make linen wid, not to feed oxen. God Almighty has give the crathers a good warm coat of their own; they neither require shifts nor shirts."

"I saw you take it, you ragged Irish vagabond, with my own eyes."

"Thin yer two eyes showed you a wicked illusion. You had betther shut up yer head, or I'll give you that for an eye-salve that shall make you see thrue for the time to come."

Relying upon his great size, and thinking that the slight stripling, who, by-the-by, was all bones and sinews, was no match for him, Uncle Joe struck Monaghan over the head with the pitchfork. In a moment the active lad was upon him like a wild cat, and in spite of the difference of his age and weight, gave the big man such a thorough dressing that he was fain to roar aloud for mercy.

"Own that you are a thief and a liar, or I'll murder you!"

"I'll own to anything whilst your knee is pressing me into a pancake. Come now—there's a good lad—let me get up." Monaghan felt irresolute, but after extorting from Uncle Joe a promise never to purloin any of the hay again, he let him rise.

"For shure," he said, "he began to turn so black in the face, I thought he'd burst intirely."

The fat man neither forgot nor forgave this injury; and though he dared not attack John personally, he set the children to insult and affront him upon all occasions. The boy was without socks, and I sent him to old Mrs. H[arris], to inquire of her what she would charge for knitting him two pairs of socks. The reply was, a dollar. This was agreed to, and dear enough they were; but the weather was very cold, and the lad was barefooted, and there was no other alternative than either to accept her offer, or for him to go without.

In a few days, Monaghan brought them home; but I found upon inspecting them that they were old socks new-footed. This was rather too glaring a cheat, and I sent the lad back with them, and told him to inform Mrs. H[arris] that as he had agreed to give the price for new socks, he expected them to be new altogether.

The avaricious old woman did not deny the fact, but she fell to cursing and swearing in an awful manner, and wished so much evil to the lad, that, with the superstitious fear so common to the natives of his country, he left her under the impression that she was gifted with the evil eye, and was an "owld witch." He never went out of the yard with the waggon and horses, but she rushed to the door, and cursed him for a bare-heeled Irish blackguard, and wished that he might overturn the waggon, kill the horses, and break his own worthless neck.

"Ma'arm," said John to me one day, after returning from C[obourg] with the team, "it would be betther for me to lave the masther intirely; for shure if I do not, some mischief will befall me or the crathers. That wicked owld wretch! I cannot thole her curses. Shure it's in purgatory I am all the while."

"Nonsense, Monaghan! you are not a Catholic, and need not fear purgatory. The next time the old woman commences her reprobate conduct, tell her to hold her tongue, and mind her own business, for curses, like chickens, come home to roost."

The boy laughed heartily at the old Turkish proverb, but did not reckon much on its efficacy to still the clamorous tongue of the ill-natured old jade. The next day he had to pass her door with the horse. No sooner did she hear the sound of the wheels, than out she hobbled, and commenced her usual anathemas.

"Bad luck to yer croaking, yer ill-conditioned owld raven. It is not me you are desthroying shure, but yer own poor miserable sinful sowl. The owld one has the grief of ye already, for 'curses, like chickens, come home to roost;' so get in wid ye, and hatch them to yerself in the chimley corner. They'll all be roosting wid ye by-and-by; and a nice warm nest they'll make for you, considering the brave brood that belongs to you."

Whether the old woman was as superstitious as John, I know not; or whether she was impressed with the moral truth of the proverb—for, as I have before stated, she was no fool—is difficult to tell; but she shrunk back into her den, and never attacked the lad again.

Poor John bore no malice in his heart, not he; for, in spite of all the ill-natured things he had to endure from Uncle Joe and his family, he never attempted to return evil for evil. In proof of this, he was one day chopping firewood in the bush, at some distance from Joe, who was engaged in the same employment with another man. A tree in falling caught upon another, which, although a very large maple, was hollow, and very much decayed, and liable to be blown down by the least shock of the wind. The tree hung directly over the path that Uncle Joe was obliged to traverse daily with his team. He looked up, and perceived, from the situation it occupied, that it was necessary for his own safety to cut it down; but he lacked courage to undertake so hazardous a job, which might be attended, if the supporting tree gave way during the operation, with very serious consequences. In a careless tone, he called to his companion to cut down the tree.

"Do it yourself, H[arris]," said the axe man with a grin.[5] "My wife and children want their man as much as your Hannah wants you."

"I'll not put axe to it," quoth Joe. Then, making signs to his comrade to hold his tongue, he shouted to Monaghan, "Hollo, boy! you're wanted here to cut down this tree. Don't you see that your master's cattle might be killed if they should happen to pass under it, and it should fall upon them."

"Thrue for you, Masther Joe; but your own cattle would have the first chance. Why should I risk my life and limbs, by cutting down the tree, when it was yerself that threw it so awkwardly over the other?"

"Oh, but you are a boy, and have no wife and children to depend upon you for bread," said Joe, gravely. "We are both family men. Don't you see that 'tis your duty to cut down the tree?"

The lad swung the axe to and fro in his hand, eyeing Joe and the tree alternately; but the natural kind-heartedness of the creature, and his reckless courage, overcame all idea of self-preservation, and raising aloft his slender but muscular arm, he cried out, "If it's a life that must be sacrificed, why not mine as well as another? Here goes! and the Lord have mercy on my sinful sowl!"

The tree fell, and, contrary to their expectations, without any injury to John. The knowing Yankee burst into a loud laugh. "Well, if you aren't a tarnation soft fool, I never saw one."

"What do you mane?" exclaimed John, his dark eyes flashing fire. "If 'tis to insult me for doing that which neither of you dared to do, you had better not thry that same. You have just seen the strength of my spirit. You had better not thry again the strength of my arm, or, may be, you and the tree would chance to share the same fate;" and, shoul-

---

5. Likely Ned Layton, who was a friend of Joe Harris. The Hamilton Township Assessment Rolls list him as William Laytham, the owner of Lot 20, Concession 9. He had served as a private in the 83rd Regiment of Foot in the War of 1812 and received his land for his services. See Chapter Ten, note 2, p. 116 and Chapter Nine, note 3, p. 110.

dering his axe, the boy strode down the hill, to get scolded by me for his foolhardiness.

The first week in March, all the people were busy making maple sugar. "Did you ever taste any maple sugar, ma'arm?" asked Monaghan, as he sat feeding Katie one evening by the fire.

"No, John."

"Well, then, you've a thrate to come; and it's myself that will make Miss Katie, the darlint, an illigant lump of that same."

Early in the morning John was up, hard at work, making troughs for the sap. By noon he had completed a dozen, which he showed me with great pride of heart. I felt a little curious about this far-famed maple sugar, and asked a thousand questions about the use to which the troughs were to be applied; how the trees were to be tapped, the sugar made, and if it were really good when made?

To all my queries, John responded, "Och! 'tis illigant. It bates all the sugar that ever was made in Jamaky. But you'll see before to-morrow night."

Moodie was away at P[eterborough],[6] and the prospect of the maple sugar relieved the dulness occasioned by his absence. I reckoned on showing him a piece of sugar of our own making when he came home, and never dreamt of the possibility of disappointment.

John tapped his trees after the most approved fashion, and set his troughs to catch the sap; but Miss Amanda and Master Ammon upset them as fast as they filled, and spilt all the sap. With great difficulty, Monaghan saved the contents of one large iron pot. This he brought in about nightfall, and made up a roaring fire, in order to boil it down into sugar. Hour after hour passed away, and the sugar-maker looked as hot and black as the stoker in a steam-boat. Many times I peeped into the large pot, but the sap never seemed to diminish.

"This is a tedious piece of business," thought I, but seeing the lad so anxious, I said nothing. About twelve o'clock, he asked me, very mysteriously, for a piece of pork to hang over the sugar.

"Pork!" said I, looking into the pot, which was half full of a very black-looking liquid; "what do you want with pork?"

"Shure, an' 'tis to keep the sugar from burning."

"But, John, I see no sugar!"

"Och, but 'tis all sugar, only 'tis molasses jist now. See how it sticks to the ladle. Aha! but Miss Katie will have the fine lumps of sugar when she awakes in the morning."

I grew so tired and sleepy that I left John to finish his job, went to bed and soon forgot all about the maple sugar. At breakfast I observed a small plate upon the table, placed in a very conspicuous manner on the tea-tray, the bottom covered with a hard, black substance, which very much resembled pitch. "What is that dirty-looking stuff, John?"

"Shure an 'tis the maple sugar."

6. Likely the fledgling town of Peterborough. John Moodie was gone overnight and was probably looking into purchasing more land in Douro adjacent to his military land grant. Sam Strickland's encouragement and advice would have been crucial to his investigations.

"Can people eat that?"

"By dad, an' they can; only thry it, ma'arm."

"Why, 'tis so hard, I cannot cut it."

With some difficulty, and not without cutting his finger, John broke a piece off, and stuffed it into the baby's mouth. The poor child made a horrible face, and rejected it as if it had been poison. For my own part, I never tasted anything more nauseous. It tasted like a compound of pork grease and tobacco juice. "Well, Monaghan, if this be maple sugar, I never wish to taste any again."

"Och, bad luck to it!" said the lad, flinging it away, plate and all. "It would have been first-rate but for the dirthy pot, and the blackguard cinders, and its burning to the bottom of the pot. That owld hag, Mrs. H[arris], bewitched it with her evil eye."

"She is not so clever as you think, John," said I, laughing. "You have forgotten how to make the sugar since you left D[ummer]; but let us forget the maple sugar, and think of something else. Had you not better get old Mrs. H[arris] to mend that jacket for you; it is too ragged."

"Ay, dad! an' it's mysel' is the illigant tailor. Wasn't I brought up to the thrade in the Foundling Hospital?"

"And why did you quit it?"

"Because it's a low, mane thrade for a jintleman's son."

"But, John, who told you that you were a gentleman's son?"

"Och! but I'm shure of it, thin. All my propensities are gintale. I love horses, and dogs, and fine clothes, and money. Och! that I was but a jintleman! I'd show them what life is intirely, and I'd challenge Masther William, and have my revenge out of him for the blows he gave me."

"You had better mend your trousers," said I, giving him a tailor's needle, a pair of scissors, and some strong thread.

"Shure, an' I'll do that same in a brace of shakes," and sitting down upon a ricketty three-legged stool of his own manufacturing, he commenced his tailoring by tearing off a piece of his trousers to patch the elbows of his jacket. And this trifling act, simple as it may appear, was a perfect type of the boy's general conduct, and marked his progress through life. The present for him was everything; he had no future. While he supplied stuff from the trousers to repair the fractures in the jacket, he never reflected that both would be required on the morrow. Poor John! in his brief and reckless career, how often have I recalled that foolish act of his. It now appears to me that his whole life was spent in tearing his trousers to repair his jacket.

In the evening John asked me for a piece of soap.

"What do you want with soap, John?"

"To wash my shirt, ma'arm. Shure an I'm a baste to be seen, as black as the pots. Sorra a shirt have I but the one, an' it has stuck on my back so long that I can thole it no longer."

I looked at the wrists and collar of the condemned garment, which was all of it that John allowed to be visible. They were much in need of soap and water.

"Well, John, I will leave you the soap; but can you wash?"

"Och, shure, an' I can thry. If I soap it enough, and rub long enough, the shirt must come clane at last."

I thought the matter rather doubtful; but when I went to bed I left what he required, and soon saw through the chinks in the boards a roaring fire, and heard John whistling over the tub. He whistled and rubbed, and washed and scrubbed, but as there seemed no end to the job, and he was as long washing this one garment as Bell would have been performing the same operation on fifty, I laughed to myself, and thought of my own abortive attempts in that way, and went fast asleep. In the morning John came to his breakfast, with his jacket buttoned up to his throat.

"Could you not dry your shirt by the fire, John? You will get cold wanting it."

"Aha, by dad! it's dhry enough now. The divil has made tinder of it long afore this."

"Why, what has happened to it? I heard you washing all night."

"Washing! Faith, an' I did scrub it till my hands were all ruined in-tirely, and thin I took the brush to it; but sorra a bit of the dirth could I get out of it. The more I rubbed the blacker it got, until I had used up all the soap, and the perspiration was pouring off me like rain. 'You dirthy owld bit of a blackguard of a rag,' says I, in an exthremity of rage, 'you're not fit for the back of a dacent lad an' a jintleman. The divil may take ye to cover one of his imps;' an' wid that I sthirred up the fire, and sent it plump into the middle of the blaze."

"And what will you do for a shirt?"

"Faith, do as many a betther man has done afore me, go widout."

I looked up two old shirts of my husband's, which John received with an ecstacy of delight. He retired instantly to the stable, but soon returned, with as much of the linen breast of the garment displayed as his waistcoat would allow. No peacock was ever prouder of his tail than the wild Irish lad was of the old shirt.

John had been treated very much like a spoiled child, and, like most spoiled children, he was rather fond of having his own way. Moodie had set him to do something which was rather contrary to his own in-clinations; he did not object to the task in words, for he was rarely saucy to his employers, but he left the following stave upon the table, written in pencil upon a scrap of paper torn from the back of an old letter:—

> "A man alive, an ox may drive
>   Unto a springing well;
> To make him drink, as he may think,
>   No man can him compel."
>   "John Monaghan"

THE EMIGRANT'S BRIDE.[7]
A Canadian Ballad.

The waves that girt my native isle,
    The parting sunbeams tinged with red;
And far to seaward, many a mile,
    A line of dazzling glory shed.
But, ah! upon that glowing track,
    No glance my aching eyeballs threw;
As I my little bark steer'd back
    To bid my love a last adieu.

Upon the shores of that lone bay,
    With folded arms the maiden stood;
And watch'd the white sails wing their way
    Across the gently heaving flood.
The summer breeze her raven hair
    Swept lightly from her snowy brow;
And there she stood, as pale and fair
    As the white foam that kiss'd my prow.

My throbbing heart with grief swell'd high,
    A heavy tale was mine to tell;
For once I shunn'd the beauteous eye,
    Whose glance on mine so fondly fell.
My hopeless message soon was sped,
    My father's voice my suit denied;
And I had promised not to wed,
    Against his wish, my island bride.

She did not weep, though her pale face
    The trace of recent sorrow wore;
But, with a melancholy grace,
    She waved my shallop from the shore.
She did not weep; but, oh! that smile
    Was sadder than the briny tear
That trembled on my cheek the while
    I bade adieu to one so dear.

She did not speak—no accents fell
    From lips that breathed the balm of May;
In broken words I strove to tell
    All that my broken heart would say.
She did not speak—but to my eyes
    She raised the deep light of her own.
As breaks the sun through cloudy skies,
    My spirit caught a brighter tone.

---

7. This poem probably first appeared in *The Literary Garland* (Montreal) 2:5 (April 1840),
p. 218, and is thus a later poem than those included by Susanna in previous chapters; it
seems to have been reprinted elsewhere only once.

"Dear girl!" I cried, "we ne'er can part,
　My angry father's wrath I'll brave;
He shall not tear thee from my heart.
　Fly, fly with me across the wave!"
My hand convulsively she press'd,
　Her tears were mingling fast with mine;
And, sinking trembling on my breast,
　She murmur'd out, "For ever thine!"

Nine

Phoebe H[arris], and Our Second Moving

She died in early womanhood,
Sweet scion of a stem so rude;
A child of Nature, free from art,
With candid brow and open heart;
The flowers she loved now gently wave
Above her low and nameless grave.

It was during the month of March that Uncle Joe's eldest daughter, Phoebe, a very handsome girl, and the best of the family, fell sick. I went over to see her. The poor girl was very depressed, and stood but a slight chance for her life, being under the medical treatment of three or four old women, who all recommended different treatment and administered different nostrums. Seeing that the poor girl was dangerously ill, I took her mother aside, and begged her to lose no time in procuring proper medical advice. Mrs. Joe listened to me very sullenly, and said there was no danger; that Phoebe had caught a violent cold by going hot from the wash-tub to fetch a pail of water from the spring; that the neighbours knew the nature of her complaint, and would soon cure her.

The invalid turned upon me her fine dark eyes, in which the light of fever painfully burned, and motioned me to come near her. I sat down by her, and took her burning hand in mine.

"I am dying, Mrs. Moodie, but they won't believe me. I wish you would talk to mother to send for the doctor."

"I will. Is there anything I can do for you?—anything I can make for you, that you would like to take?"

She shook her head. "I can't eat. But I want to ask you one thing, which I wish very much to know." She grasped my hand tightly between her own. Her eyes looked darker, and her feverish cheek paled. "What becomes of people when they die?"

"Good heavens!" I exclaimed involuntarily, "can you be ignorant of a future state?"

"What is a future state?"

I endeavoured, as well as I was able, to explain to her the nature of the soul, its endless duration, and responsibility to God for the actions done in the flesh; its natural depravity and need of a Saviour; urging her, in the gentlest manner, to lose no time in obtaining forgiveness of her sins, through the atoning blood of Christ.

The poor girl looked at me with surprise and horror. These things were all new to her. She sat like one in a dream; yet the truth seemed to flash upon her at once.

"How can I speak to God, who never knew Him? How can I ask Him to forgive me?"

"You must pray to Him."

"Pray! I don't know how to pray. I never said a prayer in my life. Mother; can you teach me how to pray?"

"Nonsense!" said Mrs. Joe, hurrying forward. "Why should you trouble yourself about *such things*? Mrs. Moodie, I desire you not to put such thoughts into my daughter's head. We don't want to know anything about Jesus Christ here."

"Oh, mother, don't speak so to the lady! Do, Mrs. Moodie, tell me more about God and my soul. I never knew until now that I had a soul."

Deeply compassionating the ignorance of the poor girl, in spite of the menaces of the heathen mother—for she was no better, but rather worse, seeing that the heathen worships in ignorance a false God, while this woman lived without acknowledging a God at all, and therefore considered herself free from all moral restraint—I bid Phoebe good-by, and promised to bring my bible, and read to her the next day.

The gratitude manifested by this sick girl was such a contrast to the rudeness and brutality of the rest of the family, that I soon felt a powerful interest in her fate.

The mother did not actually forbid me the house, because she saw that my visits raised the drooping spirits of her child, whom she fiercely loved, and, to save her life, would cheerfully have sacrificed her own. But she never failed to make all the noise she could to disturb my reading and conversation with Phoebe. She could not be persuaded that her daughter was really in any danger, until the doctor told her that her case was hopeless; then the grief of the mother burst forth, and she gave way to the most frantic and impious complainings.

The rigour of the winter began to abate. The beams of the sun during the day were warm and penetrating, and a soft wind blew from the south. I watched, from day to day, the snow disappearing from the earth, with indescribable pleasure, and at length it wholly vanished; not even a solitary patch lingered under the shade of the forest trees; but Uncle Joe gave no sign of removing his family.

"Does he mean to stay all the summer?" thought I. "Perhaps he never intends going at all. I will ask him, the next time he comes to borrow whiskey."

In the afternoon he walked in to light his pipe, and, with some anxiety, I made the inquiry.

"Well, I guess we can't be moving afore the end of May. My missus expects to be confined the fore part of the month, and I shan't move till she be quite smart agin."

"You are not using us well, in keeping us out of the house so long."

"Oh, I don't care a curse about any of you. It is my house as long as I choose to remain in it, and you may put up with it the best way you can;" and, humming a Yankee tune, he departed.

I had borne patiently the odious, cribbed-up place during the winter, but now the hot weather was coming, it seemed almost insupportable, as we were obliged to have a fire in the close room, in order to cook our provisions. I consoled myself as well as I could by roaming about the fields and woods, and making acquaintance with every wild flower as it blossomed, and in writing long letters to home friends, in which I abused one of the finest countries in the world as the worst that God ever called out of chaos. I can recall to memory, at this moment, the few lines of a poem which commenced in this strain; nor am I sorry that the rest of it has passed into oblivion:—

> Oh! land of waters, how my spirit tires,
>   In the dark prison of thy boundless woods;
> No rural charm poetic thought inspires,
>   No music murmurs in thy mighty floods;
> Though vast the features that compose thy frame,
> Turn where we will, the landscape's still the same.
>
> The swampy margin of thy inland seas,
>   The eternal forest girdling either shore,
> Its belt of dark pines sighing in the breeze,
>   And rugged fields, with rude huts dotted o'er,
> Show cultivation unimproved by art,
> That sheds a barren chillness on the heart.

How many home-sick emigrants, during their first winter in Canada, will respond to this gloomy picture! Let them wait a few years; the sun of hope will arise and beautify the landscape, and they will proclaim the country one of the finest in the world.

The middle of May at length arrived, and, by the number of long, lean women, with handkerchiefs of all colours tied over their heads, who passed my door, and swarmed into Mrs. Joe's house, I rightly concluded that another young one had been added to the tribe; and, shortly after, Uncle Joe himself announced the important fact, by putting his jolly red face in at the door, and telling me, that "his missus had got a chopping boy; and he was right glad of it, for he was tired of so many gals, and that he should move in a fortnight, if his woman did kindly."[1]

I had been so often disappointed that I paid very little heed to him, but this time he kept his word.

The *last* day of May, they went, bag and baggage, the poor sick Phoebe, who still lingered on, and the new-born infant; and right joyfully I sent a Scotch girl (another Bell, whom I had hired in lieu of her I had lost), and Monaghan, to clean out the Augean stable.[2] In a few minutes John returned, panting with indignation.

---

1. Joseph Harris, Joe and Hannah Harris's second son, was born in May 1833.
2. Susanna refers to the mythical stables, which Hercules cleaned as one of his labors.

"The house," he said, "was more filthy than a pig-sty." But that was not the worst of it: Uncle Joe, before he went, had undermined the brick chimney, and let all the water into the house. "Oh, but if he comes here agin," he continued, grinding his teeth and doubling his fist, "I'll thrash him for it. And thin, ma'arm, he has girdled round all the best graft apple-trees, the murtherin' owld villain, as if it could spile his digestion our ating them."

"It would require a strong stomach to digest apple trees, John; but never mind, it can't be helped, and we may be very thankful that these people are gone at last."

John and Bell scrubbed at the house all day, and in the evening they carried over the furniture, and I went to inspect our new dwelling.

It looked beautifully clean and neat. Bell had white-washed all the black, smoky walls and boarded ceilings, and scrubbed the dirty window-frames, and polished the fly spotted panes of glass, until they actually admitted a glimpse of the clear air and the blue sky. Snow-white fringed curtains, and a bed, with furniture to correspond, a carpeted floor, and a large pot of green boughs on the hearth-stone, gave an air of comfort and cleanliness to a room which, only a few hours before, had been a loathsome den of filth and impurity.

This change would have been very gratifying, had not a strong, disagreeable odour almost deprived me of my breath as I entered the room. It was unlike anything I had ever smelt before, and turned me so sick and faint that I had to cling to the door-post for support.

"Where does this dreadful smell come from?"

"The guidness knows, ma'am; John and I have searched the house from the loft to the cellar, but we canna find out the cause of thae stink."

"It must be in the room, Bell; and it is impossible to remain here, or live in this house, until it is removed."

Glancing my eyes all round the place, I spied what seemed to me a little cupboard, over the mantel-shelf, and I told John to see if I was right. The lad mounted upon a chair, and pulled open a small door, but almost fell to the ground with the dreadful stench which seemed to rush from the closet.

"What is it, John?" I cried from the open door.

"A skunk! ma'arm, a skunk! Shure, I thought the divil had scorched his tail, and left the grizzled hair behind him. What a strong perfume it has!" he continued, holding up the beautiful but odious little creature by the tail.

"By dad! I know all about it now. I saw Ned Layton,[3] only two days ago, crossing the field with Uncle Joe, with his gun on his shoulder, and this wee bit baste in his hand. They were both laughing like sixty. 'Well, if this does not stink the Scotchman out of the house,' said Joe, 'I'll be contint to be tarred and feathered;' and thin they both laughed until they stopped to draw breath."

I could hardly help laughing myself; but I begged Monaghan to con-

---

3. See Chapter Eight, note 5, p. 102.

vey the horrid creature away, and putting some salt and sulphur into a tin plate, and setting fire to it, I placed it on the floor in the middle of the room, and closed all the doors for an hour, which greatly assisted in purifying the house from the skunkification. Bell then washed out the closet with strong ley, and in a short time no vestige remained of the malicious trick that Uncle Joe had played off upon us.

The next day, we took possession of our new mansion, and no one was better pleased with the change than little Katie. She was now fifteen months old, and could just begin to prattle, but she dared not venture to step alone, although she would stand by a chair all day, and even climb upon it. She crept from room to room, feeling and admiring everything, and talking to it in her baby language. So fond was the dear child of flowers, that her father used to hold her up to the apple-trees, then rich in their full spring beauty, that she might kiss the blossoms. She would pat them with her soft white hands, murmuring like a bee among the branches. To keep her quiet whilst I was busy, I had only to give her a bunch of wild flowers. She would sit as still as a lamb, looking first at one and then at another, pressing them to her little breast in a sort of ecstacy as if she comprehended the worth of this most beautiful of God's gifts to man.

She was a sweet, lovely flower herself, and her charming infant graces reconciled me, more than aught else, to a weary lot. Was she not purely British? Did not her soft blue eyes, and sunny curls, and bright rosy cheeks for ever remind me of her Saxon origin, and bring before me dear forms and faces I could never hope to behold again?

The first night we slept in the new house, a demon of unrest had taken possession of it in the shape of a countless swarm of mice. They scampered over our pillows, and jumped upon our faces, squeaking and cutting a thousand capers over the floor. I never could realise the true value of Whittington's invaluable cat until that night.[4] At first we laughed until our sides ached, but in reality it was no laughing matter. Moodie remembered that we had left a mouse trap in the old house; he went and brought it over, baited it, and set it on the table near the bed. During the night no less than fourteen of the provoking vermin were captured; and for several succeeding nights the trap did equal execution. How Uncle Joe's family could have allowed such a nuisance to exist astonished me; to sleep with these creatures continually running over us was impossible; and they were not the only evils in the shape of vermin we had to contend with. The old logs which composed the walls of the house were full of bugs and large black ants; and the place, owing to the number of dogs that always had slept under the beds with the children, was infested with fleas. It required the utmost care to rid the place of these noisome and disgusting tenants.

Arriving in the country in the autumn, we had never experienced any inconvenience from the mosquitoes, but after the first moist, warm spring days, particularly after the showers, these tormenting insects annoyed us greatly. The farm lying in a valley cut up with little

4. See Chapter Four, note 4, p. 50.

streams in every direction made us more liable to their inflictions. The hands, arms, and face of the poor babe were covered every morning with red inflamed bumps, which often threw out blisters.

The banks of the little streams abounded with wild strawberries, which although small, were of a delicious flavour. Thither Bell and I, and the baby, daily repaired to gather the bright red berries of Nature's own providing. Katie, young as she was, was very expert at helping herself, and we used to seat her in the middle of a fine bed, whilst we gathered farther on. Hearing her talking very lovingly to something in the grass, which she tried to clutch between her white hands, calling it "Pitty, pitty;" I ran to the spot, and found that it was a large garter-snake that she was so affectionately courting to her embrace. Not then aware that this formidable-looking reptile was perfectly harmless, I snatched the child up in my arms, and ran with her home; never stopping until I gained the house, and saw her safely seated in her cradle.

It had been a very late, cold spring, but the trees had fully expanded into leaf, and the forest world was glorious in its beauty. Every patch of cleared land presented a vivid green to the eye; the brook brawled in the gay sunshine, and the warm air was filled with soft murmurs. Gorgeous butterflies floated about like winged flowers, and feelings allied to poetry and gladness once more pervaded my heart. In the evening we wandered through the woodland paths, beneath the glowing Canadian sunset, and gathered rare specimens of strange plants and flowers. Every object that met my eyes was new to me, and produced that peculiar excitement which has its origin in a thirst for knowledge, and a love of variety.

We had commenced gardening, too, and my vegetables did great credit to my skill and care; and, when once the warm weather sets in, the rapid advance of vegetation in Canada is astonishing.

Not understanding much about farming, especially in a climate like Canada, Moodie was advised by a neighbouring settler to farm his farm upon shares. This advice seemed very reasonable; and had it been given disinterestedly, and had the persons recommended (a man and his wife) been worthy or honest people, we might have done very well. But the farmer had found out their encroaching ways, was anxious to get rid of them himself, and saw no better way of doing so than by palming them upon us.

From our engagement with these people commenced that long series of losses and troubles to which their conduct formed the prelude. They were to live in the little shanty that we had just left, and work the farm. Moodie was to find them the land, the use of his implements and cattle, and all the seed for the crops; and to share with them the returns. Besides this, they unfortunately were allowed to keep their own cows, pigs, and poultry. The produce of the orchard, with which they had nothing to do, was reserved for our own use.

For the first few weeks, they were civil and obliging enough; and had the man been left to himself, I believe we should have done pretty well; but the wife was a coarse-minded, bold woman, who instigated him to every mischief. They took advantage of us in every way they could, and were constantly committing petty depredations.

From our own experience of this mode of farming, I would strenuously advise all new settlers never to embrace any such offer, without they are well acquainted with the parties, and can thoroughly rely upon their honesty; or else, like Mrs. O——,[5] they may impudently tell you that they can cheat you as they please, and defy you to help yourself. All the money we expended upon the farm was entirely for these people's benefit, for by their joint contrivances very little of the crops fell to our share; and when any division was made, it was always when Moodie was absent from home; and there was no person present to see fair play. They sold what apples and potatoes they pleased, and fed their hogs *ad libitum*.[6] But even their roguery was more tolerable than the irksome restraint which their near vicinity, and constantly having to come in contact with them, imposed. We had no longer any privacy, our servants were cross-questioned, and our family affairs canvassed by these gossiping people, who spread about a thousand falsehoods regarding us. I was so much disgusted with this shareship, that I would gladly have given them all the proceeds of the farm to get rid of them, but the bargain was for twelve months, and bad as it was, we could not break our engagement.

One little trick of this woman's will serve to illustrate her general conduct. A neighbouring farmer's wife had presented me with some very pretty hens, who followed to the call of old Betty Fye's handsome game-cock. I was always fond of fowls, and the innocent Katie delighted in her chicks, and would call them round her to the sill of the door to feed from her hand. Mrs. O—— had the same number as I had, and I often admired them when marshalled forth by her splendid black rooster. One morning I saw her eldest son chop off the head of the fine bird; and I asked his mother why she had allowed him to kill the beautiful creature. She laughed, and merely replied that she wanted it for the pot. The next day my sultan walked over to the widowed hens, and took all his seraglio with him. From that hour I never gathered a single egg; the hens deposited all their eggs in Mrs. O——'s hen-house. She used to boast of this as an excellent joke among her neighbours.

On the 9th of June, my dear little Agnes was born. A few days after this joyful event, I heard a great bustle in the room adjoining to mine, and old Dolly Rowe, my Cornish nurse, informed me that it was occasioned by the people who came to attend the funeral of Phoebe H[arris]. She only survived the removal of the family a week; and at her own request had been brought all the way from the [Rice L]ake plains

5. The O——s have not been identified, but it is clear that after agreeing to farm on shares with the Moodies, the O——s were annoying and antagonistic, cheating the Moodies and invading their privacy. Indeed, the O——s were likely the most important factor in the Moodies' decision to move north to Douro Township in February 1834. Clearly, Susanna did not find them amusing in the least, neither in their eccentricities nor in their mischief. The fact that Mrs. O—— was an Englishwoman and not a Yankee no doubt contributed to Susanna's sense of betrayal and disappointment.
6. Latin: At their pleasure.

to be interred in the burying ground on the hill which overlooked the stream.[7]

As I lay upon my pillow I could distinctly see the spot, and mark the long funeral procession, as it wound along the banks of the brook. It was a solemn and imposing spectacle, that humble funeral. When the waggons reached the rude enclosure, the coffin was carefully lifted to the ground, the door in the lid opened, and old and young approached, one after another, to take a last look at the dead, before consigning her to the oblivion of the grave.

Poor Phoebe! Gentle child of coarse, unfeeling parents, few shed more sincerely a tear for thy early fate than the stranger whom they hated and despised. Often have I stood beside that humble mound, when the song of the lark was above me, and the bee murmuring at my feet, and thought that it was well for thee that God opened the eyes of thy soul, and called thee out of the darkness of ignorance and sin to glory in His marvellous light. Sixteen years have passed away since I heard anything of the family, or what had become of them, when I was told by a neighbour of theirs, whom I accidentally met last winter, that the old woman, who now nearly numbers a hundred years, is still living, and inhabits a corner of her son's barn, as she still quarrels too much with his wife to reside with Joe; that the girls are all married and gone; and that Joe himself, although he does not know a letter, has commenced travelling preacher. After this, who can doubt the existence of miracles in the nineteenth century?

THE FAITHFUL HEART THAT LOVES THEE STILL.[8]

> I kneel beside the cold grey stone
> That tells me, dearest, thou are gone
> To realms more bless'd—and left me still
> To struggle with this world of ill.
> But oft from out the silent mound
> Delusive fancy breathes a sound;
> My pent-up heart within me burns,
> And all the blessed past returns.
> Thy form is present to mine eye,
>   Thy voice is whispering in mine ear,
> The love that spake in days gone by;
>   And rapture checks the starting tear
> Thy deathless spirit wakes to fill
> The faithful heart that loves thee still.
>
> For thee the day's bright glow is o'er,
> And summer's roses bloom no more;
> The song of birds in twilight bowers,
> The breath of spring's delicious flowers,
> The towering wood and mountain height,

---

7. The Harris burying ground, just off what is now called McClelland Road, is designated by an historical plaque.
8. This poem first appeared in *The Literary Garland* (Montreal) 2:7 (June 1840), p. 351.

The glorious pageantry of night;
Which fill'd thy soul with musings high,
And lighted up thy speaking eye;
The mournful music of the wave
Can never reach thy lonely grave.
Thou dost but sleep! It cannot be
   That ardent heart is silent now—
That death's dark door has closed on thee;
   And made thee cold to all below,
Ah, no! the flame death could not chill,
Thy tender love survives thee still.

That love within my breast enshrined,
In death alone shall be resign'd;
And when the eve thou lovest so well
Pours on my soul its soothing spell,
I leave the city's busy scene
To seek thy dwelling, cold and green,—
In quiet sadness here to shed
Love's sacred tribute o'er the dead—
To dream again of days gone by,
   And hold sweet converse here with thee;
In the soft air to feel thy sigh,
    Whilst winds and waters answer me.
Yes!—though resign'd to Heaven's high will,
My joy shall be to love thee still!

Ten

Brian, the Still-Hunter[1]

O'er memory's glass I see his shadow flit,
Though he was gathered to the silent dust
Long years ago. A strange and wayward man,
That shunn'd companionship, and lived apart;
The leafy covert of the dark brown woods,
The gleamy lakes, hid in their gloomy depths,
Whose still, deep waters never knew the stroke
Of cleaving oar, or echoed to the sound
Of social life, contained for him the sum
Of human happiness. With dog and gun,
Day after day he track'd the nimble deer
Through all the tangled mazes of the forest.

It was early day. I was alone in the old shanty, preparing breakfast, and now and then stirring the cradle with my foot, when a tall, thin, middle-aged man walked into the house, followed by two large, strong dogs.

---

1. Still-hunting is hunting that involves moving slowly through cover, stopping every couple of steps, watching and listening. It is a method for hunting deer and other wildlife that differs from hunting from a stand.

Placing the rifle he had carried on his shoulder, in a corner of the room, he advanced to the hearth, and without speaking, or seemingly looking at me, lighted his pipe, and commenced smoking. The dogs, after growling and snapping at the cat, who had not given the strangers a very courteous reception, sat down on the hearth-stone on either side of their taciturn master, eyeing him from time to time, as if long habit had made them understand all his motions. There was a great contrast between the dogs. The one was a brindled bulldog of the largest size, a most formidable and powerful brute; the other a staghound, tawny, deep-chested, and strong-limbed. I regarded the man and his hairy companions with silent curiosity.

He was between forty and fifty years of age; his head, nearly bald, was studded at the sides with strong, coarse, black curling hair. His features were high, his complexion brightly dark, and his eyes, in size, shape, and colour, greatly resembled the eyes of a hawk. The face itself was sorrowful and taciturn; and his thin, compressed lips looked as if they were not much accustomed to smile, or often to unclose to hold social communion with any one. He stood at the side of the huge hearth, silently smoking, his eyes bent on the fire, and now and then he patted the heads of his dogs, reproving their exuberant expressions of attachment, with—"Down, Music; down, Chance!"

"A cold, clear morning," said I, in order to attract his attention and draw him into conversation.

A nod, without raising his head, or withdrawing his eyes from the fire, was his only answer; and, turning from my unsociable guest, I took up the baby, who just then awoke, sat down on a low stool by the table, and began feeding her. During this operation, I once or twice caught the stranger's hawk-eye fixed upon me and the child, but word spoke he none; and presently, after whistling to his dogs, he resumed his gun, and strode out.

When Moodie and Monaghan came in to breakfast, I told them what a strange visitor I had had; and Moodie laughed at my vain attempt to induce him to talk.

"He is a strange being," I said; "I must find out who and what he is."

In the afternoon an old soldier, called Layton,[2] who had served during the American war, and got a grant of land about a mile in the rear of our location, came in to trade for a cow. Now, this Layton was a perfect ruffian; a man whom no one liked, and whom all feared. He was a deep drinker, a great swearer, in short, a perfect reprobate; who never cultivated his land, but went jobbing about from farm to farm, trading horses and cattle, and cheating in a pettifogging way. Uncle Joe had employed him to sell Moodie a young heifer, and he had brought her over for him to look at. When he came in to be paid, I described the stranger of the morning; and as I knew that he was familiar with every one in the neighbourhood, I asked if he knew him.

"No one should know him better than myself," he said; " 'tis old

---

2. For Ned Layton, see Chapter Eight, note 5, p. 102.

Brian B[ouskill],[3] the still-hunter, and a near neighbour of your'n. A sour, morose, queer chap he is, and as mad as a March hare! He's from Lancashire, in England, and came to this country some twenty years ago, with his wife, who was a pretty young lass in those days, and slim enough then, though she's so awful fleshy now. He had lots of money, too, and he bought four hundred acres of land, just at the corner of the concession line, where it meets the main road. And excellent land it is; and a better farmer, while he stuck to his business, never went into the bush, for it was all bush here then. He was a dashing, handsome fellow, too, and did not hoard the money either; he loved his pipe and his pot too well; and at last he left off farming, and gave himself to them altogether. Many a jolly booze he and I have had, I can tell you. Brian was an awful passionate man, and, when the liquor was in, and the wit was out, as savage and as quarrelsome as a bear. At such times there was no one but Ned Layton dared go near him. We once had a pitched battle, in which I was conqueror; and ever arter he yielded a sort of sulky obedience to all I said to him. Arter being on the spree for a week or two, he would take fits of remorse, and return home to his wife; would fall down at her knees, and ask her forgiveness, and cry like a child. At other times he would hide himself up in the woods, and steal home at night, and get what he wanted out of the pantry, without speaking a word to any one. He went on with these pranks for some years, till he took a fit of the blue devils.

" 'Come away, Ned, to the [Rice] lake, with me,' said he; 'I am weary of my life, and I want a change.'

" 'Shall we take the fishing-tackle?' says I. 'The black bass are in prime season, and F[oe][4] will lend us the old canoe. He's got some capital rum up from Kingston. We'll fish all day, and have a spree at night.'

" 'It's not to fish I'm going,' says he.

" 'To shoot, then? I've bought Rockwood's new rifle.'

" 'It's neither to fish nor to shoot, Ned; it's a new game I'm going to try; so come along.'

"Well, to the [Rice] lake we went. The day was very hot, and our path lay through the woods, and over those scorching plains, for eight long miles. I thought I should have dropped by the way; but during our long walk my companion never opened his lips. He strode on before me, at a half-run, never once turning his head.

" 'The man must be the devil!' says I, 'and accustomed to a warmer place, or he must feel this. Hollo, Brian! Stop there! Do you mean to kill me?'

" 'Take it easy,' says he; 'you'll see another day arter this—I've business on hand, and cannot wait.'

3. Brian Bouskill's attempted suicide in August 1831 at Rice Lake was reported in the Cobourg *Star* (August 16, 1831, pp. 5–6) under the title "Attempt at Suicide." It offers a different account of the event, placing the blame on Bouskill's delusions and "temporary insanity." Later in this sketch, Susanna alludes to three further suicide attempts. Layton's account describes events that occurred twelve years prior to Susanna's account, in the early 1820s.

4. A Mr. Foe kept a tavern near the Rice Lake Plains (Cobourg *Star*, August 2, 1837).

"Well, on we went, at the same awful rate, and it was mid-day when we got to the little tavern on the lake shore, kept by one F[oe] who had a boat for the convenience of strangers who came to visit the place. Here we got our dinner, and a glass of rum to wash it down. But Brian was moody, and to all my jokes he only returned a sort of grunt; and while I was talking with F[oe], he steps out, and a few minutes arter we saw him crossing the lake in the old canoe.

" 'What's the matter with Brian?' says F[oe]; 'all does not seem right with him, Ned. You had better take the boat, and look arter him.'

" 'Pooh!' says I; 'he's often so, and grows so glum now-a-days that I will cut his acquaintance altogether if he does not improve.'

" 'He drinks awful hard,' says F[oe]; 'may be he's got a fit of the delirium-tremulous. There is no telling what he may be up to at this minute.'

"My mind misgave me too, so I e'en takes the oars, and pushes out, right upon Brian's track; and, by the Lord Harry! if I did not find him, upon my landing on the opposite shore, lying wallowing in his blood, with his throat cut. 'Is that you, Brian?' says I, giving him a kick with my foot, to see if he was alive or dead. 'What upon earth tempted you to play me and F[oe] such a dirty, mean trick, as to go and stick yourself like a pig, bringing such a discredit upon the house?—and you so far from home and those who should nurse you.'

"I was so mad with him, that (saving your presence, ma'am) I swore awfully, and called him names that would be ondacent to repeat here; but he only answered with groans and a horrid gurgling in his throat. 'It's choking you are,' said I; 'but you shan't have your own way, and die so easily either, if I can punish you by keeping you alive.' So I just turned him upon his stomach, with his head down the steep bank; but he still kept choking and growing black in the face."

Layton then detailed some particulars of his surgical practice which it is not necessary to repeat.[5] He continued:

"I bound up his throat with my handkerchief, and took him neck and heels, and threw him into the bottom of the boat. Presently he came to himself a little, and sat up in the boat; and—would you believe it?—made several attempts to throw himself into the water. 'This will not do,' says I; 'you've done mischief enough already by cutting your weasand! If you dare to try that again, I will kill you with the oar.' I held it up to threaten him; he was scared, and lay down as quiet as a lamb. I put my foot upon his breast. 'Lie still, now! or you'll catch it.' He looked piteously at me; he could not speak, but his eyes seemed to say, 'Have pity upon me, Ned; don't kill me.'

"Yes, ma'am; this man, who had just cut his throat, and twice arter that tried to drown himself, was afraid that I should knock him on the head and kill him. Ha! ha! I never shall forget the work that F[oe] and I had with him arter I got him up to the house.

"The doctor came, and sewed up his throat; and his wife—poor crit-

---

5. Susanna offered a much more graphic description of Layton's "surgical practice" in the first version of this sketch, published in *The Literary Garland* in 1847.

tur!—came to nurse him. Bad as he was, she was mortal fond of him! He lay there, sick and unable to leave his bed, for three months, and did nothing but pray to God to forgive him, for he thought the devil would surely have him for cutting his own throat; and when he got about again, which is now twelve years ago, he left off drinking entirely, and wanders about the woods with his dogs, hunting. He seldom speaks to any one, and his wife's brother carries on the farm for the family. He is so shy of strangers that 'tis a wonder he came in here. The old wives are afraid of him; but you need not heed him—his troubles are to himself, he harms no one."

Layton departed, and left me brooding over the sad tale which he had told in such an absurd and jesting manner. It was evident from the account he had given of Brian's attempt at suicide, that the hapless hunter was not wholly answerable for his conduct—that he was a harmless maniac.

The next morning, at the very same hour, Brian again made his appearance; but instead of the rifle across his shoulder, a large stone jar occupied the place, suspended by a stout leather thong. Without saying a word, but with a truly benevolent smile, that flitted slowly over his stern features, and lighted them up, like a sunbeam breaking from beneath a stormy cloud, he advanced to the table, and unslinging the jar, set it down before me, and in a low and gruff, but by no means an unfriendly voice, said, "Milk, for the child," and vanished.

"How good it was of him! How kind!" I exclaimed, as I poured the precious gift of four quarts of pure new milk out into a deep pan. I had not asked him—had never said that the poor weanling wanted milk. It was the courtesy of a gentleman—of a man of benevolence and refinement.

For weeks did my strange, silent friend steal in, take up the empty jar, and supply its place with another replenished with milk. The baby knew his step, and would hold out her hands to him and cry "Milk!" and Brian would stoop down and kiss her, and his two great dogs lick her face.

"Have you any children, Mr. B[ouskill]?"

"Yes, five; but none like this."

"My little girl is greatly indebted to you for your kindness."

"She's welcome, or she would not get it. You are strangers; but I like you all. You look kind, and I would like to know more about you."

Moodie shook hands with the old hunter, and assured him that we should always be glad to see him. After this invitation, Brian became a frequent guest. He would sit and listen with delight to Moodie while he described to him elephant-hunting at the Cape; grasping his rifle in a determined manner, and whistling an encouraging air to his dogs. I asked him one evening what made him so fond of hunting.

" 'Tis the excitement," he said; "it drowns thought, and I love to be alone. I am sorry for the creatures, too, for they are free and happy; yet I am led by an instinct I cannot restrain to kill them. Sometimes the sight of their dying agonies recalls painful feelings; and then I lay aside the gun, and do not hunt for days. But 'tis fine to be alone with

God in the great woods—to watch the sunbeams stealing through the thick branches, the blue sky breaking in upon you in patches, and to know that all is bright and shiny above you, in spite of the gloom that surrounds you."

After a long pause, he continued, with much solemn feeling in his look and tone:

"I lived a life of folly for years, for I was respectably born and educated, and had seen something of the world, perhaps more than was good, before I left home for the woods; and from the teaching I had received from kind relatives and parents I should have known how to have conducted myself better. But, madam, if we associate long with the depraved and ignorant, we learn to become even worse than they are. I felt deeply my degradation—felt that I had become the slave to low vice; and in order to emancipate myself from the hateful tyranny of evil passions, I did a very rash and foolish thing. I need not mention the manner in which I transgressed God's holy laws; all the neighbours know it, and must have told you long ago. I could have borne reproof, but they turned my sorrow into indecent jests, and, unable to bear their coarse ridicule, I made companions of my dogs and gun, and went forth into the wilderness. Hunting became a habit. I could no longer live without it, and it supplies the stimulant which I lost when I renounced the cursed whiskey bottle.

"I remember the first hunting excursion I took alone in the forest. How sad and gloomy I felt! I thought that there was no creature in the world so miserable as myself. I was tired and hungry, and I sat down upon a fallen tree to rest. All was still as death around me, and I was fast sinking to sleep, when my attention was aroused by a long, wild cry. My dog, for I had not Chance then, and he's no hunter, pricked up his ears, but instead of answering with a bark of defiance, he crouched down, trembling, at my feet. 'What does this mean?' I cried, and I cocked my rifle and sprang upon the log. The sound came nearer upon the wind. It was like the deep baying of a pack of hounds in full cry. Presently a noble deer rushed past me, and fast upon his trail—I see them now, like so many black devils—swept by a pack of ten or fifteen large, fierce wolves, with fiery eyes and bristling hair, and paws that seemed hardly to touch the ground in their eager haste. I thought not of danger, for, with their prey in view, I was safe; but I felt every nerve within me tremble for the fate of the poor deer. The wolves gained upon him at every bound. A close thicket intercepted his path, and, rendered desperate, he turned at bay. His nostrils were dilated, and his eyes seemed to send forth long streams of light. It was wonderful to witness the courage of the beast. How bravely he repelled the attacks of his deadly enemies, how gallantly he tossed them to the right and left, and spurned them from beneath his hoofs; yet all his struggles were useless, and he was quickly overcome and torn to pieces by his ravenous foes. At that moment he seemed more unfortunate even than myself, for I could not see in what manner he had deserved his fate. All his speed and energy, his courage and fortitude, had been exerted in vain. I had tried to destroy myself; but he, with every effort vigorously made for self-preservation, was doomed to meet the fate he dreaded! Is God just to his creatures?"

With this sentence on his lips, he started abruptly from his seat and left the house.

One day he found me painting some wild flowers,[6] and was greatly interested in watching the progress I made in the group. Late in the afternoon of the following day he brought me a large bunch of splendid spring flowers.

"Draw these," said he; "I have been all the way to the R[ice] [L]ake plains to find them for you."

Little Katie, grasping them one by one, with infantile joy, kissed every lovely blossom.

"These are God's pictures," said the hunter, "and the child, who is all nature, understands them in a minute. Is it not strange that these beautiful things are hid away in the wilderness, where no eyes but the birds of the air, and the wild beasts of the wood, and the insects that live upon them, ever see them? Does God provide, for the pleasure of such creatures, these flowers? Is His benevolence gratified by the admiration of animals whom we have been taught to consider as having neither thought nor reflection? When I am alone in the forest, these thoughts puzzle me."

Knowing that to argue with Brian was only to call into action the slumbering fires of his fatal malady, I turned the conversation by asking him why he called his favourite dog Chance?

"I found him," he said, "forty miles back in the bush. He was a mere skeleton. At first I took him for a wolf, but the shape of his head undeceived me. I opened my wallet, and called him to me. He came slowly, stopping and wagging his tail at every step, and looking me wistfully in the face. I offered him a bit of dried venison, and he soon became friendly, and followed me home, and has never left me since. I called him Chance, after the manner I happened with him; and I would not part with him for twenty dollars."

Alas, for poor Chance! he had, unknown to his master, contracted a private liking for fresh mutton, and one night he killed no less than eight sheep that belonged to Mr. D[ean],[7] on the front road; the culprit, who had been long suspected, was caught in the very act, and this *mischance* cost him his life. Brian was sad and gloomy for many weeks after his favourite's death.

"I would have restored the sheep fourfold," he said, "if he would but have spared the life of my dog."

My recollections of Brian seem more particularly to concentrate in the adventures of one night, when I happened to be left alone, for the first time since my arrival in Canada. I cannot now imagine how I

6. Susanna Moodie took up flower and bird painting as Susanna Strickland in Suffolk. When time allowed, she sold her work in nearby towns. Her teacher was the wife of the Reverend James Ritchie of the Congregational Church in Wrentham. It was Ritchie who converted Susanna from Anglicanism in 1830.
7. Mr. D—— was likely Samuel or Weston Dean, who owned several properties on Concession 3 in Hamilton Township.

could have been such a fool as to give way for four-and-twenty hours to such childish fears; but so it was, and I will not disguise my weakness from my indulgent reader.

Moodie had bought a very fine cow of a black man, named Mollineux, for which he was to give twenty-seven dollars. The man lived twelve miles back in the woods; and one fine frosty spring day—(don't smile at the term frosty, thus connected with the genial season of the year; the term is perfectly correct when applied to the Canadian spring, which, until the middle of May, is the most dismal season of the year)—he and John Monaghan took a rope, and the dog, and sallied forth to fetch the cow home. Moodie said that they should be back by six o'clock in the evening, and charged me to have something cooked for supper when they returned, as he doubted not their long walk in the sharp air would give them a good appetite. This was during the time that I was without a servant, and living in old Mrs. [Harris's] shanty.

The day was so bright and clear, and Katie was so full of frolic and play, rolling upon the floor, or toddling from chair to chair, that the day passed on without my feeling remarkably lonely. At length the evening drew nigh, and I began to expect my husband's return, and to think of the supper that I was to prepare for his reception. The red heifer that we had bought of Layton, came lowing to the door to be milked; but I did not know how to milk in those days, and, besides this, I was terribly afraid of cattle. Yet, as I knew that milk would be required for the tea, I ran across the meadow to Mrs. Joe, and begged that one of her girls would be so kind as to milk for me. My request was greeted with a rude burst of laughter from the whole set.

"If you can't milk," said Mrs. Joe, "it's high time you should learn. My girls are above being helps."

"I would not ask you but as a great favour; I am afraid of cows."

"*Afraid of cows!* Lord bless the woman! A farmer's wife, and afraid of cows!"

Here followed another laugh at my expense; and, indignant at the refusal of my first and last request, when they had all borrowed so much from me, I shut the inhospitable door, and returned home.

After many ineffectual attempts, I succeeded at last, and bore my half-pail of milk in triumph to the house. Yes! I felt prouder of that milk than many an author of the best thing he ever wrote, whether in verse or prose; and it was doubly sweet when I considered that I had procured it without being under any obligation to my ill-natured neighbours. I had learned a useful lesson of independence, to which in after-years I had often again to refer.

I fed little Katie and put her to bed, made the hot cakes for tea, boiled the potatoes, and laid the ham, cut in nice slices, in the pan, ready to cook the moment I saw the men enter the meadow, and arranged the little room with scrupulous care and neatness. A glorious fire was blazing on the hearth, and everything was ready for their supper; and I began to look out anxiously for their arrival.

The night had closed in cold and foggy, and I could no longer distinguish any object at more than a few yards from the door. Bringing in as much wood as I thought would last me for several hours, I closed the door; and for the first time in my life I found myself at night in a house entirely alone. Then I began to ask myself a thousand torturing questions as to the reason of their unusual absence. Had they lost their way in the woods? Could they have fallen in with wolves (one of my early bugbears)? Could any fatal accident have befallen them? I started up, opened the door, held my breath, and listened. The little brook lifted up its voice in loud, hoarse wailing, or mocked, in its babbling to the stones, the sound of human voices. As it became later, my fears increased in proportion. I grew too superstitious and nervous to keep the door open. I not only closed it, but dragged a heavy box in front, for bolt there was none. Several ill-looking men had, during the day, asked their way to Toronto.[8] I felt alarmed lest such rude wayfarers should come to-night and demand a lodging, and find me alone and unprotected. Once I thought of running across to Mrs. Joe, and asking her to let one of the girls stay with me until Moodie returned; but the way in which I had been repulsed in the evening prevented me from making a second appeal to their charity.

Hour after hour wore away, and the crowing of the cocks proclaimed midnight, and yet they came not. I had burnt out all my wood, and I dared not open the door to fetch in more. The candle was expiring in the socket, and I had not courage to go up into the loft and procure another before it went finally out. Cold, heart-weary, and faint, I sat and cried. Every now and then the furious barking of the dogs at the neighbouring farms, and the loud cackling of the geese upon our own, made me hope that they were coming; and then I listened till the beating of my own heart excluded all other sounds. Oh, that unwearied brook! how it sobbed and moaned like a fretful child;—what unreal terrors and fanciful illusions my too active mind conjured up, whilst listening to its mysterious tones!

Just as the moon rose, the howling of a pack of wolves, from the great swamp in our rear, filled the whole air. Their yells were answered by the barking of all the dogs in the vicinity, and the geese, unwilling to be behind-hand in the general confusion, set up the most discordant screams. I had often heard, and even been amused, during the winter, particularly on thaw nights, with hearing the howls of these formidable wild beasts; but I had never before heard them alone, and when one dear to me was abroad amid their haunts. They were directly in the track that Moodie and Monaghan must have taken; and I now made no doubt that they had been attacked and killed on their return through the woods with the cow, and I wept and sobbed until the cold grey dawn peered in upon me through the small dim windows. I have passed many a long cheerless night, when my dear husband was away from me during the rebellion,[9] and I was left in my forest home

8. In 1833, the year of this sketch, Toronto was still known as York. The formal name change occurred in 1834.
9. In 1838 and 1839, while John was serving in militia units during the aftermath of the Rebellion, for six months at a time Susanna was alone with her children and Jenny Buchanan on their bush farm.

with five little children, and only an old Irish woman to draw and cut wood for my fire, and attend to the wants of the family, but that was the saddest and longest night I ever remember.

Just as the day broke, my friends the wolves set up a parting bene-diction, so loud, and wild, and near to the house, that I was afraid lest they should break through the frail windows, or come down the low, wide chimney, and rob me of my child. But their detestable howls died away in the distance, and the bright sun rose up and dispersed the wild horrors of the night, and I looked once more timidly around me. The sight of the table spread, and the uneaten supper, renewed my grief, for I could not divest myself of the idea that Moodie was dead. I opened the door, and stepped forth into the pure air of the early day. A solemn and beautiful repose still hung like a veil over the face of Na-ture. The mists of night still rested upon the majestic woods, and not a sound but the flowing of the waters went up in the vast stillness. The earth had not yet raised her matin hymn to the throne of the Creator. Sad at heart, and weary and worn in spirit, I went down to the spring and washed my face and head, and drank a deep draught of its icy wa-ters. On returning to the house, I met, near the door, old Brian the hunter, with a large fox dangling across his shoulder, and the dogs fol-lowing at his heels.

"Good God! Mrs. Moodie, what is the matter? You are early abroad this morning, and look dreadful ill. Is anything wrong at home? Is the baby or your husband sick?"

"Oh!" I cried, bursting into tears, "I fear he is killed by the wolves."

The man stared at me, as if he doubted the evidence of his senses, and well he might; but this one idea had taken such strong possession of my mind that I could admit no other. I then told him, as well as I could find words, the cause of my alarm, to which he listened very kindly and patiently.

"Set your heart at rest; your husband is safe. It is a long journey on foot to Mollineux, to one unacquainted with a blazed path in a bush road. They have staid all night at the black man's shanty, and you will see them back at noon."

I shook my head and continued to weep.

"Well, now, in order to satisfy you, I will saddle my mare, and ride over to the nigger's, and bring you word as fast as I can."

I thanked him sincerely for his kindness, and returned, in somewhat better spirits, to the house. At ten o'clock my good messenger returned with the glad tidings that all was well.

The day before, when half the journey had been accomplished, John Monaghan let go the rope by which he led the cow, and she had bro-ken away through to the woods, and returned to her old master; and when they again reached his place, night had set in, and they were obliged to wait until the return of the day. Moodie laughed heartily at all my fears; but indeed I found them no joke.

Brian's eldest son, a lad of fourteen, was not exactly an idiot, but what, in the old country, is very expressively termed by the poor people a "natural." He could feed and assist himself, had been taught imperfectly to read and write, and could go to and from the town on errands, and carry a message from one farm-house to another; but he was a strange, wayward creature, and evidently inherited, in no small degree, his father's malady.

During the summer months he lived entirely in the woods, near his father's dwelling, only returning to obtain food, which was generally left for him in an outhouse. In the winter, driven home by the severity of the weather, he would sit for days together moping in the chimney-corner, without taking the least notice of what was passing around him. Brian never mentioned this boy—who had a strong, active figure, a handsome, but very inexpressive face—without a deep sigh; and I feel certain that half his own dejection was occasioned by the mental aberration of his child.

One day he sent the lad with a note to our house, to know if Moodie would purchase the half of an ox that he was going to kill. There happened to stand in the corner of the room an open wood box, into which several bushels of fine apples had been thrown; and, while Moodie was writing an answer to the note, the eyes of the idiot were fastened, as if by some magnetic influence, upon the apples. Knowing that Brian had a very fine orchard, I did not offer the boy any of the fruit. When the note was finished, I handed it to him. The lad grasped it mechanically, without removing his fixed gaze from the apples.

"Give that to your father, Tom."

The boy answered not—his ears, his eyes, his whole soul, were concentrated in the apples. Ten minutes elapsed, but he stood motionless, like a pointer at a dead set.

"My good boy, you can go."

He did not stir.

"Is there anything you want?"

"I want," said the lad, without moving his eyes from the objects of his intense desire, and speaking in a slow, pointed manner, which ought to have been heard to be fully appreciated, "I want ap-ples!"

"Oh, if that's all, take what you like."

The permission once obtained, the boy flung himself upon the box with the rapacity of a hawk upon its prey, after being long poised in the air, to fix its certain aim; thrusting his hands to the right and left, in order to secure the finest specimens of the devoted fruit, scarcely allowing himself time to breathe until he had filled his old straw hat and all his pockets with apples. To help laughing was impossible; while this new Tom o' Bedlam[1] darted from the house, and scampered across the field for dear life, as if afraid that we should pursue him, to rob him of his prize.

It was during the winter that our friend Brian was left a fortune of three hundred pounds per annum; but it was necessary for him to return to his native country, in order to take possession of the property.

---

1. Tom O'Bedlam, like Tom Fool, were names given to the male inmates of Bedlam Asylum. "Tom O'Bedlam's Song" or "Mad Tom's Song" (c. 1615) had a brief popularity but the name become synonymous with madness in later centuries.

This he positively refused to do; and when we remonstrated with him on the apparent imbecility of this resolution, he declared that he would not risk his life, in crossing the Atlantic twice, for twenty times that sum. What strange inconsistency was this, in a being who had three times attempted to take away that which he dreaded so much to lose accidentally!

I was much amused with an account which he gave me, in his quaint way, of an excursion he went upon with a botanist, to collect specimens of the plants and flowers of Upper Canada.

"It was a fine spring day, some ten years ago, and I was yoking my oxen to drag in some oats I had just sown, when a little, fat, punchy man, with a broad, red, good-natured face, and carrying a small black leathern wallet across his shoulder, called to me over the fence, and asked me if my name was Brian B[ouskill]? I said, 'Yes; what of that?'

" 'Only, you are the man I want to see. They tell me that you are better acquainted with the woods than any person in these parts; and I will pay you anything in reason if you will be my guide for a few days.'

" 'Where do you want to go?' said I.

" 'Nowhere in particular,' says he. 'I want to go here and there, in all directions, to collect plants and flowers.'

"That is still-hunting with a vengeance, thought I. 'Today I must drag in my oats. If to-morrow will suit, we will be off.'

" 'And your charge?' said he. 'I like to be certain of that.'

" 'A dollar a-day. My time and labour upon my farm, at this busy season, is worth more than that.'

" 'True,' said he. 'Well, I'll give you what you ask. At what time will you be ready to start?'

" 'By daybreak, if you wish it.'

"Away he went; and by daylight next morning he was at my door, mounted upon a stout French pony. 'What are you going to do with that beast?' said I. 'Horses are no use on the road that you and I are to travel. You had better leave him in my stable.'

" 'I want him to carry my traps,' said he; 'it may be some days that we shall be absent.'

"I assured him that he must be his own beast of burthen, and carry his axe, and blanket, and wallet of food upon his own back. The little body did not much relish this arrangement; but as there was no help for it, he very good-naturedly complied. Off we set, and soon climbed the steep ridge at the back of your farm, and got upon [Rice L]ake plains. The woods were flush with flowers; and the little man grew into such an ecstacy, that at every fresh specimen he uttered a yell of joy, cut a caper in the air, and flung himself down upon them, as if he was drunk with delight. 'Oh, what treasures! what treasures!' he cried. 'I shall make my fortune!'

"It is seldom I laugh," quoth Brian, "but I could not help laughing at this odd little man; for it was not the beautiful blossoms, such as you delight to paint, that drew forth these exclamations, but the queer little plants, which he had rummaged for at the roots of old trees, among the moss and long grass. He sat upon a decayed trunk, which lay in our path, I do believe for a long hour, making an oration over some greyish things, spotted with red, that grew upon it, which looked more like mould than plants, declaring himself repaid for all the trouble and expense he had been at, if it were only to obtain a sight of them. I gathered him a beautiful blossom of the lady's slipper; but he pushed it back when I presented it to him, saying, 'Yes, yes; 'tis very fine. I have seen that often before; but these lichens are splendid.'

"The man had so little taste that I thought him a fool, and so I left him to talk to his dear plants, while I shot partridges for our supper. We spent six days in the woods, and the little man filled his black wallet with all sorts of rubbish, as if he wilfully shut his eyes to the beautiful flowers, and chose only to admire ugly, insignificant plants that everybody else passes by without noticing, and which, often as I had been in the woods, I never had observed before. I never pursued a deer with such earnestness as he continued his hunt for what he called 'specimens.'

"When we came to the Cold Creek[2] which is pretty deep in places, he was in such a hurry to get at some plants that grew under the water, that in reaching after them he lost his balance and fell head over heels into the stream. He got a thorough ducking, and was in a terrible fright; but he held on to the flowers which had caused the trouble, and thanked his stars that he had saved them as well as his life. Well, he was an innocent man," continued Brian; "a very little made him happy, and at night he would sing and amuse himself like a child. He gave me ten dollars for my trouble, and I never saw him again; but I often think of him, when hunting in the woods that we wandered through together, and I pluck the wee plants that he used to admire, and wonder why he preferred them to fine flowers."

When our resolution was formed to sell our farm, and take up our grant of land in the backwoods, no one was so earnest in trying to persuade us to give up this ruinous scheme as our friend Brian B[ouskill], who became quite eloquent in his description of the trials and sorrows that awaited us. During the last week of our stay in the township of H[amilton], he visited us every evening, and never bade us good-night without a tear moistening his cheek. We parted with the hunter as with an old friend; and we never met again. His fate was a sad one. After we left that part of the country, he fell into a moping melancholy, which ended in self-destruction.[3] But a kinder or warmer-hearted man, while he enjoyed the light of reason, has seldom crossed our path.

THE DYING HUNTER TO HIS DOG.[4]

Lie down, lie down, my noble hound!
    That joyful bark give o'er;
It wakes the lonely echoes round,
    But rouses me no more.

2. Perhaps Cold Creek near the town of Frankford, Ontario, southeast of the Rice Lake Plains.
3. Bouskill finally succeeded in committing suicide in 1837.
4. This poem first appeared in *The Literary Garland* (Montreal), NS 1:12 (December 1843), p. 548.

Thy lifted ears, thy swelling chest,
    Thine eye so keenly bright,
No longer kindle in my breast
    The thrill of fierce delight;
As following thee, on foaming steed,
My eager soul outstripp'd thy speed.

Lie down, lie down, my faithful hound!
    And watch this night with me.
For thee again the horn shall sound,
    By mountain, stream, and tree;
And thou, along the forest glade,
    Shalt track the flying deer
When, cold and silent, I am laid
    In chill oblivion here.
Another voice shall cheer thee on,
And glory when the chase is won.

Lie down, lie down, my gallant hound!
    Thy master's life is sped;
And, couch'd upon the dewy ground,
    'Tis thine to watch the dead.
But when the blush of early day
    Is kindling in the sky,
Then speed thee, faithful friend, away,
    And to my Agnes hie;
And guide her to this lonely spot,
Though my closed eyes behold her not.

Lie down, lie down, my trusty hound!
    Death comes, and now we part.
In my dull ear strange murmurs sound—
    More faintly throbs my heart;
The many twinkling lights of Heaven
    Scarce glimmer in the blue—
Chill round me falls the breath of even,
    Cold on my brow the dew;
Earth, stars, and heavens are lost to sight—
The chase is o'er!—brave friend, good-night!

Eleven

The Charivari

Our fate is seal'd! 'Tis now in vain to sigh
    For home, or friends, or country left behind.
Come, dry those tears, and lift the downcast eye
    To the high heaven of hope, and be resign'd;
Wisdom and time will justify the deed,
The eye will cease to weep, the heart to bleed.

Love's thrilling sympathies, affections pure,
　　All that endear'd and hallow'd your lost home,
Shall on a broad foundation, firm and sure,
　　Establish peace; the wilderness become
Dear as the distant land you fondly prize,
Or dearer visions that in memory rise.

The moan of the wind tells of the coming rain that it bears upon its wings; the deep stillness of the woods, and the lengthened shadows they cast upon the stream, silently but surely foreshow the bursting of the thunder-cloud; and who that has lived for any time upon the coast, can mistake the language of the waves—that deep prophetic surging that ushers in the terrible gale? So it is with the human heart—it has its mysterious warnings, its fits of sunshine and shade, of storm and calm, now elevated with anticipations of joy, now depressed by dark presentiments of ill.

All who have ever trodden this earth, possessed of the powers of thought and reflection, of tracing effects back to their causes, have listened to these voices of the soul, and secretly acknowledged their power; but few, very few, have had courage boldly to declare their belief in them: the wisest and the best have given credence to them, and the experience of every day proves their truth; yea, the proverbs of past ages abound with allusions to the same subject, and though the worldly may sneer, and the good man reprobate the belief in a theory which he considers dangerous, yet the former, when he appears led by an irresistible impulse to enter into some fortunate, but until then unthought-of speculation; and the latter, when he devoutly exclaims that God has met him in prayer, unconsciously acknowledge the same spiritual agency. For my own part, I have no doubts upon the subject, and have found many times, and at different periods of my life, that the voice in the soul speaks truly; that if we gave stricter heed to its mysterious warnings, we should be saved much after-sorrow.[1]

Well do I remember how sternly and solemnly this inward monitor warned me of approaching ill, the last night I spent at home; how it strove to draw me back as from a fearful abyss, beseeching me not to leave England and emigrate to Canada, and how gladly would I have obeyed the injunction had it still been in my power. I had bowed to a superior mandate, the command of duty; for my husband's sake, for the sake of the infant, whose little bosom heaved against my swelling heart, I had consented to bid adieu for ever to my native shores, and it seemed both useless and sinful to draw back.

Yet, by what stern necessity were we driven forth to seek a new home amid the western wilds? We were not compelled to emigrate. Bound to England by a thousand holy and endearing ties, surrounded by a circle of chosen friends, and happy in each other's love, we possessed all that the world can bestow of good—but *wealth*. The half-pay

---

1. Susanna's interest in what we now call extrasensory perception (ESP) underlies her remarks here. Such leanings led her in the 1850s to personal involvement in the lore and practice of Spiritualism.

of a subaltern officer, managed with the most rigid economy, is too small to supply the wants of a family; and if of a good family, not enough to maintain his original standing in society. True, it may find his children bread, it may clothe them indifferently, but it leaves nothing for the indispensable requirements of education, or the painful contingencies of sickness and misfortune. In such a case, it is both wise and right to emigrate; Nature points it out as the only safe remedy for the evils arising out of an over dense population, and her advice is always founded upon justice and truth.

Up to the period of which I now speak, we had not experienced much inconvenience from our very limited means. Our wants were few, and we enjoyed many of the comforts and even some of the luxuries of life; and all had gone on smoothly and lovingly with us until the birth of our first child. It was then that prudence whispered to the father, "You are happy and contented now, but this cannot always last; the birth of that child whom you have hailed with as much rapture as though she were born to inherit a noble estate, is to you the beginning of care. Your family may increase, and your wants will increase in proportion; out of what fund can you satisfy their demands? Some provision must be made for the future, and made quickly, while youth and health enable you to combat successfully with the ills of life. When you married for inclination, you knew that emigration must be the result of such an act of imprudence in over-populated England. Up and be doing, while you still possess the means of transporting yourself to a land where the industrious can never lack bread, and where there is a chance that wealth and independence may reward virtuous toil."

Alas! that truth should ever whisper such unpleasant realities to the lover of ease—to the poet, the author, the musician, the man of books, of refined taste and gentlemanly habits. Yet he took the hint, and began to bestir himself with the spirit and energy so characteristic of the glorious North, from whence he sprung.[2]

"The sacrifice," he said, "must be made, and the sooner the better. My dear wife, I feel confident that you will respond to the call of duty; and hand-in-hand and heart-in-heart we will go forth to meet difficulties, and, by the help of God, to subdue them."

Dear husband! I take shame to myself that my purpose was less firm, that my heart lingered so far behind yours in preparing for this great epoch in our lives; that, like Lot's wife,[3] I still turned and looked back, and clung with all my strength to the land I was leaving. It was not the hardships of an emigrant's life I dreaded. I could bear mere physical privations philosophically enough; it was the loss of the society in which I had moved, the want of congenial minds, of persons engaged in congenial pursuits, that made me so reluctant to respond to my husband's call.

I was the youngest in a family remarkable for their literary attain-

2. John Moodie came from the Island of Hoy in the Orkney Islands, off the northeast coast of Scotland.
3. In Genesis, Lot's wife is following her husband out of Sodom when she looks back, against God's command. She immediately turns into a pillar of salt.

ments;[4] and, while yet a child, I had seen riches melt away from our once prosperous home, as the Canadian snows dissolve before the first warm days of spring, leaving the verdureless earth naked and bare.

There was, however, a spirit in my family that rose superior to the crushing influences of adversity. Poverty, which so often degrades the weak mind, became their best teacher, the stern but fruitful parent of high resolve and ennobling thought. The very misfortunes that overwhelmed, became the source from whence they derived both energy and strength, as the inundation of some mighty river fertilises the shores over which it first spreads ruin and desolation. Without losing aught of their former position in society, they dared to be poor; to place mind above matter, and make the talents with which the great Father had liberally endowed them, work out their appointed end. The world sneered, and summer friends forsook them; they turned their backs upon the world, and upon the ephemeral tribes that live but in its smiles.

From out the solitude in which they dwelt, their names went forth through the crowded cities of that cold, sneering world, and their names were mentioned with respect by the wise and good; and what they lost in wealth, they more than regained in well-earned reputation.

Brought up in this school of self-denial, it would have been strange indeed if all its wise and holy precepts had brought forth no corresponding fruit. I endeavoured to reconcile myself to the change that awaited me, to accommodate my mind and pursuits to the new position in which I found myself placed.

Many a hard battle had we to fight with old prejudices, and many proud swellings of the heart to subdue, before we could feel the least interest in the land of our adoption, or look upon it as our home.

All was new, strange, and distasteful to us; we shrank from the rude, coarse familiarity of the uneducated people among whom we were thrown; and they in return viewed us as innovators, who wished to curtail their independence by expecting from them the kindly civilities and gentle courtesies of a more refined community. They considered us proud and shy, when we were only anxious not to give offence. The semi-barbarous Yankee squatters, who had "left their country for their country's good,"[5] and by whom we were surrounded in our first settlement, detested us, and with them we could have no feeling in common. We could neither lie nor cheat in our dealings with them; and they despised us for our ignorance in trading and our want of smartness.

The utter want of that common courtesy with which a well-brought-up European addresses the poorest of his brethren, is severely felt at first by settlers in Canada. At the period of which I am now speaking,

---

4. By 1848, Susanna could write confidently about the literary successes of her sisters. Five of the six were published writers of some reputation. In particular, Agnes (and Eliza, Agnes's silent partner) had gained international acclaim for their multivolume series *The Lives of the Queens of England*. Susanna did not hesitate to dedicate *Roughing It in the Bush* to Agnes, trading on her most important family connection.
5. See Chapter Five, note 3, p. 70.

the titles of "sir" or "madam" were very rarely applied by inferiors. They entered your house without knocking; and while boasting of their freedom, violated one of its dearest laws, which considers even the cottage of the poorest labourer his castle, and his privacy sacred.

"Is your man to hum?"—"Is the woman within?" were the general inquiries made to me by such guests, while my bare-legged, ragged Irish servants were always spoken to as "sir" and "*mem*," as if to make the distinction more pointed.

Why they treated our claims to their respect with marked insult and rudeness, I never could satisfactorily determine, in any way that could reflect honour on the species, or even plead an excuse for its brutality, until I found that this insolence was more generally practised by the low, uneducated emigrants from Britain, who better understood your claims to their civility, than by the natives themselves. Then I discovered the secret.

The unnatural restraint which society imposes upon these people at home forces them to treat their more fortunate brethren with a servile deference which is repugnant to their feelings, and is thrust upon them by the dependent circumstances in which they are placed. This homage to rank and education is not sincere. Hatred and envy lie rankling at their heart, although hidden by outward obsequiousness. Necessity compels their obedience; they fawn, and cringe, and flatter the wealth on which they depend for bread. But let them once emigrate, the clog which fettered them is suddenly removed; they are free; and the dearest privilege of this freedom is to wreak upon their superiors the long-locked-up hatred of their hearts. They think they can debase you to their level by disallowing all your claims to distinction; while they hope to exalt themselves and their fellows into ladies and gentlemen by sinking you back to the only title you received from Nature—plain "man" and "woman." Oh, how much more honourable than their vulgar pretensions!

I never knew the real dignity of these simple epithets until they were insultingly thrust upon us by the working-classes of Canada.

But from this folly the native-born Canadian is exempt; it is only practised by the low-born Yankee, or the Yankeefied British peasantry and mechanics. It originates in the enormous reaction springing out of a sudden emancipation from a state of utter dependence into one of unrestrained liberty. As such, I not only excuse, but forgive it, for the principle is founded in nature; and, however disgusting and distasteful to those accustomed to different treatment from their inferiors, it is better than a hollow profession of duty and attachment urged upon us by a false and unnatural position. Still, it is very irksome until you think more deeply upon it; and then it serves to amuse rather than to irritate.

And here I would observe, before quitting this subject, that of all follies, that of taking out servants from the old country is one of the greatest, and is sure to end in the loss of the money expended in their passage, and to become the cause of deep disappointment and mortification to yourself.

They no sooner set foot upon the Canadian shores than they become possessed with this ultra-republican spirit. All respect for their employers, all subordination, is at an end; the very air of Canada severs the tie of mutual obligation which bound you together. They fancy themselves not only equal to you in rank, but that ignorance and vulgarity give them superior claims to notice. They demand in terms the highest wages, and grumble at doing half the work, in return, which they cheerfully performed at home. They demand to eat at your table, and to sit in your company; and if you refuse to listen to their dishonest and extravagant claims, they tell you that "they are free; that no contract signed in the old country is binding in 'Meriky;' that you may look out for another person to fill their place as soon as you like; and that you may get the money expended in their passage and outfit in the best manner you can."

I was unfortunately persuaded to take out a woman with me as a nurse for my child during the voyage, as I was in very poor health; and her conduct, and the trouble and expense she occasioned, were a perfect illustration of what I have described.[6]

When we consider the different position in which servants are placed in the old and new world, this conduct, ungrateful as it then appeared to me, ought not to create the least surprise. In Britain, for instance, they are too often dependent upon the caprice of their employers for bread. Their wages are low; their moral condition still lower. They are brought up in the most servile fear of the higher classes, and they feel most keenly their hopeless degradation, for no effort on their part can better their condition. They know that if once they get a bad character, they must starve or steal; and to this conviction we are indebted for a great deal of their seeming fidelity and long and laborious service in our families, which we owe less to any moral perception on their part of the superior kindness or excellence of their employers, than to the mere feeling of assurance, that as long as they do their work well, and are cheerful and obedient, they will be punctually paid their wages, and well housed and fed.

Happy is it for them and their masters when even this selfish bond of union exists between them!

But in Canada the state of things in this respect is wholly reversed. The serving class, comparatively speaking, is small, and admits of little competition. Servants that understand the work of the country are not easily procured, and such always can command the highest wages. The possession of a good servant is such an addition to comfort, that they are persons of no small consequence, for the dread of starving no longer frightens them into servile obedience. They can live without you, and they well know that you cannot do without them. If you attempt to practice upon them that common vice of English mistresses, to scold them for any slight omission or offence, you rouse into active operation all their new-found spirit of freedom and opposition. They turn upon you with a torrent of abuse; they demand their wages, and

---

6. Hannah's errant and indulgent behaviour is more fully documented in *Flora Lyndsay*.

declare their intention of quitting you instantly. The more inconvenient the time for you, the more bitter become their insulting remarks. They tell you, with a high hand, that "they are as good as you; that they can get twenty better places by the morrow, and that they don't care a snap for your anger." And away they bounce, leaving you to finish a large wash, or a heavy job of ironing, in the best way you can.

When we look upon such conduct as the reaction arising out of their former state, we cannot so much blame them, and are obliged to own that it is the natural result of a sudden emancipation from former restraint. With all their insolent airs of independence, I must confess that I prefer the Canadian to the European servant. If they turn out good and faithful, it springs more from real respect and affection, and you possess in your domestic a valuable assistant and friend; but this will never be the case with a servant brought out with you from the old country, for the reasons before assigned. The happy independence enjoyed in this highly-favoured land is nowhere better illustrated than in the fact that no domestic can be treated with cruelty or insolence by an unbenevolent or arrogant master.

Seventeen years has made as great a difference in the state of society in Canada as it has in its commercial and political importance. When we came to the Canadas, society was composed of elements which did not always amalgamate in the best possible manner.

We were reckoned no addition to the society of C[obourg]. Authors and literary people they held in supreme detestation; and I was told by a lady, the very first time I appeared in company, that "she heard that I wrote books, but she could tell me that they did not want a Mrs. Trollope in Canada."[7]

I had not then read Mrs. Trollope's work on America, or I should have comprehended at once the cause of her indignation; for she was just such a person as would have drawn forth the keen satire of that far-seeing observer of the absurdities of our nature, whose witty exposure of American affectation has done more towards producing a reform in that respect, than would have resulted from a thousand grave animadversions soberly written.

Another of my self-constituted advisers informed me, with great asperity in her look and tone, that "it would be better for me to lay by the pen, and betake myself to some more useful employment; that she thanked her God that she could make a shirt, and see to the cleaning of her house!"

These remarks were perfectly gratuitous, and called forth by no observation of mine; for I tried to conceal my blue stockings[8] beneath the long conventional robes of the tamest commonplace, hoping to cover the faintest tinge of the objectionable colour. I had spoken to neither of these women in my life, and was much amused by their re-

7. Frances Trollope's *Domestic Manners of the Americans* (London, 1832) was enormously popular in Britain, confirming many British biases about Americans and making its author a hated figure in the United States.
8. "Blue stockings" alludes to authorship and a style of dress that became associated with women who write or are intellectual in their tastes.

marks; particularly as I could both make a shirt, and attend to the domestic arrangement of my family, as well as either of them.

I verily believe that they expected to find an author one of a distinct
species from themselves; that they imagined the aforesaid biped
should neither eat, drink, sleep, nor talk like other folks;—a proud,
useless, self-conceited, affected animal, that deserved nothing but
kicks and buffets from the rest of mankind.

Anxious not to offend them, I tried to avoid all literary subjects. I
confined my conversation to topics of common interest; but this gave
greater offence than the most ostentatious show of learning, for they
concluded that I would not talk on such subjects, because I thought
them incapable of understanding me. This was more wounding to
their self-love than the most arrogant assumption on my part; and they
regarded me with a jealous, envious stand-aloofishness, that was so intolerable that I gave up all ideas of visiting them. I was so accustomed
to hear the whispered remark, or to have it retailed to me by others,
"Oh, yes; she can write, but she can do nothing else," that I was made
more diligent in cultivating every branch of domestic usefulness; so
that these ill-natured sarcasms ultimately led to my acquiring a great
mass of most useful practical knowledge. Yet—such is the contradiction inherent in our poor fallen nature—these people were more annoyed by my proficiency in the common labours of a household, than
they would have been by any displays of my unfortunate authorship.
Never was the fable of the old man and his ass so truly verified.[9]

There is very little of the social, friendly visiting among the Canadians which constitutes the great charm of home. Their hospitality is
entirely reserved for those monster meetings in which they vie with
each other in displaying fine clothes and costly furniture. As these
large parties are very expensive, few families can afford to give more
than one during the visiting season, which is almost exclusively confined to the winter. The great gun once fired, you meet no more at the
same house around the social board until the ensuing year, and would
scarcely know that you had a neighbour, were it not for a formal morning call made now and then, just to remind you that such individuals
are in the land of the living, and still exist in your near vicinity.

I am speaking of visiting in the towns and villages. The manners and
habits of the European settlers in the country are far more simple and
natural, and their hospitality more genuine and sincere. They have not
been sophisticated by the hard, worldly wisdom of a Canadian town,[1]
and still retain a warm remembrance of the kindly humanities of home.

Among the women, a love of dress exceeds all other passions. In public they dress in silks and satins, and wear the most expensive ornaments, and they display considerable taste in the arrangement and
choice of colours. The wife of a man in moderate circumstances,
whose income does not exceed two or three hundred pounds a-year,

9. A fable attributed to Aesop, the moral of which is "Try to please all and you will end up
pleasing none."
1. In casting judgement upon "the hard, worldly wisdom of a Canadian town," Susanna draws
more on her experience of Belleville after 1840 than on Cobourg.

does not hesitate in expending ten or fifteen pounds upon one article of outside finery, while often her inner garments are not worth as many sous; thus sacrificing to outward show all the real comforts of life.

The aristocracy of wealth is bad enough; but the aristocracy of dress is perfectly contemptible. Could Raphael visit Canada in rags, he would be nothing in their eyes beyond a common sign-painter.[2]

Great and manifold, even to the ruin of families, are the evils arising from this inordinate love for dress. They derive their fashions from the French and Americans—seldom from the English, whom they far surpass in the neatness and elegance of their costume.

The Canadian women, while they retain the bloom and freshness of youth, are exceedingly pretty; but these charms soon fade, owing, perhaps, to the fierce extremes of their climate, or the withering effect of the dry, metallic air of stoves, and their going too early into company and being exposed, while yet children, to the noxious influence of late hours, and the sudden change from heated rooms to cold, biting, bitter winter blast.

Though small of stature, they are generally well and symmetrically formed, and possess a graceful, easy carriage. The early age at which they marry and are introduced into society, takes from them all awkwardness and restraint. A girl of fourteen can enter a crowded ballroom with as much self-possession, and converse with as much confidence, as a matron of forty. The blush of timidity and diffidence is, indeed, rare upon the cheek of a Canadian beauty.

Their education is so limited and confined to so few accomplishments, and these not very perfectly taught, that their conversation seldom goes beyond a particular discussion on their own dress, or that of their neighbours, their houses, furniture, and servants, sometimes interlarded with a *little harmless gossip*, which, however, tells keenly upon the characters of their dear friends.

Yet they have abilities, excellent practical abilities, which, with a little mental culture, would render them intellectual and charming companions. At present, too many of these truly lovely girls remind one of choice flowers half buried in weeds.

Music and dancing are their chief accomplishments. In the former they seldom excel. Though possessing an excellent general taste for music, it is seldom in their power to bestow upon its study the time which is required to make a really good musician. They are admirable proficients in the other art, which they acquire readily, with the least instruction, often without any instruction at all, beyond that which is given almost intuitively by a good ear for time, and a quick perception of the harmony of motion.

The waltz is their favourite dance, in which old and young join with the greatest avidity; it is not unusual to see parents and their grown-up children dancing in the same set in a public ball-room.

Their taste in music is not for the sentimental; they prefer the light,

2. Raphael (Raffaello Sanzio, 1483–1520) was considered by many to be Europe's outstanding painter, especially of religious scenes.

lively tunes of the Virginian minstrels[3] to the most impassioned strains of Bellini.[4]

On entering one of the public ball-rooms, a stranger would be delighted with such a display of pretty faces and neat figures. I have hardly ever seen a really plain Canadian girl in her teens; and a downright ugly one is almost unknown.

The high cheek-bones, wide mouth, and turned-up nose of the Saxon race, so common among the lower classes in Britain, are here succeeded in the next generation, by the small oval face, straight nose, and beautifully-cut mouth of the American; while the glowing tint of the Albion rose pales before the withering influence of late hours and stove-heat.

They are naturally a fine people, and possess capabilities and talents, which when improved by cultivation will render them second to no people in the world; and that period is not far distant.

Idiots and mad people are so seldom met with among natives of the colony, that not one of this description of unfortunates has ever come under my own immediate observation.

To the benevolent philanthropist, whose heart has bled over the misery and pauperism of the lower classes in Great Britain, the almost entire absence of mendicity from Canada would be highly gratifying. Canada has few, if any, native beggars; her objects of charity are generally imported from the mother country, and these are never suffered to want food or clothing. The Canadians are a truly charitable people; no person in distress is driven with harsh and cruel language from their doors; they not only generously relieve the wants of suffering strangers cast upon their bounty, but they nurse them in sickness, and use every means in their power to procure them employment. The number of orphan children yearly adopted by wealthy Canadians, and treated in every respect as their own, is almost incredible.

It is a glorious country for the labouring classes, for while blessed with health they are always certain of employment, and certain also to derive from it ample means of support for their families. An industrious, hard-working man in a few years is able to purchase from his savings a homestead of his own; and in process of time becomes one of the most important and prosperous class of settlers in Canada, her free and independent yeomen, who form the bones and sinews of this rising country, and from among whom she already begins to draw her senators, while their educated sons become the aristocrats of the rising generation.

It has often been remarked to me by people long resident in the colony, that those who come to the country destitute of means, but able and willing to work, invariably improve their condition and be-

3. The Virginia Minstrels specialized in evenings of imitation Negro music. Organized in the early 1840s and led by Daniel Decatur Emmett, the group of four white men performed in blackface and became the model for later touring groups that dominated popular entertainment in North America for decades.

4. Vincenzo Bellini (1801–1835), one of the era's most popular operatic composers. A leader in the "bel canto" tradition, his successes included *I Capuletie*, *I Montecchi*, *Norma*, and *La Sonnambula*.

come independent; while the gentleman who brings out with him a small capital is too often tricked and cheated out of his property, and drawn into rash and dangerous speculations which terminate in his ruin. His children, neglected and uneducated, yet brought up with ideas far beyond their means, and suffered to waste their time in idleness, seldom take to work, and not unfrequently sink down to the lowest class.

But I have dwelt long enough upon these serious subjects; and I will leave my husband, who is better qualified than myself, to give a more accurate account of the country, while I turn to matters of a light and livelier cast.[5]

It was towards the close of the summer of 1833, which had been unusually cold and wet for Canada, while Moodie was absent at D[ouro], inspecting a portion of his government grant of land,[6] that I was startled one night, just before retiring to rest, by the sudden firing of guns in our near vicinity, accompanied by shouts and yells, the braying of horns, the beating of drums, and the barking of all the dogs in the neighbourhood. I never heard a more stunning uproar of discordant and hideous sounds.

What could it all mean? The maid-servant, as much alarmed as myself, opened the door and listened.

"The goodness defend us!" she exclaimed, quickly closing it, and drawing a bolt seldom used. "We shall be murdered. The Yankees must have taken Canada, and are marching hither."

"Nonsense! that cannot be it. Besides they would never leave the main road to attack a poor place like this. Yet the noise is very near. Hark! they are firing again. Bring me the hammer and some nails, and let us secure the windows."

The next moment I laughed at my folly in attempting to secure a log hut, when the application of a match to its rotten walls would consume it in a few minutes. Still, as the noise increased, I was really frightened. My servant, who was Irish (for my Scotch girl, Bell, had taken to herself a husband, and I had been obliged to hire another in her place, who had been only a few days in the country), began to cry and wring her hands, and lament her hard fate in coming to Canada.

Just at this critical moment, when we were both self-convicted of an arrant cowardice which would have shamed a Canadian child of six years old, Mrs. O—— tapped at the door, and although generally a most unwelcome visitor, from her gossiping, mischievous propensities, I gladly let her in.[7]

"Do tell me," I cried, "the meaning of this strange uproar?"

"Oh, 'tis nothing," she replied, laughing; "you and Mary look as white as a sheet; but you need not be alarmed. A set of wild fellows

5. John Moodie contributed two chapters to complete Volume I of the book. His command of statistics and his travels in Canada made him "better qualified" than his wife to generalize on certain "serious subjects."
6. John Moodie had gone north to Duoro to look over the land grant arranged for him by Sam Strickland, and to investigate the possibility of moving north to join the fledgling bush community where Sam and Susanna's sister, Catharine Parr, were already settled.
7. See Chapter Nine, note 5, p. 113.

have met to charivari Old Satan, who has married his fourth wife to-night, a young gal of sixteen. I should not wonder if some mischief happens among them, for they are a bad set, made up of all the idle loafers about Port H[ope] and C[obourg]."

"What is a charivari?" said I. "Do, pray, enlighten me."

"Have you been nine months in Canada, and ask that question? Why, I thought you knew everything! Well, I will tell you what it is. The charivari is a custom that the Canadians got from the French, in the Lower Province, and a queer custom it is. When an old man marries a young wife, or an old woman a young husband, or two old people, who ought to be thinking of their graves, enter for the second or third time into the holy estate of wedlock, as the priest calls it, all the idle young fellows in the neighbourhood meet together to charivari them. For this purpose they disguise themselves, blackening their faces, putting their clothes on hind part before, and wearing horrible masks, with grotesque caps on their heads, adorned with cocks' feathers and bells. They then form in a regular body, and proceed to the bridegroom's house, to the sound of tin kettles, horns, and drums, cracked fiddles, and all the discordant instruments they can collect together. Thus equipped, they surround the house where the wedding is held, just at the hour when the happy couple are supposed to be about to retire to rest—beating upon the door with clubs and staves, and demanding of the bridegroom admittance to drink the bride's health, or in lieu thereof to receive a certain sum of money to treat the band at the nearest tavern.

"If the bridegroom refuses to appear and grant their request, they commence the horrible din you hear, firing guns charged with peas against the doors and windows, rattling old pots and kettles, and abusing him for his stinginess in no measured terms. Sometimes they break open the doors, and seize upon the bridegroom; and he may esteem himself a very fortunate man, under such circumstances, if he escapes being ridden upon a rail, tarred and feathered, and otherwise maltreated. I have known many fatal accidents arise out of an imprudent refusal to satisfy the demands of the assailants. People have even lost their lives in the fray; and I think the government should interfere, and put down these riotous meetings. Surely it is very hard that an old man cannot marry a young gal, if she is willing to take him, without asking the leave of such a rabble as that. What right have they to interfere with his private affairs?"[8]

"What, indeed?" said I, feeling a truly British indignation at such a lawless infringement upon the natural rights of man.

"I remember," continued Mrs. O——, who had got fairly started upon a favourite subject, "a scene of this kind, that was acted two years ago, at——, when old Mr. P—— took his third wife. He was a

---

8. The French custom of *charivari* has pagan origins; friends and relatives of newlyweds would beat on drums and make noise to scare off any evil spirits that might plague the couple. By the time the custom reached Canada and other locations in the French diaspora, including Louisiana, it had degenerated into the ceremony Mrs. O—— describes, in which the newlyweds were hounded and teased for money and gifts.

very rich storekeeper, and had made during the war a great deal of money.[9] He felt lonely in his old age, and married a young, handsome widow, to enliven his house. The lads in the village were determined to make him pay for his frolic. This got wind, and Mr. P—— was advised to spend the honeymoon in Toronto; but he only laughed, and said that 'he was not going to be frightened from his comfortable home by the threats of a few wild boys.' In the morning, he was married at the church, and spent the day at home, where he entertained a large party of his own and the bride's friends. During the evening all the idle chaps in the town collected round the house, headed by a mad young bookseller, who had offered himself for their captain, and, in the usual forms, demanded a sight of the bride, and liquor to drink her health. They were very good-naturedly received by Mr. P——, who sent a friend down to them to bid them welcome, and to inquire on what terms they would consent to let him off, and disperse.

"The captain of the band demanded sixty pounds, as he, Mr. P——, could well afford to pay it.

" 'That's too much, my fine fellows!' cried Mr. P—— from the open window. 'Say twenty-five, and I will send you down a cheque upon the bank of Montreal for the money.'

" 'Thirty! thirty! thirty! old boy!' roared a hundred voices. 'Your wife's worth that. Down with the cash, and we will give you three cheers, and three times three for the bride, and leave you to sleep in peace. If you hang back, we will raise such a 'larum about your ears that you shan't know that your wife's your own for a month to come!'

" 'I'll give you twenty-five,' remonstrated the bridegroom, not the least alarmed at their threats, and laughing all the time in his sleeve.

" 'Thirty; not one copper less!' Here they gave him such a salute of diabolical sounds that he ran from the window with his hands to his ears, and his friend came down stairs to the verandah, and gave them the sum they required. They did not expect that the old man would have been so liberal, and they gave him the 'Hip, hip, hip, hurrah!' in fine style, and marched off to finish the night and spend the money at the tavern."

"And do people allow themselves to be bullied out of their property by such ruffians?"

"Ah, my dear! 'tis the custom of the country, and 'tis not so easy to put it down. But I can tell you that a charivari is not always a joke.

"There was another affair that happened, just before you came to the place, that occasioned no small talk in the neighborhood; and well it might, for it was a most disgraceful piece of business, and attended with very serious consequences. Some of the charivari party had to fly, or they might have ended their days in the penitentiary.

"There was a runaway nigger from the States came to the village, and set up a barber's poll, and settled among us. I am no friend to the

---

9. Possibly Ebenezer Perry, a prosperous Cobourg merchant who, after his wife died in 1832, married a widow named Susannah Spencer. His story made for exciting local gossip. See the Cobourg *Star* June 6, 1832, p. 5, and November 7, 1832, p. 7. Perry had made his early fortune during the War of 1812 and thrived as one of the controllers of Cobourg Harbour.

blacks; but really Tom Smith was such a quiet, good-natured fellow, and so civil and obliging, that he soon got a good business. He was clever, too, and cleaned old clothes until they looked almost as good as new. Well, after a time he persuaded a white girl to marry him. She was not a bad-looking Irishwoman, and I can't think what bewitched the creature to take him.

"Her marriage with the black man created a great sensation in the town. All the young fellows were indignant at his presumption and her folly, and they determined to give them the charivari in fine style, and punish them both for the insult they had put upon the place.

"Some of the young gentlemen in the town joined in the frolic. They went so far as to enter the house, drag the poor nigger from his bed, and in spite of his shrieks for mercy, they hurried him out into the cold air—for it was winter—and almost naked as he was, rode him upon a rail, and so ill-treated him that he died under their hands.

"They left the body, when they found what had happened, and fled. The ringleaders escaped across the lake to the other side; and those who remained could not be sufficiently identified to bring them to trial. The affair was hushed up; but it gave great uneasiness to several respectable families whose sons were in the scrape."

"Good heavens! are such things permitted in a Christian country? But scenes like these must be of rare occurrence?"

"They are more common than you imagine. A man was killed up at W—— the other day, and two others dangerously wounded, at a charivari. The bridegroom was a man in middle life, a desperately resolute and passionate man, and he swore that if such riff-raff dared to interfere with him, he would shoot at them with as little compunction as he would at so many crows. His threats only increased the mischievous determination of the mob to torment him; and when he refused to admit their deputation, or even to give them a portion of the wedding cheer, they determined to frighten him into compliance by firing several guns, loaded with peas, at his door. Their salute was returned from the chamber window, by the discharge of a double-barrelled gun, loaded with buck-shot. The crowd gave back with a tremendous yell. Their leader was shot through the heart, and two of the foremost in the scuffle dangerously wounded. They vowed they would set fire to the house, but the bridegroom boldly stepped to the window, and told them to try it, and before they could light a torch he would fire among them again, as his gun was reloaded, and he would discharge it at them as long as one of them dared to remain on his premises.

"They cleared off; but though Mr. A—— was not punished for the *accident*, as it was called, he became a marked man, and lately left the colony, to settle in the United States.

"Why, Mrs. Moodie, you look quite serious. I can, however, tell you a less dismal tale. A charivari would seldom be attended with bad consequences if people would take it as a joke, and join in the spree."

"A very dignified proceeding, for a bride and bridegroom to make themselves the laughing-stock of such people!"

"Oh, but custom reconciles us to everything; and 'tis better to give up a little of our pride than endanger the lives of our fellow-creatures. I have been told a story of a lady in the Lower Province, who took for her second husband a young fellow, who, as far as his age was concerned, might have been her son. The mob surrounded her house at night, carrying her effigy in an open coffin, supported by six young lads, with white favours in their hats; and they buried the poor bride, amid shouts of laughter, and the usual accompaniments, just opposite her drawing-room windows. The widow was highly amused by the whole of their proceedings, but she wisely let them have their own way. She lived in a strong stone house, and she barred the doors, and closed the iron shutters, and set them at defiance.

" 'As long as she enjoyed her health,' she said, 'they were welcome to bury her in effigy as often as they pleased; she was really glad to be able to afford amusement to so many people.'

"Night after night, during the whole of that winter, the same party beset her house with their diabolical music; but she only laughed at them.

"The leader of the mob was a young lawyer from these parts, a sad mischievous fellow; the widow became aware of this, and she invited him one evening to take tea with a small party at her house. He accepted the invitation, was charmed with her hearty and hospitable welcome, and soon found himself quite at home; but only think how ashamed he must have felt, when the same 'larum commenced, at the usual hour, in front of the lady's house!

"Oh,' said Mrs. R——, smiling to her husband, 'here come our friends. Really, Mr. K——, they amuse us so much of an evening that I should feel quite dull without them.'

"From that hour the charivari ceased, and the old lady was left to enjoy the society of her young husband in quiet.

"I assure you, Mrs. Moodie, that the charivari often deters old people from making disgraceful marriages, so that it is not wholly without its use."

A few days after the charivari affair, Mrs. D——[1] stepped in to see me. She was an American; a very respectable old lady, who resided in a handsome frame-house on the main road. I was at dinner, the servant-girl, in the meanwhile, nursing my child at a distance. Mrs. D—— sat looking at me very seriously until I concluded my meal, her dinner having been accomplished several hours before. When I had finished, the girl gave me the child, and then removed the dinner-service into an outer room.

"You don't eat with your helps," said my visitor. "Is not that something like pride?"

"It is custom," said I; "we were not used to do so at home, and I think that keeping a separate table is more comfortable for both parties."

"Are you not both of the same flesh and blood? The rich and poor meet together, and the Lord is the maker of them all."

---

1. Possibly one of the Dean women who lived on the "front" road. See Chapter Ten, note 7, p. 121.

"True. Your quotation is just, and I assent to it with all my heart. There is no difference in the flesh and blood; but education makes a difference in the mind and manners, and, till these can assimilate, it is better to keep apart."

"Ah! you are not a good Christian, Mrs. Moodie. The Lord thought more of the poor than He did of the rich, and He obtained more followers from among them. Now, *we* always take our meals with our people."

Presently after, while talking over the affairs of our households, I happened to say that the cow we had bought of Mollineaux had turned out extremely well, and gave a great deal of milk.

"That man lived with us several years," she said; "he was an excellent servant, and D—— paid him his wages in land. The farm that he now occupies formed a part of our U.E. grant. But, for all his good conduct, I never could abide him, for being a *black*."

"Indeed! Is he not the same flesh and blood as the rest?"

The colour rose into Mrs. D——'s sallow face, and she answered, with much warmth,

"What! do you mean to compare *me* with a *nigger*?"

"Not exactly. But, after all, the colour makes the only difference between him and uneducated men of the same class."

"Mrs. Moodie!" she exclaimed, holding up her hands in pious horror; "they are the children of the devil! God never condescended to make a nigger."

"Such an idea is an impeachment of the power and majesty of the Almighty: How can you believe in such an ignorant fable?"

"Well, then," said my monitress, in high dudgeon, "if the devil did not make them, they are descended from Cain."

"But all Cain's posterity perished in the flood."

My visitor was puzzled.

"The African race, it is generally believed, are the descendants of Ham, and to many of their tribes the curse pronounced against him seems to cling. To be the servant of servants is bad enough, without our making their condition worse by our cruel persecutions. Christ came to seek and to save that which was lost; and in proof of this inestimable promise, he did not reject the Ethiopian eunuch who was baptised by Philip, and who was, doubtless, as black as the rest of his people. Do you not admit Mollineux to your table with other helps?"

"Good God! do you think that I would sit down at the same table with a nigger? My helps would leave the house if I dared to put such an affront upon them. Sit down with a dirty black indeed!"

"Do you think, Mrs. D——, that there will be any negroes in heaven?"

"Certainly not, or I, for one, would never wish to go there;" and out of the house she sallied in high disdain.

Yet this was the woman who had given me such a plausible lecture on pride. Alas, for our fallen nature! Which is more subversive of peace and Christian fellowship—ignorance of our own characters, or of the characters of others?

Our departure for the woods became now a frequent theme of conversation. My husband had just returned from an exploring expedition to the backwoods, and was delighted with the prospect of removing thither. The only thing I listened to in their praise, with any degree of interest, was a lively little song, which he had written during his brief sojourn at Douro:—

TO THE WOODS!—TO THE WOODS!

To the woods!—to the woods!—The sun shines bright,
    The smoke rises high in the clear frosty air;
Our axes are sharp, and our hearts are light,
    Let us toil while we can and drive away care.
Though homely our food, we are merry and strong,
    And labour is wealth, which no man can deny;
At eve we will chase the dull hours with a song,
    And at grey peep of dawn let this be our cry,

      To the woods!—to the woods!—&c.

Hark! how the trees crack in the keen morning blast,
    And see how the rapids are cover'd with steam;
Thaw your axes, my lads, the sun rises fast,
    And gilds the pine tops with his bright golden beam.

      To the woods!—to the woods!—&c.

Come, chop away, lads! the wild woods resound,
    Let your quick-falling strokes in due harmony ring;
See, the lofty tree shivers—it falls to the ground!
    Now with voices united together we'll sing—
To the woods!—to the woods!—The sun shines bright,
    The smoke rises high in the clear frosty air;
Our axes are sharp, and our hearts are light,
    Let us toil while we can, and drive away care,
      And drive away care.

                J. W. D. M.

Twelve

The Village Hotel

(An Intermediate Chapter, by J. W. D. Moodie.)

Well, stranger, here you are all safe and sound;
    You're now on shore. Methinks you look aghast,—
As if you'd made some slight mistake, and found
    A land you liked not. Think not of the past;
Your leading-strings are cut; the mystic chain
    That bound you to your fair and smiling shore

Is sever'd now, indeed. 'Tis now in vain
To sigh for joys that can return no more.

Emigration, however necessary as the obvious means of providing for
the increasing population of early-settled and over-peopled countries,
is indeed a very serious matter to the individual emigrant and his family. He is thrown adrift, as it were, on a troubled ocean, the winds and
currents of which are unknown to him. His past experience, and his
judgment founded on experience, will be useless to him in this new
sphere of action. In an old country, where generation after generation
inhabits the same spot, the mental dispositions and prejudices of our
ancestors become in a manner hereditary, and descend to their children with their possessions. In a new colony, on the contrary, the
habits and associations of the emigrant having been broken up for
ever, he is suddenly thrown on his own internal resources, and compelled to act and decide at once; not unfrequently under pain of misery or starvation. He is surrounded with dangers, often without the
ordinary means which common-sense and prudence suggest of avoiding them,—because the *experience* on which these common qualities
are founded is wanting. Separated for ever from those warm-hearted
friends, who in his native country would advise or assist him in his
first efforts, and surrounded by people who have an interest in mis-
leading and imposing upon him, every-day experience shows that no
amount of natural sagacity or prudence, founded on experience in
other countries, will be an effectual safeguard against deception and
erroneous conclusions.

It is a fact worthy of observation, that among emigrants possessing
the qualities of industry and perseverance so essential to success in all
countries, those who possess the smallest share of original talent and
imagination, and the least of a speculative turn of mind, are usually
the most successful. They follow the beaten track and prosper. However humbling this reflection may be to human vanity, it should oper-
ate as a salutary check on presumption and hasty conclusions. After a
residence of sixteen years in Canada, during which my young and
helpless family have been exposed to many privations, while we toiled
incessantly and continued to hope even against hope, these reflections
naturally occur to our minds, not only as the common-sense view of
the subject, but as the fruit of long and daily-bought experience.

After all this long probation in the backwoods of Canada, I find myself brought back in circumstances nearly to the point from whence I
started, and am compelled to admit that had I only followed my own
unassisted judgment, when I arrived with my wife and child in
Canada, and quietly settled down on the cleared farm I had purchased, in a well-settled neighbourhood, and with the aid of the
means I then possessed, I should now in all probability have been in
easy if not in affluent circumstances.

Native Canadians, like Yankees, will make money where people
from the old country would almost starve. Their intimate knowledge of

the country, and of the circumstances of the inhabitants, enables them to turn their money to great advantage; and I must add, that few people from the old country, however avaricious, can bring themselves to stoop to the unscrupulous means of acquiring property which are too commonly resorted to in this country. These reflections are a rather serious commencement of a sketch which was intended to be of a more lively description; one of my chief objects in writing this chapter being to afford a connecting link between my wife's sketches, and to account for some circumstances connected with our situation, which otherwise would be unintelligible to the reader. Before emigrating to Canada, I had been settled as a bachelor in South Africa for about twelve years.[1] I use the word *settled*, for want of a better term—for a bachelor can never, properly, be said to be settled. He has no object in life—no aim. He is like a knife without a blade, or a gun without a barrel. He is always in the way, and nobody cares for him. If he work on a farm, as I did, for I never could look on while others were working without lending a hand, he works merely for the sake of work. He benefits nobody by his exertions, not even himself; for he is restless and anxious, has a hundred indescribable ailments, which no one but himself can understand; and for want of the legitimate cares and anxieties connected with a family, he is full of cares and anxieties of his own creating. In short, he is in a false position, as every man must be who presumes to live alone when he can do better.

This was my case in South Africa. I had plenty of land, and of all the common necessaries of life; but I lived for years without companionship, for my nearest English neighbour was twenty-five miles off. I hunted the wild animals of the country, and had plenty of books to read; but, from talking broken Dutch for months together, I almost forgot how to speak my own language correctly. My very ideas (for I had not entirely lost the reflecting faculty) became confused and limited, for want of intellectual companions to strike out new lights, and form new combinations in the regions of thought; clearly showing that man was not intended to live alone. Getting, at length, tired of this solitary and unproductive life, I started for England, with the resolution of placing my domestic matters on a more comfortable footing. By a happy accident, at the house of a literary friend in London,[2] I became acquainted with one to whose cultivated mind, devoted affection, and untiring energy of character, I have been chiefly indebted for many happy hours, under the most adverse circumstances, as well as for much of that hope and firm reliance upon Providence which have enabled me to bear up against overwhelming misfortunes. I need not here repeat what has been already stated respecting the motives which induced us to emigrate to Canada. I shall merely observe that when I

1. John Moodie and his brother Donald farmed their respective land grants in the Groote Valley. John bought Donald's farm in 1828. Donald stayed in South Africa and became a prominent politician.
2. Thomas Pringle (1789–1834), who lived in Pentonville (London), and his wife had known Moodie as a fellow emigrant to South Africa. A well-regarded poet, editor and authority on South Africa, Pringle had taken an avuncular liking to young Susanna Strickland and welcomed her to his house when she was in London. It was there that Susanna and John met.

left South Africa it was with the intention of returning to that colony, where I had a fine property, to which I was attached in no ordinary degree, on account of the beauty of the scenery and delightful climate. However, Mrs. Moodie, somehow or other, had imbibed an invincible dislike to that colony, for some of the very reasons that I liked it myself. The wild animals were her terror, and she fancied that every wood and thicket was peopled with elephants, lions, and tigers, and that it would be utterly impossible to take a walk without treading on dangerous snakes in the grass. Unfortunately, she had my own book on South Africa to quote triumphantly in confirmation of her vague notions of danger; and, in my anxiety to remove these exaggerated impressions, I would fain have retracted my own statements of the hair-breadth escapes I had made, in conflicts with wild animals, respecting which the slightest insinuation of doubt from another party would have excited my utmost indignation.

In truth, before I became familiarised with such dangers, I had myself entertained similar notions, and my only wonder, in reading such narratives before leaving my own country, was how the inhabitants of the country managed to attend to their ordinary business in the midst of such accumulated dangers and annoyances. Fortunately, these hair-breadth escapes are of rare occurrence; but travellers and book-makers, like cooks, have to collect high-flavoured dishes, from far and near, the better to please the palates of their patrons. So it was with my South African adventures; I threw myself in the way of danger from the love of strong excitement, and I collected all my adventures together, and related them in pure simplicity, without very particularly informing the reader over what space of time or place my narrative extended, or telling him that I could easily have kept out of harm's way had I felt so inclined. All these arguments, however, had little influence on my good wife, for I could not deny that I had seen such animals in abundance in South Africa; and she thought she never should be safe among such neighbours. At last, between my wife's fear of the wild animals of Africa, and a certain love of novelty, which formed a part of my own character, I made up my mind, as they write on stray letters in the post-office, to "try Canada." So here we are, just arrived at the village of C[obourg], situated on the northern shore of Lake Ontario.

Mrs. Moodie has already stated that we procured lodgings at a certain hotel in the village of C[obourg] kept by S[trong], a truly excellent and obliging American. The British traveller is not a little struck, and in many instances disgusted, with a certain air of indifference in the manners of such persons in Canada, which is accompanied with a tone of equality and familiarity exceedingly unlike the limber and oily obsequiousness of tavern-keepers in England. I confess I felt at the time not a little annoyed with Mr. S[trong]'s free-and-easy manner, and apparent coolness and indifference when he told us he had no spare room in his house to accommodate our party. We endeavoured to procure lodgings at another tavern, on the opposite side of the street; but soon learned that, in consequence of the arrival of an unusual number of immigrants, all the taverns in the village were already filled to overflowing. We returned to Mr. S[trong], and after some further conversation, he seemed to have taken a kind of liking to us, and became more complaisant in his manner, until our arrangement with Tom Wilson, as already related, relieved us from further difficulty.

I *now* perfectly understand the cause of this apparent indifference on the part of our host. Of all people, Englishmen, when abroad, are the most addicted to the practice of giving themselves arrogant airs towards those persons whom they look upon in the light of dependents on their bounty; and they forget that an American tavern-keeper holds a very different position in society from one of the same calling in England. The manners and circumstances of new countries are utterly opposed to anything like pretension in any class of society; and our worthy host, and his excellent wife—who had both held a respectable position in the society of the United States—had often been deeply wounded in their feelings by the disgusting and vulgar arrogance of English *gentlemen* and *ladies*, as they are called. Knowing from experience the truth of the saying that "what cannot be cured must be endured," we were particularly civil to Mr. S[trong]; and it was astonishing how quickly his manners thawed. We had not been long in the house before we were witnesses of so many examples of the purest benevolence, exhibited by Mr. S[trong] and his amiable family, that it was impossible to regard them with any feeling but that of warm regard and esteem. S[trong] was, in truth, a noble-hearted fellow. Whatever he did seemed so much a matter of habit, that the idea of selfish design or ostentation was utterly excluded from the mind. I could relate several instances of the disinterested benevolence of this kind-hearted tavern-keeper. I shall just mention one, which came under my own observation while I lived near C[obourg].

I had frequently met a young Englishman, of the name of M[oore],[3] at Mr. S[trong]'s tavern. His easy and elegant manners, and whole deportment, showed that he had habitually lived in what is called the best society. He had emigrated to Canada with £3,000 or £4,000, had bought horses, run races, entertained many of the wealthy people of Toronto, or York, as it was then called, and had done a number of other exceedingly foolish things. Of course his money was soon absorbed by the thirsty Canadians, and he became deeply involved in debt. M[oore] had spent a great deal of money at S[trong]'s tavern, and owed him £70 or £80. At length he was arrested for debt by some other party, was sent to the district gaol, which was nearly two miles from C[obourg], and was compelled at first to subsist on the gaol allowance. What greatly aggravated the misfortunes of poor M[oore], a man without suspicion or guile, was a bitter disappointment in another quarter. He had an uncle in England, who was very rich, and who intended to leave him all his property. Some kind friend, to whom M[oore] had confided his expectations, wrote to England, informing

---

3. Possibly William Moore who was, according to court records, imprisoned for debt in the Amherst Jail for nearly four months beginning on November 23, 1832. Amherst was a village just east of Cobourg.

the old man of his nephew's extravagance and hopes. The uncle thereupon cast him off, and left his property, when he died, to another relative.

As soon as the kind-hearted tavern-keeper heard of the poor fellow's imprisonment, he immediately went to see him, and, though he had not the slightest hope of ever being paid one farthing of his claim, Mr. S[trong], for many months that poor M[oore] lay in gaol, continued to send him an excellent dinner every day from his tavern, to which he always added a bottle of wine; for as Mr. S[trong] remarked, "Poor M[oore], I guess, is accustomed to live well."

As soon as Mr. S[trong] found that we did not belong to that class of people who fancy they exalt themselves by insulting others, there were no bounds to the obligingness of his disposition. As I had informed him that I wished to buy a cleared farm near Lake Ontario, he drove me out every day in all directions, and wherever he thought farms were to be had cheap.

Before proceeding further in my account of the inhabitants, I shall endeavour to give the reader some idea of the appearance of the village and the surrounding country. Of course, from the existence of a boundless forest, only partially cleared, there is a great sameness and uniformity in Canadian scenery.

We had a stormy passage from Kingston to C[obourg], and the wind being directly ahead, the plunging of the steamboat between the sharp seas of Lake Ontario produced a "motion" which was decidedly "unconstitutional;" and, for the first time since we left England, we experienced a sensation which strongly reminded us of sea-sickness. The general appearance of the coast from the lake was somewhat uninviting. The land appeared to be covered everywhere with the dense unbroken forest, and though there were some gently sloping hills and slight elevations, showing the margin of extensive clearings, there was a general want of a background of high hills or mountains, which imparts so much interest to the scenery of every country. On reaching C[obourg], however, we found that we had been much deceived as to the features of the country, when viewed at a less distance.

Immediately on the shores of the great lake, the land is generally flat for two or three miles inland; and as the farms are there measured out in long, narrow strips, a mile and a quarter long, and a quarter of a mile wide, the back parts of the lots, which are reserved for firewood, are only visible at a distance. This narrow belt of the primeval forest, which runs along the rear of all the lots in the first line of settlements, or *concession* as it is here called, necessarily conceals the houses and clearings of the next concession, unless the land beyond rises into hills. This arrangement, however convenient, tends greatly to mar the beauty of Canadian scenery.

The unvarying monotony of rail-fences and quadrangular enclosures, occasions a tiresome uniformity in the appearance of the country, which is increased by the almost total absence of those little graceful ornaments in detail, in the immediate neighbourhood of the homesteads, which give such a charm to English rural scenery.

The day after our arrival, we had an opportunity to examine the town, or rather village, of C[obourg]. It then consisted chiefly of one long street, parallel with the shore of the lake, and the houses, with very few exceptions, were built of wood; but they were all finished, and painted with such a degree of neatness, that their appearance was showy, and in some instances elegant, from the symmetry of their proportions. Immediately beyond the bounds of the village, we, for the first time, witnessed the operation of clearing up a thick cedar-swamp. The soil looked black and rich, but the water stood in pools, and the trunks and branches of the cedars were leaning in all directions, and at all angles, with their thick foliage and branches intermingled in wild confusion. The roots spread along the uneven surface of the ground so thickly that they seemed to form a vast net-work, and apparently covered the greater part of the surface of the ground. The task of clearing such a labyrinth seemed utterly hopeless. My heart almost sickened at the prospect of clearing such land, and I was greatly confirmed in my resolution of buying a farm cleared to my hand.

The clearing process, however, in this unpromising spot, was going on vigorously. Several acres had been chopped down, and the fire had run through the prostrate trees, consuming all the smaller branches and foliage, and leaving the trunks and ground as black as charcoal could make them. Among this vast mass of ruins, four or five men were toiling with yoke of oxen. The trees were cut into manageable lengths, and were then dragged by the oxen together, so that they could be thrown up into large log-heaps to burn. The men looked, with their bare arms, hands, and faces begrimed with charcoal, more like negroes than white men; and were we, like some shallow people, to compare their apparent condition with that of the negro slaves in more favoured regions, we should be disposed to consider the latter the happier race. But this disgusting work was the work of freemen, high-spirited and energetic fellows, who feared neither man nor wild beast, and trusted to their own strong arms to conquer all difficulties, while they could discern the light of freedom and independence glimmering through the dark woods before them.

A few years afterwards, I visited C[obourg], and looked about for the dreadful cedar-swamp which struck such a chill into my heart, and destroyed the illusion which had possessed my mind of the beauty of the Canadian woods. The trees were gone, the tangled roots were gone, and the cedar-swamp was converted into a fair grassy meadow, as smooth as a bowling-green. About sixteen years after my first visit to this spot, I saw it again, and it was covered with stone and brick houses; and one portion of it was occupied by a large manufactory, five or six stories high with steam-engines, spinning-jennies, and all the machinery for working up the wool of the country into every description of clothing. This is civilisation! This is freedom!

The sites of towns and villages in Canada are never selected at random. In England, a concurrence of circumstances has generally led to the gradual formation of hamlets, villages, and towns. In many instances, towns have grown up in barbarous ages around a place of refuge during war; around a fortalice or castle, and more frequently around the ford over a river, where the detention of travellers has led to the establishment of a place of entertainment, a blacksmith's or carpenter's shop. A village or town never grows to any size in Canada without a saw or a grist mill, both which require a certain amount of water-power to work the machinery. Whenever there is a river or stream available for such purposes, and the surrounding country is fertile, the village rapidly rises to be a considerable town. Frame-houses are so quickly erected, and the materials are so easily procured near a saw-mill, that, in the first instance, no other description of houses is to be found in our incipient towns. But as the town increases, brick and stone houses rapidly supplant these less substantial edifices, which seldom remain good for more than thirty or forty years.

Mr. S[trong]'s tavern, or hotel, was an extensive frame-building of the kind common in the country. All the lodgers frequent the same long table at all their meals, at one end of which the landlord generally presides. Mr. S[trong], however, usually preferred the company of his family in another part of the house; and some one of the gentlemen who boarded at the tavern, and who possessed a sufficiently large organ of self-esteem, voted himself into the post of honour, without waiting for an invitation from the rest of the company. This happy individual is, generally some little fellow, with a long, protruding nose; some gentleman who can stretch his neck and backbone almost to dislocation, and who has a prodigious deal of talk, all about nothing.

The taverns in this country are frequented by all single men, and by many married men without children, who wish to avoid the trouble and greater expense of keeping house. Thus a large portion of the population of the towns take all their meals at the hotels or taverns, in order to save both expense and time. The extraordinary despatch used at meals in the United States has often been mentioned by travellers. The same observation equally applies to Canada, and for the same reason. Wages are high, and time is, therefore, valuable in both countries, and as one clerk is waiting in the shop while another is bolting his dinner, it would of course be exceedingly unkind to protract unnecessarily the sufferings of the hungry expectant; no one possessing any bowels of compassion could act so cruelly. For the same reason, every one is expected to take care of himself first, and to help himself, without minding his neighbours. At times a degree of compassion is extended by some naturalised old countryman towards some diffident, over-scrupulous new comer, by offering to help him first; but such marks of consideration, except to ladies, to whom all classes in Canada are attentive, are never continued a bit longer than is thought sufficient for becoming acquainted with the ways of the country.

Soon after our arrival at C[obourg], I remember asking a person, who was what the Canadians call "a hickory Quaker," from the north of Ireland,[4] to help me to a bit of very nice salmon-trout, which was vanishing alarmingly fast from the breakfast-table.

4. A flexible, hence unorthodox, Quaker.

Obadiah very considerately lent a deaf ear to my repeated entreaties, pretending to be intently occupied with his own plate of fish;
then, transferring the remains of the salmon-trout to his own place, he
turned round to me with the most innocent face imaginable, saying
very coolly, "I beg your pardon, friend, did you speak to me? There is
such a noise at the table, I cannot hear very well."

Between meals there is "considerable of drinking," among the idlers
about the tavern, of the various ingenious Yankee inventions resorted
to in this country to disturb the brain. In the evening the plot thick-
ens, and a number of young and middle-aged men drop in, and are
found in little knots in the different public rooms.

The practice of "treating" is almost universal in this country, and,
though friendly and sociable in its way, is the fruitful source of much
dissipation. It is almost impossible, in travelling, to steer clear of this
evil habit. Strangers are almost invariably drawn into it in the course
of business.

The town of C[obourg] being the point where a large number of emigrants landed on their way to the backwoods of this part of the colony,
it became for a time a place of great resort, and here a number of
land-jobbers were established, who made a profitable trade of buying
lands from private individuals, or at the government sales of wild land,
and selling them again to the settlers from the old country. Though my
wife had some near relatives settled in the backwoods, about forty
miles inland,[5] to the north of C[obourg], I had made up my mind to
buy a cleared farm near Lake Ontario, if I could get one to my mind,
and the price of which would come within my limited means.

A number of the recent settlers in the backwoods, among whom
were several speculators, resorted frequently to C[obourg]; and as
soon as a new batch of settlers arrived on the lake shore, there was a
keen contest between the land-jobbers of C[obourg] and those of the
backwoods to draw the new comer into their nets. The demand created by the continual influx of immigrants had caused a rapid increase
in the price of lands, particularly of wild lands, and the grossest imposition was often practised by these people, who made enormous profits by taking advantage of the ignorance of the new settlers and of
their anxiety to settle themselves at once.

I was continually cautioned by these people against buying a farm in
any other locality than the particular one they themselves represented
as most eligible, and their rivals were always represented as unprincipled land-jobbers. Finding these accusations to be mutual, I naturally
felt myself constrained to believe both parties to be alike.

Sometimes I got hold of a quiet farmer, hoping to obtain something
like disinterested advice; but in nine cases out of ten, I am sorry to say,
I found that the rage for speculation and trading in land, which was so
prevalent in all the great thoroughfares, had already poisoned their
minds also, and I could rarely obtain an opinion or advice which was

---

5. Susanna's brother Sam Strickland had settled in Douro Township on Lake Katchewanook, a
    broadening of the Otonabee River north of Peterborough, in 1831. His sister, Catharine Parr
    Traill, and her husband, Thomas, soon joined him on land to the north.

utterly free from self-interest. They generally had some lot of land to sell—or, probably, they would like to have a new comer for a neighbour, in the hope of selling him a span of horses or some cows at a higher price than they could obtain from the older settlers. In mentioning this unamiable trait in the character of the farmers near C[obourg], I by no means intend to give it as characteristic of the farmers in general. It is, properly speaking, a *local* vice, produced by the constant influx of strangers unacquainted with the ways of the country, which tempts the farmers to take advantage of their ignorance.

STANZAS.

Where is religion found? In what bright sphere
    Dwells holy love, in majesty serene
    Shedding its beams, like planet o'er the scene;
The steady lustre through the varying year
    Still glowing with the heavenly rays that flow
    In copious streams to soften human woe?

It is not 'mid the busy scenes of life,
    Where careworn mortals crowd along the way
    That leads to gain—shunning the light of day;
In endless eddies whirl'd, where pain and strife
    Distract the soul, and spread the shades of night,
    Where love divine should dwell in purest light.

Short-sighted man!—go seek the mountain's brow,
    And cast thy raptured eye o'er hill and dale;
    The waving woods, the ever-blooming vale,
Shall spread a feast before thee, which till now
    Ne'er met thy gaze—obscured by passion's sway;
    And Nature's works shall teach thee how to pray.

Or wend thy course along the sounding shore,
    Where giant waves resistless onward sweep
    To join the awful chorus of the deep—
Curling their snowy manes with deaf'ning roar,
    Flinging their foam high o'er the trembling sod,
    And thunder forth their mighty song to God!

J. W. D. M.

Thirteen

The Land-Jobber

Some men, like greedy monsters of the deep,
Still prey upon their kind;—their hungry maws
Engulph their victims like the rav'nous shark

That day and night unretiring plies around
The foamy bubbling wake of some great ship;
And when the hapless mariner aloft
Hath lost his hold, and down he falls
Amidst the gurgling waters on her lee,
Then, quick as thought, the ruthless felon-jaws
Close on his form;—the sea is stain'd with blood—
One sharp wild shriek is heard—and all is still!
The lion, tiger, alligator, shark—
The wily fox, the bright enamelled snake—
All seek their prey by force or stratagem;
But when—their hunger sated—languor creeps
Around their frames, they quickly sink to rest.
Not so with man—*he* never hath enough;
He feeds on all alike; and, wild or tame,
He's but a cannibal. He burns, destroys,
And scatters death to sate his morbid lust
For empty fame. But when the love of gain
Hath struck its roots in his vile, sordid heart,—
Each gen'rous impulse chill'd,—like vampire, now,
He sucks the life-blood of his friends or foes
Until he viler grows than savage beast.
And when, at length, stretch'd on his bed of death,
And powerless, friendless, o'er his clammy brow
The dark'ning shades descend, strong to the last
His avarice lives; and while he feebly plucks
His wretched coverlet, he gasps for breath,
And thinks he gathers gold!

J. W. D. M.

I had a letter of introduction to a gentleman of large property, at C[obourg], who, knowing that I wished to purchase a farm, very kindly drove me out to several lots of land in the immediate neighbourhood. He showed me seven or eight very eligible lots of cleared land, some of them with good houses and orchards; but somehow or other, on inquiry, I found they all belonged to himself, and, moreover, the prices were beyond my limited means. For one farm he asked £1000; for another, £1500, and so on. After inquiring in other quarters, I saw I had no chance of getting a farm in that neighbourhood for the price I could afford to pay down, which was only about £300. After satisfying myself as to this fact, I thought it the wiser course at once to undeceive my very obliging friend, whose attentions were obviously nicely adjusted to the estimate he had formed in his own mind of my pecuniary resources.

On communicating this discouraging fact, my friend's countenance instantly assumed a cold and stony expression, and I almost expected that he would have stopped his horses and set me down, to walk with other poor men. As may well be supposed, I was never afterwards honoured with a seat in his carriage. He saw just what I was worth, and I saw what his friendship was worth; and thus our brief acquaintance terminated.

Having thus let the cat out of the bag, when I might, according to the usual way of the world, have sported for awhile in borrowed plumage, and rejoiced in the reputation of being in more prosperous circumstances without fear of detection, I determined to pursue the same course, and make use of the little insight I had obtained into the ways of the land-jobbers of Canada, to procure a cleared farm on more reasonable terms.

It is not uncommon for the land speculators to sell a farm to a respectable settler at an unusually low price, in order to give a character to a neighbourhood where they hold other lands, and thus to use him as a decoy duck for friends or countrymen.

There was a very noted character at C[obourg], Mr. [Clark], a great land-jobber,[1] who did a large business in this way on his own account, besides getting through a great deal of dirty work for other more respectable speculators, who did not wish to drink at taverns and appear personally in such matters. To Mr. [Clark] I applied, and effected a purchase of a farm of one hundred and fifty acres, about fifty of which were cleared, for £300, as I shall mention more particularly in the sequel. In the meantime, the character of this distinguished individual was—for he has long gone to give an account of his misdeeds in the other world—so remarkable, that I must endeavour to describe it for the edification of the reader. [Clark] kept a shop, or store, in C[obourg]; but he left the principal management of this establishment to his clerks; while, taking advantage of the influx of emigrants, he pursued, with unrivalled success, the profitable business of land-jobbing.

In his store, before taking to this business, he had been accustomed for many years to retail goods to the farmers at high prices, on the usual long credit system. He had thus got a number of farmers deeply in his debt, and, in many cases, in preference to suing them, had taken mortgages on their farms. By this means, instead of merely recovering the money owing to him by the usual process of law, he was enabled, by threatening to foreclose the mortgages, to compel them to sell their farms nearly on his own terms, whenever an opportunity occurred to re-sell them advantageously to new comers. Thus, besides making thirty or forty per cent. on his goods, he often realised more than a hundred per cent. on his land speculations.

In a new country, where there is no great competition in mercantile business, and money is scarce, the power and profits of store-keepers are very great. Mr. [Clark] was one of the most grasping of this class. His heart was case-hardened, and his conscience like gum-elastic; it would readily stretch, on the shortest notice, to any required extent, while his well-tutored countenance betrayed no indication of what was passing in his mind. But I must not forget to give a sketch of the appearance, or outward man, of this highly-gifted individual.

He was about the middle size, thin and limber, and somewhat loose

1. For an unknown reason John Moodie identified Charles Clark as Mr. Q—— in his sketch. The editors of the book in London seem not to have noticed the change from Susanna's designation of Mr. C——. In this Norton Critical Edition, all references to Q—— are changed to [Clark]. A land-jobber was a speculator in lands, a self-appointed dealer in real estate.

in his lower joints, like most of the native Canadians and Yankees. He had a slight stoop in his shoulders, and his long, thin neck was continually stretched out before him, while his restless little cunning eyes were roaming about in search of prey. His face, when well watched, was an index to his selfish and unfeeling soul. Complexion he had none, except that sempiternally enduring red-and-tawny mixture which is acquired by exposure and hard drinking. His cheeks and the corners of his eyes were marked by an infinity of curved lines, and, like most avaricious and deceitful men, he had a long, crooked chin, and that peculiar prominent and slightly aquiline nose, which, by people observant of such indications, has been called "the rogue's nose." But how shall I describe his eye—that small hole through which you can see an honest man's heart? [Clark]'s eye was like no other eye I had ever seen. His face and mouth could assume a good-natured expression, and smile; but his eye was still the same—*it* never smiled, but remained cold, hard, dry, and inscrutable. If it had any expression at all, it was an unhappy one. Such were the impressions created by his appearance, when the observer was unobserved by him; for he had the art of concealing the worst traits of his character in an extraordinary degree, and when he suspected that the curious hieroglyphics which Nature had stamped on his visage were too closely scanned, he knew well how to divert the investigator's attention to some other object.

He was a humorist, besides, in his way, because he found that jokes and fun admirably served his turn. They helped to throw people off their guard, and to conceal his hang-dog look.

He had a hard head, as well as hard heart, and could stand any quantity of drink. His drinking, however, like everything else about him, had a motive; and, instead of trying to appear sober, like other drunkards, he rather wished to appear a little elevated. In addition to his other acquirements, [Clark] was a most accomplished gambler. In short, no virtuous man, who employs every passing moment of his short life in doing good to his fellow creatures, could be more devoted and energetic in his endeavours to serve God and mankind, than [Clark] was in his endeavours to ease them of their spare cash.

He possessed a great deal of that free-and-easy address and tact which distinguish the Canadians; and, in addition to the current coin of vulgar flattery which is found so useful in all countries, his quick eye could discover the high-minded gentleman by a kind of instinct, which did not seem quite natural to his sordid character; and, knowing that such men are not to be taken by vulgar adulation, he could address them with deferential respect; against which no minds are entirely secure. Thus he wriggled himself into their good graces. After a while the unfavourable impression occasioned by his sinister countenance would become more faint, while his well-feigned kindness and apparent indulgence to his numerous debtors would tell greatly in his favour.

My first impression of this man was pretty nearly such as I have described; and, though I suspected and shunned him, I was sure to meet him at every turn. At length this unfavourable feeling wore off in some degree, and finding him in the best society of the place, I began to think that his countenance belied him, and I reproached myself for my ungenerous suspicions.

Feeling a certain security in the smallness of my available capital, I did not hesitate in applying to Mr. [Clark] to sell me a farm, particularly as I was aware of his anxiety to induce me to settle near C[obourg], for the reasons already stated. I told him that £300 was the very largest sum I could give for a farm, and that, if I could not get one for that price, I should join my friends in the backwoods.

[Clark], after scratching his head, and considering for a few minutes, told me that he knew a farm which he could sell me for that price, particularly as he wished to get rid of a set of Yankee rascals who prevented emigrants from settling in that neighbourhood. We afterwards found that there was but too good reason for the character he gave of some our neighbours.

[Clark] held a mortgage for £150 on a farm belonging to a certain Yankee settler, named Joe H[arris], as security for a debt incurred for goods at his store, in C[obourg]. The idea instantly struck [Clark] that he would compel Joe H[arris] to sell him his farm, by threatening to foreclose the mortgage. I drove out with Mr. C[lark] next day to see the farm in question. It was situated in a pretty retired valley, surrounded by hills, about eight miles from C[obourg], and about a mile from the great road leading to Toronto. There was an extensive orchard upon the farm, and two log houses, and a large frame-barn. A considerable portion of the cleared land was light and sandy; and the uncleared part of the farm, situated on the flat, rocky summit of a high hill, was reserved for "a sugar bush," and for supplying fuel. On the whole, I was pleased with the farm, which was certainly cheap at the price of £300; and I therefore at once closed the bargain with Mr. [Clark].

At that time I had not the slightest idea but that the farm actually belonged to the land-jobber; and I am, to this day, unable to tell by what means he succeeded in getting Mr. H[arris] to part with his property.

The father of Joe H[arris] had cleared the farm, and while the soil was new it gave good crops; but as the rich surface, or "black muck," as it is called, became exhausted by continual cropping, nothing but a poor, meagre soil remained.

The early settlers were wretched farmers; they never ploughed deep enough, and never thought of manuring the land. After working the land for several years, they would let it lie waste for three or four years without sowing grass-seeds, and then plough it up again for wheat. The greater part of the hay raised on these farms was sold in the towns, and the cattle were fed during the long severe winter on wheat-straw. The natural result of this poor nourishment was, that their cattle continually degenerated, and great numbers died every spring of a disease called the "hollow horn," which appears to be peculiar to this country.[2] When the lands became sterile, from this exhausting treat-

---

2. "Hollow horn" was a faulty designation of bovine illness applied by untrained "cow doctors" who believed that horns were hollow only when a cow was ill, and that the horns were the source of the illness. The treatments, which involved drilling into the horn, were painful.

ment, they were called "worn-out farms;" and the owners generally sold them to new settlers from the old country, and with the money they received, bought a larger quantity of wild lands, to provide for their sons; by whom the same improvident process was recommended. These early settlers were, in fact, only fit for pioneers to a more thrifty class of settlers.

Joe H[arris], or "Uncle Joe," as the country people call any acquaintance, after a fashion borrowed, no doubt, from the Dutch settlers of the State of New York, was, neither by his habits nor industry, likely to become more prosperous than his neighbours of the same thoughtless class. His father had worked hard in his time, and Uncle Joe thought he had a good right to enjoy himself. The nearest village was only five miles from his place,[3] and he was never without some excuse for going thither every two or three days. His horse wanted shoeing, or his plough or waggon wanted "to be fixed" by the blacksmith or carpenter. As a matter of course, he came home "pretty high;" for he was in the constant habit of pouring a half-tumbler of whiskey down his throat, standing bolt upright at the bar of the tavern, after which he would drink about the same quantity of cold water to wash it down. These habits together with bad farming, and a lazy, slovenly helpmate, in a few years made Joe as poor as he could desire to be; and at last he was compelled to sell his farm to Mr. [Clark].

After we had got settled down on this farm, I had often occasion to drive into C[obourg], for the purpose of buying groceries and other necessaries, as we then thought them, at the store of Mr. [Clark]. On these occasions I always took up my quarters, for the time, at the tavern of our worthy Yankee friend, Mr. S[trong]. As I drove up to the door, I generally found S[trong] walking about briskly on the boarded platform, or "stoop," in front of the house, welcoming his guests in his own peculiar free-and-easy style, looking after their horses, and seeing that his people were attentive to their duties. I think I see him now before me with his thin, erect, lathy figure, his snub nose, and puckered-up face, wriggling and twisting himself about, in his desire to please his customers.

On stopping in front of the tavern, shortly after our settlement on the farm, Mr. S[trong] stepped up to me, in the most familiar manner imaginable, holding out his hand quite condescendingly,—"Ah, Mister Moodie, ha-a-w do you do?—and ha-a-w's *the old woman?*"

At first I could not conceive whom he meant by this very homely appelation; and I very simply asked him what person he alluded to, as I had no old woman in my establishment.

"Why, *your* old woman, to be sure—your missus—Mrs. Moodie, I guess. You don't quite understand our language yet."

"O! now I understand you; she's quite well, I thank you; and how is our friend Mrs. S[trong]?" I replied, laying a slight emphasis on the *Mrs.*, by way of a gentle hint for his future guidance.

"Mrs. S[trong], I guess she's smart, pret-ty *con*-siderable. She'll be

3. The nearest village, Port Hope, was four miles from the Harris-Moodie farm.

right glad to see you, for you're pretty considerable of a favour-*ite* with her, I tell you; but now tell me what you will drink?—for it's *my treat*."

As he said these words, he strutted into the tavern before me, throwing his head and shoulders back, and rising on his tiptoes at every step.

Mrs. S[trong] had been a very handsome woman, and still retained much of her good looks. She was a most exemplary housewife and manager. I was often astonished to witness the incessant toil she had to ensure in attending to the wants of such a numerous household.

She had plenty of Irish "helps" in the kitchen; but they knew as much of cookery as they did of astronomy, and poor Mrs. S[trong]'s hands, as well as her head, were in constant requisition.

She had two very pretty daughters, whom she would not suffer to do any rough work which would spoil their soft white hands. Mrs. S[trong], no doubt, foresaw that she could not expect to keep such fair creatures long in such a marrying country as Canada, and, according to the common caution of divines, she held these blessings with a loose hand.

There was one sweet little girl, whom I had often seen in her father's arms, with her soft dark eyes, and her long auburn ringlets hanging in wild profusion over his shoulders.

"I guess she likes pa, *some*," Mr. S[trong] would say when I remarked her fondness for him.

This little fairy had a natural genius for music, and though she was only four years old, she would sit for an hour at a time at the door of our room to hear me play on the flute, and would afterwards sing all the airs she picked up, with the sweetest voice in the world.

Humble as the calling of a tavern-keeper may be considered in England, it is looked upon in the United States, where Mrs. S[trong] was "raised," as extremely respectable; and I have never met with women, in any class of society elsewhere, who possessed more of the good feeling and unobtrusive manners which should belong to ladies than in the family of this worthy tavern-keeper.

When I contrast their genuine kindness and humanity with the haughty, arrogant airs assumed by some ladies of a higher standing in society from England who sojourned in their house at the same time with ourselves—when I remember their insolent way of giving their orders to Mrs. S[trong], and their still more wounding condescension—I confess I cannot but feel ashamed of my countrywomen. All these patronising airs, I doubt not, were assumed purposely to impress the minds of those worthy people with an idea of their vast superiority. I have sometimes, I confess, been a little annoyed with the familiarity of the Americans, Canadians as well as Yankees; but I must say that experience has taught me to blame myself at least as much as them. If, instead of sending our youthful aristocracy to the continent of Europe, to treat the natives with contempt and increase the unpopularity of the British abroad, while their stock of native arrogance is augmented by the cringing complaisance of those who only bow to their superiority in wealth, they were sent to the United States, or even to

Canada, they would receive a lesson or two which would be of infinite service to them; some of their most repulsive prejudices and peculiarities would soon be rubbed off by the rough towel of democracy.

It is curious to observe the remarkable diversity in the accounts given by recent emigrants to this country of their treatment, and of the manners and character of the people, in the United States and in Canada. Some meet with constant kindness, others with nothing but rudeness and brutality. Of course there is truth in both accounts; but strangers from an aristocratical country do not usually make sufficient allowance for the habits and prejudices of a people of a land, in which, from the comparatively equal distribution of property, and the certain prosperity attendant on industry, the whole constitution of society is necessarily democratical, irrespectively of political institutions. Those who go to such a country with the notion that they will carry everything before them by means of pretence and assumption, will find themselves grievously deceived. To use a homely illustration, it is just as irrational to expect to force a large body through a small aperture. In both cases they will meet with unyielding resistance.

When a poor and industrious mechanic, farmer, or labourer comes here without pretensions of any kind, no such complaints are to be heard. He is treated with respect, and every one seems willing to help him forward. If after-years the manners of such a settler should grow in importance with his prosperity—which is rarely the case—his pretensions would be much more readily tolerated than those of any unknown or untried individual in a higher class of society.

The North Americans generally are much more disposed to value people according to the estimate they form of their industry, and other qualities which more directly lead to the acquisition of property, and to the benefit of the community, than for their present and actual wealth. While they pay a certain mock homage to a wealthy immigrant, when they have a motive in doing so, they secretly are more inclined to look on him as a well-fledged goose who has come to America to be plucked. In truth, many of them are so dexterous in this operation that the unfortunate victim is often stripped naked before he is aware that he has lost a feather.

There seems to be a fatality attending riches imported into Canada. They are sure to make to themselves wings and flee away, while wealth is no less certain to adhere to the poor and industrious settler. The great fault of the Canadian character is an unwillingness to admit the just claims of education and talent, however unpretending, to some share of consideration. In this respect the Americans of the United States are greatly superior to the Canadians, because they are better educated and their country longer settled. These genuine Republicans, when their theory of the original and natural equality among them is once cheerfully admitted, are ever ready to show respect to *mental* superiority, whether natural or acquired.

My evenings on visiting C[obourg] were usually spent at Mr. S[trong]'s tavern, where I was often much amused with the variety of characters who were there assembled, and who, from the free-and-

easy familiarity of the colonial manners, had little chance of concealing their peculiarities from an attentive observer.

Mr. [Clark], of course, was always to be found there, drinking,
smoking cigars, and cracking jokes. To a casual observer he appeared
to be a regular boon companion, without an object but that of enjoying the passing hour. Among his numerous accomplishments, he had
learnt a number of sleight-of-hand tricks from the travelling conjurors
who visit the country, and are generally willing to sell their secrets
singly, at a regulated price. This seemed a curious investment for
[Clark], but he knew how to turn everything to account. By such
means he was enabled to contribute to the amusement of the company, and thus became a kind of favourite. If he could not manage to
sell a lot of land to an immigrant or speculator, he would carelessly
propose to some of the company to have a game at whist or loo,[4] to
pass the time away; and he never failed to conjure most of their money
into his pockets.

At this time a new character made his appearance at C[obourg], a
Mr. B——, an English farmer of the true yeoman breed. He was a
short-legged, long-bodied, corpulent little man. He wore a brown coat,
with ample skirts, and a vast expanse of vest, with drab-coloured
small-clothes and gaiters. B—— was a jolly, good-natured looking
man, with an easy blunt manner which might easily pass for honesty.

[Clark] had sold him a lot of wild land in some out-of-the-way township, by making Mr. B—— believe that he could sell it again very soon,
with a handsome profit. Of course his bargain was not a good one. He
soon found from its situation that the land was quite unsaleable, there
being no settlements in the neighbourhood. Instead of expressing any
resentment, he fairly acknowledged that [Clark] was his master at a
bargain, and gave him full credit for his address and cunning, and
quite resolved in his own mind to profit by the lesson he had received.

Now, with all their natural acuteness and habitual dexterity in such
matters, the Canadians have one weak point; they are too ready to believe that Englishmen are made of money. All that an emigrant has to
do to acquire the reputation of having money, is to seem quite easy,
and free from care or anxiety for the future, and to maintain a certain
degree of reserve in talking of his private affairs. Mr. B—— perfectly
understood how to play his cards with the land-jobber; and his fat,
jolly physiognomy, and rustic, provincial manners and accent, greatly
assisted him in the deception.

Every day [Clark] drove him out to look at different farms. B——
talked carelessly of buying some large "block" of land, that would have
cost him some £3000 or £4000, providing he could only find the kind
of soil he particularly liked for farming purposes. As he seemed to be
in no hurry in making his selection, [Clark] determined to make him
useful, in the meantime, in promoting his views with respect to others.
He therefore puffed Mr. B—— up to everybody as a Norfolk farmer of

4. A popular card game in England from the seventeenth century to the nineteenth. It is best
played by five to seven players who bet and play for tricks.

large capital, and always appealed to him to confirm the character he gave of any farm he wished to sell to a new comer. B——, on his side, was not slow in playing into [Clark]'s hand on these occasions, and without being at all suspected of collusion.

In the evening, Mr. B—— would walk into the public room of the tavern, apparently fatigued with his exertions through the day; fling himself carelessly on a sofa, and unbutton his gaiters and the knees of his small-clothes. He took little notice of anybody unless he was spoken to, and his whole demeanour seemed to say, as plainly as words, "I care for nobody, nobody cares for me." This was just the kind of man for [Clark]. He instantly saw that he would be an invaluable ally and coadjutor, without seeming to be so. When B—— made his appearance in the evening, [Clark] was seldom at the tavern, for *his* time had not yet come. In the meanwhile, B—— was sure to be drawn gradually into conversation by some emigrants, who, seeing that he was a practical farmer, would be desirous of getting his opinion respecting certain farms which they thought of purchasing. There was such an appearance of blunt simplicity of character about him, that most of these inquirers thought he was forgetting his own interest in telling them so much as he did. In the course of conversation, he would mention several farms he had been looking at with the intention of purchasing, and he would particularly mention some one of them as possessing extraordinary advantages, but which had some one disadvantage which rendered it ineligible for him; such as being too small, a circumstance which, in all probability, would recommend it to another description of settler.

It is hard to say whether [Clark] was or was not deceived by B——; but though he used him for the present as a decoy, he no doubt expected ultimately to sell him some of his farms, with a very handsome profit. B——, however, whose means were probably extremely small, fought shy of buying; and after looking at a number of farms, he told [Clark] that, on mature reflection, he thought he could employ his capital more profitably by renting a number of farms, and working them in the English manner, which he felt certain would answer admirably in Canada, instead of sinking his capital at once in the purchase of lands. [Clark] was fairly caught; and B—— hired some six or seven farms from him, which he worked for some time, no doubt greatly to his own advantage, for he neither paid rent nor wages.

Occasionally, other land-speculators would drop into the tavern, when a curious game would be played between [Clark] and them. One of the speculators would ask another if he did not own some land in a particular part of the country, as he had bought some lots in the same quarter, without seeing them, and would like to know if they were good. The other would answer in the affirmative, and pretend to desire to purchase the lots mentioned. The former, in his turn, would pretend reluctance, and make a similar offer of buying. All this cunning manoeuvring would be continued for a time, in the hope of inducing some third party or stranger to make an offer for the land, which would be accepted. It often happened that some other person, who had hitherto taken no part in the course of these conversations, and who appeared to have no personal interest in the matter, would quietly inform the stranger that he knew the land in question, and that it was all of the very best quality.

It would be endless to describe all the little artifices practised by these speculators to induce persons to purchase from them.

Besides a few of these unprincipled traders in land, some of whom are found in most of the towns, there are a large number of land-speculators who own both wild and improved farms in all parts of the colony who do not descend to these discreditable arts, but wait quietly until their lands become valuable by the progress of improvement in their neighbourhood, when they readily find purchasers—or, rather, the purchasers find them out, and obtain their lands at reasonable prices.

In 1832, when we came to Canada, a great speculation was carried on in the lands of the U.E. (or United Empire) Loyalists. The sons and daughters of these loyalists, who had fled to Canada from the United States at the time of the revolutionary war, were entitled to free grants of lots of wild land. Besides these, few free grants of land were made by the British Government, except those made to half-pay officers of the army and navy, and of course there was a rapid rise in their value.

Almost all the persons entitled to such grants had settled in the eastern part of the Upper Province,[5] and as the large emigration which had commenced to Canada had chiefly flowed into the more western part of the colony, they were, in general, ignorant of the increased value of their lands, and were ready to sell them for a mere trifle. They were bought by the speculators at from 2s. 6d. to 3s. 9d. per acre,[6] and often for much less, and were sold again, with an enormous profit, at from 5s. to 20s., and sometimes even 40s. per acre, according to their situation.

As to personally examining these lands, it was a thing never thought of, for their price was so low that it was almost impossible to lose by the purchase. The supply of U.E. Loyalists' lands, or claims for land, for a long time seemed to be almost inexhaustible; for the loyal refugees appear to have been prolific beyond all precedent, and most of those who held office at the capital of the province, or who could command a small capital, became speculators, and throve prodigiously. Many persons, during the early days of the colony, were thus enriched, without risk or labour, from the inexhaustible "quivers" of the U.E. Loyalists.

Though the bulk of the speculators bought lands at hap-hazard, certain parties who found favour at the government offices managed to secure the best lands which were for sale or location, before they were exposed to fair competition at the periodical public sales in the differ-

5. Upper Canada (now Ontario) was the Upper Province. Given his limited travels, John Moodie had no sense of the number of United Empire Loyalists who sought refuge and land in the Maritime provinces such as Nova Scotia.
6. "2 s[hillings], 6 d [the short form for 'pennies']"—British currency prevailed in Upper Canada but accommodation had necessarily to be made for American currency.

ent districts. Thus a large portion of the wild lands in the colony were and are still held: the absentee proprietors profiting from the increased value given to their property by the improvements of the actual settlers, while they contribute little or nothing to the cultivation of the country. The progress of the colony has thus been retarded, and its best interests sacrificed, to gratify the insatiable cupidity of a clique[7] who boasted the exclusive possession of all the loyalty in the country; and every independent man who dared to raise his voice against such abuses was branded as a Republican.

Mr. [Clark] dealt largely in these "U.E. Rights," as they were called, and so great was the emigration in 1832 that the lands he bought at 2s. 6d. per acre he could readily sell again to emigrants and Canadians at from 5s. to 15s. per acre, according to situation and the description of purchasers he met with. I have stated that the speculators generally buy lands at hap-hazard. By this I mean as to the quality of the lands. All colonists accustomed to observe the progress of settlement, and the local advantages which hasten improvement, acquire a peculiar sagacity in such matters. Unfortunately for many old countrymen, they are generally entirely destitute of this kind of knowledge, which is only acquired by long observation and experience in colonies.

The knowledge of the causes which promote the rapid settlement of a new country, and of those in general which lead to the improvement of the physical condition of mankind, may be compared to the knowledge of a language. The inhabitant of a civilised and long-settled country may speak and write his own language with the greatest purity, but very few ever reflect on the amount of thought, metaphor, and ingenuity which has been expended by their less civilised ancestors in bringing that language to perfection. The barbarian first feels the disadvantage of a limited means of communicating his ideas, and with great labour and ingenuity devises the means, from time to time, to remedy the imperfections of his language. He is compelled to analyse and study it in its first elements, and to augment the modes of expression in order to keep pace with the increasing number of his wants and ideas.

A colony bears the same relation to an old-settled country that a grammar does to a language. In a colony, society is seen in its first elements, the country itself is in its rudest and simplest form. The colonist knows them in this primitive state, and watches their progress step by step. In this manner he acquires an intimate knowledge of the philosophy of improvement, which is almost unattainable by an individual who has lived from his childhood in a highly-complex and artificial state of society, where everything around him was formed and arranged long before he came into the world; he sees the *effects*, the *causes* existed long before his time. His place in society—his portion of the wealth of the country—his prejudices—his religion itself, if he has any, are all more or less hereditary. He is in some measure a mere ma-

---

7. The clique alluded to is the Family Compact, an informal group centred in York (Toronto) that sought to gain personal advantage by calculatingly supporting British government interests in the colony.

chine, or rather a part of one. He is a creature of education, rather than of original thought.

The colonist has to create—he has to draw on his own stock of ideas, and to rouse up all his latent energies to meet all his wants in his new position. Thus his thinking principle is strengthened, and he is more energetic. When a moderate share of education is added to these advantages—for they are advantages in one sense—he becomes a superior being.

I have indulged in these reflections, with manifest risk of being thought somewhat prosy by my more lively readers, in order to guard my countrymen, English, Scotch, and Irish, against a kind of presumption which is exceedingly common among them when they come to Canada—of fancying that they are as capable of forming correct opinions on local matters as the Canadians themselves. It is always somewhat humbling to our self-love to be compelled to confess what may be considered an error of judgment, but my desire to guard future settlers against similar mistakes overpowers my reluctance to own that I fell into the common error of many of my countrymen, of purchasing wild land, on speculation, with a very inadequate capital. This was one of the chief causes of much suffering, in which for many years my family became involved; but through which, supported by trust in Providence, and the energy of a devoted partner, I continued by her aid to struggle, until, when least expected, the light of hope at length dawned upon us.[8]

In reflecting on this error—for error and imprudence it was, even though the result had been fortunate—I have still this poor comfort, that there was not one in a hundred of persons similarly situated but fell into the same mistake, of trusting too much to present appearances, without sufficient experience in the country.

I had, as I have already stated, about £300 when I arrived in Canada. This sum was really advantageously invested in a cleared farm, which possessed an intrinsic and not a merely speculative value. Afterwards a small legacy of about £700 fell into my hands,[9] and had I contented myself with this farm, and purchased two adjoining cleared farms, containing two hundred acres of land of the finest quality, which were sold far below their value by the thriftless owners, I should have done well, or at all events have invested my money profitably. But the temptation to buy wild land at 5s. an acre, which was expected to double in value in a few months, with the example of many instances of similar speculation proving successful which came under my notice, proved irresistible.

In 1832 emigration was just at its height, and a great number of emigrants, several of whom were of the higher class, and possessed of considerable capital, were directed to the town of C[obourg], in the

8. In November 1839, Governor General Sir George Arthur appointed John Moodie the Sheriff of Victoria County, ostensibly for Moodie's loyal military service, but partly because Arthur had been impressed by Susanna's patriotic poetry, which had appeared in *The Palladium*, a Toronto newspaper, in the wake of the Rebellion.
9. The 700 pound legacy came from one of Susanna's relatives.

rear of which extensive tracts of land were offered to settlers at the provincial government sales. Had this extensive emigration continued, I should have been enabled to double my capital, by selling my wild lands to settlers; but, unfortunately, the prevalence of cholera during that year, and other causes, gave such a serious check to emigration to Canada that it has never been renewed to the same extent since that time. Besides the chance of a check to emigration generally, the influx of strangers is often extremely capricious in the direction it takes, flowing one year into one particular locality, and afterwards into another. Both these results, neither of which was foreseen by any one, unfortunately for me, ensued just at that time. It seemed natural that emigrants should flow into a fertile tract of land, and emigration was confidently expected steadily to increase; these were our anticipations, but neither of them was realised. Were it suitable to the character of these sketches, I would enter into the subject of emigration and the progress of improvement in Canada, respecting which my judgment has been matured by experience and observation; but such considerations would be out of place in volumes like the present, and I shall therefore proceed with my narrative.

I had obtained my cleared farm on easy terms, and, in so far as the probability of procuring a comfortable subsistence was concerned, we had no reason to complain; but comfort and happiness do not depend entirely on a sufficiency of the necessaries of life. Some of our neighbours were far from being agreeable to us. Being fresh from England, it could hardly be expected that we could at once accommodate ourselves to the obtrusive familiarity of persons who had no conception of any differences in taste or manners arising from education and habits acquired in a more refined state of society. I allude more particularly to some rude and demoralised American farmers from the United States, who lived in our immediate neighbourhood. Our neighbours from the same country were worthy, industrious people; but, on the whole, the evil greatly predominated over the good amongst them.

At a few miles' distance from our farm, we had some intelligent English neighbours, of a higher class; but they were always so busily occupied with their farming operations that they had little leisure or inclination for that sort of easy intercourse to which we had been accustomed. If we called in the forenoon, we generally found our neighbour hard at work in the fields, and his wife over head and ears in her domestic occupations. We had to ring the bell repeatedly before we could gain admittance, to allow her time to change her ordinary dress. Long before this could be effected, or we could enter the door, sundry reconnoitring parties of the children would peep at us round the corners of the house, and then scamper off to make their reports.

It seems strange that sensible people should not at once see the necessity of accommodating their habits to their situation and circumstances, and receive their friends without appearing to be ashamed of their employments. This absurdity, however, is happily confined to the would-be-genteel people in the country, who visit in the towns, and occasionally are ambitious enough to give large parties to the aristocracy of the towns. The others, who do not pretend to vie with the townspeople in such follies, are a great deal more easy and natural in their manners, and more truly independent and hospitable.

Now that we are better acquainted with the country, we much prefer the conversation of the intelligent and unpretending class of farmers, who, though their education has been limited, often possess a rich fund of strong common sense and liberality of sentiment, and not unfrequently great observation and originality of mind. At the period I refer to, a number of the American settlers from the United States, who composed a considerable part of the population, regarded British settlers with an intense feeling of dislike, and found a pleasure in annoying and insulting them when any occasion offered. They did not understand us, nor did we them, and they generally mistook the reserve which is common with the British towards strangers for pride and superciliousness.

"You Britishers are too *superstitious*," one of them told me on a particular occasion.

It was some time before I found out what he meant by the term "*superstitious*," and that it was generally used by them for "supercilious."

New settlers of the lower classes were then in the habit of imitating their rudeness and familiarity, which they mistook for independence. To a certain extent, this feeling still exists amongst the working class from Europe, but they have learnt to keep it within prudent bounds for their own sakes; and the higher class have learnt to moderate their pretensions, which will not be tolerated here, where labourers are less dependent on them for employment. The character of both classes, in fact, has been altered very much for the better, and a better and healthier feeling exists between them—much more so, indeed, than in England.

The labouring class come to this country, too often with the idea that the higher class are their tyrants and oppressors; and, with a feeling akin to revenge, they are often inclined to make their employers in Canada suffer in their turn. This feeling is the effect of certain depressing causes, often remote and beyond the reach of legislation, but no less real on that account; and just in proportion to the degree of poverty and servility which exists among the labouring class in the particular part of the United Kingdom from which they come, will be the reaction here. When emigrants have been some years settled in Canada, they find out their particular and just position, as well as their duties and interests, and then they begin to feel truly happy. The fermentation arising from the strange mixture of discordant elements and feelings gradually subsides, but until this takes place, the state of society is anything but agreeable or satisfactory.

Such was its state at C[obourg], in 1832; and to us it was distasteful, that though averse, for various reasons, to commence a new settlement, we began to listen to the persuasions of our friends, who were settled in the township of D[ouro], about forty miles from C[obourg], and who were naturally anxious to induce us to settle among them.

Mrs. Moodie's brother, S[am Strickland], had recently formed a settlement in that township, and just before our arrival in Canada had been joined by an old brother officer and countryman of mine, Mr. T[raill], who was married to Mrs. Moodie's sister. The latter, who like myself, was a half-pay officer, had purchased a lot of wild land,[1] close to the farm occupied by S[trickland].

Mr. S[am] S[trickland] had emigrated to Canada while quite a youth,[2] and was thoroughly acquainted with the backwoods, and with the use of the felling-axe, which he wielded with all the ease and dexterity of a native.

I had already paid some flying visits to the backwoods,[3] and found the state of society, though rude and rough, more congenial to our European tastes and habits; for several gentlemen of liberal education were settled in the neighbourhood, among whom there was a constant interchange of visits and good offices. All these gentlemen had recently arrived from England, Ireland, or Scotland, and all the labouring class were also fresh from the old country, and consequently very little change had taken place in the manners or feelings of either class. There we felt we could enjoy the society of those who could sympathise with our tastes and prejudices, and who, from inclination as well as necessity, were inclined to assist each other in their farming operations.

There is no situation in which men feel more the necessity of mutual assistance than in clearing land.

Alone, a man may fell the trees on a considerable extent of woodland; but without the assistance of two or three others, he cannot pile up the logs previous to burning. Common labours and common difficulties, as among comrades during a campaign, produce a social unity of feeling among backwoodsmen. There is, moreover, a peculiar charm in the excitement of improving a wilderness for the benefit of children and posterity; there is in it, also, that consciousness of usefulness which forms so essential an ingredient in true happiness. Every tree that falls beneath the axe opens a wider prospect, and encourages the settler to persevere in his efforts to attain independence.

Mr. S[trickland] had secured for me a portion of the military grant of four hundred acres, which I was entitled to as a half-pay officer, in his immediate neighbourhood. Though this portion amounted to only sixty acres, it was so far advantageous to me as being in a settled part of the country. I bought a clergy reserve of two hundred acres,[4] in the rear of the sixty acres for £1 per acre, for which immediately after-

1. Lt. Thomas Traill (1793–1859) had purchased Lot 19, Concession 7, just north of Sam Strickland's land in Douro.
2. Samuel Strickland (1805–1867) had emigrated to Upper Canada in 1825 as a seventeen-year-old, joining family friends the Blacks near Darlington (present-day Bowmanville). Strickland bought land near Peterborough, worked for several years for the Canada Company, and eventually settled on land he purchased near present-day Lakefield in Douro Township. In 1831–32 his prospects were excellent, and he did all he could to persuade John Moodie and Thomas Traill to join him there and to engage in various projects and speculations.
3. John Moodie made at least two visits to Douro from his Hamilton Township farm.
4. Clergy reserves were lands designated originally for the use of the Church of England, but which under certain conditions could be sold to private buyers.

wards I was offered £2 per acre, for at that period there was such an influx of settlers into that locality that lands had risen rapidly to a fictitious price. I had also purchased one hundred acres more for £1 10s. per acre, from a private individual; this also was considered cheap at the time.

These lots, forming altogether a compact farm of three hundred and sixty acres, were situated on the sloping banks of a beautiful lake,[5] or, rather, expansion of the river Otonabee, about half-a-mile wide, and studded with woody islets. From this lake I afterwards procured many a good meal for my little family, when all other means of obtaining food had failed us. I thus secured a tract of land which was amply sufficient for the comfortable subsistence of a family, had matters gone well with me.

It should be distinctly borne in mind by the reader, that uncleared land in a remote situation from markets possesses, properly speaking, no intrinsic value, like cleared land, for a great deal of labour or money must be expended before it can be made to produce anything to sell. My half-pay, which amounted to about £100 per annum of Canadian currency, was sufficient to keep us supplied with food, and to pay for clearing a certain extent of land, say ten acres every year, for wheat, which is immediately afterwards sown with grass-seeds to supply hay for the cattle during winter. Unfortunately, at this period, a great change took place in my circumstances, which it was impossible for the most prudent or cautious to have foreseen.

An intimation from the War-office appeared in all the newspapers, calling on half-pay officers either to sell their commissions or to hold themselves in readiness to join some regiment. This was a hard alternative, as many of these officers were situated; for a great many of them had been tempted to emigrate to Canada by the grants of land which were offered them by government, and had expended all their means in improving these grants, which were invariably given to them in remote situations, where they were worse than worthless to any class of settlers but those who could command sufficient labour in their own families to make the necessary clearings and improvements.

Rather than sell my commission, I would at once have made up my mind to join a regiment in any part of the world; but, when I came to think of the matter, I recollected that the expense of an outfit, and of removing my family—to say nothing of sacrificing my property in the colony—would render it utterly impossible for me to accept this unpleasant alternative after being my own master for eighteen years, and after effectually getting rid of all the habits which render a military life attractive to a young man. Under these circumstances, I too hastily determined to sell out of the army.[6] This, of course, was easily man-

5. Lake Katchewanook is a widening of the Otonabee River between present-day Lakefield and Young's Point, and part of the Trent-Severn Waterway, which connects Lake Ontario at Trenton with Georgian Bay and the Great Lakes to the west. It is about ten miles north of Peterborough.
6. The sale of Moodie's half-pay pension was formally announced by the British War-Office on February 21, 1834.

aged. I expected to get about £600 for my commission; and, before the transaction was concluded, I was inquiring anxiously for some mode of investing the proceeds, as to yield a yearly income.

Unfortunately, as it turned out, I made a bargain with Mr. [Clark] for twenty-five shares, of £25 each, in a fine steamer,[7] which had just been built at C[obourg] and which was expected to pay at least twenty-five per cent. to the shareholders. This amount of stock [Clark] offered me for the proceeds of my commission, whatever amount it might be sold for; offering at the same time to return all he should receive above £600 sterling. As I had nothing but his word for this part of the agreement, he did not recollect it when he obtained £700, which was £100 more than I expected.

Some boats on Lake Ontario, while the great emigration lasted, and there was less competition, yielded more than thirty per cent.; and there seemed then no reason to doubt that the new boat would be equally profitable.

It is possible that [Clark] foresaw what actually happened; or, more probably, he thought he could employ his money better in land speculations. As soon as the steamer began to run, a quarrel took place between the shareholders who resided at C[obourg], where she was built, and those who lived at the capital of the Upper Province—York, as it was then called. The consequence was that she remained idle a long time, and at last she came under the entire control of the shareholders at York, who managed the boat as they liked, and to suit their own interests. Afterwards, though the boat continued to be profitably employed, somehow or other all her earnings were consumed in repairs, &c., and for several years I never received a penny for my shares. At last the steamer was sold, and I only received about a fourth part of my original stock. This, as may be supposed, was a bitter disappointment to me; for I had every reason to think that I had not only invested my money well, but very profitably, judging from the profits of the other boats on the lake. Had I received the proceeds of my commission, and bought bank stock in the colony—which then and still yields eight per cent.—my £700 sterling, equal to £840 currency, would have given me £60 per annum, which, with my own labour, would have kept my family tolerably well, have helped to pay servants, and have saved us all much privation and harrassing anxiety.

Having thus supplied the painful details of a transaction, a knowledge of which was necessary to explain many circumstances in our situation, otherwise unintelligible, I shall proceed with my narrative.

The government did not carry out its intention with respect to half-pay officers in the colonies; but many officers, like myself, had already sold their commissions, under the apprehension of being compelled to accept this hard alternative. I was suddenly thrown on my own resources, to support a helpless and increasing family, without any regu-

---

7. The steamboat was named the *Cobourg*. Capitalized at 7,500 pounds (300 shares at 25 pounds each), its troubled story is accurately recounted by John Moodie. He was much disadvantaged by struggles among its ownership.

lar income. I had this consolation, however, under my misfortune, that I had acted from the best motives, and without the most remote idea that I was risking the comfort and happiness of those depending upon me. I found very soon, that I had been too precipitate, as people often are in extraordinary positions; though, had the result been more fortunate, most people would have commended my prudence and foresight. We determined, however, to bear up manfully against our ill-fortune, and trust to that Providence which never deserts those who do not forget their own duties in trying circumstances.

It is curious how, on such occasions, some stray stanzas, which hang about the outskirts of the memory, will suddenly come to our aid. Thus, I often caught myself humming over some of the verses of that excellent moral song, "The Pilot," and repeating, with a peculiar emphasis, the concluding lines of each stanza,

> "Fear not! but trust in Providence,
> Wherever thou may'st be."[8]

Such songs do good; and a peculiar blessing seems to attend every composition, in prose or verse, which inculcates good moral sentiments, or tends to strengthen our virtuous resolutions. This fine song, I feel assured, will live embalmed in the memory of mankind long after the sickly, affected, and unnatural ditties of its author have gone to their merited oblivion. Sometimes, however, in spite of my good resolutions, when left alone, the dark clouds of despondency would close around me, and I could not help contrasting the happy past in our life with my gloomy anticipations of the future. Sleep, which should bring comfort and refreshment, often only aggravated my painful regrets, by recalling scenes which had nearly escaped my waking memory. In such a mood the following verses were written:—

OH, LET ME SLEEP!

> Oh, let me sleep! nor wake to sadness
> The heart that, sleeping, dreams of gladness;
> For sleep is death, without the pain—
> Then wake me not to life again.
> Oh, let me sleep! nor break the spell
> That soothes the captive in his cell;
> That bursts his chains, and sets him free,
> To revel in his liberty.
>
> Loved scenes, array'd in tenderest hue,
> Now rise in beauty to my view;
> And long-lost friends around me stand,
> Or, smiling, grasp my willing hand.
> Again I seek my island home;[9]

8. "The Pilot" by Thomas Haynes Bayly; see *Songs and Ballads, Grave and Gay, By Thomas Haynes Bayly. With a Memoir of the Author* (Philadelphia: Carey and Hart, 1844), p. 42.

9. John Moodie was born at Melsetter, the family estate on the Island of Hoy in the Orkneys. His poem first appeared in the *Palladium of British America*, a Toronto newspaper, on 7 February 1838.

Along the silent bays I roam,
Or, seated on the rocky shore,
I hear the angry surges roar.

And oh, how sweet the music seems
I've heard amid my blissful dreams!
But of the sadly pleasing strains,
Nought save the thrilling sense remains.
Those sounds so loved in scenes so dear,
Still—still they murmur in my ear:
But sleep alone can bless the sight
With forms that face with morning's light.

                                        J. W. D. M.

Fourteen

A Journey to the Woods[1]

'Tis well for us poor denizens of earth
That God conceals the future from our gaze;
Or Hope, the blessed watcher on Life's tower,
Would fold her wings, and on the dreary waste
Close the bright eye that through the murky clouds
Of blank Despair still sees the glorious sun.

It was a bright frosty morning when I bade adieu to the farm, the birthplace of my little Agnes, who, nestled beneath my cloak, was sweetly sleeping on my knee, unconscious of the long journey before us into the wilderness. The sun had not as yet risen. Anxious to get to our place of destination before dark, we started as early as we could. Our own fine team had been sold the day before for forty pounds; and one of our neighbours, a Mr. D——,[2] was to convey us and our household goods to Douro for the sum of twenty dollars. During the week he had made several journeys, with furniture and stores; and all that now remained was to be conveyed to the woods in two large lumber-sleighs, one driven by himself, the other by a younger brother.

It was not without regret that I left Melsetter,[3] for so my husband had called the place, after his father's estate in Orkney. It was a beautiful, picturesque spot; and, in spite of the evil neighbourhood, I had learned to love it; indeed, it was much against my wish that it was sold. I had a great dislike to removing, which involves a necessary loss, and is apt to give to the emigrant roving and unsettled habits. But all regrets were now useless; and happily unconscious of the life of toil

1. In the first printings of *Roughing It in the Bush*, this chapter began Volume II.
2. Mr. D—— was likely Mr. Belcher. The Belcher family ran a flourishing carriage and livery business serving the Cobourg area.
3. Melsetter, John Moodie's Orkney home, was the name the Moodies gave to the former Harris home in Hamilton Township once they took possession of it.

and anxiety that awaited us in those dreadful woods, I tried my best to be cheerful, and to regard the future with a hopeful eye.

Our driver was a shrewd, clever man, for his opportunities. He took charge of the living cargo, which consisted of my husband, our maid-servant, the two little children, and myself—besides a large hamper, full of poultry, a dog, and a cat. The lordly sultan of the imprisoned seraglio thought fit to conduct himself in a very eccentric manner, for at every barn-yard we happened to pass, he clapped his wings, and crowed so long and loud that it afforded great amusement to the whole party, and doubtless was very edifying to the poor hens, who lay huddled together as mute as mice.

"That 'ere rooster thinks he's on the top of the heap," said our driver, laughing. "I guess he's not used to travelling in a close con-veyance. Listen! How all the crowers in the neighbourhood give him back a note of defiance! But he knows that he's safe enough at the bottom of the basket."

The day was so bright for the time of the year, (the first week in Feb-ruary), that we suffered no inconvenience from the cold. Little Katie was enchanted with the jingling of the sleigh-bells, and nestled among the packages, kept singing or talking to the horses in her baby lingo. Trifling as these little incidents were, before we had proceeded ten miles on our long journey, they revived my drooping spirits, and I be-gan to feel a lively interest in the scenes through which we were pass-ing.

The first twenty miles of the way was over a hilly and well-cleared country; and as in winter the deep snow fills up the inequalities, and makes all roads alike, we glided as swiftly and steadily along as if they had been the best highways in the world. Anon, the clearings began to diminish, and tall woods arose on either side of the path; their solemn aspect, and the deep silence that brooded over their vast solitudes, in-spiring the mind with a strange awe. Not a breath of wind stirred the leafless branches, whose huge shadows—reflected upon the dazzling white covering of snow—lay so perfectly still, that it seemed as if Na-ture had suspended her operations, that life and motion had ceased, and that she was sleeping in her winding-sheet, upon the bier of death.

"I guess you will find the woods pretty lonesome," said our driver, whose thoughts had been evidently employed on the same subject as our own. "We were once in the woods, but emigration has stepped ahead of us, and made our'n a cleared part of the country. When I was a boy, all this country, for thirty miles on every side of us, was bush land. As to Peterborough, the place was unknown; not a settler had ever passed through the great swamp, and some of them believed that it was the end of the world."

"What swamp is that?" asked I.

"Oh, the great Cavan swamp.[4] We are just two miles from it; and I

4. The Cavan Swamp in Cavan Township remains a geographical feature southwest of Peter-borough.

tell you that the horses will need a good rest, and ourselves a good dinner, by the time we are through it. Ah! Mrs. Moodie, if ever you travel that way in summer, you will know something about corduroy roads. I was 'most jolted to death last fall; I thought it would have been no bad notion to have insured my teeth before I left C[obourg]. I really expected that they would have been shook out of my head before we had done manoeuvring over the big logs."

"How will my crockery stand it in the next sleigh?" quoth I. "If the road is such as you describe, I am afraid that I shall not bring a whole plate to Douro."

"Oh! the snow is a great leveller—it makes all rough places smooth. But with regard to this swamp, I have something to tell you. About ten years ago, no one had ever seen the other side of it; and if pigs or cattle strayed away into it, they fell a prey to the wolves and bears, and were seldom recovered.

"An old Scotch emigrant, who had located himself on this side of it, so often lost his beasts that he determined during the summer season to try and explore the place, and see if there were any end to it. So he takes an axe on his shoulder, and a bag of provisions for a week, not forgetting a flask of whiskey, and off he starts all alone, and tells his wife that if he never returned, she and little Jock must try and carry on the farm without him; but he was determined to see the end of the swamp, even if it led to the other world. He fell upon a fresh cattle-track, which he followed all that day; and towards night he found himself in the heart of a tangled wilderness of bushes, and himself half eaten up with mosquitoes and black-flies. He was more than tempted to give in, and return home by the first glimpse of light.

"The Scotch are a tough people; they are not easily daunted—a few difficulties only seem to make them more eager to get on; and he felt ashamed the next moment, as he told me, of giving up. So he finds out a large thick cedar-tree for his bed, climbs up, and coiling himself among the branches like a bear, he was soon fast asleep.

"The next morning, by daylight, he continued his journey, not forgetting to blaze with his axe the trees to the right and left as he went along. The ground was so spongy and wet that at every step he plunged up to his knees in water, but he seemed no nearer the end of the swamp than he had been the day before. He saw several deer, a raccoon, and a ground-hog, during his walk, but was unmolested by bears or wolves. Having passed through several creeks, and killed a great many snakes, he felt so weary towards the close of the second day that he determined to go home the next morning. But just as he began to think his search was fruitless he observed that the cedars and tamaracks which had obstructed his path became less numerous, and were succeeded by bass and soft maple. The ground, also, became less moist, and he was soon ascending a rising slope, covered with oak and beech, which shaded land of the very best quality. The old man was now fully convinced that he had cleared the great swamp; and that, instead of leading to the other world, it had conducted him to a country that would yield the very best returns for cultivation. His favourable report led to the formation of the road that we are about to cross, and to the settlement of Peterborough, which is one of the most promising new settlements in this district, and is surrounded by a splendid back country."

We were descending a very steep hill, and encountered an ox-sleigh, which was crawling slowly up it in a contrary direction. Three people were seated at the bottom of the vehicle upon straw, which made a cheap substitute for buffalo robes. Perched, as we were, upon the crown of the height, we looked completely down into the sleigh, and during the whole course of my life I never saw three uglier mortals collected into such a narrow space. The man was blear-eyed, with a hare-lip, through which protruded two dreadful yellow teeth that resembled the tusks of a boar. The woman was long-faced, high cheek-boned, red-haired, and freckled all over like a toad. The boy resembled his hideous mother, but with the addition of a villanous obliquity of vision which rendered him the most disgusting object in this singular trio.

As we passed them, our driver gave a knowing nod to my husband, directing, at the same time, the most quizzical glance towards the strangers, as he exclaimed, "We are in luck, sir! I think that 'ere sleigh may be called Beauty's egg-basket!"

We made ourselves very merry at the poor people's expense, and Mr. D——, with his odd stories and Yankeefied expressions, amused the tedium of our progress through the great swamp, which in summer presents for several miles one uniform bridge of rough and unequal logs, all laid loosely across huge sleepers, so that they jump up and down, when pressed by the wheels, like the keys of a piano. The rough motion and jolting occasioned by this collision is so distressing that it never fails to entail upon the traveller sore bones and an aching head for the rest of the day. The path is so narrow over these logs that two waggons cannot pass without great difficulty, which is rendered more dangerous by the deep natural ditches on either side of the bridge, formed by broad creeks that flow out of the swamp, and often terminate in mud-holes of very ominous dimensions. The snow, however, hid from us all the ugly features of the road, and Mr. D—— steered us through in perfect safety, and landed us at the door of a little log house which crowned the steep hill on the other side of the swamp, and which he dignified with the name of a tavern.

It was now two o'clock. We had been on the road since seven; and men, women, and children were all ready for the good dinner that Mr. D—— had promised us at this splendid house of entertainment, where we were destined to stay for two hours, to refresh ourselves and rest the horses.

"Well, Mrs. J[ohnston],[5] what have you got for our dinner?" said our driver, after he had seen to the accommodation of his teams.

"Pritters and pork, sir. Nothing else to be had in the woods. Thank God, we have enough of that!"

---

5. Jane Johnston (or Johnson) kept an "Inn and house of entertainment" in Cavan Township, according to tavern and shop licensing records for the Cobourg area.

D—— shrugged his shoulders, and looked at us.

"We've plenty of that same at home. But hunger's good sauce. Come, be spry, widow, and see about it, for I am very hungry."

I inquired for a private room for myself and the children, but there were no private rooms in the house. The apartment we occupied was like the cobbler's stall in the old song, and I was obliged to attend upon them in public.

"You have much to learn, ma'am, if you are going to the woods," said Mrs. J[ohnston].

"To unlearn, you mean," said Mr. D——. "To tell you the truth, Mrs. Moodie, ladies and gentlemen have no business in the woods. Eddication spoils man or woman for that location. So, widow (turning to our hostess), you are not tired of living alone yet?"

"No, sir; I have no wish for a second husband. I had enough of the first. I like to have my own way—to lie down mistress, and get up master."

"You don't like to be put out of your *old* way," returned he, with a mischievous glance.

She coloured very red; but it might be the heat of the fire over which she was frying the pork for our dinner.

I was very hungry, but I felt no appetite for the dish she was preparing for us. It proved salt, hard, and unsavoury.

D—— pronounced it very bad, and the whiskey still worse, with which he washed it down.

I asked for a cup of tea and a slice of bread. But they were out of tea, and the hop-rising had failed, and there was no bread in the house. For this disgusting meal we paid at the rate of a quarter of a dollar a-head.

I was glad when the horses being again put to, we escaped from the rank odour of the fried pork, and were once more in the fresh air.

"Well, mister; did not you grudge your money for that bad meat?" said D——, when we were once more seated in the sleigh. "But in these parts, the worse the fare the higher the charge."

"I would not have cared," said I, "If I could have got a cup of tea."

"Tea! it's poor trash. I never could drink tea in my life. But I like coffee, when 'tis boiled till it's quite black. But coffee is not good without plenty of trimmings."

"What do you mean by trimmings?"

He laughed. "Good sugar, and sweet cream. Coffee is not worth drinking without trimmings."

Often in after-years have I recalled the coffee trimmings, when endeavouring to drink the vile stuff which goes by the name of coffee in the houses of entertainment in the country.

We had now passed through the narrow strip of clearing which surrounded the tavern, and again entered upon the woods. It was near sunset, and we were rapidly descending a steep hill, when one of the traces that held our sleigh suddenly broke. D—— pulled up in order to repair the damage. His brother's team was close behind, and our unexpected stand-still brought the horses upon us before J. D——

could stop them. I received so violent a blow from the head of one of them, just in the back of the neck, that for a few minutes I was stunned and insensible. When I recovered, I was supported in the arms of my husband, over whose knees I was leaning, and D—— was rubbing my hands and temples with snow.

"There, Mr. Moodie, she's coming-to. I thought she was killed. I have seen a man before now killed by a blow from a horse's head in the like manner." As soon as we could, we resumed our places in the sleigh; but all enjoyment of our journey, had it been otherwise possible, was gone.

When we reached Peterborough, Moodie wished us to remain at the inn all night,[6] as we had still eleven miles of our journey to perform, and that through a blazed forest-road, little travelled, and very much impeded by fallen trees and other obstacles; but D—— was anxious to get back as soon as possible to his own home, and he urged us very pathetically to proceed.

The moon arose during our stay at the inn, and gleamed upon the straggling frame-houses which then formed the now populous and thriving town of Peterborough. We crossed the wild, rushing, beautiful Otonabee river by a rude bridge, and soon found ourselves journeying over the plains or level heights beyond the village, which were thinly wooded with picturesque groups of oak and pine, and very much resembled a gentleman's park at home.

Far below, to our right (for we were upon the Smithtown side)[7] we heard the rushing of the river, whose rapid waters never receive curb from the iron chain of winter. Even while the rocky banks are coated with ice, and the frost-king suspends from every twig and branch the most beautiful and fantastic crystals, the black waters rush foaming along, a thick steam rising constantly above the rapids, as from a boiling pot. The shores vibrate and tremble beneath the force of the impetuous flood, as it whirls round cedar-crowned islands and opposing rocks, and hurries on to pour its tribute into the Rice Lake, to swell the calm, majestic grandeur of the Trent, till its waters are lost in the beautiful bay of Quinté, and finally merged in the blue ocean of Ontario.

The most renowned of our English rivers dwindle into little muddy rills when compared with the sublimity of the Canadian waters. No language can adequately express the solemn grandeur of her lake and river scenery; the glorious islands that float, like visions from fairy land, upon the bosom of these azure mirrors of her cloudless skies. No dreary breadth of marshes, covered with flags, hides from our gaze the expanse of heaven-tinted waters; no foul mud-banks spread their unwholesome exhalations around. The rocky shores are crowned with the cedar, the birch, the alder, and soft maple, that dip their long tresses in the pure stream; from every crevice in the limestone the hare-bell and Canadian rose wave their graceful blossoms.

6. Likely the same inn, McFadden's Hotel, in Peterborough where the Traills stayed when they
   passed through town in 1832.
7. Arriving from the south, the Moodies crossed the bridge at Peterborough to the north side of
   the Otonabee River, then advanced into Smith Township on their trip northward.

The fiercest droughts of summer may diminish the volume and power of these romantic streams, but it never leaves their rocky channels bare, nor checks the mournful music of their dancing waves.

Through the openings in the forest, we now and then caught the silver gleam of the river tumbling on in moonlight splendour, while the hoarse chiding of the wind in the lofty pines above us gave a fitting response to the melancholy cadence of the waters.

The children had fallen asleep. A deep silence pervaded the party. Night was above us with her mysterious stars. The ancient forest stretched around us on every side, and a foreboding sadness sunk upon my heart. Memory was busy with the events of many years. I retraced step by step the pilgrimage of my past life, until arriving at that passage in its sombre history, I gazed through tears upon the singularly savage scene around me, and secretly marvelled, "What brought me here?"

"Providence," was the answer which the soul gave. "Not for your own welfare, perhaps, but for the welfare of your children, the unerring hand of the Great Father has led you here. You form a connecting link in the destinies of many. It is impossible for any human creature to live for himself alone. It may be your lot to suffer, but others will reap a benefit from your trials. Look up with confidence to Heaven, and the sun of hope will yet shed a cheering beam through the forbidding depths of this tangled wilderness."

The road now became so bad that Mr. D—— was obliged to dismount, and lead his horses through the more intricate passages. The animals themselves, weary with their long journey and heavy load, proceeded at footfall. The moon, too, had deserted us, and the only light we had to guide us through the dim arches of the forest was from the snow and the stars, which now peered down upon us, through the leafless branches of the trees, with uncommon brilliancy.

"It will be past midnight before we reach your brother's clearing" (where we expected to spend the night), said D——. "I wish, Mr. Moodie, we had followed your advice, and staid at Peterborough. How fares it with you, Mrs. Moodie, and the young ones? It is growing very cold."

We were now in the heart of a dark cedar swamp, and my mind was haunted with visions of wolves and bears; but beyond the long, wild howl of a solitary wolf, no other sound awoke the sepulchral silence of that dismal-looking wood.

"What a gloomy spot!" said I to my husband. "In the old country, superstition would people it with ghosts."

"Ghosts! There are no ghosts in Canada!" said Mr. D——. "The country is too new for ghosts. No Canadian is afeard of ghosts. It is only in old countries, like your'n, that are full of sin and wickedness, that people believe in such nonsense. No human habitation has ever been erected in this wood through which you are passing. Until a very few years ago, few white persons had ever passed through it; and the Red Man would not pitch his tent in such a place as this. Now, ghosts, as I understand the word, are the spirits of bad men, that are not allowed by Providence to rest in their graves, but, for a punishment, are made to haunt the spots where their worst deeds were committed. I don't believe in all this; but, supposing it to be true, bad men must have died here before their spirits could haunt the place. Now, it is more than probable that no person ever ended his days in this forest, so that it would be folly to think of seeing his ghost."

This theory of Mr. D——'s had the merit of originality, and it is not improbable that the utter disbelief in supernatural appearances which is common to most native-born Canadians, is the result of the same very reasonable mode of arguing. The unpeopled wastes of Canada must present the same aspect to the new settler that the world did to our first parents after their expulsion from the Garden of Eden; all the sin which could defile the spot, or haunt it with the association of departed evil, is concentrated in their own persons. Bad spirits cannot be supposed to linger near a place where crime has never been committed. The belief in ghosts, so prevalent in old countries, must first have had its foundation in the consciousness of guilt.

After clearing this low, swampy portion of the wood, with much difficulty, and the frequent application of the axe, to cut away the fallen timber that impeded our progress, our ears were assailed by a low, roaring, rushing sound, as of the falling of waters.

"That is Herriot's Falls,"[8] said our guide. "We are within two miles of our destination."

Oh, welcome sound! But those two miles appeared more lengthy than the whole journey. Thick clouds, that threatened a snow-storm, had blotted out the stars, and we continued to grope our way through a narrow, rocky path, upon the edge of the river, in almost total darkness. I now felt the chilliness of the midnight hour, and the fatigue of the long journey, with double force, and envied the servant and children, who had been sleeping ever since we left Peterborough. We now descended the steep bank, and prepared to cross the rapids.

Dark as it was, I looked with a feeling of dread upon the foaming waters as they tumbled over their bed of rocks, their white crests flashing, life-like, amid the darkness of the night.

"This is an ugly bridge over such a dangerous place," said D——, as he stood up in the sleigh and urged his tired team across the miserable, insecure log bridge where darkness and death raged below, and one false step of his jaded horses would have plunged us into both. I must confess I drew a freer breath when the bridge was crossed, and D—— congratulated us on our safe arrival in Douro.

We now continued our journey along the left bank of the river, but when in sight of Mr. S[trickland]'s clearing, a large pine-tree, which had newly fallen across the narrow path, brought the teams to a stand-still.

8. Herriott's Falls was then the name of the crossing of the Otonabee River at what is now called Lakefield. Here the Moodies crossed the bridge from Smith Township into Douro Township on the eastern shore of the Otonabee River and Lake Katchewanook. James Herriott was a young Scot who had recently built the crude bridge there and set up a mill to take advantage of the falls below the narrowing of Lake Katchewanook. The bridge collapsed later in 1834, taking Herriott's fortunes with it.

The mighty trunk which had lately formed one of the stately pillars in the sylvan temple of Nature, was of too large dimensions to chop in two with axes; and after about half-an-hour's labour, which to me, poor, cold, weary wight! seemed an age, the males of the party abandoned the task in despair. To go round it was impossible; its roots were concealed in an impenetrable wall of cedar-jungle on the right-hand side of the road, and its huge branches hung over the precipitous bank of the river.

"We must try and make the horses jump over it," said D——. "We may get an upset, but there is no help for it; we must either make the experiment, or stay here all night, and I am too cold and hungry for that—so here goes." He urged his horses to leap the log; restraining their ardour for a moment as the sleigh rested on the top of the formidable barrier, but so nicely balanced, that the difference of a straw would almost have overturned the heavily-laden vehicle and its helpless inmates. We, however, cleared it in safety. He now stopped, and gave directions to his brother to follow the same plan that he had adopted; but whether the young man had less coolness, or the horses in his team were more difficult to manage, I cannot tell: the sleigh, as it hung poised upon the top of the log, was overturned with a loud crash, and all my household goods and chattels were scattered over the road.

Alas, for my crockery and stone china! scarcely one article remained unbroken.

"Never fret about the china," said Moodie; "thank God, the man and the horses are uninjured."

I should have felt more thankful had the crocks been spared too; for, like most of my sex, I had a tender regard for china, and I knew that no fresh supply could be obtained in this part of the world. Leaving his brother to collect the scattered fragments, D—— proceeded on his journey. We left the road, and were winding our way over a steep hill, covered with heaps of brush and fallen timber, and as we reached the top, a light gleamed cheerily from the windows of a log house, and the next moment we were at my brother's door.

I thought my journey was at an end; but here I was doomed to fresh disappointment. His wife was absent on a visit to her friends,[9] and it had been arranged that we were to stay with my sister, Mrs. T[raill], and her husband.[1] With all this I was unacquainted; and I was about to quit the sleigh and seek the warmth of the fire when I was told that I had yet further to go. Its cheerful glow was to shed no warmth on me, and, tired as I was, I actually buried my face and wept upon the neck of a hound which Moodie had given to Mr. S[trickland], and which sprang up upon the sleigh to lick my face and hands. This was my first halt in that weary wilderness, where I endured so many bitter years of toil and sorrow. My brother-in-law and his family had retired to rest,

9. Sam Strickland's clearing was one mile north of Herriott's bridge. Sam's second wife, Mary (Reid), was away, perhaps visiting her family, who lived several miles to the south in Douro.
1. Catharine Parr Strickland and her husband Thomas Traill, whom Susanna had not seen since they left England in the spring of 1832.

but they instantly rose to receive the way-worn travellers; and I never enjoyed more heartily a warm welcome after a long day of intense fatigue, than I did that night of my first sojourn in the backwoods.

THE OTONABEE.[2]

Dark, rushing, foaming river!
I love the solemn sound
That shakes thy shores around,
And hoarsely murmurs, ever,
As thy waters onward bound,
Like a rash, unbridled steed
Flying madly on its course;
That shakes with thundering force
The vale and trembling mead.
So thy billows downward sweep,
Nor rock nor tree can stay
Their fierce, impetuous way;
Now in eddies whirling deep,
Now in rapids white with spray.

I love thee, lonely river!
Thy hollow restless roar,
Thy cedar-girded shore;
The rocky isles that sever
The waves that round them pour.
Katchawanook[3] basks in light,
But thy currents woo the shade
By the lofty pine-trees made,
That cast a gloom like night,
Ere day's last glories fade.
Thy solitary voice
The same bold anthem sung
When Nature's frame was young.
No longer shall rejoice
The woods where erst it rung!

Lament, lament, wild river!
A hand is on thy mane[4]
That will bind thee in a chain
No force of thine can sever.
Thy furious headlong tide,
In murmurs soft and low,
Is destined yet to glide

2. First published in *The Literary Garland* (Montreal) 1:6 (May 1839), p. 275, when Susanna was still living on the bush farm in Douro.
3. The Indian name for one of the many expansions of this beautiful river. [*Author's note.*]
4. Alluding to the projected improvements on the Trent, of which the Otonabee is a continuation. Fifteen years have passed away since this little poem was written; but the Otonabee still rushes on its own wild strength. Some idea of the rapidity of this river may be formed from the fact that heavy rafts of timber are floated down from Herriot's Falls, a distance of nine miles from Peterborough, in less than an hour. The shores are bold and rocky, and abound in beautiful and picturesque views. [*Author's note.*]

To meet the lake below;
And many a bark shall ride
Securely on thy breast,
To waft across the main
Rich stores of golden grain
From the valleys of the West.

Fifteen

The Wilderness, and Our Indian Friends

Man of strange race! stern dweller of the wild!
Nature's free-born, untamed, and daring child!

The clouds of the preceding night, instead of dissolving in snow, brought on a rapid thaw. A thaw in the middle of winter is the most disagreeable change that can be imagined. After several weeks of clear, bright, bracing, frosty weather, with a serene atmosphere and cloudless sky, you awake one morning surprised at the change in the temperature; and, upon looking out of the window, behold the woods obscured by a murky haze—not so dense as an English November fog, but more black and lowering—and the heavens shrouded in a uniform covering of leaden-coloured clouds, deepening into a livid indigo at the edge of the horizon. The snow, no longer hard and glittering, has become soft and spongy, and the foot slips into a wet and insidiously-yielding mass at every step. From the roof pours down a continuous stream of water, and the branches of the trees, collecting the moisture of the reeking atmosphere, shower it upon the earth from every dripping twig. The cheerless and uncomfortable aspect of things without never fails to produce a corresponding effect upon the minds of those within, and casts such a damp upon the spirits that it appears to destroy for a time all sense of enjoyment. Many persons (and myself among the number) are made aware of the approach of a thunder-storm by an intense pain and weight about the head; and I have heard numbers of Canadians complain that a thaw always made them feel bilious and heavy, and greatly depressed their animal spirits.

I had a great desire to visit our new location, but when I looked out upon the cheerless waste, I gave up the idea, and contented myself with hoping for a better day on the morrow; but many morrows came and went before a frost again hardened the road sufficiently for me to make the attempt.

The prospect from the windows of my sister's log hut was not very prepossessing. The small lake in front,[1] which formed such a pretty object in summer, now looked like an extensive field covered with snow, hemmed in from the rest of the world by a dark belt of sombre

---

1. At low water levels, Lake Katchewanook seemed to be comprised of three small lakes. The Traill house fronted on one of these, and the Moodies' fronted on another. The largest part of the lake was to the north of the Moodies.

pine-woods. The clearing round the house was very small, and only just reclaimed from the wilderness, and the greater part of it covered with piles of brushwood, to be burnt the first dry days of spring. The charred and blackened stumps on the few acres that had been cleared during the preceding year were everything but picturesque, and I concluded, as I turned, disgusted, from the prospect before me, that there was very little beauty to be found in the backwoods. But I came to this decision during a Canadian thaw, be it remembered, when one is wont to view every object with jaundiced eyes.

Moodie had only been able to secure sixty-six acres of his government grant upon the Upper Katchawanook Lake, which, being interpreted, means in English, the "Lake of the Waterfalls," a very poetical meaning, which most Indian names have. He had, however, secured a clergy reserve of two hundred acres adjoining; and he afterwards purchased a fine lot, which likewise formed part of the same block, one hundred acres, for £150.[2] This was an enormously high price for wild land; but the prospect of opening the Trent and Otonabee for the navigation of steam-boats and other small craft, was at that period a favourite speculation, and its practicability, and the great advantages to be derived from it, were so widely believed as to raise the value of the wild lands along these remote waters to an enormous price; and settlers in the vicinity were eager to secure lots, at any sacrifice, along their shores.

Our government grant was upon the lake shore, and Moodie had chosen for the site of his log house a bank that sloped gradually from the edge of the water, until it attained to the dignity of a hill. Along the top of this ridge, the forest-road ran, and midway down the hill, our humble home, already nearly completed, stood, surrounded by the eternal forest. A few trees had been cleared in the immediate vicinity, just sufficient to allow the workmen to proceed, and to prevent the fall of any tree injuring the building, or the danger of its taking fire during the process of burning the fallow.

A neighbour had undertaken to build this rude dwelling by contract, and was to have it ready for us by the first week in the new year. The want of boards to make the divisions in the apartments alone hindered him from fulfilling his contract. These had lately been procured, and the house was to be ready for our reception in the course of a week. Our trunks and baggage had already been conveyed thither by Mr. D——; and in spite of my sister's kindness and hospitality, I longed to find myself once more settled in a home of my own.

The day after our arrival, I was agreeably surprised by a visit from Monaghan, whom Moodie had once more taken into his service. The poor fellow was delighted that his nurse-child, as he always called lit-

---

2. After a lapse of fifteen years, we have been glad to sell these lots of land, after considerable clearings had been made upon them for less than they originally cost us. [*Author's note.*]

   Susanna refers to the four lots that made up Moodie's military land grant. While he held sixty-six acres on the Douro shore of Lake Katchewanook (parts of Lot 21, Concession 6 and Lot 17, Concession 3), he also owned parcels of land in Verulam and Fenelon Townships, making a total of 400 acres.

tle Katie, had not forgotten him, but evinced the most lively satisfaction at the sight of her dark friend.

Early every morning, Moodie went off to the house; and the first fine day, my sister undertook to escort me through the wood, to inspect it. The proposal was joyfully accepted; and although I felt *rather* timid when I found myself with only my female companion in the vast forest, I kept my fears to myself, lest I should be laughed at. This foolish dread of encountering wild beasts in the woods I never could wholly shake off, even after becoming a constant resident in their gloomy depths, and accustomed to follow the forest-path, alone, or attended with little children, daily. The cracking of an old bough, or the hooting of the owl, was enough to fill me with alarm, and try my strength in a precipitate flight. Often have I stopped and reproached myself for want of faith in the goodness of Providence, and repeated the text, "The wicked are afraid when no man pursueth: but the righteous are as bold as a lion,"[3] as if to shame myself into courage. But it would not do; I could not overcome the weakness of the flesh. If I had one of my infants with me, the wish to protect the child from any danger which might beset my path gave me for a time a fictitious courage; but it was like love fighting with despair.

It was in vain that my husband assured me that no person had ever been attacked by wild animals in the woods, that a child might traverse them even at night in safety; whilst I knew that wild animals existed in those woods, I could not believe him, and my fears on this head rather increased than diminished.

The snow had been so greatly decreased by the late thaw, that it had been converted into a coating of ice, which afforded a dangerous and slippery footing. My sister, who had resided for nearly twelve months in the woods,[4] was provided for her walk with Indian moccasins, which rendered her quite independent; but I stumbled at every step. The sun shone brightly, the air was clear and invigorating, and, in spite of the treacherous ground and my foolish fears, I greatly enjoyed my first walk in the woods. Naturally of a cheerful, hopeful disposition, my sister was enthusiastic in her admiration of the woods. She drew such a lively picture of the charms of a summer residence in the forest that I began to feel greatly interested in her descriptions, and to rejoice that we, too, were to be her near neighbours and dwellers in the woods; and this circumstance not a little reconciled me to the change.

Hoping that my husband would derive an income equal to the one he had parted with from the investment of the price of his commission in the steam-boat stock, I felt no dread of want. Our legacy of £700 had afforded us means to purchase land, build our house, and give out a large portion of land to be cleared, and, with a considerable sum of

3. Proverbs 28:1.
4. The Traills had come to Peterborough in August 1832 but had not settled on their farm site until the winter of 1832–33. Their home took several months to contract and build; in the interim they stayed with various friends, including Thomas and Frances Stewart, who lived in Douro, within two miles of Peterborough.

money still in hand, our prospects for the future were in no way discouraging.

When we reached the top of the ridge that overlooked our cot, my sister stopped, and pointed out a log-house among the trees. "There, S[usanna]," she said, "is your home. When that black cedar swamp is cleared away, that now hides the lake from us, you will have a very pretty view." My conversation with her had quite altered the aspect of the country, and predisposed me to view things in the most favourable light. I found Moodie and Monaghan employed in piling up heaps of bush near the house, which they intended to burn off by hand previous to firing the rest of the fallow, to prevent any risk to the building from fire. The house was made of cedar logs, and presented a superior air of comfort to most dwellings of the same kind. The dimensions were thirty-six feet in length, and thirty-two in breadth, which gave us a nice parlour, a kitchen, and two small bed-rooms, which were divided by plank partitions. Pantry or store-room there was none; some rough shelves in the kitchen, and a deal cupboard in a corner of the parlour, being the extent of our accommodations in that way.

Our servant, Mary Tate, was busy scrubbing out the parlour and bed-room; but the kitchen, and the sleeping-room off it, were still knee-deep in chips, and filled with the carpenter's bench and tools, and all our luggage. Such as it was, it was a palace when compared to Old Satan's log hut, or the miserable cabin we had wintered in during the severe winter of 1833, and I regarded it with complacency as my future home.

While we were standing outside the building, conversing with my husband, a young gentleman of the name of Morgan,[5] who had lately purchased land in that vicinity, went into the kitchen to light his pipe at the stove, and, with true backwood carelessness, let the hot cinder fall among the dry chips that strewed the floor. A few minutes after, the whole mass was in a blaze, and it was not without great difficulty that Moodie and Mr. R[eid] succeeded in putting out the fire.[6] Thus were we nearly deprived of our home before we had taken up our abode in it.

The indifference to the danger of fire in a country where most of the dwellings are composed of inflammable materials, is truly astonishing. Accustomed to see enormous fires blazing on every hearth-stone, and to sleep in front of these fires, his bedding often riddled with holes made by hot particles of wood flying out during the night, and igniting beneath his very nose, the sturdy backwoodsman never dreads an enemy in the element that he is used to regard as his best friend. Yet what awful accidents, what ruinous calamities arise, out of this criminal negligence, both to himself and others!

5. An English emigrant of respectable family, James Morgan shared with Thomas Traill and William Wood a deed on Lot 21, Concession 5. He later drowned.
6. Robert Reid, the father of Sam Strickland's wife Mary, lived in Douro but to the south. He was one of the earliest settlers in Douro and had played a part in convincing the Moodies to emigrate by visiting them in Southwold during a trip home to Ireland and England in 1831 (see *Letters of a Lifetime*, p. 63).

A few days after this adventure, we bade adieu to my sister, and took possession of our new dwelling, and commenced "a life in the woods."

The first spring we spent in comparative ease and idleness. Our cows had been left upon our old place during the winter. The ground had to be cleared before it could receive a crop of any kind, and I had little to do but to wander by the lake shore, or among the woods, and amuse myself.

These were the halcyon days of the bush. My husband had purchased a very light cedar canoe, to which he attached a keel and a sail; and most of our leisure hours, directly the snows melted, were spent upon the water.

These fishing and shooting excursions were delightful. The pure beauty of the Canadian water, the sombre but august grandeur of the vast forest that hemmed us in on every side and shut us out from the rest of the world, soon cast a magic spell upon our spirits, and we began to feel charmed with the freedom and solitude around us. Every object was new to us. We felt as if we were the first discoverers of every beautiful flower and stately tree that attracted our attention, and we gave names to fantastic rocks and fairy isles, and raised imaginary houses and bridges on every picturesque spot which we floated past during our aquatic excursions. I learned the use of the paddle, and became quite a proficient in the gentle craft.

It was not long before we received visits from the Indians, a people whose beauty, talents, and good qualities have been somewhat overrated, and invested with a poetical interest which they scarcely deserve. Their honesty and love of truth are the finest traits in characters otherwise dark and unlovely. But these are two God-like attributes, and from them spring all that is generous and ennobling about them.

There never was a people more sensible of kindness, or more grateful for any little act of benevolence exercised towards them. We met them with confidence; our dealings with them were conducted with the strictest integrity; and they became attached to our persons, and in no single instance ever destroyed the good opinion we entertained of them.

The tribes that occupy the shores of all these inland waters, back of the great lakes, belong to the Chippewa or Missasagua Indians,[7] perhaps the least attractive of all these wild people, both with regard to their physical and mental endowments.

The men of this tribe are generally small of stature, with very coarse and repulsive features. The forehead is low and retreating, the observing faculties large, the intellectual ones scarcely developed; the ears large, and standing off from the face, the eyes looking towards the

7. The Chippewa and Missassauga Indians (Ojibway) frequented the lakes north of Peterborough in the early 1830s, setting up hunting camps in both winter and summer close to water. Various families for whom Mud Lake (later Chemong Lake) was their home base, including the Nogans, Cows, Muskrats and Irons, camped in a clearing near the Moodies' "dry cedar swamp" and close to the shore of Lake Katchewanook. These families had all been converted to Christianity, likely through the ministry of Peter Jones at Rice Lake, prior to the Moodies' arrival.

temples, keen, snake-like, and far apart; the cheek-bones prominent; the nose long and flat, the nostrils very round; the jaw-bone projecting, massy, and brutal; the mouth expressing ferocity and sullen determination; the teeth large, even, and dazzlingly white. The mouth of the female differs widely in expression from that of the male; the lips are fuller, the jaw less projecting, and the smile is simple and agreeable. The women are a merry, light-hearted set, and their constant laugh and incessant prattle form a strange contrast to the iron taciturnity of their grim lords.

Now I am upon the subject, I will recapitulate a few traits and sketches of these people, as they came under my own immediate observation.

A dry cedar-swamp, not far from the house, by the lake shore, had been their usual place of encampment for many years.[8] The whole block of land was almost entirely covered with maple-trees, and had originally been an Indian sugar-bush. Although the favourite spot had now passed into the hands of strangers, they still frequented the place, to make canoes and baskets, to fish and shoot, and occasionally to follow their old occupation.

Scarcely a week passed away without my being visited by the dark strangers; and as my husband never allowed them to eat with the servants (who viewed them with the same horror that Mrs. D[ean] did black Mollineux), but brought them to his own table, they soon grew friendly and communicative, and would point to every object that attracted their attention, asking a thousand questions as to its use, the material of which it was made, and if we were inclined to exchange it for their commodities?

With a large map of Canada they were infinitely delighted. In a moment they recognised every bay and headland in Ontario, and almost screamed with delight when, following the course of the Trent with their fingers, they came to their own lake.

How eagerly each pointed out the spot to his fellows; how intently their black heads were bent down, and their dark eyes fixed upon the map! What strange, uncouth exclamations of surprise burst from their lips as they rapidly repeated the Indian names for every lake and river on this wonderful piece of paper!

The old chief, Peter Nogan,[9] begged hard for the coveted treasure. He would give "Canoe, venison, duck, fish, for it; and more by-and-by."

I felt sorry that I was unable to gratify his wishes; but the map had cost upwards of six dollars, and was daily consulted by my husband, in reference to the names and situations of localities in the neighbourhood.

8. The site of the Moodie log home remains very much as it was. They built on a low ridge above the lake and were separated from it by a heavy stand of cedars. Now cottages rim the lakeshore but the dense cedars remain, as does the poor-quality farmland above, which is now grazing acreage for a herd of cows. The log house is no longer there, but was the site of several digs in the late 1990s by field schools run by the Anthropology Department at Trent University.
9. Peter Nogan, the "old chief" of the Missassaugas of Mud Lake, had a large family, many members of which figure prominently in Susanna's personalized anecdotes.

I had in my possession a curious Japanese sword,[1] which had been given to me by an uncle of Tom Wilson's—a strange gift to a young lady; but it was on account of its curiosity, and had no reference to my warlike propensities. This sword was broad, and three-sided in the blade, and in shape resembled a moving snake. The hilt was formed of a hideous carved image of one of their war-gods; and a more villain-ous-looking wretch was never conceived by the most distorted imagi-nation. He was represented in a sitting attitude, the eagle's claws, that formed his hands, resting upon his knees; his legs terminated in lion's paws; and his face was a strange compound of beast and bird—the up-per part of his person being covered with feathers, the lower with long, shaggy hair. The case of this awful weapon was made of wood, and in spite of its serpentine form, fitted it exactly. No trace of a join could be found in this scabbard, which was of hard wood, and highly polished.

One of my Indian friends found this sword lying upon the book-shelf, and he hurried to communicate the important discovery to his companions. Moodie was absent, and they brought it to me to demand an explanation of the figure that formed the hilt.

I told them that it was a weapon that belonged to a very fierce peo-ple who lived in the East, far over the Great Salt Lake; that they were not Christians as we were, but said their prayers to images made of sil-ver, and gold, and ivory, and wood, and that this was one of them; that before they went into battle they said their prayers to that hideous thing, which they had made with their own hands.

The Indians were highly amused by this relation, and passed the sword from one to the other, exclaiming, "A god!—Owgh!—A god!"

But, in spite of these outward demonstrations of contempt, I was sorry to perceive that this circumstance gave the weapon a great value in their eyes, and they regarded it with a sort of mysterious awe.

For several days they continued to visit the house, bringing along with them some fresh companion to look at Mrs. Moodie's god!—until, vexed and annoyed by the delight they manifested at the sight of the eagle-beaked monster, I refused to gratify their curiosity, by not producing him again.

The manufacture of the sheath, which had caused me much per-plexity, was explained by old Peter in a minute. " 'Tis burnt out," he said. "Instrument made like sword—heat red-hot—burnt through—polished outside."

Had I demanded a whole fleet of canoes for my Japanese sword, I am certain they would have agreed to the bargain.

The Indian possesses great taste, which is displayed in the carving of his paddles, in the shape of his canoes, in the elegance and symme-try of his bows, in the cut of his leggings and moccasins, the sheath of his hunting-knife, and in all the little ornaments in which he delights. It is almost impossible for a settler to imitate to perfection an Indian's

---

1. In February 1839 Susanna reported that she gave the Japanese "dagger" to George Craw-ford, a Douro neighbour whose wife had been a friend and help to her when she was alone in the bush during John's military service (see *Letters of Love and Duty*, p. 127).

cherry-wood paddle. My husband made very creditable attempts, but still there was something wanting—the elegance of the Indian finish was not there. If you show them a good print, they invariably point out the most natural, and the best-executed figure in the group. They are particularly delighted with pictures, examine them long and carefully, and seem to feel an artist-like pleasure in observing the effect produced by light and shade.

I had been showing John Nogan, the eldest son of old Peter, some beautiful coloured engravings of celebrated females; and to my astonishment he pounced upon the best, and grunted out his admiration in the most approved Indian fashion. After having looked for a long time at all the pictures very attentively, he took his dog Sancho upon his knee, and showed him the pictures, with as much gravity as if the animal really could have shared in his pleasure.

The vanity of these grave men is highly amusing. They seem perfectly unconscious of it themselves; and it is exhibited in the most child-like manner.

Peter and his son John were taking tea with us, when we were joined by my brother, Mr. S[trickland]. The latter was giving us an account of the marriage of Peter Jones, the celebrated Indian preacher.[2]

"I cannot think," he said, "how any lady of property and education could marry such a man as Jones. Why, he's as ugly as Peter here."

This was said, not with any idea of insulting the red-skin on the score of his beauty, of which he possessed not the smallest particle, but in total forgetfulness that our guest understood English. Never shall I forget the red flash of that fierce dark eye as it glared upon my unconscious brother. I would not have received such a fiery glance for all the wealth that Peter Jones obtained with his Saxon bride. John Nogan was highly amused by his father's indignation. He hid his face behind the chief; and though he kept perfectly still, his whole frame was convulsed with suppressed laughter.

A plainer human being than poor Peter could scarcely be imagined; yet he certainly deemed himself handsome. I am inclined to think that their ideas of personal beauty differ very widely from ours.

Tom Nogan, the chief's brother, had a very large, fat, ugly squaw for his wife. She was a mountain of tawny flesh; and, but for the innocent, good-natured expression which, like a bright sunbeam penetrating a swarthy cloud, spread all around a kindly glow, she might have been termed hideous.

This woman they considered very handsome, calling her "a fine squaw—clever squaw—a much good woman;" though in what her superiority consisted, I never could discover, often as I visited the wigwam. She was very dirty, and appeared quite indifferent to the claims of common decency (in the disposal of the few filthy rags that covered

2. Peter Jones, the son of a white father and a mother who was a daughter of a Mississauga chief, converted to Methodism in the 1820s. He became a preacher at Rice Lake, where he converted many Indians of the region to the Christian faith. In 1833, after a trip to Britain, he married an Englishwoman named Eliza Field before returning to his missionary work.

her). She was, however, very expert in all Indian craft. No Jew could drive a better bargain than Mrs. Tom; and her urchins, of whom she was the happy mother of five or six, were as cunning and avaricious as herself.

One day she visited me, bringing along with her a very pretty covered basket for sale. I asked her what she wanted for it, but could obtain from her no satisfactory answer. I showed her a small piece of silver. She shook her head. I tempted her with pork and flour, but she required neither. I had just given up the idea of dealing with her, in despair, when she suddenly seized upon me, and, lifting up my gown, pointed exultingly to my quilted petticoat, clapping her hands, and laughing immoderately.

Another time she led me all over the house, to show me what she wanted in exchange for *basket*. My patience was well nigh exhausted in following her from place to place, in her attempt to discover the coveted article, when, hanging upon a peg in my chamber, she espied a pair of trousers belonging to my husband's logging-suit. The riddle was solved. With a joyful cry she pointed to them, exclaiming "Take basket.—Give them!" It was with no small difficulty that I rescued the indispensables from her grasp.

From this woman I learned a story of Indian coolness and courage which made a deep impression on my mind. One of their squaws, a near relation of her own, had accompanied her husband on a hunting expedition into the forest. He had been very successful, and having killed more deer than they could well carry home, he went to the house of a white man to dispose of some of it, leaving the squaw to take care of the rest until his return. She sat carelessly upon the log with his hunting-knife in her hand, when she heard the breaking of branches near her, and turning round, beheld a great bear only a few paces from her.

It was too late to retreat; and seeing that the animal was very hungry, and determined to come to close quarters, she rose, and placed her back against a small tree, holding her knife close to her breast, and in a straight line with the bear. The shaggy monster came on. She remained motionless, her eyes steadily fixed upon her enemy, and as his huge arms closed around her, she slowly drove the knife into his heart. The bear uttered a hideous cry, and sank dead at her feet. When the Indian returned, he found the courageous woman taking the skin from the carcass of the formidable brute. What iron nerves these people must possess, when even a woman could dare and do a deed like this!

The wolf they hold in great contempt, and scarcely deign to consider him as an enemy. Peter Nogan assured me that he never was near enough to one in his life to shoot it; that, except in large companies, and when greatly pressed by hunger, they rarely attack men. They hold the lynx, or wolverine,[3] in much dread, as they often spring from trees upon their prey, fastening upon the throat with their sharp

---

3. Susanna here confuses the lynx and wolverine. The lynx is a predatory member of the cat family, and the wolverine is a dark, shaggy coated member of the weasel family noted for its shyness, viciousness and alarming cry.

teeth and claws, from which a person in the dark could scarcely free himself without first receiving a dangerous wound. The cry of this animal is very terrifying, resembling the shrieks of a human creature in mortal agony.

My husband was anxious to collect some of the native Indian airs, and they all sing well, and have a fine ear for music, but all his efforts proved abortive. "John," he said to young Nogan (who played very creditably on the flute, and had just concluded the popular air of "Sweet Home"),[4] cannot you play me one of your own songs?"

"Yes,—but no good."

"Leave me to be the judge of that. Cannot you give me a war-song?"

"Yes,—but no good," with an ominous shake of the head.

"A hunting song?"

"No fit for white man,"—with an air of contempt.—"No good, no good!"

"Do, John, sing us a love-song," said I, laughing, "if you have such a thing in your language."

"Oh! much love-song—very much—bad—bad—no good for Christian man. Indian song no good for white ears." This was very tantalising, as their songs sounded very sweetly from the lips of their squaws, and I had a great desire and curiosity to get some of them rendered into English.

To my husband they gave the name of "the musician," but I have forgotten the Indian word. It signified the maker of sweet sounds. They listened with intense delight to the notes of his flute, maintaining a breathless silence during the performance; their dark eyes flashing into fierce light at a martial strain, or softening with the plaintive and tender.

The cunning which they display in their contests with their enemies, in their hunting, and in making bargains with the whites (who are too apt to impose on their ignorance), seems to spring more from a law of necessity, forced upon them by their isolated position and precarious mode of life, than from any innate wish to betray. The Indian's face, after all, is a perfect index of his mind. The eye changes its expression with every impulse and passion, and shows what is passing within as clearly as the lightning in a dark night betrays the course of the stream. I cannot think that deceit forms any prominent trait in the Indian's character. They invariably act with the strictest honour towards those who never attempt to impose upon them. It is natural for a deceitful person to take advantage of the credulity of others. The genuine Indian never utters a falsehood, and never employs flattery (that powerful weapon in the hands of the insidious), in his communications with the whites.

His worst traits are those which he has in common with the wild an-

---

4. The popular song is from an opera entitled *Clari; or, the Maid of Milan* (1823) by John Howard Payne and Henry R. Bishop. Its still well-known lines include

> " 'Mid pleasures and palaces though we may roam,
> Be it ever so humble, there's *no* place like home."

imals of the forest, and which his intercourse with the lowest order of civilised men (who, in point of moral worth, are greatly his inferiors), and the pernicious effects of strong drink, have greatly tended to inflame and debase.

It is a melancholy truth, and deeply to be lamented, that the vicinity of European settlers has always produced a very demoralising effect upon the Indians. As a proof of this, I will relate a simple anecdote.

John, of Rice Lake,[5] a very sensible, middle-aged Indian, was conversing with me about their language, and the difficulty he found in understanding the books written in Indian for their use. Among other things, I asked him if his people ever swore, or used profane language towards the Deity.

The man regarded me with a sort of stern horror, as he replied, "Indian, till after he knew your people, never swore—no bad word in Indian. Indian must learn your words to swear and take God's name in vain."

Oh, what a reproof to Christian men! I felt abashed, and degraded in the eyes of this poor savage—who, ignorant as he was in many respects, yet possessed that first great attribute of the soul, a deep reverence for the Supreme Being. How inferior were thousands of my countrymen to him in this important point!

The affection of Indian parents to their children, and the deference which they pay to the aged, is another beautiful and touching trait in their character.

One extremely cold, wintry day, as I was huddled with my little ones over the stove, the door softly unclosed, and the moccasined foot of an Indian crossed the floor. I raised my head, for I was too much accustomed to their sudden appearance at any hour to feel alarmed, and perceived a tall woman standing silently and respectfully before me, wrapped in a large blanket. The moment she caught my eye she dropped the folds of her covering from around her, and laid at my feet the attenuated figure of a boy, about twelve years of age, who was in the last stage of consumption.

"Papouse die," she said, mournfully clasping her hands against her breast, and looking down upon the suffering lad with the most heartfelt expression of maternal love, while large tears trickled down her dark face. "Moodie's squaw save papouse—poor Indian woman much glad."

Her child was beyond all human aid. I looked anxiously upon him, and knew, by the pinched-up features and purple hue of his wasted cheek, that he had not many hours to live. I could only answer with tears her agonising appeal to my skill.

"Try and save him! All die but him." (She held up five of her fingers.) "Brought him all the way from Mutta Lake[6] upon my back, for white squaw to cure."

5. Occasionally Indians from Rice Lake, possibly from the north shore (what would become the Hiawatha reserve) or Alderville on the south shore, set up hunting camps on Lake Katchewanook.
6. Mud Lake, or Lake *Shemong*, in Indian. [*Author's note.*]

"I cannot cure him, my poor friend. He is in God's care; in a few hours he will be with Him.

The child was seized with a dreadful fit of coughing, which I expected every moment would terminate his frail existence. I gave him a teaspoonful of currant-jelly, which he took with avidity, but could not retain a moment on his stomach.

"Papouse die," murmured the poor woman; "alone—alone! No papouse; the mother all alone."

She began re-adjusting the poor sufferer in her blanket. I got her some food, and begged her to stay and rest herself; but she was too much distressed to eat, and too restless to remain. She said little, but her face expressed the keenest anguish; she took up her mournful load, pressed for a moment his wasted, burning hand in hers, and left the room.

My heart followed her a long way on her melancholy journey. Think what this woman's love must have been for that dying son, when she had carried a lad of his age six miles, through the deep snow, upon her back, on such a day, in the hope of my being able to do him some good. Poor heart-broken mother! I learned from Joe Muskrat's squaw some days after that the boy died a few minutes after Elizabeth Iron, his mother, got home.

They never forget any little act of kindness. One cold night, late in the fall, my hospitality was demanded by six squaws, and puzzled I was how to accommodate them all. I at last determined to give them the use of the parlour floor during the night. Among these women there was one very old, whose hair was as white as snow. She was the only grey-haired Indian I ever saw, and on that account I regarded her with peculiar interest. I knew that she was the wife of a chief, by the scarlet embroidered leggings which only the wives and daughters of chiefs are allowed to wear. The old squaw had a very pleasing countenance, but I tried in vain to draw her into conversation. She evidently did not understand me; and the Muskrat squaw, and Betty Cow, were laughing at my attempts to draw her out. I administered supper to them with my own hands, and after I had satisfied their wants (which is no very easy task, for they have great appetites), I told our servant to bring in several spare mattresses and blankets for their use. "Now mind, Jenny,[7] and give the old squaw the best bed." I said; "the others are young, and can put up with a little inconvenience."

The old Indian glanced at me with her keen, bright eye; but I had no idea that she comprehended what I said.

Some weeks after this, as I was sweeping over my parlour floor, a slight tap drew me to the door. On opening it I perceived the old squaw, who immediately slipped into my hand a set of beautifully-embroidered bark trays, fitting one within the other, and exhibiting the

---

The use of the word "Mutta" may be either an attempt to catch the pronunciation of the lake's name as Susanna heard it or is a misinterpretation by the compositors in England. The Curve Lake reserve is located at the join of Chemong and Buckhorn Lakes.

7. Jenny Buchanan. This anecdote must date from 1838, when Jenny entered into service with the Moodies.

very best sample of the porcupine quill-work. While I stood wondering what this might mean, the good old creature fell upon my neck, and kissing me, exclaimed, "You remember old squaw—make her comfortable! Old squaw no forget you. Keep them for her sake," and before I could detain her she ran down the hill with a swiftness which seemed to bid defiance to years. I never saw this interesting Indian again, and I concluded that she died during the winter, for she must have been of a great age.

My dear reader, I am afraid I shall tire you with my Indian stories; but you must bear with me patiently whilst I give you a few more. The real character of a people can be more truly gathered from such seemingly trifling incidents than from any ideas we may form of them from the great facts in their history and this is my reason for detailing events which might otherwise appear insignificant and unimportant.

A friend was staying with us, who wished much to obtain a likeness of Old Peter. I promised to try and make a sketch of the old man the next time he paid us a visit. That very afternoon he brought us some ducks in exchange for pork, and Moodie asked him to stay and take a glass of whiskey with him and his friend Mr. K——. The old man had arrayed himself in a new blanket-coat, bound with red, and the seams all decorated with the same gay material. His leggings and moccasins were new, and elaborately fringed; and, to cap the climax of the whole, he had a blue cloth conical cap upon his head, ornamented with a deer's tail dyed blue, and several cock's feathers.

He was evidently very much taken up with the magnificence of his own appearance, for he often glanced at himself in a small shaving-glass that hung opposite, with a look of grave satisfaction. Sitting apart, that I might not attract his observation, I got a tolerably faithful likeness of the old man, which after slightly colouring, to show more plainly his Indian finery, I quietly handed over to Mr. K——.[8] Sly as I thought myself, my occupation and the object of it had not escaped the keen eye of the old man. He rose, came behind Mr. K——'s chair, and regarded the picture with a most affectionate eye. I was afraid that he would be angry at the liberty I had taken. No such thing! He was as pleased as Punch.

"That Peter?" he grunted. "Give me—put up in wigwam—make dog too! Owgh! owgh!" and he rubbed his hands together, and chuckled with delight. Mr. K—— had some difficulty in coaxing the picture from the old chief; so pleased was he with this rude representation of himself. He pointed to every particular article of his dress, and dwelt with peculiar glee on the cap and blue deer's tail.

A few days after this, I was painting a beautiful little snow-bird, that our man had shot out of a large flock that alighted near the door. I was so intent upon my task, to which I was putting the finishing strokes, that I did not observe the stealthy entrance (for they all walk like cats)

---

8. Though an accomplished watercolorist, Susanna specialized in still-lifes of flowers and birds; she attempted in this instance a human figure, evidently with some success. A likeness of Old Peter appeared as the frontispiece of Catharine Parr Traill's *The Backwoods of Canada* (1836). Whether it is the picture sketched by Susanna is not known.

of a stern-looking red man, till a slender, dark hand was extended over my paper to grasp the dead bird from which I was copying, and which as rapidly transferred it to the side of the painted one, accompanying the act with the deep guttural note of approbation, the unmusical, savage "Owgh."

My guest then seated himself with the utmost gravity in a rocking-chair, directly fronting me, and made the modest demand that I should paint a likeness of him, after the following quaint fashion.

"Moodie's squaw know much—make Peter Nogan toder day on pa-pare—make Jacob to-day—Jacob young—great hunter—give much duck—venison—to squaw."

Although I felt rather afraid of my fierce-looking visitor, I could scarcely keep my gravity; there was such an air of pompous self-approbation about the Indian, such a sublime look of conceit in his grave vanity.

"Moodie's squaw cannot do everything; she cannot paint young men," said I, rising, and putting away my drawing-materials, upon which he kept his eye intently fixed, with a hungry, avaricious expression. I thought it best to place the coveted objects beyond his reach. After sitting for some time, and watching all my movements, he withdrew, with a sullen, disappointed air.

This man was handsome, but his expression was vile. Though he often came to the house, I never could reconcile myself to his countenance.

Late one very dark, stormy night, three Indians begged to be allowed to sleep by the kitchen stove. The maid was frightened out of her wits at the sight of these strangers, who were Mohawks from the Indian woods upon the Bay of Quinté, and they brought along with them a horse and cutter. The night was so stormy, that, after consulting our man—Jacob Faithful, as we usually called him[9]—I consented to grant their petition, although they were quite strangers, and taller and fiercer-looking than our friends the Missasaguas.

I was putting my children to bed, when the girl came rushing in, out of breath. "The Lord preserve us, madam, if one of these wild men has not pulled off his trousers, and is a-sitting mending them behind the stove! and what shall I do?"

"Do?—why, stay with me, and leave the poor fellow to finish his work."

The simple girl had never once thought of this plan of pacifying her outraged sense of propriety.

Their sense of hearing is so acute that they can distinguish sounds at an incredible distance, which cannot be detected by a European at all. I myself witnessed a singular exemplification of this fact. It was mid-winter; the Indians had pitched their tent, or wigwam, as usual, in our swamp. All the males were absent on a hunting expedition up the country, and had left two women behind to take care of the camp

---

9. Susanna makes an allusion to the narrator and protagonist of Captain Frederick Marryat's popular 1834 novel of the same name. Young Jacob was an Englishman, likely from one of the Wiltshire emigrant families in Dummer.

and its contents, Mrs. Tom Nogan and her children, and Susan Moore, a young girl of fifteen, and the only truly beautiful squaw I ever saw. There was something interesting about this girl's history, as well as her appearance. Her father had been drowned during a sudden hurricane, which swamped his canoe on Stony Lake; and the mother, who witnessed the accident from the shore, and was near her confinement with this child, boldly swam out to his assistance. She reached the spot where he sank, and even succeeded in recovering the body; but it was too late; the man was dead.

The soul of an Indian that has been drowned is reckoned accursed, and he is never permitted to join his tribe on the happy hunting-grounds, but his spirit haunts the lake or river in which he lost his life. His body is buried on some lonely island, which the Indians never pass without leaving a small portion of food, tobacco, or ammunition, to supply his wants; but he is never interred with the rest of his people.

His children are considered unlucky, and few willingly unite themselves to the females of the family, lest a portion of the father's curse should be visited on them.

The orphan Indian girl generally kept aloof from the rest, and seemed so lonely and companionless, that she soon attracted my attention and sympathy, and a hearty feeling of good-will sprang up between us. Her features were small and regular, her face oval, and her large, dark, loving eyes were full of tenderness and sensibility, but as bright and shy as those of the deer. A rich vermilion glow burnt upon her olive cheek and lips, and set off the dazzling whiteness of her even and pearly teeth. She was small of stature, with delicate little hands and feet, and her figure was elastic and graceful. She was a beautiful child of nature, and her Indian name signified "the voice of angry waters." Poor girl, she had been a child of grief and tears from her birth! Her mother was a Mohawk, from whom she, in all probability, derived her superior personal attractions; for they are very far before the Missasaguas in this respect.

My friend and neighbour, Emilia S[hairp], the wife of a naval officer, who lived about a mile distant from me, through the bush, had come to spend the day with me; and hearing that the Indians were in the swamp, and the men away, we determined to take a few trifles to the camp, in the way of presents, and spend an hour in chatting with the squaws.

What a beautiful moonlight night it was, as light as day!—the great forest sleeping tranquilly beneath the cloudless heavens—not a sound to disturb the deep repose of nature but the whispering of the breeze, which, during the most profound calm, creeps through the lofty pine tops. We bounded down the steep bank to the lake shore. Life is a blessing, a precious boon indeed, in such an hour, and we felt happy in the mere consciousness of existence—the glorious privilege of pouring out the silent adoration of the heart to the Great Father in his universal temple.

On entering the wigwam, which stood within a few yards of the clearing, in the middle of a thick group of cedars, we found Mrs. Tom alone with her elvish children, seated before the great fire that burned in the centre of the camp; she was busy boiling some bark in an iron spider. The little boys, in red flannel shirts which were their only covering, were tormenting a puppy, which seemed to take their pinching and pommelling in good part, for it neither attempted to bark nor to bite, but, like the eels in the story, submitted to the infliction because it was used to it. Mrs. Tom greeted us with a grin of pleasure, and motioned to us to sit down upon a buffalo-skin, which, with a courtesy so natural to the Indians, she had placed near her for our accommodation.

"You are all alone," said I, glancing round the camp.

"Ye'es; Indian away hunting—Upper Lakes. Come home with much deer."

"And Susan, where is she?"

"By-and-by," (meaning that she was coming). "Gone to fetch water —ice thick—chop with axe—take long time."

As she ceased speaking, the old blanket that formed the door of the tent was withdrawn, and the girl, bearing two pails of water, stood in the open space, in the white moonlight. The glow of the fire streamed upon her dark, floating locks, danced in the black, glistening eye, and gave a deeper blush to the olive cheek! She would have made a beautiful picture; Sir Joshua Reynolds would have rejoiced in such a model[1]—so simply graceful and unaffected, the very *beau idéal* of savage life and unadorned nature. A smile of recognition passed between us. She put down her burden beside Mrs. Tom, and noiselessly glided to her seat.

We had scarcely exchanged a few words with our favourite, when the old squaw, placing her hand against her ear, exclaimed, "Whist! whist!"

"What is it?" cried Emilia and I, starting to our feet. "Is there any danger?"

"A deer—a deer—in bush!" whispered the squaw, seizing a rifle that stood in a corner. "I hear sticks crack—a great way off. Stay here!"

A great way off the animal must have been, for though Emilia and I listened at the open door, an advantage which the squaw did not enjoy, we could not hear the least sound: all seemed still as death. The squaw whistled to an old hound, and went out.

"Did you hear anything, Susan?"

She smiled, and nodded.

"Listen; the dog has found the track."

The next moment the discharge of a rifle, and the deep baying of the dog, woke up the sleeping echoes of the woods; and the girl started off to help the old squaw to bring in the game that she had shot.

The Indians are great imitators, and possess a nice tact in adopting the customs and manners of those with whom they associate. An Indian is Nature's gentleman—never familiar, coarse, or vulgar. If he

---

1. From her time in London, Susanna was familiar with the works and fame of Sir Joshua Reynolds (1723–1792) as a portrait painter.

takes a meal with you, he waits to see how you make use of the implements on the table, and the manner in which you eat, which he imitates with a grave decorum, as if he had been accustomed to the same usages from childhood. He never attempts to help himself, or demand more food, but waits patiently until you perceive what he requires. I was perfectly astonished at this innate politeness, for it seems natural to all the Indians with whom I have had any dealings.

There was one old Indian, who belonged to a distant settlement, and only visited our lakes occasionally on hunting parties. He was a strange, eccentric, merry old fellow, with a skin like red mahogany, and a wiry, sinewy frame, that looked as if it could bid defiance to every change of temperature.

Old Snow-storm,[2] for such was his significant name, was rather too fond of the whiskey-bottle, and when he had taken a drop too much, he became an unmanageable wild beast. He had a great fancy for my husband, and never visited the other Indians without extending the same favour to us. Once upon a time, he broke the nipple of his gun; and Moodie repaired the injury for him by fixing a new one in its place, which little kindness quite won the heart of the old man, and he never came to see us without bringing an offering of fish, ducks, partridges, or venison, to show his gratitude.

One warm September day, he made his appearance bare-headed, as usual, and carrying in his hand a great checked bundle.

"Fond of grapes?" said he, putting the said bundle into my hands. "Fine grapes—brought them from island, for my friend's squaw and papouses."

Glad of the donation, which I considered quite a prize, I hastened into the kitchen to untie the grapes and put them into a dish. But imagine my disappointment, when I found them wrapped up in a soiled shirt, only recently taken from the back of the owner. I called Moodie, and begged him to return Snow-storm his garment, and to thank him for the grapes.

The mischievous creature was highly diverted with the circumstance, and laughed immoderately.

"Snow-storm," said he, "Mrs. Moodie and the children are obliged to you for your kindness in bringing them the grapes; but how came you to tie them up in a dirty shirt?"

"Dirty!" cried the old man, astonished that we should object to the fruit on that score. "It ought to be clean; it has been washed often enough. Owgh! You see, Moodie," he continued, "I have no hat—never wear hat—want no shade to my eyes—love the sun—see all around me—up and down—much better widout hat. Could not put grapes in hat—blanket-coat too large, crush fruit, juice run out. I had nothing but my shirt, so I takes off shirt, and brings grape safe over the water on my back. Papouse no care for dirty shirt; their *lee-tel bellies have no eyes.*"

---

2. In his memoir *Twenty-seven Years in Canada West* (1854), Sam Strickland describes a fight between Tom Nogan and "old Jacob Snowstorm of Rice Lake" (Volume 2, p. 74). Old Jacob is reputed to have married the widow of one of the Cow family.

In spite of this eloquent harangue, I could not bring myself to use the grapes, ripe and tempting as they looked, or give them to the children. Mr. W[ood][3] and his wife happening to step in at that moment fell into such an ecstacy at the sight of the grapes, that, as they were perfectly unacquainted with the circumstance of the shirt, I very *generously* gratified their wishes by presenting them with the contents of the large dish; and they never ate a bit less sweet for the novel mode in which they were conveyed to me!

The Indians, under their quiet exterior, possess a deal of humour. They have significant names for everything, and a nickname for every one, and some of the latter are laughably appropriate. A fat, pompous, ostentatious settler in our neighbourhood they called *Muckakee*, "the bull frog." Another, rather a fine young man, but with a very red face, they named *Segoskee*, "the rising sun." Mr. Wood, who had a farm above ours, was a remarkably slender young man, and to him they gave the appellation of *Metiz*, "thin stick." A woman, that occasionally worked for me, had a disagreeable squint; she was known in Indian by the name of *Sachábó*, "cross eye." A gentleman with a very large nose was *Choojas*, "big or ugly nose." My little Addie,[4] who was a fair, lovely creature, they viewed with great approbation, and called *Anoonk*, "a star;" while the rosy Katie was *Nogesigook*, "the northern lights." As to me, I was *Nonocosiqui*, a "humming-bird;" a ridiculous name for a tall woman, but it had reference to the delight I took in painting birds. My friend, Emilia, was "blue cloud;" my little Donald, "frozen face;"[5] young C[addy],[6] "the red-headed woodpecker," from the colour of his hair; my brother, *Chippewa*, and "the bald-headed eagle." He was an especial favourite among them.

The Indians are often made a prey of and cheated by the unprincipled settlers, who think it no crime to overreach a red-skin. One anecdote will fully illustrate this fact. A young squaw, who was near becoming a mother, stopped at a Smith-town settler's house to rest herself.[7] The woman of the house, who was Irish, was peeling for dinner some large white turnips, which her husband had grown in their garden. The Indian had never seen a turnip before, and the appearance of the firm, white, juicy root gave her such a keen craving to taste it that she very earnestly begged for a small piece to eat. She had purchased at Peterborough a large stone-china bowl, of a very handsome pattern (or, perhaps, got it at the store in exchange for *basket*), the worth of which might be half-a-dollar. If the poor squaw longed for the turnip, the value of which could scarcely reach a copper, the covetous European had fixed as longing a glance upon the china bowl, and she was deter-

3. Mr. William Wood owned land on Lot 22, Concession 5 of Douro, and later purchased Lot 21, Concession 5.
4. Addie is Agnes Moodie, Susanna's second daughter.
5. The first mention of Donald Moodie, Susanna's second son, born May 21, 1836. Her first son, Dunbar, was born in the backwoods on August 20, 1834. The jumbled chronology of the anecdotes collected in this sketch leads to some surprising interjections.
6. Young C—— is likely Cyprian Caddy, who often visited his neighbours, the Moodies. The large family of Lieutenant Colonel John Thomas Caddy figure in later sketches.
7. Smith-town is Smith Township, across the lake from the Moodie homestead.

mined to gratify her avaricious desire and obtain it on the most easy terms. She told the squaw, with some disdain, that her man did not grow turnips to give away to "Injuns," but she would sell her one. The squaw offered her four coppers, all the change she had about her. This the woman refused with contempt. She then proferred a basket; but that was not sufficient; nothing would satisfy her but the bowl. The Indian demurred; but opposition had only increased her craving for the turnip in a tenfold degree; and, after a short mental struggle, in which the animal propensity overcame the warnings of prudence, the squaw gave up the bowl, and received in return *one turnip*! The daughter of this woman told me this anecdote of her mother as a very clever thing. What ideas some people have of moral justice!

I have said before that the Indian never forgets a kindness. We had a thousand proofs of this, when overtaken by misfortune, and withering beneath the iron grasp of poverty, we could scarcely obtain bread for ourselves and our little ones; then it was that the truth of the Eastern proverb was brought home to our hearts, and the goodness of God fully manifested towards us, "Cast thy bread upon the waters, and thou shalt find it after many days."[8] During better times we had treated these poor savages with kindness and liberality, and when dearer friends looked coldly upon us they never forsook us. For many a good meal I have been indebted to them, when I had nothing to give in return, when the pantry was empty, and "the hearth-stone growing cold," as they term the want of provisions to cook at it. And their delicacy in conferring these favours was not the least admirable part of their conduct. John Nogan, who was much attached to us, would bring a fine bunch of ducks, and drop them at my feet "for the papouse," or leave a large muskinonge on the sill of the door, or place a quarter of venison just within it, and slip away without saying a word, thinking that receiving a present from a poor Indian might hurt our feelings, and he would spare us the mortification of returning thanks.

Often have I grieved that people with such generous impulses should be degraded and corrupted by civilised men; that a mysterious destiny involves and hangs over them, pressing them back into the wilderness, and slowly and surely sweeping them from the earth.

Their ideas of Christianity appeared to me vague and unsatisfactory. They will tell you that Christ died for men, and that He is the Saviour of the World, but they do not seem to comprehend the spiritual character of Christianity, nor the full extent of the requirements and application of the law of Christian love. These imperfect views may not be entertained by all Christian Indians, but they were very common amongst those with whom I conversed. Their ignorance upon theological, as well as upon other subjects, is, of course, extreme. One Indian asked me very innocently if I came from the land where Christ was born, and if I had ever seen Jesus. They always mention the name of the Persons in the Trinity with great reverence.

8. Ecclesiastes 11:1.

They are a highly imaginative people. The practical meaning of their names, and their intense admiration for the beauties of Nature, are proof of this. Nothing escapes their observing eyes. There is not a flower that blooms in the wilderness, a bird that cuts the air with its wings, a beast that roams the wood, a fish that stems the water, or the most minute insect that sports in the sunbeams, but it has an Indian name to illustrate its peculiar habits and qualities. Some of their words convey the direct meaning of the thing implied—thus, *ché-charm*, "to sneeze," is the very sound of that act; *toó-me-duh*, "to churn," gives the noise made by the dashing of the cream from side to side; and many others.

They believe in supernatural appearances—in spirits of the earth, the air, the waters. The latter they consider evil, and propitiate, before undertaking a long voyage, by throwing small portions of bread, meat, tobacco, and gunpowder into the water.

When an Indian loses one of his children, he must keep a strict fast for three days, abstaining from food of any kind. A hunter, of the name of Young,[9] told me a curious story of their rigid observance of this strange rite.

"They had a chief," he said, "a few years ago, whom they called 'Handsome Jack'—whether in derision, I cannot tell, for he was one of the ugliest Indians I ever saw.[1] The scarlet fever got into the camp—a terrible disease in this country, and doubly terrible to those poor creatures who don't know how to treat it.[2] His eldest daughter died. The chief had fasted two days when I met him in the bush. I did not know what had happened, but I opened my wallet, for I was on a hunting expedition, and offered him some bread and dried venison. He looked at me reproachfully.

" 'Do white men eat bread the first night their papoose is laid in the earth?'

"I then knew the cause of his depression, and left him."

On the night of the second day of his fast another child died of the fever. He had now to accomplish three more days without tasting food. It was too much even for an Indian. On the evening of the fourth, he was so pressed by ravenous hunger, that he stole into the woods, caught a bull-frog, and devoured it alive. He imagined himself alone; but one of his people, suspecting his intention, had followed him, unperceived, to the bush. The act he had just committed was a hideous crime in their eyes, and in a few minutes the camp was in an uproar.

9. Likely Francis Young, an Irish emigrant to Douro in 1825 and progenitor of a large family that settled at the waterfall between Lake Katchewanook and Clear Lake immediately to the north. With the help of his sons Patrick and Matthew, Francis Young built at that site a mill, which the Moodies used, and he oversaw travel between the two lakes. Eventually a lock was built at Young's Point near the site of the Young homestead. See Chapter Eighteen, beginning on p. 219.

1. "Handsome Jack" Cow may have preceded John Nogan as chief of the Missassaugas. According to local legend, his daughter Polly Cow was buried near the northern end of Lake Katchewanook, on a small island that still bears her name. Jack died soon after his daughter.

2. Epidemics were frequent in the backwoods. In her letters and in *Roughing It in the Bush*, Susanna recounts instances of typhus and scarlet fever. In 1839, she worried that the fever would take away two of her children despite her diligent care. See *Letters of Love and Duty*, pp. 129–30.

The chief fled for protection to Young's house. When the hunter demanded the cause of his alarm, he gave for answer, "There are plenty of flies at my house. To avoid their stings I come to you."

It required all the eloquence of Mr. Young, who enjoyed much popularity among them, to reconcile the rebellious tribe to their chief.

They are very skilful in their treatment of wounds, and many diseases. Their knowledge of the medicinal qualities of their plants and herbs is very great. They make excellent poultices from the bark of the bass and the slippery elm. They use several native plants in their dyeing of baskets and porcupine quills. The inner bark of the swampalder, simply boiled in water, makes a beautiful red. From the root of the black briony they obtain a fine salve for sores, and extract a rich yellow dye. The inner bark of the root of the sumach, roasted, and reduced to powder, is a good remedy for the ague; a teaspoonful given between the hot and cold fit. They scrape the fine white powder from the large fungus that grows upon the bark of the pine, into whiskey, and take it for violent pains in the stomach. The taste of this powder strongly reminded me of quinine.

I have read much of the excellence of Indian cookery, but I never could bring myself to taste anything prepared in their dirty wigwams. I remember being highly amused in watching the preparation of a mess, which might have been called the Indian hotch-potch. It consisted of a strange mixture of fish, flesh, and fowl, all boiled together in the same vessel. Ducks, partridges, muskinonge, venison, and muskrats, formed a part of this delectable compound. These were literally smothered in onions, potatoes, and turnips, which they had procured from me. They very hospitably offered me a dishful of the odious mixture, which the odour of the muskrats rendered everything but savoury; but I declined, simply stating that I was not hungry. My little boy tasted it, but quickly left the camp to conceal the effect it produced upon him.

Their method of broiling fish, however, is excellent. They take a fish, just fresh out of the water, cut out the entrails, and, without removing the scales, wash it clean, dry it in a cloth, or in grass, and cover it all over with clear hot ashes. When the flesh will part from the bone, they draw it out of the ashes, strip off the skin, and it is fit for the table of the most fastidious epicure.

The deplorable want of chastity that exists among the Indian women of this tribe seems to have been more the result of their intercourse with the settlers in the country than from any previous disposition to this vice. The jealousy of their husbands has often been exercised in a terrible manner against the offending squaws; but this has not happened of late years. The men wink at these derelictions in their wives, and share with them the price of their shame.

The mixture of European blood adds greatly to the physical beauty of the half-race, but produces a sad falling-off from the original integrity of the Indian character. The half-caste is generally a lying, vicious rogue, possessing the worst qualities of both parents in an eminent degree. We have many of these half-Indians in the penitentiary, for crimes of the blackest dye.

The skill of the Indian in procuring his game, either by land or water, has been too well described by better writers than I could ever hope to be to need any illustration from my pen, and I will close this long chapter with a droll anecdote which is told of a gentleman in this neighbourhood.

The early loss of his hair obliged Mr. —— to procure the substitute of a wig. This was such a good imitation of nature, that none but his intimate friends and neighbours were aware of the fact.

It happened that he had had some quarrel with an Indian, which had to be settled in one of the petty courts. The case was decided in favour of Mr.——, which so aggrieved the savage, who considered himself the injured party, that he sprang upon him with a furious yell, tomahawk in hand, with the intention of depriving him of his scalp. He twisted his hand in the locks which adorned the cranium of his adversary, when—horror of horrors!—the treacherous wig came off in his hand, "Owgh! owgh!" exclaimed the affrighted savage, flinging it from him, and rushing from the court as if he had been bitten by a rattle-snake. His sudden exit was followed by peals of laughter from the crowd, while Mr. —— coolly picked up his wig, and drily remarked that it had saved his head.

THE INDIAN FISHERMAN'S LIGHT. [3]

The air is still, the night is dark,
　　No ripple breaks the dusky tide;
From isle to isle the fisher's bark
　　Like fairy meteor seems to glide;
Now lost in shade—now flashing bright
　　On sleeping wave and forest tree;
We hail with joy the ruddy light,
Which far into the darksome night
　　Shines red and cheerily!

With spear high poised, and steady hand,
　　The centre of that fiery ray,
Behold the Indian fisher stand
　　Prepared to strike the finny prey;
Hurrah! the shaft has sped below—
　　Transfix'd the shining prize I see;
On swiftly darts the birch canoe;
Yon black rock shrouding from my view
　　Its red light gleaming cheerily!

Around yon bluff, whose pine crest hides
　　The noisy rapids from our sight,
Another bark—another glides—

---

3. Subtitled "A Canadian Song," this poem first appeared in *The Literary Garland* (Montreal) NS 1:2 (February 1843), p. 63. It has often been anthologized since. Certain of its details suggest the experience of fishing at night near the rapids at the south end of Lake Katchewanook.

Red meteors of the murky night.
The bosom of the silent stream
With mimic stars is dotted free;
The waves reflect the double gleam,
The tall woods lighten in the beam,
Through darkness shining cheerily!

Sixteen

Burning the Fallow

There is a hollow roaring in the air—
The hideous hissing of ten thousand flames,
That from the centre of yon sable cloud
Leap madly up, like serpents in the dark,
Shaking their arrowy tongues at Nature's heart.

It is not my intention to give a regular history of our residence in the bush, but merely to present to my readers such events as may serve to illustrate a life in the woods.[1]

The winter and spring of 1834 had passed away. The latter was uncommonly cold and backward; so much so that we had a very heavy fall of snow upon the 14th and 15th of May, and several gentlemen drove down to Cobourg in a sleigh, the snow lying upon the ground to the depth of several inches.

A late, cold spring in Canada is generally succeeded by a burning hot summer; and the summer of '34 was the hottest I ever remember. No rain fell upon the earth for many weeks, till nature drooped and withered beneath one bright blaze of sunlight; and the ague and fever in the woods, and the cholera in the large towns and cities, spread death and sickness through the country.

Moodie had made during the winter a large clearing of twenty acres around the house. The progress of the workmen had been watched by me with the keenest interest. Every tree that reached the ground opened a wider gap in the dark wood, giving us a broader ray of light and a clearer glimpse of the blue sky. But when the dark cedar-swamp fronting the house fell beneath the strokes of the axe, and we got a first view of the lake, my joy was complete; a new and beautiful object was now constantly before me, which gave me the greatest pleasure. By night and day, in sunshine or in storm, water is always the most sublime feature in a landscape, and no view can be truly grand in which it is wanting. From a child, it always had the most powerful effect upon my mind, from the great ocean rolling in majesty, to the tinkling forest rill, hidden by the flowers and rushes along its banks. Half the solitude of my forest home vanished when the lake unveiled its bright face to the blue heavens, and I saw sun, and moon, and stars,

---

1. The Moodies lived on their farm in the backwoods from mid-February 1834 until the end of December 1839. This sketch focuses on events of summer 1834.

and waving trees reflected there. I would sit for hours at the window as the shades of evening deepened round me, watching the massy foliage of the forests pictured in the waters, till fancy transported me back to England, and the songs of birds and the lowing of cattle were sounding in my ears. It was long, very long, before I could discipline my mind to learn and practise all the menial employments which are necessary in a good settler's wife.

The total absence of trees about the doors in all new settlements had always puzzled me, in a country where the intense heat of summer seems to demand all the shade that can be procured. My husband had left several beautiful rock-elms (the most picturesque tree in the country) near our dwelling, but, alas! the first high gale prostrated all my fine trees, and left our log cottage entirely exposed to the fierce rays of the sun.

The confusion of an uncleared fallow spread around us on every side.[2] Huge trunks of trees and piles of brush gave a littered and uncomfortable appearance to the locality, and as the weather had been very dry for some weeks, I heard my husband daily talking with his choppers as to the expediency of firing the fallow. They still urged him to wait a little longer, until he could get a good breeze to carry the fire well through the brush.

Business called him suddenly to Toronto, but he left a strict charge with old Thomas and his sons,[3] who were engaged in the job, by no means to attempt to burn it off until he returned, as he wished to be upon the premises himself, in case of any danger. He had previously burnt all the heaps immediately about the doors.

While he was absent, old Thomas and his second son fell sick with the ague, and went home to their own township, leaving John, a surly, obstinate young man, in charge of the shanty, where they slept, and kept their tools and provisions.

Monaghan I had sent to fetch up my three cows, as the children were languishing for milk, and Mary and I remained alone in the house with the little ones.

The day was sultry, and towards noon a strong wind sprang up that roared in the pine tops like the dashing of distant billows, but without in the least degree abating the heat. The children were lying listlessly upon the floor for coolness, and the girl and I were finishing sunbonnets, when Mary suddenly exclaimed, "Bless us, mistress, what a smoke!" I ran immediately to the door, but was not able to distinguish ten yards before me. The swamp immediately below us was on fire, and the heavy wind was driving a dense black cloud of smoke directly towards us.

"What can this mean?" I cried. "Who can have set fire to the fallow?"

---

2. The fallow here refers to the brush and logs gathered into crude piles after the clearing of the land.
3. Thomas Thomas, one of the Wiltshire settlers from England who came to Dummer Township in 1831. He and his sons lived in the Moodies' lumbering shanty while employed to clear land for the fall wheat planting.

As I ceased speaking, John Thomas stood pale and trembling before me. "John, what is the meaning of this fire?"

"Oh, ma'am, I hope you will forgive me; it was I set fire to it, and I would give all I have in the world if I had not done it."

"What is the danger?"

"Oh, I'm terribly afear'd that we shall all be burnt up," said the fellow, beginning to whimper.

"Why did you run such a risk, and your master from home, and no one on the place to render the least assistance?"

"I did it for the best," blubbered the lad. "What shall we do?"

"Why, we must get out of it as fast as we can, and leave the house to its fate."

"We can't get out," said the man, in a low, hollow tone, which seemed the concentration of fear; "I would have got out of it if I could; but just step to the back door, ma'am, and see."

I had not felt the least alarm up to this minute; I had never seen a fallow burnt, but I had heard of it as a thing of such common occurrence that I had never connected with it any idea of danger. Judge then, my surprise, my horror, when, on going to the back door, I saw that the fellow, to make sure of his work, had fired the field in fifty different places. Behind, before, on every side, we were surrounded by a wall of fire, burning furiously within a hundred yards of us, and cutting off all possibility of retreat; for could we have found an opening through the burning heaps, we could not have seen our way through the dense canopy of smoke; and, buried as we were in the heart of the forest, no one could discover our situation till we were beyond the reach of help.

I closed the door, and went back to the parlour. Fear was knocking loudly at my heart, for our utter helplessness annihilated all hope of being able to effect our escape—I felt stupified. The girl sat upon the floor by the children, who, unconscious of the peril that hung over them, had both fallen asleep. She was silently weeping; while the fool who had caused the mischief was crying aloud.

A strange calm succeeded my first alarm; tears and lamentations were useless; a horrible death was impending over us, and yet I could not believe that we were to die. I sat down upon the step of the door, and watched the awful scene in silence. The fire was raging in the cedar-swamp, immediately below the ridge on which the house stood, and it presented a spectacle truly appalling. From out the dense folds of a canopy of black smoke, the blackest I ever saw, leaped up continually red forks of lurid flame as high as the tree tops, igniting the branches of a group of tall pines that had been left standing for saw-logs.[4]

A deep gloom blotted out the heavens from our sight. The air was filled with fiery particles, which floated even to the door-step—while the crackling and roaring of the flames might have been heard at a

---

4. The tall pines were likely white pines and were much valued by lumber merchants. Their great height, often over 100 feet, helps explain the sense of the looming forest that so affected the Moodies once they came to the backwoods.

great distance. Could we have reached the lake shore, where several canoes were moored at the landing, by launching out into the water we should have been in perfect safety; but, to attain this object, it was necessary to pass through this mimic hell; and not a bird could have flown over it with unscorched wings. There was no hope in that quarter, for, could we have escaped the flames, we should have been blinded and choked by the thick, black, resinous smoke.

The fierce wind drove the flames at the sides and back of the house up the clearing; and our passage to the road, or to the forest, on the right and left, was entirely obstructed by a sea of flames. Our only ark of safety was the house, so long as it remained untouched by the consuming element. I turned to young Thomas, and asked him, how long he thought that would be.

"When the fire clears this little ridge in front, ma'am. The Lord have mercy upon us, then, or we must all go!"

"Cannot *you*, John, try and make your escape, and see what can be done for us and the poor children?"

My eye fell upon the sleeping angels, locked peacefully in each other's arms, and my tears flowed for the first time.[5]

Mary, the servant-girl,[6] looked piteously up in my face. The good, faithful creature had not uttered one word of complaint, but now she faltered forth,

"The dear, precious lambs!—Oh! such a death!"

I threw myself down upon the floor beside them, and pressed them alternately to my heart, while inwardly I thanked God that they were asleep, unconscious of danger, and unable by their childish cries to distract our attention from adopting any plan which might offer to effect their escape.

The heat soon became suffocating. We were parched with thirst, and there was not a drop of water in the house, and none to be procured nearer than the lake. I turned once more to the door, hoping that a passage might have been burnt through to the water. I saw nothing but a dense cloud of fire and smoke—could hear nothing but the crackling and roaring of the flames, which were gaining so fast upon us that I felt their scorching breath in my face.

"Ah," thought I—and it was a most bitter thought—"what will my beloved husband say when he returns and finds that his poor Susy and his dear girls have perished in this miserable manner? But God can save us yet."

The thought had scarcely found a voice in my heart before the wind rose to a hurricane, scattering the flames on all sides into a tempest of burning billows. I buried my head in my apron, for I thought that our time was come, and that all was lost, when a most terrific crash of thunder burst over our heads, and, like the breaking of a water-spout, down came the rushing torrent of rain which had been pent up for so many weeks.

5. At this point, Susanna's children were Katie, age three, and Agnes, age one.
6. Mary Tate of Cavan Township.

In a few minutes the chip-yard was all afloat, and the fire effectually checked. The storm which unnoticed by us, had been gathering all day, and which was the only one of any note we had that summer, continued to rage all night, and before morning had quite subdued the cruel enemy, whose approach we had viewed with such dread.

The imminent danger in which we had been placed struck me more forcibly after it was past than at the time, and both the girl and myself sank upon our knees, and lifted up our hearts in humble thanksgiving to that God who had saved us by an act of His Providence from an awful and sudden death. When all hope from human assistance was lost, His hand was mercifully stretched forth, making His strength more perfectly manifested in our weakness:—

> "He is their stay when earthly help is lost,
> The light and anchor of the tempest-toss'd."[7]

There was one person unknown to us, who had watched the progress of that rash blaze, and had even brought his canoe to the landing, in the hope of getting off. This was an Irish pensioner named Dunn,[8] who had cleared a few acres on his government grant, and had built a shanty on the opposite shore of the lake.

"Faith, madam! an' I thought the captain was stark, staring mad to fire his fallow on such a windy day, and that blowing right from the lake to the house. When Old Wittals came in and towld us that the masther was not to the fore,[9] but only one lad, an' the wife an' the chilther at home,—thinks I, there's no time to be lost, or the crathurs will be burnt up intirely. We started instanther, but, by Jove! we were too late. The swamp was all in a blaze when we got to the landing, and you might as well have thried to get to Heaven by passing through the other place."

This was the eloquent harangue with which the honest creature informed me the next morning of the efforts he had made to save us, and the interest he had felt in our critical situation. I felt comforted for my past anxiety, by knowing that one human being, however humble, had sympathised in our probable fate; while the providential manner in which we had been rescued will ever remain a theme of wonder and gratitude.

The next evening brought the return of my husband, who listened to the tale of our escape with a pale and disturbed countenance; not a little thankful to find his wife and children still in the land of the living.

For a long time after the burning of that fallow, it haunted me in my dreams. I would awake with a start, imagining myself fighting with the flames, and endeavouring to carry my little children through them to the top of the clearing, when invariably their garments and my own took fire just as I was within reach of a place of safety.

---

7. This couplet may be of Susanna's making or from an unidentified hymn.
8. Ned or John Dunn, a commissioned pensioner and former soldier from Ireland who owned Lot 31, Concession 10 in Smith Township.
9. Edward Sibbon, described by Catharine Parr Traill as "a Suffolk settler of small degree & great appetite" (see *I Bless You in My Heart*, p. 41) lived on the north half of Lot 22, Concession 5 in Douro. He often worked for Sam Strickland and was locally renowned for using the phrase "devouring wittles" (victuals).

THE FORGOTTEN DREAM.[1]

Ere one ruddy streak of light
Glimmer'd o'er the distant height,
Kindling with its living beam
Frowning wood and cold grey stream,
I awoke with sudden start,
Clammy brow and beating heart,
Trembling limbs, convulsed and chill,
Conscious of some mighty ill;
Yet unable to recall
Sights that did my sense appal;
Sounds that thrill'd my sleeping ear
With unutterable fear;
Forms that to my sleeping eye
Presented some strange phantasy—
Shadowy, spectral, and sublime,
That glance upon the sons of time
At moments when the mind, o'erwrought,
Yields reason to mysterious thought,
And night and solitude in vain
Bind the free spirit in their chain.
Such the vision wild that press'd
On tortur'd brain and heaving chest;
But sight and sound alike are gone,
I woke, and found myself alone;
With choking sob and stifled scream
To bless my God 'twas but a dream!
To smooth my damp and stiffen'd hair,
And murmur out the Saviour's prayer—
The first to grateful memory brought,
The first a gentle mother taught,
When, bending o'er her children's bed,
She bade good angels guard my head;
Then paused, with tearful eyes, and smiled
On the calm slumbers of her child—
As God himself had heard her prayer,
And holy angels worshipp'd there.

Seventeen

Our Logging-Bee

There was a man in our town,
In our town, in our town—
There was a man in our town,
He made a logging-bee;

---

1. This has not been identified as a separately published poem.

And he bought lots of whiskey,
To make the loggers frisky—
To make the loggers frisky
At his logging-bee.

The Devil sat on a log heap,
A log heap, a log heap—
A red hot burning log heap—
A-grinning at the bee;

And there was lots of swearing,
Of boasting and of daring,
Of fighting and of tearing,
At that logging-bee.

J. W. D. M.

A logging-bee followed the burning of the fallow, as a matter of course. In the bush, where hands are few, and labour commands an enormous rate of wages, these gatherings are considered indispensable, and much has been written in their praise; but to me, they present the most disgusting picture of a bush life. They are noisy, riotous, drunken meetings, often terminating in violent quarrels, sometimes even in bloodshed. Accidents of the most serious nature often occur, and very little work is done when we consider the number of hands employed, and the great consumption of food and liquor.

I am certain, in our case, had we hired with the money expended in providing for the bee, two or three industrious, hard-working men, we should have got through twice as much work, and have had it done well, and have been the gainers in the end.

People in the woods have a craze for giving and going to bees, and run to them with as much eagerness as a peasant runs to a race-course or a fair; plenty of strong drink and excitement making the chief attraction of the bee.

In raising a house or barn, a bee may be looked upon as a necessary evil, but these gatherings are generally conducted in a more orderly manner than those for logging. Fewer hands are required; and they are generally under the control of the carpenter who puts up the frame, and if they get drunk during the raising they are liable to meet with very serious accidents.

Thirty-two men, gentle and simple, were invited to our bee, and the maid and I were engaged for two days preceding the important one, in baking and cooking for the entertainment of our guests. When I looked at the quantity of food we had prepared, I thought that it never could be all eaten, even by thirty-two men. It was a burning hot day towards the end of July,[1] when our loggers began to come in, and the "gee!" and "ha!" of the oxen resounded on every side.

---

1. A logging bee is the gathering of men to fell and cut trees for the purpose of clearing forested land. In late July 1834, the Moodies' first summer in the backwoods, they held three logging bees, during which sixteen acres were cleared. Susanna was eight months pregnant at the time of the bee she describes here.

There was my brother S[am Strickland], with his frank English face, a host in himself; Lieutenant —— in his blouse, wide white trousers, and red sash, his broad straw hat shading a dark manly face that would have been a splendid property for a bandit chief; the four gay, reckless, idle sons of——, famous at any spree, but incapable of the least mental or physical exertion, who considered hunting and fishing as the sole aim and object of life. These young men rendered very little assistance themselves, and their example deterred others who were inclined to work.

There were the two R[eid]s, who came to work and to make others work;[2] my good brother-in-law, who had volunteered to be the Grog Bos[3], and a host of other settlers, among whom I recognised Moodie's old acquaintance, Dan Simpson,[4] with his lank red hair and long freckled face; the Youngs, the hunters, with their round, black, curly heads and rich Irish brogue;[5] poor C—— with his long, spare, consumptive figure, and thin, sickly face. Poor fellow, he has long since been gathered to his rest!

There was the ruffian squatter P[helan], from Clear Lake,[6]—the dread of all honest men; the brutal M——, who treated oxen as if they had been logs, by beating them with handspikes; and there was Old Wittals, with his low forehead and long nose, a living witness of the truth of phrenology, if his large organ of acquisitiveness and his want of conscientiousness could be taken in evidence. Yet in spite of his derelictions from honesty, he was a hard-working, good-natured man, who, if he cheated you in a bargain, or took away some useful article in mistake from your homestead, never wronged his employer in his day's work.[7]

He was a curious sample of cunning and simplicity—quite a character in his way—and the largest eater I ever chanced to know. From this ravenous propensity, for he ate his food like a famished wolf, he had obtained his singular name of "Wittals."

During the first year of his settlement in the bush, with a very large family to provide for, he had been often in want of food. One day he came to my brother, with a very long face.

" 'Fore God! Mr. S[trickland] I'm no beggar, but I'd be obliged to you for a loaf of bread. I declare to you on my honour that I have not had a bit of wittals to devour for two whole days."

He came to the right person with his petition. Mr. S[trickland] with a liberal hand relieved his wants, but he entailed upon him the name of "Old Wittals," as part payment.

---

2. The eldest sons of Robert Reid (see Chapter Fifteen, note 6, p. 185).
3. Thomas Traill was the Grog Boss; that is, as the dispenser of the alcohol to the working party after their labors.
4. Robert Simpson was an Irishman and a retired soldier living on Lot 19, Concession 4 of Douro with his wife Judy and children. John Moodie memorialized him in his sketch "The 'Ould Dhragoon' " (see Chapter Nineteen, beginning on p. 230).
5. Francis Young and his two sons, Patrick and Matthew (see Chapter Fifteen, note 9, p. 201).
6. Patrick Phelan, as an Irishman and former sergeant in the 88th Regiment of Foot, had settled on Lot 22, Concession 3 of Douro on Clear Lake, petitioning for ownership of it in 1838 on the basis of his prior military service. The Moodies had strained relations with him (see p. 224 and especially 240).
7. See Chapter Sixteen, note 9, p. 208.

His daughter, who was a very pretty girl, had stolen a march upon him into the wood, with a lad whom he by no means regarded with a favourable eye. When she returned, the old man confronted her and her lover with this threat, which I suppose he considered "the most awful" punishment that he could devise.

"March into the house, Madam 'Ria (Maria); and if ever I catch you with that scamp again, I'll tie you up to a stump all day, and give you no wittals."

I was greatly amused by overhearing a dialogue between Old Wittals and one of his youngest sons, a sharp, Yankeefied-looking boy, who had lost one of his eyes, but the remaining orb looked as if it could see all ways at once.

"I say, Sol, how came you to tell that tarnation tearing lie to Mr. S[trickland] yesterday? Didn't you expect that you'd catch a good wallopping for the like of that? Lying may be excusable in a man, but 'tis a terrible bad habit in a boy."

"Lor', father, that worn't a lie. I told Mr. S[trickland], our cow worn't in his peas. Nor more she wor; she was in his wheat."

"But she was in the peas all night, boy."

"That wor nothing to me; she worn't in just then. Sure I won't get a licking for that?"

"No, no, you are a good boy; but mind what I tell you, and don't bring me into a scrape with any of your real lies."

Prevarication, the worst of falsehoods, was a virtue in his eyes. So much for the old man's morality.

Monaghan was in his glory, prepared to work or fight, whichever should come uppermost; and there was old Thomas and his sons, the contractors for the clearing,[8] to expedite whose movements the bee was called. Old Thomas was a very ambitious man in his way. Though he did not know A from B, he took it into his head that he had received a call from Heaven to convert the heathen in the wilderness; and every Sunday he held a meeting in our loggers' shanty, for the purpose of awakening sinners, and bringing over "Injun pagans" to the true faith. His method of accomplishing this object was very ingenious. He got his wife, Peggy—or "my Paggy," as he called her—to read aloud to him a text from the Bible, until he knew it by heart; and he had, as he said truly, "a good remembrancer," and never heard a striking sermon but he retained the most important passages, and retailed them secondhand to his bush audience.

I must say that I was not a little surprised at the old man's eloquence when I went one Sunday over to the shanty to hear him preach. Several wild young fellows had come on purpose to make fun of him; but his discourse, which was upon the text, "We shall all meet before the judgment seat of Christ,"[9] was rather too serious a subject to turn into a jest, with even old Thomas for the preacher. All went on

---

8. See Chapter Sixteen, note 3, p. 205.
9. Old Thomas likely drew his text from two Biblical sources involving the words of Paul—Romans 14:10 and 2 Corinthians 5:10.

very well until the old man gave out a hymn, and led off in such a loud, discordant voice, that my little Katie, who was standing between her father's knees, looked suddenly up, and said, "Mamma, what a noise old Thomas makes!" This remark led to a much greater noise, and the young men, unable to restrain their long-suppressed laughter, ran tumultuously from the shanty.

I could have whipped the little elf; but small blame could be attached to a child of two years old, who had never heard a preacher, especially such a preacher as the old backwoodsman, in her life. Poor man! he was perfectly unconscious of the cause of the disturbance, and remarked to us, after the service was over.

"Well, ma'am, did not we get on famously? Now, worn't that a *bootiful* discourse?"

"It was, indeed; much better than I expected."

"Yes, yes; I knew it would please you. It had quite an effect on those wild fellows. A few more such sermons will teach them good behaviour. Ah! the bush is a bad place for young men. The farther in the bush, say I, the farther from God, and the nearer to hell. I told that wicked Captain L[loyd] of Dummer[1] so the other Sunday; 'an',' says he, 'if you don't hold your confounded jaw, you old fool, I'll kick you there.' Now, ma'am—now, sir, was not that bad manners in a gentleman, to use such *appropriate epitaphs* to a humble servant of God, like I?"

And thus the old man ran on for an hour, dilating upon his own merits and the sins of his neighbours.

There was John R——, from Smith-town, the most notorious swearer in the district; a man who esteemed himself clever, nor did he want for natural talent, but he had converted his mouth into such a sink of iniquity that it corrupted the whole man, and all the weak and thoughtless of his own sex who admitted him into their company. I had tried to convince John R—— (for he often frequented the house under the pretence of borrowing books) of the great crime that he was constantly committing, and of the injurious effect it must produce upon his own family, but the mental disease had taken too deep a root to be so easily cured. Like a person labouring under some foul disease, he contaminated all he touched. Such men seem to make an ambitious display of their bad habits in such scenes, and if they afford a little help, they are sure to get intoxicated and make a row. There was my friend, old Ned Dunn, who had been so anxious to get us out of the burning fallow. There was a whole group of Dummer Pines:[2] Levi, the little wiry, witty poacher; Cornish Bill, the honest-

---

1. Captain Frederick Lloyd, a discharged Marine of Anglo-Irish descent who had received a large land grant in Dummer Township and settled his family there in the summer of 1831. A notorious drinker prone to violent outbursts, he abandoned his wife Louisa on occasion, finally decamping with his eldest son to the United States in 1838. It is Louisa who Susanna and Emilia Shairp visit in Chapter Twenty-seven, "The Walk to Dummer"; there she is identified as "Mrs. N——." Jenny Buchanan escaped Captain Lloyd's tyrannical behaviour to work for the Moodies in 1838.
2. There were six families of Pines (Paynes) in Dummer Township. Like the Thomases, they were English emigrants from Wiltshire. Levi's daughter Mary Payne later worked for the Moodies.

hearted old peasant, with his stalwart figure and uncouth dialect; and David, and Ned—all good men and true; and Malachi Chroak,[3] a queer, withered-up, monkey-man, that seemed like some mischievous elf, flitting from heap to heap to make work and fun for the rest; and many others were at that bee who have since found a rest in the wilderness: Adam T——, H——, J. M——, H. N——.[4] These, at different times, lost their lives in those bright waters in which, on such occasions as these, they used to sport and frolic to refresh themselves during the noonday heat. Alas! how many, who were then young and in their prime, that river and its lakes have swept away!

Our men worked well until dinner-time, when, after washing in the lake, they all sat down to the rude board which I had prepared for them, loaded with the best fare that could be procured in the bush. Pea-soup, legs of pork, venison, eel, and raspberry pies, garnished with plenty of potatoes, and whiskey to wash them down, besides a large iron kettle of tea. To pour out the latter, and dispense it round, devolved upon me. My brother and his friends, who were all temperance men, and consequently the best workers in the field, kept me and the maid actively employed in replenishing their cups.

The dinner passed off tolerably well; some of the lower order of the Irish settlers were pretty far gone, but they committed no outrage upon our feelings by either swearing or bad language, a few harmless jokes alone circulating among them.

Some one was funning Old Wittals for having eaten seven large cabbages at Mr. T[raill]'s bee, a few days previous. His son, Sol, thought himself as in duty bound to take up the cudgel for his father.

"Now, I guess that's a lie, anyhow. Father was sick that day, and I tell you he only ate five."

This announcement was followed by such an explosion of mirth that the boy looked fiercely round him, as if he could scarcely believe the fact that the whole party were laughing at him.

Malachi Chroak, who was good-naturedly drunk, had discovered an old pair of cracked bellows in a corner, which he placed under his arm, and applying his mouth to the pipe, and working his elbows to and fro, pretended that he was playing upon the bagpipes, every now and then letting the wind escape in a shrill squeak from this novel instrument.

"Arrah, ladies and jintlemen, do jist turn your swate little eyes upon me whilst I play for your iddifications the last illigant tune which my owld grandmother taught me. Och hone! 'tis a thousand pities that such musical owld crathers should be suffered to die, at all at all, to be poked away into a dirthy, dark hole, when their canthles shud be

---

3. Malachi Croak was the Traills' hired man at the time.
4. Among the men who drowned in the Otonabee or adjacent lakes during the 1830s and early 1840s were John M—— (Morgan, or possibly James Morgan——; see Chapter Fifteen, note 5, p. 185), who in June 1835 drowned in Stony Lake during a "pleasure party" involving Alexander Shairp and Sam Strickland. Morgan was the third son of Richard Morgan of Chapelfield, Norwich, England. Another victim was H——, James Hague of Lot 11, Concession 8, Douro, who drowned in the Otonabee in 1843. The Hagues were friends of the Moodies (see Chapter Twenty-six, note 1, p. 315).

burnin' a-top of a bushel, givin' light to the house. An' then it is she that was the illigant dancer, stepping out so lively and frisky, just so." And here he minced to and fro, affecting the airs of a fine lady. The supposititious bagpipe gave an uncertain, ominous howl, and he flung it down, and started back with a ludicrous expression of alarm.

"Alive, is it ye are? Ye croaking owld divil, is that the tune you taught your son?

> "Och! my owld granny taught me, but now she is dead,
> That a dhrop of nate whiskey is good for the head;
> It would make a man spake when jist ready to dhie,
> If you doubt it—my boys!—I'd advise you to thry.
>
> Och! my owld granny sleeps with her head on a stone,—
> 'Now, Malach, don't throuble the galls when I'm gone!'
> I thried to obey her; but, och, I am shure,
> There's no sorrow on earth that the angels can't cure.
>
> Och! I took her advice—I'm a bachelor still;
> And I dance and I play, with such excellent skill,
> *(Taking up the bellows, and beginning to dance.)*
> That the dear little crathurs are striving in vain
> Which first shall my hand or my fortin' obtain."

"Malach!" shouted a laughing group. "How was it that the old lady taught you to go a-courting?"

"Arrah, that's a secret! I don't let out owld granny's sacrets," said Malachi, gracefully waving his head to and fro to the squeaking of the bellows; then, suddenly tossing back the long, dangling black elf-locks that curled down the sides of his lank yellow cheeks, and winking knowingly with his comical little deep-seated black eyes, he burst out again—

> "Wid the blarney I'd win the most dainty proud dame,
> No gal can resist the soft sound of that same;
> Wid the blarney, my boys—if you'd doubt it, go thry—
> But hand here the bottle, my whistle is dhry."

The men went back to the field, leaving Malachi to amuse those who remained in the house; and we certainly did laugh our fill at his odd capers and conceits.

Then he would insist upon marrying our maid.[5] There could be no refusal—have her he would. The girl, to keep him quiet, laughingly promised that she would take him for her husband. This did not satisfy him. She must take her oath upon the Bible to that effect. Mary pretended that there was no bible in the house, but he found an old spelling-book upon a shelf in the kitchen, and upon it he made her swear, and called upon me to bear witness to her oath, that she was now his betrothed, and he would go next day with her to the "praist."

---

5. See Chapter Sixteen, note 6, p. 207.

Poor Mary had reason to repent her frolic, for he stuck close to her the whole evening, tormenting her to fulfil her contract.

After the sun went down, the logging-band came in to supper, which was all ready for them. Those who remained sober ate the meal in peace, and quietly returned to their own homes; while the vicious and the drunken stayed to brawl and fight.

After having placed the supper on the table, I was so tired with the noise, and heat, and fatigue of the day, that I went to bed, leaving to Mary and my husband the care of the guests.

The little bed-chamber was only separated from the kitchen by a few thin boards; and, unfortunately for me and the girl, who was soon forced to retreat thither, we could hear all the wickedness and profanity going on in the next room. My husband, disgusted with the scene, soon left it, and retired into the parlour, with the few of the loggers who at that hour remained sober. The house rang with the sound of unhallowed revelry, profane songs, and blasphemous swearing. It would have been no hard task to have imagined these miserable, degraded beings, fiends instead of men. How glad I was when they at last broke up; and we were once more left in peace to collect the broken glasses and cups, and the scattered fragments of that hateful feast!

We were obliged to endure a second and a third repetition of this odious scene, before sixteen acres of land were rendered fit for the reception of our fall crop of wheat.

My hatred to these tumultuous, disorderly meetings was not in the least decreased by my husband being twice seriously hurt while attending them. After the second injury he received, he seldom went to them himself, but sent his oxen and servant in his place. In these odious gatherings, the sober, moral, and industrious man is more likely to suffer than the drunken and profane, as during the delirium of drink these men expose others to danger as well as themselves.

The conduct of many of the settlers, who considered themselves gentlemen, and would have been very much affronted to have been called otherwise, was often more reprehensible than that of the poor Irish emigrants, to whom they should have set an example of order and sobriety. The behaviour of these young men drew upon them the severe but just censures of the poorer class, whom they regarded in every way as their inferiors.

"That blackguard calls himself a gentleman. In what respect is he better than us?" was an observation too frequently made use of at these gatherings. To see a bad man in the very worst point of view, follow him to a bee: be he profane, licentious, quarrelsome, or a rogue, all his native wickedness will be fully developed there.

Just after the last of these logging-bees, we had to part with our good servant Mary, and just at a time when it was the heaviest loss to me. Her father, who had been a dairy-man in the north of Ireland, an honest, industrious man, had brought out upwards of one hundred pounds to this country. With more wisdom than is generally exercised by Irish emigrants, instead of sinking all his means in buying a bush farm, he hired a very good farm in Cavan, stocked it with cattle, and returned to his old avocation. The services of his daughter, who was an excellent dairymaid, were required to take the management of the cows; and her brother brought a waggon and horses all the way from the front to take her home.

This event was perfectly unexpected, and left me without a moment's notice to provide myself with another servant, at a time when servants were not to be had, and I was perfectly unable to do the least thing. My little Addie was sick almost to death with the summer complaint,[6] and the eldest still too young to take care of herself.

This was but the beginning of trouble.

Ague and lake fever had attacked our new settlement. The men in the shanty were all down with it; and my husband was confined to his bed on each alternate day, unable to raise hand or foot, and raving in the delirium of the fever.

In my sister and brother's families, scarcely a healthy person remained to attend upon the sick; and at Herriot's Falls, nine persons were stretched upon the floor of one log cabin, unable to help themselves or one another. After much difficulty, and only by offering enormous wages, I succeeded in procuring a nurse to attend upon me during my confinement. The woman had not been a day in the house before she was attacked by the same fever. In the midst of this confusion, and with my precious little Addie lying insensible on a pillow at the foot of my bed—expected every moment to breathe her last sigh—on the night of the 26th of August the boy I had so ardently coveted was born.[7] The next day, old Pine carried his wife (my nurse) away upon his back, and I was left to struggle through, in the best manner I could, with a sick husband, a sick child, and a new-born babe.

It was a melancholy season, one of severe mental and bodily suffering. Those who have drawn such agreeable pictures of a residence in the backwoods never dwell upon the periods of sickness, when, far from medical advice, and often, as in my case, deprived of the assistance of friends by adverse circumstances, you are left to languish, unattended, upon the couch of pain.

The day that my husband was free of the fit, he did what he could for me and his poor sick babes, but, ill as he was, he was obliged to sow the wheat to enable the man to proceed with the drag, and was therefore necessarily absent in the field the greater part of the day.

I was very ill, yet for hours at a time I had no friendly voice to cheer me, to proffer me a drink of cold water, or to attend to the poor babe; and worse, still worse, there was no one to help that pale, marble child, who lay so cold and still, with half-closed violet eye, as if death had already chilled her young heart in his iron grasp.

There was not a breath of air in our close, burning bed-closet; and the weather was sultry beyond all that I have since experienced. How

---

6. The "summer complaint" is ague, a recurrent malarial fever that prostrated many emigrants for lengthy periods of time. It was passed on to humans by mosquitoes.

7. Susanna's first son and third child, John Alexander Dunbar Moodie, was born on August 20, 1834, under stressful conditions. The erroneous date in the text likely was an error in the composition of the text in London.

I wished that I could be transported to an hospital at home, to enjoy the common care that in such places is bestowed upon the sick! Bitter tears flowed continually from my eyes over those young children. I had asked of Heaven a son, and there he lay helpless by the side of his almost equally helpless mother, who could not lift him up in her arms, or still his cries; while the pale, fair angel, with her golden curls, who had lately been the admiration of all who saw her, no longer recognised my voice, or was conscious of my presence. I felt that I could almost resign the long and eagerly hoped for son, to win one more smile from that sweet suffering creature. Often did I weep myself to sleep, and wake to weep again with renewed anguish.

And my poor little Katie, herself under three years of age, how patiently she bore the loss of my care, and every comfort! How earnestly the dear thing strove to help me! She would sit on my sick-bed, and hold my hand, and ask me to look at her and speak to her; would inquire why Addie slept so long, and when she would awake again. Those innocent questions went like arrows to my heart.

Lieutenant S[hairp], the husband of my dear Emilia, at length heard of my situation. His inestimable wife was from home, nursing her sick mother;[8] but he sent his maid-servant up every day for a couple of hours, and the kind girl despatched a messenger nine miles through the woods to Dummer, to fetch her younger sister, a child of twelve years old.

Oh, how grateful I felt for these signal mercies! for my situation for nearly a week was one of the most pitiable that could be imagined. The sickness was so prevalent that help was not to be obtained for money; and without the assistance of that little girl, young as she was, it is more than probable that neither myself nor my children would ever have risen from that bed of sickness.

The conduct of our man Jacob,[9] during this trying period, was marked with the greatest kindness and consideration. On the days that his master was confined to his bed with the fever, he used to place a vessel of cold water and a cup by his bedside, and then put his honest English face in at my door to know if he could make a cup of tea, or toast a bit of bread for the mistress, before he went into the field.

Katie was indebted to him for her meals. He baked, and cooked, and churned, milked the cows, and made up the butter, as well and as carefully as the best female servant could have done. As to poor John Monaghan, he was down with the fever in the shanty, where four other men were all ill with the same terrible complaint.

I was obliged to leave my bed and endeavour to attend to the wants of my young family long before I was really able. When I made my first attempt to reach the parlour I was so weak, that, at every step, I felt as if I should pitch forward to the ground, which seemed to undulate beneath my feet like the floor of a cabin in a storm at sea. My husband continued to suffer for many weeks with the ague; and when he was

8. Emilia Shairp's parents lived in Peterborough at their villa named Endsleigh.
9. See Chapter Fifteen, note 9, p. 195.

convalescent, all the children, even the poor babe, were seized with it; nor did it leave us until late in the spring of 1835.

THE EMIGRANT'S FAREWELL.[1]

Rise, Mary! meet me on the shore,
And tell our tale of sorrow o'er,
There must we meet to part no more—
    Rise, Mary, rise!

Come, dearest, come! though all in vain;
Once more beside yon summer main
We'll plight our hopeless vows again—
    Unclose thine eyes.

My bark amidst the surge is toss'd;
I go, by evil fortunes cross'd,
My earthly hopes for ever lost—
    Love's dearest prize.

But when thy hand is clasp'd in mine,
I'll laugh at fortune, nor repine;
In life, in death, for ever thine—
    Then check these sighs.

They move a bosom steel'd to bear
Its own unwonted load of care,
That will not bend beneath despair—
    Rise, dearest, rise!

Life's but a troubled dream at best;
There comes a time when grief shall rest;
Kind, faithful hearts shall yet be bless'd
    'Neath brighter skies!

Eighteen

A Trip to Stony Lake

Oh Nature! in thy ever-varying face,
    By rocky shore, or 'neath the forest tree,
What love divine, what matchless skill, I trace!
    My full warm heart responsive thrills to thee.
Yea, in my throbbing bosom's inmost core,
    Thou reign'st supreme; and, in thy sternest mood,
Thy votary bends in rapture to adore
    The Mighty Maker, who pronounced thee good.

1. This poem was originally published as "Rise, Mary! And Meet Me on the Shore" in *The Literary Garland* (Montreal) 2:4 (March 1840), p. 164.

> Thy broad, majestic brow still bears His seal;
> And when I cease to love, oh, may I cease to feel!

My husband had long promised me a trip to Stony Lake, and in the summer of 1835, before the harvest commenced, he gave Mr. Y[oung], who kept the mill at the rapids below Clear Lake, notice of our intention, and the worthy old man and his family made due preparation for our reception. The little girls were to accompany us.

We were to start at sunrise, to avoid the heat of the day, to go up as far as Mr. Y[oung]'s in our canoe, re-embark with his sons above the rapids in birch-bark canoes, go as far up the lake as we could accomplish by daylight, and return at night; the weather being very warm, and the moon at full. Before six o'clock we were all seated in the little raft, which spread her white sail to a foaming breeze, and sped merrily over the blue waters. The lake on which our clearing stood was about a mile and a half in length, and about three quarters of a mile in breadth; a mere pond, when compared with the Bay of Quinté, Ontario, and the inland seas of Canada. But it was *our* lake, and, consequently, it had ten thousand beauties in our eyes, which would scarcely have attracted the observation of a stranger.

At the head of the Katchawanook, the lake is divided by a long neck of land, that forms a small bay on the right-hand side, and a very brisk rapid on the left.[1] The banks are formed of large masses of limestone; and the cardinal-flower and the tiger-lily seem to have taken an especial fancy to this spot, and to vie with each other in the display of their gorgeous colours.

It is an excellent place for fishing; the water is very deep close to the rocky pavement that forms the bank, and it has a pebbly bottom. Many a magic hour, at rosy dawn, or evening grey, have I spent with my husband on this romantic spot; our canoe fastened to a bush, and ourselves intent upon ensnaring the black bass, a fish of excellent flavour that abounds in this place.

Our paddles soon carried us past the narrows, and through the rapid water, the children sitting quietly at the bottom of the boat, enchanted with all they heard and saw, begging papa to stop and gather water-lilies, or to catch one of the splendid butterflies that hovered over us; and often the little Addie darted her white hand into the wa-

---

1. The fishing site at "the head of the Katchawanook" that Susanna describes here lies to the south of the Moodies' clearing and below the narrows where their lake joined the small lake they called "Bessikákoon." Because of lower water levels, Lake Katchewanook, as it is known today, seemed to settlers in 1834 to be comprised of three small lakes connected by narrows, through which the water flowed in rapids, because of the strong current flowing south. In 1872, Susanna saw their old clearing from the water and observed that the scenery was much changed:

> Our old place I should never have recognized. The woods about it are all gone, and a new growth of small cedars fringes the shore in front. There is a tolerable looking modern cottage on the spot, that the old log house once occupied, and the old barn survives on the same spot on which it was built, more than 30 years ago, but the woods that framed it in, are all down, and it has a bare desolate look, and is used as a place for feeding young cattle. The back waters from the mill dams have drowned all the trees on Moodie's Island which still bears the name, and it has become a very ugly place to what it was in the hand of Nature (*Letters of Love and Duty,* p. 337).

ter to grasp at the shadow of the gorgeous insects as they skimmed along the waves.

After passing the rapids, the river widened into another small lake, perfectly round in form, and having in its centre a tiny green island, in the midst of which stood, like a shattered monument of bygone storms, one blasted, black ash-tree.

The Indians call this lake *Bessikákoon*, but I do not know the exact meaning of the word. Some say that it means "the Indian's grave," others "the lake of the one island." It is certain that an Indian girl is buried beneath that blighted tree; but I never could learn the particulars of her story, and perhaps there was no tale connected with it. She might have fallen a victim to disease during the wanderings of her tribe, and been buried on that spot; or she might have been drowned, which would account for her having been buried away from the rest of her people.

This little lake lies in the heart of the wilderness. There is but one clearing upon its shores, and that had been made by lumberers many years before; the place abounded with red cedar. A second growth of young timber had grown up in this spot, which was covered also with raspberry-bushes—several hundred acres being entirely overgrown with this delicious berry.

It was here annually that we used to come in large picnic parties, to collect this valuable fruit for our winter preserves, in defiance of black-flies, mosquitoes, snakes, and even bears; all which have been encountered by berry-pickers upon this spot, as busy and as active as themselves, gathering an ample repast from Nature's bounteous lap.

And, oh! what beautiful wild shrubs and flowers grew up in that neglected spot! Some of the happiest hours I spent in the bush are connected with reminiscences of "Irving's shanty," for so the raspberry-grounds were called. The clearing could not be seen from the shore. You had to scramble through a cedar-swamp to reach the sloping ground which produced the berries.

The mill at the Clear Lake rapids was about three miles distant from our own clearing; and after stemming another rapid, and passing between two beautiful wooded islands, the canoe rounded a point, and the rude structure was before us.

A wilder and more romantic spot than that which the old hunter had chosen for his homestead in the wilderness could scarcely be imagined. The waters of Clear Lake[2] here empty themselves through a narrow, deep, rocky channel, not exceeding a quarter of a mile in length, and tumble over a limestone ridge of ten or twelve feet in height, which extends from one bank of the river to the other.[3] The shores on either side are very steep, and the large oak-trees which have anchored their roots in every crevice of the rock, throw their fan-

2. Clear Lake contrasts sharply to Lake Katchewanook below and Stony Lake above, being without islands and very deep. Seen on a map it appears to be as much a widening of the Otonabee River as it does a long, narrow lake.

3. Young's mill and its pristine waterfall were much altered by the building of a lock to facilitate boating along the Otonabee system. As Susanna described it in 1872:

tastic arms far over the foaming waterfall, the deep green of their massy foliage forming a beautiful contrast with the white, flashing waters that foam over the shoot at least fifty feet below the brow of the limestone rock. By a flight of steps cut in the banks we ascended to the platform above the river on which Mr. Y[oung]'s house stood.

It was a large, rough-looking, log building, surrounded by barns and sheds of the same primitive material. The porch before the door was covered with hops, and the room of general resort, into which it immediately opened, was of large dimensions, the huge fire-place forming the most striking feature. On the hearth-stone, hot as was the weather, blazed a great fire, encumbered with all sorts of culinary apparatus, which, I am inclined to think, had been called into requisition for our sole benefit and accommodation.

The good folks had breakfasted long before we started from home, but they would not hear of our proceeding to Stony Lake until after we had dined. It was only eight o'clock A.M., and we had still four hours to dinner, which gave us ample leisure to listen to the old man's stories, ramble round the premises, and observe all the striking features of the place.

Mr. Y[oung] was a Catholic, and the son of a respectable farmer from the south of Ireland. Some few years before, he had emigrated with a large family of seven sons and two daughters, and being fond of field sports, and greatly taken with the beauty of the locality in which he had pitched his tent in the wilderness, he determined to raise a mill upon the dam which Nature had provided to his hands, and wait patiently until the increasing immigration should settle the townships of Smith and Douro, render the property valuable, and bring plenty of grist to the mill.

He was not far wrong in his calculations; and though, for the first few years, he subsisted entirely by hunting, fishing, and raising what potatoes and wheat he required for his own family, on the most fertile spots he could find on his barren lot, very little corn passed through the mill.

At the time we visited his place, he was driving a thriving trade, and all the wheat that was grown in the neighbourhood was brought by water to be ground at Y[oung]'s mill.

He had lost his wife a few years after coming to the country; but his two daughters, Betty and Norah, were excellent housewives, and amply supplied her loss. From these amiable women we received a most kind and hearty welcome, and every comfort and luxury within their reach.

They appeared a most happy and contented family. The sons—a fine, hardy, independent set of fellows—were regarded by the old man

---

These drowned lands spoil the once pretty shores of the upper Katchewanook Lake and the scene is greatly changed all the way up the Young's old place. The falls there have been blasted out to make the canal into Clear Lake, and the great beauty of the place, while in the wilderness, is greatly diminished, but a pretty Catholic church and burying ground, and a small picturesque group of cottages, gives an air of civilization to the once romantic place (*Letters of Love and Duty*, p. 337).

with pride and affection. Many were his anecdotes of their prowess in hunting and fishing.

His method of giving them an aversion to strong drink while very young amused me greatly, but it is not every child that could have stood the test of his experiment.

"When they were little chaps, from five to six years of age, I made them very drunk," he said; "so drunk that it brought on severe headache and sickness, and this so disgusted them with liquor, that they never could abide the sight of it again. I have only one drunkard among the seven; and he was such a weak, puling crathur, that I dared not try the same game with him, lest it should kill him. 'Tis his nature, I suppose, and he can't help it; but the truth is, that to make up for the sobriety of all the rest, he is killing himself with drink."

Norah gave us an account of her catching a deer that had got into the enclosure the day before.

"I went out," she said, "early in the morning, to milk the cows, and I saw a fine young buck struggling to get through a pale of the fence, in which having entangled his head and horns, I knew, by the desperate efforts he was making to push aside the rails, that if I was not quick in getting hold of him, he would soon be gone."

"And did you dare to touch him?"

"If I had had Mat's gun I would have shot him, but he would have made his escape long before I could run to the house for that, so I went boldly up to him and got him by the hind legs; and though he kicked and struggled dreadfully, I held on till Mat heard me call, and ran to my help, and cut his throat with his hunting-knife. So you see," she continued, with a good-natured laugh, "I can beat our hunters hollow—they hunt the deer, but I can catch a buck with my hands."

While we were chatting away, great were the preparations making by Miss Betty and a very handsome American woman, who had recently come thither as a help. One little barefooted garsoon was shelling peas in an Indian basket, another was stringing currants into a yellow pie-dish, and a third was sent to the rapids with his rod and line, to procure a dish of fresh fish to add to the long list of bush dainties that were preparing for our dinner.

It was in vain that I begged our kind entertainers not to put themselves to the least trouble on our account, telling them that we were now used to the woods, and contented with anything; they were determined to exhaust all their stores to furnish forth the entertainment. Nor can it be wondered at, that, with so many dishes to cook, and pies and custards to bake, instead of dining at twelve, it was past two o'clock before we were conducted to the dinner-table. I was vexed and disappointed at the delay, as I wanted to see all I could of the spot we were about to visit before night and darkness compelled us to return.

The feast was spread in a large outhouse, the table being formed of two broad deal boards laid together, and supported by rude carpenter's stools. A white linen cloth, a relic of better days, concealed these arrangements. The board was covered with an indescribable variety of roast and boiled, of fish, flesh, and fowl. My readers should see a table laid out in a wealthy Canadian farmer's house before they can have any idea of the profusion displayed in the entertainment of two visitors and their young children.

Besides venison, pork, chickens, ducks, and fish of several kinds, cooked in a variety of ways, there was a number of pumpkin, raspberry, cherry, and currant pies, with fresh butter and green cheese (as the new cream-cheese is called), molasses, preserves, and pickled cucumbers, besides tea and coffee—the latter, be it known, I had watched the American woman boiling in the *frying-pan*. It was a black-looking compound, and I did not attempt to discuss its merits. The vessel in which it had been prepared had prejudiced me, and rendered me very sceptical on that score.

We were all very hungry, having tasted nothing since five o'clock in the morning, and contrived, out of the variety of good things before us, to make an excellent dinner.

I was glad, however, when we rose, to prosecute our intended trip up the lake. The old man, whose heart was now thoroughly warmed with whiskey, declared that he meant to make one of the party, and Betty, too, was to accompany us; her sister Norah kindly staying behind to take care of the children.

We followed a path along the top of the high ridge of limestone rock, until we had passed the falls and the rapids above, when we found Pat and Mat Y[oung] waiting for us on the shore below, in two beautiful new birch-bark canoes, which they had purchased the day before from the Indians.[4]

Miss Betty, Mat, and myself, were safely stowed into one, while the old miller, and his son Pat, and my husband, embarked in the other, and our steersmen pushed off into the middle of the deep and silent stream; the shadow of the tall woods, towering so many feet above us, casting an inky hue upon the waters.

The scene was very imposing, and after paddling for a few minutes in shade and silence, we suddenly emerged into light and sunshine, and Clear Lake, which gets its name from the unrivalled brightness of its waters, spread out its azure mirror before us. The Indians regard this sheet of water with peculiar reverence. It abounds in the finest sorts of fish, the salmon-trout, the delicious white fish, muskenongé, and black and white bass. There is no island in this lake, no rice beds, nor stick nor stone to break its tranquil beauty, and, at the time we visited it, there was but one clearing upon its shores.

The log hut of the squatter P[helan], commanding a beautiful prospect up and down the lake, stood upon a bold slope fronting the water; all the rest was unbroken forest.

We had proceeded about a mile on our pleasant voyage, when our

---

4. Patrick Young seems to have been the most outgoing and jolly of Francis's seven sons. Susanna met him again in 1872 when he was Lockmaster at Young's Point. They reminisced about the Moodies' visit in 1834, and Pat was delighted to learn that the two little Moodie girls whom he had carried down to the canoes late that night had both married Irishmen, and that little Katie was the mother of nine children (*Letters of Love and Duty*, p. 337).

attention was attracted by a singular natural phenomenon, which Mat Y[oung] called the battery.

On the right-hand side of the shore rose a steep, perpendicular wall of limestone, that had the appearance of having been laid by the hand of man, so smooth and even was its surface. After attaining a height of about fifty feet, a natural platform of eight or ten yards broke the perpendicular line of the rock, when another wall, like the first, rose to a considerable height, terminating in a second and third platform of the same description.

Fire, at some distant period, had run over these singularly beautiful terraces, and a second growth of poplars and balm-of-gileads, relieved, by their tender green and light, airy foilage, the sombre indigo tint of the heavy pines that nodded like the plumes of a funeral hearse over the fair young dwellers on the rock.

The water is forty feet deep at the base of this precipice, which is washed by the waves. After we had passed the battery, Mat Y[oung] turned to me and said, "That is a famous place for bears; many a bear have I shot among those rocks."

This led to a long discussion on the wild beasts of the country.

"I do not think that there is much danger to be apprehended from them," said he; "but I once had an ugly adventure with a wolf, two winters ago, on this lake."

I was all curiosity to hear the story, which sounded doubly interesting told on the very spot, and while gliding over those lovely waters.

"We were lumbering, at the head of Stony Lake, about eight miles from here, my four brothers, myself, and several other hands. The winter was long and severe; although it was the first week in March, there was not the least appearance of a thaw, and the ice on these lakes was as firm as ever. I had been sent home to fetch a yoke of oxen to draw the saw-logs down to the water, our chopping being all completed, and the logs ready for rafting.

"I did not think it necessary to encumber myself with my rifle, and was, therefore, provided with no weapon of defence but the long gad I used to urge on the cattle. It was about four o'clock in the afternoon when I rounded Sandy Point, that long point which is about a mile a-head of us on the left shore, when I first discovered that I was followed, but at a great distance, by a large wolf. At first, I thought little of the circumstance, beyond a passing wish that I had brought my gun. I knew that he would not attack me before dark, and it was still two long hours to sundown; so I whistled, and urged on my oxen, and soon forgot the wolf—when, on stopping to repair a little damage to the peg of the yoke, I was surprised to find him close at my heels. I turned, and ran towards him, shouting as loud as I could, when he slunk back, but showed no inclination to make off. Knowing that he must have companions near, by his boldness, I shouted as loud as I could, hoping that my cries might be heard by my brothers, who would imagine that the oxen had got into the ice, and would come to my assistance. I was now winding my way through the islands in Stony Lake; the sun was setting red before me, and I had still three miles of my journey to accomplish. The wolf had become so impudent that I kept him off by pelting him with snowballs; and once he came so near that I struck him with the gad. I now began to be seriously alarmed, and from time to time, shouted with all my strength; and you may imagine my joy when these cries were answered by the report of a gun. My brothers had heard me, and the discharge of a gun, for a moment, seemed to daunt the wolf. He uttered a long howl, which was answered by the cries of a large pack of the dirty brutes from the wood. It was only just light enough to distinguish objects, and I had to stop and face my enemy, to keep him at bay.

"I saw the skeleton forms of half-a-dozen more of them slinking among the bushes that skirted a low island; and tired and cold, I gave myself and the oxen up for lost, when I felt the ice tremble on which I stood, and heard men running at a little distance. 'Fire your guns!' I cried out, as loud as I could. My order was obeyed, and such a yelling and howling immediately filled the whole forest as would have chilled your very heart. The thievish varmints instantly fled away into the bush.

"I never felt the least fear of wolves until that night; but when they meet in large bands, like cowardly dogs, they trust to their numbers, and grow fierce. If you meet with one wolf, you may be certain that the whole pack is at no great distance."

We were fast approaching Sandy Point, a long white ridge of sand, running half across the lake, and though only covered with scattered groups of scrubby trees and brush, it effectually screened Stony Lake from our view.[5] There were so many beautiful flowers peeping through the dwarf, green bushes, that, wishing to inspect them nearer, Mat kindly ran the canoe ashore, and told me that he would show me a pretty spot, where an Indian, who had been drowned during a storm off that point, was buried. I immediately recalled the story of Susan Moore's father, but Mat thought that he was interred upon one of the islands farther up.

"It is strange," he said, "that they are such bad swimmers. The Indian, though unrivalled by us whites in the use of the paddle, is an animal that does not take readily to the water, and those among them who can swim seldom use it as a recreation."

Pushing our way through the bushes, we came to a small opening in

---

5. Beyond Sandy Point, Stony Lake and its myriad islands begin. In June 1872, Susanna Moodie took part in a pleasure cruise by steamer from the town of Lakefield on Lake Katchewanook to Stony Lake, passing through the lock at Young's Point. In a letter to her son-in-law John Vickers, she described "the grand scenery of Stoney Lake."

> That is just the same, and its Islands, there are 1200 in it, must remain as they now appear to the end of time. Great bare red granite rocks crowned with scrub oak and pine. Some are many 100 feet high and heave up like the bare bones of some ancient world. It is quite a labyrinth of Islands, how people can find their way through them is the wonder. How I wished that Katie could have seen them. It is a wonderful place, so vast, so wild and lonely, the waters so blue, the dark woods frowning down upon them from their lofty granite ridges that towered far far above us.

Prophetically, she concluded, "The time will come when this will be one of the sight seeing places in Canada" (*Letters of Love and Duty*, p. 337). Stony Lake (a debate continues as to its correct spelling) is frequented by both Canadian and American cottagers, and is one of the most popular cottaging locales in Ontario.

the underwood, so thickly grown over with wild Canadian roses, in full blossom, that the air was impregnated with a delightful odour. In the centre of this bed of sweets rose the humble mound that protected the bones of the red man from the ravenous jaws of the wolf and the wild cat. It was completely covered with stones and from among the crevices had sprung a tuft of blue harebells, waving as wild and free as if they grew among the bonny red heather on the glorious hills of the North, or shook their tiny bells to the breeze on the broom-encircled commons of England.

The harebell had always from a child been with me a favourite flower; and the first sight of it in Canada, growing upon that lonely grave, so flooded my soul with remembrances of the past, that, in spite of myself, the tears poured freely from my eyes. There are moments when it is impossible to repress those outgushings of the heart—

> "Those flood-gates of the soul that sever,
> In passion's tide to part for ever."

If Mat and his sister wondered at my tears, they must have suspected the cause, for they walked to a little distance, and left me to the indulgence of my feelings. I gathered those flowers, and placed them in my bosom, and kept them for many a day; they had become holy, when connected with sacred home recollections, and the never-dying affections of the heart which the sight of them recalled.

A shout from our companions in the other canoe made us retrace our steps to the shore. They had already rounded the point, and were wondering at our absence.

Oh, what a magnificent scene of wild and lonely grandeur burst upon us as we swept round the little peninsula, and the whole majesty of Stony Lake broke upon us at once; another Lake of the Thousand Isles, in miniature, and in the heart of the wilderness! Imagine a large sheet of water, some fifteen miles in breadth and twenty-five in length, taken up by islands of every size and shape, from the lofty naked rock of red granite to the rounded hill, covered with oak-trees to its summit; while others were level with the waters, and of a rich emerald green, only fringed with a growth of aquatic shrubs and flowers. Never did my eyes rest on a more lovely or beautiful scene. Not a vestige of man, or of his works, was there. The setting sun, that cast such a gorgeous flood of light upon this exquisite panorama, bringing out some of these lofty islands in strong relief, and casting others into intense shade, shed no cheery beam upon church spire or cottage pane. We beheld the landscape, savage and grand in its primeval beauty.

As we floated among the channels between these rocky picturesque isles, I asked Mat how many of them there were.

"I never could succeed," he said, "in counting them all. One Sunday, Pat and I spent a whole day in going from one to the other, to try and make out how many there were, but we could only count up to one hundred and forty before we gave up the task in despair. There are a great many of them; more than any one would think—and, what is very singular, the channel between them is very deep, sometimes above forty feet, which accounts for the few rapids to be found in this lake. It is a glorious place for hunting; and the waters, undisturbed by steam-boats, abound in all sorts of fish.

"Most of these islands are covered with huckleberries; while grapes, high and low-bush cranberries, blackberries, wild cherries, gooseberries, and several sorts of wild currants grow here in profusion. There is one island among these groups (but I never could light upon the identical one) where the Indians yearly gather their wampum-grass. They come here to collect the best birch-bark for their canoes, and to gather wild onions. In short, from the game, fish, and fruit which they collect among the islands of this lake, they chiefly depend for their subsistence. They are very jealous of the settlers in the country coming to hunt and fish here, and tell many stories of wild beasts and rattlesnakes that abound along its shores; but I, who have frequented the lake for years, was never disturbed by anything, beyond the adventure with the wolf, which I have already told you. The banks of this lake are all steep and rocky, and the land along the shore is barren, and totally unfit for cultivation.

"Had we time to run up a few miles further, I could have showed you some places well worth a journey to look at; but the sun is already down, and it will be dark before we get back to the mill."

The other canoe now floated alongside, and Pat agreed with his brother that it was high time to return. With reluctance I turned from this strangely fascinating scene. As we passed under one bold rocky island, Mat said, laughingly, "That is Mount Rascal."

"How did it obtain that name?"

"Oh, we were out here berrying, with our good priest, Mr. B——. This island promised so fair, that we landed upon it, and, after searching for an hour, we returned to the boat without a single berry, upon which Mr. B—— named it 'Mount Rascal.' "

The island was so beautiful, it did not deserve the name, and I christened it "Oak Hill," from the abundance of oak-trees which clothed its steep sides. The wood of this oak is so heavy and hard that it will not float in the water, and it is in great request for the runners of lumber-sleighs, which have to pass over very bad roads.

The breeze, which had rendered our sail up the lakes so expeditious and refreshing, had stiffened into a pretty high wind, which was dead against us all the way down. Betty now knelt in the bow and assisted her brother, squaw fashion, in paddling the canoe; but, in spite of all their united exertions, it was past ten o'clock before we reached the mill. The good Norah was waiting tea for us. She had given the children their supper four hours ago, and the little creatures, tired with using their feet all day, were sound asleep upon her bed.

After supper, several Irish songs were sung, while Pat played upon the fiddle, and Betty and Mat enlivened the company with an Irish jig.

It was midnight when the children were placed on my cloak at the bottom of the canoe, and we bade adieu to this hospitable family. The wind being dead against us, we were obliged to dispense with the sail, and take to our paddles. The moonlight was as bright as day, the air warm and balmy; and the aromatic, resinous smell exuded by the heat from the balm-of-gilead and the pine-trees in the forest, added greatly to our sense of enjoyment as we floated past scenes so wild and lonely— isles that assumed a mysterious look and character in that witching hour. In moments like these, I ceased to regret my separation from my native land; and, filled with the love of Nature, my heart forgot for the time the love of home. The very spirit of peace seemed to brood over the waters, which were broken into a thousand ripples of light by every breeze that stirred the rice blossoms, or whispered through the shivering aspen-trees. The far-off roar of the rapids, softened by distance, and the long, mournful cry of the night-owl, alone broke the silence of the night. Amid these lonely wilds the soul draws nearer to God, and is filled to overflowing by the overwhelming sense of His presence.

It was two o'clock in the morning when we fastened the canoe to the landing, and Moodie carried up the children to the house. I found the girl still up with my boy, who had been very restless during our absence. My heart reproached me, as I caught him to my breast, for leaving him so long; in a few minutes he was consoled for past sorrows, and sleeping sweetly in my arms.

A CANADIAN SONG.[6]

Come, launch the light canoe;
   The breeze is fresh and strong;
The summer skies are blue,
   And 'tis joy to float along;
     Away o'er the waters,
     The bright-glancing waters,
     The many-voiced waters,
As they dance in light and song.

When the great Creator spoke,
   On the long unmeasured night
The living day-spring broke,
   And the waters own'd His might;
     The voice of many waters,
     Of glad, rejoicing waters,
     Of living, leaping waters,
First hail'd the dawn of light.

Where foaming billows glide
   To earth's remotest bound;
The rushing ocean tide
   Rolls on the solemn sound;
     God's voice is in the waters;
     The deep, mysterious waters,
     The sleepless, dashing waters,
Still breathe its tones around.

6. This poem was first published as "The Waters. A Canadian Song" in *The Literary Garland* 2:8 (July 1840), p. 360.

Nineteen

The "Ould Dhragoon"[1]
or, a Visit to the Beaver Meadow.

—Behold that man, with lanky locks,
Which hang in strange confusion o'er his brow;
And nicely scan his garments, rent and patch'd,
In colours varied, like a pictured map;
And watch his restless glance—now grave, now gay—
As saddening thought, or merry humour's flash
Sweeps o'er the deep-mark'd lines which care hath left;
As when the world is steep'd in blackest night,
The forked lightning flashes through the sky,
And all around leaps into life and light,
To sink again in darkness blacker still.
Yes! look upon that face lugubrious, long,
As thoughtfully he stands with folded arms
Amid his realm of charr'd and spectral stumps,
Which once were trees, but now, with sprawling roots,
Cling to the rocks which peep above the soil.
——Ay! look again,
And say if you discern the faintest trace
Of warrior bold;—the gait erect and proud,
The steady glance that speaks the fearless soul,
Watchful and prompt to do what man can do
When duty calls. All wreck'd and reckless now;—
But let the trumpet's soul-inspiring sound
Wake up the brattling echoes of the woods,
Then watch his kindling eye—his eagle glance—
While thoughts of glorious fields, and battles won,
And visions bright of joyous, hopeful youth
Sweep o'er his soul. A soldier now once more—
Touch'd by the magic sound, he rears his head,
Responsive to the well-known martial note,
And stands again a hero 'mid his rags.

It is delightful to observe a feeling of contentment under adverse circumstances. We may smile at the rude and clumsy attempts of the remote and isolated backwoodsman to attain something like comfort, but happy he who, with the buoyant spirits of the light-hearted Irishman, contrives to make himself happy even when all others would be miserable.

A certain degree of dissatisfaction with our present circumstances is necessary to stimulate us to exertion, and thus to enable us to secure future comfort; but where the delusive prospect of future happiness is too remote for any reasonable hope of ultimate attainment, then surely it is true wisdom to make the most of the present, and to cultivate a spirit of happy contentment with the lot assigned to us by Providence.

1. I am indebted to my husband for this sketch. [*Author's note.*]

"Ould Simpson," or the "Ould Dhragoon,"[2] as he was generally called, was a good sample of this happy character; and I shall proceed to give the reader a sketch of his history, and a description of his establishment. He was one of that unfortunate class of discharged soldiers who are tempted to sell their pensions often far below their true value, for the sake of getting a lot of land in some remote settlement, where it is only rendered valuable by the labour of the settler, and where they will have the unenviable privilege of expending the last remains of their strength in clearing a patch of land for the benefit of some grasping storekeeper who has given them credit while engaged in the work.

The old dragoon had fixed his abode on the verge of an extensive beaver-meadow, which was considered a sort of natural curiosity in the neighbourhood; and where he managed, by cutting the rank grass in the summer time, to support several cows, which afforded the chief subsistence of his family. He had also managed, with the assistance of his devoted partner, Judy, to clear a few acres of poor rocky land on the sloping margin of the level meadow, which he planted year after year with potatoes. Scattered over this small clearing, here and there might be seen the butt-end of some half-burnt hemlock tree, which had escaped the general combustion of the log heaps, and now formed a striking contrast to the white limestone rocks which showed their rounded surfaces above the meagre soil.

The "ould dhragoon" seemed, moreover, to have some taste for the picturesque, and by way of ornament, had left standing sundry tall pines and hemlocks neatly girdled to destroy their foliage, the shade of which would have been detrimental to the "blessed praties" which he designed to grow in his clearing, but which, in the meantime, like martyrs at the stake, stretched their naked branches imploringly towards the smiling heavens. As he was a kind of hermit, from choice, and far removed from other settlers, whose assistance is so necessary in new settlements, old Simpson was compelled to resort to the most extraordinary contrivances while clearing his land. Thus, after felling the trees, instead of chopping them into lengths, for the purpose of facilitating the operation of piling them preparatory to burning, which would have cost him too much labour, he resorted to the practice of "niggering," as it is called; which is simply laying light pieces of round timber across the trunks of the trees, and setting fire to them at the point of contact, by which means the trees are slowly burned through.

It was while busily engaged in this interesting operation that I first became acquainted with the subject of this sketch.

Some twenty or thirty little fires were burning briskly in different parts of the blackened field, and the old fellow was watching the slow progress of his silent "niggers," and replacing them from time to time as they smouldered away. After threading my way among the uncouth logs, blazing and smoking in all directions, I encountered the old man,

2. See Chapter Seventeen, note 4, p. 211. A dragoon is a heavily armed mounted soldier. The spelling here (the added "h") reflects one way in which vernacular Irish pronunciation was indicated in print.

attired in an old hood, or bonnet, of his wife Judy, with his patched canvas trousers rolled up to his knees; one foot bare, and the other furnished with an old boot, which from its appearance had once belonged to some more aristocratic foot. His person was long, straight, and sinewy, and there was a light springiness and elasticity in his step which would have suited a younger man, as he skipped along with a long handspike over his shoulder. He was singing a stave from the "Enniskillen Dragoon" when I came up with him,

> "With his silver-mounted pistols, and his long carbine,
> Long life to the brave Inniskillen dragoon."[3]

His face would have been one of the most lugubrious imaginable, with his long, tangled hair hanging confusedly over it, in a manner which has been happily compared to a "bewitched haystack," had it not been for a certain humorous twitch or convulsive movement, which affected one side of his countenance, whenever any droll idea passed through his mind. It was with a twitch of this kind, and a certain indescribable twinkle of his somewhat melancholy eye, as he seemed intuitively to form a hasty conception of the oddity of his appearance to a stranger unused to the bush, that he welcomed me to his clearing. He instantly threw down his handspike, and leaving his "niggers" to finish their work at their leisure, insisted on our going to his house to get something to drink.

On the way, I explained to him the object of my visit, which was to mark out, or "blaze," the sidelines of a lot of land I had received as part of a military grant, immediately adjoining the beaver-meadow,[4] and I asked him to accompany me, as he was well acquainted with the different lots.

"Och! by all manner of manes, and welcome; the dhevil a foot of the way but I know as well as my own clearing; but come into the house, and get a dhrink of milk, an' a bite of bread an' butther, for sorrow a dhrop of the whiskey has crossed my teeth for the last month; an' it's but poor intertainment for man or baste I can offer you, but shure you're heartily welcome."

The precincts of the homestead were divided and subdivided into an infinity of enclosures, of all shapes and sizes. The outer enclosure was a bush fence, formed of trees felled on each other in a row, and the gaps filled up with brushwood. There was a large gate, swung with wooden hinges, and a wooden latch to fasten it; the smaller enclosures were made with round poles, tied together with bark. The house was of the rudest description of "shanty," with hollowed basswood logs, fitting into each other somewhat in the manner of tiles for a roof, instead of shingles. No iron was to be seen, in the absence of which

3. Several songs commemorate the "Enniskillen" (or Inniskillen) Dragoons, whose fame dated from their fighting on behalf of William of Orange. A loose parallel is found in Charles Lever's novel *Charles O'Malley The Irish Dragoon* (1841), though it is likely that Lever himself was drawing on an oral song tradition that celebrated these soldiers.

4. A beaver meadow is a flat grassland in the woods created by a beaver dam. The backwoods are often marked by such surprising clearings. They were at first small ponds that, when dried out to some extent, became a combination of dry and soggy turf.

there was plenty of leathern hinges, wooden latches for locks, and bark-strings instead of nails. There was a large fire-place at one end of the shanty, with a chimney, constructed of split laths, plastered with a mixture of clay and cow-dung. As for windows, these were luxuries which could well be dispensed with; the open door was an excellent substitute for them in the daytime, and at night none were required. When I ventured to object to this arrangement, that he would have to keep the door shut in the winter time, the old man replied, in the style so characteristic of his country, "Shure it will be time enough to think of that when the could weather sets in." Everything about the house wore a Robinson Crusoe aspect, and though there was not any appearance of original plan or foresight, there was no lack of ingenious contrivance to meet every want as it arose.

Judy dropped us a low curtsey as we entered, which was followed by a similar compliment from a stout girl of twelve, and two or three more of the children, who all seemed to share the pleasure of their parents in receiving strangers in their unpretending tenement. Many were the apologies that poor Judy offered for the homely cheer she furnished us, and great was her delight at the notice we took of the "childher." She set little Biddy, who was the pride of her heart, to reading the Bible; and she took down a curious machine from a shelf, which she had "conthrived out of her own head," as she said, for teaching the children to read. This was a flat box, or frame, filled with sand, which saved paper, pens, and ink. Poor Judy had evidently seen better days, but, with a humble and contented spirit, she blessed God for the food and scanty raiment their labour afforded them. Her only sorrow was the want of "idication" for the children.

She would have told us[5] long story about her trials and sufferings, before they had attained their present comparative comfort and independence, but, as we had a tedious scramble before us, through cedar-swamps, beaver-meadows, and piny ridges, the "ould dhragoon" cut her short, and we straightway started on our toilsome journey.

Simpson, in spite of a certain dash of melancholy in his composition, was one of those happy fellows of the "light heart and thin pair of breeches" school,[6] who, when they meet with difficulty or misfortune, never stop to measure its dimensions, but hold in their breath and run lightly over, as in crossing a bog, where to stand still is to sink.

Off, then, we went, with the "ould dhragoon" skipping and bounding on before us, over fallen trees and mossy rocks; now ducking under the low, tangled branches of the white cedar, then carefully piloting us along rotten logs, covered with green moss, to save us from the discomfort of wet feet. All this time he still kept one of his feet

5. Oddly, John Moodie shifts at this point to the plural, suggesting that he was accompanied by a friend on his excursion to Dan Simpson's land grant and curious abode.
6. From a well-known seventeenth-century song entitled "The Sailor's Ballad," the chorus of which reads:

Then why shou'd we quarrel for Riches,
Or any such glittering Toy;
A light Heart, and a thin Pair of Breeches,
Goes thorough the World, brave Boy.

safely ensconced in the boot, while the other seemed to luxuriate in the water, as if there was something amphibious in his nature.

We soon reached the beaver-meadow, which extended two or three miles; sometimes contracting into a narrow gorge, between the wooded heights, then spreading out again into an ample field of verdure, and presenting everywhere the same unvarying level surface, surrounded with rising grounds, covered with the dense unbroken forest, as if its surface had formerly been covered by the waters of a lake; which in all probability has been the case at some not very remote period. In many places the meadow was so wet that it required a very large share of faith to support us in passing over its surface; but our friend, the dragoon, soon brought us safe through all dangers to a deep ditch, which he had dug to carry off the superfluous water from the part of the meadow which he owned. When we had obtained firm footing on the opposite side, we sat down to rest ourselves before commencing the operation of "blazing," or marking the trees with our axes, along the side-line of my lot. Here the mystery of the boot was explained. Simpson very coolly took it off from the hitherto favoured foot, and drew it on the other.

He was not a bit ashamed of his poverty, and candidly owned that this was the only boot he possessed, and he was desirous of giving each of his feet fair play.

Nearly the whole day was occupied in completing our job, in which the "dhragoon" assisted us, with the most hearty good-will, enlivening us with his inexhaustible fund of good-humour and drollery. It was nearly dark when we got back to his "shanty," where the kind-hearted Judy was preparing a huge pot of potatoes and other "combustibles," as Simpson called the other eatables, for our entertainment.

Previous to starting on our surveying expedition,[7] we had observed Judy very earnestly giving some important instructions to one of her little boys, on whom she seemed to be most seriously impressing the necessity of using the utmost diligence. The happy contentment which now beamed in poor Judy's still comely countenance bespoke the success of the messenger. She could not "call up spirits from the vasty deep" of the cellar,[8] but she had procured some whiskey from her next-door neighbour—some five or six miles off; and there it stood somewhat ostentatiously on the table in a "greybeard," with a "corn cob," or ear of Indian corn stripped of its grain, for a cork, smiling most benevolently on the family circle, and looking a hundred welcomes to the strangers.

An indescribably enlivening influence seemed to exude from every pore of that homely earthen vessel, diffusing mirth and good-humour in all directions. The old man jumped and danced about on the rough floor of the "shanty;" and the children sat giggling and nudging each other in a corner, casting a timid look, from time to time, at their mother, for fear she might check them for being "over bould."

7. Surveying in the back townships was still primitive, in part because of the difficulties in travel and access.
8. A phrase from Shakespeare's *Henry IV*, Part I, III.i.52.

"Is it crazy ye are intirely, ye ould omadhawn!"[9] said Judy, whose notions of propriety were somewhat shocked with the undignified levity
of her partner; "the likes of you I never seed; ye are too foolidge intirely. Have done now wid your diviltries, and set the stools for the
gintlemens, while I get the supper for yes."

Our plentiful though homely meal was soon discussed, for hunger,
like a good conscience, can laugh at luxury; and the "greybeard" made
its appearance, with the usual accompaniments of hot water and
maple sugar, which Judy had scraped from the cake, and placed in a
saucer on the table before us.

The "ould dhragoon," despising his wife's admonitions, gave way
freely to his feelings, and knew no bounds to his hilarity. He laughed
and joked, and sang snatches of old songs picked up in the course of his
service at home and abroad. At length Judy, who looked on him as a
"raal janius," begged him to "sing the gintlemens the song he made
when he first came to the counthry." Of course we ardently seconded
the motion, and nothing loth, the old man, throwing himself back on his
stool, and stretching out his long neck, poured forth the following ditty,
with which I shall conclude my hasty sketch of the "ould dhragoon."

> Och! it's here I'm intirely continted,[1]
>   In the wild woods of swate 'Mericay;
> God's blessing on him that invinted
>   Big ships for our crossing the say!
>
> Here praties grow bigger nor turnips;
>   And though cruel hard is our work,
> In ould Ireland we'd nothing but praties,
>   But here we have praties and pork.
>
> I live on the banks of a meadow,
>   Now see that my maning you take;
> It bates all the bogs of ould Ireland—
>   Six months in the year it's a lake.
>
> Bad luck to the beavers that dammed it!
>   I wish them all kilt for their pains;
> For shure though the craters are clever,
>   'Tis sartin they've drown'd my domains.
>
> I've built a log hut of the timber
>   That grows on my charmin' estate;
> And an illigant root-house erected,
>   Just facing the front of my gate.
>
> And I've made me an illigant pig-sty,
>   Well litter'd wid straw and wid hay;

9. "Omadhawn" is an Irish term meaning a fool, an idiot.
1. John Moodie's poem was printed several times, often under the title of its first line, "Och!
    It's here I'm intirely continted."

And it's there, free from noise of the chilther,
    I sleep in the heat of the day.

It's there I'm intirely at aise, sir,
    And enjoy all the comforts of home;
I stretch out my legs as I plase, sir,
    And dhrame of the pleasures to come.

Shure, it's pleasant to hear the frogs croakin',
    When the sun's going down in the sky,
And my Judy sits quietly smokin'
    While the praties are boil'd till they're dhry.

Och! thin, if you love indepindence,
    And have money your passage to pay,
You must quit the ould counthry intirely,
    And start in the middle of May.

J. W. D. M.

Twenty

Disappointed Hopes

Stern Disappointment, in thy iron grasp
The soul lies stricken. So the timid deer,
Who feels the foul fangs of the felon wolf
Clench'd in his throat, grown desperate for life,
Turns on his foes, and battles with the fate
That hems him in—and only yields in death.

The summer of '35 was very wet; a circumstance so unusual in
Canada that I have seen no season like it during my sojourn in the
country. Our wheat crop promised to be both excellent and abundant;
and the clearing and seeding sixteen acres, one way or another, had
cost us more than fifty pounds; still, we hoped to realise something
handsome by the sale of the produce; and, as far as appearances went,
all looked fair. The rain commenced about a week before the crop was
fit for the sickle, and from that time until nearly the end of September
was a mere succession of thunder showers; days of intense heat, succeeded by floods of rain. Our fine crop shared the fate of all other fine
crops in the country; it was totally spoiled; the wheat grew in the
sheaf, and we could scarcely save enough to supply us with bad, sticky
bread; the rest was exchanged at the distillery for whiskey, which was
the only produce which could be obtained for it. The storekeepers
would not look at it, or give either money or goods for such a damaged
article.

My husband and I had worked hard in the field; it was the first time
I had ever tried my hand at field-labour, but our ready money was ex-

hausted, and the steam-boat stock had not paid us one farthing; we could not hire, and there was no help for it. I had a hard struggle with my pride before I would consent to render the least assistance on the farm, but reflection convinced me that I was wrong—that Providence had placed me in a situation where I was called upon to work—that it was not only my duty to obey that call, but to exert myself to the utmost to assist my husband, and help to maintain my family.

Ah, glorious poverty! thou art a hard taskmaster, but in thy soul-ennobling school I have received more godlike lessons, have learned more sublime truths, than ever I acquired in the smooth highways of the world!

The independent in soul can rise above the seeming disgrace of poverty, and hold fast their integrity, in defiance of the world and its selfish and unwise maxims. To them, no labour is too great, no trial too severe; they will unflinchingly exert every faculty of mind and body, before they will submit to become a burden to others.

The misfortunes that now crowded upon us were the result of no misconduct or extravagance on our part, but arose out of circumstances which we could not avert nor control.[1] Finding too late the error into which we had fallen, in suffering ourselves to be cajoled and plundered out of our property by interested speculators, we braced our minds to bear the worst, and determined to meet our difficulties calmly and firmly, nor suffer our spirits to sink under calamities which energy and industry might eventually repair. Having once come to this resolution, we cheerfully shared together the labours of the field. One in heart and purpose, we dared remain true to ourselves, true to our high destiny as immortal creatures, in our conflict with temporal and physical wants.

We found that manual toil, however distasteful to those unaccustomed to it, was not after all such a dreadful hardship; that the wilderness was not without its rose, the hard face of poverty without its smile. If we occasionally suffered severe pain, we as often experienced great pleasure, and I have contemplated a well-hoed ridge of potatoes on that bush farm, with as much delight as in years long past I had experienced in examining a fine painting in some well-appointed drawing-room.

I can now look back with calm thankfulness on that long period of trial and exertion—with thankfulness that the dark clouds that hung over us, threatening to blot us from existence, when they did burst upon us, were full of blessings. When our situation appeared perfectly desperate, then were we on the threshold of a new state of things, which was born out of that very distress.

In order more fully to illustrate the necessity of a perfect and child-like reliance upon the mercies of God—who, I most firmly believe never deserts those who have placed their trust in Him—I will give a brief sketch of our lives during the years 1836 and 1837.

---

1. The years 1835 to 1837 were difficult for the Moodies, especially as their small capital eroded and their family needs increased.

Still confidently expecting to realise an income, however small, from the steam-boat stock, we had involved ourselves considerably in debt, in order to pay our servants and obtain the common necessaries of life; and we owed a large sum to two Englishmen in Dummer, for clearing ten more acres upon the farm.[2] Our utter inability to meet these demands weighed very heavily upon my husband's mind. All superfluities in the way of groceries were now given up, and we were compelled to rest satisfied upon the produce of the farm. Milk, bread, and potatoes during the summer became our chief, and often, for months, our only fare. As to tea and sugar, they were luxuries we would not think of, although I missed the tea very much; we rang the changes upon peppermint and sage, taking the one herb at our breakfast, the other at our tea, until I found an excellent substitute for both in the root of the dandelion.

The first year we came to this country, I met with an account of dandelion coffee, published in the *New York Albion*, given by a Dr. Harrison, of Edinburgh, who earnestly recommended it as an article of general use.[3]

"It possesses," he says, "all the fine flavour and exhilarating properties of coffee, without any of its deleterious effects. The plant being of a soporific nature, the coffee made from it when drunk at night produces a tendency to sleep, instead of exciting wakefulness, and may be safely used as a cheap and wholesome substitute for the Arabian berry, being equal in substance and flavour to the best Mocha coffee."

I was much struck with this paragraph at the time, and for several years felt a great inclination to try the Doctor's coffee; but something or other always came in the way, and it was put off till another opportunity. During the fall of '35, I was assisting my husband in taking up a crop of potatoes in the field, and observing a vast number of fine dandelion roots among the potatoes, it brought the dandelion coffee back to my memory, and I determined to try some for our supper. Without saying anything to my husband, I threw aside some of the roots, and when we left work, collecting a sufficient quantity for the experiment, I carefully washed the roots quite clean, without depriving them of the fine brown skin which covers them; and which contains the aromatic flavour, which so nearly resembles coffee that it is difficult to distinguish it from it while roasting.

I cut my roots into small pieces, the size of a kidney-bean, and roasted them on an iron baking-pan in the stove-oven, until they were as brown and crisp as coffee. I then ground and transferred a small cupful of the powder to the coffee-pot, pouring upon it scalding water, and boiling it for a few minutes briskly over the fire. The result was

2. The Moodies owed money to James and Stephen Jory of Dummer for clearing additional acres of the bush farm.
3. The *Albion*, the weekly paper published in New York City by John Sherrin Bartlett, provided news from home to emigrants in America and Canada. The Moodies subscribed to it when possible, and both of them published their poetry in the paper on occasion. The recipe for dandelion coffee has not been located.

beyond my expectations. The coffee proved excellent—far superior to the common coffee we procured at the stores.

To persons residing in the bush, and to whom tea and coffee are very expensive articles of luxury, the knowledge of this valuable property in a plant scattered so abundantly through their fields, would prove highly beneficial. For years we used no other article; and my Indian friends who frequented the house gladly adopted the root, and made me show them the whole process of manufacturing it into coffee.

Experience taught me that the root of the dandelion is not so good when applied to this purpose in the spring as it is in the fall. I tried it in the spring, but the juice of the plant, having contributed to the production of leaves and flowers, was weak, and destitute of the fine bitter flavour so peculiar to coffee. The time of gathering in the potato crop is the best suited for collecting and drying the roots of the dandelion; and as they always abound in the same hills, both may be accomplished at the same time. Those who want to keep a quantity for winter use may wash and cut up the roots, and dry them on boards in the sun. They will keep for years, and can be roasted when required.

Few of our colonists are acquainted with the many uses to which this neglected but most valuable plant may be applied. I will point out a few which have come under my own observation, convinced as I am that the time will come when this hardy weed, with its golden flowers and curious seed-vessels, which form a constant plaything to the little children rolling about and luxuriating among the grass, in the sunny month of May, will be transplanted into our gardens, and tended with due care.

The dandelion planted in trenches, and blanched to a beautiful cream-colour with straw, makes an excellent salad, quite equal to endive, and is more hardy and requires less care.

In many parts of the United States, particularly in new districts where vegetables are scarce, it is used early in the spring, and boiled with pork as a substitute for cabbage. During our residence in the bush we found it, in the early part of May, a great addition to the dinner-table. In the township of Dummer, the settlers boil the tops, and add hops to the liquor, which they ferment, and from which they obtain excellent beer. I have never tasted this simple beverage, but I have been told by those who use it that it is equal to the table-beer used at home.

Necessity has truly been termed the mother of invention, for I contrived to manufacture a variety of dishes almost out of nothing, while living in her school. When entirely destitute of animal food, the different variety of squirrels supplied us with pies, stews, and roasts. Our barn stood at the top of the hill near the bush, and in a trap set for such "small deer," we often caught from ten to twelve a day.

The flesh of the black squirrel is equal to that of the rabbit, and the red, and even the little chipmunk, is palatable when nicely cooked. But from the lake, during the summer, we derived the larger portion of our food. The children called this piece of water "Mamma's pantry;" and many a good meal has the munificent Father given to his poor dependent children from its well-stored depths. Moodie and I used to rise by daybreak, and fish for an hour after sunrise, when we returned, he to the field, and I to dress the little ones, clean up the house, assist with the milk, and prepare the breakfast.

Oh, how I enjoyed these excursions on the lake; the very idea of our dinner depending upon our success added double zest to our sport!

One morning we started as usual before sunrise; a thick mist still hung like a fine veil upon the water when we pushed off, and anchored at our accustomed place. Just as the sun rose, and the haze parted and drew up like a golden sheet of transparent gauze, through which the dark woods loomed out like giants, a noble buck dashed into the water, followed by four Indian hounds.

We then discovered a canoe, full of Indians, just below the rapids, and another not many yards from us, that had been concealed by the fog. It was a noble sight, that gallant deer exerting all his energy, and stemming the water with such matchless grace, his branching horns held proudly aloft, his broad nostrils distended, and his fine eye fixed intently upon the opposite shore. Several rifle-balls whizzed past him, the dogs followed hard upon his track, but my very heart leaped for joy when, in spite of all his foes, his glossy hoofs spurned the opposite bank and he plunged headlong into the forest.

My beloved partner was most skilful in trolling for bass and muskinongé. His line he generally fastened to the paddle, and the motion of the oar gave a life-like vibration to the queer-looking mice and dragonflies I used to manufacture from squirrel fur, or scarlet and white cloth, to tempt the finny wanderers of the wave.

When too busy himself to fish for our meals, little Katie and I ventured out alone in the canoe, which we anchored in any promising fishing spot, by fastening a harrow tooth to a piece of rope, and letting it drop from the side of the little vessel. By the time she was five years old, my little mermaid could both steer and paddle the light vessel, and catch small fish, which were useful for soup.

During the winter of '36, we experienced many privations. The ruffian squatter P[helan],[4] from Clear Lake, drove from the barn a fine young bull we were rearing, and for several weeks all trace of the animal was lost. We had almost forgotten the existence of poor Whiskey, when a neighbour called and told Moodie that his yearling was at P[helan]'s, and that he would advise him to get it back as soon as possible.

Moodie had to take some wheat to Y[oung]'s mill, and as the squatter lived only a mile further, he called at his house; and there, sure enough, he found the lost animal. With the greatest difficulty he succeeded in regaining his property, but not without many threats of vengeance from the parties who had stolen it. To these he paid no regard; but a few days after, six fat hogs, on which we depended for all our winter store of animal food, were driven into the lake, and destroyed.

4. See Chapter Seventeen, note 6, p. 211; see also p. 224.

The death of these animals deprived us of three barrels of pork, and half-starved us through the winter. That winter of '36, how heavily it wore away! The grown flour, frosted potatoes, and scant quantity of animal food rendered us all weak, and the children suffered much from the ague.

One day, just before the snow fell, Moodie had gone to Peterborough for letters; our servant was sick in bed with the ague, and I was nursing my little boy, Dunbar, who was shaking with the cold fit of his miserable fever, when Jacob put his honest, round, rosy face in at the door.[5]

"Give me the master's gun, ma'am; there's a big buck feeding on the rice-bed near the island."

I took down the gun, saying, "Jacob, you have no chance; there is but one charge of buck-shot in the house."

"One chance is better nor none," said Jacob, as he commenced loading the gun. "Who knows what may happen to oie? Mayhap oie may chance to kill 'un; and you and the measter and the wee bairns may have zummut zavory for zupper yet."

Away walked Jacob with Moodie's "Manton" over his shoulder. A few minutes after, I heard the report of the gun, but never expected to see anything of the game; when Jacob suddenly bounced into the room, half-wild with delight.

"Thae beast iz dead az a door-nail. Zure, how the measter will laugh when he zees the fine buck that oie a 'zhot."

"And have you really shot him?"

"Come and zee! 'Tis worth your while to walk down to the landing to look at 'un."

Jacob got a rope, and I followed him to the landing, where, sure enough, lay a fine buck, fastened in tow of the canoe. Jacob soon secured him by the hind legs to the rope he had brought; and, with our united efforts, we at last succeeded in dragging our prize home. All the time he was engaged in taking off the skin, Jacob was anticipating the feast that we were to have; and the good fellow chuckled with delight when he hung the carcass quite close to the kitchen door, that his "measter" might run against it when he came home at night. This event actually took place. When Moodie opened the door, he struck his head against the dead deer.

"What have you got here?"

"A fine buck, zur," said Jacob, bringing forward the light, and holding it up in such a manner that all the merits of the prize could be seen at a glance.

"A fine one, indeed! How did we come by it?"

"It was zhot by oie," said Jacob, rubbing his hands in a sort of ecstacy. "Thae beast iz the first oi eever zhot in my life. He! he! he!"

"You shot that fine deer, Jacob?—and there was only one charge in the gun! Well done; you must have taken a good aim."

"Why, zur, oie took no aim at all. Oie just pointed the gun at the

---

5. See Chapter Fifteen, note 9, p. 195.

deer, and zhut my oeys an let fly at 'un. 'Twas Providence kill'd 'un, not oie."

"I believe you," said Moodie; "Providence has hitherto watched over us and kept us from actual starvation."

The flesh of the deer, and the good broth that I was able to obtain from it, greatly assisted in restoring our sick to health; but long before that severe winter terminated we were again out of food. Mrs. ——[6] had given to Katie, in the fall, a very pretty little pig, which she had named Spot. The animal was a great favourite with Jacob and the children, and he always received his food from their hands at the door, and followed them all over the place like a dog. We had a noble hound called Hector, between whom and the pet pig there existed the most tender friendship. Spot always shared with Hector the hollow log which served him for a kennel, and we often laughed to see Hector lead Spot round the clearing by his ear. After bearing the want of animal food until our souls sickened at the bad potatoes and grown flour bread, we began—that is, the eldest of the family—to cast very hungry eyes upon Spot; but no one liked to propose having him killed. At last Jacob spoke his mind upon the subject.

"Oi've heard, zur, that the Jews never eat pork; but we Christians dooz, and are right glad ov the chance. Now, zur, oi've been thinking that 'tis no manner ov use our keeping that beast Spot. If he wor a zow, now, there might be zome zenze in the thing; and we all feel weak for a morzel of meat. S'poze I kill him? He won't make a bad piece of pork."

Moodie seconded the move; and, in spite of the tears and prayers of Katie, her uncouth pet was sacrificed to the general wants of the family; but there were two members of the house who disdained to eat a morsel of the victim; poor Katie and the dog Hector. At the self-denial of the first I did not at all wonder, for she was a child full of sensibility and warm affections, but the attachment of the brute creature to his old playmate filled us all with surprise. Jacob first drew our attention to the strange fact.

"That dog," he said, as we were passing through the kitchen while he was at dinner, "do teach uz Christians a lesson how to treat our friends. Why, zur, he'll not eat a morsel of Spot. Oie have tried and tempted him in all manner ov ways, and he only do zneer and turn up his nose when oie hould him a bit to taste." He offered the animal a rib of the fresh pork as he finished speaking, and the dog turned away with an expression of aversion, and on a repetition of the act, walked from the table.

Human affection could scarcely have surpassed the love felt by this poor animal for his playfellow. His attachment to Spot, that could overcome the pangs of hunger—for, like the rest of us, he was half-starved—must have been strong indeed.

Jacob's attachment to us, in its simplicity and fidelity, greatly resem-

---

6. Possibly Mrs. Emilia Shairp, whose generosity to Susanna and affection for her children were often evident during these troubled years.

bled that of the dog; and sometimes, like the dog, he would push himself in where he was not wanted, and gratuitously give his advice, and make remarks which were not required.

Mr. K——, from Cork, was asking Moodie many questions about the partridges of the country; and, among other things, he wanted to know by what token you were able to discover their favourite haunts. Before Moodie could answer this last query a voice responded, through a large crack in the boarded wall which separated us from the kitchen, "They always bides where they's drum." This announcement was received with a burst of laughter that greatly disconcerted the natural philosopher in the kitchen.

On the 21st of May of this year, my second son, Donald, was born. The poor fellow came in hard times. The cows had not calved, and our bill of fare, now minus the deer and Spot, only consisted of bad potatoes and still worse bread. I was rendered so weak by want of proper nourishment that my dear husband, for my sake, overcame his aversion to borrowing, and procured a quarter of mutton from a friend. This, with kindly presents from neighbours—often as badly off as ourselves—a loin of a young bear, and a basket, containing a loaf of bread, some tea, some fresh butter, and oatmeal, went far to save my life.

Shortly after my recovery, Jacob—the faithful, good Jacob—was obliged to leave us, for we could no longer afford to pay wages. What was owing to him had to be settled by sacrificing our best cow, and a great many valuable articles of clothing from my husband's wardrobe. Nothing is more distressing than being obliged to part with articles of dress which you know that you cannot replace. Almost all my clothes had been appropriated to the payment of wages, or to obtain garments for the children, excepting my wedding dress, and the beautiful baby-linen which had been made by the hands of dear and affectionate friends for my first-born. These were now exchanged for coarse, warm flannels, to shield her from the cold.

Moodie and Jacob had chopped eight acres during the winter, but these had to be burnt off and logged-up before we could put in a crop of wheat for the ensuing fall. Had we been able to retain this industrious, kindly English lad, this would have been soon accomplished; but his wages, at the rate of thirty pounds per annum, were now utterly beyond our means.

Jacob had formed an attachment to my pretty maid, Mary Pine,[7] and before going to the Southern States, to join an uncle who resided in Louisville, an opulent tradesman, who had promised to teach him his business, Jacob thought it as well to declare himself. The declaration took place on a log of wood near the back-door, and from my chamber window I could both hear and see the parties, without being myself observed. Mary was seated very demurely at one end of the

---

7. See Chapter Seventeen, note 2, p. 213. Mary did in fact marry "old Ralph T——h" (Tully) and his mare rather than the absent Jacob. Ralph Tully farmed Lot 3, Concession 2 in Smith Township and married Mary at St. John's Anglican Church in Peterborough on September 7, 1837.

log, twisting the strings of her checked apron, and the loving Jacob
was busily whittling the other extremity of their rustic seat. There
was a long silence. Mary stole a look at Jacob, and he heaved a
tremendous sigh, something between a yawn and a groan. "Meary,"
he said, "I must go."

"I knew that afore," returned the girl.

"I had zummat to zay to you, Meary. Do you think you will miss
oie?" (looking very affectionately and twitching nearer.)

"What put that into your head, Jacob?" This was said very demurely.

"Oie thowt, may be, Meary, that your feelings might be zummat
loike my own. I feel zore about the heart, Meary, and it's all com' of
parting with you. Don't you feel queerish, too?"

"Can't say that I do, Jacob. I shall soon see you again," (pulling violently at her apron-string.)

"Meary, oi'm afear'd you don't feel like oie."

"P'r'aps not—women can't feel like men. I'm sorry that you are going, Jacob, for you have been very kind and obliging, and I wish you
well."

"Meary," cried Jacob, growing desperate at her coyness, and getting
quite close up to her, "will you marry oie? Say yeez or noa?"

This was coming close to the point. Mary drew farther from him,
and turned her head away.

"Meary," said Jacob, seizing upon the hand that held the apron-
string. "Do you think you can better yoursel'? If not—why, oie'm your
man. Now, do just turn about your head and answer oie."

The girl turned round, and gave him a quick, shy glance, then burst
out into a simpering laugh.

"Meary, will you take oie?" (jogging her elbow.)

"I will," cried the girl, jumping up from the log and running into the
house.

"Well, that bargain's made," said the lover, rubbing his hands; "and
now, oie'll go and bid measter and missus good-buoy."

The poor fellow's eyes were full of tears, for the children, who loved
him very much, clung, crying, about his knees. "God bless yees all,"
sobbed the kind-hearted creature. "Doan't forget Jacob, for he'll
neaver forget you. Good-buoy!"

Then turning to Mary, he threw his arms round her neck, and bestowed upon her fair cheek the most audible kiss I ever heard.

"And doan't you forget me, Meary. In two years oie will be back to
marry you; and may be oie may come back a rich man."

Mary, who was an exceedingly pretty girl, shed some tears at the
parting; but in a few days she was as gay as ever, and listening with
great attention to the praises bestowed upon her beauty by an old
bachelor, who was her senior by five-and-twenty years. But then he
had a good farm, a saddle mare, and plenty of stock, and was reputed
to have saved money. The saddle mare seemed to have great weight in
old Ralph T——h's wooing; and I used laughingly to remind Mary of
her absent lover, and beg her not to marry Ralph T——h's mare.

THE CANADIAN HUNTER'S SONG.[8]

The northern lights are flashing,
    On the rapids' restless flow;
And o'er the wild waves dashing,
    Swift darts the light canoe.
        The merry hunters come.
        "What cheer?—what cheer?"—
        "We've slain the deer!"
        "Hurrah!—You're welcome home!"

The blithesome horn is sounding,
    And the woodman's loud halloo;
And joyous steps are bounding
    To meet the birch canoe.
        "Hurrah!—The hunters come."
        And the woods ring out
        To their merry shout
    As they drag the dun deer home!

The hearth is brightly burning,
    The rustic board is spread;
To greet the sire returning
    The children leave their bed.
        With laugh and shout they come—
        That merry band—
        To grasp his hand,
    And bid him welcome home!

Twenty-one

The Little Stumpy Man

There was a little man—
I'll sketch him if I can,
For he clung to mine and me
Like the old man of the sea;
And in spite of taunt and scoff
We could not pitch him off,
For the cross-grained, waspish elf
Cared for no one but himself.[1]

Before I dismiss for ever the troubles and sorrows of 1836, I would
fain introduce to the notice of my readers some of the odd characters
with whom we became acquainted during that period. The first that

8. First published in *The Literary Garland* (Montreal) 1:2 (January 1843), p. 63.
1. In volume 3 of *The Thousand and One Nights*, Sinbad the Sailor, shipwrecked on an island,
   meets an old man who needs help to cross a river. Sinbad carries him across on his shoulders, but once across the old man refuses to release his grip. He becomes a burden for many
   days until Sinbad manages to trick him into releasing his grip.

starts vividly to my recollection is the picture of a short, stumpy, thick-set man—a British sailor, too—who came to stay one night under our roof, and took quiet possession of his quarters for nine months, and whom we were obliged to tolerate from the simple fact that we could not get rid of him.

During the fall, Moodie had met this individual (whom I will call Mr. Malcolm)[2] in the mail-coach, going up to Toronto. Amused with his eccentric and blunt manners, and finding him a shrewd, clever fellow in conversation, Moodie told him that if ever he came into his part of the world he should be glad to renew their acquaintance. And so they parted, with mutual good-will, as men often part who have travelled a long journey in good fellowship together, without thinking it probable they should ever meet again.

The sugar season had just commenced with the spring thaw;[3] Jacob had tapped a few trees in order to obtain sap to make molasses for the children, when his plans were frustrated by the illness of my husband, who was again attacked with the ague. Towards the close of a wet, sloppy night, while Jacob was in the wood, chopping, and our servant gone to my sister, who was ill, to help to wash, as I was busy baking bread for tea, my attention was aroused by a violent knocking at the door, and the furious barking of our dog, Hector. I ran to open it, when I found Hector's teeth clenched in the trousers of a little, dark, thickset man, who said in a gruff voice,

"Call off your dog. What the devil do you keep such an infernal brute about the house for? Is it to bite people who come to see you?"

Hector was the best-behaved, best-tempered animal in the world; he might have been called a gentlemanly dog. So little was there of the unmannerly puppy in his behaviour, that I was perfectly astonished at his ungracious conduct. I caught him by the collar, and not without some difficulty, succeeded in dragging him off.

"Is Captain Moodie within?" said the stranger.

"He is, sir. But he is ill in bed—too ill to be seen."

"Tell him a friend" (he laid a strong stress upon the last word), "a particular friend must speak to him."

I now turned my eyes to the face of the speaker with some curiosity. I had taken him for a mechanic, from his dirty, slovenly appearance; and his physiognomy was so unpleasant that I did not credit his assertion that he was a friend of my husband, for I was certain that no man who possessed such a forbidding aspect could be regarded by Moodie as a friend. I was about to deliver his message, but the moment I let go Hector's collar, the dog was at him again.

---

2. "Mr. Malcolm" was a former British sailor named Malcolm Ramsay. His identity is confirmed in a fascinating entry in John Moodie's Spiritualism journal (December 28, 1857). He records a séance in which Susanna, as medium, received a message from Ramsay, who speaks from hell and begs apology for his behaviour as the Moodies' guest and his "mis-spent life," blaming his mother ("an old jade") for his own "bad passions." He compares hell with "hoeing potatoes with Moodie under the broiling sun of Canada tormented by those damned Devils—black flies." "I know no blacker Demons here," he adds. See OONL, PHEC, Series II, Manuscript Box 5, Spiritualism Album, pp. 72–73.

3. The nine-month stay of Malcolm Ramsay began in the early spring of 1836 and lasted until Christmas Eve of that year.

"Don't strike him with your stick," I cried, throwing my arms over the faithful creature. "He is a powerful animal, and if you provoke him, he will kill you."

I at last succeeded in coaxing Hector into the girl's room, where I shut him up, while the stranger came into the kitchen, and walked to the fire to dry his wet clothes.

I immediately went into the parlour, where Moodie was lying upon a bed near the stove, to deliver the stranger's message; but before I could say a word, he dashed in after me, and going up to the bed, held out his broad, coarse hand, with, "How are you, Mr. Moodie? You see I have accepted your kind invitation sooner than either you or I expected. If you will give me house-room for the night, I shall be obliged to you."

This was said in a low, mysterious voice; and Moodie, who was still struggling with the hot fit of his disorder, and whose senses were not a little confused, stared at him with a look of vague bewilderment. The countenance of the stranger grew dark.

"You cannot have forgotten me—my name is Malcolm."

"Yes, yes; I remember you now," said the invalid, holding out his burning, feverish hand. "To my home, *such as it is,* you are welcome."

I stood by in wondering astonishment, looking from one to the other, as I had no recollection of ever hearing my husband mention the name of the stranger; but as he had invited him to share our hospitality, I did my best to make him welcome, though in what manner he was to be accommodated puzzled me not a little. I placed the arm-chair by the fire, and told him that I would prepare tea for him as soon as I could.

"It may be as well to tell you, Mrs. Moodie," said he sulkily, for he was evidently displeased by my husband's want of recognition on his first entrance, "that I have had no dinner."

I sighed to myself, for I well knew that our larder boasted of no dainties; and from the animal expression of our guest's face, I rightly judged that he was fond of good living.

By the time I had fried a rasher of salt pork, and made a pot of dandelion coffee, the bread I had been preparing was baked; but grown flour will not make light bread, and it was unusually heavy. For the first time I felt heartily ashamed of our humble fare. I was sure that he for whom it was provided was not one to pass it over in benevolent silence. "He might be a gentleman," I thought, "but he does not look like one;" and a confused idea of who he was, and where Moodie had met with him, began to float through my mind. I did not like the appearance of the man, but I consoled myself that he was only to stay for one night, and I could give up my bed for that one night, and sleep on a bed on the floor by my sick husband. When I re-entered the parlour to cover the table, I found Moodie fallen asleep, and Mr. Malcolm reading. As I placed the tea-things on the table, he raised his head, and regarded me with a gloomy stare. He was a strange-looking creature; his features were tolerably regular, his complexion dark, with a good colour, his very broad and round head was covered with a perfect mass of close, black, curling hair, which, in growth, texture, and hue, resembled the wiry, curly hide of a water-dog. His eyes and mouth were both well-shaped, but gave, by their sinister expression, an odious and doubtful meaning to the whole of his physiognomy. The eyes were cold, insolent, and cruel, and as green as the eyes of a cat. The mouth bespoke a sullen, determined, and sneering disposition, as if it belonged to one brutally obstinate, one who could not by any gentle means be persuaded from his purpose. Such a man in a passion would have been a terrible wild beast; but the current of his feelings seemed to flow in a deep, sluggish channel, rather than in a violent or impetuous one; and, like William Penn,[4] when he reconnoitred his unwelcome visitors through the keyhole of the door, I looked at my strange guest, and liked him not. Perhaps my distant and constrained manner made him painfully aware of the fact, for I am certain that, from that first hour of our acquaintance, a deep-rooted antipathy existed between us, which time seemed rather to strengthen than diminish.

He ate of his meal sparingly, and with evident disgust; the only remarks which dropped from him were:

"You make bad bread in the bush. Strange, that you can't keep your potatoes from the frost! I should have thought that you could have had things more comfortable in the woods."

"We have been very unfortunate," I said, "since we came to the woods. I am sorry that you should be obliged to share the poverty of the land. It would have given me much pleasure could I have set before you a more comfortable meal."

"Oh, don't mention it. So that I get good pork and potatoes I shall be contented."

What did these words imply?—an extension of his visit? I hoped that I was mistaken; but before I could lose any time in conjecture my husband awoke. The fit had left him, and he rose and dressed himself, and was soon chatting cheerfully with his guest.

Mr. Malcolm now informed him that he was hiding from the sheriff of the N—— district's officers,[5] and that it would be conferring upon him a great favour if he would allow him to remain at his house for a few weeks.

"To tell you the truth, Malcolm," said Moodie, "we are so badly off that we can scarcely find food for ourselves and the children. It is out of our power to make you comfortable, or to keep an additional hand, without he is willing to render some little help on the farm. If you can do this, I will endeavour to get a few necessaries on credit, to make your stay more agreeable."

To this proposition Malcolm readily assented, not only because it released him from all sense of obligation, but because it gave him a privilege to grumble.

Finding that his stay might extend to an indefinite period, I got Jacob to construct a rude bedstead out of two large chests that had

4. Penn (1644–1718) was the founder of Pennsylvania. No source has been found.
5. Probably the Newcastle District.

transported some of our goods across the Atlantic, and which he put up in a corner of the parlour. This I provided with a small hair-mattress, and furnished with what bedding I could spare.

For the first fortnight of his sojourn, our guest did nothing but lie upon that bed, and read, and smoke, and drink whiskey-and-water from morning until night. By degrees he let out part of his history; but there was a mystery about him which he took good care never to clear up. He was the son of an officer in the navy, who had not only attained a very high rank in the service, but, for his gallant conduct, had been made a Knight-Companion of the Bath.

He had himself served his time as a midshipman on board his father's flag-ship, but had left the navy and accepted a commission in the Buenos-Ayrean service during the political struggles in that province; he had commanded a sort of privateer under the government, to whom, by his own account, he had rendered many very signal services. Why he left South America and came to Canada he kept a profound secret. He had indulged in very vicious and dissipated courses since he came to the province, and by his own account had spent upwards of four thousand pounds, in a manner not over cred-itable to himself. Finding that his friends would answer his bills no longer, he took possession of a grant of land obtained through his fa-ther's interest, up in Harvey, a barren township on the shores of Stony Lake; and, after putting up his shanty, and expending all his remaining means, he found that he did not possess one acre out of the whole four hundred that would yield a crop of potatoes. He was now consid-erably in debt, and the lands, such as they were, had been seized, with all his effects, by the sheriff, and a warrant was out for his own appre-hension, which he contrived to elude during his sojourn with us. Money he had none; and, beyond the dirty fearnought blue seaman's jacket which he wore, a pair of trousers of the coarse cloth of the country, an old black vest that had seen better days, and two blue-checked shirts, clothes he had none. He shaved but once a week, never combed his hair, and never washed himself. A dirtier or more slovenly creature never before was dignified by the title of a gentle-man. He was, however, a man of good education, of excellent abilities, and possessed a bitter, sarcastic knowledge of the world; but he was selfish and unprincipled in the highest degree.

His shrewd observations and great conversational powers had first attracted my husband's attention, and, as men seldom show their bad qualities on a journey, he thought him a blunt, good fellow, who had travelled a great deal, and could render himself a very agreeable com-panion by a graphic relation of his adventures. He could be all this, when he chose to relax from his sullen, morose mood; and, much as I disliked him, I have listened with interest for hours to his droll de-scriptions of South American life and manners.

Naturally indolent, and a constitutional grumbler, it was with the greatest difficulty that Moodie could get him to do anything beyond bringing a few pails of water from the swamp for the use of the house, and he has often passed me carrying water up from the lake without offering to relieve me of the burden. Mary, the betrothed of Jacob, called him a perfect "beast;" but he, returning good for evil, considered *her* a very pretty girl, and paid her so many uncouth attentions that he roused the jealousy of honest Jake, who vowed that he would give him a good "loomping" if he only dared to lay a finger upon his sweetheart. With Jacob to back her, Mary treated the "zea-bear," as Jacob termed him, with vast disdain, and was so saucy to him that, forgetting his admiration, he declared he would like to serve her as the Indians had done a scolding woman in South America. They attacked her house during the absence of her husband, cut out her tongue, and nailed it to the door, by way of knocker; and he thought that all women who could not keep a civil tongue in their head should be served in the same manner.

"And what should be done to men who swear and use ondacent language?" quoth Mary, indignantly. "Their tongues should be slit, and given to the dogs. Faugh! You are such a nasty fellow that I don't think Hector would eat your tongue."

"I'll kill that beast," muttered Malcolm, as he walked away.

I remonstrated with him on the impropriety of bandying words with our servants. "You see," I said, "the disrespect with which they treat you; and if they presume upon your familiarity, to speak to our guest in this contemptuous manner, they will soon extend the same conduct to us."

"But, Mrs Moodie, you should reprove them."

"I cannot, sir, while you continue, by taking liberties with the girl, and swearing at the man, to provoke them to retaliation."

"Swearing! What harm is there in swearing? A sailor cannot live without oaths."

"But a gentleman might, Mr. Malcolm. I should be sorry to consider you in any other light."

"Ah, you are such a prude—so methodistical—you make no allowance for circumstances! Surely, in the woods we may dispense with the hypocritical, conventional forms of society, and speak and act as we please."

"So you seem to think; but you see the result."

"I have never been used to the society of ladies, and I cannot fashion my words to please them; and I won't, that's more!" he muttered to himself as he strode off to Moodie in the field. I wished from my very heart that he was once more on the deck of his piratical South American craft.

One night he insisted on going out in the canoe to spear muskinongé with Moodie. The evening turned out very chill and foggy, and, before twelve, they returned, with only one fish, and half frozen with cold. Malcolm had got twinges of rheumatism, and he fussed, and sulked, and swore, and quarrelled with everybody and everything, until Moodie, who was highly amused by his petulance, advised him to go to his bed, and pray for the happy restoration of his temper.

"Temper!" he cried, "I don't believe there's a good-tempered person in the world. It's all hypocrisy! I never had a good-temper! My mother was an ill-tempered woman, and ruled my father, who was a confoundedly severe, domineering man. I was born in an ill-temper. I was an ill-tempered child; I grew up an ill-tempered man. I feel worse than ill-tempered now, and when I die it will be in an ill-temper."

"Well," quoth I, "Moodie has made you a tumbler of hot punch, which may help to drive out the cold and the ill-temper, and cure the rheumatism."

"Ay; your husband's a good fellow, and worth two of you, Mrs. Moodie. He makes some allowance for the weakness of human nature, and can excuse even my ill-temper."

I did not choose to bandy words with him, and the next day the unfortunate creature was shaking with the ague. A more intractable, outrageous, *im*-patient I never had the ill-fortune to nurse. During the cold fit, he did nothing but swear at the cold, and wished himself roasting; and during the fever, he swore at the heat, and wished that he was sitting, in no other garment than his shirt, on the north side of an iceberg. And when the fit at last left him, he got up, and ate such quantities of fat pork, and drank so much whiskey-punch, that you would have imagined he had just arrived from a long journey, and had not tasted food for a couple of days.

He would not believe that fishing in the cold night-air upon the water had made him ill, but raved that it was all my fault for having laid my baby down on his bed while it was shaking with the ague.

Yet, if there were the least tenderness mixed up in his iron nature, it was the affection he displayed for that young child. Dunbar was just twenty months old,[6] with bright, dark eyes, dimpled cheeks, and soft, flowing, golden hair, which fell round his infant face in rich curls. The merry, confiding little creature formed such a contrast to his own surly, unyielding temper, that, perhaps, that very circumstance made the bond of union between them. When in the house, the little boy was seldom out of his arms, and whatever were Malcolm's faults, he had none in the eyes of the child, who used to cling around his neck, and kiss his rough, unshaven cheeks with the greatest fondness.

"If I could afford it, Moodie," he said one day to my husband, "I should like to marry. I want some one upon whom I could vent my affections." And wanting that some one in the form of woman, he contented himself with venting them upon the child.

As the spring advanced, and after Jacob left us, he seemed ashamed of sitting in the house doing nothing, and therefore undertook to make us a garden, or "to make garden," as the Canadians term preparing a few vegetables for the season. I procured the necessary seeds, and watched with no small surprise the industry with which our strange visitor commenced operations. He repaired the broken fence, dug the ground with the greatest care, and laid it out with a skill and neatness of which I had believed him perfectly incapable. In less than three weeks, the whole plot presented a very pleasing prospect, and he was really elated by his success.

6. John Alexander Dunbar Moodie was born in August 1834, thus dating this episode to April 1836. Jacob (Faithful) left the Moodies' service in late spring.

"At any rate," said he, "we shall no longer be starved on bad flour and potatoes. We shall have peas, and beans, and beets, and carrots, and cabbage in abundance; besides, the plot I have reserved for cucumbers and melons."

"Ah," thought I; "does he, indeed, mean to stay with us until the melons are ripe?" and my heart died within me, for he not only was a great additional expense, but he gave a great deal of additional trouble, and entirely robbed us of all privacy, as our very parlour was converted into a bedroom for his accommodation; besides that, a man of his singularly dirty habits made a very disagreeable inmate.

The only redeeming point in his character, in my eyes, was his love for Dunbar. I could not entirely hate a man who was so fondly attached to my child. To the two little girls he was very cross, and often chased them from him with blows.

He had, too, an odious way of finding fault with everything. I never could cook to please him; and he tried in the most malicious way to induce Moodie to join in his complaints. All his schemes to make strife between us, however, failed, and were generally visited upon himself. In no way did he ever seek to render me the least assistance. Shortly after Jacob left us, Mary Pine was offered higher wages by a family at Peterborough, and for some time I was left with four little children, and without a servant. Moodie always milked the cows, because I never could overcome my fear of cattle; and though I had occasionally milked when there was no one else in the way, it was in fear and trembling.

Moodie had to go down to Peterborough; but before he went, he begged Malcolm to bring me what water and wood I required, and to stand by the cattle while I milked the cows, and he would himself be home before night.

He started at six in the morning, and I got the pail to go and milk. Malcolm was lying upon his bed, reading.

"Mr. Malcolm, will you be so kind as to go with me to the fields for a few minutes while I milk?"

"Yes!" (then, with a sulky frown,) "but I want to finish what I am reading."

"I will not detain you long."

"Oh, no! I suppose about an hour. You are a shocking bad milker."

"True; I never went near a cow until I came to this country; and I have never been able to overcome my fear of them."

"More shame for you! A farmer's wife, and afraid of a cow! Why, these little children would laugh at you."

I did not reply, nor would I ask him again. I walked slowly to the field, and my indignation made me forget my fear. I had just finished milking, and with a brimming pail was preparing to climb the fence and return to the house, when a very wild ox we had came running with headlong speed from the wood. All my fears were alive again in a moment. I snatched up the pail, and, instead of climbing the fence and getting to the house, I ran with all the speed I could command down the steep hill towards the lake shore; my feet caught in a root of the many stumps in the path, and I fell to the ground, my pail rolling many yards ahead of me. Every drop of my milk was spilt upon the grass. The ox passed on. I gathered myself up and returned home. Malcolm was very fond of new milk, and he came to meet me at the door.

"Hi! hi!—Where's the milk?"

"No milk for the poor children to-day," said I showing him the inside of the pail, with a sorrowful shake of the head, for it was no small loss to them and me.

"How the devil's that? So you were afraid to milk the cows. Come away, and I will keep off the buggaboos."

"I did milk them—no thanks to your kindness, Mr. Malcolm—but—"

"But what?"

"The ox frightened me, and I fell and spilt all the milk."

"Whew! Now don't go and tell your husband that it was all my fault; if you had had a little patience, I would have come when you asked me, but I don't choose to be dictated to, and I won't be made a slave by you or any one else."

"Then why do you stay, sir, where you consider yourself so treated?" said I. "We are all obliged to work to obtain bread; we give you the best share—surely the return we ask for it is but small."

"You make me feel my obligations to you when you ask me to do anything; if you left it to my better feelings we should get on better."

"Perhaps you are right. I will never ask you to do anything for me in future."

"Oh, now, that's all mock humility. In spite of the tears in your eyes, you are as angry with me as ever; but don't go make mischief between me and Moodie. If you'll say nothing about my refusing to go with you, I'll milk the cows for you myself to-night."

"And can you milk?" said I, with some curiosity.

"Milk! Yes; and if I were not so confoundedly low-spirited and—lazy, I could do a thousand other things too. But now, don't say a word about it to Moodie."

I made no promise; but my respect for him was not increased by his cowardly fear of reproof from Moodie, who treated him with a kindness and consideration which he did not deserve.

The afternoon turned out very wet, and I was sorry that I should be troubled with his company all day in the house. I was making a shirt for Moodie from some cotton that had been sent me from home, and he placed himself by the side of the stove, just opposite, and continued to regard me for a long time with his usual sullen stare. I really felt half afraid of him.

"Don't you think me mad?" said he. "I have a brother deranged; he got a stroke of the sun in India, and lost his senses in consequence; but sometimes I think it runs in the family."

What answer could I give to this speech, but mere evasive commonplace!

"You won't say what you really think," he continued; "I know you hate me, and that makes me dislike you. Now what would you say if I told you I had committed a murder, and that it was the recollection of that circumstance that made me at times so restless and unhappy?"

I looked up in his face, not knowing what to believe.

" 'Tis fact," said he, nodding his head; and I hoped that he would not go mad, like his brother, and kill me.

"Come, I'll tell you all about it; I know the world would laugh at me for calling such an act *murder*; and yet I have been such a miserable man ever since that I *feel* it was.

"There was a noted leader among the rebel Buenos-Ayreans, whom the government wanted much to get hold of. He was a fine, dashing, handsome fellow; I had often seen him, but we never came to close quarters. One night, I was lying wrapped up in my poncho at the bottom of my boat, which was rocking in the surf, waiting for two of my men, who were gone on shore. There came to the shore, this man and one of his people, and they stood so near the boat, which I suppose they thought empty, that I could distinctly hear their conversation. I suppose it was the devil who tempted me to put a bullet through that man's heart. He was an enemy to the flag under which I fought, but he was no enemy to me—I had no right to become his executioner; but still the desire to kill him, for the mere devilry of the thing, came so strongly upon me that I no longer tried to resist it. I rose slowly upon my knees; the moon was shining very bright at the time, both he and his companion were too earnestly engaged to see me, and I deliberately shot him through the body. He fell with a heavy groan back into the water; but I caught the last look he threw up to the moonlight skies before his eyes glazed in death. Oh, that look!—so full of despair, of unutterable anguish; it haunts me yet—it will haunt me for ever. I would not have cared if I had killed him in strife—but in cold blood, and he so unsuspicious of his doom! Yes, it was murder; I know by this constant tugging at my heart that it was murder. What do you say to it?"

"I should think as you do, Mr. Malcolm. It is a terrible thing to take away the life of a fellow-creature without the least provocation."

"Ah, I knew you would blame me; but he was an enemy after all; I had a right to kill him; I was hired by the government under whom I served to kill him; and who shall condemn me?"

"No one more than your own heart."

"It is not the heart, but the brain, that must decide in questions of right and wrong," said he. "I acted from impulse, and shot that man; had I reasoned upon it for five minutes, the man would be living now. But what's done cannot be undone. Did I ever show you the work I wrote upon South America?"

"Are you an author," said I, incredulously.

"To be sure I am. Murray offered me £100 for my manuscript,[7] but I would not take it. Shall I read to you some passages from it?"

---

7. John Murray (1778–1843), a leading English publisher whose authors included Lord Byron and Jane Austen.

I am sorry to say that his behaviour in the morning was uppermost in my thoughts, and I had no repugnance in refusing.

"No, don't trouble yourself. I have the dinner to cook, and the children to attend to, which will cause a constant interruption; you had better defer it to some other time."

"I shan't ask you to listen to me again," said he, with a look of offended vanity; but he went to his trunk, and brought out a large MS., written on foolscap, which he commenced reading to himself with an air of great self-importance, glancing from time to time at me, and smiling disdainfully. Oh, how glad I was when the door opened, and the return of Moodie broke up this painful *tête-à-tête*.

From the sublime to the ridiculous is but a step. The very next day, Mr. Malcolm made his appearance before me, wrapped in a great-coat belonging to my husband, which literally came down to his heels. At this strange apparition, I fell a-laughing.

"For God's sake, Mrs. Moodie, lend me a pair of inexpressibles. I have met with an accident in crossing the fence, and mine are torn to shreds—gone to the devil entirely."

"Well, don't swear. I'll see what can be done for you."

I brought him a new pair of fine, drab-coloured kerseymere trousers that had never been worn. Although he was eloquent in his thanks, I had no idea that he meant to keep them for his sole individual use from that day thenceforth. But after all, what was the man to do? He had no trousers, and no money, and he could not take to the woods. Certainly his loss was not our gain. It was the old proverb reversed.

The season for putting in the potatoes had now arrived. Malcolm volunteered to cut the sets, which was easy work that could be done in the house, and over which he could lounge and smoke; but Moodie told him that he must take his share in the field, that I had already sets enough saved to plant half-an-acre, and would have more prepared by the time they were required. With many growls and shrugs, he felt obliged to comply; and he performed his part pretty well, the execrations bestowed upon the musquitoes and black-flies forming a sort of safety-valve to let off the concentrated venom of his temper. When he came in to dinner, he held out his hands to me.

"Look at these hands."

"They are blistered with the hoe."

"Look at my face."

"You are terribly disfigured by the black-flies. But Moodie suffers just as much, and says nothing."

"Bah!—The only consolation one feels for such annoyances is to complain. Oh, the woods!—the cursed woods!—how I wish I were out of them." The day was very warm, but in the afternoon I was surprised by a visit from an old maiden lady, a friend of mine from C[obourg].[8]

---

8. Susanna's maiden-lady friend from Cobourg was likely one of the Miss Browns, possibly Susan Brown, a sister of the widow of her close London friend, Thomas Pringle. Susan was staying with the Pringles when Susanna was there and co-signed a letter verifying the authenticity and reliability of "The History of Mary Prince" that Susanna had transcribed for Pringle.

She had walked up with a Mr. Crowe, from Peterborough, a young, brisk-looking farmer, in breeches and top-boots, just out from the old country, who, naturally enough, thought he would like to roost among the woods.

He was a little, lively, good-natured manny, with a real Anglo-Saxon face,—rosy, high cheek-boned, with full lips, and a turned-up nose; and like most little men, was a great talker, and very full of himself. He had belonged to the secondary class of farmers, and was very vulgar, both in person and manners. I had just prepared tea for my visitors, when Malcolm and Moodie returned from the field. There was no affectation about the former. He was manly in his person, and blunt even to rudeness, and I saw by the quizzical look which he cast upon the spruce little Crowe that he was quietly quizzing him from head to heel. A neighbour had sent me a present of maple molasses, and Mr. Crowe was so fearful of spilling some of the rich syrup upon his drab shorts that he spread a large pocket-handkerchief over his knees, and tucked another under his chin. I felt very much inclined to laugh, but restrained the inclination as well as I could—and if the little creature would have sat still, I could have quelled my rebellious propensity altogether; but up he would jump at every word I said to him, and make me a low, jerking bow, often with his mouth quite full, and the treacherous molasses running over his chin.

Malcolm sat directly opposite to me and my volatile next-door neighbour. He saw the intense difficulty I had to keep my gravity, and was determined to make me laugh out. So, coming slyly behind my chair, he whispered in my ear, with the gravity of a judge, "Mrs. Moodie, that must have been the very chap who first jumped Jim Crowe."[9]

This appeal obliged me to run from the table. Moodie was astonished at my rudeness; and Malcolm, as he resumed his seat, made the matter worse, by saying, "I wonder what is the matter with Mrs. Moodie; she is certainly very hysterical this afternoon."

The potatoes were planted, and the season of strawberries, green-peas, and young potatoes come, but still Malcolm remained our constant guest. He had grown so indolent, and gave himself so many airs, that Moodie was heartily sick of his company, and gave him many gentle hints to change his quarters; but our guest was determined to take no hint. For some reason best known to himself, perhaps out of sheer contradiction, which formed one great element in his character, he seemed obstinately bent upon remaining where he was.

Moodie was busy under-bushing for a full fallow. Malcolm spent much of his time in the garden, or lounging about the house. I had baked an eel-pie for dinner, which if prepared well is by no means an unsavoury dish. Malcolm had cleaned some green-peas and washed the first young potatoes we had drawn that season, with his own

9. An allusion to the odd little dance reputedly performed by an old negro and observed by Thomas Dartmouth "Daddy" Rice, who adapted it for performance in the 1820s. The song and dance number, entitled "Jim Crow," became "the first international song hit from America," according to Irving Sablosky in *American Music* (Chicago, 1969), p. 48.

hands, and he was reckoning upon the feast he should have on the potatoes with childish glee. The dinner at length was put upon the table. The vegetables were remarkably fine, and the pie looked very nice.

Moodie helped Malcolm, as he always did, very largely, and the other covered his plate with a portion of peas and potatoes, when, lo and behold! my gentleman began making a very wry face at the pie.

"What an infernal dish!" he cried, pushing away his plate with an air of great disgust. "These eels taste as if they had been stewed in oil. Moodie, you should teach your wife to be a better cook."

The hot blood burnt upon Moodie's cheek. I saw indignation blazing in his eye.

"If you don't like what is prepared for you, sir, you may leave the table, and my house, if you please. I will put up with your ungentlemanly and ungrateful conduct to Mrs. Moodie no longer."

Out stalked the offending party. I thought, to be sure, we had got rid of him; and though he deserved what was said to him, I was sorry for him. Moodie took his dinner, quietly remarking, "I wonder he could find it in his heart to leave those fine peas and potatoes."

He then went back to his work in the bush, and I cleared away the dishes, and churned, for I wanted butter for tea.

About four o'clock, Mr. Malcolm entered the room. "Mrs. Moodie," said he, in a more cheerful voice than usual, "where's the boss?"

"In the wood, under-bushing." I felt dreadfully afraid that there would be blows between them.

"I hope, Mr. Malcolm, that you are not going to him with any intention of a fresh quarrel."

"Don't you think I have been punished enough by losing my dinner?" said he, with a grin. "I don't think we shall murder one another." He shouldered his axe, and went whistling away.

After striving for a long while to stifle my foolish fears, I took the baby in my arms, and little Dunbar by the hand, and ran up to the bush where Moodie was at work.

At first I only saw my husband, but the strokes of an axe at a little distance soon guided my eyes to the spot where Malcolm was working away, as if for dear life. Moodie smiled, and looked at me significantly.

"How could the fellow stomach what I said to him? Either great necessity or great meanness must be the cause of his knocking under. I don't know whether most to pity or despise him."

"Put up with it, dearest, for this once. He is not happy, and must be greatly distressed."

Malcolm kept aloof, ever and anon casting a furtive glance towards us; at last little Dunbar ran to him, and held up his arms to be kissed. The strange man snatched him to his bosom, and covered him with caresses. It might be love to the child that had quelled his sullen spirit, or he might really have cherished an affection for us deeper than his ugly temper would allow him to show. At all events, he joined us at tea as if nothing had happened, and we might truly say that he had obtained a new lease of his long visit.

But what could not be effected by words or hints of ours was brought about a few days after by the silly observation of a child. He asked Katie to give him a kiss, and he would give her some raspberries he had gathered in the bush.

"I don't want them. Go away; I don't like you, *you little stumpy man!*"

His rage knew no bounds. He pushed the child from him, and vowed that he would leave the house that moment—that she could not have thought of such an expression herself; she must have been taught it by us. This was an entire misconception on his part; but he would not be convinced that he was wrong. Off he went, and Moodie called after him, "Malcolm, as I am sending to Peterborough tomorrow, the man shall take in your trunk." He was too angry even to turn and bid us good-by; but we had not seen the last of him yet.

Two months after, we were taking tea with a neighbour, who lived a mile below us on the small lake. Who should walk in but Mr. Malcolm? He greeted us with great warmth for him, and when we rose to take leave, he rose and walked home by our side. "Surely the little stumpy man is not returning to his old quarters?" I am still a babe in the affairs of men. Human nature has more strange varieties than any one menagerie can contain, and Malcolm was one of the oddest of her odd species.

That night he slept in his old bed below the parlour window, and for three months afterwards he stuck to us like a beaver.

He seemed to have grown more kindly, or we had got more used to his eccentricities, and let him have his own way; certainly he behaved himself much better.

He neither scolded the children nor interfered with the maid, nor quarrelled with me. He had greatly discontinued his bad habit of swearing, and he talked of himself and his future prospects with more hope and self-respect. His father had promised to send him a fresh supply of money, and he proposed to buy of Moodie the clergy reserve, and that they should farm the two places on shares. This offer was received with great joy, as an unlooked-for means of paying our debts, and extricating ourselves from present and overwhelming difficulties, and we looked upon the little stumpy man in the light of a benefactor.

So matters continued until Christmas-eve, when our visitor proposed walking into Peterborough, in order to give the children a treat of raisins to make a Christmas pudding.

"We will be quite merry to-morrow," he said. "I hope we shall eat many Christmas dinners together, and continue good friends."

He started after breakfast, with the promise of coming back at night; but night came, the Christmas passed away, months and years fled away, but we never saw the little stumpy man again!

He went away that day with a stranger in a wagon from Peterborough, and never afterwards was seen in that part of Canada. We afterwards learned that he went to Texas, and it is thought that he was killed at St. Antonio; but this is mere conjecture. Whether dead or living, I feel convinced that

"We ne'er shall look upon his like again."[1]

OH, THE DAYS WHEN I WAS YOUNG!

Oh, the days when I was young,
   A playful little boy,
When my piping treble rung
   To the notes of early joy.
Oh, the sunny days of spring,
   When I sat beside the shore,
And heard the small birds sing;—
   Shall I never hear them more?

And the daisies scatter'd round,
   Half hid amid the grass,
Lay like gems upon the ground,
   Too gay for me to pass.
How sweet the milkmaid sung,
   As she sat beside her cow,
How clear her wild notes rung;—
   There's no music like it now.

As I watch'd the ship's white sail
   'Mid the sunbeams on the sea,
Spreading canvas to the gale—
   How I long'd with her to be.
I thought not of the storm,
   Nor the wild cries on her deck,
When writhed her graceful form
   'Mid the hurricane and wreck.

And I launch'd my little ship,
   With her sails and hold beneath;
Deep laden on each trip,
   With berries from the heath.
Ah, little did I know,
   When I long'd to be a man,
Of the gloomy cares and woe,
   That meet in life's brief span.

Oh, the happy nights I lay
   With my brothers in our beds,
Where we soundly slept till day
   Shone brightly o'er our heads.
And the blessed dreams that came
   To fill my heart with joy.
Oh, that I now could dream,
   As I dreamt, a little boy.

1. See *Hamlet* 1.ii.188.

The sun shone brighter then,
   And the moon more soft and clear;
For the wiles of crafty men,
   I had not learn'd to fear;
But all seem'd fair and gay
   As the fleecy clouds above;
I spent my hours in play,
   And my heart was full of love.

I loved the heath-clad hill,
   And I loved the silent vale,
With its dark and purling rill
   That murmur'd in the gale.
Of sighs I'd none to share,
   They were stored for riper years,
When I drain'd the dregs of care
   With many bitter tears.

My simple daily fare,
   In my little tiny mug,
How fain was I to share
   With Cato on the rug.
Yes, he gave his honest paw,
   And he lick'd my happy face,
He was true to Nature's law,
   And I thought it no disgrace.

There's a voice so soft and clear,
   And a step so gay and light,
That charms my listening ear
   In the visions of the night.
And my father bids me haste,[1]
   In the deep, fond tones of love,
And leave this dreary waste,
   For brighter realms above.

Now I am old and grey,
   My bones are rack'd with pain,
And time speeds fast away—
   But why should I complain?
There are joys in life's young morn
   That dwell not with the old,
Like the flowers the wind hath torn,
   From the stem, all bleak and cold.

The weary heart may mourn
   O'er the wither'd hopes of youth,
But the flowers so rudely shorn

---

1. It may appear strange in this poem that no allusions are made by Mr. M. to his mother; but
he unfortunately lost her in the first early days of infancy. [*Author's note.*]

Still leave the seeds of truth.
And there's hope for hoary men
    When they're laid beneath the sod;
For we'll all be young again
    When we meet around our God.

J. W. D. M.

Twenty-two

The Fire

Now, Fortune, do thy worst! For many years,
Thou, with relentless and unsparing hand,
Hast sternly pour'd on our devoted heads
The poison'd phials of thy fiercest wrath.

The early part of the winter of 1837, a year never to be forgotten in the annals of Canadian history,[1] was very severe. During the month of February, the thermometer often ranged from eighteen to twenty-seven degrees below zero. Speaking of the coldness of one particular day, a genuine brother Jonathan remarked,[2] with charming simplicity, that it was thirty degrees below zero that morning, and it would have been much colder if the thermometer had been longer.

The morning of the seventh was so intensely cold that everything liquid froze in the house. The wood that had been drawn for the fire was green, and it ignited too slowly to satisfy the shivering impatience of women and children; I vented mine in audibly grumbling over the wretched fire, at which I in vain endeavoured to thaw frozen bread, and to dress crying children.

It so happened that an old friend, the maiden lady before alluded to, had been staying with us for a few days. She had left us for a visit to my sister, and as some relatives of hers were about to return to Britain by the way of New York, and had offered to convey letters to friends at home, I had been busy all the day before preparing a packet for England.

It was my intention to walk to my sister's with this packet, directly the important affair of breakfast had been discussed; but the extreme cold of the morning had occasioned such delay that it was late before the breakfast-things were cleared away.

After dressing, I found the air so keen that I could not venture out without some risk to my nose, and my husband kindly volunteered to go in my stead.

I had hired a young Irish girl the day before.[3] Her friends were only just located in our vicinity, and she had never seen a stove until she came to our house. After Moodie left, I suffered the fire to die away in

---

1. "Never to be forgotten" because of the Rebellions that occurred in both Lower and Upper Canada late in the year, effectively challenging the political operations of the colony.
2. Susanna's adopted phrase for a typical American.
3. The unnamed Irish servant replaced Mary Pine who had taken a job in Peterborough. She had left before Jenny Buchanan joined the Moodie household in May.

the Franklin stove in the parlour, and went into the kitchen to prepare bread for the oven.

The girl, who was a good-natured creature, had heard me complain bitterly of the cold, and the impossibility of getting the green wood to burn, and she thought that she would see if she could not make a good fire for me and the children, against my work was done. Without saying one word about her intention, she slipped out through a door that opened from the parlour into the garden, ran round to the wood-yard, filled her lap with cedar chips, and, not knowing the nature of the stove, filled it entirely with the light wood.

Before I had the least idea of my danger I was aroused from the com-pletion of my task by the crackling and roaring of a large fire, and a suf-focating smell of burning soot. I looked up at the kitchen cooking-stove. All was right there. I knew I had left no fire in the parlour stove; but not being able to account for the smoke and smell of burning, I opened the door, and to my dismay found the stove red-hot, from the front plate to the topmost pipe that let out the smoke through the roof.

My first impulse was to plunge a blanket, snatched from the ser-vant's bed, which stood in the kitchen, into cold water. This I thrust into the stove, and upon it I threw water, until all was cool below. I then ran up to the loft, and by exhausting all the water in the house, even to that contained in the boilers upon the fire, contrived to cool down the pipes which passed through the loft. I then sent the girl out of doors to look at the roof, which, as a very deep fall of snow had taken place the day before, I hoped would be completely covered, and safe from all danger of fire.

She quickly returned, stamping and tearing her hair, and making a variety of uncouth outcries, from which I gathered that the roof was in flames.

This was terrible news, with my husband absent, no man in the house, and a mile and a quarter from any other habitation. I ran out to ascertain the extent of the misfortune, and found a large fire burning in the roof between the two stone pipes. The heat of the fires had melted off all the snow, and a spark from the burning pipe had already ignited the shingles. A ladder, which for several months had stood against the house, had been moved two days before to the barn, which was at the top of the hill, near the road; there was no reaching the fire through that source. I got out the dining-table, and tried to throw wa-ter upon the roof by standing on a chair placed upon it, but I only ex-pended the little water that remained in the boiler, without reaching the fire. The girl still continued weeping and lamenting.

"You must go for help," I said. "Run as fast as you can to my sister's and fetch your master."

"And lave you, ma'arm, and the childher alone wid the burnin' house?"

"Yes, yes! Don't stay one moment."

"I have no shoes, ma'arm, and the snow is so deep."

"Put on your master's boots; make haste, or we shall be lost before help comes."

The girl put on the boots and started, shrieking "Fire!" the whole way. This was utterly useless, and only impeded her progress by exhausting her strength. After she had vanished from the head of the clearing into the wood, and I was left quite alone, with the house burning over my head, I paused one moment to reflect what had best be done.

The house was built of cedar logs; in all probability it would be consumed before any help could arrive. There was a brisk breeze blowing up from the frozen lake, and the thermometer stood at eighteen degrees below zero. We were placed between the two extremes of heat and cold, and there was as much danger to be apprehended from the one as the other. In the bewilderment of the moment, the direful extent of the calamity never struck me: we wanted but this to put the finishing stroke to our misfortunes, to be thrown, naked, houseless, and penniless, upon the world. "*What shall I save first?*" was the thought just then uppermost in my mind. Bedding and clothing appeared the most essentially necessary and without another moment's pause, I set to work with a right good will to drag all that I could from my burning home.

While little Agnes, Dunbar, and baby Donald filled the air with their cries, Katie, as if fully conscious of the importance of exertion, assisted me in carrying out sheets and blankets, and dragging trunks and boxes some way up the hill, to be out of the way of the burning brands when the roof should fall in.

How many anxious looks I gave to the head of the clearing as the fire increased, and large pieces of burning pine began to fall through the boarded ceiling, about the lower rooms where we were at work. The children I had kept under a large dresser in the kitchen, but it now appeared absolutely necessary to remove them to a place of safety. To expose the young, tender things to the direful cold was almost as bad as leaving them to the mercy of the fire. At last I hit upon a plan to keep them from freezing. I emptied all the clothes out of a large, deep chest of drawers, and dragged the empty drawers up the hill; these I lined with blankets, and placed a child in each drawer, covering it well over with the bedding, giving to little Agnes the charge of the baby to hold between her knees, and keep well covered until help should arrive. Ah, how long it seemed coming!

The roof was now burning like a brush-heap, and, unconsciously, the child and I were working under a shelf, upon which were deposited several pounds of gun-powder which had been procured for blasting a well, as all our water had to be brought up hill from the lake. This gun-powder was in a stone jar, secured by a paper stopper; the shelf upon which it stood was on fire, but it was utterly forgotten by me at the time; and even afterwards, when my husband was working on the burning loft over it.

I found that I should not be able to take many more trips for goods. As I passed out of the parlour for the last time, Katie looked up at her father's flute, which was suspended upon two brackets, and said,

"Oh, dear mamma! do save papa's flute; he will be so sorry to lose it."

God bless the dear child for the thought! the flute was saved; and, as I succeeded in dragging out a heavy chest of clothes, and looked up once more despairingly to the road, I saw a man running at full speed. It was my husband. Help was at hand, and my heart uttered a deep thanksgiving as another and another figure came upon the scene.

I had not felt the intense cold, although without cap, or bonnet, or shawl; with my hands bare and exposed to the bitter, biting air. The intense excitement, the anxiety to save all I could, had so totally diverted my thoughts from myself, that I had felt nothing of the danger to which I had been exposed; but now that help was near, my knees trembled under me, I felt giddy and faint, and dark shadows seemed dancing before my eyes.

The moment my husband and brother-in-law entered the house, the latter[4] exclaimed,

"Moodie, the house is gone; save what you can of your winter stores and furniture."

Moodie thought differently. Prompt and energetic in danger, and possessing admirable presence of mind and coolness when others yield to agitation and despair, he sprang upon the burning loft and called for water. Alas, there was none!

"Snow, snow; hand me up pailfuls of snow!"

Oh! it was bitter work filling those pails with frozen snow; but Mr. T[raill] and I worked at it as fast as we were able.

The violence of the fire was greatly checked by covering the boards of the loft with this snow. More help had now arrived. Young B[ird][5] and S[am Strickland] had brought the ladder down with them from the barn, and were already cutting away the burning roof, and flinging the flaming brands into the deep snow.

"Mrs. Moodie, have you any pickled meat?"

"We have just killed one of our cows, and salted it for winter stores."

"Well, then, fling the beef into the snow, and let us have the brine."

This was an admirable plan. Wherever the brine wetted the shingles, the fire turned from it, and concentrated into one spot.

But I had not time to watch the brave workers on the roof. I was fast yielding to the effects of overexcitement and fatigue, when my brother's team dashed down the clearing, bringing my excellent old friend, Miss B[rown], and the servant-girl.

My brother sprang out, carried me back into the house, and wrapped me up in one of the large blankets scattered about. In a few minutes I was seated with the dear children in the sleigh, and on the way to a place of warmth and safety.

Katie alone suffered from the intense cold. The dear little creature's feet were severely frozen, but were fortunately restored by her uncle discovering the fact before she approached the fire, and rubbing them well with snow.

In the meanwhile, the friends we had left so actively employed at

4. Thomas Traill.
5. James Bird was the teenaged son of James and Emma Bird of Yoxford, Suffolk. He had accompanied the Moodies on their trans-Atlantic voyage on the *Anne* and had headed for the backwoods soon after their arrival in Cobourg, taking up work for Sam Strickland on his farm on Lake Katchewanook.

the house succeeded in getting the fire under before it had destroyed the walls. The only accident that occurred was to a poor dog, that Moodie had called Snarleyowe. He was struck by a burning brand thrown from the house, and crept under the barn and died.

Beyond the damage done to the building, the loss of our potatoes and two sacks of flour, we had escaped in a manner almost miraculous. This fact shows how much can be done by persons working in union, without bustle and confusion, or running in each other's way. Here were six men, who, without the aid of water, succeeded in saving a building, which, at first sight, almost all of them had deemed past hope. In after-years, when entirely burnt out in a disastrous fire that consumed almost all we were worth in the world, some four hundred persons were present, with a fire-engine to second their endeavours, yet all was lost. Every person seemed in the way; and though the fire was discovered immediately after it took place, nothing was done beyond saving some of the furniture.

Our party was too large to be billetted upon one family. Mrs. T[raill] took compassion upon Moodie, myself, and the baby, while their uncle received the three children to his hospitable home.

It was some weeks before Moodie succeeded in repairing the roof, the intense cold preventing any one from working in such an exposed situation.

The news of our fire travelled far and wide. I was reported to have done prodigies, and to have saved the greater part of our household goods before help arrived. Reduced to plain prose, these prodigies shrink into the simple, and by no means marvellous fact, that during the excitement I dragged out chests which, under ordinary circumstances, I could not have moved; and that I was unconscious, both of the cold and the danger to which I was exposed while working under a burning roof, which, had it fallen, would have buried both the children and myself under its ruins.

These circumstances appeared far more alarming, as all real danger does, after they were past. The fright and over-exertion gave my health a shock from which I did not recover for several months, and made me so fearful of fire, that from that hour it haunts me like a nightmare. Let the night be ever so serene, all stoves must be shut up, and the hot embers covered with ashes, before I dare retire to rest; and the sight of a burning edifice, so common a spectacle in large towns in this country, makes me really ill. This feeling was greatly increased after a second fire, when, for some torturing minutes, a lovely boy, since drowned, was supposed to have perished in the burning house.[6]

Our present fire led to a new train of circumstances, for it was the means of introducing to Moodie a young Irish gentleman, who was staying at my brother's house. John E[vans][7] was one of the best and gentlest of human beings. His father, a captain in the army, had died

6. This second fire occurred in Belleville in December 1840. See *Life in the Clearings* (1853).
7. John Evans stayed with the Moodies for some nine months in 1837, working the farm on shares and hoping to find the means to buy some of that land for himself.

while his family were quite young, and had left his widow with scarcely any means beyond the pension she received at her husband's death, to bring up and educate a family of five children. A handsome, showy woman, Mrs. E[vans] soon married again; and the poor lads were thrown upon the world. The eldest, who had been educated for the Church, first came to Canada in the hope of getting some professorship in the college, or of opening a classical school. He was a handsome, gentlemanly, well-educated young man, but constitutionally indolent—a natural defect which seemed common to all the males of the family, and which was sufficiently indicated by their soft, silky, fair hair and milky complexions. R—— had the good sense to perceive that Canada was not the country for him. He spent a week under our roof, and we were much pleased with his elegant tastes and pursuits; but my husband strongly advised him to try and get a situation as a tutor in some family at home. This he afterwards obtained. He became tutor and travelling companion to the young Lord M——; and has since got an excellent living.

John, who had followed his brother to Canada without the means of transporting himself back again, was forced to remain, and was working with Mr. S[trickland] for his board. He proposed to Moodie working his farm upon shares; and as we were unable to hire a man, Moodie gladly closed with his offer; and, during the time he remained with us, we had every reason to be pleased with the arrangement.

It was always a humiliating feeling to our proud minds, that hirelings should witness our dreadful struggles with poverty, and the strange shifts we were forced to make in order to obtain even food. But John E[vans] had known and experienced all that we had suffered, in his own person, and was willing to share our home with all its privations. Warmhearted, sincere, and truly affectionate—a gentleman in word, thought, and deed—we found his society and cheerful help a great comfort. Our odd meals became a subject of merriment, and the peppermint and sage tea drank with a better flavour when we had one who sympathised in all our trials, and shared all our toils, to partake of it with us.

The whole family soon became attached to our young friend; and after the work of the day was over, greatly we enjoyed an hour's fishing on the lake. John E[vans] said that we had no right to murmur, as long as we had health, a happy home, and plenty of fresh fish, milk, and potatoes. Early in May, we received an old Irishwoman into our service, who for four years proved a most faithful and industrious creature. And what with John E[vans] to assist my husband on the farm, and old Jenny to help me to nurse the children, and manage the house, our affairs, if they were no better in a pecuniary point of view, at least presented a more pleasing aspect at home. We were always cheerful, and sometimes contented and even happy.

How great was the contrast between the character of our new inmate and that of Mr. Malcolm! The sufferings of the past year had been greatly increased by the intolerable nuisance of his company, while many additional debts had been contracted in order to obtain luxuries for him which we never dreamed of purchasing for ourselves.

Instead of increasing my domestic toils, John did all in his power to lessen them; and it always grieved him to see me iron a shirt, or wash the least article of clothing for him. "You have too much to do already; I cannot bear to give you the least additional work," he would say. And he generally expressed the greatest satisfaction at my method of managing the house, and preparing our simple fare. The little ones he treated with the most affectionate kindness, and gathered the whole flock about his knees the moment he came in to his meals.

On a wet day, when no work could be done abroad, Moodie took up his flute, or read aloud to us, while John and I sat down to work. The young emigrant, early cast upon the world and his own resources, was an excellent hand at the needle. He would make or mend a shirt with the greatest precision and neatness, and cut out and manufacture his canvass trousers and loose summer-coats with as much adroitness as the most experienced tailor; darn his socks, and mend his boots and shoes, and often volunteered to assist me in knitting the coarse yarn of the country into socks for the children, while he made them moccasins from the dressed deer-skins that we obtained from the Indians.

Scrupulously neat and clean in his person, the only thing which seemed to ruffle his calm temper was the dirty work of logging; he hated to come in from the field with his person and clothes begrimed with charcoal and smoke. Old Jenny used to laugh at him for not being able to eat his meals without first washing his hands and face.

"Och! my dear heart, yer too particular intirely; we've no time in the woods to be clane." She would say to him, in answer to his request for soap and a towel, "An' is it soap yer a wantin'? I tell yer that same is not to the fore; bating the throuble of makin', it's little soap that the misthress can get to wash the clothes for us and the childher, widout yer wastin' it in makin' yer purty skin as white as a leddy's. Do, darlint, go down to the lake and wash there; that basin is big enough, any how." And John would laugh, and go down to the lake to wash, in order to appease the wrath of the old woman. John had a great dislike to cats, and even regarded with an evil eye our old pet cat, Peppermint, who had taken a great fancy to share his bed and board.

"If I tolerate our own cat," he would say, "I will not put up with such a nuisance as your friend Emilia sends us in the shape of her ugly Tom. Why, where in the world do you think I found that beast sleeping last night?"

I expressed my ignorance.

"In our potato-pot. Now, you will agree with me that potatoes dressed with cat's hair is not a very nice dish. The next time I catch Master Tom in the potato-pot, I will kill him."

"John, you are not in earnest. Mrs. [Shairp] would never forgive any injury done to Tom, who is a great favourite."

"Let her keep him at home, then. Think of the brute coming a mile through the woods to steal from us all he can find, and then sleeping off the effects of his depredations in the potato-pot."

I could not help laughing, but I begged John by no means to annoy Emilia by hurting her cat.

The next day, while sitting in the parlour at work, I heard a dreadful squall, and rushed to the rescue. John was standing, with a flushed cheek, grasping a large stick in his hand, and Tom was lying dead at his feet.

"Oh, the poor cat!"

"Yes, I have killed him; but I am sorry for it now. What will Mrs. [Shairp] say?"

"She must not know it. I have told you the story of the pig that Jacob killed. You had better bury it with the pig."

John was really sorry for having yielded, in a fit of passion, to do so cruel a thing; yet a few days after he got into a fresh scrape with Mrs. [Shairp]'s animals.

The hens were laying, up at the barn. John was very fond of fresh eggs, but some strange dog came daily and sucked the eggs. John had vowed to kill the first dog he found in the act. Mr. [Shairp] had a very fine bulldog, which he valued very highly; but with Emilia, Chowder was an especial favourite. Bitterly had she bemoaned the fate of Tom, and many were the inquiries she made of us as to his sudden disappearance.

One afternoon John ran into the room. "My dear Mrs. Moodie, what is Mrs. [Shairp]'s dog like?"

"A large bull-dog, brindled black and white."

"Then, by Jove, I've shot him!"

"John, John! you mean me to quarrel in earnest with my friend. How could you do it?"

"Why, how the deuce should I know her dog from another? I caught the big thief in the very act of devouring the eggs from under your sitting hen, and I shot him dead without another thought. But I will bury him, and she will never find it out a bit more than she did who killed the cat."

Some time after this, Emilia returned from a visit at P[eterborough]. The first thing she told me was the loss of the dog. She was so vexed at it, she had had him advertised, offering a reward for his recovery.

I, of course, was called upon to sympathise with her, which I did with a very bad grace. "I did not like the beast," I said; "he was cross and fierce, and I was afraid to go up to her house while he was there."

"Yes; but to lose him so. It is so provoking; and him such a valuable animal. I could not tell how deeply she felt the loss. She would give four dollars to find out who had stolen him."

How near she came to making the grand discovery the sequel will show.

Instead of burying him with the murdered pig and cat, John had scratched a shallow grave in the garden, and concealed the dead brute.

After tea, Emilia requested to look at the garden; and I, perfectly unconscious that it contained the remains of the murdered Chowder, led the way. Mrs. [Shairp], whilst gathering a handful of fine green-peas, suddenly stooped, and looking earnestly at the ground, called to me,

"Come here, Susanna, and tell me what has been buried here. It looks like the tail of a dog."

She might have added, "of my dog." Murder, it seems, will out. By some strange chance, the grave that covered the mortal remains of Chowder had been disturbed, and the black tail of the dog was sticking out.

"What can it be?" said I, with an air of perfect innocence. "Shall I call Jenny, and dig it up?"

"Oh, no, my dear; it has a shocking smell, but it does look very much like Chowder's tail."

"Impossible! How could it come among my peas?"

"True. Besides, I saw Chowder, with my own eyes, yesterday, following a team; and George C[addy] hopes to recover him for me."[7]

"Indeed! I am glad to hear it. How these musquitoes sting. Shall we go back to the house?"

While we returned to the house, John, who had overheard the whole conversation, hastily disinterred the body of Chowder, and placed him in the same mysterious grave with Tom and the pig.

Moodie and his friend finished logging-up the eight acres which the former had cleared the previous winter; besides putting in a crop of peas and potatoes, and an acre of Indian corn, reserving the fallow for fall wheat, while we had the promise of a splendid crop of hay off the sixteen acres that had been cleared in 1834. We were all in high spirits, and everything promised fair, until a very trifling circumstance again occasioned us much anxiety and trouble, and was the cause of our losing most of our crop.

Moodie was asked to attend a bee, which was called to construct a corduroy-bridge over a very bad piece of road. He and J. E[vans] were obliged to go that morning with wheat to the mill, but Moodie lent his yoke of oxen for the work.

The driver selected for them at the bee was the brutal M——y, a savage Irishman, noted for his ill-treatment of cattle, especially if the animals did not belong to him. He gave one of the oxen such a severe blow over the loins with a handspike that the creature came home perfectly disabled, just as we wanted his services in the hay-field and harvest.

Moodie had no money to purchase, or even to hire a mate for the other ox; but he and John hoped that by careful attendance upon the injured animal he might be restored to health in a few days. They conveyed him to a deserted clearing, a short distance from the farm, where he would be safe from injury from the rest of the cattle; and early every morning we went in the canoe to carry poor Duke a warm mash, and to watch the progress of his recovery.

Ah! ye who revel in this world's wealth, how little can you realise the importance which we, in our poverty, attached to the life of this valuable animal! Yes, it even became the subject of prayer, for the bread for

7. George William Caddy, the fourth son of a neighbouring family in Douro, would marry Emilia Shairp's sister, Maryanne, in Peterborough on April 19, 1838.

ourselves and our little ones depended greatly upon his recovery. We were doomed to disappointment. After nursing him with the greatest attention and care for some weeks, the animal grew daily worse, and suffered such intense agony, as he lay groaning upon the ground, unable to rise, that John shot him to put him out of pain.

Here, then, were we left without oxen to draw in our hay, or secure our other crops. A neighbour, who had an odd ox, kindly lent us the use of him, when he was not employed on his own farm; and John and Moodie gave their own work for the occasional loan of a yoke of oxen for a day. But with all these drawbacks, and in spite of the assistance of old Jenny and myself in the field, a great deal of the produce was damaged before it could be secured. The whole summer we had to labour under this disadvantage. Our neighbours were all too busy to give us any help, and their own teams were employed in saving their crops. Fortunately, the few acres of wheat we had to reap were close to the barn, and we carried the sheaves thither by hand; old Jenny proving an invaluable help, both in the harvest and hay-field.

Still, with all these misfortunes, Providence watched over us in a signal manner. We were never left entirely without food. Like the widow's cruise of oil,[8] our means though small, were never suffered to cease entirely. We had been for some days without meat, when Moodie came running in for his gun. A great she-bear was in the wheat-field at the edge of the wood, very busily employed in helping to harvest the crop. There was but one bullet, and a charge or two of buck-shot, in the house; but Moodie started to the wood with the single bullet in his gun, followed by a little terrier dog that belonged to John E[vans]. Old Jenny was busy at the wash-tub, but the moment she saw her master running up the clearing, and knew the cause, she left her work, and, snatching up the carving-knife, ran after him, that in case the bear should have the best of the fight, she would be there to help "the masther." Finding her shoes incommode[d] her, she flung them off, in order to run faster. A few minutes after, came the report of the gun, and I heard Moodie halloo to E[vans], who was cutting stakes for a fence in the wood. I hardly thought it possible that he could have killed the bear, but I ran to the door to listen. The children were all excitement, which the sight of the black monster, borne down the clearing upon two poles, increased to the wildest demonstrations of joy. Moodie and John were carrying the prize, and old Jenny, brandishing her carving-knife, followed in the rear.

The rest of the evening was spent in skinning, and cutting up, and salting the ugly creature, whose flesh filled a barrel with excellent meat, in flavour resembling beef, while the short grain and juicy nature of the flesh gave to it the tenderness of mutton. This was quite a Godsend, and lasted us until we were able to kill two large fat hogs, in the fall.

A few nights after, Moodie and I encountered the mate of Mrs.

---

8. 2 Kings 4:1–7: Fearing that her sons would be sold into slavery, a widow is advised to take her pot of oil, borrow many empty vessels from her neighbours, and shut herself in a room. Miraculously, the oil from the single pot fills all the vessels, allowing her to pay her debts and save her sons.

Bruin, while returning from a visit to Emilia, in the depth of the wood. We had been invited to meet our friend's father and mother,[9] who had come up on a short visit to the woods; and the evening passed away so pleasantly that it was near midnight before the little party of friends separated. The moon was down. The wood, through which we had to return, was very dark; the ground being low and swampy, and the trees thick and tall. There was, in particular, one very ugly spot, where a small creek crossed the road. This creek could only be passed by foot-passengers scrambling over a fallen tree, which, in a dark night, was not very easy to find.

I begged a torch of Mr. [Shairp]; but no torch could be found. Emilia laughed at my fears; still, knowing what a coward I was in the bush of a night, she found up about an inch of candle, which was all that remained from the evening's entertainment. This she put into an old lanthorn.

"It will not last you long, but it will carry you over the creek."

This was something gained, and off we set.

It was so dark in the bush, that our dim candle looked like a solitary red spark in the intense surrounding darkness, and scarcely served to show us the path.

We went chatting along, talking over the news of the evening, Hector running on before us, when I saw a pair of eyes glare upon us from the edge of the swamp, with the green, bright light emitted by the eyes of a cat.

"Did you see those terrible eyes, Moodie?" and I clung, trembling, to his arm.

"What eyes?" said he, feigning ignorance. "It's too dark to see anything. The light is nearly gone, and, if you don't quicken your pace, and cross the tree before it goes out, you will, perhaps, get your feet wet by falling into the creek."

"Good Heavens! I saw them again; and do just look at the dog."

Hector stopped suddenly, and, stretching himself along the ground, his nose resting between his forepaws, began to whine and tremble. Presently he ran back to us, and crept under our feet. The cracking of branches, and the heavy tread of some large animal, sounded close beside us.

Moodie turned the open lanthorn in the direction from whence the sounds came, and shouted as loud as he could at the same time endeavouring to urge forward the fear-stricken dog, whose cowardice was only equalled by my own.

Just at that critical moment the wick of the candle flickered a moment in the socket, and expired. We were left, in perfect darkness, alone with the bear—for such we supposed the animal to be.

My heart beat audibly; a cold perspiration was streaming down my face, but I neither shrieked nor attempted to run. I don't know how Moodie got me over the creek. One of my feet slipped into the water,

9. Emilia Shairp's parents, Major Alexander Shairp and his wife, of Endsleigh Cottage in Peterborough. See Chapter Twenty, note 6, p. 242 and Chapter Seventeen, note 8, p. 218.

but, expecting, as I did every moment, to be devoured by master Bruin, that was a thing of no consequence. My husband was laughing at my fears, and every now and then he turned towards our companion, who continued following us at no great distance, and gave him an encouraging shout. Glad enough was I when I saw the gleam of the light from our little cabin window shine out among the trees; and, the moment I got within the clearing I ran, without stopping until I was safely within the house. John was sitting up for us, nursing Donald. He listened with great interest to our adventure with the bear, and thought that Bruin was very good to let us escape without one affectionate hug.

"Perhaps it would have been otherwise had he known, Moodie, that you had not only killed his good lady, but were dining sumptuously off her carcass every day."

The bear was determined to have something in return for the loss of his wife. Several nights after this, our slumbers were disturbed, about midnight, by an awful yell, and old Jenny shook violently at our chamber door.

"Masther, masther, dear!—Get up wid you this moment, or the bear will desthroy the cattle intirely."

Half asleep, Moodie sprang from his bed, seized his gun, and ran out. I threw my large cloak round me, struck a light, and followed him to the door. The moment the latter was unclosed, some calves that we were rearing rushed into the kitchen, closely followed by the larger beasts, who came bellowing headlong down the hill, pursued by the bear.

It was a laughable scene, as shown by that paltry tallow-candle. Moodie, in his night-shirt, taking aim at something in the darkness, surrounded by the terrified animals; old Jenny, with a large knife in her hand, holding on to the white skirts of her master's garment, making outcry loud enough to frighten away all the wild beasts in the bush—herself almost in a state of nudity.

"Och, maisther, dear! don't timpt the ill-conditioned crathur wid charging too near; think of the wife and the childher. Let me come at the rampaging baste, an' I'll stick the knife into the heart of him."

Moodie fired. The bear retreated up the clearing, with a low growl. Moodie and Jenny pursued him some way, but it was too dark to discern any object at a distance. I, for my part, stood at the open door, laughing until the tears ran down my cheeks, at the glaring eyes of the oxen, their ears erect, and their tails carried gracefully on a level with their backs, as they stared at me and the light, in blank astonishment. The noise of the gun had just roused John E[vans] from his slumbers. He was no less amused than myself, until he saw that a fine yearling heifer was bleeding, and found, upon examination, that the poor animal, having been in the claws of the bear, was dangerously, if not mortally hurt.

"I hope," he cried, "that the brute has not touched my foal!" I pointed to the black face of the filly peeping over the back of an elderly cow.

"You see, John, that Bruin preferred veal; there's your 'horsey,' as Dunbar calls her, safe, and laughing at you."

Moodie and Jenny now returned from the pursuit of the bear.

E[vans] fastened all the cattle into the back yard, close to the house. By daylight he and Moodie had started in chase of Bruin, whom they tracked by his blood some way into the bush; but here he entirely escaped their search.

THE BEARS OF CANADA.

Oh! *bear* me from this savage land of *bears*,
    For 'tis indeed *unbearable* to me;
I'd rather cope with vilest worldly cares,
    Or writhe with cruel sickness of the sea.
Oh! *bear* me to my own *bare* land of hills,[1]
    Where I'd be sure brave *bare*-legg'd lads to see—
Bear cakes, *bare* rocks, and whiskey stills,
    And *bare*-legg'd nymphs, to smile once more on me.

I'd *bear* the heat, I'd *bear* the freezing air
    Of equatorial realm or Arctic Sea,
I'd sit all *bare* at night, and watch the Northern *Bear*,
    And bless my soul that he was far from me.
I'd *bear* the poor-rates, tithes, and all the ills
    John Bull must *bear*, (who takes them all, poor sinner!
As patients do, when forced to gulp down pills,
    And water-gruel drink in lieu of dinner).

I'd *bear* the *bareness* of all barren lands
    Before I'd *bear* the *bearishness* of this;
Bare head, *bare* feet, *bare* legs, *bare* hands,
    Bear everything, but want of social bliss.
But should I die in this drear land of *bears*,
    Oh! ship me off, my friends, discharge the sable wearers,
For if you don't, in spite of priests and prayers,
    The *bears* will come, and eat up corpse and *bearers*.

J. W. D. M.

Twenty-three

The Outbreak

    Can a corrupted stream pour through the land
    Health-giving waters? Can the slave, who lures
    His wretched followers with the hope of gain,
    Feel in his bosom the immortal fire
    That bound a Wallace[1] to his country's cause,
    And bade the Thracian shepherd[2] cast away

1. The Orkney Isles. [*Author's note.*]
1. William Wallace (c. 1270–1305), the heroic defender of Scottish independence and an important heroic figure to Susanna Moodie.
2. Spartacus was "the Thracian shepherd" and another of Moodie's heroes; her first published book, *Spartacus* (1822), was aimed at a youthful British audience.

Rome's galling yoke; while the astonish'd world—
Rapt into admiration at the deed—
Paused, ere she crush'd, with overwhelming force,
The man who fought to win a glorious grave?[3]

The long-protracted harvest was at length brought to a close. Moodie
had procured another ox from Dummer, by giving a note at six months
date for the payment; and he and John E[vans] were in the middle of
sowing their fall crop of wheat, when the latter received a letter from
the old country, which conveyed to him intelligence of the death of his
mother, and of a legacy of two hundred pounds. It was necessary for
him to return to claim the property, and though we felt his loss severely, we could not, without great selfishness, urge him to stay. John
had formed an attachment to a young lady in the country, who, like
himself, possessed no property. Their engagement, which had existed
several years, had been dropped, from its utter hopelessness, by mutual consent. Still the young people continued to love each other, and
to look forward to better days, when their prospects might improve so
far that E[vans] would be able to purchase a bush-farm; and raise a
house, however lowly, to shelter his Mary.

He, like our friend Malcolm, had taken a fancy to buy a part of our
block of land, which he could cultivate in partnership with Moodie,
without being obliged to hire, when the same barn, cattle, and implements would serve for both. Anxious to free himself from the thraldom
of debts which pressed him sore, Moodie offered to part with two hundred acres at less than they cost us, and the bargain was to be considered as concluded directly the money was forthcoming.

It was a sorrowful day when our young friend left us; he had been a
constant inmate in the house for nine months, and not one unpleasant word had ever passed between us. He had rendered our sojourn in
the woods more tolerable by his society, and sweetened our bitter lot
by his friendship and sympathy. We both regarded him as a brother,
and parted with him with sincere regret. As to old Jenny, she lifted up
her voice and wept, consigning him to the care and protection of all
the saints in the Irish calendar.

For several days after John left us, a deep gloom pervaded the
house. Our daily toil was performed with less cheerfulness and
alacrity; we missed him at the evening board, and at the evening fire;
and the children asked each day, with increasing earnestness, when
dear E[vans] would return.

Moodie continued sowing his fall wheat. The task was nearly completed, and the chill October days were fast verging upon winter, when
towards the evening of one of them he contrived—I know not how—to
crawl down from the field at the head of the hill, faint and pale, and in
great pain. He had broken the small bone of his leg. In dragging among
the stumps, the heavy machine (which is made in the form of the let-

3. These lines are drawn from Susanna Moodie's poem "On Reading the Proclamation Delivered by William Lyon Mackenzie, on Navy Island," *The Palladium of British America*, 1:5
   (January 17, 1838).

ter V, and is supplied with large iron teeth) had hitched upon a stump, and being swung off again by the motion of the oxen, had come with great force against his leg. At first he was struck down, and for some time was unable to rise; but at length he contrived to unyoke the team, and crawled partly on his hands and knees down the clearing.

What a sad, melancholy evening that was! Fortune seemed never tired of playing us some ugly trick. The hope which had so long sustained me seemed about to desert me altogether; when I saw him on whom we all depended for subsistence, and whose kindly voice ever cheered us under the pressure of calamity, smitten down helpless, all my courage and faith in the goodness of the Divine Father seemed to forsake me, and I wept long and bitterly.

The next morning I went in search of a messenger to send to Peterborough for the doctor; but though I found and sent the messenger, the doctor never came. Perhaps he did not like to incur the expense of a fatiguing journey, with small chance of obtaining a sufficient remuneration.

Our dear sufferer contrived, with assistance, to bandage his leg; and after the first week of rest had expired, he amused himself with making a pair of crutches, and in manufacturing Indian paddles for the canoe, axe-handles, and yokes for the oxen. It was wonderful with what serenity he bore this unexpected affliction.

Buried in the obscurity of those woods, we knew nothing, heard nothing of the political state of the country, and were little aware of the revolution which was about to work a great change for us and for Canada.

The weather continued remarkably mild. The first great snow, which for years had ordinarily fallen between the 10th and 15th of November, still kept off. November passed on; and as all our firewood had to be chopped by old Jenny during the lameness of my husband, I was truly grateful to God for the continued mildness of the weather.

On the 4th of December—that great day of the outbreak—Moodie was determined to take advantage of the open state of the lake to carry a large grist up to Y[oung]'s mill. I urged upon him the danger of a man attempting to manage a canoe in rapid water, who was unable to stand without crutches; but Moodie saw that the children would need bread, and he was anxious to make the experiment.

Finding that I could not induce him to give up the journey, I determined to go with him. Old Wittals,[4] who happened to come down that morning, assisted in placing the bags of wheat in the little vessel, and help to place Moodie at the stern. With a sad, foreboding spirit, I assisted to push off from the shore.

The air was raw and cold, but our sail was not without its pleasure.

The lake was very full from the heavy rains, and the canoe bounded over the waves with a free, springy motion. A slight frost had hung every little bush and spray along the shores with sparkling crystals. The red pigeon-berries, shining through their coating of ice, looked

4. See Chapter Sixteen, note 9, p. 208.

like cornelian beads set in silver, and strung from bush to bush. We found the rapids at the entrance of Bessikakoon Lake very hard to stem, and were so often carried back by the force of the water that, cold as the air was, the great exertion which Moodie had to make use of to obtain the desired object brought the perspiration out in big drops upon his forehead. His long confinement to the house and low diet had rendered him very weak.

The old miller received us in the most hearty and hospitable manner; and complimented me upon my courage in venturing upon the water in such cold, rough weather. Norah was married, but the kind Betty provided us an excellent dinner, while we waited for the grist to be ground.

It was near four o'clock when we started on our return. If there had been danger in going up the stream, there was more in coming down. The wind had changed, the air was frosty, keen, and biting, and Moodie's paddle came up from every dip in to the water, loaded with ice. For my part, I had only to sit still at the bottom of the canoe, as we floated rapidly down with wind and tide. At the landing we were met by old Jenny, who had a long story to tell us, of which we could make neither head nor tail—how some gentleman had called during our absence, and left a large paper, all about the Queen and the Yankees; that there was war between Canada and the States; that Toronto had been burnt, and the governor killed, and I know not what other strange and monstrous statements. After much fatigue, Moodie climbed the hill, and we were once more safe by our own fireside. Here we found the elucidation of Jenny's marvellous tales: a copy of the Queen's proclamation,[5] calling upon all loyal gentlemen to join in putting down the unnatural rebellion.

A letter from my sister explained the nature of the outbreak, and the astonishment with which the news had been received by all the settlers in the bush. My brother and my sister's husband had already gone off to join some of the numerous bands of gentlemen who were collecting from all quarters to march to the aid of Toronto, which it was said was besieged by the rebel force. She advised me not to suffer Moodie to leave home in his present weak state; but the spirit of my husband was aroused, he instantly obeyed what he considered the imperative call of duty, and told me to prepare him a few necessaries, that he might be ready to start early in the morning.

Little sleep visited our eyes that night. We talked over the strange news for hours; our coming separation, and the probability that if things were as bad as they appeared to be, we might never meet again. Our affairs were in such a desperate condition that Moodie anticipated that any change must be for the better; it was impossible for them to be worse. But the poor, anxious wife thought only of a parting which to her put a finishing stroke to all her misfortunes.

5. The proclamation, in the name of Queen Victoria, was issued in Toronto by Sir Francis Bond Head, the Lieutenant Governor of Upper Canada, on December 7, 1837. It encouraged all citizens of Upper Canada to unite to suppress "this unnatural Rebellion." Susanna's dating is here slightly off.

Before the cold, snowy morning broke, we were all stirring. The children, who had learned that their father was preparing to leave them, were crying and clinging around his knees. His heart was too deeply affected to eat; the meal passed over in silence, and he rose to go. I put on my hat and shawl to accompany him through the wood as far as my sister Mrs. T[raill]'s. The day was like our destiny, cold, dark, and lowering. I gave the dear invalid his crutches, and we commenced our sorrowful walk. Then old Jenny's lamentations burst forth, as, flinging her arms round my husband's neck, she kissed and blessed him after the fashion of her country.

"Och hone! och hone!" she cried, wringing her hands, "masther dear, why will you lave the wife and the childher? The poor crathur is breakin' her heart intirely at partin' wid you. Shure an' the war is nothin' to you, that you must be goin' into danger; an' you wid a broken leg. Och hone! och hone! come back to your home—you will be kilt, and thin what will become of the wife and the wee bairns?"

Her cries and lamentations followed us into the wood. At my sister's, Moodie and I parted; and with a heavy heart I retraced my steps through the wood. For once, I forgot all my fears. I never felt the cold. Sad tears were flowing over my cheeks; when I entered the house, hope seemed to have deserted me, and for upwards of an hour I lay upon the bed and wept.

Poor Jenny did her best to comfort me, but all joy had vanished with him who was my light of life.

Left in the most absolute uncertainty as to the real state of public affairs, I could only conjecture what might be the result of this sudden outbreak. Several poor settlers called at the house during the day, on their way down to Peterborough; but they brought with them the most exaggerated accounts. There had been a battle, they said, with the rebels, and the loyalists had been defeated; Toronto was besieged by sixty thousand men, and all the men in the backwoods were ordered to march instantly to the relief of the city.

In the evening, I received a note from Emilia, who was at Peterborough, in which she informed me that my husband had borrowed a horse of Mr. S[hairp], and had joined a large party of two hundred volunteers, who had left that morning for Toronto; that there had been a battle with the insurgents; that Colonel Moodie had been killed,[6] and the rebels had retreated; and that she hoped my husband would return in a few days.

The honest backwoodsmen, perfectly ignorant of the abuses that had led to the present position of things,[7] regarded the rebels as a set of monsters, for whom no punishment was too severe, and obeyed the call to arms with enthusiasm. The leader of the insurgents must have been astonished at the rapidity with which a large force was collected,

---

6. Colonel Robert Moodie, a veteran of the War of 1812, was killed near Montgomery's Tavern on Yonge Street, north of Toronto, while trying to warn officials of the rebellious activity.
7. Susanna's comments here provide an apology of sorts for having been so overly sympathetic to Bond Head and so critical of the rebels in her Rebellion poems, three of which she includes in this chapter. William Lyon Mackenzie was the leader of the rebels.

as if by magic, to repel his designs. A great number of these volunteers were half-pay officers, many of whom had fought in the continental wars with the armies of Napoleon, and would have been found a host in themselves. I must own that my British spirit was fairly aroused, and as I could not aid in subduing the enemies of my beloved country with my arm, I did what little I could to serve the good cause with my pen. It may probably amuse my readers, to give them a few specimens of these loyal staves, which were widely circulated through the colony at the time.

AN ADDRESS TO THE FREEMEN OF CANADA.[8]

Canadians! will you join the band—
　　The factious band—who dare oppose
The regal power of that bless'd land
　　From whence your boasted freedom flows?
Brave children of a noble race,
　　Guard well the altar and the hearth;
And never by your deeds disgrace
　　The British sires who gave you birth.

What though your bones may never lie
　　Beneath dear Albion's hallow'd sod,
Spurn the base wretch who dare defy,
　　In arms, his country and his God!
Whose callous bosom cannot feel
　　That he who acts a traitor's part,
Remorselessly uplifts the steel
　　To plunge it in a parent's heart.

Canadians! will you see the flag,
　　Beneath whose folds your fathers bled,
Supplanted by the vilest rag[9]
　　That ever host to rapine led?
Thou emblem of a tyrant's sway,
　　Thy triple hues are dyed in gore;
Like his, thy power has pass'd away—
　　Like his, thy short-lived triumph's o'er.

Ay! let the trampled despot's fate
　　Forewarn the rash, misguided band
To sue for mercy ere too late,
　　Nor scatter ruin o'er the land.
The baffled traitor, doomed to bear
　　A people's hate, his colleagues' scorn,

8. This poem appeared in the *Palladium of British America* as "Canadians! Will You Join the Band. A Loyal Song," 1:1 (December 20, 1837). While in Toronto arranging for his military position as a captain in the Queen's Own Regiment, John Moodie placed this poem and others that followed it with Charles Fothergill, an old acquaintance and the editor of this new Toronto newspaper. It was reprinted in at least seven Canadian newspapers.
9. The tri-coloured flag assumed by the rebels. [*Author's note.*]

Defeated by his own despair,
  Will curse the hour that he was born!

By all the blood for Britain shed
  On many a glorious battle-field,
To the free winds her standard spread,
  Nor to these base insurgents yield.
With loyal bosoms beating high,
  In your good cause securely trust;
"God and Victoria!" be your cry,
  And crush the traitors to the dust.

This outpouring of a national enthusiasm, which I found it impossible to restrain, was followed by

THE OATH OF THE CANADIAN VOLUNTEERS.[1]

Huzza for England!—May she claim
  Our fond devotion ever;
And, by the glory of her name,
Our brave forefathers' honest fame,
  We swear—no foe shall sever
Her children from their parent's side;
  Though parted by the wave,
In weal or woe, what'er betide,
  We swear to die, or save
Her honour from the rebel band
Whose crimes pollute our injured land!

Let the foe come—we will not shrink
  To meet them if they dare;
Well must they fight, ere rashly think
To rend apart one sacred link
  That binds our country fair
To that dear isle, from whence we sprung,
  Which gave our fathers birth;
Whose glorious deeds her bards have sung;
  The unrivall'd of the earth,
The highest privilege we claim,
To own her sway—to bear her name.

Then, courage, loyal volunteers!
  God will defend the right;
That thought will banish slavish fears,
That blessed consciousness still cheers
  The soldier in the fight.
The stars for us shall never burn,
  The stripes may frighten slaves,

---

1. This poem may have appeared first in the *Palladium of British America* (no complete run is extant), but it definitely appeared in *The Literary Garland* (Montreal) 1:6 (May 1839), p. 281. It was reprinted thereafter in at least four Canadian newspapers.

> The Briton's eye will proudly turn
> Where Britain's standard waves.
> Beneath its folds, if Heaven requires,
> We'll die, as died of old our sires!

In a week, Moodie returned. So many volunteers had poured into Toronto that the number of friends was likely to prove as disastrous as that of enemies, on account of the want of supplies to maintain them all. The companies from the back townships had been remanded, and I received with delight my own again. But this re-union did not last long. Several regiments of militia were formed to defend the colony,[2] and to my husband was given the rank of captain in one of those then stationed in Toronto.

On the 20th of January, 1838, he bade us a long adieu. I was left with old Jenny and the children to take care of the farm. It was a sad, dull time. I could bear up against all trials with him to comfort and cheer me, but this long-continued absence cast a gloom upon my spirit not easily to be shaken off. Still his very appointment to this situation was a signal act of mercy. From his full pay, he was enabled to liquidate many pressing debts, and to send home from time to time sums of money to procure necessaries for me and the little ones. These remittances were greatly wanted; but I demurred before laying them out for comforts which we had been so long used to dispense with. It seemed almost criminal to purchase any article of luxury, such as tea and sugar, while a debt remained unpaid.

The [Jory]'s[3] were very pressing for the thirty pounds that we owed them for the clearing; but they had such a firm reliance upon the honour of my husband, that, poor and pressed for money as they were, they never sued us. I thought it would be a pleasing surprise to Moodie, if, with the sums of money which I occasionally received from him, I could diminish this debt, which had always given him the greatest uneasiness; and, my resolution once formed, I would not allow any temptation to shake it.

The money was always transmitted to Dummer. I only reserved the sum of two dollars a-month, to pay a little lad to chop wood for us. After a time, I began to think the [Jory]'s were gifted with second-sight; for I never received a money-letter but the very next day I was sure to see some of the family.

Just at this period I received a letter from a gentleman requesting me to write for a magazine (the *Literary Garland*),[4] just started in Montreal, with promise to remunerate me for my labours. Such an application was like a gleam of light springing up in the darkness; it seemed to promise the dawning of a brighter day. I had never been

---

2. John Moodie was granted a captaincy in the newly-formed Queen's Own Regiment, which trained in Toronto until early March 1838.
3. James and Stephen Jory of Dummer Township. See Chapter Twenty, note 2, p. 238.
4. Montreal publisher John Lovell had begun *The Literary Garland*, a monthly magazine, in December 1838. He made the magazine one of the finest in Canada for its time. Susanna Moodie was among his most prolific contributors as a poet and writer of serialized fiction. A number of the sketches included in *Roughing It in the Bush* first appeared in the *Literary Garland* in 1847.

able to turn my thoughts towards literature during my sojourn in the bush. When the body is fatigued with labour, unwonted and beyond its strength, the mind is in no condition for mental occupation.

The year before, I had been requested by an American author, of great merit, to contribute to the *North American Review*, published for several years in Philadelphia;[5] and he promised to remunerate me in proportion to the success of the work. I had contrived to write several articles after the children were asleep, though the expense even of the stationery and the postage of the manuscripts was severely felt by one so destitute of means; but the hope of being of the least service to those dear to me cheered me to the task. I never realised anything from that source; but I believe it was not the fault of the editor. Several other American editors had written to me to furnish them with articles; but I was unable to pay the postage of heavy packets to the States, and they could not reach their destination without being paid to the frontier. Thus, all chance of making anything in that way had been abandoned. I wrote to Mr. L[ovell], and frankly informed him how I was situated. In the most liberal manner he offered to pay the postage on all manuscripts to his office, and left me to name my own terms of remuneration. This opened up a new era in my existence; and for many years I have found in this generous man, to whom I am still personally unknown, a steady friend. I actually shed tears of joy over the first twenty-dollar bill I received from Montreal. It was my own; I had earned it with my own hand; and it seemed to my delighted fancy to form the nucleus out of which a future independence for my family might arise. I no longer retired to bed when the labours of the day were over. I sat up, and wrote by the light of a strange sort of candles, that Jenny called "sluts," and which the old woman manufactured out of pieces of old rags, twisted together and dipped in pork lard, and stuck in a bottle. They did not give a bad light, but it took a great many of them to last me for a few hours.

The faithful old creature regarded my writings with a jealous eye. "An', sure, it's killin' yerself that you are intirely. You were thin enough before you took to the pen; scribblin' an' scrabblin' when you should be in bed an' asleep. What good will it be to the childhren, dear heart! if you die afore your time, by wastin' your strength afther that fashion?"

Jenny never could conceive the use of books. "Shure; we can live and die widout them. It's only a waste of time botherin' your brains wid the like of them; but, thank goodness! the lard will soon be all done, an' thin we shall hear you spakin' again, instead of sittin' there doubled up all night, desthroying your eyes wid porin' over the dirthy writin'."

As the sugar-making season drew near, Jenny conceived the bold thought of making a good *lump* of sugar, that the "childher" might

---

5. Sumner Lincoln Fairfield was a poet who edited *The North American Quarterly Magazine*. He reviewed Moodie's book of poems, *Enthusiasm, and Other Poems* (1831), in the December 1834 issue of the magazine and in later issues published several of her poems and stories. See *Letters of a Lifetime*, pp. 75–76 and 92–94. The magazine folded in 1836.

have something to "ate" with their bread during the summer. We had no sugar-kettle, but a neighbour promised to lend us his, and to give us twenty-eight troughs, on condition that we gave him half the sugar we made. These terms were rather hard, but Jenny was so anxious to fulfil the darling object that we consented. Little Sol[6] and the old woman made some fifty troughs more, the trees were duly tapped, a shanty in the bush was erected of small logs and brush, and covered in at the top with straw; and the old woman and Solomon, the hired boy, commenced operations.

The very first day, a terrible accident happened to us; a large log fell upon the sugar-kettle—the borrowed sugar-kettle—and cracked it, spilling all the sap, and rendering the vessel, which had cost four dollars, useless. We were all in dismay. Just at that time Old Wittals happened to pass, on his way to Peterborough. He very good-naturedly offered to get the kettle repaired for us; which, he said, could be easily done by a rivet and an iron hoop. But where was the money to come from? I thought awhile. Katie had a magnificent coral and bells, the gift of her godfather;[7] I asked the dear child if she would give it to buy another kettle for Mr. T[raill].[8] She said, "I would give ten times as much to help mamma."

I wrote a little note to Emilia, who was still at her father's; and Mr. W——,[9] the storekeeper, sent us a fine sugar-kettle back by Wittals, and also the other mended, in exchange for the useless piece of finery. We had now two kettles at work, to the joy of Jenny, who declared that it was a lucky fairy who had broken the old kettle.

While Jenny was engaged in boiling and gathering the sap in the bush, I sugared off the syrup in the house; an operation watched by the children with intense interest. After standing all day over the hot stove-fire, it was quite a refreshment to breathe the pure air at night. Every evening I ran up to see Jenny in the bush, singing and boiling down the sap in the front of her little shanty. The old woman was in her element, and afraid of nothing under the stars; she slept beside her kettles at night, and snapped her fingers at the idea of the least danger. She was sometimes rather despotic in her treatment of her attendant, Sol. One morning, in particular, she bestowed upon the lad a severe cuffing.

I ran up the clearing to the rescue, when my ears were assailed by the "boo-hooing" of the boy.

"What has happened? Why do you beat the child, Jenny?"

"It's jist, thin, I that will bate him—the unlucky omadhawn! Has not he spilt and spiled two buckets of syrup, that I have been the live-long night bilin'. Sorra wid him; I'd like to strip the skin of him, I would! Musha! but 'tis enough to vex a saint."

---

6. Little Sol, one of the six children of Edward Sibbon (Old Wittals). Susanna paid him sixpence a day to chop and draw firewood for the family (see *Letters of Love and Duty*, p. 117).
7. Katie's godfather was James Bird, the Yoxford poet and close friend of many of the Strickland girls. His poem to Katie appeared in the Cobourg *Star* (September 19, 1832), p. 5.
8. Thomas Traill.
9. Mr. A. Warke kept a general store in Peterborough and advertised in the Cobourg *Star* (July 16, 1834), p. 2.

"Ah, Jenny!" blubbered the poor boy, "but you have no mercy. You forget that I have but one eye, and that I could not see the root which caught my foot and threw me down."

"Faix! An' 'tis a pity that you have the one eye, when you don't know how to make a better use of it," muttered the angry dame, as she picked up the pails, and pushing him on before her, beat a retreat into the bush.

I was heartily sick of the sugar-making, long before the season was over; however, we were well paid for our trouble. Besides one hundred and twelve pounds of fine soft sugar, as good as Muscovado, we had six gallons of molasses, and a keg containing six gallons of excellent vinegar.

Fifty pounds went to Mr. T[raill], for the use of his kettle; and the rest (with the exception of a cake for Emilia, which I had drained in a wet flannel bag until it was almost as white as loaf sugar), we kept for our own use. There was no lack, this year, of nice preserves and pickled cucumbers, dainties found in every native Canadian establishment.

Besides gaining a little money with my pen, I practised a method of painting birds and butterflies upon the white velvety surface of the large fungi that grow plentifully upon the bark of the sugar-maple. These had an attractive appearance; and my brother, who was a captain in one of the provisional regiments,[1] sold a great many of them among the officers, without saying by whom they were painted. One rich lady in Peterborough, long since dead, ordered two dozen to send as curiosities to England. These, at one shilling each, enabled me to buy shoes for the children, who, during our bad times, had been forced to dispense with these necessary coverings. How often, during the winter season, have I wept over their little chapped feet, literally washing them with my tears! But these days were to end; Providence was doing great things for us; and Hope raised at last her drooping head to regard with a brighter glance the far-off future.

Slowly the winter rolled away; but he to whom every thought turned was still distant from his humble home. The receipt of an occasional letter from him was my only solace during his long absence, and we were still too poor to indulge often in this luxury. My poor Katie was as anxious as her mother to hear from her father; and when I did get the long-looked-for prize, she would kneel down before me, her little elbows resting on my knees, her head thrown back, and the tears trickling down her innocent cheeks, eagerly drinking in every word.

The spring brought us plenty of work; we had potatoes and corn to plant, and the garden to cultivate. By lending my oxen for two days' work, I got Wittals, who had no oxen, to drag me in a few acres of oats, and to prepare the land for potatoes and corn. The former I dropped into the earth, while Jenny covered them up with the hoe.

Our garden was well dug and plentifully manured, the old woman

<hr>

1. Sam Strickland was Lieutenant in the Second Northumberland Provisional Battalion then training in Peterborough for post-Rebellion duty.

bringing the manure, which had lain for several years at the barn door, down to the plot, in a large Indian basket placed upon a hand-sleigh. We had soon every sort of vegetable sown, with plenty of melons and cucumbers, and all our beds promised a good return. There were large flights of ducks upon the lake every night and morning; but though we had guns, we did not know how to use them. However, I thought of a plan, which I flattered myself might prove successful; I got Sol to plant two stakes in the shallow water, near the rice beds, and to these I attached a slender rope made by braiding long strips of the inner bark of the basswood together; to these again I fastened, at regular intervals, about a quarter of a yard of whipcord, headed by a strong perch-hook. These hooks I baited with fish offal, leaving them to float just under the water. Early next morning, I saw a fine black duck fluttering upon the line. The boy ran down with the paddles, but before he could reach the spot, the captive got away by carrying the hook and line with him. At the next stake he found upon the hooks a large eel and a catfish.

I had never before seen one of those whiskered, toad-like natives of the Canadian waters (so common to the Bay of Quinté, where they grow to a great size), that I was really terrified at the sight of the hideous beast, and told Sol to throw it away. In this I was very foolish, for they are esteemed good eating in many parts of Canada; but to me, the sight of the reptile-like thing is enough—it is uglier, and far more disgusting-looking than a toad.

When the trees came into leaf, and the meadows were green, and flushed with flowers, the poor children used to talk constantly to me of their father's return; their innocent prattle made me very sad. Every evening we walked into the wood, along the path that he must come whenever he did return home, to meet him; and though it was a vain hope, and the walk was taken just to amuse the little ones, I used to be silly enough to feel deeply disappointed when we returned alone. Donald, who was a mere baby when his father left us, could just begin to put words together. "Who is papa?" "When will he come?" "Will he come by the road?" "Will he come in a canoe?" The little creature's curiosity to see this unknown father was really amusing; and oh! how I longed to present the little fellow, with his rosy cheeks and curling hair, to his father; he was so fair; so altogether charming in my eyes. Emilia had called him Cedric the Saxon; and he well suited the name, with his frank, honest disposition, and large, loving blue eyes.

June had commenced; the weather was very warm, and Mr. T[raill] had sent for the loan of old Jenny to help him for a day with his potatoes. I had just prepared dinner when the old woman came shrieking like a mad thing down the clearing, and waving her hands towards me. I could not imagine what had happened.

"Ninny's mad!" whispered Dunbar; "she's the old girl for making a noise."

"Joy! joy!" bawled out the old woman, now running breathlessly towards us. "The masther's come—the masther's come!"

"Where?—where?"

"Jist above in the wood. Goodness gracious! I have run to let you know—so fast—that my heart—is like to—break."

Without stopping to comfort poor Jenny, off started the children and myself, at the very top of our speed; but I soon found that I could not run—I was too much agitated. I got to the head of the bush, and sat down upon a fallen tree. The children sprang forward like wild kids, all but Donald, who remained with his old nurse. I covered my face with my hands; my heart, too, was beating audibly; and now that he was come, and was so near me, I scarcely could command strength to meet him. The sound of happy young voices roused me up; the children were leading him along in triumph; and he was bending down to them, all smiles, but hot and tired with his long journey. It was almost worth our separation, that blissful meeting. In a few minutes he was at home, and the children upon his knees. Katie stood silently holding his hand, but Addie and Dunbar had a thousand things to tell him. Donald was frightened at his military dress, but he peeped at him from behind my gown, until I caught and placed him in his father's arms.

His leave of absence only extended to a fortnight. It had taken him three days to come all the way from Lake Erie,[2] where his regiment was stationed, at Point Abino; and the same time would be consumed in his return. He could only remain with us eight days. How soon they fled away! How bitter was the thought of parting with him again! He had brought money to pay the [Jory]'s. How surprised he was to find their large debt more than half liquidated. How gently did he chide me for depriving myself and the children of the little comforts he had designed for us, in order to make this sacrifice. But never was self-denial more fully rewarded; I felt happy in having contributed in the least to pay a just debt to kind and worthy people. You must become poor yourself before you can fully appreciate the good qualities of the poor—before you can sympathise with them, and fully recognise them as your brethren in the flesh. Their benevolence to each other, exercised amidst want and privation, as far surpasses the munificence of the rich towards them, as the exalted philanthropy of Christ and his disciples does the Christianity of the present day. The rich man gives from his abundance; the poor man shares with a distressed comrade his all.

One short, happy week too soon fled away, and we were once more alone. In the fall, my husband expected the regiment in which he held his commission would be reduced, which would again plunge us into the same distressing poverty. Often of a night I revolved these things in my mind, and perplexed myself with conjectures as to what in future was to become of us. Although he had saved all he could from his pay, it was impossible to pay several hundreds of pounds of debt; and the steam-boat stock still continued a dead letter. To remain much longer in the wood was impossible, for the returns from the farm

2. John Moodie had been posted in the Niagara area, mostly on the north shore of Lake Erie, keeping a close eye on Buffalo.

scarcely fed us; and but for the clothing sent us by friends from home, who were not aware of our real difficulties, we should have been badly off indeed.

I pondered over every plan that thought could devise; at last, I prayed to the Almighty to direct me as to what would be the best course for us to pursue. A sweet assurance stole over me, and soothed my spirit, that God would provide for us, as He had hitherto done— that a great deal of our distress arose from want of faith. I was just sinking into a calm sleep when the thought seemed whispered into my soul, "Write to the Governor;[3] tell him candidly all you have suffered during your sojourn in this country; and trust to God for the rest."

At first I paid little heed to this suggestion; but it became so importunate that at last I determined to act upon it as if it were a message sent from heaven. I rose from my bed, struck a light, sat down, and wrote a letter to the Lieutenant-Governor, Sir George Arthur, a simple statement of facts, leaving it to his benevolence to pardon the liberty I had taken in addressing him.

I asked of him to continue my husband in the militia service, in the same regiment in which he now held the rank of captain, which, by enabling him to pay our debts, would rescue us from our present misery. Of the political character of Sir George Arthur I knew nothing. I addressed him as a man and a Christian; and I acknowledge, with the deepest and most heartfelt gratitude, the generous kindness of his conduct towards us.

Before the day dawned, my letter was ready for the post. The first secret I ever had from my husband was the writing of that letter; and, proud and sensitive as he was, and averse to asking the least favour of the great, I was dreadfully afraid that the act I had just done would be displeasing to him; still, I felt resolutely determined to send it. After giving the children their breakfast, I walked down and read it to my brother-in-law, who was not only much pleased with its contents, but took it down himself to the post-office.

Shortly after, I received a letter from my husband, informing me that the regiment had been reduced, and that he should be home in time to get in the harvest. Most anxiously I awaited a reply to my application to the Governor; but no reply came.

The first week in August our dear Moodie came home, and brought with him, to our no small joy, J. E[vans], who had just returned from Ireland. E[vans] had been disappointed about the money, which was subject to litigation; and, tired of waiting at home until the tedious process of the law should terminate, he had come back to the woods, and, before night, was reinstated in his old quarters.

3. Susanna wrote to Sir George Arthur, the new Lieutenant Governor of Upper Canada, in June 1838. The letter has not been found among Arthur's papers. However, a second letter she sent to Arthur, dated December 18, 1838, has been located in the Upper Canada Sundries files, National Library of Canada. In the letter, Susanna thanks Arthur for his kindness to her husband in appointing him as Paymaster to the Victoria District, in effect offering him a second military appointment. It is also clear from Arthur's papers that he was impressed by Susanna's loyal Rebellion poems, which he had read in *The Palladium* and other papers.

His presence made Jenny all alive; she dared him at once to a trial of skill with her in the wheat-field, which E[vans] prudently declined. He did not expect to stay longer in Canada than the fall, but, whilst he did stay, he was to consider our house his home.

That harvest was the happiest we ever spent in the bush. We had enough of the common necessaries of life. A spirit of peace and harmony pervaded our little dwelling, for the most affectionate attachment existed among its members. We were not troubled with servants, for the good old Jenny we regarded as an humble friend, and were freed, by that circumstance, from many of the cares and vexations of a bush life. Our evening excursions on the lake were doubly enjoyed after the labours of the day, and night brought us calm and healthful repose.

The political struggles that convulsed the country were scarcely echoed in the depths of those old primeval forests, though the expulsion of Mackenzie from Navy Island, and the burning of the Caroline by Captain Drew,[4] had been discussed on the farthest borders of civilisation. With a tribute to the gallant conduct of that brave officer, I will close this chapter:—

THE BURNING OF THE CAROLINE.[5]

A sound is on the midnight deep—
    The voice of waters vast;
And onward, with resistless sweep,
    The torrent rushes past—
In frantic chase, wave after wave,
The crowding surges press, and rave
    Their mingled might to cast
Adown Niagara's giant steep;
The fretted billows foaming leap
    With wild tumultuous roar;
The clashing din ascends on high,
In deaf'ning thunders to the sky,
    And shakes the rocky shore.

Hark! what strange sounds arise—
'Tis not stern Nature's voice—
    In mingled chorus to the skies!
The waters in their depth rejoice.
    Hark! on the midnight air
    A frantic cry uprose;

---

4. William Lyon Mackenzie had fled Toronto in the wake of the failed Rebellion, setting up camp on Navy Island in the Niagara River above Niagara Falls. There he regrouped and made plans for an invasion into Canada. A crucial event in countering his plans was the destruction of his supply ship, the *Caroline*, in an attack led by Captain Andrew Drew. Spectacularly, the damaged ship went over the falls. Continuing bombardment of Navy Island by British troops and Canadian militia led Mackenzie to escape into Upper New York state rather than face arrest and possible death.

5. Susanna's poem was written for *The Palladium of British America* and was published there sometime in October 1838. It also appeared in *The Literary Garland* 3:4 (March 1841), p. 176.

The yell of fierce despair,
　　The shout of mortal foes;
And mark yon sudden glare,
　　Whose red, portentous gleam
　　Flashes on rock and stream
With strange, unearthly light;
　　What passing meteor's beam
Lays bare the brow of night?

From yonder murky shore
　　What demon vessel glides,
　　Stemming the unstemm'd tides,
Where maddening breakers roar
　　In hostile surges round her path,
Or hiss, recoiling from her prow,
　　That reeling, staggers to their wrath;
While distant shores return the glow
　　That brightens from her burning frame,
And all above—around—below—
　　Is wrapt in ruddy flame?

Sail on!—sail on!—No mortal hand
　　Directs that vessel's blazing course;
The vengeance of an injured land
　　Impels her with resistless force
'Midst breaking wave and fiery gleam,
　　O'er-canopied with clouds of smoke;
Midway she stems the raging stream,
　　And feels the rapids' thundering stroke;
Now buried deep, now whirl'd on high,
　　She struggles with her awful doom,—
With frantic speed now hurries by
　　To find a watery tomb.

Lo, poised upon the topmost surge,
　　She shudders o'er the dark abyss;
The foaming waters round her hiss
　　And hoarse waves ring her funeral dirge;
The chafing billows round her close;
　　But ere her burning planks are riven,
Shoots up one ruddy spout of fire,—
　　Her last farewell to earth and heaven.
Down, down to endless night she goes!
　　So may the traitor's hope expire,
So perish all our country's foes!

Destruction's blazing star
　　Has vanish'd from our sight;
The thunderbolt of war
　　Is quench'd in endless night;
Nor sight, nor sound of fear

Startles the listening ear;
   Naught but the torrent's roar,
The dull, deep, heavy sound,
From out the dark profound,
   Echoes from shore to shore.
Where late the cry of blood
   Rang on the midnight air,
The mournful lapsing of the flood,
The wild winds in the lonely wood,
   Claim sole dominion there.

To thee, high-hearted Drew!
   And thy victorious band
Of heroes tried and true
A nation's thanks are due.
   Defender of an injured land!
Well hast thou taught the dastard foe
   That British honour never yields
To democratic influence, low,
   The glory of a thousand fields.

Justice to traitors, long delay'd,
   This night was boldly dealt by thee;
The debt of vengeance thou hast paid,
   And may the deed immortal be.
Thy outraged country shall bestow
   A lasting monument of fame,
The highest meed of praise below—
   A British patriot's deathless name!

Twenty-four

The Whirlwind[1]

Dark, heavy clouds were gathering in the west,
   Wrapping the forest in funereal gloom;
Onward they roll'd, and rear'd each livid crest,
   Like Death's murk shadows frowning o'er earth's tomb.
From out the inky womb of that deep night
   Burst livid flashes of electric flame.
Whirling and circling with terrific might,
   In wild confusion on the tempest came.
Nature, awakening from her still repose,
   Shudders responsive to the whirlwind's shock,
Feels at her mighty heart convulsive throes;
   Her groaning forests to earth's centre rock.

---

1. For the poem that heads this chapter, I am indebted to my brother, Mr. Strickland, of Douro, C. W. [*Author's note*.] Sam Strickland supplied the poem and eight paragraphs of description for this chapter. Upper Canada became Canada West (C.W.) in 1841.

But hark!—What means that hollow, rushing sound,
  That breaks the death-like stillness of the morn?
Red forked lightnings fiercely glare around,
  Sharp, crashing thunders on the winds are borne,
And see you spiral column, black as night,
  Rearing triumphantly its wreathing form;
Ruin's abroad, and through the murky light,—
  Drear desolation marks the spirit of the storm.

S. S.

The 19th of August came, and our little harvest was all safely housed.[2]
Business called Moodie away for a few days to Cobourg. Jenny had
gone to Dummer, to visit her friends, and J. E[vans] had taken a grist
of the new wheat, which he and Moodie had threshed the day before,
to the mill. I was consequently left alone with the children, and had a
double portion of work to do. During their absence it was my lot to
witness the most awful storm I ever beheld, and a vivid recollection of
its terrors was permanently fixed upon my memory.

The weather had been intensely hot during the three preceding
days, although the sun was entirely obscured by a blueish haze, which
seemed to render the unusual heat of the atmosphere more oppressive. Not a breath of air stirred the vast forest, and the waters of the
lake assumed a leaden hue. After passing a sleepless night, I arose, a
little after day-break, to superintend my domestic affairs. E[vans] took
his breakfast, and went off to the mill, hoping that the rain would
keep off until after his return.

"It is no joke," he said, "being upon these lakes in a small canoe,
heavily laden, in a storm."

Before the sun rose, the heavens were covered with hard-looking
clouds, of a deep blue and black cast, fading away to white at their
edges, and in form resembling the long, rolling waves of a heavy sea—
but with this difference, that the clouds were perfectly motionless,
piled in long curved lines, one above the other, and so remained until
four o'clock in the afternoon. The appearance of these clouds, as the
sun rose above the horizon, was the most splendid that can be imagined, tinged up to the zenith with every shade of saffron, gold, rose-
colour, scarlet, and crimson, fading away into the deepest violet.
Never did the storm-fiend shake in the face of day a more gorgeous
banner; and, pressed as I was for time, I stood gazing like one en-
tranced upon the magnificent pageant.

As the day advanced, the same blue haze obscured the sun, which
frowned redly through his misty veil. At ten o'clock the heat was suffocating, and I extinguished the fire in the cooking-stove, determined to
make our meals upon bread and milk, rather than add to the oppressive heat. The thermometer in the shade ranged from ninety-six to
ninety-eight degrees, and I gave over my work and retired with the little ones to the coolest part of the house. The young creatures

---

2. The storm, or "hurricane," or tornado, occurred on August 19, 1837.

stretched themselves upon the floor, unable to jump about or play; the dog lay panting in the shade; the fowls half-buried themselves in the dust, with open beaks and outstretched wings. All nature seemed to droop beneath the scorching heat.

Unfortunately for me, a gentleman arrived about one o'clock from Kingston, to transact some business with my husband. He had not tasted food since six o'clock, and I was obliged to kindle the fire to prepare his dinner. It was one of the hardest tasks I ever performed; I almost fainted with the heat, and most inhospitably rejoiced when his dinner was over, and I saw him depart. Shortly after, my friend Mrs. C[addy] and her brother called in, on their way from Peterborough.[3]

"How do you bear the heat?" asked Mrs. C[addy]. "This is one of the hottest days I ever remember to have experienced in this part of the province. I am afraid that it will end in a hurricane, or what the Lower Canadians term 'L'Orage.' "

About four o'clock they rose to go. I urged them to stay longer. "No," said Mrs. C[addy], "the sooner we get home the better. I think we can reach it before the storm breaks."

I took Donald in my arms, and my eldest boy by the hand, and walked with them to the brow of the hill, thinking that the air would be cooler in the shade. In this I was mistaken. The clouds over our heads hung so low, and the heat was so great, that I was soon glad to retrace my steps.

The moment I turned round to face the lake, I was surprised at the change that had taken place in the appearance of the heavens. The clouds, that had before lain so motionless, were now in rapid motion, hurrying and chasing each other round the horizon. It was a strangely awful sight. Before I felt a breath of the mighty blast that had already burst on the other side of the lake, branches of trees, leaves, and clouds of dust were whirled across the lake, whose waters rose in long sharp furrows, fringed with foam, as if moved in their depths by some unseen but powerful agent.

Panting with terror, I just reached the door of the house as the hurricane swept up the hill, crushing and overturning everything in its course. Spell-bound, I stood at the open door, with clasped hands, unable to speak, rendered dumb and motionless by the terrible grandeur of the scene; while little Donald, who could not utter many intelligible words, crept to my feet, appealing to me for protection, and his rosy cheeks paled even to marble whiteness. The hurrying clouds gave to the heavens the appearance of a pointed dome, round which the lightning played in broad ribbons of fire. The roaring of the thunder, the rushing of the blast, the impetuous down-pouring of the rain, and the crash of falling trees were perfectly deafening; and in the midst of this

3. Hannah Godard Caddy, the wife of Colonel Caddy, and her brother John Godard. The Caddys were the Moodies' nearest neighbours to the northeast and had lived previously in Quebec City. The widowed Godard and his three sons also lived nearby. Susanna spoke sadly of "poor old Godard," who lost his position in the Commisariat but was rescued from financial difficulties by his son, who had success in the timber trade. Another of his sons, Cyprian Godard, did some work for the Moodies and was welcome in their home (*Letters of Love and Duty*, p. 125).

uproar of the elements, old Jenny burst in, drenched with wet, and half-dead with fear.

"The Lord preserve us!" she cried, "this surely is the day of judgment. Fifty trees fell across my very path, between this an' the creek. Mrs. C[addy] just reached her brother's clearing a few minutes before a great oak fell on her very path. What thunther!—what lightning! Misthress, dear!—it's turn'd so dark, I can only jist see yer face."

Glad enough was I of her presence, for to be alone in the heat of the great forest, in a log hut, on such a night, was not a pleasing prospect. People gain courage by companionship, and in order to re-assure each other, struggle to conceal their fears.

"And where is Mr. E[vans]?"

"I hope not on the lake. He went early this morning to get the wheat ground at the mill."

"Och, the crathur! He's surely drowned. What boat could stan' such a scrimmage as this?"

I had my fears for poor John; but as the chance that he had to wait at the mill till others were served was more than probable, I tried to still my apprehensions for his safety.

The storm soon passed over, after having levelled several acres of wood near the house, and smitten down in its progress two gigantic pines in the clearing, which must have withstood the force of a thousand winters. Talking over the effects of this whirlwind with my brother, he kindly sent me the following very graphic description of a whirlwind which passed through the town of Guelph in the summer of 1829.[4]

"In my hunting excursions and rambles through the Upper Canadian forests, I had frequently met with extensive wind-falls; and observed with some surprise that the fallen trees lay strewn in a succession of circles, and evidently appeared to have been twisted off the stumps. I also remarked that these wind-falls were generally narrow, and had the appearance of a road slashed through the forest. From observations made at the time, and since confirmed, I have no doubt that Colonel Reid's theory of storms is a correct one, viz., that all wind-storms move in a circular direction, and the nearer the centre the more violent the force of the wind.[5] Having seen the effects of several similar hurricanes since my residence in Canada West, I shall proceed to describe one which happened in the township of Guelph during the early part of the summer of 1829.

"The weather, for the season of the year (May), had been hot and sultry, with scarcely a breath of wind stirring. I had heard distant

---

4. Written by Mr. Strickland, of Douro. [*Author's note.*] In the late 1820s, Sam Strickland had worked for John Galt's Canada Company helping to lay out the town sites for both Guelph and Goderich, the chief towns in what was called "the Huron [Lake Huron] Tract." See *Twenty-Seven Years in Canada West*. Susanna defers here to her brother's wider experience of summers in Upper Canada.
5. Lieutenant-Colonel William Reid of the Royal Engineers published a paper in 1838 entitled *An Attempt to Develop the Law of Storms*. It was often reprinted. Reid was particularly attentive to the fact that storms are most violent at their centers.

thunder from an early hour in the morning, which, from the eastward, is rather an unusual occurrence. About 10 A.M., the sky had a most singular, and I must add a most awful appearance, presenting to the view a vast arch of rolling blackness, which seemed to gather strength and density as it approached the zenith. All at once the clouds began to work round in circles, as if chasing one another through the air. Suddenly the dark arch of clouds appeared to break up into detached masses, whirling and mixing through each other in dreadful commotion. The forked lightning was incessant, accompanied by heavy thunder. In a short time, the clouds seemed to converge to a point, which approached very near the earth, still whirling with great rapidity directly under this point; and apparently from the midst of the woods arose a black column, in the shape of a cone, which instantly joined itself to the depending cloud. The sight was now grand, and awful in the extreme. Picture to your imagination a vast column of smoke, of inky blackness, reaching from earth to heaven, gyrating with fearful velocity—bright lightnings issuing from the vortex; the roar of thunder—the rushing of the blast—the crash of timber—the limbs of trees, leaves, and rubbish, mingled with clouds of dust, whirling through the air,—you then have a faint idea of the scene.

"I had ample time for observation, as the hurricane commenced its devastating course about two miles from the town, through the centre of which it took its way, passing within fifty yards of where a number of persons, myself among the rest, were standing, watching its fearful progress.

"As the tornado approached, the trees seemed to fall like a pack of cards before its irresistible current. After passing through the clearing made around the village, the force of the wind gradually abated, and in a few minutes died away entirely.

"As soon as the storm was over, I went to see the damage it had done. From the point where I first observed the black column to rise from the woods and join the cloud, the trees were twisted in every direction. A belt of timber had been levelled to the ground about two miles in length, and about one hundred yards in breadth. At the entrance of the town it crossed the river Speed, and uprooted about six acres of wood, which had been thinned out, and left by Mr. Galt (late superintendent of the Canada Company),[6] as an ornament to his house.

"The Eremosa road was completely blocked up for nearly half-a-mile, in the wildest confusion possible. In its progress through the town the storm unroofed several houses, levelled many fences to the ground, and entirely demolished a frame barn. Windows were dashed in; and, in one instance, the floor of a log house was carried through the roof. Some hair-breadth escapes occurred; but, luckily, no lives were lost.

"About twelve years since a similar storm occurred in the north part

6. John Galt (1779–1839) was both a well-known Scottish author and superintendent of the Canada Company. He lived near Guelph until 1829.

of the township of Douro, but was of much less magnitude. I heard an intelligent settler, who resided some years in the township of Madoc, state that, during his residence in that township, a similar hurricane to the one I have described, though of a much more awful character, passed through a part of Marmora and Madoc, and had been traced, in a north-easterly direction, upwards of forty miles into the unsurveyed lands; the uniform width of which appeared to be three quarters of a mile.

"It is very evident, from the traces which they have left behind them, that storms of this description have not been unfrequent in the wooded districts of Canada; and it becomes a matter of interesting consideration whether the clearing of our immense forests will not, in a great measure, remove the cause of these phenomena."

A few minutes after our household had retired to rest, my first sleep was broken by the voice of J. E[vans], speaking to old Jenny in the kitchen. He had been overtaken by the storm, but had run his canoe ashore upon an island before its full fury burst, and turned it over the flour; while he had to brave the terrors of the pitiless tempest— buffeted by the wind, and drenched with torrents of rain. I got up and made him a cup of tea, while Jenny prepared a rasher of bacon and eggs for his supper.

Shortly after this, J. E[vans] bade a final adieu to Canada, with his cousin C. W——. He volunteered into the Scotch Greys, and we never saw him more; but I have been told that he was so highly respected by the officers of the regiment that they subscribed for his commission; that he rose to the rank of lieutenant; accompanied the regiment to India, and was at the taking of Cabul;[7] but from himself we never heard again.

The 16th of October, my third son was born; and a few days after, my husband was appointed pay-master to the militia regiments in the V[ictoria] District, with the rank and full pay of captain.[8]

This was Sir George Arthur's doing. He returned no answer to my application, but he did not forget us.

As the time that Moodie might retain this situation was very doubtful, he thought it advisable not to remove me and the family until he could secure some permanent situation; by so doing, he would have a better opportunity of saving the greater part of his income to pay off his old debts.

This winter of 1839 was one of severe trial to me. Hitherto I had enjoyed the blessing of health; but both the children and myself were now doomed to suffer from dangerous attacks of illness. All the little things had malignant scarlet fever, and for several days I thought it would please the Almighty to take from me my two girls. This fever is

7. During the first Anglo-Afghan War (1839–42), a British army entered Kabul in 1839.
8. John Moodie was appointed "paymaster to the Militia force stationed at Presque Isle, the Trent, Belleville, Bath, & Amherst Island" on December 21, 1838. The general area was called the Victoria District, with its center at the town of Belleville, where the officers were stationed.

so fatal to children in Canada that none of my neighbours dared approach the house. For three weeks Jenny and I were never undressed; our whole time was taken up in nursing the five little helpless creatures through the successive stages of their alarming disease. I sent for Dr. Taylor;[9] but he did not come, and I was obliged to trust to the mercy of God, and my own judgment and good nursing. Though I escaped the fever, mental anxiety and fatigue brought on other illness, which for nearly ten weeks rendered me perfectly helpless. When I was again able to creep from my sick bed, the baby was seized with an illness, which Dr. B[ird] pronounced mortal.[1] Against all hope, he recovered, but these severe mental trials rendered me weak and nervous, and more anxious than ever to be re-united to my husband. To add to these troubles, my sister and her husband sold their farm, and removed from our neighbourhood.[2] Mr. S[hairp] had returned to England, and had obtained a situation in the customs; and his wife, my friend Emilia, was keeping a school in the village; so that I felt more solitary than ever, thus deprived of so many kind, sympathising friends.

A SONG OF PRAISE TO THE CREATOR.

Oh, thou great God! from whose eternal throne
    Unbounded blessings in rich bounty flow,
Like thy bright sun in glorious state alone,
    Thou reign'st supreme, while round thee as they go,
Unnumber'd worlds, submissive to thy sway,
With solemn pace pursue their silent way.

Benignant God! o'er every smiling land,
    Thy handmaid, Nature, meekly walks abroad,
Scattering thy bounties with unsparing hand,
    While flowers and fruits spring up along her road.
How can thy creatures their weak voices raise
To tell thy deeds in their faint songs of praise?

9. Dr. Taylor of Peterborough was for a time a partner of Dr. John Hutchison. Neither doctor was particularly keen to answer calls so far north of the town, especially for those who did not subscribe to their services. Moreover, in times of illness and epidemic, such travels were less important than immediate needs closer to home. Dr. Hutchison made one visit to the Moodies' cabin in December 1837 to treat Susanna for a dangerous case of mastitis. During the first half of 1838, Taylor was attached to the Queen's Own Regiment, in which John Moodie served as captain.

1. Doctor George Gwynne Bird was an English doctor who in 1833 came to Peterborough, where he tried farming and set up a pharmacy. In a letter to John on March 6, 1839, Susanna wrote that after she had tried twice to get Dr. Hutchison to visit her dangerously ill children, her messenger, Cyprian Godard, managed to persuade Dr. Bird to come up "inspite of the bad roads and the dreadful night. Good old dear how kind he was—He told me, that without medical aid the child must have died. That he was still in great danger, though the remidies [sic] we had applied had prolonged his life—'I am an old man,' he said[, ']to come thus far, through such weather, but I did it to serve Mr. Moodie, when I heard Hutchison would not come, I was determined that the child should not be lost if I could save it.' " See *Letters of Love and Duty*, p. 131.

2. The Traills had been advertising their farm for several years. They sold it in March 1839 for 200 pounds and moved to Ashburnham, or East Peterborough. Emilia Shairp had moved to Peterborough, where she started a school.

When, darkling o'er the mountain's summit hoar,
    Portentous hangs the black and sulph'rous cloud,
When lightnings flash, and awful thunders roar,
    Great Nature sings to thee her anthem loud.
The rocks reverberate her mighty song,
And crashing woods the pealing notes prolong.

The storm is pass'd; o'er fields and woodlands gay,
    Gemm'd with bright dew-drops from the eastern sky,
The morning sun now darts his golden ray,
    The lark on fluttering wing is poised on high;
Too pure for earth, he wings his way above,
To pour his grateful song of joy and love.

Hark! from the bowels of the earth, a sound
    Of awful import! From the central deep
The struggling lava rends the heaving ground,
    The ocean-surges roar—the mountains leap—
They shoot aloft.—Oh, God! the fiery tide
Has burst its bounds, and rolls down Etna's side.

Thy will is done, great God! the conflict's o'er,
    The silver moonbeams glance along the sea;
The whispering waves half ripple on the shore,
    And lull'd creation breathes a prayer to thee!
The night-flower's incense to their God is given,
And grateful mortals raise their thoughts to heaven.

J. W. D. M.

Twenty-five

The Walk to Dummer

We trod a weary path, through silent woods,
Tangled and dark, unbroken by a sound
Of cheerful life. The melancholy shriek
Of hollow winds careering o'er the snow,
Or tossing into waves the green pine tops,
Making the ancient forest groan and sigh
Beneath their mocking voice, awoke alone
The solitary echoes of the place.

Reader! Have you ever heard of a place situated in the forest-depths of
this far western wilderness, called Dummer?[1] Ten years ago, it might
not inaptly have been termed "The *last* clearing in the world." Nor to

---

1. Dummer Township lies to the immediate east of Douro; it includes the town of Warsaw and
   stretches to the southern shores of lower Stony Lake. It seemed remote to Susanna, given
   her limited travels around the Peterborough area.

this day do I know of any in that direction which extends beyond it. Our bush-farm was situated on the border-line of a neighbouring township, only one degree less wild, less out of the world, or near to the habitations of civilisation than the far-famed "English Line,"[2] the boast and glory of this *terra incognita*.

This place, so named by the emigrants who had pitched their tents in that solitary wilderness, was a long line of cleared land, extending upon either side for some miles through the darkest and most interminable forest. The English Line was inhabited chiefly by Cornish miners, who, tired of burrowing like moles underground, had determined to emigrate to Canada, where they could breathe the fresh air of Heaven, and obtain the necessaries of life upon the bosom of their mother earth. Strange as it may appear, these men made good farmers, and steady, industrious colonists, working as well above ground as they had toiled in their early days beneath it. All our best servants came from Dummer; and although they spoke a language difficult to be understood, and were uncouth in their manners and appearance, they were faithful and obedient, performing the tasks assigned to them with patient perseverance; good food and kind treatment rendering them always cheerful and contented.

My dear old Jenny, that most faithful and attached of all humble domestic friends, came from Dummer, and I was wont to regard it with complacency for her sake. But Jenny was not English; she was a generous, warm-hearted daughter of the Green Isle—the Emerald gem set in the silver of ocean. Yes, Jenny was one of the poorest children of that impoverished but glorious country where wit and talent seem indigenous, springing up spontaneously in the rudest and most uncultivated minds; showing what the land could bring forth in its own strength, unaided by education, and unfettered by the conventional rules of society. Jenny was a striking instance of the worth, noble self-denial, and devotion which are often met with—and, alas! but too often disregarded—in the poor and ignorant natives of that deeply-injured, and much abused land. A few words about my old favourite may not prove uninteresting to my readers.

Jenny Buchanan, or as she called it, Bohánon, was the daughter of a petty exciseman, of Scotch extraction (hence her industry) who, at the time of her birth, resided near the old town of Inniskillen. Her mother died a few months after she was born; and her father, within the twelve months, married again. In the meanwhile the poor orphan babe had been adopted by a kind neighbour, the wife of a small farmer in the vicinity.

In return for coarse food and scanty clothing, the little Jenny became a servant-of-all-work. She fed the pigs, herded the cattle, assisted in planting potatoes and digging peat from the bog, and was undisputed mistress of the poultry-yard. As she grew up to womanhood, the importance of her labours increased. A better reaper in the

---

2. The English Line separated the first and second concessions of Dummer, and was likely named for the predominance of English settlers in its vicinity.

harvest-field, or footer of turf in the bog, could not be found in the district, or a woman more thoroughly acquainted with the management of cows and the rearing of young cattle; but here poor Jenny's accomplishments terminated.

Her usefulness was all abroad. Within the house she made more dirt than she had the inclination or the ability to clear away. She could neither read, nor knit, nor sew; and although she called herself a Protestant, and a Church of England woman, she knew no more of religion, as revealed to man through the Word of God, than the savage who sinks to the grave in ignorance of a Redeemer. Hence she stoutly resisted all idea of being a sinner, or of standing the least chance of receiving hereafter the condemnation of one.

"Och, shure thin," she would say, with simple earnestness of look and manner, almost irresistible. "God will never throuble Himsel' about a poor, hard-working crathur like me, who never did any harm to the manest of His makin.' "

One thing was certain, that a benevolent Providence had "throubled Himsel' " about poor Jenny in times past, for the warm heart of this neglected child of nature contained a stream of the richest benevolence, which, situated as she had been, could not have been derived from any other source. Honest, faithful, and industrious, Jenny became a law unto herself, and practically illustrated the golden rule of her blessed Lord, "to do unto others as we would they should do unto us." She thought it was impossible that her poor services could ever repay the debt of gratitude that she owed to the family who had brought her up, although the obligation must have been entirely on their side. To them she was greatly attached—for them she toiled unceasingly; and when evil days came, and they were not able to meet the rent-day, or to occupy the farm, she determined to accompany them in their emigration to Canada, and formed one of the stout-hearted band that fixed its location in the lonely and unexplored wilds now known as the township of Dummer.

During the first year of their settlement, the means of obtaining the common necessaries of life became so precarious, that, in order to assist her friends with a little ready money, Jenny determined to hire out into some wealthy house as a servant. When I use the term wealth as applied to any bush-settler, it is of course only comparatively; but Jenny was anxious to obtain a place with settlers who enjoyed a small income independent of their forest means.

Her first speculation was a complete failure. For five long, hopeless years she served a master from whom she never received a farthing of her stipulated wages. Still her attachment to the family was so strong, and had become so much the necessity of her life, that the poor creature could not make up her mind to leave them. The children whom she had received into her arms at their birth, and whom she had nursed with maternal tenderness, were as dear to her as if they had been her own; she continued to work for them although her clothes were worn to tatters, and her own friends were too poor to replace them.

Her master, Captain [Lloyd],[3] a handsome, dashing officer, who had served many years in India, still maintained the carriage and appearance of a gentleman, in spite of his mental and moral degradation arising from a constant state of intoxication; he still promised to remunerate at some future day her faithful services; and although all his neighbours well knew that his means were exhausted, and that that day would never come, yet Jenny, in the simplicity of her faith, still toiled on, in the hope that the better day he spoke of would soon arrive.

And now a few words respecting this master, which I trust may serve as a warning to others. Allured by the bait that has been the ruin of so many of his class, the offer of a large grant of land, Captain [Lloyd] had been induced to form a settlement in this remote and untried township; laying out much, if not all, of his available means in building a log house, and clearing a large extent of barren and stony land. To this uninviting home he conveyed a beautiful young wife, and a small and increasing family. The result may be easily anticipated. The want of society—a dreadful want to a man of his previous habits—the total absence of all the comforts and decencies of life, produced inaction, apathy, and at last, despondency, which was only alleviated by a constant and immoderate use of ardent spirits. As long as Captain [Lloyd] retained his half-pay, he contrived to exist. In an evil hour he parted with this, and quickly trod the down-hill path to ruin.

And here I would remark that it is always a rash and hazardous step for any officer to part with his half-pay; although it is almost every day done, and generally followed by the same disastrous results. A certain income, however small, in a country where money is so hard to be procured, and where labour cannot be attained but at a very high pecuniary remuneration, is invaluable to a gentleman unaccustomed to agricultural employment; who, without this reserve to pay his people, during the brief but expensive seasons of seed-time and harvest, must either work himself or starve. I have known no instance in which such sale has been attended with ultimate advantage; but, alas! too many in which it has terminated in the most distressing destitution. These government grants of land, to half-pay officers, have induced numbers of this class to emigrate to the backwoods of Canada, who are totally unfit for pioneers; but, tempted by the offer of finding themselves landholders of what, on paper, appear to them fine estates, they resign a certainty, to waste their energies, and die half-starved and brokenhearted in the depths of the pitiless wild.

If a gentleman so situated would give up all idea of settling on his grant, but hire a good farm in a favourable situation—that is, not too far from a market—and with his half-pay hire efficient labourers, of

3. The alcoholic Captain Frederick Lloyd, who Susanna refers to as Captain N——, and his wife Louisa had several children, including Ella or Eloise, who was Jenny Buchanan's favourite. See Chapter Seventeen, note 1, p. 213.

which plenty are now to be had, to cultivate the land, with common prudence and economy, he would soon obtain a comfortable subsistence for his family. And if the males were brought up to share the burthen and heat of the day, the expense of hired labour, as it yearly diminished, would add to the general means and well-being of the whole, until the hired farm became the real property of the industrious tenants. But the love of show, the vain boast of appearing richer and better-dressed than our neighbours, too often involves the emigrant's family in debt, from which they are seldom able to extricate themselves without sacrificing the means which would have secured their independence.

This, although a long digression, will not, I hope, be without its use; and if this book is regarded not as a work of amusement but one of practical experience, written for the benefit of others, it will not fail to convey some useful hints to those who have contemplated emigration to Canada; the best country in the world for the industrious and well-principled man, who really comes out to work, and to better his condition by the labour of his hands; but a gulf of ruin to the vain and idle, who only set foot upon these shores to accelerate their ruin.

But to return to Captain [Lloyd]. It was at this disastrous period that Jenny entered his service. Had her master adapted his habits and expenditure to his altered circumstances, much misery might have been spared, both to himself and his family. But he was a proud man—too proud to work, or to receive with kindness the offers of service tendered to him by his half-civilised, but well-meaning neighbours.

"Hang him!" cried an indignant English settler (Captain [Lloyd] was an Irishman), whose offer of drawing wood had been rejected with unmerited contempt. "Wait a few years, and we shall see what his pride will do for him. I *am* sorry for his poor wife and children; but for himself, I have no pity for him."

This man had been uselessly insulted, at the very moment when he was anxious to perform a kind and benevolent action; when, like a true Englishman, his heart was softened by witnessing the sufferings of a young, delicate female and her infant family. Deeply affronted by the captain's foolish conduct, he now took a malignant pleasure in watching his arrogant neighbour's progress to ruin.

The year after the sale of his commission, Captain [Lloyd] found himself considerably in debt, "Never mind, Ella," he said to his anxious wife; "the crops will pay all."

The crops were a failure that year. Creditors pressed hard; the captain had no money to pay his workmen, and he would not work himself. Disgusted with his location, but unable to change it for a better; without friends in his own class (for he was the only gentleman then resident in the new township), to relieve the monotony of his existence with their society, or to afford him advice or assistance in his difficulties, the fatal whiskey-bottle became his refuge from gloomy thoughts.

His wife, an amiable and devoted creature, well-born, well-educated, and deserving of a better lot, did all in her power to wean him from the growing vice. But, alas! the pleadings of an angel, in such circumstances, would have had little effect upon the mind of such a man. He loved her as well as he could love anything, and he fancied that he loved his children, while he was daily reducing them, by his favourite vice, to beggary.

For awhile, he confined his excesses to his own fireside, but this was only for as long a period as the sale of his stock and land would supply him with the means of criminal indulgence. After a time, all these resources failed, and his large grant of eight hundred acres of land had been converted into whiskey, except the one hundred acres on which his house and barn stood, embracing the small clearing from which the family derived their scanty supply of wheat and potatoes. For the sake of peace, his wife gave up all her ornaments and household plate, and the best articles of a once handsome and ample wardrobe, in the hope of hiding her sorrows from the world, and keeping her husband at home.

The pride, that had rendered him so obnoxious to his humbler neighbours, yielded at length to the inordinate craving for drink; the man who had held himself so high above his honest and industrious fellow-settlers, could now unblushingly enter their cabins and beg for a drop of whiskey. The feeling of shame once subdued, there was no end to his audacious mendicity. His whole time was spent in wandering about the country, calling upon every new settler, in the hope of being asked to partake of the coveted poison. He was even known to enter by the window of an emigrant's cabin, during the absence of the owner, and remain drinking in the house while a drop of spirits could be found in the cupboard. When driven forth by the angry owner of the hut, he wandered on to the distant town of P[eterborough], and lived there in a low tavern, while his wife and children were starving at home.

"He is the filthiest beast in the township," said the afore-mentioned neighbour to me; "it would be a good thing for his wife and children if his worthless neck were broken in one of his drunken sprees."

This might be the melancholy fact, but it was not the less dreadful on that account. The husband of an affectionate wife—the father of a lovely family—and his death to be a matter of rejoicing!—a blessing, instead of being an affliction!—an agony not to be thought upon without the deepest sorrow.

It was at this melancholy period of her sad history that Mrs. [Lloyd] found, in Jenny Buchanan, a help in her hour of need. The heart of the faithful creature bled for the misery which involved the wife of her degraded master, and the children she so dearly loved. Their want and destitution called all the sympathies of her ardent nature into active operation; they were long indebted to her labour for every morsel of food which they consumed. For them, she sowed, she planted, she reaped. Every block of wood which shed a cheering warmth around their desolate home was cut from the forest by her own hands, and brought up a steep hill to the house upon her back. For them, she coaxed the neighbours, with whom she was a general favourite, out of many a mess of eggs for their especial benefit; while with her cheerful songs, and hearty, hopeful disposition, she dispelled much of the cramping despair which chilled the heart of the unhappy mother in her deserted home.

For several years did this great, poor woman keep the wolf from the door of her beloved mistress, toiling for her with the strength and energy of a man. When was man ever so devoted, so devoid of all self-ishness, so attached to employers, yet poorer than herself, as this un-educated Irishwoman?

A period was at length put to her unrequited services. In a fit of in-toxication her master beat her severely with the iron ramrod of his gun, and turned her, with abusive language from his doors. Oh, hard return for all her unpaid labours of love! She forgave this outrage for the sake of the helpless beings who depended upon her care. He re-peated the injury, and the poor creature returned almost heart-broken to her former home.

Thinking that his spite would subside in a few days, Jenny made a third effort to enter his house in her usual capacity; but Mrs. [Lloyd] told her, with many tears, that her presence would only enrage her husband, who had threatened herself with the most cruel treatment if she allowed the faithful servant again to enter the house. Thus ended her five years' service to this ungrateful master. Such was her reward!

I heard of Jenny's worth and kindness from the Englishman who had been so grievously affronted by Captain [Lloyd], and sent for her to come to me. She instantly accepted my offer, and returned with my messenger. She had scarcely a garment to cover her. I was obliged to find her a suit of clothes before I could set her to work. The smiles and dimples of my curly-headed, rosy little Donald, then a baby-boy of fifteen months, consoled the old woman for her separation from Ellie [Lloyd]; and the good-will with which all the children (now four in number) regarded the kind old body, soon endeared to her the new home which Providence had assigned to her.

Her accounts of Mrs. [Lloyd], and her family, soon deeply interested me in her fate; and Jenny never went to visit her friends in Dummer without an interchange of good wishes passing between us.

The year of the Canadian rebellion came, and brought with it sor-row into many a bush dwelling. Old Jenny and I were left alone with the little children, in the depths of the dark forest, to help ourselves in the best way we could. Men could not be procured in that thinly-settled spot for love nor money, and I now fully realised the extent of Jenny's usefulness. Daily she yoked the oxen, and brought down from the bush fuel to maintain our fires, which she felled and chopped up with her own hands. She fed the cattle, and kept all things snug about the doors; not forgetting to load her master's two guns, "in case," as she said, "the rebels should attack us in our retrate."

The months of November and December of 1838 had been unnatu-rally mild for this iron climate;[4] but the opening of the ensuing January

4. Susanna Moodie's dating is off here—the actual walk occurred in January 1838. The text should read, "The months of November and December of 1837 had been unnaturally mild . . ." The chapter would be more accurately placed earlier, perhaps just after "The Outbreak."

brought a short but severe spell of frost and snow. We felt very lonely in our solitary dwelling, crouching round the blazing fire, that scarcely chased the cold from our miserable log-tenement, until this dreary period was suddenly cheered by the unexpected presence of my beloved friend, Emilia, who came to spend a week with me in my forest home.

She brought her own baby-boy with her, and an ample supply of buffalo robes, not forgetting a treat of baker's bread, and "sweeties" for the children. Oh, dear Emilia! best and kindest of women, though absent in your native land, long, long shall my heart cherish with affectionate gratitude all your visits of love, and turn to you as to a sister, tried, and found most faithful, in the dark hour of adversity, and, amidst the almost total neglect of those from whom nature claimed a tenderer and holier sympathy.[5]

Great was the joy of Jenny at this accession to our family-party; and after Mrs. S[hairp] was well warmed, and had partaken of tea—the only refreshment we could offer her—we began to talk over the news of the place.

"By-the-bye, Jenny," said she, turning to the old servant, who was undressing the little boy by the fire, "have you heard lately from poor Mrs. [Lloyd]? We have been told that she and the family are in a dreadful state of destitution. That worthless man has left them for the States, and it is supposed that he has joined Mackenzie's band of ruffians on Navy island; but whether this be true or false, he has deserted his wife and children, taking his eldest son along with him (who might have been of some service at home), and leaving them without money or food."

"The good Lord! What will become of the crathers?" responded Jenny, wiping her wrinkled cheek with the back of her hard, brown hand. "An' thin they have not a sowl to chop and draw them firewood; an' the weather so oncommon savare. Och, hone! What has not that *baste* of a man to answer for?"

"I heard," continued Mrs. S[hairp], "that they have tasted no food but potatoes for the last nine months, and scarcely enough of them to keep soul and body together; that they have sold their last cow; and the poor young lady and her second brother, a lad of only twelve years old, bring all the wood for the fire from the bush on a hand-sleigh."

"Oh, dear!—oh, dear!" sobbed Jenny; "an' I not there to hilp them! An' poor Miss Mary the tinder thing! Oh, tis hard, terribly hard upon the crathers, an they not used to the like."

"Can nothing be done for them?" said I.

"That is what we want to know," returned Emilia, "and that was one of my reasons for coming up to D[ouro]. I wanted to consult you and Jenny upon the subject. You, who are an officer's wife, and I, who am both an officer's wife and daughter, ought to devise some plan of rescuing this unfortunate lady and her family from her present forlorn situation."

5. This passage can be read as a soft indictment of Susanna's sister and brother and their families.

The tears sprang to my eyes, and I thought, in the bitterness of my heart, upon my own galling poverty, that my pockets did not contain even a single copper, and that I had scarcely garments enough to shield me from the inclemency of the weather. By unflinching industry, and taking my part in the toil of the field, I had bread for myself and family, and this was more than poor Mrs. [Lloyd] possessed; but it appeared impossible for me to be of any assistance to the unhappy sufferer, and the thought of my incapacity gave me severe pain. It was only in moments like the present that I felt the curse of poverty.

"Well," continued my friend, "you see, Mrs. Moodie, that the ladies of P[eterborough] are all anxious to do what they can for her; but they first want to learn if the miserable circumstances in which she is said to be placed are true. In short, my dear friend, they want you and me to make a pilgrimage to Dummer, to see the poor lady herself; and then they will be guided by our report."

"Then let us lose no time in going upon our own mission of mercy."

"Och, my dear heart, you will be lost in the woods!" said old Jenny. "It is nine long miles to the first clearing, and that through a lonely, blazed path. After you are through the beaver-meadow, there is not a single hut for you to rest or warm yourselves. It is too much for the both of yees; you will be frozen to death on the road."

"No fear," said my benevolent friend, "God will take care of us, Jenny. It is on His errand we go; to carry a message of hope to one about to perish."

"The Lord bless you for a darlint," cried the old woman, devoutly kissing the velvet cheek of the little fellow sleeping upon her lap. "May your own purty child never know the want and sorrow that is around her."

Emilia and I talked over the Dummer scheme until we fell asleep. Many were the plans we proposed for the immediate relief of the unfortunate family. Early the next morning, my brother-in-law, Mr. T[raill], called upon my friend. The subject next our heart was immediately introduced, and he was called into the general council. His feelings, like our own, were deeply interested; and he proposed that we should each provide something from our own small stores to satisfy the pressing wants of the distressed family; while he promised to bring his cutter the next morning, and take us through the beaver-meadow, and to the edge of the great swamp, which would shorten four miles, at least, of our long and hazardous journey.

We joyfully acceded to his proposal, and set cheerfully to work to provide for the morrow. Jenny baked a batch of her very best bread, and boiled a large piece of beef; and Mr. T[raill] brought with him, the next day, a fine cooked ham, in a sack, into the bottom of which he stowed the beef and loaves, besides some sugar and tea, which his own kind wife, the author of "the Backwoods of Canada," had sent.[6] I had some misgivings as to the manner in which these good things could be intro-

6. Susanna's only mention of Catharine Parr Traill's *The Backwoods of Canada* (1836), published in London by Charles Knight for the Society for the Diffusion of Useful Knowledge. Her sister's book was very successful and served as a prototype for Susanna to use and work against in writing her own account of life in the bush.

duced to the poor lady, who, I had heard, was reserved and proud.

"Oh, Jenny," I said, "how shall I be able to ask her to accept provisions from strangers? I am afraid of wounding her feelings."

"Oh, darlint, never fear that! She is proud, I know; but 'tis not a stiff pride, but jist enough to consale her disthress from her ignorant English neighbours, who think so manely of poor folk like her who were once rich. She will be very thankful to you for your kindness, for she has not experienced much of it from the Dummer people in her throuble, though she may have no words to tell you so. Say that old Jenny sent the bread to dear wee Ellie, 'cause she knew she would like a loaf of Jenny's bakin'.'"

"But the meat."

"Och, the mate, is it? May be, you'll think of some excuse for the mate when you get there."

"I hope so; but I'm a sad coward with strangers, and I have lived so long out of the world that I am at a great loss what to do. I will try and put a good face on the matter. Your name, Jenny, will be no small help to me."

All was now ready. Kissing our little bairns who crowded around us with eager and inquiring looks, and charging Jenny for the hundredth time to take especial care of them during our absence, we mounted the cutter, and set off, under the care and protection of Mr. T[raill], who determined to accompany us on the journey.

It was a black, cold day; no sun visible in the grey dark sky; a keen, cutting wind, and hard frost. We crouched close to each other.

"Good heavens, how cold it is!" whispered Emilia. "What a day for such a journey!"

She had scarcely ceased speaking, when the cutter went upon a stump which lay concealed under the drifted snow; and we, together with the ruins of our conveyance, were scattered around.

"A bad beginning," said my brother-in-law, with a rueful aspect, as he surveyed the wreck of the cutter from which we had promised ourselves so much benefit. "There is no help for it but to return home."

"Oh, no," said Mrs. S[hairp]; "bad beginnings make good endings, you know. Let us go on; it will be far better walking than riding such a dreadful day. My feet are half-frozen already with sitting still."

"But, my dear madam," expostulated Mr. T[raill], "consider the distance, the road, the dark, dull day, and our imperfect knowledge of the path. I will get the cutter mended to-morrow; and the day after we may be able to proceed."

"Delays are dangerous," said the pertinacious Emilia, who, woman-like, was determined to have her own way. "Now, or never. While we wait for the broken cutter, the broken-hearted Mrs. [Lloyd] may starve. We can stop at Colonel C[addy]'s and warm ourselves,[7] and you can leave the cutter at his house until our return."

7. Colonel John Caddy and his wife, Hannah Godard Caddy, had a large family, six members of which settled in Canada with them. They were George (b. 1813), Edward (b. 1815), Henry and James (twins, b. 1818), Agnes (b. 1823), and Cyprian (b. 1825). See *The Chronicle of the Caddy Family*, a privately published family history by Gordon H. Roper. See also Chapter Twenty-four, note 3, p. 291.

"It was upon your account that I proposed the delay," said the good Mr. T[raill], taking the sack, which was no inconsiderable weight, upon his shoulder, and driving his horse before him into neighbour W——'s stable. "Where you go, I am ready to follow."

When we arrived, Colonel C[addy]'s family were at breakfast, of which they made us partake; and after vainly endeavouring to dissuade us from what appeared to them our Quixotic expedition, Mrs. C[addy] added a dozen fine white fish to the contents of the sack, and sent her youngest son to help Mr. T[raill] along with his burthen, and to bear us company on our desolate road.

Leaving the Colonel's hospitable house on our left we again plunged into the woods, and after a few minutes' brisk walking, found ourselves upon the brow of a steep bank that overlooked the beaver-meadow, containing within its area several hundred acres.

There is no scenery in the bush that presents such a novel appearance as those meadows, or openings, surrounded, as they invariably are, by dark, intricate forests; their high, rugged banks covered with the light, airy tamarack and silver birch. In summer they look like a lake of soft, rich verdure, hidden in the bosom of the barren and howling waste. Lakes they certainly have been, from which the waters have receded, "ages, ages long ago;"[8] and still the whole length of these curious level valleys is traversed by a stream of no inconsiderable dimensions.

The waters of the narrow, rapid creek, which flowed through the meadow we were about to cross, were of sparkling brightness, and icy cold. The frost-king had no power to check their swift, dancing movements, or stop their perpetual song. On they leaped, sparkling and flashing beneath their ice-crowned banks, rejoicing as they revelled on in their lonely course. In the prime of the year, this is a wild and lovely spot, the grass is of the richest green, and the flowers of the most gorgeous dyes. The gayest butterflies float above them upon painted wings; and the whip-poor-will pours forth from the neighbouring woods, at close of dewy eve, his strange but sadly plaintive cry. Winter was now upon the earth, and the once green meadow looked like a small forest lake covered with snow.

The first step we made into it plunged us up to the knees in the snow, which was drifted to a great height in the open space. Mr. T[raill] and our young friend C[addy] walked on ahead of us, in order to break a track through the untrodden snow. We soon reached the cold creek; but here a new difficulty presented itself. It was too wide to jump across, and we could see no other way of passing to the other side.

"There must be some sort of a bridge here about," said young C[addy],[9] "or how can the people from Dummer pass constantly during the winter to and fro. I will go along the bank, and halloo to you if I find one."

8. Compare to John Keats's "The Eve of St. Agnes" (1820), line 370: "And they are gone: ay, ages long ago."
9. Young Caddy is likely Cyprian Caddy, then thirteen years old.

In a few minutes he gave the desired signal, and on reaching the spot, we found a round, slippery log flung across the stream by way of bridge. With some trouble, and after various slips, we got safely on the other side. To wet our feet would have been to ensure their being frozen; and as it was, we were not without serious apprehension on that score. After crossing the bleak, snowy plain, we scrambled over another brook, and entered the great swamp which occupied two miles of our dreary road.

It would be vain to attempt giving any description of this tangled maze of closely-interwoven cedars, fallen trees, and loose-scattered masses of rock. It seemed the fitting abode of wolves and bears, and every other unclean beast. The fire had run through it during the summer, making the confusion doubly confused. Now we stooped, half-doubled, to crawl under fallen branches that hung over our path, then again we had to clamber over prostrate trees of great bulk, descending from which we plumped down into holes in the snow, sinking mid-leg into the rotten trunk of some treacherous, decayed pine-tree. Before we were half through the great swamp, we began to think ourselves sad fools, and to wish that we were safe again by our own firesides. But, then, a great object was in view,—the relief of a distressed fellow-creature, and like the "full of hope, misnamed forlorn,"[1] we determined to overcome every difficulty, and toil on.

It took us an hour at least to clear the great swamp, from which we emerged into a fine wood, composed chiefly of maple-trees. The sun had, during our immersion in the dark shades of the swamp, burst through his leaden shroud, and cast a cheery gleam along the rugged boles of the lofty trees. The squirrel and chipmunk occasionally bounded across our path; the dazzling snow which covered it reflected the branches above us in an endless variety of dancing shadows. Our spirits rose in proportion. Young C[addy] burst out singing, and Emilia and I laughed and chatted as we bounded along our narrow road. On, on for hours, the same interminable forest stretched away to the right and left, before and behind us.

"It is past twelve," said my brother T[raill] thoughtfully; "if we do not soon come to a clearing, we may chance to spend the night in the forest."

"Oh, I am dying with hunger," cried Emilia. "Do, C[yprian], give us one or two of the cakes your mother put into the bag for us to eat upon the road."

The ginger-cakes were instantly produced. But where were the teeth to be found that could masticate them? The cakes were frozen as hard as stones; this was a great disappointment to us tired and hungry wights; but it only produced a hearty laugh. Over the logs we went again; for it was a perpetual stepping up and down, crossing the fallen trees that obstructed our path. At last we came to a spot where two distinct blazed roads diverged.

---

1. From Byron's *The Siege of Corinth. A Poem* (1816), line 191: "The full of hope, misnamed 'forlorn', / Who hold the thought of death in scorn."

"What are we to do now?" said Mr. T[raill].

We stopped, and a general consultation was held, and without one dissenting voice we took the branch to the right, which, after pursuing for about half-a-mile, led us to a log hut of the rudest description.

"Is this the road to Dummer?" we asked a man, who was chopping wood outside the fence.

"I guess you are in Dummer," was the answer.

My heart leaped for joy, for I was dreadfully fatigued.

"Does this road lead through the English Line?"

"That's another thing," returned the woodman. "No, you turned off from the right path when you came up here." We all looked very blank at each other. "You will have to go back, and keep the other road, and that will lead you straight to the English Line."

"How many miles is it to Mrs. [Lloyd]'s?"

"Some four, or thereabouts," was the cheering rejoinder. " 'Tis one of the last clearings on the line. If you are going back to Douro to-night, you must look sharp."

Sadly and dejectedly we retraced our steps. There are few trifling failures more bitter in our journey through life than that of a tired traveller mistaking his road. What effect must that tremendous failure produce upon the human mind, when at the end of life's unretraceable journey, the traveller finds that he has fallen upon the wrong track through every stage, and instead of arriving at a land of blissful promise, sinks for ever into the gulf of despair!

The distance we had trodden in the wrong path, while led on by hope and anticipation, now seemed to double in length, as with painful steps we toiled on to reach the right road. This object once attained, soon led us to the dwellings of men.

Neat, comfortable log houses, surrounded by well-fenced patches of clearing, arose on either side of the forest road; dogs flew out and barked at us, and children ran shouting in-doors to tell their respective owners that strangers were passing their gates; a most unusual circumstance, I should think, in that location.

A servant who had hired two years with my brother-in-law, we knew must live somewhere in this neighbourhood, at whose fireside we hoped not only to rest and warm ourselves, but to obtain something to eat. On going up to one of the cabins to inquire for Hannah J[ory],[2] we fortunately happened to light upon the very person we sought. With many exclamations of surprise, she ushered us into her neat and comfortable log dwelling.

A blazing fire, composed of two huge logs, was roaring up the wide chimney, and the savoury smell that issued from a large pot of pea-soup was very agreeable to our cold and hungry stomachs. But, alas, the refreshment went no further! Hannah most politely begged us to take seats by the fire, and warm and rest ourselves; she even knelt down and assisted in rubbing our half-frozen hands; but she never once made mention of the hot soup, or of the tea, which was drawing

---

2. One of the Jory clan living on the English line in Dummer.

in a tin teapot upon the hearth-stone, or of a glass of whiskey, which would have been thankfully accepted by our male pilgrims.

Hannah was not an Irishwoman, no, nor a Scotch lassie, or her very first request would have been for us to take "a pickle of soup,": or "a sup of thae warm broths." The soup was no doubt cooking for Hannah's husband and two neighbours, who were chopping for him in the bush; and whose want of punctuality she feelingly lamented.

As we left her cottage, and jogged on, Emilia whispered, laughing, "I hope you are satisfied with your good dinner? Was not the pea-soup excellent?—and that cup of nice hot tea!—I never relished anything more in my life. I think we should never pass that house without giving Hannah a call, and testifying our gratitude for her good cheer."

Many times did we stop to inquire the way to Mrs. L[loyd]'s, before we ascended the steep, bleak hill upon which her house stood. At the door, Mr. T[raill] deposited the sack of provisions, and he and young C[addy] went across the road to the house of an English settler (who, fortunately for them, proved more hospitable than Hannah J[ory]), to wait until our errand was executed.

The house before which Emilia and I were standing had once been a tolerably comfortable log dwelling. It was larger than such buildings generally are, and was surrounded by dilapidated barns and stables, which were not cheered by a solitary head of cattle. A black pine-forest stretched away to the north of the house, and terminated in a dismal, tangled cedar-swamp, the entrance to the house not having been constructed to face the road.

The spirit that had borne me up during the journey died within me. I was fearful that my visit would be deemed an impertinent intrusion. I knew not in what manner to introduce myself, and my embarrassment had been greatly increased by Mrs. S[hairp] declaring that I must break the ice, for she had not courage to go in. I remonstrated, but she was firm. To hold any longer parley was impossible. We were standing on the top of a bleak hill, with the thermometer many degrees below zero, and exposed to the fiercest biting of the bitter, cutting blast. With a heavy sigh, I knocked slowly but decidedly at the crazy door. I saw the curly head of a boy glance for a moment against the broken window. There was a stir within, but no one answered our summons. Emilia was rubbing her hands together, and beating a rapid tattoo with her feet upon the hard and glittering snow, to keep them from freezing.

Again I appealed to the inhospitable door, with a vehemence which seemed to say, "We are freezing, good people; in mercy let us in!"

Again, there was a stir, and a whispered sound of voices, as if in consultation, from within; and after waiting a few minutes longer— which, cold as we were, seemed an age—the door was cautiously opened by a handsome, dark-eyed lad of twelve years of age, who was evidently the owner of the curly head that had been sent to reconnoitre us through the window. Carefully closing the door after him, he stepped out upon the snow, and asked us coldly but respectfully what we wanted. I told him that we were two ladies, who had walked all the way from Douro to see his mamma, and that we wished very much to speak to her. The lad answered us, with the ease and courtesy of a gentleman, that he did not know whether his mamma could be seen by strangers, but he would go in and see. So saying he abruptly left us, leaving behind him an ugly skeleton of a dog, who, after expressing his disapprobation at our presence in the most disagreeable and unequivocal manner, pounced like a famished wolf upon the sack of good things which lay at Emilia's feet; and our united efforts could scarcely keep him off.

"A cold, doubtful reception this!" said my friend, turning her back to the wind, and hiding her face in her muff. "This is worse than Hannah's liberality, and the long, weary walk."

I thought so too, and began to apprehend that our walk had been in vain, when the lad again appeared, and said that we might walk in, for his mother was dressed.

Emilia, true to her determination, went no farther than the passage. In vain were all my entreating looks and mute appeals to her benevolence and friendship; I was forced to enter alone the apartment that contained the distressed family.

I felt that I was treading upon sacred ground, for a pitying angel hovers over the abode of suffering virtue, and hallows all its woes. On a rude bench, before the fire, sat a lady, between thirty and forty years of age, dressed in a thin, coloured muslin gown, the most inappropriate garment for the rigour of the season, but, in all probability, the only decent one that she retained. A subdued melancholy looked forth from her large, dark, pensive eyes. She appeared like one who, having discovered the full extent of her misery, had proudly steeled her heart to bear it. Her countenance was very pleasing, and, in early life (but she was still young), she must have been eminently handsome. Near her, with her head bent down, and shaded by her thin, slender hand, her slight figure scarcely covered by her scanty clothing, sat her eldest daughter, a gentle, sweet-looking girl, who held in her arms a baby brother whose destitution she endeavoured to conceal. It was a touching sight; that suffering girl, just stepping into womanhood hiding against her young bosom the nakedness of the little creature she loved. Another fine boy, whose neatly-patched clothes had not one piece of the original stuff apparently left in them, stood behind his mother with dark, glistening eyes fastened upon me, as if amused, and wondering who I was, and what business I could have there. A pale and attenuated, but very pretty, delicately-featured little girl was seated on a low stool before the fire. This was old Jenny's darling, Ellie, or Eloise. A rude bedstead, of home manufacture, in a corner of the room, covered with a coarse woollen quilt, contained two little boys, who had crept into it to conceal their wants from the eyes of the stranger. On the table lay a dozen peeled potatoes, and a small pot was boiling on the fire, to receive this their scanty and only daily meal. There was such an air of patient and enduring suffering in the whole group, that, as I gazed heart-stricken upon it, my fortitude quite gave way, and I burst into tears.

Mrs. [Lloyd] first broke the painful silence, and, rather proudly, asked me to whom she had the pleasure of speaking. I made a desperate effort to regain my composure, and told her, but with much embarrassment, my name; adding that I was so well acquainted with her and her children, through Jenny, that I could not consider her as a stranger; that I hoped that, as I was the wife of an officer, and, like her, a resident in the bush, and well acquainted with all its trials and privations, she would look upon me as a friend.

She seemed surprised and annoyed, and I found no small difficulty in introducing the object of my visit; but the day was rapidly declining, and I knew that not a moment was to be lost. At first she coldly rejected all offers of service, and said that she was contented, and wanted for nothing.

I appealed to the situation in which I beheld herself and her children, and implored her, for their sakes, not to refuse help from friends who felt for her distress. Her maternal feelings triumphed over her assumed indifference, and when she saw me weeping, for I could no longer restrain my tears, her pride yielded, and for some minutes not a word was spoken. I heard the large tears, as they slowly fell from her daughter's eyes, drop one by one upon her garments.

At last the poor girl sobbed out, "Dear mamma, why conceal the truth? You know that we are nearly naked, and starving."

Then came the sad tale of domestic woes: the absence of the husband and eldest son; the uncertainty as to where they were, or in what engaged; the utter want of means to procure the common necessaries of life; the sale of the only remaining cow that used to provide the children with food. It had been sold for twelve dollars, part to be paid in cash, part in potatoes; the potatoes were nearly exhausted, and they were allowanced to so many a day. But the six dollars she had retained as their last resource. Alas! she had sent the eldest boy the day before to P[eterborough], to get a letter out of the post-office, which she hoped contained some tidings of her husband and son. She was all anxiety and expectation —but the child returned late at night without the letter which they had longed for with such feverish impatience. The six dollars upon which they had depended for a supply of food were in notes of the Farmer's Bank,[3] which at that time would not pass for money, and which the roguish purchaser of the cow had passed off upon this distressed family.

Oh! imagine, ye who revel in riches—who can daily throw away a large sum upon the merest toy—the cruel disappointment, the bitter agony of this poor mother's heart, when she received this calamitous news, in the midst of her starving children. For the last nine weeks they had lived upon a scanty supply of potatoes;—they had not tasted raised bread or animal food for eighteen months.

"Ellie," said I, anxious to introduce the sack, which had lain like a nightmare upon my mind, "I have something for you; Jenny baked some loaves last night, and sent them to you with her best love."

3. The Farmers' Joint Banking Company had opened for business in Upper Canada in 1835 as a small private bank. During the aftermath of the Rebellion and its ensuing financial uncertainty, it had suspended specie payments for two months.

The eyes of all the children grew bright. "You will find the sack with the bread in the passage," said I to one of the boys. He rushed joyfully out, and returned with Mrs. [Shairp] and the sack. Her bland and affectionate greeting restored us all to tranqúility.

The delighted boy opened the sack. The first thing he produced was the ham.

"Oh," said I, "that is a ham that my sister sent to Mrs. [Lloyd]; 'tis of her own curing, and she thought that it might be acceptable.

Then came the white fish, nicely packed in a clean cloth. "Mrs. C[addy] thought fish might be a treat to Mrs. [Lloyd], as she lived so far from the great lakes." Then came Jenny's bread, which had already been introduced. The beef, and tea, and sugar, fell upon the floor without any comment. The first scruples had been overcome, and the day was ours.

"And now, ladies," said Mrs. [Lloyd], with true hospitality, "since you have brought refreshments with you, permit me to cook something for your dinner."

The scene I had just witnessed had produced such a choking sensation that all my hunger had vanished. Before we could accept or refuse Mrs. [Lloyd]'s kind offer, Mr. T[raill] arrived, to hurry us off.

It was two o'clock when we descended the hill in front of the house, that led by a side-path round to the road, and commenced our homeward route. I thought the four miles of clearings would never be passed; and the English Line appeared to have no end. At length we entered once more the dark forest.

The setting sun gleamed along the ground; the necessity of exerting our utmost speed, and getting through the great swamp before darkness surrounded us, was apparent to all. The men strode vigorously forward, for they had been refreshed with a substantial dinner of potatoes and pork, washed down with a glass of whiskey, at the cottage in which they had waited for us; but poor Emilia and I, faint, hungry, and foot-sore, it was with the greatest difficulty we could keep up. I thought of Rosalind,[4] as our march up and down the fallen logs recommenced, and often exclaimed with her, "Oh, Jupiter! how weary are my legs!"

Night closed in just as we reached the beaver-meadow. Here our ears were greeted with the sound of well-known voices. James and Henry C[addy] had brought the ox-sleigh to meet us at the edge of the bush. Never was splendid equipage greeted with such delight. Emilia and I, now fairly exhausted with fatigue, scrambled into it, and lying down on the straw which covered the bottom of the rude vehicle, we drew the buffalo robes over our faces, and actually slept soundly until we reached Colonel C[addy]'s hospitable door.

An excellent supper of hot fish and fried venison was smoking on the table, with other good cheer, to which we did ample justice. I, for

---

4. Banished from the court in the forest of Arden, Shakespeare's Rosalind exclaims, "O Jupiter, how [weary] are my spirits!" Touchstone, her companion, replies, "I care not for my spirits, if my legs were not weary." *As You Like It*, II.iv.1.

one, never was so hungry in my life. We had fasted for twelve hours, and that on an intensely cold day, and had walked during that period upwards of twenty miles. Never, never shall I forget that weary walk to Dummer; but a blessing followed it.

It was midnight when Emilia and I reached my humble home; our good friends the oxen being again put in requisition to carry us there. Emilia went immediately to bed, from which she was unable to rise for several days. In the meanwhile I wrote to Moodie an account of the scene I had witnessed, and he raised a subscription among the officers of the regiment for the poor lady and her children, which amounted to forty dollars.[5] Emilia lost no time in making a full report to her friends at P[eterborough]; and before a week passed away, Mrs. [Lloyd] and her family were removed thither by several benevolent individuals in the place. A neat cottage was hired for her; and, to the honour of Canada be it spoken, all who could afford a donation gave cheerfully. Farmers left at her door, pork, beef, flour, and potatoes; the storekeepers sent groceries, and goods to make clothes for the children; the shoemakers contributed boots for the boys; while the ladies did all in their power to assist and comfort the gentle creature thus thrown by Providence upon their bounty.

While Mrs. [Lloyd] remained at P[eterborough] she did not want for any comfort. Her children were clothed and her rent paid by her benevolent friends, and her house supplied with food and many comforts from the same source. Respected and beloved by all who knew her, it would have been well had she never left the quiet asylum where for several years she enjoyed tranquillity and a respectable competence from her school; but in an evil hour she followed her worthless husband to the Southern States, and again suffered all the woes which drunkenness inflicts upon the wives and children of its degraded victims.

THE CONVICT'S WIFE.[6]

Pale matron! I see thee in agony steep
The pillow on which thy young innocents sleep;
Their slumbers are tranquil, unbroken their rest,
They know not the grief that convulses thy breast;
They mark not the glance of that red, swollen eye,
That must weep till the fountain of sorrow is dry;
They guess not thy thoughts in this moment of dread,
Thou desolate widow, but not of the dead!

Ah, what are thy feelings, whilst gazing on those,
Who unconsciously smile in their balmy repose,—
The pangs which thy grief-stricken bosom must prove
Whilst gazing through tears on those pledges of love,

5. Writing to Susanna from the Niagara District on April 17, 1838, John Moodie told Susanna that he had "left the subscription paper for poor Mrs. Lloyd" in Toronto with a friend. See *Letters of Love and Duty*, p. 79.
6. This poem first appeared in the short-lived *Canadian Literary Magazine* 1:1 (April 1833), p. 44. It later appeared in *The Literary Garland* in April 1841.

Who murmur in slumber the dear, cherish'd name
Of that sire who has cover'd his offspring with shame,—
Of that husband whom justice has wrench'd from thy side
Of the wretch, who the laws of his country defied?

Poor, heart-broken mourner! thy tears faster flow,
Time can bring no oblivion to banish thy woe;
The sorrows of others are soften'd by years.
Ah, what now remains for thy portion but tears?
Anxieties ceaseless, renew'd day by day,
While thy heart yearns for one who is ever away.
No hope speeds thy thoughts as they traverse the wave
To the far-distant land of the exile and slave.

And those children, whose birth with such rapture was hail'd,
When the holiest feelings of nature prevail'd,
And the bright drops that moisten'd the father's glad cheek
Could alone the deep transport of happiness speak;
When he turn'd from his first-born with glances of pride,
In grateful devotion to gaze on his bride,
The loved and the loving, who, silent with joy,
Alternately gazed from the sire to his boy.

Ah! what could induce the young husband to fling
Love's garland away in life's beautiful spring,
To scatter the roses Hope wreath'd for her brow
In the dust, and abandon his partner to woe?
The wine-cup can answer. The Bacchanal's bowl
Corrupted life's chalice, and poison'd his soul.
It chill'd the warm heart, added fire to the brain,
Gave to pleasure and passion unbridled the rein;
Till the gentle endearments of children and wife
Only roused the fell demon to anger and strife.

By conscience deserted, by law unrestrain'd,
A felon convicted, unblushing, and chain'd;
Too late from the dark dream of ruin he woke
To remember the wife whose fond heart he had broke;
The children abandon'd to sorrow and shame,
Their deepest misfortune the brand of his name.
Oh, dire was the curse he invoked on his soul,
Then gave his last mite for a draught of the bowl!

Twenty-six

A Change in Our Prospects

The future flower lies folded in the bud,—
Its beauty, colour, fragrance, graceful form,
Carefully shrouded in that tiny cell;

Till time and circumstance, and sun and shower,
Expand the embryo blossom—and it bursts
Its narrow cerements, lifts its blushing head,
Rejoicing in the light and dew of heaven.
But if the canker-worm lies coil'd around
The heart o' the bud, the summer sun and dew
Visit in vain the sear'd and blighted flower.

During my illness, a kind neighbour, who had not only frequently come to see me, but had brought me many nourishing things made by her own fair hands, took a great fancy to my second daughter, who, lively and volatile, could not be induced to remain quiet in the sick chamber. The noise she made greatly retarded my recovery, and Mrs. H[ague][1] took her home with her, as the only means of obtaining for me necessary rest. During that winter, and through the ensuing summer, I only received occasional visits from my little girl, who, fairly established with her new friends, looked upon their house as her home.

This separation, which was felt as a great benefit at the time, greatly estranged the affections of the child from her own people. She saw us so seldom that she almost regarded us, when she did meet, as strangers; and I often deeply lamented the hour when I had unwittingly suffered the threefold cord of domestic love to be unravelled by absence, and the flattering attentions which fed the vanity of a beautiful child, without strengthening her moral character. Mrs. H[ague], whose husband was wealthy,[2] was a generous, warm-hearted girl of eighteen. Lovely in person, and fascinating in manners, and still too young to have any idea of forming the character of a child, she dressed the little creature expensively; and, by constantly praising her personal appearance, gave her an idea of her own importance which it took many years to eradicate.

It is a great error to suffer a child, who has been trained in the hard school of poverty and self-denial, to be transplanted suddenly into the hot-bed of wealth and luxury. The idea of the child being so much happier and better off blinds her fond parents to the dangers of her situation, where she is sure to contract a dislike to all useful occupation, and to look upon scanty means and plain clothing as a disgrace. If the re-action is bad for a grown-up person, it is almost destructive to a child who is incapable of moral reflection. Whenever I saw little Addie, and remarked the growing coldness of her manner towards us, my heart reproached me for having exposed her to temptation.

Still, in the eye of the world, she was much better situated than she could possibly be with us. The heart of the parent could alone understand the change.

1. Mary Hague, the daughter of Lieutenant Colonel Walter Crawford and wife of James Hague, had given birth to a daughter in October of 1838. Nevertheless, she was enchanted by little Agnes Moodie and eager to help Susanna by taking her daughter off her hands in January 1839, during Susanna's prolonged illness. The Hagues were quite generous to Susanna in her troubles, sending her "a gallon of old port wine, and so many nice things." See Susanna's letter to John Moodie of January 11, 1839, in *Letters of Love and Duty*, p. 115.
2. A Scotsman, James Hague drowned in the Otonabee River in 1843. See also Chapter Seventeen, note 4, p. 214.

So sensible was her father of this alteration, that the first time he paid us a visit he went and brought home his child.

"If she remain so long away from us, at her tender years," he said, "she will cease to love us. All the wealth in the world would not compensate me for the love of my child."

The removal of my sister rendered my separation from my husband doubly lonely and irksome. Sometimes the desire to see and converse with him would press so painfully on my heart that I would get up in the night, strike a light, and sit down and write him a long letter, and tell him all that was in my mind; and when I had thus unburdened my spirit, the letter was committed to the flames, and after fervently commending him to the care of the Great Father of mankind, I would lay down my throbbing head on my pillow beside our first-born son, and sleep tranquilly.

It is a strange fact that many of my husband's letters to me were written at the very time when I felt those irresistible impulses to hold communion with him. Why should we be ashamed to admit openly our belief in this mysterious intercourse between the spirits of those who are bound to each other by the tender ties of friendship and affection, when the experience of every day proves its truth! Proverbs, which are the wisdom of ages collected into a few brief words, tell us in one pithy sentence that "if we talk of the devil he is sure to appear." While the name of a long-absent friend is in our mouth, the next moment brings him into our presence. How can this be, if mind did not meet mind, and the spirit had not a prophetic consciousness of the vicinity of another spirit, kindred with its own? This is an occurrence so common that I never met with any person to whom it had not happened; few will admit it to be a spiritual agency, but in no other way can they satisfactorily explain its cause. If it were a mere coincidence, or combination of ordinary circumstances, it would not happen so often, and people would not be led to speak of the long-absent always at the moment when they are just about to present themselves before them. My husband was no believer in what he termed my fanciful, speculative theories; yet at the time when his youngest boy and myself lay dangerously ill, and hardly expected to live, I received a letter, written in great haste, which commenced with this sentence: "Do write to me, dear S[usie], when you receive this. I have felt very uneasy about you for some days past, and am afraid that all is not right at home."[3]

Whence came this sudden fear? Why at that particular time did his thoughts turn so despondingly towards those so dear to him? Why did the dark cloud in his mind hang so heavily above his home? The burden of my weary and distressed spirit had reached him; and without knowing of our sufferings and danger, his own responded to the call.

3. In his letter to Susanna from Belleville of March 16, 1839, John spoke of a "kind of foreboding" about the health of Susanna and the children, urging her to "Write me dearest whenever you have an opportunity and relieve me from my anxiety" (*Letters of Love and Duty,* p. 134). His concern was less a matter of "spiritual agency" or ESP than a response to her monthly letters, in which she detailed the illnesses she and the children had suffered.

The holy and mysterious nature of man is yet hidden from himself; he is still a stranger to the movements of that inner life, and knows little of its capabilities and powers. A purer religion, a higher standard of moral and intellectual training may in time reveal all this. Man still remains a half-reclaimed savage; the leaven of Christianity is slowly and surely working its way, but it has not yet changed the whole lump, or transformed the deformed into the beauteous child of God. Oh, for that glorious day! It is coming. The dark clouds of humanity are already tinged with the golden radiance of the dawn, but the sun of righteousness has not yet arisen upon the world with healing on his wings; the light of truth still struggles in the womb of darkness, and man stumbles on to the fulfilment of his sublime and mysterious destiny.

This spring I was not a little puzzled how to get in the crops. I still continued so weak that I was quite unable to assist in the field, and my good old Jenny was sorely troubled with inflamed feet, which required constant care. At this juncture, a neighbouring settler, who had recently come among us, offered to put in my small crop of peas, potatoes, and oats, in all not comprising more than eight acres, if I would lend him my oxen to log-up a large fallow of ten acres, and put in his own crops. Trusting to his fair dealing, I consented to this arrangement; but he took advantage of my isolated position, and not only logged-up his fallow, but put in all his spring crops before he sowed an acre of mine. The oxen were worked down so low that they were almost unfit for use, and my crops were put in so late, and with such little care, that they all proved a failure. I should have felt this loss more severely had it happened in any previous year; but I had ceased to feel that deep interest in the affairs of the farm, from a sort of conviction in my own mind that it would not long remain my home.

Jenny and I did our best in the way of hoeing and weeding; but no industry on our part could repair the injury done to the seed by being sown out of season.

We therefore confined our attention to the garden, which, as usual, was very productive, and with milk, fresh butter, and eggs, supplied the simple wants of our family. Emilia enlivened our solitude by her company, for several weeks during the summer, and we had many pleasant excursions on the water together.

My knowledge of the use of the paddle, however, was not entirely without its danger.

One very windy Sunday afternoon, a servant-girl, who lived with my friend Mrs. C[addy],[4] came crying to the house, and implored the use of my canoe and paddle, to cross the lake to see her dying father. The request was instantly granted; but there was no man upon the place to ferry her across, and she could not manage the boat herself—in short, had never been in a canoe in her life.

The girl was deeply distressed. She said that she had got word that her father could scarcely live till she could reach Smith-town; that if

---

4. Either Hannah Godard Caddy or Marianne (Shairp) Caddy.

she went round by the bridge, she must walk five miles, while if she crossed the lake she could be home in half-an-hour.

I did not much like the angry swell upon the water, but the poor creature was in such grief that I told her, if she was not afraid of venturing with me, I would try and put her over.

She expressed her thanks in the warmest terms, accompanied by a shower of blessings; and I took the paddles and went down to the landing. Jenny was very averse to my *tempting Providence*, as she termed it, and wished that I might get back as safe as I went. However, the old woman launched the canoe for me, pushed us from the shore, and away we went. The wind was in my favour, and I found so little trouble in getting across that I began to laugh at my own timidity. I put the girl on shore, and endeavoured to shape my passage home. But this I found was no easy task. The water was rough, and the wind high, and the strong current, which runs through that part of the lake to the Smith rapids, was dead against me. In vain I laboured to cross this current; it resisted all my efforts, and at each repulse, I was carried farther down towards the rapids, which were full of sunken rocks, and hard for the strong arm of a man to stem—to the weak hand of a woman their safe passage was impossible. I began to feel rather uneasy at the awkward situation in which I found myself placed, and for some time I made desperate efforts to extricate myself, by paddling with all my might. I soon gave this up, and contented myself by steering the canoe in the path that it thought fit to pursue. After drifting down with the current for some little space, until I came opposite a small island, I put out all my strength to gain the land. In this I fortunately succeeded, and getting on shore, I contrived to drag the canoe so far round the headland that I got her out of the current. All now was smooth sailing, and I joyfully answered old Jenny's yells from the landing, that I was safe, and would join her in a few minutes.

This fortunate manoeuvre stood me in good stead upon another occasion, when crossing the lake, some weeks after this, in company with a young female friend, during a sudden storm.

Two Indian women, heavily laden with their packs of dried venison, called at the house to borrow the canoe, to join their encampment upon the other side. It so happened that I wanted to send to the mill that afternoon, and the boat could not be returned in time without I went over with the Indian women and brought it back. My young friend was delighted at the idea of the frolic, and as she could both steer and paddle, and the day was calm and bright, though excessively warm, we both agreed to accompany the squaws to the other side, and bring back the canoe.

Mrs. Muskrat had fallen in love with a fine fat kitten, whom the children had called "Buttermilk," and she begged so hard for the little puss, that I presented it to her, rather marvelling how she would contrive to carry it so many miles through the woods, and she loaded with such an enormous pack; when, lo! the squaw took down the bundle, and, in the heart of the piles of dried venison, she deposited the cat in a small basket, giving it a thin slice of the meat to console it for its close confinement. Puss received the donation with piteous mews; it was evident that mice and freedom were preferred by her to venison and the honour of riding on a squaw's back.

The squaws paddled us quickly across, and we laughed and chatted as we bounded over the blue waves, until we were landed in a dark cedar-swamp, in the heart of which we found the Indian encampment.

A large party were lounging around the fire, superintending the drying of a quantity of venison which was suspended on forked sticks. Besides the flesh of the deer, a number of musk-rats were skinned and extended as if standing bolt upright before the fire, warming their paws. The appearance they cut was most ludicrous. My young friend pointed to the musk-rats, as she sank down, laughing, upon one of the skins.

Old Snow-storm, who was present, imagined that she wanted one of them to eat, and very gravely handed her the unsavoury beast, stick and all.

"Does the old man take me for a cannibal?" she said. "I would as soon eat a child."

Among the many odd things cooking at that fire there was something that had the appearance of a bull-frog.

"What can that be?" she said, directing my eyes to the strange monster. "Surely they don't eat bull-frogs!"

This sally was received by a grunt of approbation from Snow-storm; and, though Indians seldom forget their dignity so far as to laugh, he for once laid aside his stoical gravity, and, twirling the thing round with a stick, burst into a hearty peal.

"*Muckakee*? Indian eat *muckakee*?—Ha! ha! Indian no eat *muckakee*! Frenchmans eat his hind legs; they say the speckled beast much good. This no *muckakee*!—the liver of deer, dried—very nice—Indian eat him."

"I wish him much joy of the delicate morsel," said the saucy girl, who was intent upon quizzing and examining everything in the camp.

We had remained the best part of an hour, when Mrs. Muskrat laid hold of my hand, and leading me through the bush to the shore, pointed up significantly to a cloud, as dark as night, that hung loweringly over the bush.

"Thunder in that cloud—get over the lake—quick, quick, before it breaks." Then motioning for us to jump into the canoe, she threw in the paddles, and pushed us from the shore.

We saw the necessity of haste, and both plied the paddle with diligence to gain the opposite bank, or at least the shelter of the island, before the cloud poured down its fury upon us. We were just in the middle of the current when the first peal of thunder broke with startling nearness over our heads. The storm frowned darkly upon the woods; the rain came down in torrents; and there were we exposed to its utmost fury in the middle of a current too strong for us to stem.

"What shall we do? We shall be drowned!" said my young friend, turning her pale, tearful face towards me.

"Let the canoe float down the current till we get close to the island; then run her into the land. I saved myself once before by this plan."

We did so, and were safe; but there we had to remain, wet to our skins, until the wind and the rain abated sufficiently for us to manage our little craft. "How do you like being upon the lake in a storm like this?" I whispered to my shivering, dripping companion.

"Very well in romance, but terribly dull in reality. We cannot, however, call it a dry joke," continued she, wringing the rain from her dress. "I wish we were suspended over Old Snow-storm's fire with the bull-frog, for I hate a shower-bath with my clothes on."

I took warning by this adventure, never to cross the lake again without a stronger arm than mine in the canoe to steer me safely through the current.

I received much kind attention from my new neighbour, the Rev. W. W[olseley],[5] a truly excellent and pious clergy-man of the English Church. The good, white-haired old man expressed the kindest sympathy in all my trials, and strengthened me greatly with his benevolent counsels and gentle charity. Mr. W[olseley] was a true follower of Christ. His Christianity was not confined to his own denomination; and every Sabbath his log cottage was filled with attentive auditors, of all persuasions, who met together to listen to the word of life delivered to them by a Christian minister in the wilderness.

He had been a very fine preacher, and though considerably turned of seventy, his voice was still excellent, and his manner solemn and impressive.

His only son, a young man of twenty-eight years of age, had received a serious injury in the brain by falling upon a turf-spade from a loft window when a child, and his intellect had remained stationary from that time. Poor Harry was an innocent child; he loved his parents with the simplicity of a child, and all who spoke kindly to him he regarded as friends. Like most persons of his caste of mind, his predilection for pet animals was a prominent instinct. He was always followed by two dogs, whom he regarded with especial favour. The moment he caught your eye, he looked down admiringly upon his four-footed attendants, patting their sleek necks, and murmuring, "Nice dogs—nice dogs." Harry had singled out myself and my little ones as great favourites. He would gather flowers for the girls, and catch butterflies for the boys; while to me he always gave the title of "dear aunt."

It so happened that one fine morning I wanted to walk a couple of miles through the bush, to spend the day with Mrs. C[addy];[6] but the woods were full of the cattle belonging to the neighbouring settlers, and of these I was terribly afraid. While I was dressing the little girls to accompany me, Harry W[olseley] came in with a message from his mother. "Oh, thought I, here is Harry W[olseley]. He will walk with us through the bush, and defend us from the cattle."

The proposition was made, and Harry was not a little proud of being invited to join our party. We had accomplished half the distance with-

5. The Reverend Henry Hulbert Wolseley bought the Traills' farm (Lot 19, Concession 7, Douro) in March 1839. He occasionally took services at St. John's (Anglican) Church in Peterborough and was buried there in 1841 after his death at the age of sixty-five.
6. Either Hannah Caddy or her daughter-in-law Marianne Caddy, but likely the latter.

out seeing a single hoof; and I was beginning to congratulate myself upon our unusual luck, when a large red ox, maddened by the stings of the gad-flies, came headlong through the brush, tossing up the withered leaves and dried moss with his horns, and making directly towards us. I screamed to my champion for help; but where was he?— running like a frightened chipmunk along the fallen timber, shouting to my eldest girl, at the top of his voice.

"Run, Katty, run!—The bull, the bull! Run, Katty!—The bull, the bull!"—leaving us poor creatures far behind in the chase.

The bull, who cared not one fig for us, did not even stop to give us a passing stare, and was soon lost among the trees; while our valiant knight never stopped to see what had become of us, but made the best of his way home. So much for taking an innocent for a guard.

The next month most of the militia regiments were disbanded. My husband's services were no longer required at B[elleville], and he once more returned to help to gather in our scanty harvest. Many of the old debts were paid off by his hard-saved pay; and though all hope of continuing in the militia service was at an end,[7] our condition was so much improved that we looked less to the dark than to the sunny side of the landscape.

The potato crop was gathered in, and I had collected my store of dandelion-roots for our winter supply of coffee, when one day brought a letter to my husband from the Governor's secretary, offering him the situation of sheriff of the V[ictoria] district. Though perfectly unacquainted with the difficulties and responsibilities of such an important office, my husband looked upon it as a gift sent from heaven to remove us from the sorrows and poverty with which we were surrounded in the woods.

Once more he bade us farewell; but it was to go and make ready a home for us, that we should no more be separated from each other.

Heartily did I return thanks to God that night for all his mercies to us; and Sir George Arthur was not forgotten in those prayers.[8]

From B[elleville], my husband wrote to me to make what haste I could in disposing of our crops, household furniture, stock, and farming implements; and to prepare myself and the children to join him on the first fall of snow that would make the roads practicable for sleighing. To facilitate this object, he sent me a box of clothing, to make up for myself and children.

For seven years I had lived out of the world entirely; my person had been rendered coarse by hard work and exposure to the weather. I looked double the age I really was, and my hair was already thickly

7. John Moodie had been stationed at Belleville. By the summer of 1839, concerns about the Rebellion and a Mackenzie-led invasion of Canada by American forces had diminished, so special militia units were being disbanded.
8. The Victoria District centered at Belleville. Sir George Arthur remained interested in helping the Moodies, not only because of Susanna's patriotic poetry and letters to him but also because of John Moodie's excellent service as captain and paymaster. John was held in high regard by George, Baron de Rottenburg, his immediate superior in Belleville. De Rottenburg, who had been for a time Arthur's private secretary, recommended him for a new civil position. For his part, John quietly applied for the available position (see *Letters of Love and Duty*, p. 156).

sprinkled with grey. I clung to my solitude. I did not like to be dragged from it to mingle in gay scenes, in a busy town, and with gaily-dressed people. I was no longer fit for the world; I had lost all relish for the pursuits and pleasures which are so essential to its votaries; I was contented to live and die in obscurity.

My dear Emilia rejoiced, like a true friend, in my changed prospects, and came up to help me to cut clothes for the children, and to assist me in preparing them for the journey.

I succeeded in selling off our goods and chattels much better than I expected. My old friend, Mr. W[olseley], who was a new comer, became the principal purchaser, and when Christmas arrived I had not one article left upon my hands save the bedding, which it was necessary to take with us.

THE MAGIC SPELL.

The magic spell, the dream is fled,
    The dream of joy sent from above;
The idol of my soul is dead,
    And naught remains but hopeless love.
The song of birds, the scent of flowers,
    The tender light of parting day—
Unheeded now the tardy hours
    Steal sadly, silently away.

But welcome now the solemn night,
    When watchful stars are gleaming high,
For though thy form eludes my sight,
    I know thy gentle spirit's nigh.
O! dear one, now I feel thy power,
    'Tis sweet to rest when toil is o'er,
But sweeter far that blessed hour
    When fond hearts meet to part no more.

J. W. D. M.

Twenty-seven

Adieu to the Woods

Adieu!—adieu!—when quivering lips refuse
    The bitter pangs of parting to declare;
And the full bosom feels that it must lose
    Friends who were wont its inmost thoughts to share;
When hands are tightly clasp'd, 'mid struggling sighs
And streaming tears, those whisper'd accents rise,
    Leaving to God the objects of our care
    In that short, simple, comprehensive prayer—

ADIEU!

Never did eager British children look for the first violets and primroses of spring with more impatience than my baby boys and girls watched, day after day, for the first snow-flakes that were to form the road to convey them to their absent father.

"Winter never means to come this year. It will never snow again!" exclaimed my eldest boy, turning from the window on Christmas-day, with the most rueful aspect that ever greeted the broad, gay beams of the glorious sun. It was like a spring day. The little lake in front of the window glittered like a mirror of silver, set in its dark frame of pine woods.

I, too, was wearying for the snow, and was tempted to think that it did not come as early as usual, in order to disappoint us. But I kept this to myself, and comforted the expecting child with the oft-repeated assertion that it would certainly snow upon the morrow.

But the morrow came and passed away, and many other morrows, and the same mild, open weather prevailed. The last night of the old year was ushered in with furious storms of wind and snow; the rafters of our log cabin shook beneath the violence of the gale, which swept up from the lake like a lion roaring for its prey, driving the snow-flakes through every open crevice, of which there were not a few, and powdering the floor until it rivalled in whiteness the ground without.

"Oh, what a dreadful night!" we cried, as we huddled, shivering, around the old broken stove. "A person abroad in the woods to-night would be frozen. Flesh and blood could not long stand this cutting wind."

"It reminds me of the commencement of a laughable extempore ditty," said I to my young friend, A. C[addy],[1] who was staying with me, "composed by my husband, during the first very cold night we spent in Canada:"

> Oh, the cold of Canada nobody knows,
> The fire burns our shoes without warming our toes;
> Oh, dear, what shall we do?
> Our blankets are thin, and our noses are blue—
> Our noses are blue, and our blankets are thin,
> It's at zero without, and we're freezing within!
> (*Chorus*). Oh, dear, what shall we do?

"But, joking apart, my dear A[gnes], we ought to be very thankful that we are not travelling this night to B[elleville]."

"But to-morrow," said my eldest boy, lifting up his curly head from my lap. "It will be fine to-morrow, and we shall see dear papa again."

In this hope he lay down on his little bed upon the floor, and was soon fast asleep; perhaps dreaming of that eagerly-anticipated journey, and of meeting his beloved father.

Sleep was a stranger to my eyes. The tempest raged so furiously

---

1. Likely Agnes Caddy, the sixteen-year old daughter of Colonel and Hannah Caddy. She was visiting during the day, knowing that Susanna and the children were soon to depart. She is likely the "young friend" who accompanied Susanna by canoe to the Indian encampment (see Chapter Twenty-six).

without that I was fearful the roof would be carried off the house, or that the chimney would take fire. The night was far advanced when old Jenny and myself retired to bed.

My boy's words were prophetic; that was the last night I ever spent in the bush—in the dear forest home which I had loved in spite of all the hardships which we had endured since we pitched our tent in the backwoods. It was the birthplace of my three boys, the school of high resolve and energetic action in which we had learned to meet calmly, and successfully to battle with the ills of life. Nor did I leave it without many regretful tears, to mingle once more with a world to whose usages, during my long solitude, I had become almost a stranger, and to whose praise or blame I felt alike indifferent.

When the day dawned, the whole forest scenery lay glittering in a mantle of dazzling white; the sun shone brightly, the heavens were intensely blue, but the cold was so severe that every article of food had to be thawed before we could get our breakfast. The very blankets that covered us during the night were stiff with our frozen breath. "I hope the sleighs won't come to-day," I cried; "we should be frozen on the long journey."

About noon two sleighs turned into our clearing. Old Jenny ran screaming into the room, "The masther has sent for us at last! The sleighs are come! Fine large sleighs, and illigant teams of horses! Och, and it's a cowld day for the wee things to lave the bush."

The snow had been a week in advance of us at B[elleville], and my husband had sent up the teams to remove us. The children jumped about, and laughed aloud for joy. Old Jenny did not know whether to laugh or cry, but she set about helping me to pack up trunks and bedding as fast as our cold hands would permit.

In the midst of the confusion, my brother arrived, like a good genius, to our assistance, declaring his determination to take us down to B[elleville] himself in his large lumber-sleigh. This was indeed joyful news. In less than three hours he despatched the hired sleighs with their loads, and we all stood together in the empty house, striving to warm our hands over the embers of the expiring fire.

How cold and desolate every object appeared! The small windows, half blocked up with snow, scarcely allowed a glimpse of the declining sun to cheer us with his serene aspect. In spite of the cold, several kind friends had waded through the deep snow to say, "God bless you!—Good-bye;" while a group of silent Indians stood together, gazing upon our proceedings with an earnestness which showed that they were not uninterested in the scene. As we passed out to the sleigh, they pressed forward, and silently held out their hands, while the squaws kissed me and the little ones with tearful eyes. They had been true friends to us in our dire necessity, and I returned their mute farewell from my very heart.

Mr. S[trickland] sprang into the sleigh. One of our party was missing. "Jenny!" shouted my brother, at the top of his voice, "it is too cold to keep your mistress and the little children waiting."

"Och, shure thin, it is I that am comin'!" returned the old body, as she issued from the house.

Shouts of laughter greeted her appearance. The figure she cut upon that memorable day I shall never forget. My brother dropped the reins upon the horses' necks, and fairly roared. Jenny was about to commence her journey to the front in three hats. Was it to protect her from the cold? Oh, no; Jenny was not afraid of the cold! She could have eaten her breakfast on the north side of an iceberg, and always dispensed with shoes, during the most severe of our Canadian winters. It was to protect these precious articles from injury.

Our good neighbour, Mrs. W[olseley], had presented her with an old sky-blue drawn-silk bonnet, as a parting benediction. This, by way of distinction, for she never had possessed such an article of luxury as a silk bonnet in her life, Jenny had placed over the coarse calico cap, with its full furbelow of the same yellow, ill-washed, homely material, next to her head; over this, as second in degree, a sun-burnt straw hat, with faded pink ribbons, just showed its broken rim and tawdry trimmings; and to crown all, and serve as a guard to the rest, a really serviceable grey-beaver bonnet, once mine, towered up as high as the celebrated crown in which brother Peter figures in Swift's "Tale of a Tub."[2]

"Mercy, Jenny! Why, old woman, you don't mean to go with us that figure?"

"Och, my dear heart! I've no band-box to kape the cowld from desthroying my illigant bonnets," returned Jenny, laying her hand upon the side of the sleigh.

"Go back, Jenny; go back," cried my brother. "For God's sake take all that tom-foolery from off your head. We shall be the laughing-stock of every village we pass through."

"Och, shure now, Mr. S[trickland], who'd think of looking at an owld crathur like me! It's only yersel' that would notice the like."

"All the world, everybody would look at you, Jenny. I believe that you put on those hats to draw the attention of all the young fellows that we shall happen to meet on the road. Ha, Jenny!"

With an air of offended dignity, the old woman returned to the house to re-arrange her toilet, and provide for the safety of her "illigant bonnets," one of which she suspended to the strings of her cloak, while she carried the third dangling in her hand; and no persuasion of mine would induce her to put them out of sight.

Many painful and conflicting emotions agitated my mind, but found no utterance in words, as we entered the forest path, and I looked my last upon that humble home consecrated by the memory of a thousand sorrows. Every object had become endeared to me during my long exile from civilised life. I loved the lonely lake, with its magnificent belt of dark pines sighing in the breeze; the cedar-swamp, the

2. Susanna refers to Jonathan Swift's *A Tale of a Tub* (1704), in which "poor Peter," in a distracted state, places three hats on his head.

summer home of my dark Indian friends; my own dear little garden, with its rugged snake-fence which I had helped Jenny to place with my own hands, and which I had assisted the faithful woman in cultivating for the last three years, where I had so often braved the tormenting musquitoes, black-flies, and intense heat, to provide vegetables for the use of the family. Even the cows, that had given a breakfast for the last time to my children, were now regarded with mournful affection. A poor labourer stood in the doorway of the deserted house, holding my noble water-dog, Rover, on a string. The poor fellow gave a joyous bark as my eyes fell upon him.

"James J[ory], take care of my dog."[3]

"Never fear, ma'am, he shall bide with me as long as he lives."

"He and the Indians at least feel grieved for our departure," I thought. Love is so scarce in this world that we ought to prize it, however lowly the source from whence it flows.

We accomplished only twelve miles of our journey that night. The road lay through the bush, and along the banks of the grand, rushing, foaming Otonabee river, the wildest and most beautiful of forest streams. We slept at the house of kind friends, and early in the morning resumed our long journey, but minus one of our party. Our old favourite cat, Peppermint, had made her escape from the basket in which she had been confined, and had scampered off, to the great grief of the children.

As we passed Mrs. H[ague]'s house, we called for dear Addie. Mr. H[ague] brought her in his arms to the gate, well wrapped up in a large fur cape and a warm woollen shawl.

"You are robbing me of my dear little girl," he said. "Mrs. H[ague] is absent; she told me not to part with her if you should call; but I could not detain her without your consent. Now that you have seen her, allow me to keep her for a few months longer?"

Addie was in the sleigh. I put my arm about her. I felt I had my child again, and I secretly rejoiced in the possession of my own. I sincerely thanked him for his kindness, and Mr. S[trickland] drove on.

At Mr. R[eid]'s, we found a parcel from dear Emilia, containing a plum-cake and other good things for the children. Her kindness never flagged.[4]

We crossed the bridge over the Otonabee, in the rising town of Peterborough, at eight o'clock in the morning. Winter had now set in fairly. The children were glad to huddle together in the bottom of the sleigh, under the buffalo skins and blankets; all but my eldest boy, who, just turned of five years old, was enchanted with all he heard and saw, and continued to stand up and gaze around him. Born in the forest, which he had never quitted before, the sight of a town was such a

---

3. Susanna gave James Jory the dog she had received from Louisa Lloyd, a gift for her kindness in bringing food to her in a time of great need. James had agreed to take the farm as a tenant, looking after it and paying the taxes. John Moodie planned to sell it but had no prospective buyer at the time. See *Letters of Love and Duty*, pp. 159–60.
4. On the journey to Peterborough along the Douro side of the Otonabee River, the Moodies would first have passed the Hagues' home and then the Reids'. It is not clear where they stayed on that first night.

novelty that he could find no words wherewith to express his astonishment.

"Are the houses come to see one another?" he asked. "How did they all meet here?"

The question greatly amused his uncle, who took some pains to explain to him the difference between town and country. During the day, we got rid of old Jenny and her bonnets, whom we found a very refractory travelling companion; as wilful, and far more difficult to manage than a young child. Fortunately, we overtook the sleighs with the furniture, and Mr. S[trickland] transferred Jenny to the care of one of the drivers; an arrangement that proved satisfactory to all parties.

We had been most fortunate in obtaining comfortable lodgings for the night. The evening had closed in so intensely cold that although we were only two miles from C[obourg], Addie was so much affected by it that the child lay sick and pale in my arms, and, when spoken to, seemed scarcely conscious of our presence.

My brother jumped from the front seat, and came round to look at her. "That child is ill with the cold; we must stop somewhere to warm her, or she will hardly hold out till we get to the inn at C[obourg]."

We were just entering the little village of A[mherst], in the vicinity of the court-house,[5] and we stopped at a pretty green cottage, and asked permission to warm the children. A stout, middle-aged woman came to the sleigh, and in the kindest manner requested us to alight.

"I think I know that voice," I said. "Surely it cannot be Mrs. S[trong], who once kept the [Steamboat] hotel at C[obourg]?"

"Mrs. Moodie, you are welcome," said the excellent woman, bestowing upon me a most friendly embrace; "you and your children. I am heartily glad to see you again after so many years. God bless you all!"

Nothing could exceed the kindness and hospitality of this generous woman; she would not hear of our leaving her that night, and, directing my brother to put up his horses in her stable, she made up an excellent fire in a large bed-room, and helped me to undress the little ones who were already asleep, and to warm and feed the rest before we put them to bed.

This meeting gave me real pleasure. In their station of life, I seldom have found a more worthy couple than this American and his wife; and, having witnessed so many of their acts of kindness, both to ourselves and others, I entertained for them a sincere respect and affection, and truly rejoiced that Providence had once more led me to the shelter of their roof.

Mr. S[trong] was absent, but I found little Mary—the sweet child who used to listen with such delight to Moodie's flute—grown up into a beautiful girl; and the baby that was, a fine child of eight years old. The next morning was so intensely cold that my brother would not resume the journey until past ten o'clock, and even then it was a hazardous experiment.

---

5. Amherst, a village close to Cobourg, was where the courthouse for Hamilton Township had been built.

We had not proceeded four miles before the horses were covered with icicles. Our hair was frozen as white as old Time's solitary fore-lock, our eyelids stiff, and every limb aching with cold.

"This will never do," said my brother, turning to me; "the children will freeze. I never felt the cold more severe than this."

"Where can we stop?" said I; "we are miles from C[obourg], and I see no prospect of the weather becoming milder."

"Yes, yes; I know, by the very intensity of the cold, that a change is at hand. We seldom have more than three very severe days running, and this is the third. At all events, it is much warmer at night in this country than during the day; the wind drops, and the frost is more bearable. I know a worthy farmer who lives about a mile a-head; he will give us house-room for a few hours; and we will resume our jour-ney in the evening. The moon is at full; and it will be easier to wrap the children up, and keep them warm when they are asleep. Shall we stop at Old Woodruff's?"

"With all my heart." My teeth were chattering with the cold, and the children were crying over their aching fingers at the bottom of the sleigh.

A few minutes' ride brought us to a large farm-house, surrounded by commodious sheds and barns. A fine orchard opposite, and a yard well-stocked with fat cattle and sheep, sleek geese, and plethoric-looking swine, gave promise of a land of abundance and comfort. My brother ran into the house to see if the owner was at home, and presently returned, accompanied by the staunch Canadian yeoman and his daughter, who gave us a truly hearty welcome, and assisted in removing the children from the sleigh to the cheerful fire, that made all bright and cozy within.

Our host was a shrewd, humorous-looking Yorkshireman. His red, weather-beaten face, and tall, athletic figure, bent as it was with hard labour, gave indications of great personal strength; and a certain knowing twinkle in his small, clear grey eyes, which had been acquired by long dealing with the world, with a quiet, sarcastic smile that lurked around the corners of his large mouth, gave you the idea of a man who could not easily be deceived by his fellows; one who, though no rogue himself, was quick in detecting the roguery of others. His manners were frank and easy, and he was such a hospitable enter-tainer that you felt at home with him in a minute.

"Well, how are you, Mr. S[trickland]?" cried the farmer, shaking my brother heartily by the hand. "Toiling in the bush still, eh?"

"Just in the same place."

"And the wife and children?"

"Hearty. Some half-dozen have been added to the flock since you were our way."

"So much the better—so much the better. The more the merrier, Mr. S[trickland]; children are riches in this country."

"I know not how that may be; I find it hard to clothe and feed mine."

"Wait till they grow up; they will be brave helps to you then. The price of labour—the price of labour, Mr. S[trickland], is the destruction of the farmer."

"It does not seem to trouble you much, Woodruff," said my brother, glancing round the well-furnished apartment.

"My son and S—— do it all," cried the old man. "Of course the girls help in busy times, and take care of the dairy, and we hire occasionally; but small as the sum is which is expended in wages during seed-time and harvest, I feel it, I can tell you."

"You are married again, Woodruff?"

"No, sir," said the farmer, with a peculiar smile; "not yet:" which seemed to imply the probability of such an event. "That tall gal is my eldest daughter; she manages the house, and an excellent housekeeper she is. But I cannot keep her for ever." With a knowing wink, "Gals will think of getting married, and seldom consult the wishes of their parents upon the subject when once they have taken the notion into their heads. But 'tis natural, Mr. S[trickland], it is natural; we did just the same when we were young."

My brother looked laughingly toward the fine, handsome young woman, as she placed upon the table hot water, whiskey, and a huge plate of plum-cake, which did not lack a companion, stored with the finest apples which the orchard could produce.

The young girl looked down, and blushed.

"Oh, I see how it is, Woodruff! You will soon lose your daughter. I wonder that you have kept her so long. But who are these young ladies?" he continued, as three girls very demurely entered the room.

"The two youngest are my darters, by my last wife, who, I fear, mean soon to follow the bad example of their sister. The other *lady*," said the old man, with a reverential air, "is a *particular* friend of my eldest darter's."

My brother laughed slily, and the old man's cheek took a deeper glow as he stooped forward to mix the punch.

"You said that these two young ladies, Woodruff, were by your last wife. Pray how many wives have you had?"

"Only three. It is impossible, they say in my country, to have too much of a good thing."

"So I suppose you think," said my brother, glancing first at the old man and then towards Miss Smith. "Three wives! You have been a fortunate man, Woodruff, to survive them all."

"Ay, have I not, Mr. S[trickland]? But to tell you the truth, I have been both lucky and unlucky in the wife way," and then he told us the history of his several ventures in matrimony, with which I shall not trouble my readers.[6]

When he had concluded, the weather was somewhat milder, the sleigh was ordered to the door, and we proceeded on our journey, rest-

6. The story of Old Woodruff's three wives was cut in the text of *Roughing It in the Bush*, likely because Susanna feared a negative reaction from genteel readers to Woodruff's callous and self-serving behaviour as a husband. The full text can be found in the sketch entitled "Old Woodruff and His Three Wives: A Canadian Sketch," published in *The Literary Garland* (Montreal) NS 5:1 (January 1847), pp. 13–18. See Appendices, pp. 373–82.

ing for the night at a small village about twenty miles from B[elleville], rejoicing that the long distance which separated us from the husband and father was diminished to a few miles, and that, with the blessing of Providence, we should meet on the morrow.

About noon we reached the distant town, and were met at the inn by him whom one and all so ardently longed to see. He conducted us to a pretty, neat cottage, which he had prepared for our reception, and where we found old Jenny already arrived. With great pride the old woman conducted me over the premises, and showed me the furniture "the masther" had bought; especially recommending to my notice a china tea-service, which she considered the most wonderful acquisition of the whole.

"Och! who would have thought, a year ago, misthress dear, that we should be living in a mansion like this, and ating off raal chaney? It is but yestherday that we were hoeing praties in the field."

"Yes, Jenny, God has been very good to us, and I hope that we shall never learn to regard with indifference the many benefits which we have received at His hands."

Reader! It is not my intention to trouble you with the sequel of our history. I have given you a faithful picture of life in the backwoods of Canada, and I leave you to draw from it your own conclusions. To the poor, industrious working man it presents many advantages; to the poor gentleman, *none!* The former works hard, puts up with coarse, scanty fare, and submits, with a good grace, to hardships that would kill a domesticated animal at home. Thus he becomes independent, inasmuch as the land that he has cleared finds him in the common necessaries of life; but it seldom, if ever, in remote situations, accomplishes more than this. The gentleman can neither work so hard, live so coarsely, nor endure so many privations as his poorer but more fortunate neighbour. Unaccustomed to manual labour, his services in the field are not of a nature to secure for him a profitable return. The task is new to him, he knows not how to perform it well; and, conscious of his deficiency, he expends his little means in hiring labour, which his bush-farm can never repay. Difficulties increase, debts grow upon him, he struggles in vain to extricate himself, and finally sees his family sink into hopeless ruin.

If these sketches should prove the means of deterring one family from sinking their property, and shipwrecking all their hopes, by going to reside in the backwoods of Canada, I shall consider myself amply repaid for revealing the secrets of the prison-house, and feel that I have not toiled and suffered in the wilderness in vain.

THE MAPLE-TREE.
A Canadian Song.[7]

Hail to the pride of the forest—hail
To the maple, tall and green;

---

7. This poem was written for the book's conclusion. It first appeared in print in *The Literary Garland* (Montreal) NS 7:5 (April 1849), p. 214.

It yields a treasure which ne'er shall fail
  While leaves on its boughs are seen.
    When the moon shines bright,
    On the wintry night,
And silvers the frozen snow;
    And echo dwells
    On the jingling bells
As the sleighs dart to and fro;
    Then it brightens the mirth
    Of the social hearth
With its red and cheery glow.

Afar, 'mid the bosky forest shades,
  It lifts its tall head on high;
When the crimson-tinted evening fades
  From the glowing saffron sky;
    When the sun's last beams
    Light up woods and streams,
And brighten the gloom below;
    And the deer springs by
    With his flashing eye,
And the shy, swift-footed doe;
    And the sad winds chide
    In the branches wide,
With a tender plaint of woe.

The Indian leans on its rugged trunk,
  With the bow in his red right-hand,
And mourns that his race, like a stream, has sunk
  From the glorious forest land.
    But, blythe and free,
    The maple-tree,
Still tosses to sun and air
    Its thousand arms,
    While in countless swarms
The wild bee revels there;
    But soon not a trace
    Of the red man's race
Shall be found in the landscape fair.

When the snows of winter are melting fast,
  And the sap begins to rise,
And the biting breath of the frozen blast
  Yields to the spring's soft sighs,
    Then away to the wood,
    For the maple, good,
Shall unlock its honied store;
    And boys and girls,
    With their sunny curls,
Bring their vessels brimming o'er
    With the luscious flood

Of the brave tree's blood,
Into cauldrons deep to pour.

The blaze from the sugar-bush gleams red;
    Far down in the forest dark,
A ruddy glow on the trees is shed,
    That lights up their rugged bark;
        And with merry shout,
        The busy rout
Watch the sap as it bubbles high;
        And they talk of the cheer
        Of the coming year,
And the jest and the song pass by;
        And brave tales of old
        Round the fire are told,
That kindle youth's beaming eye.

Hurrah! for the sturdy maple-tree!
    Long may its green branch wave;
In native strength sublime and free,
    Meet emblem for the brave.
        May the nation's peace
        With its growth increase,
And its worth be widely spread;
        For it lifts not in vain
        To the sun and rain
Its tall, majestic head.
        May it grace our soil,
        And reward our toil,
Till the nation's heart is dead.

Choice of Text and Editing Strategy

Roughing It in the Bush appeared in numerous editions in London, New York and Toronto. There were thus several candidates for the text to be chosen for the Norton Critical Edition. They are, in chronological order:

A. The first English edition (London), published in two volumes in February 1852 by Richard Bentley.

B. The second English edition (London), published in two volumes in July 1852 by Bentley, with some added material and editorial emendations.

C. The pirated edition, edited by C. F. B. (Charles Franco Briggs), and published in one volume in New York by George Putnam in July 1852.

D. The first Canadian edition, published in one volume by Hunter, Rose (Toronto) in 1871 as well as by Dawson Brothers in Montreal and Thomas Maclear (Toronto). This edition was used by subsequent Canadian publishers Bell and Cockburn in 1913 and McClelland and Stewart in 1923.

E. The scholarly edition, edited by Carl Ballstadt for the Centre for the Editing of Early Canadian Texts (CEECT) and published by Carleton University Press (Ottawa) in 1988. In this edition Ballstadt includes all the material that Moodie intended for the book, even though, given the distance between the backwoods and London, some of the sketches arrived too late for textual inclusion. For readers interested in the intricacies of the text itself (line-end hyphenated compounds and historical collation) and its detailed publishing history, the CEECT edition provides a comprehensive study of the book's evolution and of Susanna Moodie's intentions in writing it. It also supplies a complete record of the various editions, issues and reprints undertaken by publishers in Canada, Britain, the United States and France. The Ballstadt edition is invaluable as a resource and has been an important reference in preparing this new edition.

Like several other editors, I have chosen the second English edition as a copytext because it offers some corrections to the first edition (made in England) and adds selected material Susanna belatedly sent from Canada. While some of those sketches ("Jeanie Burns" and "Lost Children") could not be fit in due to the advanced state of the typesetting of the text, John Moodie's "Canadian Sketches" was included by Bentley as it was written to be positioned at the end of Volume II.

I have also compared the second edition with the CEECT edition and have made a number of silent corrections based on that comparison.

To American readers, it might seem appropriate to have chosen the 1852 Putnam text since it was edited to conform to Charles Franco Briggs' and George Putnam's sense of what an American audience would have wished to see. Putnam and Briggs were particularly conscious of the pro-British and anti-American biases inherent in Susanna's point of view and sought to soften their effects by excisions. Moreover, they were also concerned to publish a shorter, one-volume book. Hence, Briggs cut what he deemed to be superfluous material (many of Susanna and John Moodie's poems) to reduce the length of the text. As such, Briggs altered the text in ways that stretched well beyond a mere cutting back of what he saw as Susanna Moodie's British biases.

In the interests of providing a readable and useful text, I have decided to exercise what may seem an unusual editorial prerogative. I have elected to cut from the text proper John Moodie's long and analytical concluding essay for Volume II, entitled "Canadian Sketches." I have included it instead in "Backgrounds." This essay, aimed generally at male readers, was added to the second Bentley edition to provide an informative and statistical account useful to those who were thinking of emigrating to Canada. In its emphasis on progress and its descriptive account of Canadian society of the early 1850s, it differs significantly from the sketches that comprise most of the book. As a concluding chapter it does balance John's two sketches that close Volume I, but, unlike those sketches, it adds little to the Moodies' personal story. It is often bypassed by contemporary readers of the text who find it an unwanted and unwarranted extension of the more personalized book they thought they were reading. A few paragraphs convince them that they need read no more. As an appendix, the sketch remains accessible to interested readers.

My other conspicuous intervention has been, where possible, to fill in the blanks that mark the pages of *Roughing It in the Bush* by means of square-bracketed names. Like many of her contemporaries, Susanna Moodie practised this genteel convention of avoiding specifics, especially when it came to the inclusion in her sketches of actual place names and the names of living individuals. In this regard consistency was not her forte, but she did use blanks on many occasions. Those blanks have frustrated many past readers of the book. Research undertaken by Carl Ballstadt, Elizabeth Hopkins, and myself in the 1980s and 1990s revealed the identities of many of the individuals whom Susanna included in her sketches. Where there is no doubt as to the actual place or person in question, I have included in square brackets the full names of those locales and characters. Footnotes also address some of these identities. Readers will thus be better informed as to the individual in question, even as they are aware of my editorial intervention.

BACKGROUNDS

Susanna Strickland as a young woman, c. 1825. Cameo sketch by Thomas
Cheesman. Library and Archives Canada, NL 15658.

Reydon Hall, near Southwold, Suffolk. Photograph courtesy of Elizabeth Hopkins.

The view from above the Moodie property, Lake Katchewanook, Upper Canada, ca. 1900. Courtesy of Kathy Hooke.

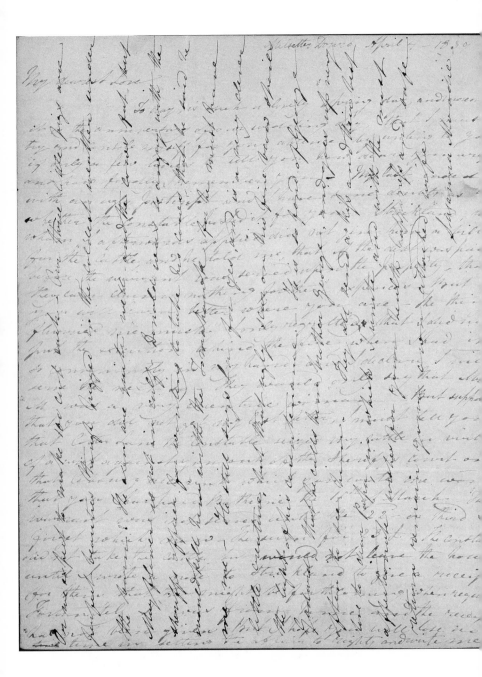

A sample letter from the backwoods, April 4, 1830; the cross-writing shows the struggle to save paper and postage costs. Library and Archives Canada, NL 15559.

Susanna Moodie in the 1850s. Library and Archives Canada, C007043.

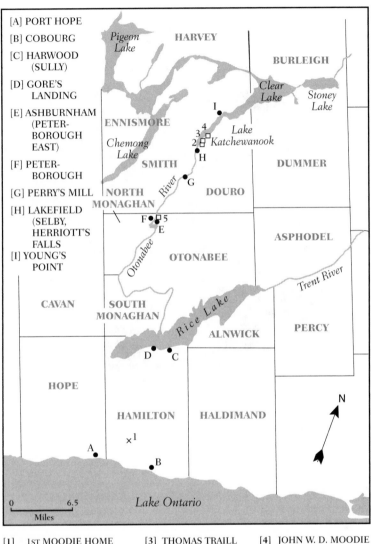

[A] PORT HOPE

[B] COBOURG

[C] HARWOOD (SULLY)

[D] GORE'S LANDING

[E] ASHBURNHAM (PETER-BOROUGH EAST)

[F] PETER-BOROUGH

[G] PERRY'S MILL

[H] LAKEFIELD (SELBY, HERRIOTT'S FALLS

[I] YOUNG'S POINT

[1] 1ST MOODIE HOME (HAMILTON TOWNSHIP) 'Melsetter I'

[2] SAMUEL STRICKLAND 'Homestead'

[3] THOMAS TRAILL 'Westove' 1832–1839

[4] JOHN W. D. MOODIE 'Melsetter II' 1834–1899

[5] THOMAS TRAILL 1839–1843

The Upper Canada area north of Cobourg, including the two sites of settlement by the Moodies. *Based on a map by Gordon C. Dibb, redrawn by John McAusland.*

Advertisement for the First Edition†

In justice to Mrs. Moodie, it is right to state that being still resident in the far-west of Canada, she has not been able to superintend this work whilst passing through the press. From this circumstance some verbal mistakes and oversights may have occurred, but the greatest care has been taken to avoid them.

Although well known as an authoress in Canada, and a member of a family which has enriched English literature with works of very high popularity, Mrs. Moodie is chiefly remembered in this country by a volume of Poems published in 1831, under her maiden name of Susanna Strickland. During the rebellion in Canada, her loyal lyrics, prompted by strong affection for her native country, were circulated and sung throughout the colony, and produced a great effect in rousing an enthusiastic feeling in favour of law and order. Another of her lyrical compositions, the charming Sleigh Song, printed in the present work,[1] has been extremely popular in Canada. The warmth of feeling which beams through every line, and the touching truthfulness of its details, won for it a reception there as universal as it was favourable.

The glowing narrative of personal incident and suffering which she gives in the present work, will no doubt attract general attention. It would be difficult to point out delineations of fortitude under privation, more interesting or more pathetic than those contained in her second volume.

LONDON,
January 22, 1852.

---

† This note was included by the publisher in the first English edition (February 1852).
1. See "The Sleigh-Bells," pp. 95–96.

C. F .B. [CHARLES FREDERICK BRIGGS]

Preface to *Roughing It in the Bush*†

Roughing It in the Bush is a work of so much merit, the scenes and adventures it describes are so full of freshness, truth and humour, the tone that pervades its entertaining pages is so healthy, and the lessons it teaches are so profitable, that it was thought a pity for its wide circulation to be endangered by the retention of any extraneous matter that would increase its bulk and its cost without adding to its value. The accomplished and heroic author will not, therefore, be disposed to complain that her work should have undergone a careful excision of certain passages of a purely personal or political character, which could have possessed no interest for the American reader, and the loss of which will be compensated by the gain of a larger audience than she could have otherwise hoped for.

Mrs. Moodie is a true heroine, and her simple narrative is a genuine romance, which has all the interest of an imaginative creation. Her sister, Miss Agnes Strickland, who has written the histories of the Queens of England, has never recorded the life of a more noble-hearted and heroic woman, one more devoted to her duties, or more courageous in their fulfilment, than will be found developed in the following pages.

The London Edition of "Roughing it in the Bush" contains several poems by Mrs. Moodie and her husband, which have been excluded, because they rather retarded the flow of the narrative, and did not possess sufficient interest in themselves to serve as an apology for their presence.

SUSANNA MOODIE

Introduction to the 1871 Edition

Canada. A Contrast.‡

In the year 1832 I landed with my husband, J. W. Dunbar Moodie, in Canada. Mr. Moodie was the youngest son of Major Moodie, of Mellsetter, in the Orkney Islands; he was a lieutenant in the 21st regiment of Fusileers, and had been severely wounded in the night-attack upon Bergen-op-Zoom, in Holland.

Not being overgifted with the good things of this world—the younger sons of old British families seldom are—he had, after mature deliberation, determined to try his fortunes in Canada, and settle

---

† The Preface to *Roughing It in the Bush* (New York: Putnam, 1852).
‡ Susanna Moodie's preface to the first Canadian edition, Toronto, 1871.

upon the grant of 400 acres of land, ceded by the Government to officers upon half-pay.

Emigration, in most cases—and ours was no exception to the general rule—is a matter of necessity, not of choice. It may, indeed, generally be regarded as an act of duty performed at the expense of personal enjoyment, and at the sacrifice of all those local attachments which stamp the scenes in which our childhood grew in imperishable characters upon the heart.

Nor is it, until adversity has pressed hard upon the wounded spirit of the sons and daughters of old, but impoverished, families, that they can subdue their proud and rebellious feelings, and submit to make the trial.

This was our case, and our motive for emigrating to one of the British colonies can be summed up in a few words.

The emigrant's hope of bettering his condition, and securing a sufficient competence to support his family, to free himself from the slighting remarks, too often hurled at the poor gentleman by the practical people of the world, which is always galling to a proud man, but doubly so, when he knows that the want of wealth constitutes the sole difference between him and the more favored offspring of the same parent stock.

In 1830 the tide of emigration flowed westward, and Canada became the great land-mark for the rich in hope and poor in purse. Public newspapers and private letters teemed with the almost fabulous advantages to be derived from a settlement in this highly favored region. Men, who had been doubtful of supporting their families in comfort at home, thought that they had only to land in Canada to realize a fortune. The infection became general. Thousands and tens of thousands from the middle ranks of British society, for the space of three or four years, landed upon these shores. A large majority of these emigrants were officers of the army and navy, with their families; a class perfectly unfitted, by their previous habits and standing in society, for contending with the stern realities of emigrant life in the backwoods. A class formed mainly from the younger scions of great families, naturally proud, and not only accustomed to command, but to receive implicit obedience from the people under them, are not men adapted to the hard toil of the woodman's life. Nor will such persons submit cheerfully to the saucy familiarity of servants, who, republicans at heart, think themselves quite as good as their employers.

Too many of these brave and honest men took up their grants of wild land in remote and unfavorable localities, far from churches, schools, and markets, and fell an easy prey to the land speculators, that swarmed in every rising village on the borders of civilization.

It was to warn such settlers as these last mentioned, not to take up grants and pitch their tents in the wilderness, and by so doing, reduce themselves and their families to hopeless poverty, that my work "*Roughing it in the Bush*" was written.

I gave the experience of the first seven years we passed in the woods, attempting to clear a bush farm, as a warning to others, and the number of persons who have since told me, that my book "told the history" of their own life in the woods, ought to be the best proof to every candid mind that I spoke the truth. It is not by such feeble instruments as the above that Providence works, when it seeks to reclaim the waste places of the earth, and make them subservient to the wants and happiness of its creatures. The great Father of the souls and bodies of men knows the arm which wholesome labour from infancy has made strong, the nerves that have become iron by patient endurance, and he chooses such to send forth into the forest to hew out the rough paths for the advance of civilization.

These men become wealthy and prosperous, and are the bones and sinews of a great and rising country. Their labour is wealth, not exhaustion; it produces content, not home sickness and despair.

What the backwoods of Canada are to the industrious and ever-to-be-honored sons of honest poverty, and what they are to the refined and polished gentleman, these sketches have endeavored to show.

The poor man is in his native element; the poor gentleman totally unfitted, by his previous habits and education, to be a hewer of the forest, and a tiller of the soil. What money he brought out with him is lavishly expended during the first two years, in paying for labour to clear and fence lands, which, from his ignorance of agricultural pursuits, will never make him the least profitable return, and barely find coarse food for his family. Of clothing we say nothing. Bare feet and rags are too common in the bush.

Now, had the same means and the same labour been employed in the cultivation of a leased farm, or one purchased for a few hundred dollars, near a village, how different would have been the results, not only to the settler, but it would have added greatly to the wealth and social improvement of the country.

I am well aware that a great, and, I must think, a most unjust prejudice has been felt against my book in Canada, because I dared to give my opinion freely on a subject which had engrossed a great deal of my attention; nor do I believe that the account of our failure in the bush ever deterred a single emigrant from coming to the country, as the only circulation it ever had in the colony, was chiefly through the volumes that often formed a portion of their baggage. The many, who have condemned the work without reading it, will be surprised to find that not one word has been said to prejudice intending emigrants from making Canada their home. Unless, indeed, they ascribe the regret expressed at having to leave my native land, so natural in the painful home-sickness which, for several months, preys upon the health and spirits of the dejected exile, to a deep-rooted dislike to the country.

So far from this being the case, my love for the country has steadily increased, from year to year, and my attachment to Canada is now so strong, that I cannot imagine any inducement, short of absolute necessity, which could induce me to leave the colony, where, as a wife and mother, some of the happiest years of my life have been spent.

Contrasting the first years of my life in the bush, with Canada as

she now is, my mind is filled with wonder and gratitude at the rapid
strides she has made towards the fulfilment of a great and glorious
destiny.

What important events have been brought to pass within the narrow
circle of less than forty years! What a difference since *now* and *then*.
The country is the same only in name. Its aspect is wholly changed.
The rough has become smooth, the crooked has been made straight, the
forests have been converted into fruitful fields, the rude log cabin of the
woodsman has been replaced by the handsome, well appointed homestead, and large populous cities have pushed the small clap-boarded village into the shade.

The solitary stroke of the axe, that once broke the uniform silence
of the vast woods, is only heard in remote districts, and is superseded
by the thundering tread of the iron horse, and the ceaseless panting of
the steam engine in our saw mills and factories.

Canada is no longer a child, sleeping in the arms of nature, dependent for her very existence on the fostering care of her illustrious
mother. She has outstepped infancy, and is in the full enjoyment of a
strong and vigorous youth. What may not we hope for her maturity ere
another forty summers have glided down the stream of time. Already
she holds in her hand the crown of one of the mightiest empires that
the world has seen, or is yet to see.

Look at her vast resources—her fine healthy climate—her fruitful
soil—the inexhaustible wealth of her pine forests—the untold treasures hidden in her unexplored mines. What other country possesses
such an internal navigation for transporting its products from distant
Manitoba to the sea, and from thence to every port in the world!

If an excellent Government, defended by wise laws, a loyal people,
and a free Church can make people happy and proud of their country,
surely we have every reason to rejoice in our new Dominion.

When we first came to the country it was a mere struggle for bread
to the many, while all the offices of emolument and power were held
by a favored few. The country was rent to pieces by political factions,
and a fierce hostility existed between the native born Canadians—the
first pioneers of the forest—and the British emigrants, who looked
upon each other as mutual enemies who were seeking to appropriate
the larger share of the new country.

Those who had settled down in the woods, were happily unconscious
that these quarrels threatened to destroy the peace of the colony.

The insurrection of 1837 came upon them like a thunder clap; they
could hardly believe such an incredible tale. Intensely loyal, the emigrant officers rose to a man to defend the British flag, and chastise the
rebels and their rash leader.

In their zeal to uphold British authority, they made no excuse for the
wrongs that the dominant party had heaped upon a clever and high-
spirited man. *To them he was a traitor*; and as such, a public enemy. Yet
the blow struck by that injured man, weak as it was, without money,
arms, or the necessary munitions of war, and defeated and broken in its

first effort, gave freedom to Canada, and laid the foundation of the excellent constitution that we now enjoy.[1] It drew the attention of the Home Government to the many abuses then practised in the colony; and made them aware of its vast importance in a political point of view; and ultimately led to all our great national improvements.

The settlement of the long vexed clergy reserves question, and the establishment of common schools, was a great boon to the colony. The opening up of new townships, the making of roads, the establishment of municipal councils in all the old districts, leaving to the citizens the free choice of their own members in the council for the management of their affairs, followed in rapid succession.

These changes of course took some years to accomplish, and led to others equally important. The Provincial Exhibitions have done much to improve the agricultural interests, and have led to better and more productive methods of cultivation, than were formerly practised in the Province. The farmer gradually became a wealthy and intelligent land owner, proud of his improved flocks and herds, of his fine horses, and handsome homestead. He was able to send his sons to college and his daughters to boarding school, and not uncommonly became an honorable member of the Legislative Council.

While the sons of poor gentlemen have generally lost caste, and sunk into useless sots, the children of these honest tillers of the soil have steadily risen to the highest class; and have given to Canada some of her best and wisest legislators.

Men who rest satisfied with the mere accident of birth for their claims to distinction, without energy and industry to maintain their position in society, are sadly at discount in a country, which amply rewards the worker, but leaves the indolent loafer to die in indigence and obscurity.

Honest poverty is encouraged, not despised, in Canada. Few of her prosperous men have risen from obscurity to affluence without going through the mill, and therefore have a fellow-feeling for those who are struggling to gain the first rung on the ladder.

Men are allowed in this country a freedom enjoyed by few of the more polished countries in Europe; freedom in religion, politics, and speech; freedom to select their own friends and to visit with whom they please, without consulting the Mrs. Grundys of society; and they can lead a more independent social life than in the mother country, because less restricted by the conventional prejudices that govern older communities.

Few people who have lived many years in Canada, and return to England to spend the remainder of their days, accomplish the fact. They almost invariably come back, and why? They feel more independent and happier here; they have no idea what a blessed country it is to live in until they go back and realize the want of social freedom. I

---

1. William Lyon Mackenzie. Compare to Moodie's account in "The Outbreak" (Chapter 23). Her initial poetic responses were decidedly loyal and vehemently against Mackenzie and the rebels. See also pp. 536–57.

have heard this from so many educated people, persons of taste and refinement, that I cannot doubt the truth of their statements.

Forty years has accomplished as great a change in the habits and tastes of the Canadian people, as it has in the architecture of their fine cities, and the appearance of the country. A young Canadian gentleman is as well educated as any of his compeers across the big water, and contrasts very favourably with them. Social and unaffected, he puts on no airs of offensive superiority, but meets a stranger with the courtesy and frankness best calculated to shorten the distance between them, and to make his guest feel perfectly at home.

Few countries possess a more beautiful female population. The women are elegant in their tastes, graceful in their manners, and naturally kind and affectionate in their dispositions. Good housekeepers, sociable neighbours, and lively and active in speech and movement; they are capital companions, and make excellent wives and mothers. Of course there must be exceptions to every rule; but cases of divorce, or desertion of their homes, are so rare an occurrence, that it speaks volumes for their domestic worth. Numbers of British officers have chosen their wives in Canada, and I never heard that they had cause to repent of their choice.

In common with our American neighbours, we find that the worst members of our community are not Canadian born, but importations from other countries.

The Dominion and Local Governments are now doing much to open up the resources of Canada, by the Intercolonial and projected Pacific Railways, and other Public Works, which, in time, will make a vast tract of land available for cultivation, and furnish homes for multitudes of the starving populations of Europe.

And again, the Government of the flourishing Province of Ontario,—of which the Hon. J. Sandfield Macdonald is premier—has done wonders during the last four years by means of its Immigration policy, which has been most successfully carried out by the Hon. John Carling, the Commissioner, and greatly tended to the development of the country. By this policy liberal provision is made for free grants of land to actual settlers, for general education, and for the encouragement of the industrial Arts and Agriculture; by the construction of public roads, and the improvement of the internal navigable waters of the Province; and by the assistance now given to an economical system of railways connecting these interior waters with the leading railroads and ports on the frontier; and not only are free grants of land given in the districts extending from the eastern to the western extremity of the Province, but one of the best of the new townships has been selected in which the Government is now making roads, and upon each lot is clearing five acres and erecting thereon a small house, which will be granted to heads of families, who, by six annual instalments, will be required to pay back to the Government the cost of these improvements—not exceeding $200, or £40 sterling—when a free patent (or deed) of the land will be given, without any charge whatever, under a protective Homestead Act. This wise and liberal policy would have astonished the Colonial Legislature of 1832; but will, no doubt, speedily give to the Province a noble and progressive back country, and add much to its strength and prosperity.

Our busy factories and foundries—our copper, silver and plumbago mines—our salt and petroleum—the increasing exports of native produce—speak volumes for the prosperity of the Dominion, and for the government of those who are at the head of affairs. It only requires the loyal co-operation of an intelligent and enlightened people, to render this beautiful and free country the greatest and the happiest upon the face of the earth.

When we contrast forest life in Canada forty years ago, with the present state of the country, my book will not be without interest and significance. We may truly say, old things have passed away, all things have become new.

What an advance in the arts and sciences, and in the literature of the country has been made during the last few years. Canada can boast of many good and even distinguished authors, and the love of books and book-lore is daily increasing.

Institutes and literary associations for the encouragement of learning are now to be found in all the cities and large towns in the Dominion. We are no longer dependent upon the States for the reproduction of the works of celebrated authors; our own publishers, both in Toronto and Montreal, are furnishing our handsome book stores with volumes that rival, in cheapness and typographical excellence, the best issues from the large printing establishments in America. We have no lack of native talent or books, or of intelligent readers to appreciate them.

Our print shops are full of the well-executed designs of native artists. And the grand scenery of our lakes and forests, transferred to canvas, adorns the homes of our wealthy citizens.

We must not omit in this slight sketch to refer to the number of fine public buildings, which meet us at every turn, most of which have been designed and executed by native architects. Montreal can point to her Victoria Bridge, and challenge the world to produce its equal. This prodigy of mechanical skill should be a sufficient inducement to strangers from other lands to visit our shores, and though designed by the son of the immortal George Stephenson, it was Canadian hands that helped him to execute his great project—to raise that glorious monument to his fame, which, we hope, will outlast a thousand years.

Our new Houses of Parliament, our churches, banks, public halls, asylums for the insane, the blind, and the deaf and dumb, are buildings which must attract the attention of every intelligent traveller; and when we consider the few brief years that have elapsed since the Upper Province was reclaimed from the wilderness, our progress in mechanical arts, and all the comforts which pertain to modern civilization, is unprecedented in the history of older nations.

If the Canadian people will honestly unite in carrying out measures proposed by the Government, for the good of the country, irrespective of self-interest and party prejudices, they must, before the close of the present century, become a great and prosperous people, bearing their own flag, and enjoying their own nationality. May the blessing of God rest upon Canada and the Canadian people!

SUSANNA MOODIE.
BELLEVILLE, 1871

JOHN MOODIE

Canadian Sketches†

The preceding sketches of Canadian life, as the reader may well suppose, are necessarily tinctured with somewhat somber hues, imparted by the difficulties and privations with which, for so many years the writer had to struggle; but we should be sorry should these truthful pictures of scenes and characters, observed fifteen or twenty years ago, have the effect of conveying erroneous impressions of the present state of a country, which is manifestly destined, at no remote period, to be one of the most prosperous in the world. Had we merely desired to please the imagination of our readers, it would have been easy to have painted the country and the people rather as we could have wished them to be, than as they actually were, at the period to which our description refers; and, probably, what is thus lost in truthfulness, it would have gained in popularity with that class of readers who peruse books more for amusement than instruction.

When I say that Canada is destined to be one of the most prosperous countries in the world, let it not be supposed that I am influenced by any unreasonable partiality for the land of my adoption. Canada may not possess mines of gold or silver, but she possesses all those advantages of climate, geological structure, and position, which are essential to greatness and prosperity. Her long and severe winter, so disheartening to her first settlers, lays up, amidst the forests of the West, inexhaustible supplies of fertilising moisture for the summer, while it affords the farmer the very best of natural roads to enable him to carry his wheat and other produce to market. It is a remarkable fact, that hardly a lot of land containing two hundred acres, in British America, can be found without an abundant supply of water at all seasons of the year; and a very small proportion of the land itself is naturally unfit for cultivation. To crown the whole, where can a country be pointed out which possesses such an extent of internal navigation? A chain of river navigation and navigable inland seas, which, with the canals recently constructed, gives to the countries bordering on them all the advantages of an extended sea-coast, with a greatly diminished risk of loss from shipwreck!

Little did the modern discoverers of America dream, when they

† From the second English edition (Chapter 28).

called this country "Canada," from the exclamation of one of the exploring party, "Aca nada,"—"there is nothing here," as the story goes,[1]
that Canada would far outstrip those lands of gold and silver, in which
their imaginations revelled, in that real wealth of which gold and silver
are but the portable representatives. The interminable forests—that
most gloomy and forbidding feature in its scenery to the European
stranger, should have been regarded as the most certain proof of its
fertility.

The severity of the climate, and the incessant toil of clearing the land
to enable the first settlers to procure the mere necessaries of life, have
formed in its present inhabitants an indomitable energy of character,
which, whatever may be their faults, must be regarded as a distinguish-
ing attribute of the Canadians, in common with our neighbours of the
United States. When we consider the progress of the Northern races of
mankind, it cannot be denied, that while the struggles of the hardy
races of the North with their severe climate, and their forests, have
gradually endowed them with an unconquerable energy of character,
which has enabled them to become the masters of the world; the inhabitants of more favoured climates, where the earth almost spontaneously yields all the necessaries of life, have remained comparatively
feeble and inactive, or have sunk into sloth and luxury. It is unnecessary to quote any other instances in proof of this obvious fact, than the
progress of Great Britain and the United States of America, which have
conquered as much by their industry as by their swords.

Our neighbours of the United States are in the habit of attributing
their wonderful progress in improvements of all kinds of their republican institutions. This is no doubt quite natural in a people who have
done so much for themselves in so short a time; but when we consider
the subject in all its bearings, it may be more truly asserted that, with
any form of government not absolutely despotic, the progress of North
America, peopled by a civilised and energetic race, with every motive
to industry and enterprise in the nature of the country itself, must
necessarily have been rapid. An unbounded extent of fertile soil, with
an increasing population, were circumstances which of themselves
were sufficient to create a strong desire for the improvement of internal communications; as, without common roads, rail-roads, or canals,
the interior of the country would have been unfit to be inhabited by
any but absolute barbarians. All the first settlers of America wanted
was to be left to themselves.

When we compare the progress of Great Britain with that of North
America, the contrast is sufficiently striking to attract our attention.
While the progress of the former has been the work of ages, North
America has sprung into wealth and power almost within a period
which we can remember. But the colonists of North America should

---

1. The origin of Canada's name is uncertain, but it is most likely derived from the Huron-
   Iroquois word *kanata*—"village" or "settlement." Moodie refers to the apocryphal story of
   Spanish cartographers or Portuguese explorers dismissing the northern region of Canada as
   having "nothing there."

recollect, when they indulge in such comparisons, that their British ancestors took many centuries to civilise themselves, before they could send free and intelligent settlers to America. The necessity for improvements in the internal communications is vastly more urgent in a widely-extended continent than in an island, no part of which is far removed from the sea-coast; and patriotism, as well as self-interest, would readily suggest such improvements to the minds of a people who inherited the knowledge of their ancestors, and were besides stimulated to extraordinary exertions by their recently-acquired independence. As the political existence of the United States commenced at a period when civilisation had made great progress in the mother-country, their subsequent improvement would, for various reasons, be much more rapid than that of the country from which they originally emigrated. To show the influence of external circumstances on the characters of men, let us just suppose two individuals, equal in knowledge and natural capacity, to be placed, the one on an improved farm in England, with the necessary capital and farm-stock, and the other in the wilds of America, with no capital but his labour, and the implements required to clear the land for his future farm. In which of these individuals might we reasonably expect to find the most energy, ingenuity, and general intelligence on subjects connected with their immediate interests? No one who has lived for a few years in the United States or Canada can hesitate for a reply.

The farmer in the more improved country generally follows the beaten track, the example of his ancestors, or the successful one of his more intelligent contemporaries; he is rarely compelled to draw upon his individual mental resources. Not so with the colonist. He treads in tracks but little known; he has to struggle with difficulties on all sides. Nature looks sternly on him, and in order to preserve his own existence, he must conquer Nature, as it were, by his perseverance and ingenuity. Each fresh conquest tends to increase his vigour and intelligence, until he becomes a new man, with faculties of mind which, but for his severe lessons in the school of adversity, might have lain for ever dormant.

While America presents the most forbidden aspect to the new settler, it at the same time offers the richest rewards to stimulate his industry. On the one hand, there is want and misery; on the other, abundance and prosperity. There is no middle course for the settler; he must work or starve. In North America there is another strong incentive to improvement, to be found in the scarcity of labour; and still more, therefore, than in Europe must every mechanical contrivance which supersedes manual labour tend to increase the prosperity of the inhabitants. When these circumstances are duly considered, we need no longer wonder at the rapid improvements in labour-saving machinery, and in the means of internal communication throughout the United States. But for the steam-engine, canals, and railroads, North America would have remained for ages a howling wilderness of endless forests, and instead of the busy hum of men, and the sound of the mill and steam-engine, we should now have heard nothing but

"The melancholy roar of unfrequented floods."

The scenes and characters presented to the reader in the preceding pages, belong, in some measure, rather to the past than the present state of Canada. In the last twenty years great changes have taken place, as well in the external appearance of the country, as in the general character of its inhabitants. In many localities where the land was already under the plough, the original occupants of the soil have departed to renew their endless wars with the giants of the forest, in order to procure more land for their increasing families where it could be obtained at a cheaper price. In the back-woods, forests have been felled, the blackened stumps have disappeared, and regular furrows are formed by the ploughman, where formerly he had not time or inclination to whistle at his work. A superior class of farmers has sprung up, whose minds are as much improved by cultivation as their lands, and who are comfortably settled on farms supposed to be exhausted of their fertility by their predecessors. As the breadth of land recovered from the forest is increased, villages, towns, and cities have grown up and increased in population and wealth in proportion to the productiveness of the surrounding country.

In Canada, it is particularly to be noted, that there is hardly any intermediate stage between the rude toil and privation of the back-woods, and the civilisation, comfort, and luxury of the towns and cities, many of which are to all outward appearance entirely European, with the encouraging prospect of a continual increase in the value of fixed property. When a colony, capable, from the fertility of the soil and abundance of moisture, of supporting a dense population, has been settled by a civilised race, they are never long in establishing a communication with the sea-coast and with other countries. When such improvements have been effected, the inhabitants may be said at once to take their proper place among civilised nations. The elements of wealth and power are already there, and time and population only are required fully to develope the resources of the country.

Unhappily the natural progress of civilised communities in our colonies is too often obstructed by the ignorance of governments, and unwise or short-sighted legislation; and abundance of selfish men are always to be found in the colonies themselves, who, destitute of patriotism, greedily avail themselves of this ignorance, in order to promote their private interests at the expense of the community. Canada has been greatly retarded in its progress by such causes, and this will in a great measure account for its backwardness when compared with the United States, without attributing the difference to the different forms of government. It was manifestly the intention of the British government, in conferring representative institutions on Canada, that the people should enjoy all the privileges of their fellow-subjects in the mother-country. The more to assimilate our government to that of its great original, the idea was for some time entertained of creating a titled and hereditary aristocracy, but it was soon found that though

"The King can make a belted knight,
    A marquis, duke, an' a' that,"[2]

it was not in his power to give permanency to an institution which, in
its origin, was as independent as royalty itself, arising naturally out of
the feudal system: but which was utterly inconsistent with the genius
and circumstances of a modern colony. The sovereign might endow
the members of such an aristocracy with grants of the lands of the
crown to support their dignity, but what benefit could such grant be,
even to the recipients, in a country covered with boundless forests and
nearly destitute of inhabitants? It is obvious that no tenants could be
found to pay rents for such lands, or indeed even to occupy them,
while lands could be purchased on easy terms in the United States, or
in Canada itself. Had this plan been carried out, Canada would have
been a doomed country for centuries.

The strongest incitements to industry are required, those of propri-
etorship and ultimate independence, to induce settlers to encounter all
the privations and toil of a new settlement in such a country. A genuine
aristocracy can only exist in a country already peopled, and which has
been conquered and divided among the conquerors. In such a state of
things, aristocracy, though artificial in its origin, becomes naturalised,
if I may use the expression, and even, as in Great Britain, when restrained within proper limits, highly beneficial in advancing civilisation.
Be it for good or be it for evil, it is worse than useless to disguise the
fact that the government of a modern colony, where every conquest is
made from the forest by little at a time, must be essentially republican.

Any allusion to political parties is certainly foreign to the object of
the preceding sketches; but it is impossible to make the British reader
acquainted with the various circumstances which retarded the
progress of this fine colony, without explaining how the patronage of
the local government came formerly to be so exclusively bestowed on
one class of the population,—thus creating a kind of spurious aristocracy which disgusted the colonists, and drove emigration from our
shores to those of the United States.

After the American Revolution, considerable numbers of loyalists in
the United States voluntarily relinquished their homesteads and property, and came to Canada, which then, even on the shores of Lake Ontario, was a perfect wilderness. Lands were of course granted to them
by the government, and very naturally these settlers were peculiarly
favoured by the local authorities. These loyalists were generally known
by the name of "tories," to distinguish them from the republicans, and
forming the great mass of the population. Any one who called himself
a reformer was regarded with distrust and suspicion, as a concealed
republican or rebel. It must not, however, be supposed that these loyalists were really tories in their political principles. Their notions on
such subjects were generally crude and undefined, and living in a
country where the whole construction of society and habits of feeling
were decidedly republican, the term tory, when adopted by them, was

2. From the poem "For a' that an a' that" by the Scottish poet Robert Burns (1759–1796).

certainly a misnomer. However, hated by, and hating as cordially, the republican party in the United States, they by no means unreasonably considered that their losses and their attachment to British institutions, gave them an almost exclusive claim to the favour of the local government in Canada. Thus the name of U.E. (United Empire) Loyalist or Tory came to be considered an indispensable qualification for every office in the colony.

This was all well enough so long as there was no other party in the country. But gradually a number of other American settlers flowed into Canada from the United States, who had no claim to the title of tories or loyalists, but who in their feelings and habits were probably not much more republican than their predecessors. These were of course regarded with peculiar jealousy by the older or loyalist settlers from the same country. It seemed to them as if a swarm of locusts had come to devour their patrimony. This will account for the violence of party feeling which lately prevailed in Canada.

There is nothing like a slight infusion of self-interest to give point and pungency to party feeling. The British immigrants, who afterwards flowed into this colony in greater numbers, of course brought with them their own particular political predilections. They found what was called toryism and high churchism in the ascendant, and self-interest or prejudice induced most of the more early settlers of this description to fall in with the more powerful and favoured party; while influenced by the representations of the old loyalist party, they shunned the other American settlers as republicans. In the meantime, however, the descendants of the original loyalists were becoming numerous, while the government became unable to satisfy them all according to their own estimation of their merits; and as high churchism was, unfortunately for the peace of society, associated with toryism, every shade of religious dissent as well as political difference of opinion generally added to the numbers and power of the reform party, which was now beginning to be known in the colony. Strange to say, the great bulk of the present reform party is composed of the descendants of these U.E. Loyalists, while many of our most ultra tories are the descendants of republican settlers from the United States.

As may be supposed, thirty years of increasing emigration from the mother-country has greatly strengthened the reform party, and they now considerably out-number the conservatives. While the mass of the people held tory, or, I should rather call them, *conservative* principles, our government seemed to work as well as any representative government may be supposed to work without the necessary check of a constitutional opposition. Favouritism was, of course, the order of the day; and the governor, for the time being, filled up all offices according to his will and pleasure, without many objections being made by the people as to the qualifications of the favourite parties, provided the selections for office were made from the powerful party. Large grants of land were given to favoured individuals in the colony, or to immigrants who came with recommendations from the home government. In such a state of matters the people certainly possessed the external form of a free government, but as an opposition party gradually acquired an ascendancy in the lower House of Parliament, they were unable to carry the measures adopted by their majority into operation, in consequence of the systematic opposition of the legislative and executive councils, which were generally formed exclusively from the old conservative party. Whenever the conservatives obtained the majority in the House of Assembly, the reformers, in retaliation, as systematically opposed every measure. Thus a constant bickering was kept up between the parties in Parliament; while the people, amidst these contentions, lost sight of the true interests of the country, and improvements of all kinds came nearly to a stand-still. As matters were then conducted, it would have been much better had the colony been ruled by a governor and council; for, in that case, beneficial measures might have been carried into effect. Such a state of things could not last long; and the discontent of a large portion of the people, terminating, through the indiscretion of an infatuated local government, in actual rebellion, soon produced the remedy. The party generally most powerful in the Legislative Assembly, and the members of which had been so long and so unconstitutionally excluded from holding offices under the government, at once obtained the position to which they were entitled, and the people being thus given the power of governing by their majorities in Parliament, improvements of all kinds are steadily advancing up to the present moment, and their prosperity and contentment have increased in an equal proportion.

Had the first settlement of Canada been conducted on sound and philosophical principles, much hardship and privation, as well as loss of capital in land speculations, would have been saved to its first settlers, and the country, improved and improving as it *now* is, would have presented a very different aspect at the present time. With the best intentions, the British government may be justly accused of gross ignorance of the true principles of colonisation, and the local governments are still more open to the accusation of squandering the resources of the colony—its lands—in building up the fortunes of a would-be aristocracy, who being non-resident proprietors of wild lands, necessarily obstructed the progress of improvement, while the people were tantalised with the empty semblance of a free government.

No sooner did emigrants from Great Britain begin to pour into Upper Canada, so as to afford a prospect of the wild lands becoming saleable, then a system of land speculation was resorted to by many of the old colonists. This land speculation has no doubt enriched many individuals, but more than any other abuse has it retarded the natural progress of the country, and the interests of the many have thus been sacrificed to those of the few. Almost all other speculations may be said, in one shape or another, to do good; but land speculation has been an unmitigated curse to Canada, because it occasions a monopoly of the soil, and prevents it from being cleared and rendered productive, until the speculators can obtain their own price for it.

The lands granted to soldiers and sailors who had served in Canada, and those granted to the U.E. Loyalists, were bought up, often at merely nominal prices, from the original grantees and their children, and sold again with an immense profit to new settlers from the old country, or retained for many years in an unproductive state. A portion of the lands granted to the U.E. Loyalists was, of course, occupied by the heads of families; but the lands to which their children became entitled, under the same benevolent provision of the government, were generally drawn in remote situations. By far the larger portion of these grants, however, were not located or rendered available by the grantees, but remained in the shape of U.E. rights, which were purchased at very low prices by the speculators. These U.E. rights were bought at the rate of 1s. 3d., 2s. 6d., or 3s. 9d. per acre; and it was by no means uncommon for old soldiers to sell one hundred acres of land for two or three dollars, or even for a bottle of rum, so little value did they set on such grants in the then state of Canada. These grants, though well meant, and with respect to the U.E. Loyalists, perhaps, unavoidable, have been most injurious to the country.

The great error in this matter, and which *could* have been avoided, was the opening of too great an extent of land *at once* for settlement. A contrary system, steadily pursued, would have produced a concentrated population; and the resources of such a population would have enabled the colonists, by uniting their labour and capital, to make the means of communication, in some degree, keep pace with the settlement of the lands; and Upper Canada would now have been as well provided with canals and railroads as the United States. The same abuses, no doubt, existed formerly to as great an extent in that country, but, being longer settled, it has outgrown the evil. Enough has been said on this subject to show some of the causes which have retarded improvements in Canada.

Another chief cause of the long and helpless torpor in which the country lay, was the absence of municipal governments in the various rural localities. It indeed seems strange, that such a simple matter as providing the means of making roads and bridges by local assessment could not have been conceded to the people, who, if we suppose them to be gifted with common sense, are much more capable of understanding and managing their own parish business, than any government, however well disposed to promote their interests.

Formerly the government of Upper Canada was deluged with petitions for grants of money from Parliament to be expended in improvements in this or that locality, of the reasonableness of which claims the majority of the legislators were, of course, profoundly ignorant. These money grants became subjects of a species of jobbing, or manoeuvering, among the members of the House of Assembly; and he was considered the best member who could get the most money for his county. Commissioners resident in the particular localities were appointed to superintend these public works; and as these commissioners were generally destitute of practical knowledge, these Parliamentary grants were usually expended without producing equivalent results. Nothing in the abstract is more reasonable than that any number of individuals should be allowed to associate themselves for the purpose of effecting some local improvement, which would be beneficial to others as well as to themselves; but nothing of this could be attempted without an Act of Parliament, which, of course, was attended with expense and delay, if not disappointment. The time and attention of the provincial parliament were thus occupied with a mass of parish business, which could have been much better managed by the people themselves on the spot.

When the union of the two provinces was in contemplation, it became evident that the business of such an extended colony could not be carried on in the United Parliament, were it to be encumbered and distracted with the contending claims of so many localities.[3] This consideration led to the establishment of the District (now County) Municipal Councils. These municipal councils were denounced by the conservative party at the time as a step towards republicanism! Were this true, it would only prove that the government of our republican neighbours is better than our own; for these municipal institutions have been eminently beneficial to Canada. But municipal councils are necessarily no more republican in their nature, than the House of Commons in England. However this may be, the true prosperity of Upper Canada may be mainly attributed to their influence on the minds of the people.

Possessing many of the external forms of a parliament, they are admirable political schools for a free people. The most intelligent men in the different townships are freely elected by the inhabitants, and assemble in the county town to deliberate and make by-laws, to levy taxes, and, in short, to do everything which in their judgment will promote the interest of their constituents. Having previously been solely occupied in agricultural pursuits, it might naturally be expected that their first notions would be somewhat crude, and that they would have many long-cherished prejudices to overcome. Their daily intercourse with the more educated inhabitants of the towns, however, tended to remove these prejudices, while new ideas were continually presented to their minds. The rapidity with which this species of practical education is acquired is remarkable, and also, how soon men with such limited opportunities of acquiring knowledge, learn to think and to express their views and opinions in appropriate language. These municipal councillors go home among their constituents, where they have to explain and defend their proceedings; while so engaged, they have occasion to communicate facts and opinions, which are fairly discussed, and thus enlightened views are diffused through the mass of people.

The councillors, at first, were averse to the imposition or increase of taxation, however desirable the object might be; but pride and emulation very soon overcame this natural reluctance; and the example of some neighbouring county, with that natural desire to do good, which,

3. The Union of Canada East (Lower Canada) and Canada West (Upper Canada) occurred in 1841 as a result of the Durham Report.

more or less, influences the feelings and conduct of all public men, were not long in producing their beneficial results, even with the risk of offending their constituents. When the County Municipal Councils were first established, the warden or president of the council, and also the treasurer, were appointed by the governor; but both these offices were afterwards made elective, the warden being elected by the council from their own body, and the treasurer being selected by them, without previous election by the people.

Lately, councils have been also established in each township for municipal purposes affecting the interest of the township only, the reeves, or presidents, of which minor councils form the members of the county council. This general system of municipalities, and a late act of the provincial parliament, enabling the inhabitants to form themselves into road companies, have converted the formerly torpid and inactive townships into busy hives of industry and progressive improvement.

Our agricultural societies have also played no mean part in furthering the progress of the colony. In colonies fewer prejudices are entertained on the subject of agricultural matters than on any others, and the people are ever ready to try any experiment which offers any prospect of increased remuneration for labour. Education, of late, has also made rapid advances in this province; and now, the yeomanry of the more improved townships, though they may be inferior to the yeomanry of England in the acquirements derived from common school education, are certainly far superior to them in general intelligence. Their minds are better stocked with ideas, and they are infinitely more progressive. When we consider the relative periods at which the first settlements were formed in the United States and in Upper Canada, and the accumulation of capital in the former, it will not be difficult to show that the progress of Canada has been much more rapid.

The excavation of the Erie Canal, the parent of all the subsequent improvements of a similar nature in the United States, opened up for settlement a vast country to the westward, which would otherwise for many years have remained a wilderness, unfit for the habitation of man. The boundless success of this experiment necessarily led to all the other similar undertakings. The superior advantages Canada enjoyed in her river and lake navigation, imperfect as that navigation was, operated in a manner rather to retard than to accelerate improvements of this kind; while the construction of the Erie Canal was a matter of prospective necessity, in order to provide for a rapidly increasing population and immigration. In the same manner, the recent completion of the works on the St. Lawrence, and the enlargement of the Welland Canal, connecting Lakes Erie and Ontario, will just as necessarily be followed by similar results, with the additional advantage of the whole colony being greatly benefitted by the commerce of the United States, in addition to her own.

We have now, thanks to responsible government, municipal councils, and common schools, no longer any reason to consider their institutions better calculated to develope the resources of the colony, than our own. Our interests are almost identical, and with our canals and railroads on both sides mutually beneficial, our former hostility has merged into a friendly rivalry in the march of intellect, and we may now truly say that, without wishing for any change in political institutions, which are most congenial to the feelings of the people where they exist, each country now sincerely rejoices in the prosperity of its neighbour.

Before concluding this chapter, I shall endeavour to give the reader a short description of the county of Hastings, in which I have held the office of sheriff for the last twelve years, and which, I believe, possesses many advantages as a place of settlement, over all the other places I have seen in the Upper Province. I should premise, however, lest my partiality for this part of the colony should be supposed to incline me to overrate its comparative advantages to the settler, that my statements are principally intended to show the progress of Upper Province generally; and that when I claim any superiority for this part of it, I shall give, what I trust the reader will consider, satisfactory reasons for my conclusion.

The settlement of a thickly-wooded country, when it is left to chance, is a most uncertain and capricious matter. The narrow views and interests of a clique in the colony or even of an influential individual, often direct emigration out of its natural course, involving unnecessary suffering to the settler, a waste or absolute loss of capital, and a retarding of the progress of the country. The circumstances and situation of the United States were less productive of these evils than those of Upper Canada, because settlement went on more uniformly from the seacoast towards the interior. The mighty rivers and lakes of Canada, though productive of boundless prosperity, operated in the first period of its settlement, most unfavourably on the growth of the colony, by throwing open for settlement an extensive inland coast, at that time unconnected with the ocean by means of canals. Hence numerous detached, feeble, and unprogressive settlements, came into existence, where the new settlers had to struggle for years with the most disheartening difficulties.

European settlers know but little of the value of situation. In most cases they are only desirous of acquiring a large extent of land at a low price, and thus, unless restrained by the wise regulations of a provident government, they too often ruin themselves, and waste their capital in a wilderness, where it does good to no one. When emigration from the United Kingdom began to set in to Upper Canada, the pernicious speculation in wild lands commenced in earnest. As most of the land speculators possessed shares in the steam-boats on Lake Ontario, the interests of both speculations were combined. It was, of course, the interest of the steam-boat proprietors to direct emigration as far to the westward as possible; and influenced by their interested representations and those of the land speculators settled in Toronto, Cobourg, and Hamilton, the greater portion of the emigrants possessing capital were thrown into these towns, near which they were led to expect desirable locations. In the same manner the agents of the Canada Land Company, who were to be found on every steamer, were actively employed in directing the emigrants to the Huron track.

By a simple inspection of the map of Upper Canada, it will be seen, that as the Bay of Quinté was out of the general route of the steamers, and too near the lower end of the lake navigation, it did not suit the views of the parties most interested to direct emigration to its shores. Thus the beautiful Bay of Quinté, with the most fertile land on its shores, and scenery which exceeds in variety and picturesque beauty that of any part of Upper Canada, Hamilton and Niagara alone excepted, has been passed by for years for situations much less desirable or attractive to European settlers.

The forbidding aspect of the country near Kingston, which is situated at the entrance of the bay from the St. Lawrence, where the soil has a rocky and barren appearance, has no doubt deterred emigrants from proceeding in this direction.

The shores of the Bay of Quinté were originally occupied principally by U.E. loyalists and retired officers, who had served during the late war with the United States,[4] but the emigration from Europe has chiefly consisted of the poorer class of Irish Catholics, and of Protestants from the North of Ireland, settled in two very thriving townships in the county of Hastings. There is also a sprinkling of Scotch and English in different parts of the county. Comparatively few possessing any considerable amount of capital have found their way here, as the county town, Belleville, is not in the line of the summer travel on the lakes.

The scenery along the shores of the bay is exceedingly beautiful all the way from Kingston to the head, where a large river, the Trent, discharges itself into it at a thriving village, of about a thousand inhabitants, called Trent Port.[5] A summer ride along the lower portion of this river presents scenery of a bolder and grander character than is often met with in Upper Canada, and it is enlivened by spectacles of immense rafts of timber descending the rapids, and by the merry chorus of the light-hearted lumbermen, as they pursue their toilsome and perilous voyage to Quebec.

Belleville was originally a spot reserved for the Mississagua Indians, and was laid out in 1816 for a village, when there were only two or three white men settled among them as traders in the place. It was only during the last year that the two frame farm-houses, situated about a quarter of a mile apart, were removed to make room for more substantial buildings. Belleville remained nearly stationary for several years, during which a few persons realised handsome fortunes, by means of large profits, notwithstanding the limited extent of their business. It at length began to grow in importance as the fine country in its neighbourhood was cleared and rendered productive.

In 1839, when the county of Hastings was set apart from the Midland district, under the name of the District of Victoria, and Belleville became the District town, the population of the county, including

---

4. The War of 1812.
5. Trent Port became Trenton. Located on Lake Ontario just west of Belleville, it became the outlet of the Trent-Severn Waterway,

Belleville, was about 12,000, and that of Belleville about 1500. In 1850 the population of the county had reached 23,454, of which that of Belleville was 3326. By the census just taken, on a much more correct principle than formerly, the population of Belleville in 1852 appears to be 4554, showing an increase of 1228 in two years. During the same period, from 1850 to 1852, the population of Cobourg on Lake Ontario, which town formerly enjoyed the full benefit of a large emigration, has risen from 3379 to 3867, showing an increase of only 488. The town of Dundas in the same time has increased its population from 2311 in 1850 to 3519 in 1852, showing an increase of 1208. The population of the city of Hamilton in 1850 was 10,312, and now, in 1852, it is said to exceed 13,000. In 1838 the then *town* of Hamilton contained a population of only 3116. When I first visited that place in 1832 it was a dull insignificant village, which might, I suppose, contain a population of 1200 or 1500. I can hardly describe my surprise on revisiting it in 1849, to behold a city grown up suddenly, as if by enchantment, with several handsome churches and public and private buildings of cut stone, brought from the fine freestone quarries in the precipitous mountains or table-land behind the city.

Little need be said of the capital of the province, the city of Toronto, the progress of which has been less remarkable in the same period, for the obvious reason that its merits were sooner appreciated or known by the emigrants from Europe. The population of Toronto, then called Little York, in 1826 was 1677, while that of the now city of Kingston was 2329. In 1838 the population of Toronto was 12,571, and that of Kingston 3877. In 1850 the population of Toronto was 25,166, and that of Kingston 10,097.

These few facts will enable the reader to form some idea of the comparative progress of different towns in Upper Canada, under circumstances similar in some cases and different in others. When it is considered that all of these last-mentioned towns have for many years reaped the full benefit of the influx of emigration and capital from the mother country, while the shores of the Bay of Quinté were little known or appreciated, it will appear that the progress of Belleville has been at least equal to that of any of them. The prosperity of Belleville may in fact be almost entirely attributed to the gradual development of its own internal resources, the fertility of the lands in its vicinity, and a large exportation, of late years, of lumber of all kinds to the United States.

Having no desire unnecessarily to trouble the reader with dry statistical tables, I shall merely quote the following facts and figures, kindly furnished me by G. Benjamin, Esq., the present warden of the county of Hastings, to whose business talents and public spirit the county is largely indebted for its progress in internal improvement.[6]

6. George Benjamin had been one of John Moodie's political enemies in Belleville. As the owner and editor of the *Belleville Intelligencer*, a Tory paper, he had regularly found fault with Moodie's pro-reform politics and the way he conducted his business as sheriff.

The increase of business at the port of Belleville has been most extraordinary. In 1839, the total amount of duties paid at this port amounted to 280*l*.; and in the year 1850 the amount reached 3659*l*. 12*s*. 4*d*. The total arrivals at this port from the United States are as follows:—

	No. of Vessels.	Tons.	Hands employed
British propellers	8	2,400	104
British sailing vessels	81	4,140	375
Foreign do. do.	124	12,643	730
Total	213	19,183	1209

This in addition to our daily steamers.

Our exports to the United States are			£ 52,532	17	5
And British ports below Belleville			153,411	16	6

	£	s	d.	£205,944	13	11
Total imports from United States	25,067	2	6			
Total acceptances from United States	17,435	0	0			
Total importations from lower ports, including drafts and other resources	130,294	0	0	172,796	2	6

Showing the balance of trade in favour of this port to be	£33,148	11	5

Our exports to the lower ports are made up as follows:—

3,485	barrels of Potash	£27,880	0	0
33,198	" Flour	33,198	0	0
357	bushels of Grass seed	133	17	6
1,450	" Barley	181	5	0
4,947	" Peas	594	14	0
4,349	" Rye	434	18	0
37,360	" Wheat	7,472	0	0
198	barrels of pork	396	0	0
54	" Beef	74	5	0
1,141	Sheep-skins	114	2	0
4,395,590	feet square Timber	74,903	2	6
173	kegs of Butter	540	12	6
	Furs	716	0	0
	Fatted Cattle	1,840	0	0
	High Wines	3,098	0	0
	Whiskey	1,830	0	0
		£153,411	16	6

Our exports to the United States are made up as follows:

30,686	bushels of Wheat	£6,137	4	11
3,514	" Rye	351	8	0
3,728	" Peas	466	0	0
90	" Barley	9	0	0
316	" Grass seed	118	10	0
18,756	barrels of Flour	18,756	0	0

338	"	Potash	2,366	0	0
1,000	bushels of Potatoes		62	10	0
92	M.	Shingles	23	0	0
117	M.	Laths	43	15	0
18,210	lbs.	Rags	190	0	0
9,912	lbs.	Wool	481	19	6
466	Sheep-skins		57	10	0
61	kegs of Butter		122	0	0
19,648,000	feet sawed Lumber		21,296	0	0
513	Cows		2,052	0	0
			£52,532	17	5

The River Moira passing through Belleville, where it discharges itself into the Bay of Quinté, is one principal source of its prosperity. The preceding statement will show the quantity of sawed lumber exported, most of which is furnished by the saw-mills of Belleville, or its immediate vicinity. Besides saw and flour-mills, there are cloth and paper manufactories, a manufactory of edge tools; pail manufactories, where great quantities of these useful articles are made at a low price by machinery; planing machines, several iron foundries, breweries, distilleries, &c., in almost all of which establishments steam-engines, or water-power from the river, are used. A remarkable feature in Belleville, in common with other towns in Canada, is the great number of tailoring and shoe-making establishments, when compared with towns of an equal population in Great Britain. This shows, more than anything I am aware of, the general prosperity of the people, who can afford to be large consumers of such articles.

There is very little difference to be observed in the costliness of the clothing of the different classes of society in Upper Canadian towns and cities, and much less difference in the taste with which these articles are selected, than might be expected. With the exception of the lower class of labourers, all persons are well and suitably clad, and they can afford to be so.

Twelve years ago there were not more than five or six piano-fortes in Belleville. Now there are nearly one hundred of a superior description, costing from £80 to £150.

Another remarkable circumstance in Upper Canada is the number of lawyers in all the towns. In Belleville there are about a dozen, which seems to be a large number for a town containing only 4554 inhabitants, when in an English town of the same size there is often not more than one. Of course, I do not mention this as any particular advantage, but to show the great difference in the amount of transactions, and of subjects of contention, in an old and a new country. The same may be said of the number of newspapers, as indicative of commercial activity. Two newspapers, representing the two political parties, are well-supported in Belleville, both by their subscribers, and the number of advertisements.

The mouth of the Moira River, which widens out at its junction with the Bay of Quinté, is completely covered with saw-logs and square timber of various kinds during the summer months. This river, at Belleville, is often dammed up by confused piles of timber. No sooner are these removed than its waters are covered over by vast quantities of oak staves, which are floated down separately to be rafted off like the squared lumber for the Quebec market. The greater proportion of the saw-logs are, however, cut up for exportation to the United States by the various saw-mills on the river, or by a large steam saw-mill with twenty or thirty run of saws, erected on a little island in the mouth of the river. Several large schooners are constantly loading with sawed lumber, and there are two or three steamboats always running between Belleville and Kingston, carrying passengers to and fro, and generally heavily laden with goods or produce. The Bay of Quinté offers more than common facilities in the summer months for rapid and safe communication with other places; and, in the winter time, being but slightly affected by the current of the river Trent, it affords excellent sleighing.

Large quantities of wheat and other farm produce are transported over the ice to Belleville from the neighbouring county of Prince Edward, which is an exceedingly prosperous agricultural settlement, yielding wheat of the finest quality, and particularly excellent cheese and butter. The scenery on the shores of Prince Edward is exceedingly picturesque, and there are numerous wharfs at short distances, from whence the farmers roll their barrels of flour and other articles on board the steamers on their way to market. I have seen no scenery in Upper Canada presenting the same variety and beauty as that of the shores of Prince Edward in particular.

The peninsular situation of this county is its only disadvantage— being out of the line of the land travel and of the telegraphic communication which passes through Belleville. The county of Prince Edward having nearly exhausted its exportation lumber—the people are thus freed from the evils of a trade that is always more or less demoralising in its tendency, and can now give their undivided attention to the cultivation of their farms. Certain it is, that more quiet, industrious, and prosperous settlers, are not to be found in the Province.

A few miles below Belleville, on the south side of the bay, is a very remarkable natural curiosity, called "The Stone Mills." On the summit of a table-land, rising abruptly several hundred feet above the shore of the bay, there is a lake of considerable size and very great depth, and which apparently receives a very inadequate supply from the elevated land on which it is situated. The lake has no natural outlet, and the common opinion is that it is unfathomable, and that it is supplied with water by means of a subterranean communication with Lake Huron, or some other lake at the same level. This is, of course, extremely improbable, but there can be no doubt of its great depth, and that it cannot be supplied from the Bay of Quinté, so far beneath its level. As a small rivulet runs into this lake from the flat ground in its vicinity, and as the soil of this remarkable excavation, however it may have been originally formed, is tenacious, I think we require no such improbable theory to account for its existence. Availing himself of the convenient position of this lake, a farmer in the neighbourhood erected a mill, which gives its name to the lake, on the shore of the Bay of Quinté, and which he supplied with water by making a deep cutting from the lake to the edge of the precipice, from whence it is conveyed in troughs to the mill.

There is a somewhat similar lake in the township of Sidney in the county of Hastings, covering some hundred acres. This lake is also of great depth, though situated on the summit of a range of high hills, from whence it gets the name of the "Oak Hill Pond."

The Bay of Quinté abounds in excellent fish of various kinds, affording excellent sport to those who are fond of fishing. When the ice breaks up in the spring, immense shoals of pickerel commence running up the Moira river, at Belleville, to spawn in the interior. At that time a number of young men amuse themselves with spearing them, standing on the flat rocks at the end of the bridge which crosses the river. They dart their spears into the rushing waters at hap-hazard in the darkness, bringing up a large fish at every second or third stroke. My eldest son, a youth of fifteen, sometimes caught so many fish in this manner in two or three hours, that we had to send a large wheelbarrow to fetch them home. Formerly, before so many mills were erected, the fish swarmed in incredible numbers in all our rivers and lakes.

In the back-woods there is excellent deer-hunting, and parties are often formed for this purpose by the young men, who bring home whole waggon-loads of venison.

While speaking of Belleville, I may mention, as one of its chief advantages, the long period for which the sleighing continues in this part of the country, when compared with other places on the shore of Lake Ontario. Nearly the whole winter there is excellent sleighing on the Bay of Quinté; and on the land we have weeks of good sleighing for days in most other places. This is owing to the influence of a large sheet of frozen water interposed between us and Lake Ontario, which is never frozen.

The county of Prince Edward is a peninsula connected with the main land by a narrow isthmus of low swampy land about four miles wide. Through this neck of land it has long been in contemplation to cut a canal to enable the lake steam-boats to take Belleville in their route between Kingston and Toronto, thus affording a safe navigation in stormy weather. The effect of such a work on the prosperity of the counties of Hastings and Prince Edward would be very great, as European emigrants would have an opportunity of seeing a country which has hitherto escaped their notice, from the causes already mentioned.

Besides the usual variety of churches, there is a grammar-school, and also four large common schools, which latter are free schools, being supported by assessments on the people of the town.

Every Saturday, which is the great day for business from the country, the streets are crowded with farmers' waggons or sleighs, with their wives and pretty daughters, who come in to make their little purchases of silk gowns and ribbons, and to sell their butter and eggs, which are the peculiar perquisites for the females in this country. The counties of

Hastings and Prince Edward are celebrated for female beauty, and nowhere can you see people in the same class more becomingly attired. At the same time there is nothing rustic about them, except genuine good nature and unaffected simplicity of manners. To judge by their light elastic step and rosy smiling countenances, no people on earth seem to enjoy a greater share of health and contentment.

Since the establishment of the county municipal councils, plank and macadamised roads have branched out in all directions from the various central county towns, stretching their ramifications like the veins of the human body, conveying nourishment and prosperity throughout the country, increasing the trade and the travel, connecting man with man and promoting intelligence and civilisation; while the magnetic telegraph, now traversing the whole length of the country, like the nervous system, still further stimulates the inhabitants to increased activity.

The people of this county have not been behind their neighbours in these improvements. The first plank-road which they constructed was from Belleville to Canniff's Mills, a distance of three miles over a road which at the time was often knee-deep in mud, with a solid foundation of flat limestone rock, which prevented the escape of the water. So infamous was this road, that, on some parts of it, it was a matter of serious doubt whether a boat or waggon would be the better mode of conveyance. Notwithstanding the badness of this road, it was the greatest thoroughfare in the county, as it was the only approach to a number of mills situated on the river, and to Belleville, from the back country. It was, however, with the utmost difficulty that the warden could induce the other members of the county-council to sanction the construction of a plank-road at the expense of the county; so little was then known in Canada of the effects of such works.

The profits yielded by this road are unusually large, amounting, it is said, to seven or eight per cent. This extraordinary success encouraged the people to undertake other lines, by means of joint-stock companies formed among the farmers. All these plank-roads are highly remunerative, averaging, it is stated, fourteen per cent. over and above all expenses of repair. More than thirty miles of plank-road is already constructed in the county. In a few years plank or gravel roads will be extended through every part of the country, and they will be most available as feeders to the great line of railway which will very soon be constructed through the entire length of the province, and which has been already commenced at Toronto and Hamilton.[7] A single track plank-road costs from £375 to £425 per mile, according to the value of the land to be purchased, or other local causes. The cost of a gravel road, laid twelve feet wide and nine inches deep, and twenty-two feet from out to out, is from £250 to £325, and it is much more lasting, and more easily repaired than a plank-road. Macadamised or gravel roads will no doubt entirely supersede the others.

In the present circumstances of the colony, however, plank-roads

7. The Grand Trunk Railway.

will be preferred, because they are more quickly constructed, and with less immediate outlay of money in the payment of labourers' wages, as our numerous saw-mills enable the farmers to get their own logs sawed, and they thus pay the greater portion of their instalments on the stock taken in the roads. In fact, by making arrangements with the proprietors of saw-mills they can generally manage to get several months' credit, so that they will receive the first dividends from the road before they will be required to pay any money. The mode of making these roads is exceedingly simple.

The space required for the road is first levelled, ditched, and drained, and then pieces of scantling, five or six inches square, are laid longitudinally on each side, at the proper distance for a road-way twelve feet wide, and with the ends of each piece sawn off diagonally, so as to rest on the end of the next piece, which is similarly prepared, to prevent the road from settling down unequally. The pieces of scantling thus connected are simply bedded firmly in the ground, which is levelled up to their upper edges. Pine planks, three inches thick, are then laid across with their ends resting on the scantling. The planks are closely wedged together like the flooring of a house, and secured here and there by strong wooden pins, driven into auger-holes bored through the planks into the scantling. The common way is to lay the plank-flooring at right angles with the scantling, but a much better way has been adopted in the county of Hastings. The planks are here laid diagonally, which of course requires that they should be cut several feet longer. This ensures greater durability, as the shoes of the horses cut up the planks much more when the grain of the wood corresponds in direction with their sharp edges. When a double track is required, three longitudinal courses of scantling are used, and the ends of the planks meet on the centre one. Very few, if any, iron nails are generally used.

The great advantage of a plank-road is the large load it enables the horses to draw. Whilst on a common road a farmer can only carry twenty-five bushels of wheat in his waggon, a plank-road will enable him to carry forty or fifty bushels of the same grain with a pair of horses. The principal disadvantage of the plank-roads is, that they are found by experience to be injurious to horses, particularly when they are driven quickly on them. They are best adapted for a large load drawn at a slow pace. I shall not attempt to describe the country in the neighbourhood of Belleville, or the more northern parts of the county. It will suffice to observe, that the country is generally much varied in its surface, and beautiful, and the soil is generally excellent. Within the last ten or twelve years the whole country has been studded with good substantial stone or brick houses, or good white painted frame houses, even for thirty miles back, and the farms are well fenced and cultivated, showing undeniable signs of comfort and independence. Streams and water are abundant, and there are several thriving villages and hamlets scattered through the country,—the village of Canniff's Mills, three miles from Belleville, and soon destined to form a part of it, alone containing a population of about a thousand.

In describing the progress of this county, I may be understood as describing that of most other counties in the Upper Province; the progress of all of them being rapid, though varying according to the advantages of situation or from causes already alluded to.

From what has been said, the reader will perceive that the present condition of Canada generally is exceedingly prosperous, and when the resources of the country are fully developed by the railroads now in progress of construction, and by the influx of capital and population from Europe, no rational person can doubt that it will ultimately be as prosperous and opulent as any country in the world, ancient or modern.

It may be said, "should we not then be hopeful and contented with our situation and prospects." And so the people are in the main, and the shrewd capitalists of England think so, or they would not be so ready to invest their money in our public works. But some deduction from this general state of contentment and confidence must be made for those little discontents and grumblings created by the misrepresentations of certain disappointed politicians and ambitious men of all parties, who expect to gain popularity by becoming grievance-mongers. Much has been done, and a great deal still remains to be done in the way of reform, here as elsewhere. But there never was any just cause or motive in that insane cry for "annexation" to the United States, which was raised some years ago, and by the tories, too, of all people in the world! The "annexation" mania can now only be regarded as indicative of the last expiring struggle of a domineering party—it would not be correct to call it a political party—which had so long obstructed the progress of Canada by its selfish and monopolising spirit, when it found that its reign had ceased for ever.

Great sacrifices have been, and will be made, by men of loyalty and principle in support of institutions, which are justly dear to every Briton and to every freeman; but this feeling necessarily has its limits along the mass of mankind; and the loyalty of a people must be supported by reason and justice. They should have good reason to believe that their institutions are more conducive to happiness and prosperity than those of all other countries. Without this conviction, loyalty in a people who have by any means been deprived of the power of correcting the abuses of their government, would be hardly rational. Canadians now have that power to its full extent. Why, then, should we not be loyal to the constitution of our country which has stood the test of ages, purifying itself and developing its native energies as a vigorous constitution outgrows disease in the human frame. The government of Canada is practically more republican than that of the mother country and nearly as republican as that of the United States. Our government is also notoriously much less expensive. Our public officers are also, practically, much more responsible to the people, though indirectly, because they are appointed by a Colonial Ministry who are elected by the people, and whose popularity depends in a great degree on the selections they make and upon their watchfulness over their conduct.

The government of the United States is not a cheap government, because all officers being elective by the people, the responsibility of the selections to office is divided and weakened. Moreover, the change or prospect of the electors being the elected inclines them to put up with abuses and defalcations which would be considered intolerable under another form of government. The British Government now holds the best security for the continued loyalty of the people of Canada, in their increasing prosperity. To Great Britain they are bound by the strongest ties of duty and interest; and nothing but the basest ingratitude or absolute infatuation can ever tempt them to transfer their allegiance to another country.

I shall conclude this chapter with a few verses written two years ago, and which were suggested by an indignant feeling at the cold manner with which the National Anthem was received by some persons who used to be loud in their professions of loyalty on former public occasions. Happily, this wayward and pettish, I will not call it disloyal spirit, has passed away, and most of the "Annexationists" are now heartily ashamed of their conduct.

GOD SAVE THE QUEEN.

God save the Queen. The time has been
When these charmed words, or said or sung,
Have through the welkin proudly rung;
And, heads uncovered, every tongue
    Has echoed back—"God save the Queen!"
        God save the Queen!

It was not like the feeble cry
That slaves might raise as tyrants pass'd,
With trembling knees and hearts downcast,
While dungeoned victims breathed their last
    In mingled groans of agony!
        God save the Queen!

Nor were these shouts without the will,
Which servile crowds oft send on high,
When gold and jewels meet the eye,
When pride looks down on poverty,
    And makes the poor man poorer still!
        God save the Queen!

No!—It was like the thrilling shout—
The joyous sounds of price and praise
That patriot hearts are wont to raise,
'Mid cannon's roar and bonfire's blaze,
    When Britain's foes are put to rout—
        God save the Queen!

For 'mid those sounds, to Britons dear,
No dastard selfish thoughts intrude
To mar a nation's gratitude:

But one soul moves that multitude—
To sing in accents loud and clear—
God save the Queen!

Such sounds as these in days of yore,
On war-ship's deck and battle plain,
Have rung o'er heaps of foemen slain—
And with God's help they'll ring again,
When warriors' blood shall flow no more,
God save the Queen!

God save the Queen! let patriots cry;
And palsied be the impious hand
Would guide the pen, or wield the brand,
Against our glorious Fatherland.
Let shouts of freemen rend the sky,
God save the Queen!—and Liberty!

Reader! My task is ended.

SUSANNA MOODIE

Old Woodruff and His Three Wives†

A Canadian Sketch.

This must have been an adventurous old man. Three wives! Yes; and he was actually thinking of a fourth when we became acquainted with him. There are no histories so graphic as those which people tell of themselves, for self-love is sure to embellish the most common-place occurrences with a tinge of the marvellous, and every day events become quite romantic in the mouths of some narrators. Our biographer was not one of these flighty historians. There was not a dash of romance in his composition. Had a phrenologist examined his head, I verily believe that no bump of ideality could have been discovered in the mountain range of skull-land;—all about that wondrous region, being a dead flat—the aspect of his head giving you the idea of a copper pot with the head closely screwed down. He was a shrewd, humorous looking Yorkshire man, with a sharp red weather beaten face, a pair of small keen grey eyes, glancing knowingly towards his ridgy nose, or looking obliquely back upon his high cheek bones. A large coarse good natured mouth, in a great measure relieved the upper portion of his face from the sinister expression which had been acquired by long dealing with the world, and in overcoming the knavery of his species; for Woodruff was not a rogue himself, though very expert in detecting roguery in others. His tall athletic figure, bent as it was, with hard labour, gave indication of great personal strength; and his ap-

† From *The Literary Garland* NS 5:1 (January 1847), pp. 13–18.

pearance altogether was rather pleasing than otherwise. His manners were frank and easy; and the old man was such an hospitable entertainer, that you felt at home with him in a minute.

But to begin at the beginning, for I have a little outrun my story, the picture of the old yeoman coming so forcibly before me, that I could not forbear sketching it, prior to introducing the owner to my readers. A bad precedent—but I have not time to step back, and go over the ground again.

In the year 1840, a change in my husband's circumstances removed him from a long residence in the back woods, to fill a public situation in a populous town. He went down to B[elleville], some months previous to the removal of his family, to enter upon his new office, and prepare things comfortably for their reception.

He left his forest home in October, and we were to follow with the household wares, and five little children, the first of sleighing. Never did eager British children look for the first violets and primroses of spring, with more impatience than my baby boys and girls watched, day after day, for the first snow flakes that were to form the road, to convey them to their absent father and their new home.

"Winter never means to come this year. It will never snow again!" exclaimed my eldest boy, turning from the window on Christmas day, with the most rueful aspect that ever greeted the broad gay beams of the glorious sun.

It was like a spring day. The little lake in front of the window glittering like a mirror of silver, set in its dark frame of pine woods.

I, too, was wearying for the snow; and was tempted to think that it did not come as early as usual, in order to disappoint us. But I kept this to myself, and comforted the expecting child with the oft-repeated assertion, "that it would certainly snow upon the morrow."

But the morrow came and passed away, and many other morrows; and the same mild open weather prevailed. The last night of the old year was ushered in with furious storms of wind and snow. The rafters of our log cabin shook beneath the violence of the gale, which swept up from the lake like a lion roaring for its prey, driving the snow-flakes through every open crevice, of which there were not a few, and powdering the floor till it was as white as the ground without.

"Oh! what a dreadful night," we cried, as we all huddled shivering around the stove. "A person abroad in the woods to-night, would be frozen."

"Thank God," I said, "we are not travelling this night to B[elleville]."

"But, to-morrow!" said my eldest boy, lifting up his curly head from my lap. "It will be fine to-morrow, and we shall see dear papa again."

In this hope he lay down with the rest, in his little bed upon the floor, and was soon fast asleep. The tempest raged so furiously without that I was fearful that the house would be unroofed; and the night was far advanced when my faithful old Irish servant, Jenny, and myself, retired to bed.

My boy's words were prophetic. That was the last night I ever spent in the bush—in the dear forest home, which I had loved in spite of all the hardships which I had endured since we pitched our tent in the back woods. It was the birth place of my three boys; the school of high resolve and energetic action, in which we had learned to meet calmly and battle successfully with the ills of life. I did not leave it without many regretful tears, to mingle once more with a world, to whose usages, in my long solitude, I had become almost a stranger; and to whose praise or blame I felt alike indifferent.

When the day dawned the whole forest scenery lay glittering in a mantle of dazzling white. The sun shone brightly, the heavens were intensely blue, but the cold was so severe that every article of food had to be thawed before we could get our breakfast. The very blankets that covered us during the night were stiff with our frozen breath.

"I hope the people won't come to take away the furniture to-day," I cried. "We should be frozen on the long journey."

About noon two sleighs with fine spans of horses, made their appearance at the head of the clearing. The snow had been two days in advance of us at B[elleville], and my husband had sent up the teams to remove us. The children jumped about and laughed aloud for joy— while old Jenny and myself commenced packing up trunks and boxes as fast as our cold hands would permit us. In the midst of our muddles, my brother arrived, like a good genius, to our assistance, declaring his determination of taking us down to B[elleville] himself, in his large lumber sleigh. This was indeed joyful news—and in three hours he had dispatched the two sleighs and their loads, and we all stood together in the empty house, striving to warm ourselves over the embers of the expiring fire.

How cold and desolate every object appeared. The small windows half blocked up with snow, scarcely allowed a glimpse of the declining sun to cheer us with his serene aspect. In spite of the cold, several kind friends had waded through the deep snow, to say "God bless you—Good bye!" while a group of silent Indians stood together, gazing upon our proceedings, with an earnestness which shewed that they were not uninterested in the scene. As the children and I passed out to the sleigh, each one pressed forward and silently held out a hand, while the poor squaws kissed me with tearful eyes. They had been true friends to us in our dire necessity, and I returned their mute farewell from my very heart.

Mr. S[trickland] sprang into his sleigh. One of our party was wanting. "Jenny!" shouted my brother at the top of his voice; "it is too cold to keep your mistress and the little children waiting here."

"Och! sure then, I'm after coming," returned the old body, as she issued from the house.

Shouts of laughter greeted her appearance. The figure she cut on that memorable day, I shall never forget. My brother dropped the reins upon the horses' necks, and fairly roared. Jenny was about to commence her journey in three hats. Was it to protect her from the cold? Oh! no—Jenny was not afraid of the cold. She could have ate her breakfast on the north side of an iceberg; and always dispensed with shoes during the most severe of our Canadian winters. It was to protect these precious articles from injury. Our good neighbour, Mrs. W[olseley], had presented her with an old sky-blue drawn silk bonnet, as a parting benediction. This, by way of distinction, as she never had possessed such an article of luxury as a silk bonnet in her life—Jenny had placed over the coarse calico cap with its full yellow furbelow of the same homely material, next her head. Over this, as next in degree, a sunburst straw hat, with faded pink ribbons, a bequest from Miss A[gnes Caddy], just showed its brown rim and taudry trimmings; and, to crown all, and serve as a guard to the rest—a really serviceable grey beaver bonnet of mine, towered up as high as the celebrated crown in which Brother Peter figures in the Tale of the Tub.

"Mercy, Jenny! You don't mean to go with us that figure?"

"Och! my dear heart—I have no band-box that will keep out the cold from my illigant bonnets," returned the old woman, laying her hand upon the sleigh.

"Go back, Jenny! go back"—cried my brother between suffocating peals of mirth. "For God's sake take that tomfoolerie from off your head. We shall be the laughing stock of every village we pass through."

"Och! sure now, Mr. S[trickland], who wo'd think of looking at an ould crathur like me? Its only yerself that wo'd notice the like."

"All the world. Every body would look at you. I believe you put those hats on to be stared at by all the young fellows we meet. Ha! Jenny?"

With offended dignity the old woman retired to re-arrange her toilet, and provide for the safety of her "illigant bonnets," one of which she suspended to the strings of her cloak; and no persuasion of mine could induce her to put it out of sight.

Many painful and conflicting emotions rose up in my heart, but found no utterance in words, as we entered the forest path, and I looked my last upon that humble home of many sorrows. Every object had become familiar during my long exile from civilized life. I loved the lonely lake with its magnificent belt "of dark pines sighing in the breeze;" the cedar swamp—the summer home of my dark Indian friends; my own dear little garden with its rugged fence, cultivated by my own hands, in which I had so often braved the tormenting musquitos, black-flies, and intense heat, to provide vegetables and melons for the use of the family. Even the cows, which had given a breakfast for the last time to my little ones, were regarded with mournful affection. A poor laborer stood at the deserted door, holding my noble water-dog, Rover, on a string. The poor fellow gave a joyous bark as my eyes fell upon him, and struggled to get free.

"James J[ory]," I said, "take care of my dog."

"Never fear, ma'am! he shall bide with me as long as he lives."

"He and the poor Indians, at least, feel grief for our departure," I thought. "Love is so scarce in this world that we ought to prize it, however lowly the source from whence it glows."

We accomplished only twelve miles of our journey that night, which lay through the bush along the banks of the grand, rushing, foaming Otonabee river—the wildest and most beautiful of forest streams. We slept at the house of kind friends, and in the morning resumed our long journey. Winter had now set in fairly. The children were glad to huddle together in the bottom of the sleigh, under the buffaloes and blankets; all but my eldest boy, a child of four years old, who, enchanted by all he saw, continued to stand up and gaze around him.

Born in the forest which he had never quitted before, the sight of a town was such a novelty that he could find no words wherewith to express his astonishment.

"Are the houses come to see one another?" he asked. "How did they all meet here?"

The question greatly amused his uncle, who took some pains to explain to him the difference between town and country. On putting up for the night, we rejoiced to find that truly the long distance which separated us from the husband and father was nearly accomplished. During our ride we had got rid of old Jenny and her bonnets, whom we found a very refractory travelling companion. Fortunately, we overtook the sleighs with the furniture, and Mr. S[trickland] had transferred Jenny to the care of the driver; an arrangement which proved satisfactory to all parties but little Donald, her darling pet, who was fast asleep in my lap when Jenny and her bonnets made their exit. At supper he asked for his old nurse, and his uncle, to tease him, told him that Jenny was dead and that we were going to have some of her fried for supper.

When the beef stakes were brought to table, in spite of his long day's fast, Donald cried piteously, and refused to touch a bit of them; until some fried chickens making their appearance, one of the children cried out—"See, Donald! here is more of Jenny."

"No! no," said the sobbing child, wiping his eyes and laughing once more. "Ninny is not dead, for I know she had not wings."

The next morning was so intensely cold, that out of tender consideration for our noses, Mr. S[trickland] would not resume the journey until past ten o'clock; and even then, it was a desperate experiment. We had not proceeded four miles before the horses were covered with icicles. Our hair was frozen as white as old Time's solitary forelock, and our eyelids were stiff, and every limb aching with cold.

"This will never do," said my brother, turning to me. "The children will freeze. We must put up somewhere. I never felt the cold so severe as this."

"Where can we stop?" said I. "We are miles from any inn, and I see no prospect of the weather becoming milder."

"Yes, yes, I know by the very intensity of the cold, that a change is at hand. At all events, it is much warmer at night in this country than during the day. The wind falls off, and the frost is more bearable. I know a worthy farmer who lives about a mile a-head. He will give us houseroom for a few hours, and we will resume our journey in the evening."

My teeth were chattering with the cold. The children were crying in the bottom of the sleigh, and I gladly consented to the proposal.

A few minutes' ride brought us to a large frame house, surrounded by commodious sheds and barns. A fine orchard opposite, and a yard

well stocked with fat cattle and sheep, sleek geese and plethoric looking swine, gave promise of a land of abundance and comfort. My
brother ran into the house to see if the owner was at home, and
presently returned with the gentleman, whose portrait we have already
drawn, followed by two fine young women, his daughters, who gave us
a truly warm welcome, and assisted in removing the children from the
sleigh, to the cheerful fire, that made all bright and easy within.

"Well! how are you Mr. S[trickland]?" cried the farmer, shaking my
brother heartily by the hand. "Toiling in the bush still, eh?"

"Just in the same place."

"And the wife and children?"

"Hearty. Some half dozen have been added to the flock since you
were in our parts, Woodruff."

"So much the better. The more the merrier, Mr. S[trickland]. Children are riches in this country."

"I know not how that may be. I find it dueced hard to clothe and
feed mine."

"Wait until they grow up. They will be brave helps to you then. The
price of labor—the price of labor, Mr. S[trickland], is the destruction
of the farmer."

"It does not seem to trouble you much," said my brother, glancing
round the well furnished, comfortable apartment.

"My son and I do it all," cried the old man. "Of course the girls help
in busy times, and take care of the dairy, and we hire occasionally. But
small as the sum is which is expended in hiring during seed time and
harvest, I feel it, I can tell you."

"You are not married again, Woodruff?"

"No Sir," said the old man with a peculiar smile, which did not entirely preclude the probability of such an event. "That tall girl with the
fair hair, is my eldest daughter. She manages the house, and an excellent house-keeper she is. But I cannot keep her forever," continued he
with a knowing wink. "Girls will think of getting married, and seldom
consult the wishes of their parents on the subject. But it is natural,
Mr. S[trickland]; it is natural."

My brother looked laughingly towards the fine handsome young
woman, as she placed upon the table, hot water, whisky, and a huge
plate of plum cake, which did not lack a companion stored with the
finest specimens which the orchard could produce.

The young girl looked down and blushed.

"Ah! I see how it is, Woodruff—you will soon lose your daughter. I
wonder that you have kept her so long. But who are these young
ladies?" said my brother, as three fine girls very demurely entered the
room.

"The two shortest are my galls, by my last wife," replied Woodruff,
"who I fear, mean soon to follow the bad example of their sister. The
other lady," said the old man, with a reverential air, "is a *particular*
friend of my eldest daughter."

My brother laughed slily, and the old man's cheek took a deeper
glow, as he stooped forward to mix the punch.

"You said, these two ladies were by your last wife, Woodruff. How many wives have you had?"

"Only three, Mr. S[trickland]. It is impossible, they say in my country, to have too much of a good thing."

"So I suppose you think," said my brother, again glancing towards the comely Miss Smith.

"Three wives! You have been a fortunate man to survive them all."

"Aye! have I not? But I have been both lucky and unlucky in the wife way, Mr. S[trickland]. I was quite a youngster when I married my first woman. My father died when I was quite a child, and I was brought up by an uncle who rented one of those small snug farms in the North Riding, which are now so rarely to be met with in the Old Country. He had saved a little money, and his whole family consisted of one gall and me. She was not very pretty, but she was good and industrious; and would have at his death all the old man had to bestow. She was fond of me, and I thought I could not do better than make her my wife. It is all very well to marry for love, Mr. S[trickland], if a fellow can afford it; but a little money is not to be despised; it goes a great way towards making the home comfortable. Uncle had no great objections, and so we were married. She managed the dairy and I helped upon the farm. We lived very happily together until my poor Betsy died in her confinement with that gall. Yes, Miss—you cost me a good wife, and should not be so anxious to run away and leave me in the lurch."

"Dear father," commenced the young woman.

"There, hold your tongue, Miss. The least said the soonest mended," continued the old man, smiling good humouredly—for it was not only evident, that he was extremely proud of his eldest daughter, but proud of her being the affianced wife of a gentleman in the neighbourhood.

"Well, Mr. S[trickland], I felt very lonely after Betsy died; and I had been so comfortable as a married man, that I thought the best compliment I could pay to her memory was to take another wife."

"Perhaps she would not have thought it one," said I.

"Why, to be sure, women are often a leetle unreasonable," returned Woodruff. "But as she was not there to consult upon the subject, I took the liberty to please myself. Well, Mr. S[trickland], I was always a great admirer of beauty, and so I thought I would try my luck this time with a handsome wife. There was a develish fine gall in our village, only she was a leetle flighty, or so. The lads said to me, when they saw what I was arter—'Sam, you had better carry your pigs to another market. The lass is not right in the upper works.' 'I'll take the chance of that,' says I. 'There is not a prettier gall atween this and York.' Well, my uncle did not like the match by no manner of means.

" 'If you put that madcap,' says he, 'in my poor Betsy's place, I will never leave you a shilling.' "

" 'You may do as you please,' returned I, for you must know, Mr. S[trickland], that I was desperately in love, which I had never been before in my life, 'for I mean to marry the gall right off.'

"I kept my word, and we were married."

The narrator made a long, and I thought, rather an ominous pause, and took a deep draught from a fresh brewage of hot punch.

"Well," said I, rather impatiently, "and how did this second marriage turn out?"

"Bad enough for me," said he, with the most comical expression on his hard countenance, as he turned towards my brother.

Whether he was inclined to laugh or to cry, was no easy matter to determine; but it is certain that neither my brother nor myself could well maintain our gravity, as he exclaimed:

"Well! Mr. S[trickland], would you believe it? She thought fit to cut her throat only three day's arter the wedding. What put such a thing into her head, I never could find out, but you may depend upon it, I never felt so uncomfortable in all my life."

The idea of a man telling such a dreadful circumstance, in such a calm, matter of fact manner, and declaring with the greatest philosophy, that it only made him feel uncomfortable, had in it something so irresistibly comic, that I was forced to hasten to the window to ascertain the state of the weather, in order to conceal the laugh which would come to my lips in spite of every effort to restrain it.

"No wonder that it made you feel uncomfortable, Woodruff," said my brother, casting a wicked look at me, which made me turn again to the window. "It would have been the death of some people. But you are a remarkably strong minded man, or you could not take it so coolly."

"I flatter myself I am," returned the farmer, who did not perceive that my brother was quizzing him. "What was the use of making a fuss? She preferred killing herself to living comfortably with me, and I was not going to play the fool for her. But the worst of it was, that all the galls looked suspiciously at me; and I found that I must go farther a-field, for a third wife. My uncle had a drove of cattle for the London market—I undertook the charge of them—sold the beasts advantageously for him, and returned with the money and a wife. My uncle was glad enough to get the money, but he made a sour face at the wife. She was not to his taste, but she exactly suited mine. We had a bit of a quarrel about my hasty marriage, as he called it. I got mad at the rude things he said, and we parted. I thought that he was too fond of little Betsy, to do an ill-natured thing; but I was mistaken. In order to revenge himself on me, he married his housekeeper, by whom he had soon a large young family.

"All my hopes in that quarter were now at an end. Says I to my wife, 'My dear, we can no longer depend upon my uncle—we must learn to shift for ourselves.'

"With the little property I got with my third wife, I opened a butcher's shop; and we got on comfortably enough for a few years. She was a good woman, and made me an excellent wife. She was the mother of my son and the two youngest of my galls. Suddenly our luck took a turn. My partner, (for I had been fool enough to take one,) ran off, and took along with him all my little savings, leaving me to pay his debts and my own. This was a hard blow. I felt it more than the death of either of my wives.

"To repine was useless, so I sold all my cattle and furniture, paid my creditors the last farthing, and then wrote to my uncle requesting him to lend me fifty pounds to transport myself and family to Canada. The old man knew me to be an honest, hardworking fellow, and for little Betsy's sake, for so run the letter, he sent me a draft upon his banker for fifty pounds, with a gentle hint that it would be the last I must expect from him, as children were nearer to him than grand-children. This was true enough, but I still thought that those children had no right to stand between little Betsy and him. I was very glad of the money, and I wrote him a letter of thanks, promising to repay it if ever I was able. This, with the blessing of God, I did two years ago; and the money found him in a worse state than I was when I left Old England; and I have his letter full of gratitude for the same.

"But to return to the wife. She and the children reached these shores in perfect health. It was in 1832, the year of the great cholera; and I never once imagined that it would attack us who were strangers in the country. A friend, whom I had known in England, hearing of my arrival, wrote to me from Bytown, to come up and look at a farm near him, which he wished me to hire.

"Not caring to drag my wife and children up the country, until I had seen the place myself and prepared all things for their reception, I left them in lodgings at Quebec, and proceeded up the country. I had not been two days at my friend's, and was still undecided about the farm, when I got a letter, written by my eldest gall, which informed me that my poor wife lay bad of the cholera; and if I wished to see her alive, I must start immediately.

"Off I went that very day, vexed to my heart at this untoward accident. Still, Mr. S[trickland], I had left her so well, that I did not think it possible that she could die so soon. While stopping for the boat at Montreal, to proceed on my journey, I met an old school-fellow whom I had not seen for many years, and did not know what had become of him. He had been settled for twenty years in the country, and was now a wealthy merchant in the city.

" 'Oh! Sam Woodruff,' says he; 'who would have thought of meeting with you in Canada. You must come home and dine with me—and talk over old times."

" 'With all my heart,' says I—'but my wife is sick of the cholera at Quebec, and I am waiting for the next boat, to go down and see her."

" 'That is bad,' says he; 'but a few hours cannot make much difference; there is another, and a far better and more commodious boat, starts at six in the evening. Come, don't say no. I long to have a friendly chat over a bottle of good wine.'

"Well, Mr. S[trickland], I did not think it could make much difference. It was only three hours. I should certainly be in time to see my wife—besides I felt sure that she was already better.

"I went to my friend's. We had an excellent dinner, and some of the best wine to relish it, I ever tasted. And what with hearing his adventures and telling my own, and comparing the merits of the two countries, the time slipped away very fast.

"I heard the clock strike six. 'My wife,' says I, springing to my feet. 'Depend upon it, Woodruff,' says my friend, 'that you will find her quite well, and don't forget to bring her to see me, as you pass up.'

"I was only just in time for the boat, and I reached Quebec late the next evening."

"And your wife?" said I.

"Was just dead when I arrived. If I had not gone to dine with my friend, I should have seen her alive. But who would have thought that the trifling delay could have made such a difference?"

My brother looked again at me. "What an unfeeling wretch!" thought I. "This man looks upon his wives much in the same light that he would upon a horse. His grief for their death only amounts to the inconvenience which it occasions. Heaven defend me from such a husband!"

"I wonder," said my brother, "that you could live so long without a fourth."

The old man's heart now began to warm with the punch which he had been drinking—and nodding facetiously towards Miss Smith, he said:

"All in good time, Mr. S[trickland]. I am not so old that a wife would come amiss. When my girls are married, I must get a woman to take care of the house, and make and mend my clothes. Besides, these long winter nights are cruelly cold, and blankets are very dear; depend upon it, the very best thing an old man can do, to keep himself warm and comfortable, and to prolong his days upon the earth, is to take a young wife."

The old man was as good as his word. The next time I passed through ——, I found the pretty young wife in the chimney corner, and the old man as hearty and as hale as ever.

SUSANNA MOODIE

Jeanie Burns†

"Ah, human hearts are strangely cast,
    Time softens grief and pain;
Like reeds that shiver in the blast,
    They bend to rise again.

But she in silence bowed her head,
    To none her sorrow would impart:
Earth's faithful arms enclose the dead,
    And hide for aye her broken heart."

S. M.

---

† This sketch first appeared in *Bentley's Miscellany* 32 (August 1852), pp. 143–52. It also appeared in *Graham's Magazine* 41:4 (October 1852), pp. 430–33. This text of "Jeanie Burns" is taken from Susanna Moodie's *Life in the Clearings* (Toronto: McClelland and Stewart).

While the steamboat is leaving Cobourg in the distance, and, through the hours of night and darkness, holds on her course to Toronto, I will relate another true but mournful history from the romance of real life, that was told to me during my residence in this part of the country.

One morning our man-servant, James N[oble], came to me to request the loan of one of the horses to attend a funeral. M[oodie] was absent on business at Toronto, and the horses and the man's time were both greatly needed to prepare the land for the full crop of wheat. I demurred; James looked anxious and disappointed; and the loan of the horse was at length granted, but not without a strict injunction that he should return to his work directly the funeral was over. He did not come back until late that evening.

I had just finished my tea, and was nursing my wrath at his staying out the whole day, when the door of the room (we had but one, and that was shared in common with the servants) opened, and the delinquent at last appeared. He hung up the new English saddle, and sat down before the blazing hearth without speaking a word.

"What detained you so long, James? You ought to have had half an acre of land, at least, ploughed to-day."

"Verra true, mistress; it was nae fau't o' mine. I had mista'en the hour; the funeral did na come in afore sundoon, an' I cam' awa' as sune as it was owre."

"Was it any relation of yours?"

"Na'na', jest a freend, an auld acquaintance, but nane o' mine ain kin. I never felt sae sad in a' my life as I ha'e dune this day. I ha'e seen the clods piled on mony a heid, an' never felt the saut tear in my een. But puir Jeanie! puir lass! it was a sair sight to see them thrown down upon her."

My curiosity was excited; I pushed the tea-things from me, and told Bell, my maid, to give James his supper.

"Naething for me the night, Bell. I canna' eat; my thoughts will a'run on that puir lass. Sae young, sae bonnie, an'a few months ago as blythe as a lark, an' noo a clod o' the airth. Hout! we maun a' dee when our ain time comes; but, somehow, I canna think that Jeanie ought to ha'e gane sae sune."

"Who is Jeanie Burns? Tell me, James, something about her?"

In compliance with my request, the man gave me the following story. I wish I could convey it in his own words; but though I perfectly understand the Scotch dialect when I hear it spoken, I could not write it in its charming simplicity,—that honest, truthful brevity, which is so characteristic of this noble people. The smooth tones of the blarney may flatter our vanity, and please us for the moment, but who places any confidence in those by whom it is employed? We know that it is only uttered to cajole and deceive; and when the novelty wears off, the repetition awakens indignation and disgust. But who mistrusts the blunt, straightforward speech of the land of Burns? for good or ill, it strikes home to the heart.

Jeanie Burns was the daughter of a respectable shoemaker, who gained a comfortable living by his trade in a small town of Ayrshire.

Her father, like herself, was an only child, and followed the same vocation, and wrought under the same roof that his father had done before him. The elder Burns had met with many reverses, and now,
helpless and blind, was entirely dependent upon the charity of his son.
Honest Jock had not married until late in life, that he might more
comfortably provide for the wants of his aged parents. His mother had
been dead for some years. She was a good, pious woman, and Jock
quaintly affirmed "that it had pleased the Lord to provide a better inheritance for his dear auld mither than his arm could win, proud an'
happy as he wud ha'e been to ha'e supported her, when she was nae
langer able to work for him."

Jock's filial love was repaid at last. Chance threw in his way a cannie
young lass, baith gude an' bonnie, an' wi' a hantel o' siller. They were
united, and Jeanie was the sole fruit of the marriage. But Jeanie
proved a host in herself, and grew up the best-natured, the prettiest,
and the most industrious girl in the village, and was a general favourite with young and old. She helped her mother in the house, bound
shoes for her father, and attended to all the wants of her dear old
grandfather, Saunders Burns, who was so much attached to his little
handmaid, that he was never happy when she was absent.

Happiness, however, is not a flower of long growth in this world; it
requires the dew and sunlight of heaven to nourish it, and it soon
withers, removed from its native skies. The cholera visited the remote
village; it smote the strong man in the pride of his strength, and the
matron in the beauty of her prime, while it spared the helpless and the
aged, the infant of a few days, and the patriarch of many years. Both
Jeanie's parents fell victims to the fatal disease, and the old blind
Saunders and the young Jeanie were left to fight alone a hard battle
with poverty and grief.

The truly deserving are never entirely forsaken; God may afflict
them with many trials, but he watches over them still, and often provides for their wants in a manner truly miraculous. Sympathizing
friends gathered round the orphan girl in her hour of need, and obtained for her sufficient employment to enable her to support her old
grandfather and herself, and provide for them the common necessaries of life.

Jeanie was an excellent sempstress, and what between making
waistcoats and trousers for the tailors, and binding shoes for the shoemakers,—a business that she thoroughly understood,—she soon had
her little hired room neatly furnished, and her grandfather as clean
and spruce as ever. When she led him into the kirk of a sabbath morning, all the neighbours greeted the dutiful daughter with an approving
smile, and the old man looked so serene and happy that Jeanie was
fully repaid for her labours of love.

Her industry and piety often formed the theme of conversation to
the young lads of the village. "What a guid wife Jeanie Burns wull
mak'!" cried one.

"Aye," said another; "he need na complain of ill fortin who has the
luck to get the like o' her."

"An' she's sae bonnie," would Willie Robertson add, with a sigh; "I wud na covet the wealth o' the hale world an' she were mine."

Willie Robertson was a fine active young man, who bore an excellent character, and his comrades thought it very likely that Willie was to be the fortunate man. Robertson was the son of a farmer in the neighbourhood; he had no land of his own, and he was the youngest of a very large family. From a boy he had assisted his father in working the farm for their common maintenance; but after he took to looking at Jeanie Burns at kirk, instead of minding his prayers, he began to wish that he had a homestead of his own, which he could ask Jeanie and her grandfather to share.

He made his wishes known to his father. The old man was prudent. A marriage with Jeanie Burns offered no advantages in a pecuniary view; but the girl was a good, honest girl, of whom any man might be proud. He had himself married for love, and had enjoyed great comfort in his wife.

"Willie, my lad," he said, "I canna gi'e ye a share o' the farm. It is owre sma' for the mony mouths it has to feed. I ha'e laid by a hantel o' siller for a rainy day, an' this I maun gi'e ye to win a farm for yoursel' in the woods of Canada. There is plenty o' room there, an' industry brings its ain reward. If Jeanie Burns lo'es you as weel as your dear mither did me, she will be fain to follow you there."

Willie grasped his father's hand, for he was too much elated to speak, and he ran away to tell his tale of love to the girl of his heart. Jeanie had long loved Robertson in secret, and they were not long in settling the matter. They forgot, in their first moments of joy, that old Saunders had to be consulted, for they had determined to take the old man with them. But here an obstacle occurred, of which they had not dreamed. Old age is selfish, and Saunders obstinately refused to comply with their wishes. The grave that held the remains of his wife and son, was dearer to him than all the comforts promised to him by the impatient lovers in that far foreign land. Jeanie wept, but Saunders, deaf and blind, neither heard nor saw her grief, and like a dutiful child she breathed no complaint to him, but promised to remain with him until his head rested on the same pillow with the dead.

This was a sore and great trial to Willie Robertson, but he consoled himself for the disappointment with the reflection that Saunders, in the course of nature, could not live long; and that he would go and prepare a place for his Jean, and have everything ready for her reception against the old man died.

"I was a cousin of Willie's," continued James, "by the mither's side, an' her persuaded me to go wi' him to Canada. We set sail the first o' May, an' were here in time to chop a sma' fallow for our fall crop. Willie had more o' the world's gear than I, for his father had provided him wi' sufficient funds to purchase a good lot o' wild land, which he did in the township of M——, an' I was to wark wi' him on shares. We were amang the first settlers in that place, an' we found the wark before us rough an' hard to our heart's content. Willie, however, had a strong motive for exertion, an' neever did man wark harder than he did that first year on his bush-farm, for the love o' Jeanie Burns. We built a comfortable log-house, in which we were assisted by the few neighbours we had, who likewise lent a han' in clearing ten acres we had chopped for fall crop.

"All this time Willie kept up a correspondence wi' Jeanie; an' he used to talk to me o' her comin' out, an' his future plans, every night when our wark was dune. If I had na lovit and respected the girl mysel', I sud ha'e got unco tired o' the subject.

"We had jest put in our first crop o' wheat, when a letter cam' frae Jeanie bringin' us the news o' her grandfather's death. Weel I ken the word that Willie spak' to me when he closed the letter,—'Jamie, the auld man's gane at last; an' God forgi'e me, I feel too gladsome to greet. Jeanie is willin' to come whenever I ha'e the means to bring her out; an' hout, man, I'm jest thinkin' that she winna ha'e to wait lang.'

"Guid workmen were gettin' very high wages jest then, an' Willie left the care o' the place to me, an' hired for three months wi' auld squire Jones, in the next township. Willie was an unco guid teamster, an' could put his han' to ony kind o' wark; an' when his term o' service expired, he sent Jeanie forty dollars to pay her passage out, which he hoped she would not delay longer than the spring.

"He got an answer frae Jeanie full o' love an' gratitude; but she thought that her voyage might be delayed until the fall. The guid woman with whom she had lodged sin' her parents died had jest lost her husband, an' was in a bad state o' health, an' she begged Jeanie to bide wi' her until her daughter could leave her service in Edinburg, an' come to tak' charge o' the house. This person had been a kind an' steadfast frin' to Jeanie in a' her troubles, an' had helped her to nurse the auld man in his dyin' illness. I am sure it was jest like Jeanie to act as she did; she had all her life looked more to the comforts of others than to her ain. Robertson was an angry man when he got that letter, an' he said,—'If that was a' the lo'e that Jeanie Burns had for him, to prefer an auld wife's comfort, wha was naething to her, to her betrothed husband, she might bide awa' as lang as she pleased; he would never fash himsel' to mak' screed o' a pen to her agen.'

"I could na think that the man was in earnest, an' I remonstrated wi' him on his folly an' injustice. This ended in a sharp quarrel atween us, and I left him to gang his ain gate, an' went to live with my uncle, who kept the smithy in the village.

"After a while, we heard that Willie Robertson was married to a Canadian woman, neither young nor good-looking, an' vara much his inferior every way; but she had a guid lot o' land in the rear o' his farm. Of course I thought it was a' broken aff wi' puir Jean, an' I wondered what she wud spier at the marriage.

"It was early in June, an' the Canadian woods were in their first flush o' green,—an' how green an' lightsome they be in their spring dress!—when Jeanie Burns landed in Canada. She travelled her lane up the country, wonderin' why Willie was not at Montreal to meet her, as he had promised in the last letter he sent her. It was late in the afternoon when the steamboat brought her to Cobourg, an' without waitin' to ask ony questions respectin' him, she hired a man an' cart to take her an' her luggage to M——. The road through the bush was vara heavy, an' it was night before they reached Robertson's clearin'. Wi some difficulty the driver fund his way among the charred logs to the cabin door.

"Hearin' the sound o' wheels, the wife—a coarse, ill-dressed slattern —cam' out to spier wha' could bring strangers to sic' an out-o'-the-way place at that late hour. Puir Jeanie! I can weel imagin' the flutterin' o' her heart, when she spiered o' the coarse wife 'if her ain Willie Robertson was at hame?'

" 'Yes,' answered the woman, gruffly; 'but he is not in frae the fallow yet. You maun ken him up yonder, tending the blazing logs.'

"Whiles Jeanie was strivin' to look in the direction which the woman pointed out, an' could na see through the tears that blinded her e'e, the driver jumped down frae the cart, an' asked the puir lass whar he sud leave her trunks, as it was getting late, and he must be aff.

" 'You need na bring thae big kists in here,' quoth Mistress Robertson; 'I ha'e na room in my house for strangers an' their luggage.'

" 'Your house!' gasped Jeanie, catchin' her arm. "Did ye na tell me that *he* lived here?—an' wherever Willie Robertson bides, Jeanie Burns sud be a welcome guest. Tell him,' she continued, tremblin' all owre,— for she telt me afterwards that there was somethin' in the woman's look an' tone that made the cold chills run to her heart,—'that an auld frind frae Scotland has jest come aff a lang, wearisome journey, to see him.'

" 'You may spier for yoursel',' said the woman, angrily. 'My husband is noo comin' dune the clearin'.'

"The word husband was scarcely out o' her mouth, than puir Jeanie fell as ane dead across the door-stair. The driver lifted up the unfortunat' girl, carried her into the cabin, an' placed her in a chair, regardless o' the opposition of Mistress Robertson, whose jealousy was now fairly aroused, an' she declared that the bold hizzie sud not enter her doors.

"It was a long time afore the driver succeeded in bringin' Jeanie to hersel'; an' she had only jest unclosed her een, when Willie cam' in.

" 'Wife,' he said, 'whose cart is this standin' at the door? an' what do these people want here?'

" 'You ken best,' cried the angry woman. 'That creater is nae acquaintance o' mine; an' if she is suffered to remain here, I will quit the house.'

" 'Forgi'e me, gude woman, for having unwittingly offended you,' said Jeanie, rising; 'but mercifu' Father! how sud I ken that Willie Robertson—my ain Willie—had a wife? Oh, Willie!' she cried, coverin' her face in her hands, to hide a' the agony that was in her heart, 'I ha'e come a lang way, an' a weary, to see ye, an' ye might ha'e spared me the grief, the burnin' shame o' this. Fareweel, Willie Robertson! I will never mair trouble ye nor her wi' my presence; but this cruel deed o' yours has broken my heart!'

"She went her lane weepin', an' he had na the courage to detain her, or speak ae word o' comfort in her sair distress, or attempt to gi'e ony account o' his strange conduct. Yet, if I ken him right, that must ha'e been the most sorrowfu' moment in his life.

"Jeanie was a distant connexion o' my aunt's; an' she found us out that night, on her return to the village, an' tould us a' her grief. My aunt was a kind, guid woman, an' was indignant at the treatment she had received, an' loved and cherished her as if she had been her ain bairn. For two whole weeks she kept her bed, an' was sae ill, that the doctor despaired o' her life; and when she did come amang us agen, the rose had faded aff her cheek, an' the light frae her sweet blue e'e, an' she spak' in a low, subdued voice; but she never accused him o' being the cause o' her grief. One day she called me aside and said—

" 'Jamie, you ken'd how I lo'ed an' trusted him, an' obeyed his ain wish in comin' out to this wearisome country to be his wife. But 'tis a' owre now.' An' she passed her sma' hands tightly owre her breast, to keep doon the swellin' o' her heart. 'Jamie, I ken that this is a' for the best; I lo'ed him too weel,—mair than ony creature sud lo'e a perishin' thing o' earth. But I thought that he wud be sae glad an' sae proud to see his ain Jeanie sae sune. But, oh—ah, weel; I maun na think o' that. What I wud jest say is this—and she tuk a sma' packet frae her breast, while the saut tears streamed doon her pale cheeks—'he sent me forty dollars to bring me owre the sea to him. God bless him for that! I ken he worked hard to earn it, for he lo'ed me then. I was na idle during his absence; I had saved enough to bury my dear auld grandfather, an' to pay my expenses out; an' I thought, like the guid servant in the parable, I wud return Willie his ain wi' interest, an' I hoped to see him smile at my diligence, an' ca' me his dear, bonnie lassie. Jamie, I canna keep his siller; it lies like a weight o' lead on my heart. Tak' it back to him, an' tell him frae me, that I forgi'e him a' his cruel deceit, an' pray God to grant him prosperity, an' restore to him that peace o' mind o' which he has robbed me for ever.'

"I did as she bade me. Willie Robertson looked stupified when I delivered her message. The only remark he made when I gied him back the siller was, 'I maun be gratefu', man, that she did na curse me.' The wife cam' in, an' he hid awa' the packet and slunk aff. The man looked degraded in his ain sight, an' sae wretched, that I pitied him frae my heart.

"When I cam' home, Jeanie met me at the gate. 'Tell me,' she said, in a dowie, anxious voice,—'tell me, cousin Jamie, what passed atween ye'. Had Willie nae word for me?'

" 'Naething, Jeanie. The man is lost to himsel'—to a' who ance wished him weel. He is na worth a decent body's thought.'

"She sighed sairly; an' I saw that her heart craved after some word or token frae him. She said nae mair; but pale an' sorrowfu', the verra ghaist o' her former sel', went back into the house.

"Frae that hour she never breathed his name to ony o' us; but we all ken'd that it was her lo'e for him that was wearin' out her life. The grief that has nae voice, like the canker-worm, lies ne'est the heart. Puir Jean, she held out durin' the simmer, but when the fa' cam', she jest withered awa', like a flower nipped by the early frost; an' this day we laid her in the earth.

"After the funeral was owre, an' the mourners a'gane, I stood beside her grave, thinking owre the days o' my boyhood, when she an' I were happy weans, an' used to pu' the gowans together, on the heathery hills o' dear auld Scotland. An' I tried in vain to understan' the mysterious providence o' God that had stricken her, who seem sae guid an' pure, an spared the like o' me, who was mair deservin' o' his wrath, when I heard a deep groan, an' I saw Willie Robertson standin' near me, beside the grave.

" 'You may as weel spare your grief noo,' said I, for I felt hard towards him, 'an' rejoice that the weary is at rest.'

" 'It was I killed her,' said he; 'an' the thought will haunt me to my last day. Did she remember me on her death-bed?'

" 'Her thoughts were only ken'd by Him, Willie, wha reads the secrets of a' hearts. Her end was peace; and her Saviour's blessed name was the last sound on her lips. If ever woman died o' a broken heart, there she lies.'

" 'Ah, Jeanie!' he cried, 'my ain darlin' Jeanie! my blessed lammie! I was na worthy o' yer luve. My heart, too, is breakin'. To bring ye back ance mair, I would gladly lay me doon an' dee.'

"An' he flung himsel' upon the fresh piled sods, an' greeted like a child.

"When he grew more calm, we had a long conversation about the past; an' truly I think that the man was na in his right senses, when he married yon wife. At ony rate, he is nae lang for this world; he has fretted the flesh aff his banes, an' afore mony months are owre, his heid wul lie as low as puir Jeanie Burns."

MY NATIVE LAND.

"My native land, my native land!
　How many tender ties,
Connected with thy distant strand,
　Call forth my heavy sighs!

"The rugged rock, the mountain stream,
　The hoary pine-tree's shade,
Where often in the noon-tide beam,
　A happy child I played.

"I think of thee, when early light
　Is trembling on the hill;
I think of thee at dead of night,
　When all is dark and still.

"I think of those whom I shall see
　On this fair earth no more;
And wish in vain for wings to flee
　Back to thy much-loved shore."

SUSANNA MOODIE

Lost Children†

"Oh, how I love the pleasant woods, when silence reigns around,
And the mighty shadows calmly sleep, like giants on the ground,
And the fire-fly sports her fairy lamp beside the moonlit stream,
And the lofty trees, in solemn state, frown darkly in the beam!"

S. M.

There was a poor woman on board the steamer, who was like myself in search of health, and was going to the West to see her friends, and to get rid of (if possible) a hollow, consumptive cough. She looked to me in the last stage of pulmonary consumption; but she seemed to hope everything from the change of air.

She had been for many years a resident in the woods, and had suffered great hardships; but the greatest sorrow she ever knew, she said, and what had pulled her down the most, was the loss of a fine boy, who had strayed away after her through the bush, when she went to nurse a sick neighbour; and though every search had been made for the child, he had never been found. "It is a many years ago," she said, "and he would be a fine young man now, if he were alive." And she sighed deeply, and still seemed to cling to the idea that he might possibly be living, with a sort of forlorn hope, that to me seemed more melancholy than the certainty of his death.

This brought to my recollection many tales that I had been told, while living in the bush, of persons who had perished in this miserable manner. Some of these tales may chance to interest my readers.

I was busy sewing one day for my little girl, when we lived in the township of Hamilton, when Mrs. H——,[1] a woman whose husband farmed our farm on shares, came running in quite out of breath, and cried out—

"Mrs. M[oodie], you have heard the good news?—One of the lost children is found!"

I shook my head, and looked inquiringly.

"What! did not you hear about it? Why, one of Clark's little fellows, who were lost last Wednesday in the woods, has been found."

"I am glad of it. But how were they lost?"

"Oh, 'tis a thing of very common occurrence here. New settlers, who are ignorant of the danger of going astray in the forest, are always having their children lost. I take good care never to let my boys go alone to the bush. But people are so careless in this respect, that I wonder it does not more frequently happen.

"These little chaps are the sons of a poor emigrant who came out this

---

† This sketch was first published in *Life in the Clearings* (1853), the sequel to *Roughing It in the Bush*. Like *Jeanie Burns*, it arrived in London too late for inclusion in *Roughing It*. It belongs to the period of the Moodies' stay in Hamilton Township.
1. "Mrs. H——" is actually "Mrs. O——." See Chapter Nine, note 5, p. 113. The O——s farmed Melsetter on shares with the Moodies in 1833.

summer, and took up a lot of wild land just at the back of us, towards the plains.[2] Clark is busy logging up his fallow for fall wheat, on which his family must depend for bread during the ensuing year; and he is so anxious to get it ready in time, that he will not allow himself an hour at noon to go home to get his dinner, which his wife generally sends in a basket to the woods by his eldest daughter, a girl of fourteen.

"Last Wednesday, the girl had been sent an errand by her mother, who thought that, in her absence, she might venture to trust the two boys to take the dinner to their father. The boys, who are from five to seven years old, and very smart and knowing for their age, promised to mind all her directions, and went off quite proud of the task, carrying the little basket between them.

"How they came to ramble off into the woods, the younger child, who has been just found, is too much stupified to tell, and perhaps he is too young to remember.

"At night Clark returned from his work, and scolded his wife for not sending his dinner as usual; but the poor woman, (who all day had quieted her fears with the belief that the children had stayed with their father,) instead of paying any regard to his angry words, demanded, in a tone of agony, what had become of her children?

"Tired and hungry as Clark was, he instantly comprehended the danger to which his boys were exposed, and started off in pursuit of them. The shrieks of the distracted woman soon called the neighbours together, who instantly joined in the search. It was not until this afternoon that any trace could be discovered of the lost children, when Brian, the hunter,[3] found the youngest boy, Johnnie, lying fast asleep upon the trunk of a fallen tree, fifteen miles back in the bush."

"And the brother?"

"Will never, I fear, be heard of again. They have searched for him in all directions, and have not discovered him. The story little Johnnie tells is to this effect. During the first two days of their absence, the food they had brought in the basket for their father's dinner sustained life; but to-day, it seems that little Johnnie grew very hungry, and cried continually for bread. William, the eldest boy, promised him bread if he would try and walk farther; but his feet were bleeding and sore, and he could not walk another step. For some time the other little fellow carried him upon his back; but growing tired himself, he bade Johnnie sit down upon a fallen log, (the log on which he was found,) and not stir from the place until he came back. He told the child that he would run on until he found a house, and would return as soon as he could, and bring him something to eat. He then wiped his eyes, and told him not to cry, and not to be scared, for God would take care of him till he came back, and he kissed him several times, and ran away.

"This is all the little fellow knows about his brother; and it is very probable that the generous-hearted boy has been eaten by the wolves that are very plenty in that part of the forest where the child was

2. The Rice Lake Plains.
3. See "Brian, the Still-Hunter," Chapter Ten, pp. 215–18.

found. The Indians traced him for more than a mile along the banks of the creek, when they lost his trail altogether. If he had fallen into the water, it is so shallow, that they could scarcely have failed in discovering the body; but they think that he has been dragged into some hole in the bank among the tangled cedars, and devoured.

"Since I have been in the country," continued Mrs. H——, "I have known many cases of children, and even of grown persons, being lost in the woods, who were never heard of again. It is a frightful calamity to happen to any one; for should they escape from the claws of wild animals, these dense forests contain nothing on which life can be supported for any length of time. The very boughs of the trees are placed so far from the ground, that no child could reach or climb to them; and there is so little brush and small bushes among these giant trees, that no sort of fruit can be obtained, on which they might subsist while it remained in season. It is only in clearings, or where the fire has run through the forest, that strawberries or raspberries are to be found; and at this season of the year, and in the winter, a strong man could not exist many days in the wilderness—let alone a child.

"Parents cannot be too careful in guarding their young folks against rambling alone in the bush. Persons, when once they get off the beaten track, get frightened and bewildered, and lose all presence of mind; and instead of remaining where they are when they first discover their misfortune—which is the only chance they have of being found—they plunge desperately on, running hither and thither, in the hope of getting out, while they only involve themselves more deeply among the mazes of the interminable forest.

"Some winters ago, the daughter of a settler in the remote township of Dummer (where my husband took up his grant of wild land, and in which we lived for two years) went with her father to the mill, which was four miles from their log-shanty, and the road lay entirely through the bush. For awhile the girl, who was about twelve years of age, kept up with her father, who walked briskly a-head with his bag of corn on his back; for as their path lay through a tangled swamp, he was anxious to get home before night. After some time, Sarah grew tired with stepping up and down over the fallen logs that strewed their path, and lagged a long way behind. The man felt not the least apprehensive when he lost sight of her, expecting that she would soon come up with him again. Once or twice he stopped and shouted, and she answered, 'Coming, father!' and he did not turn to look after her again. He reached the mill, saw the grist ground, resumed his burden, and took the road home, expecting to meet Sarah by the way. He trode the long path alone; but still he thought that the girl, tired with her walk in the woods, had turned back, and he should find her safe at home.

"You may imagine, Mrs. M[oodie], his consternation, and that of the family, when they found that the girl was lost.

"It was now dark, and all search for her was given up for that night as hopeless. By day-break the next morning the whole settlement, which was then confined to a few lonely log tenements, inhabited solely by Cornish miners, were roused from their sleep to assist in the search.

"The men turned out with guns and horns, and divided into parties, that started in different directions. Those who first discovered Sarah were to fire their guns, which was to be the signal to guide the rest to the spot. It was not long before they found the object of their search, seated under a tree about half a mile from the path she had lost on the preceding day.

"She had been tempted by the beauty of some wild flowers to leave the road; and, when once in the forest, she grew bewildered, and could not find her way back. At first she ran to and fro, in an agony of terror, at finding herself in the woods all alone, and uttered loud and frantic cries; but her father had by this time reached the mill, and was out of hearing.

"With a sagacity beyond her years, and not very common to her class, instead of wandering further into the labyrinth which surrounded her, she sat down under a large tree, covered her face with her apron, said the Lord's prayer—the only one she knew, and hoped that God would send her father back to find her the moment he discovered that she was lost.

"When night came down upon the forest, (and oh! how dark night is in the woods!) the poor girl said that she felt horribly afraid of being eaten by the wolves that abound in those dreary swamps; but she did not cry, for fear they should hear her. Simple girl! she did not know that the scent of a wolf is far keener than his ear; but this was her notion, and she lay down close to the ground and never once uncovered her head, for fear of seeing something dreadful standing beside her; until, overcome by terror and fatigue, she fell fast asleep, and did not awake till roused by the shrill braying of the horns, and the shouts of the party who were seeking her."

"What a dreadful situation! I am sure that I should not have had the courage of this poor girl, but should have died with fear."

"We don't know how much we can bear till we are tried. This girl was more fortunate than a boy of the same age, who was lost in the same township just as the winter set in. The lad was sent by his father, an English settler, in company with two boys of his own age, the sons of neighbours, to be measured for a pair of shoes. George Desne, who followed the double occupation of farmer and shoe-maker, lived about three miles from the clearing known as the English line. After the lads left their home, the road lay entirely through the bush. It was a path they had often travelled, both alone and with their parents, and they felt no fear.

"There had been a slight fall of snow, just enough to cover the ground, and the day was clear and frosty. The boys in this country always hail with delight the first fall of snow; and they ran races and slid over all the shallow pools, until they reached George Desne's cabin. He measured young Brown for a strong pair of winter boots, and the boys returned on their homeward path, shouting and laughing in the glee of their hearts.

"About half-way they suddenly missed their companion, and ran back nearly a mile to find him; not succeeding, they thought that he had hidden himself behind some of the trees, and, in order to frighten them, was pretending to be lost; and after shouting his name at the top of their voices, and receiving no answer, they determined to defeat his trick, and ran home without him. They knew he was well acquainted with the road, that it was still broad day, and he could easily find his way home alone. When his father inquired for George, they said he was coming, and went to their respective cabins.

"Night came on and the lad did not return, and his parents began to feel alarmed at his absence. Mr. Brown went over to the neighbouring settlements, and made the lads repeat to him all they knew about his son. The boys described the part of the road where they first missed him; but they had felt no uneasiness about him, for they concluded that he had either run home before them, or had gone back to spend the night with the young Desnes, who had been very importunate for him to stay. This account pacified the anxious father. Early the next morning he went to Desne's himself to bring home the boy, but, to his astonishment and grief, he had not been there.

"His mysterious disappearance gave rise to a thousand strange surmises. The whole settlement turned out in search of the boy. His steps were traced off the road a few yards into the bush, and entirely disappeared at the foot of a large oak tree. The tree was lofty, and the branches so far from the ground, that it was almost impossible for any boy, unassisted, to have raised himself to such a height. There was no track of any animal to be seen on the new fallen snow—no shred of garment, or stain of blood. That boy's fate will always remain a great mystery, for he was never found."

"He must have been carried up the tree by a bear, and dragged down into the hollow trunk," said I.

"If that had been the case, there would have been the track of the bear's feet in the snow. It does not, however, follow that the boy is dead, though it is more than probable. I knew of a case where two boys and a girl were sent into the woods by their mother to fetch home the cows. The children were lost. The parents mourned them for dead, for all search after them proved fruitless. At length, after seven years, the eldest son returned. The children had been overtaken and carried off by a party of Indians, who belonged to a tribe who inhabited the islands in Lake Huron, and who were out on a hunting expedition. They took them many hundred miles away from their forest home, and adopted them as their own. The girl, when she grew up, married one of the tribe; the boys followed the occupation of hunters and fishers, and, from their dress and appearance, might have passed for aborigines of the forest. The eldest boy, however, never forgot his own name, or the manner in which he had been separated from his parents. He distinctly remembered the township and the natural features of the locality, and took the first opportunity of making his escape, and travelling back to the home of his childhood.

"When he made himself known to his mother, who was a widow, but resided on the same spot, he was so dark and Indian-like that she could not believe that it was really her son, until he brought back to her mind a little incident that, forgotten by her, had never left his memory.

" 'Mother, don't you remember saying to me on that afternoon, Ned, you need not look for the cows in the swamp—they went off towards the big hill!'

"The delighted mother immediately caught him to her heart, exclaiming, 'You say truly—you are my own, my long-lost son!' "

THE CANADIAN HERD-BOY.

"Through the deep woods, at peep of day,
The careless herd-boy wends his way,
By piny ridge and forest stream,
To summon home his roving team—
Cobos! cobos![2] from distant dell
Shy echo wafts the cattle-bell.

"A blithe reply he whistles back,
And follows out the devious track,
O'er fallen tree and mossy stone—
A path to all, save him, unknown.
Cobos! cobos! far down the dell
More faintly falls the cattle-bell.

"See the dark swamp before him throws
A tangled maze of cedar boughs;
On all around deep silence broods,
In nature's boundless solitudes,
Cobos! cobos! the breezes swell.
As nearer floats the cattle-bell.

"He sees them now—beneath yon trees
His motley herd recline at ease;
With lazy pace and sullen stare,
They slowly leave their shady lair.
Cobos! cobos!—far up the dell
Quick jingling comes the cattle-bell!"

2. The phrase means "Cows! Cows!"

SUSANNA MOODIE'S LETTERS TO
HER HUSBAND, 1839†

Melsetter, Douro
Jan. 11, 1839

The receipt of your long kind letter dearest Moodie gave me great joy, as it convinced me that you were well and likely to succeed in your new and arduous situation. God bless you dearest, the children, and poor Susy, send you a thousand kisses and hope you may enjoy many happy new years.

How sorry you will be to learn, that I have been ill ever since you left us, confined chiefly to my bed obliged to send for Dr. Hutchinson, and even to have a nurse. During the Christmas week I was in great agony, and did little else but cry and groan until the following Sunday night, when kind Traill went himself after dark and brought up the Dr. at three o clock in the bitter cold morning. He put the lancet immediately into my breast, and I was able to turn and move my left arm for the first time for ten days, for I lay like a crushed snake on my back unable to move or even to be raised forward without the most piteous cries. You may imagine what I suffered when I tell you that more than half a pint of matter must have followed the cut of the lancet, and the wound has continued to discharge ever since. I was often quite out of my senses, and only recovered to weep over the probability that I might never see my beloved husband again. Poor Jenny nursed me somewhat like a she bear, her tenderest mercies were neglect. She is however behaving better now. Dr. H. seemed greatly concerned for my situation. When he looked round the forlorn, cold, dirty room feebly lighted by the wretched lamp, he said with great emphasis, 'In the name of God! Mrs Moodie get out of this.' Well, I have got through it, and am once more able to crawl about the house, but I am very weak. I have great reason to be thankful for the disinterested kindness of my female neighbors. Mrs Caddy, when she heard I was so bad, came down through a heavy snow storm, and offered to stay and nurse me herself. This I would not consent to, but she took away my noisy merry Dunny, and has kept him ever since, and more than this, she has clothed him from head to foot, and he looks so smart and handsome, and behaves himself so well. She brought him to see me one Sunday, but he would go back with dear Mamma Caddy, and is quite a plaything for the old Colonel.

She sent me fresh beef and chicken for to make broth and has been quite a Mother to me. Dear Mrs Hague and Mrs Crawford came to see me twice, and both wept much at my miserable state. Mrs H. sent me a gallon of old port wine, and so many nice things, I could not help shedding tears when I received them. She took away my poor little

† The full text of Susanna's monthly letters in 1839 to John Moodie are in *Letters of Love and Duty: The Correspondence of Susanna and John Moodie*, eds. Ballstadt, Hopkins and Peterman (University of Toronto Press, 1993). Readers are invited to compare Susanna's letters to the relevant sections of *Roughing It in the Bush*.

Aggy, and insists on keeping her through the winter. Traill tells me that they have bought her shoes and nice clothes, that Mrs H. is so fond of her and teaches her to read herself, that A. looks happy and well, and behaves quite like a little lady minding every word Mrs Hague says to her. I have not seen her since the week after you left me, but she is coming to see me on tuesday, and my heart yearns for my poor noisy little pet. So much for Aggy and Dunnie. Sweet Katie has remained to be my kind little nurse. During the period I was so very ill, she sat crying by my bed side all day, and till late into the night. To add to my sorrows Donald got a dreadful fall on the stove and laid his skull bare above the right eye. Jenny called out that he was killed, and for a moment when I saw his ghastly face, the blood pouring in a torrent from the frightful wound I thought so too. The old woman in her despair uttered only frightful cries, and I sent her away for help and took my poor bleeding boy into my lap almost as terrified or more so than he. After sometime I succeeded in staunching the blood with very warm water, and then I examined carefully his head, and I felt convinced his skull was not fractured though I saw the bone plainly, and I bound it up and got him to sleep before Strickland and Mr Traill came and dressed the wound. I have suffered much anxiety about it, often having to poultice it, but thank God he is well now, and naught remains of his wound but the ugly scar, which I think will wear away in time. He still looks pale from the loss of blood, but he says, 'dear Papa is at Bellwill,' and I am to write two kisses for him.

When my dear Mrs Shairp heard from Dr H. how ill I was she came up on New Years day, and has been with me ever since, the kindest of all kind nurses to me and sweet little Johnnie, who has suffered little from his poor Mothers illness. Surely my dear love I have bought this boy at a price. He ought to be my best child. You would not know him, he is grown such a fine creature, and laughs, and capers, and crows, and is the most lively babe I ever had. I have not weaned him, through all, but the milk has left my bad breast in all probability for ever.

* * *

Douro
Feb. 14, 1839

Good morning to you Valentine!

Dearest and best, I have been anxiously looking for an opportunity of writing to you with the books; but no such occurring, my heart is sore to write to you, and I can delay no longer. Your affectionate and welcome letter made me *very happy*, and has done more to restore me to health, than all the Doctors in Canada. God bless you for all your goodness to me. My breast is quite well now, and I am beginning to gather strength again. We have suffered dreadfully from cold, these heavy gales, not daring to put much fire into the stove on account of the bad pipes, but the worst is past, and I begin to look forward with hope to the spring. Your tenderness, reconciles me to every thing and while you continue to write me such kind letters, I could bear ten times more privations without a murmur.

* * *

Douro
March 6, 1839

My dearest Husband

I have been anxiously looking for a letter from you for some days past, and I can no longer repress the strong desire I feel to write to you. Since the date of my last, I have been occupied incessantly at the sick bed of two of our dear children, whom I expected every hour to breathe their last. You may imagine the anguish of your poor Susy, and you so far away. Poor little Donald, was first taken, with sudden inflamation on the lungs, attended with violent fever and every symptom of croup. I had to put him in a warm bath, force castor oil down his throat and apply a large blister to his chest. Poor little fellow his cries were dreadful and his entreaties for me to take all the pins out of his belly which was the violent pains in his chest and at the pit of his stomach. Dear Mrs Traill came to me at the break of day, and Traill went down to get advice from the Doctor if he could not bring him up. That night my beloved baby was struck in the same manner. Only he was to all appearance dead. It was about five in the afternoon. He had been in a heavy dose all day. I was busy doing something for Donald when I saw Johnnie throw up his hands in an unusual way. I hastened to take him up. But all sense appeared to have fled. His jaws were relaxed the foam was running from his mouth and my lovely dear's beautiful limbs fell over my arms a dead weight. I burst into an agony of tears in which I was joined by poor Katey, and putting my insensible lamb into her arms, I ran and called Jenny who was with the two young Godards in the sugar bush. Thank God she came directly, and there happened to be warm water on. We got him into the bath but it was a long time before he gave any signs of returning to life. In the mean time kind Cyprian Godard ran off for the doctor, sending up in his way Mrs Strickland and dear Catharine who was at tea at Crawfords. Neither could give me any hopes of my darlings recovery. But we did all we could for him, we put on a blister, on his white tender chest and forced some tartar emetic down his throat and put hot flannels to his cold feet, and sat down to watch through the dreary night the faint heavings of his innocent breast. In the mean time my messenger sped on to Peterboro', and met Mr. Traill who was bringing up medicines for Donald, and dear Mrs [Emilia] Shairp who would come up when she heard my dear child was so ill.

Oh what a comfort this warm hearted friend was to me in my dire distress for though she could not stop my streaming tears, she helped me nurse my poor suffering children, and shared my grief. It was four o'clock in the morning before Cyprian returned faint and tired. Dr H. would not come, but said, that he would send up Dr Dixon in the morning.

The next was a dreadfully severe day of wind, frost, and drifting snow. The dear babe was apparently worse and no Dr came, when Cyprian, again volunteered to go down for a Dr. But Dr H. would not be entreated. 'If you do not come,' Cyprian said, 'the sweet babe will die.' 'I cant help that,' was the unfeeling reply. 'The roads are too bad, and I cant leave Peterboro'.' Cyprian then went to old Dr Bird, who came up inspite of the bad roads and the dreadful night. Good old dear how kind he was—He told me, that without medical aid the child must have died. That he was still in great danger, though the remidies we had applied had prolonged his life—'I am an old man,' he said 'to come thus far, through such weather, but I did it to serve Mr. Moodie, when I heard Hutchison would not come, I was determined that the child should not be lost if I could save it.' He told me Donald was out of danger, but that I was very ill myself. I had not even felt the effects of this horrible influenza—so great was my anxiety about my children. Numbers of children have died with it.

* * *

Melsetter
March 20, 1839

My Dearest Husband,

Banish all your gloomy forbodings, our dear children are *quite* out of danger, though a cough hangs on both of them, especially my lovely Johnnie, but I do not feel uneasy about it; as the spring advances I hope they will lose it entirely. I cannot keep Donald indoors, and the poor moccasins that I can manufacture out of old cloth, keep his feet constantly wet, which is one cause of the obstinacy of his cough. Dunbar, who is no better off, is quite stout and well, and grows a very noble looking boy. His love for Agnes Caddy, is almost a passion, and he is always there. You would laugh to hear the little creature talking to her, just like a man desperately in love. He always sleeps with her, and says that he can't sleep if his head is not on his dear Addy's bosom. 'Oh my dear little Addy; I love you better than any sing in the world.' Addy is very kind to her wee pet, and makes him so docile and obedient, that he is quite a pattern to all the rest. Your kind letter was a great comfort to me. To know, that you love us, and think of us in all our sickness and privations atones for them all. How precious that love and sympathy is to your poor Susy no written language can tell. In it, is concentrated every better thought and feeling of heart and mind. Oh, that I were indeed deserving of the love and esteem I so much covet. But, then, I should be too happy and perfect happiness is no denizen of earth. * * *

* * * The dear Traills are gone—I am doubly lonely now. Many tears have I shed for their removal, we have been on such happy terms all winter. They have been so kind to me especially poor Traill. One knows not the value of a friend till one is left alone in this weary world. The poor children quite fret after their good Aunt. * * *

Melsetter Douro
July 16, 1839

My Dearest Moodie,

When I recal the date of your last letter written so many weeks ago, I know not how to still the constant enquiries of my anxious heart— 'What can keep him—why does he neither write nor send to us.' Surely dearest, we cannot have become indifferent to you that you should leave us, in this dreadful state of uncertainty as to your plans and present situation. Your long absence and silence, paralizes all exertion. I only live from day to day, in the hope of seeing you before night, or hearing from you, but night comes and no word from you, and I take poor little Johnnie into my arms and pray for his absent father and bathe his innocent face with tears. Cruel Moodie, one short sentence which would tell me you are well would remove this miserable state of anxiety. Oh do write, if but one line to me. You were to have been here, the first week in June. Here is the middle of July, and no Moodie. I will walk down to Belleville if you do not come or send to me. The poor children have ceased to talk now of your return. Katie says, 'Papa has forgotten us.' Thank God the dear children are all well and send a kiss and their best love to dear Papa. * * *

CATHARINE PARR TRAILL

A Slight Sketch of the Early Life of Mrs. Moodie†

My sister Susanna was the youngest of the six sisters and was by no means the least remarkable for talent among us. From her earliest childhood, she shewed an originality of thought, that developed itself apart from teaching, or imitation. She early shewed a lively imagination—She lived in a sort of dream-world of her own, clothing the fanciful images of her fertile brain, in language that often partook of the poetical, rather than the plain matter of fact words in which children usually express their ideas—In fact Susie was a genius. When she was about four years old, she would suddenly look up with her earnest grey eyes, and relate some wonderful romance of her own creation, which usually began, "When I was a little boy and lived in Souf America." What the stories of her childish dreams were, I cannot now remember—only I recollect she used to talk of great rivers, and big trees, and white ants, snakes and croccodiles—Sometimes she would tell the story as a dream—but more often as a fact, that she had once seen. Possibly some of these images were gathered up by the child, from our father's conversation, or passages from books of travel, read out by our parents.

---

† From Traill Family Collection, volume 7, National Archives of Canada. See also Catharine Parr Traill, *Forest and Other Gleanings*, ed. Michael A. Peterman and Carl Ballstadt (Ottawa: U of Ottawa P, 1994): 46–56.

One day Susie was found sitting on the doorstep, hugging some little thing in her lap—caressing the little dolly-like bundle, and saying—"Oh oo pity dear, I *do* love oo so!" To the horror of the nurse maid, it proved to be a lizard, that she had found and wrapped up in her pinafore. The maid snatched the strange nurseling away—The child cried for her "beautiful darling" and it was hard to comfort her. She was a great admirer of frogs and toads, of which she had no fear—They had beauty in her wondering eyes.

When Susanna was born, she was a tiny weakly baby, so much so that it was thought desirable that she should be baptized within a short time after her birth. Great was the excitement among my elder sisters about the name to be chosen for her. Elizabeth suggested Cassandra—for they were just then deep in Pope's Homer's Illiad[1]—Agnes insisted on the grand sounding name of Andromache, her hero Hector's wife, while Sarah meekly suggested Hecuba, fortunately baby escaped the infliction of being given any of these remarkable names. I remember our mother mentioning the circumstance one day in after years, when Susie was rather lamenting that she had been Christened the Jewish name of Susanna—but she was reconciled to its homliness, and quite thankful, when she heard of the escape she had had, from such out of the way names as Cassandra, Andromache and Hecuba! The last especially roused her indignation. "How could she have lived with such a heathenish name?" She might have cried out "Hecuba Strickland! Phoebus what a name."

Like the rest of her sisters she was a great reader. As early as the age of nine or ten years, she began to clothe her ideas and feelings in verse. Her facility for rhyme was great and her imagination, vivid and romantic, tinged with gloom and grandeur, rather than wit and humor,—Though in later years this element was not wanting in her writings. She and I were devoted to one another, I was not of so imaginative a disposition, our tempers and abilities were unlike, and possibly it was the contrast between us in many ways, that had the effect of binding us so closely together. Our faithful friendship was never broken—As it was in our childish days—so has it always been, through our long lives—and in our extreme old age, we clung to each other with a love and trust, that knew no change nor coldness—And now that death has called her from me—I know that the parting will not be for long—that we cannot long be severed. May the reunion be granted through our mutual faith, in the Lord of Life and light in that land where partings are no more.[2]

When our Father retired from the management of Wells and Hallets Dockyards, on the Thames (his health requiring the change, being afflicted with gout, so much so that he was obliged—as long as I can recollect—to walk with a cane or crutch.) The breaking up of the home circle—or rather the division of it, threw us more closely in

1. Alexander Pope's 1713 translation of Homer's *Iliad*, an ancient Greek epic poem.
2. Catharine wrote a draft of this sketch sometime after Susanna's death in 1885. It was part of a longer manuscript about members of her family and was not edited for publication in her lifetime.

communion with one another, as my elder sisters were more frequently with our Father at Stowe House, near the historic town of Bungay. Sometimes my Mother too would be away—leaving one of the older sisters with the servants, and such of the younger ones as were not at the city house with our Father.

Susanna was naturally of an impulsive temper, and as is often found in persons of genius, she was often elated and often oppressed, easily excited by passing events, unable to control emotions caused by either pain or pleasure—morbidly sensitive to reproof, which if conscious of fault in herself, created self-reproach—and made her for a time unhappy and miserable—but if undeserved, roused in her a spirit of resistance against what she regarded—from her point of view, as tyranny and injustice. And having made her protest against it, she retired into herself and made no concessions to the higher powers—I think I must often have acted the part of the brake, on the steep hill, for the safety of the inside passengers. The strong affection that this dear sister always felt for me, had great power in toning down the troubled spirit— A few tender words had the effect that oil poured on water has—it smoothed the waves of irritated feelings, and calmed the rising storm. Susie was controlled by love—It was the magnet that she ever obeyed—Opposition, stern remonstrance would only have produced the contrary effect. We did not always see things in the same light, yet we never quarrelled. Once indeed I remember, being provoked to anger by some unreasonable fit of obstinacy on my sister's part, I forget the exact circumstances of the case—but I was wrong, no doubt, I struck her a sharp blow. I was the oldest of the two, about twelve years old—too old to give way to such a fit of passion. I shall never forget the feelings of anguish and remorse on my part, that followed this unsisterly deed, nor the surprise and dismay of Susanna, at this unusual display of temper—coming from one who had never struck her before, under any provocation—I think she cried more from grief, than from pain—but such an outrage never occurred again, to break the love and harmony of our lives.

* * *

[FREDERICK HARDMANN]

Forest Life in Canada West†

Ladies of Britain, deftly embroidering in carpeted saloon, gracefully bending over easel or harp, pressing, with nimble finger, your piano's ivory, or joyously tripping in Cellarian circles, suspend, for a moment, your silken pursuits, and look forth into the desert at a sister's sufferings! May you never, from stern experience, learn fully to appreciate them. But, should fate have otherwise decreed, may you equal her in fortitude and courage. Meanwhile, transport yourselves, in imagina-

† From Blackwood's *Edinburgh Magazine* 71.437 (March 1852): 355–65.

tion's car, to Canada's backwoods, and behold one, gently nurtured as yourselves, cheerfully condescending to rudest toils, unrepiningly enduring hardships you never dreamed of. Not to such hardships was she born, nor educated for them. The comforts of an English home, the endearments of sisterly affection, the refinement of literary tastes, but ill prepared the emigrant's wife to work in the rugged and inclement wilderness, harder than the meanest of the domestics, whom, in her own country, she was used to command. But where are the obstacles and difficulties that shall not be overcome by a strong will, a warm heart, a trusting and cheerful spirit?—precious qualities, strikingly combined by the lady of whose countless trials and troubles we have here an affecting and remarkable record.

The Far West of Canada is so remote a residence, and there is so much oblivion in a lapse of twenty years, that it may be necessary to mention who the authoress is who now appeals (successfully, or we are much mistaken) to the favour of her countrymen, and more especially of her countrywomen. Of a family well known in literature, Mrs Moodie is a sister of Miss Agnes Strickland, the popular and accomplished historical biographer. In 1831, Miss Susanna Strickland published a volume of poems. Had she remained in England, she in time, perhaps, might have rivalled her sister's fame as one of the most distinguished female writers of the day. But it was otherwise ordained. In 1832 she sailed, as Mrs. Moodie, an emigrant to Canada. Under most unfavourable circumstances, she still from time to time took up the pen. The anxieties and accidents of her forest life, her regrets for the country she loved so well, and had left perhaps for ever, and, subsequently, the rebellion in Canada, suggested many charming songs and poems, some of which are still extremely popular in our North American colony. Years passed amidst hardships and sufferings. At last a brighter day dawned, and it is from a tranquil and happy home, as we gladly understand, that the settler's brave wife has transmitted this narrative of seven years' exertion and adventure.

All that poor Mrs Moodie endured from her reprobate neighbours, could not be told in detail within the compass of a much larger work than hers. But we may glean a tolerable idea of her constant vexations and annoyance from her first volume, which contains sketches, at once painful and humorous, of the persecutions to which she was subjected. Impudent intrusion and unscrupulous borrowings were of daily occurrence, varied occasionally by some gross act of unneighbourliness and aggression. Although evidently a person of abundant energy and spirit, Mrs Moodie, partly through terror of these semi-savages, and partly from a wish to conciliate and make friends, long submitted to insolence and extortion. The wives and daughters of the Yankee settlers—some of whom had "squatted," without leave or license, on ground to which they had no right, made a regular property of her. Every article of domestic use, kettles and pans, eatables, drinkables, and wearables, did these insatiable wretches borrow—and never return. They would walk into her house and carry off the very things she at the moment needed, or come in her absence and take her gown from the peg, or the pot from the fire. The three families from which she had most to endure were those of a red-headed American squatter, who had fled his own country for some crime; of "Uncle Joe," the former proprietor of her farm, and still the occupant of her house; and of "Old Satan," a disgusting and brutal Yankee, who had one eye gouged out in a fight, and whose face was horribly disfigured by the scars of wounds inflicted by his adversary's teeth. A pertinacious tormentor, too, was old Betty Fye, who lived in the log shanty across the creek. Having made Mrs Moodie's acquaintance, under pretence of selling her a "rooster," she became a constant and most unwelcome visitor, borrowing everything she could think of, returning nothing, and interlarding her discourse with oaths, which greatly shocked the good-tempered English lady.

Most affecting is the account . . . of hopes disappointed and hardships endured, in the years 1836 and 1837. . . . Here is a melancholy note in the diary of the emigrant's wife:—

> "On the 21st May of this year, my second son, Donald, was born. The poor fellow came in hard times. . . . I was rendered so weak by want of proper nourishment that my dear husband, for my sake, overcame his aversion to borrowing, and procured a quarter of mutton from a friend. This . . . went far to save my life."

Think of this, ye dainty dames, who, in like circumstances, heap your beds with feathers, and strew the street with straw. Think of the chilly forest, the windy log-house, the frosted potatoes, the five children, the weary, half-famished mother, the absence of all that gentle aid and comfort which wait upon your slightest ailment. Think of all these things and, if the picture move you, remember that the like sufferings and necessities abound nearer home, within scope of your charity and relief.

It is very touching to contemplate Mrs Moodie walking twenty miles through a bleak forest—the ground covered with snow, and the thermometer far below zero—to minister to the necessities of one whose sufferings were greater even than her own. Still more touching is the exquisite delicacy with which she and her friend Emilia imparted the relief they brought, and strove to bestow their charity without imposing an obligation. "The Walk to Dummer" is a chapter of Mrs Moodie's book that alone would secure her the esteem and admiration of her readers. . . . Ladies, lounging on damask cushions in your well-hung carriages, read this account of a walk through the wilderness; read the twelfth chapter of Mrs Moodie's second volume, and—having read it—you will assuredly read the whole of her book, and rise from its perusal with full hearts, and with the resolution to imitate, as far as your opportunities allow—and to none of us, who seek them with a fervent and sincere spirit, shall opportunities be wanting—her energetic and truly Christian charity.

[ANONYMOUS]

The Backwoods of Canada†

"Roughing it in the Bush" is the appropriate title to a history of a rude experience in the backwoods of Canada. Mrs. Moodie, with her husband, an officer in the British Army, emigrated to Canada in the year 1832 and for seven years endured the hardships and struggled with the trials of an emigrant's life amid the wilds of a new and uncultivated land. Hard living, wrung by hard labor, from a wilderness, the rude companionship of coarse men and women, disease, misfortune, and the bitter severity of poverty, were the severe tests of the powers of endurance with which Mrs. Moodie and her family were tried, and which were borne with heroic fortitude. In a personal narrative of her experience and trials, the authoress tells, with the effect of a skilful narrator, a story of striking incident and adventure. The narrative is full of natural, womanly feeling and wins our sympathy, that accompanies the authoress, a noble heroine, from the beginning to the end. We follow the development, of her history of a life of hardship and suffering, with a tender interest, that makes every scene and incident personal to ourselves. Deeply moved as we have been by the sad story of trials and misfortunes, we are rejoiced at the close to find a happy ending in the prosperity of a family in which Mrs. Moodie's charming book has given us so warm an interest.

The authoress, with an eye for the beauties of nature, a quiet sense of humor, a shrewd observation, and a cultivated literary skill worthy of her sister, Agnes Strickland, has heightened the interest of her personal narrative, with picturesque descriptions of the wild scenery of Canada, humorous pictures of a settler's life, and well drawn sketches of the rude and unrestrained character of the backwoods.

Mrs. Moodie would teach us the moral of her book, that a life in the backwoods of Canada, presents many advantages to the poor, industrious workingman; to the poor gentleman *none*. The authoress teaches however, in her own person, a higher moral, the triumph of a brave heart over adversity, and moreover that the sensibilities of a woman, properly cultivated, can find in the intellectual observation of life and the beauties of nature, consolation for the hard realities of poverty and misfortune.

---

† From *The Literary World* (1852), No. 285; p. 39.

[CHARLES LYNDSAY]

Misrepresentation†

In Canada, we complain, and not without reason, of being misrepresented in other countries. Say what we may, we are only a great people at home. Abroad we are positively insignificant. As regards our trade, commerce, industry, or public policy, this might be bearable; were it only generally known that we own one of the finest countries in the world—that we possess resources almost inexhaustable, and that we have ample room for millions of industrious people. Whence comes this misrepresentation of which we complain? Is it from those that know us—that have sought any means of knowing us, or that are in any way fitted to pronounce an opinion? These are questions which merit consideration. It is, first of all, no small consolation to reflect, that whoever the detractor may be he is an ignoramus! But then again, it is pitiful to consider, that no amount of ignorance will mitigate the mischief wrought by detraction and misrepresentation, and no *history* can be too absurd to gain credence among the vulgar. And, astonishing is it, that not merely the illiterate peasant, whose ideas have never travelled beyond his native parish, but the man of learning, the statesman, and most pitiable of all—the Minister of the Crown—the dictator of nearly fifty colonies—too frequently takes as standard authority the fictitious trash that is found in the literature of tourists.

The author of the fabulous stories that form the staple commodity retailed as Canadian history, is the homogeneous creature known by the apt cognomen of a *Traveller*. He travels on and on, without either acquiring wisdom himself or communicating it to others. He is one of the positive nuisances that we have to complain of, and in order that foreigners may know him and know us, it were well that he were pointed out. He comes here in his "travels," and he serves us—we will not say worse than he serves others, but in such a way, as affords us large room for complaint. Did he confine his researches and adventures to himself, his travels, if not profitable, would at least be harmless; but in this lies the mischief: the merest youth that ever escaped from the parental domicile, has no sooner caught a glimpse of foreign scenes than he must forthwith inflict a Book on the community. And a heavy infliction it is, verily—one solid jumble, in ninety-nine of every hundred cases, of exaggeration and lies. How can it be otherwise? Our modern traveller or tourist's knowledge—such select portions of it as he prints—is not even derived from personal observation. It is never gleaned from things which he has seen or on which he has studied or reflected. In most cases the pith of his wonderful narrative is to be found in some antiquated volume descriptive of men and things half a century gone by. And to give the grandfather tale a modern air, this valuable *guide* to the history of the country is interspersed at certain

---

† From the *Toronto Examiner*, June 16, 1852. Lyndsay was the *Examiner's* editor.

intervals with some wayside gossip—the extravaganzas of a loafing acquaintance.

Place beside the fabulous adventures of our Traveller, the plain, indisputable facts and figures in which Lillie or Smith have ably and triumphantly shown the progress, the capabilities and the prospects of our infant country—shew these productions to the wise men of the East, and with ready discernment they will pronounce the statements of the latter prejudiced, improbable, and unworthy of credence; while the former—the production of some literary sprig of their Modern Athens—is veritable, naked truth. And in plain fact, it is evident, that as far as public opinion is or will be regulated by the high literature of British Magazines, we bid fair to be holden as a starvation-stricken race—the denizens of an outlawed region parallel in climate and material enjoyments to the penal colonies of the Russian Czar.

This is no exaggeration. Hear *Blackwood* in March, 1852, discoursing of the "Canadian Wilderness." But let us premise (lest we heap unmerited opprobrium on the "Traveller") that *Blackwood's* Novel—for it is simply a novel—a most mischievous one, more over—is founded on the published experience of a disappointed settler—an ape of aristocracy, too poor to lie on a sofa and too proud to labour for a living. The unutterable hardships of the Canadian Settler are thus introduced to the commiseration of the fair ones of England:—

"Ladies of Britain, deftly embroidering in carpeted saloon, gracefully bending over easel or harp, pressing with nimble finger your piano's ivory, or joyously tripping in Cellerian circles, suspend for a moment your silken pursuits, and look forth into the *desert* (mark that) at a sister's sufferings. . . . The comforts of an English home, the endearments of sisterly affection, the refinement of literary tastes, but ill prepared the emigrant's wife to work in *the rugged and inclement wilderness*."

Think of that ye braggarts accustomed to dub your country the "Home of independence." Talk of cultivated farms, of pleasant Homesteads and luxuriant crops in a "desert." The thing is positively preposterous. We are dragging out a miserable existence in a "rugged and inclement wilderness," and worse than all, we seem to be ignorant that it is so. We imagine ourselves happy, poor, ignorant folks! and *Blackwood* tells the Ladies of Britain in their carpeted saloons, we are miserable beyond conception. Was ignorance ever known to be bliss before?

But we begin to be serious, and certainly not inclined to laugh, when we see writers ranked at the head of the Literature of the Empire speaking of Canada as a remote wilderness. Is it possible that the writer in *Blackwood* is ignorant that this remote "residence" is within 12 days travel of Liverpool, and the "carpeted saloons"—a journey no greater than that between the extremities of the diminutive Island of Britain some half a century ago? Or what are this wiseacre's ideas of distance? Fifty years ago, Niebuhr,[1] the great historical critic, travelled

---

1. Georg Barthold Niebuhr (1776–1831), German statesman and historian who spent 1798 in Edinburgh.

from London to the Northern metropolis, in 4 1/2 days, and records the unprecedented feat for the information of his wonder stricken countrymen. Give us a Railway from the port of Halifax—and we believe a few years will see the completion of this great undertaking—and this *remote* region may be reached in 60 hours' longer time than Niebuhr's expeditious journey through half the island of Britain.

The diffusion of sound information respecting the condition and resources of the country is a matter which could not fail to tell very powerfully on its material progress as well as on the social prosperity of the people. That such information is at the present time accessible every one must be prepared to admit. And for this reason it becomes more lamentable that British journalists and Reviewers, for the sake, it may be, of gratifying a taste for romance and novelty, are found at this moment pawning such counterfeit pictures of Canadian life as that which we have noticed, on the gullible natives of the three kingdoms. That fanciful and fabulous stories should form a standard guide book for the emigrant is a more serious matter than at first sight appears. The people of Britain will read, and what more palatable reading do they expect to find than in the pages of the great magazines of the metropolis, in which is concentrated the best talent of the country? So long, therefore, as the periodical literature of Britain is prejudiced against Colonial interests, whether willfully or through ignorance, so long these interests suffer in the eyes of those on whom they are mainly dependent for favour and furtherance. In view of this, while deploring the continued circulation of mythical treatises on Canadian affairs, we hail, as an omen for good, the manifestations given of an increased taste within the Province for scientific and literary pursuits; believing that in the cultivation of these a standard literature will be formed within the country, which will ultimately give character and tone to such foreign publications as aim at an honest and impartial transcript of Canadian history.

[ANONYMOUS]

Roughing It in the Bush†

We briefly called attention to this work in a previous number of 'The Provincial,' and now after a perusal, are enabled to make some remarks, and to present our readers with a few extracts from this interesting publication.

Mrs. Moodie, the authoress of the work in question, is by birth an English woman, and connected with a family whose genealogy can almost boast of royalty. She was a Strickland, sister of the accomplished authoress of the Lives of the Queens of England, to whom these volumes are inscribed. She was early celebrated in the literary world, hav-

---

† From *The Provincial: or, Halifax Monthly Magazine* (October 1852), pp. 383–89.

ing published a volume of poems in 1831, under her maiden name of Susannah Strickland. The associations and scenes of her early life make the contrast presented to us, in this sketch of her residence and sufferings in Canada, more striking; as the hardships she underwent there, seem to be of a character almost too aggravated for a female accustomed from childhood to labour and poverty, much less for one brought up in the elegance and refinement of English society.

* * *

* * * [N]obly indeed did this true-hearted woman fulfil her appointed task; nobly did she repay the full confidence her husband reposed in her; never did man have a more worthy helpmeet, or one more willing and able to bear with the sufferings and privations of life, than the heroic woman whose recital of her residence in the backwoods of Canada, does even more credit to her character as a woman, than it does to her reputation as a writer.

The first chapter, containing an account of her landing at Grosse Isle, and subsequent journey into the interior of the country, is written in a sprightly and graphic style, shewing her susceptibility to the humourous as well as to the grand and beautiful. Many a laughable adventure and comic character are interwoven with the details of her narrative, adding to its interest and charms. The miseries of the borrowing system so extensively practised by her impertinent neighbours, after she had found a residence in Canada, are well delineated; and we can only marvel how Mrs. Moodie's patience continued inexhaustible for so long a time. The insolence of the settlers around her was almost unbearable. They entered her house at all times, interfered with her arrangements, and appropriated her furniture to themselves. The account is laughable to peruse, but the reality must have been immensely provoking to bear with at the time.

Their first settlement in Canada was attended with much inconvenience and discomfort: but, as yet, want had been kept from their dwelling. It was only after Captain Moodie's removal to the backwoods, when, owing to an intimation from the war office, he hastily sold his commission, and invested the proceeds (£700 stg.) in steamboat stock, which never returned him a penny, that poverty made its appearance. It was difficult and expensive to procure labor; common provisions even were hard to get; and comforts absolutely necessary, were unknown. * * *

* * *

Ponder on this tale of suffering, ladies, even in our own little province, who, surrounded with physicians and nurses, and every luxury wealth and affection can procure, yet murmur at confinement and pain. Think of her as tenderly reared as the most gentle among you, in the hour of trial, alone; with sickness and death around her, and destitute of every common necessary of life; and then ask yourselves why you have deserved more than she. And yet hear how her hopeful spirit bore her up through all; how she cast all her 'care upon Him who careth for us,' and how nobly she met the torrent of evil.

* * *

But our space will not permit of further extracts. We could quote a hundred passages, exemplifying her nobleness of soul and courageous spirit, but we must leave our readers to satisfy their curiosity from the volume itself. It will amply repay the perusal: it is written with the attractiveness of a romance, and the convincing force of truth. Each successive page is turned with an eager interest, for the narrative is so vivid, that we identify ourselves with its writer, and wait with anxious hearts for each new development of her history. Trials thicken upon her as we proceed through the second volume, which almost make the soul grow faint to experience. But her high, hero[ic] spirit sustains her through all, and she bears cheerfully the lot providence has appointed her. Faithful friends rise up to cheer her in this dark wilderness; and the attachment of a servant, 'old Jenny,' is touchingly described. Two more sons were born to Mrs. Moodie during her residence in the backwoods, and each came in hard times; but Heaven sustained the fond mother through all!

Though written in a most modest and unpretending manner as regards herself, no feature in her character shines forth more strongly in her book than her devoted affection for her husband and children. Only this could have sustained her through so many difficulties, with such cheerfulness and hope; and her most severe trial appears to have been when Captain Moodie left his home to take part in active service for his Sovereign, at the time of the Canadian rebellion. Then when he whom she calls 'her light of life,' was abroad the strong heart of the loving woman sank within her. We must find space for the account of his return, for a few days, to his family.

* * *

What a lover-like picture for the wife of a dozen years! When things were at their worst Captain Moodie was appointed by the Governor, Sir George Arthur, to the situation of Sheriff of the country of V——: the result of an application from his true hearted wife. This ended their trials in the backwoods: yet so strong is habit that it was with regret that Mrs. Moodie bade adieu to the scene of so much sorrow; but it had also been the home of much happiness. With her removal to society and comfort, her story ends; and our only regret on closing the volume is, that we leave her still an exile from England. Her strong love of home prevails so in every page and her heartsick yearning for the 'daisied meadows' of her native land, which linger in her first volume, make us long to see her restored once more to the glorious land of her childhood. But she has acquired a love for her adopted country, and while she acknowledges that 'whatever is, is right,' we need not complain.

We have said so much in praise of this work, that we may be allowed to pass one censure, and it shall be brief. The only objection that strikes us, is a certain coarseness of language which sounds harshly from the pen of a lady. We may be fastidious; but when an article or event can be expressed in different terms, we prefer the most delicate. Mrs. Moodie has erred in this instance, we think, but on recalling the scenes and characters with which necessity compelled her to associate for so long a period, the marvel may be, why she has escaped so free from their vulgarity and contamination. We will, therefore, not enlarge upon this defect, but recommend 'Roughing it in the Bush,' to the attentive perusal of every emigrant, settler and *woman*. All may derive benefit and instruction from its pages, both in a pecuniary and moral point of view. Such women as Mrs. Moodie lift the reproach from the female character, and shew us how capable it is of endurance, courage, and triumphant conquest over poverty, disappointment and pain. May her sisters all profit by the bright example she has given them, and in the hour of trial, be to those who depend so much upon their exertions for success—helpmeets indeed.

[ANONYMOUS]

Review of *Roughing It in the Bush*†

A generation has passed away since Mrs. Moodie first gave to the world this interesting narrative of her experience in the back-woods. At that time, the work appears to have attracted little attention in Canada, and that little chiefly assumed the form of captious and ungenerous criticism. The bulk of the population were then living the life and practically realizing the hardships the author so graphically depicted. No description, therefore, however vivid, would impress them, except as an imperfect reflection of the toils and struggles of every-day life. The humorous side of pioneer labour, which Mrs. Moodie successfully brought out, would scarcely strike the early settler; or, if it did, the playful vein of the author might, in all probability, jar offensively upon him, in his serious and earnest moods. Moreover, the book was avowedly a story of failure, and the colonists, with characteristic sensitiveness, were not willing that such a story should go forth to the emigrating class at home. In this edition Mrs. Moodie devotes a portion of the introductory chapter to an explanation and defence of her motives in writing and publishing the work:

"In 1830 the tide of emigration flowed westward, and Canada became the great land-mark for the rich in hope and poor in purse. Public newspapers and private letters teemed with the almost fabulous advantages to be derived from a settlement in this highly favoured region. Men, who had been doubtful of supporting their families in comfort at home, thought that they had only to land in Canada to realize a fortune. The infection became general. Thousands and tens of thousands from the middle ranks of British society, for the space of three or four years, landed upon these shores. A large majority of these emigrants were officers of the army and navy, with their families; a class perfectly unfitted, by their previous habits and standing in soci-

---

† From *The Canadian Monthly and National Review*, No. 1, 1872; review of the 1871 Hunter, Rose edition (the first Canadian edition).

ety, for contending with the stern realities of emigrant life in the back-woods. A class formed mainly from the younger scions of great fami-lies, naturally proud, and not only accustomed to command, but to receive implicit obedience from the people under them, are not men adapted to the hard toil of the woodman's life.

* * *

The poor man is in his native element; the poor gentleman totally unfitted, by his previous habits and education, to be a hewer of the forest and a tiller of the soil. What money he brought out with him is lavishly expended during the first two years, in paying for labour to clear and fence lands, which, from his ignorance of agricultural pur-suits, will never make him the least profitable return, and barely find coarse food for his family. Of clothing we say nothing. Bare feet and rags are too common in the bush. Now, had the same means and the same labour been employed in the cultivation of a leased farm, pur-chased for a few hundred dollars, near a village, how different would have been the results not only to the settler, but it would have added greatly to the wealth and social improvement of the country." It was to warn "poor gentlemen" against foolishly taking up grants of wild land which they could not reduce under cultivation, and to point out the poverty and suffering which inevitably followed, that "Roughing it in the Bush" was originally written. Having taking a false step, Mrs. Moodie related her experience for the admonition of those who might be tempted to make a similar mistake. It was no part of her design to deter the able-bodied agriculturist from settling on Canadian soil; she only sought to undeceive those who fancied that bush-farming was a diversion, in which any one might comfortably and profitably indulge. Forty years' residence in Canada enables the author to give ample tes-timony regarding the substantial progress of the country, material, in-tellectual and social. With the growth of Ontario, has grown likewise her affection for it. To quote her own words:—"My love for the coun-try has steadily increased from year to year, and my attachment to Canada is now so strong, that I cannot imagine any inducement, short of absolute necessity, which could induce me to leave the colony, where, as a wife and mother, some of the happiest years of my life have been spent."

It is not our intention to follow our author and her family through all their troubles from the arrival in quarantine at Grosse Isle in the cholera year (1832) until Sir George Arthur relieved them from the consequences of their luckless experiment by the appointment of Mr. Moodie to a shrievalty. One notable episode, however, occurred during those years of trial to vary the monotony of forest labour—the rebel-lion of 1837. In the body of the work, (chap. 23) Mrs. Moodie gives us a lively impression of the alacrity with which the loyal half-pay officers obeyed the summons of the Government. "I must own," she adds, "that my own British spirit was fairly aroused, and, as I could not aid in subduing the enemies of my beloved country with my arm, I did what little I could to serve the good cause with my pen." This she did in "one of those loyal staves, which were widely circulated through the colony at the time." Mr. Moodie, though in feeble health, knew his duty too well as an old soldier—who had been severely wounded in his country's service—to hesitate, as to the side he should espouse. Mrs. Moodie seems, even at that time, notwithstanding her "British spirit" to have had some misgivings, from a political stand-point. The view she takes of the events of that period, after a lapse of thirty-five years, we shall give in her own words, from the introductory chapter:— "When we first came to the country it was a mere struggle for bread to the many, while all the offices of emolument and power were held by a favoured few. The country was rent to pieces by political factions, and a fierce hostility existed between the native-born Canadians—the first pioneers of the forest—and the British emigrants, who looked upon each other as mutual enemies who were seeking to appropriate the larger share of the new country." Notwithstanding the signs of impending strife the loyal population could not imagine that an armed outbreak was possible. "The insurrection of 1837 came upon them like a thunder clap; they could hardly believe such an incredible tale. Intensely loyal, the emigrant officers rose to a man to defend the British flag, and chastise the rebels and their rash leader. In their zeal to uphold British authority, they made no excuse for the wrongs that the dominant party had heaped upon a clever and high-spirited man. To them he was a traitor; and as such a public enemy. Yet the blow struck by that injured man, weak as it was, without money, arms, or the necessary munitions of war, and defeated and broken in its first effort, gave freedom to Canada, and laid the foundation of the excellent constitution that we now enjoy. It drew the attention of the Home Government to the many abuses then practised in the colony; and made them aware of its vast importance in a political point of view; and ultimately led to all our great national improvements." We give Mrs. Moodie's political reflections without comment as the matured views of an acute observer who, having passed through those troublous times, now ventures to sum up the results of her experience in our own. The extracts we have given are, for the most part, from the introduction, which forms no part of the work proper. It is, as we have stated, a defence of the author as well as a testimony to the progress of Ontario during a period of forty years. We hope, therefore, that our readers will not mistake the nature of "Roughing it in the Bush." It is an extremely lively book, full of incident and character. Although its primary object was to give a warning by means of an example, it is by no means a jeremiad. On the contrary, we almost lose sight of the immigrants' troubles in the ludicrous phases of human character which present themselves to view in rapid succession.

How far Mrs. Moodie has taken an artist's liberty with her *dramatis personæ* does not appear. She has evidently a keen appreciation of the humorous, and there is an air of verisimilitude about the narrative which gives a zest to its incidents and inspires the reader with confidence in the author. As an interesting picture of a by-gone time, graphically painted, we trust it will be widely circulated. Bush-life does not yet belong to the past, it is true, but to most of us a description of it seems quite as much out of the range of our knowledge, as it would if every acre of our soil had been cleared by the woodman. We may add that the work is produced in a style extremely creditable to the printers and publishers.

CRITICISM

MARGARET ATWOOD

Afterword to *The Journals of Susanna Moodie*†

These poems were generated by a dream. I dreamt I was watching an opera I had written about Susanna Moodie. I was alone in the theatre; on the empty white stage, a single figure was singing.

Although I had heard of Susanna Moodie I had never read her two books about Canada, *Roughing It in the Bush* and *Life in the Clearings*. When I did read them I was disappointed. The prose was discursive and ornamental and the books had little shape: they were collections of disconnected anecdotes. The only thing that held them together was the personality of Mrs Moodie, and what struck me most about this personality was the way in which it reflects many of the obsessions still with us.

If the national mental illness of the United States is megalomania, that of Canada is paranoid schizophrenia. Mrs Moodie is divided down the middle: she praises the Canadian landscape but accuses it of destroying her; she dislikes the people already in Canada but finds in people her only refuge from the land itself; she preaches progress and the march of civilization while brooding elegiacally upon the destruction of the wilderness; she delivers optimistic sermons while showing herself to be fascinated with deaths, murders, the criminals in Kingston Penitentiary and the incurably insane in the Toronto lunatic asylum. She claims to be an ardent Canadian patriot while all the time she is standing back from the country and criticizing it as though she were a detached observer, a stranger. Perhaps that is the way we still live. We are all immigrants to this place even if we were born here: the country is too big for anyone to inhabit completely, and in the parts unknown to us we move in fear, exiles and invaders. This country is something that must be chosen—it is so easy to leave—and if we do choose it we are still choosing a violent duality.

Once I had read the books I forgot about them. The poems occurred later, over a period of a year and a half. I suppose many of them were suggested by Mrs Moodie's books, though it was not her conscious voice but the other voice running like a counterpoint through her work that made the most impression on me. Although the poems can be read in connection with Mrs. Moodie's books, they don't have to be: they have detached themselves from the books in the same way that other poems detach themselves from the events that give rise to them.

The arrangement of the poems follows, more or less, the course of Mrs Moodie's life. Journal I begins with her arrival in Canada and her voyage up the St Lawrence, past Quebec and Montreal where a

† Afterword, "Disembarking at Quebec," and "The Double Voice" are from *The Journals of Susanna Moodie* by Margaret Atwood (Toronto: Oxford UP), 1970, pp. 62–64, 11, 42. Copyright © Oxford University Press Canada 1970. Reprinted by permission of Oxford University Press Canada and Houghton Mifflin.

cholera epidemic is raging. In Upper Canada she encounters earlier settlers who despise the Moodies as greenhorns and cheat them whenever possible. Later, on a remote bush farm, she can neither hold on to her English past nor renounce it for a belief in her Canadian future. After seven years of struggle and near starvation, and just as she is beginning to come to terms with her environment, the family moves away.

After 1840 the Moodies lived in Belleville, where Susanna's husband had been made sheriff as a result of his helping to suppress the rebellion of 1837. (Ironically, Susanna later admitted that the rebellion was probably a good thing for Canada.) Journal II contains reflections about the society Mrs Moodie finds herself in, as well as memories of the years spent in the bush. At the beginning of this section Mrs Moodie finally accepts the reality of the country she is in, and at its end she accepts also the inescapable doubleness of her own vision.

Most of Journal III was written after I had come across a little-known photograph of Susanna Moodie as a mad-looking and very elderly lady. The poems take her through an estranged old age, into death and beyond. After her death she can hear the twentieth century above her, bulldozing away her past, but she refuses to be ploughed under completely. She makes her final appearance in the present, as an old woman on a Toronto bus who reveals the city as an unexplored, threatening wilderness. Susanna Moodie has finally turned herself inside out, and has become the spirit of the land she once hated.

Disembarking at Quebec

Is it my clothes, my way of walking,
the things I carry in my hand
—a book, a bag with knitting—
the incongruous pink of my shawl

this space cannot hear

or is it my own lack
of conviction which makes
these vistas of desolation,
long hills, the swamps, the barren sand, the glare
of sun on the bone-white
driftlogs, omens of winter,
the moon alien in day—
time a thin refusal

The others leap, shout

Freedom!

The moving water will not show me
my reflection.

The rocks ignore.

I am a word
in a foreign language.

The Double Voice

Two voices
took turns using my eyes:

One had manners,
painted in watercolours,
used hushed tones when speaking
of mountains or Niagara Falls,
composed uplifting verse
and expended sentiment upon the poor.

The other voice
had other knowledge:
that men sweat
always and drink often,
that pigs are pigs
but must be eaten
anyway, that unborn babies
fester like wounds in the body,
that there is nothing to be done
about mosquitoes;

One saw through my
bleared and gradually
bleaching eyes, red leaves,
the rituals of seasons and rivers

The other found a dead dog
jubilant with maggots
half-buried among the sweet peas.

CARL BALLSTADT

Susanna Moodie and the English Sketch†

Susanna Moodie's *Roughing It in the Bush* has long been recognized
as a significant and valuable account of pioneer life in Upper Canada
in the mid-nineteenth century. From among a host of journals, diaries,
and travelogues, it is surely safe to say, her book is the one most often
quoted when the historian, literary or social, needs commentary on
backwoods people, frontier living conditions, or the difficulty of ad-

† From *Canadian Literature* 51 (Winter 1972): 32–38. Reprinted by permission of the author.

justment experienced by such upper middle-class immigrants as Mrs. Moodie and her husband.

The reasons for the pre-eminence of *Roughing It in the Bush* have also long been recognized. Mrs. Moodie's lively and humorous style, the vividness and dramatic quality of her characterization, the strength and good humour of her own personality as she encountered people and events have contributed to make her book a very readable one. For these reasons it enjoys a prominent position in any survey of our literary history, and, indeed, it has become a "touchstone" of our literary development. W. H. Magee, for example, uses *Roughing It in the Bush* as the prototype of local colour fiction against which to measure the degree of success of later Canadian local colourists.[1] More recently, Carl F. Klinck observes that Mrs. Moodie's book represents a significant advance in the development of our literature from "statistical accounts and running narratives" toward novels and romances of pioneer experience.[2] Professor Klinck, in noting the fictive aspects of Mrs. Moodie's writing, sees it as part of an inevitable, indigenous development of Canadian writing, even though, in Mrs. Moodie's case, that development was strongly conditioned by her practice as a writer of children's stories before she came to Canada, and as the author of serialized fiction with English settings for the *Literary Garland* of Montreal.

Except for passing reference, Susanna Moodie's literary practice and acquaintanceships in England have not been considered in relationship to the form and techniques of her most successful book. As a member of a literary family which drew some attention to itself amongst minor English literary circles, Susanna Strickland sought and established literary friendships, and as a writer she followed an established pattern which, even had she remained in England, would very probably have led her to produce a book similar in many respects to *Roughing It in the Bush*. At the very least, however, when Susanna emigrated to Canada, she brought with her an awareness of models for a book of sketches about a region and its people.

Susanna's early career involved three kinds of writing, the first of which was literature for children. The writing of children's books certainly gave her practice in the description of characters, in the writing of dialogue, and in the use of the rhetoric proper to religious, moral, and didactic tales, a rhetoric which she was never willing to abandon. But the children's stories were simply the first stage in a pattern followed by many young women of the early nineteenth century who tried to forge literary careers for themselves. They progressed to poems and stories for the elegant annuals and gift books, and then, perhaps, to longer forms such as romances or biographies. Such was the pattern of the careers of Mrs. S. C. Hall, or Mary Howitt,[3] or Su-

1. "Local Colour in Canadian Fiction," *University of Toronto Quarterly*, 28 (Jan. 1959), 176–89.
2. Introduction, *Roughing It in the Bush*, New Canadian Library edition, 1962.
3. Mary Howitt was the author of *Sketches of Natural History*, for children, and she later produced *Biographical Sketches of the Queens of Great Britain* (1851) in the wake of the suc-

sanna's own sisters, Eliza and Agnes, who distinguished themselves in the 1840's as the biographers of the Queens of England. It was virtually inevitable, therefore, that Susanna should proceed to contribute sentimental and religious poems to the annuals and gift books, and that these poems should be collected and brought out by subscription as *Enthusiasm and Other Poems* (1831). Her sister Agnes had done much the same before her.[4]

It is, however, another phase of Susanna Strickland's career which is most pertinent to *Roughing It in the Bush*. During the years 1827–1829, Susanna Strickland contributed a series of prose sketches to a London periodical for ladies entitled *La Belle Assemblée* which was edited by a Suffolk native and friend of the Strickland family, Thomas Harral. The series, "Sketches from the Country", consists of five pieces: "The Witch of East Cliff", "The Two Fishermen", "Naomi", "The Dead Man's Grave", and "Old Hannah, or, the Charm".[5] The first four involve Suffolk legends told to the author by elderly natives of the region. Unfortunately, they are marred by an excessively metaphorical style and are without restraint on sentiment. Only in the introduction does the author exercise economy and limit her pen to what she really knows. The fifth sketch is Susanna's personal recollection of a maidservant at Reydon Hall, the Strickland home in Suffolk, near Southwold. It reflects warmth and good humour, and, perhaps because it is personal, is characterized by a greater directness and simplicity of style than the preceding sketches.

The importance of this series of sketches is that it represents Susanna's early attempt to emulate the writing of Mary Russell Mitford and to do for Suffolk what Miss Mitford did so prolifically and so well for Berkshire. Miss Mitford in turn was an admirer of Washington Irving's *Sketch Book of Geoffrey Crayon* (1818), and, although she was also inspired by her own "hearty love of her subject",[6] shortly after the publication of Irving's book she began contributing country sketches to the *New Monthly Magazine* and to annuals and gift books. In 1824 the first volume of a five volume series, *Our Village; Sketches of Rural Character and Scenery* (1824–1837), was published in London. Her first series was followed by *Belford Regis; or Sketches of a Country Town* (3 vols., 1835).

Susanna Strickland was a reader of the annuals and of the *New Monthly Magazine*, a journal to which her sister Agnes also contributed in 1824 and 1825. Having read and admired Mitford's

cess of the Strickland sisters, Agnes and Eliza. Mrs. Samuel Hall, having begun as an author of children's stories, followed Mitford's successes with *Sketches of Irish Character* (1829) and *Lights and Shadows of Irish Life* (1838).

4. Agnes Strickland was the author of several volumes of verse, including *Worcester Field; or, The Cavalier* (1826) in the manner of Sir Walter Scott. She also produced *Old Friends and New Acquaintances* (1860 and 1861), two series of Suffolk sketches which it might have been Susanna's lot to write had she remained in England.

5. *La Belle Assemblée*, n.s. VI (1827) 15–19, 109–14, 247–51; n.s. VII (1828), 51–55; n.s. IX (1829), 21–24.

6. Preface to *Our Village*, vol. 1 (London, 1824).

sketches in these sources, she began to correspond with her in 1829, first addressing a poetic tribute to the celebrated Mitford in June of that year. Miss Mitford responded with a letter in July, 1829, and there followed an exchange of letters over the course of a year.

The published letters of Susanna to Miss Mitford clearly establish her admiration of Mitford's work:

> I had always ranked Miss Mitford as one of the first of our female writers, and though my knowledge of your writings was entirely confined to the sketches in the annuals, and to some extracts from the 'Foscari', these were sufficient to make me feel the deepest interest in your name, and even to rejoice in the success that ever attended the publication of your works.[7]

The letter in which this statement of admiration appears also contains Susanna's wish that she could visit Miss Mitford in London, as well as an invitation for the latter to visit the Strickland home in Suffolk where she would find "such sweet woodland lanes as you so inimitably describe."

Succeeding letters from Susanna to Miss Mitford include comments on her family and their literary pursuits; Susanna's own temptation to emigrate to Canada because of the attractive accounts which her brother, Samuel, had sent home; a visit to London during which she resided with her "dear adopted father", Thomas Pringle;[8] and characters and customs described in Mitford's sketches. The recurring references to these sketches and the occasional tributes to Miss Mitford's skills make it very clear, I think, that Susanna's admiration was sufficient to lead her to emulate Mitford's subjects and techniques.

Such emulation is indicated in the titles and contents of Susanna's country sketches. In the *Our Village* sketches, Miss Mitford was wont to include portraits of rural characters, accounts of country walks, and tributes to rural institutions. A few titles from her first volume give a reasonable indication of the kind of contents: "Walks in the Country: the First Primrose", "Tom Cordery", "A Village Beau", "A Great Farm House". They usually begin with a general passage of reflection or description which eases the reader into a particular topic or event, or some portion of an individual's history, including his eccentricities, dress, occupation, and perhaps some crisis in which he has been involved. The style is familiar and direct, exhibiting a fine attention to detail; the tone is delicate and quiet. They are sketches of ordinary life and the emphasis is upon the colour and charm of rural living. The introduction to

---

7. The poetic tribute and the letters of Susanna Strickland to Mary Russell Mitford are in *The Friendships of Mary Russell Mitford as Recorded in Letters from Her Literary Correspondents* edited by The Reverend A. G. L'Estrange, 2 vols. (London, 1882), vol. 1, pp. 196–98, 204–08, 212–13, 222–23. The tribute is dated June 2, 1829 and the last letter August 12, 1830. The quotation is from the first letter, July 31, 1829.

8. Thomas Pringle was another friend of the Strickland family, in fact, the person who carried the correspondence from Susanna to Mitford. Pringle was probably the man who introduced Susanna to John Dunbar Moodie. Both men had been in South Africa. At the time of Susanna's visit to London, Pringle was secretary to the Anti-Slavery Society. He was the author of *African Sketches* (1834) and *Narrative of a Residence in South Africa* (1835).

"Hannah Bint" is a good example of her loving attention to nature, as a prelude to the character and situation of a country friend:

> The Shaw, leading to Hannah Bint's habitation, is, as I perhaps have said before, a very pretty mixture of wood and coppice; that is to say, a track of thirty or forty acres covered with fine growing timber—ash, and oak, and elm—very regularly planted; and interspersed here and there with large patches of underwood, hazel, maple, birch, holly, and hawthorn, woven into almost impenetrable thickets by long wreaths of the bramble, the briony, and the briar-rose, or by the pliant and twisting garlands of the wild honey-suckle. In other parts, the Shaw is quite clear of its bosky undergrowth, and clothed only with large beds of feathery fern, or carpets of flowers, primroses, orchises, cowslips, ground-ivy, crane's-bill, cotton-grass, Solomon's seal, and forget-me-not, crowded together with a profusion and brilliancy of colour such as I have rarely seen equalled even in a garden. Here the wild hyacinth really enamels the ground with its fresh and lovely purple. . . . The variety is much greater than I have enumerated; for the ground is so unequal, now swelling in gentle ascents, now dimpling into dells and hollows, and the soil so different in different parts, that the sylvan flora is unusually extensive and complete.[9]

The same kind of introduction is employed by Susanna in her country scenes, particularly in "Old Hannah" and "The Dead Man's Grave." The latter is characterized by the similar attention to the particulars of a locale related to a specific history or event:

> Should any of the readers of La Belle Assemblée wish to become better acquainted with the spot known by the designation of The Dead Man's Grave, they may find it at the end of a long narrow lane, in the well-known village of Reydon, where four cross country roads terminate, in the entrance to Goose Green, a piece of common so called from the number of geese which are bred upon it. Each of these roads forms a pleasant summer's walk, shaded from the heat of the sun by tall hawthorn hedges full of fine old trees. The grave rises to a considerable height in the centre of a pretty waste, of a triangular form, which attracts the notice of the traveller from each of its approaches. Generally, it is covered with a soft mantle of verdure, rivaling the emerald in brightness. The ground about it is thickly studded with broom and stunted blackthorn bushes, seldom rising to the height of four feet above the turf, and affording, with their low branches, a shelter for the violets that open their deep blue eyes beneath, and grows in profusion around the grave, while the more aspiring primrose rears her pale star-like crest above the mossy mound, and encircles it with a diadem of living gems.[1]

---

9. *Sketches of English Life and Character* (London, The Weekend Library, 1928), pp. 152–53.
1. *La Belle Assemblée*, n.s. VII (1828), pp. 51–55.

In the introductions to four of her sketches and throughout her reminiscence of Old Hannah, Susanna Strickland's series reminds one of Mitford's attention to a region and its people; it is local colour fiction. It seems very likely, then, that when Susanna Moodie decided to write of her Canadian experiences near Cobourg and Peterborough, she would have thought of Miss Mitford's books on rural life and scenery. A connection seems indicated not only by her early interest in *Our Village*, but by the fact that parts of *Roughing It in the Bush* were first published as a series of "Canadian Sketches" in the *Literary Garland*.[2] That series of six sketches includes a country walk, a backwoods custom, and portraits of eccentric or peculiar characters, all categories used by Mary Mitford, and all assuming an important place in *Roughing It in the Bush* when it was published in 1852. For the British reader of the mid-nineteenth century, large sections of "Uncle Joe and his Family", "Brian the Still Hunter", "The Charivari", "The Wilderness and Our Indian Friends", and "The Walk to Dummer" would satisfy an appetite for impressions of the peculiarities of custom and character in British North America.

Of course, *Roughing It* was conditioned by other important factors and, therefore, has different components and tones than *Our Village*. Mrs. Moodie had more functions than one to fulfil in writing her book. She wished to convey information to prospective immigrants, to tell her personal story of fortunes and misfortunes, and to create impressions and descriptions. She is, therefore, the essayist as well as the story-teller, and *Roughing It* is both a didactic book, an autobiography, and a sketch-book of pioneer life.

In *Our Village* the author's personality as a unifying factor is much less important. Although the sketches which are entirely devoted to seasonal country walks express Mitford's personal delight in nature, she is generally objective and does not obtrude with her personal fortunes.

Differences in the tone and flavour of the two books are largely due to the landscape which each writer focuses on. While Miss Mitford's sketches take on the gentle and fertile character of the Berkshire countryside, Mrs. Moodie's reflect the larger dimensions of the Canadian scene and the sense of challenge which the bold extremes of Canadian climate and landscape demanded.

An interesting coincidence may serve to conclude and to support the suggestion that *Roughing It in the Bush* has connections with *Our Village*. In 1840, a book very similar to Mrs. Moodie's, *A New Home— Who'll Follow?*, was published in Boston. Its author, Caroline Kirkland, was a refined New England lady who settled with her husband in Michigan in the 1830's. Many of her attitudes and responses to the wilderness and its inhabitants are similar to Mrs. Moodie's, as are many of her disappointments. Although her prose is more pretentious

2. The sketches, "Old Woodruff and his Three Wives", "The Walk to Dummer", "Our Borrowing", "Tom Wilson's Emigration", "Uncle Joe and his Family", and "Brian, the Still Hunter", appeared in the *Literary Garland*, n.s. V (1847).

and sentimental than Susanna's, her book progresses by sketches of custom, character, and anecdote, and many of her topics are inevitably the same as those of *Roughing It*. But Mrs. Kirkland also serves to indicate the extent of Miss Mitford's influence:

> If Miss Mitford, who has given us such charming glimpses of Aberleigh . . . had by some happy chance been translated to Michigan, what would she not have made of such materials as Tinkerville, Montacute, and Turnip?[3]

Very probably Miss Mitford would have made much the same of Caroline Kirkland's backwoods towns as she herself did, or as Mrs. Moodie did of her Cobourg and Peterborough environs.

DAVID STOUCK

"Secrets of the Prison-House": Mrs. Moodie and the Canadian Imagination[†]

> "If these sketches should prove the means of deterring one family from sinking their property, and ship-wrecking all their hopes, by going to reside in the backwoods of Canada, I shall consider myself amply repaid for revealing the secrets of the prison-house, and feel that I have not toiled and suffered in the wilderness in vain."[1]

As we struggle in Canada to define our national identity in terms of a literary tradition, we repeatedly come up against Susanna Moodie's *Roughing It in the Bush*, a conceded classic, but a book which has resisted definition and critical assimilation. Part of the reason for this is formal. *Roughing It* is generically a collection of sketches, and this loose narrative form admits the inclusion of almost any kind of literary expression: landscape description, character portraits, legends and anecdotes, philosophical reflection. Mrs. Moodie accordingly lets the Crusoe-like interest of the book (her account of survival in the backwoods) be diverted for long stretches at a time by other preoccupations. But perhaps the greater reason for our confused and dislocated responses to this book lies in our learned cultural expectations. As North Americans we have been conditioned to view the pioneer experience as the heroic period of our history, as a simpler and more affirmative era in which our ancestors made creative sacrifices to ensure and enhance the lives of future generations. But *Roughing It* is no splendid celebration of pioneer life such as we find in the classic texts of American literature, no Franklinesque account of how to rise in the world; rather it is a tale of hardship and misery which culminates in

---

3. *A New Home*, p. 11.
† From *Dalhousie Review* 54 (1974): 463–72. Reprinted by permission of the author. Page numbers in brackets refer to the text in this Norton Critical Edition.
1. See p. 330. [*Editor's note.*]

withdrawal and defeat. Above all it is a book which denies the myths of renaissance and individual power in a new land. As Canadians we are now making many reversals in our thinking, and if we are willing to relinquish what ideally might have been our first account of heroic pioneer life, we will be rewarded in turn with a book which is imaginatively much richer than we might have guessed, a book more subtle, complex, devious.[2]

A collection of sketches (and Thoreau's *Walden* is a good example of this form developed to its highest literary and philosophical end) achieves its unity and interest from the personality of the writer, and it is with this aspect of *Roughing It* that I am most concerned. Formally speaking, Mrs. Moodie's journal is not a work of art; however, the personality of the narrator has an imaginative numinousness which has caught a sympathetic reflection in the contemporary sensibility (witness the collection of poems by Margaret Atwood, *The Journals of Susanna Moodie*[3]) and which is often paralleled in the work of Canadian artists in the past. What is initially so fascinating in the journals is the way Mrs. Moodie's public statements continually belie the drift of her unconscious feelings. As Margaret Atwood has put it, Mrs. Moodie speaks with two voices:[4] with one, her public voice, she attempts to affirm the myths of the pioneer experience and lauds Canada as the land of future promise; but with the other, her private voice, she inadvertently expresses negative, inadmissable feelings which invalidate her patriotic rhetoric. The fundamental opposition or tension between these two voices (between what is socially acceptable and desired and what is privately felt) gives the book an imaginative dimension which other accounts of life in the Canadian backwoods do not have.

Mrs. Moodie's imaginative conflict is most strikingly apparent in the book's style—in the contrast, for example, between the Wordsworthian response to the Canadian landscape and the writer's detailed, day-to-day observations. Nurtured on the romantic myths of early nineteenth-century England, Mrs. Moodie, on first viewing the rugged scenery along the St. Lawrence, responds in a rhapsodic manner:

> The previous day had been dark and stormy, and a heavy fog had concealed the mountain chain, which forms the stupendous background to this sublime view, entirely from our sight. As the clouds rolled away from their grey, bald brows, and cast into denser shadow the vast forest belt that girdled them round, they

2. The imaginative character of the book has teased the minds of several critics. Clara Thomas in her essay "Journeys to Freedom," *Canadian Literature* 51 (Winter 1972), writes: "The book is a bewildering, contradictory amalgam of personal moods and literary modes—sentimental, comic, tragic, didactic. It is also unmistakeably, the work of a gifted, but embryonic, novelist who, in a dozen or so characters and as many scattered scenes, moved from the raw world she lived in towards the timeless reality of a contained world of the imagination" (p. 18). Professor Thomas, however, does not go on to suggest the nature of that imaginative world to which Mrs. Moodie's vision was directed. My purpose here is to begin exploring those qualities which give the book an imaginative dimension and which suggest that Mrs. Moodie is a figure central to our literary tradition.
3. See pp. 417–19 of this edition. [*Editor's note*.]
4. Margaret Atwood, *The Journals of Susanna Moodie* (Toronto: Oxford University Press, 1970), p. 42.

loomed out like mighty giants—Titans of the earth, in all their rugged and awful beauty—a thrill of wonder and delight prevaded my mind. The spectacle floated dimly on my sight—my eyes were blinded with tears—blinded by the excess of beauty. I turned to the right and to the left, I looked up and down the glorious river, never had I beheld so many striking objects blended into one mighty whole! Nature had lavished all her noblest features in producing that enchanting scene.[5]

The landscape in this passage is scarcely described; the distant panorama yields to an idea and correspondent emotion which blinds the narrator to the actual scene itself. The idea of nature as an unfailing source of inspiration persists throughout the journal, and in her public-spirited, affirmative mood, Mrs. Moodie asserts that "Nature ever did, and I hope ever will, continue: 'To shoot marvellous strength into my heart.' " (p. 100 [90]) But that very passage is followed by a confession that her feeling for Canada was like the feeling of a condemned criminal whose only hope for escape is through the grave. In the accounts of day-to-day life there are descriptions of nature which, far from Wordsworthian rhapsody, direct us to an undercurrent of negative feeling about the country and the conditions of pioneer life:

A thaw in the middle of winter is the most disagreeable change that can be imagined. After several weeks of clear, bright, bracing, frosty weather, with a serene atmosphere and cloudless sky, you awake one morning surprised at the change in the temperature; and, upon looking out of the window, behold the woods obscured by a murky haze—not so dense as an English November fog, but more black and lowering—and the heavens shrouded in a uniform covering of leaden-coloured clouds, deepening into a livid indigo at the edge of the horizon. The snow, no longer hard and glittering, has become soft and spongy, and the foot slips into a wet and insidiously-yielding mass at every step. From the roof pours down a continuous stream of water, and the branches of the trees, collecting the moisture of the reeking atmosphere, shower it upon the earth from every dripping twig (p. 151 [182]).

In this mood the author describes not just the horizon, but the details in the foreground in a realistic, documentary style which is closer to the style of F. P. Grove[6] than to her contemporaries. This is the mood in which the author explores her genuinely imaginative feelings about Canada, though at the same time never allowing herself to abandon the nineteenth-century myths of nature, mother country and pioneer.

The conflict of styles, however, involves much more than simply a literary manner unevenly executed. The Wordsworthian stance was for

5. *Roughing It in the Bush* (Toronto: McClelland and Stewart, 1964), pp. 22–23 [17–18]. I have used the abridged New Canadian Library edition because of its ready availability to most readers. [*Author's note.*] Carl Klinck's NCL edition (1964) was the only available paperback text for many years. See Thurston, p. 436. [*Editor's note.*]

6. Frederick Philip Grove (1871–1948), Canadian novelist of German origin, whose works include *Settlers of the Marsh* (1925) and *Fruits of the Earth* (1933). [*Editor's note.*]

Mrs. Moodie not just a learned set of attitudes or an affected literary pose, but something integral to her personality—a definition of self fundamental to survival in the backwoods. What emerges in the author's account of her rude experiences is a deep-seated fear of social contact, and her *role* as a gentlewoman in the wilderness is clearly a vital defence against what she fears most. By defining herself as both a gentlewoman and a woman of letters she is able to evade a reflexive relationship with the other settlers in the area. Even more to the point she is able to evade the social failure such relationships might precipitate. Likely our first opinion of Mrs. Moodie is that she is an intolerable prude, that she is proud and affected beyond endurance. She defines her Canadian neighbours as her inferiors, both socially and intellectually, and thus explains her reluctance to participate in their society. At times we may feel like her nearest neighbour, "Mrs. Joe", who one day finds Mrs. Moodie scrubbing a tubful of clothes and says, 'Well! I am glad to see you brought to work at last. I hope you may have to work as hard as I have. I don't see, not I, why you, who are no better than me, should sit still all day, like a lady!' " (p. 101 [92]). But it is a simple truth that pride invariably has its source in feelings of self-doubt, and in order to read Mrs. Moodie's journal with any sympathy we must recognize that her role playing throughout is a bulwark against a profound sense of inadequacy. At the time of Mrs. Joe's sneering remarks, she is in fact engaged upon a task at which she is hopelessly inept: she has rubbed the skin off her wrists in her effort to wash out the baby's things. Similar situations recur throughout the narrative; one remembers especially her fear of milking cows, her fear of wild animals in the woods, her failure at baking bread.

But Mrs. Moodie's sense of failure and inadequacy, which she in part cloaks under her role of gentlewoman in the backwoods, extends further than ineptitude at frontier tasks; it is rooted deeply in her nature and finds direct expression when she reflects on her separation from England. In outbursts of homesickness she upbraids herself as a guilty, unworthy creature whose exile in Canada is a form of punishment for an unspecified crime. Consider the psychological innuendos in this frequently repeated lament:

> Dear, dear England! why was I forced by stern necessity to leave you? What heinous crime had I committed that I, who adored you, should be torn from your sacred bosom, to pine out my joyless existence in a foreign clime? Oh that I might be permitted to return and die upon your wave-encircled shores, and rest my weary head and heart beneath your daisy-covered sod at last! (p. 56 [49]).

Death is the price the writer is willing to pay in order to be reunited with the maternal land. The same bargain is metaphorically struck at least twice again in the narrative. When taking up her first residence in the backwoods her thoughts are full of England: "One simple word dwelt for ever in my heart, and swelled it to bursting—'Home!' I repeated it waking a thousand times a day, and my last prayer before I sank to sleep was still 'Home! Oh, that I could return, if only to die at home!' " (p. 67 [60])[7] Later the sound of the stream near the log cabin makes her thoughts journey back to England and she concludes that her only escape from Canada will be "through the portals of the grave" (p. 100 [91]). Although Mrs. Moodie nostalgically romanticizes the past ("the daisied meadows of England . . . the fragrant shade of her green hedgerows"), a conviction of guilt and failure is her actual legacy from the mother country, which did not provide her family with a livelihood and forced her to emigrate. When she first reaches Canada she looks upon the new country as a possible refuge, a "second Eden". As she and her husband step ashore at Grosse Isle, they instinctively draw away from "the noisy, riotous crowd" to a little secluded copse by a river. The scene inspires Mrs. Moodie with Wordsworthian content at having found a refuge from "the cold, sneering world", but the idyllic Canadian scene is spoiled by "the profane sounds" and "discordant yells" of her fellow emigrants whom she bitterly designates as "filthy beings". In spite of her Wordsworthian faith in nature and the ennobling effects of poverty, Mrs. Moodie quickly finds Canada no second Eden. Her sense of failure is reinforced by her anomolous presence in the backwoods, and she retreats into her role as a gentlewoman in exile. Nor is there escape for Mrs. Moodie through her husband, for he is a weak, unsuccessful man and during moments of crisis is invariably absent. Only through her writing can Mrs. Moodie salvage something of her life, and here she significantly evades self-confrontation and dramatizes herself as a martyr figure—a victim of unjust social conditions in England and a heroic pioneer, sacrificing personal happiness so that a new country can be formed.

But *Roughing It* is no affecting creation story with Mrs. Moodie a figure of fertility. The author remains emotionally fixated on the past ("Dear, dear England") and her creative instincts are immobilized by feelings of rejection and inadequacy. In lieu of personal achievements her narrative focuses on an impersonal image of growth—the idea of Canada, "a noble, free, and rising country" (p. 56 [49]) and the idea of mankind in general slowly but surely moving toward the fulfilment of a sublime and mysterious destiny (a sentimental vision accommodating both Victorian Christianity and something like Social Darwinism). Such statements throughout the book project an idealized and dramatic sense of self in relation to society, but one which fails to convince as a total self-image. More revealing and suggestive is the way random vignettes in the narrative—the character sketches and anecdotes—fall together to form a pattern of social aversion and a preoccupation with failure and death. All the characters that Mrs. Moodie describes at any length are, like herself, totally out of place in the backwoods. The pattern is begun with the description of the Moodies'

7. Mrs. Moodie's retreat from the world is through nostaligia. The one passage in Margaret Atwood's poetic recreation of Mrs. Moodie which fails to convince in terms of psychological verisimilitude is when the narrator withdraws into herself like an animal and grows fur. Mrs. Moodie never conceives of herself as becoming part of the primal landscape; she escapes reality through her dreams of returning "home".

friend in England, Tom Wilson. Scarcely a promising pioneer, he is described as "a man in a mist, who seemed afraid of moving about for fear of knocking his head against a tree, and finding a halter suspended to its branches—a man as helpless and as indolent as a baby" (p. 49 [43]). The mood here is deliberately comic, and yet there is a note of concern in the narrator's voice which suggests a sympathetic identification with her friend. In the same vein she writes: "Tom would have been a treasure to an undertaker. He would have been celebrated as a mute; he looked as if he has been born in a shroud, and rocked in a coffin" (p. 50 [44]). Tom has already failed as an emigrant to Australia and soon matches that adventure with a similar experience in Canada. The Moodies look after him for a while (characters like Tom Wilson are the only society they ever do entertain), but he eventually returns to England, having lost everything he started out with.

Tom Wilson belongs to a remarkable gallery of characters who are failures (often guilt-ridden, like Mrs. Moodie), and who are associated with death in some form or other. After Wilson leaves, the Moodies hire an Irish boy, John Monaghan, who is seeking refuge from a harsh master. He is a spirited youth, but dogged by misfortune which he attributes to the fact that he is an orphan. Again we hear an echo of the narrator's own preoccupation—she calls herself an "orphan of civilization"—which is underscored by Monaghan's obsession that he is actually of gentle birth. Brian, the Still-Hunter, another emigrant from Britain, is a man of genuine despair. He appears at the log-house one day without speaking and follows this visit with several more, doing little kindnesses for Mrs. Moodie. Once a man of much promise, he began drinking and as he grew more incontinent, he became self-disgusted at having betrayed his family's hopes. A first attempt at suicide (he slashed his own throat) failed, but Mrs. Moodie tells us that some years after she left the bush, she heard that he finally succeeded in taking his own life. Brian's sense of guilt and his suicidal despair seem to touch something at the quick of the narrator. The story of Phoebe [Harris], the sensitive and gentle child born to the uncouth family of "Uncle Joe", is paradigmatic of the author's own feeling of being unappreciated and unjustly treated by the world. That girl's early death moves the narrator to an outburst of grief that is coloured by self-pity: "Gentle child of coarse, unfeeling parents, few shed more sincerely a tear for thy early fate than the stranger whom they hated and despised" (p. 120 [114]).

Perhaps the most vivid of the character sketches is the portrait of Malcolm, "the Little Stumpy Man", who, uninvited, stays with the Moodies for nine months. Mrs. Moodie's unyielding social manner is nowhere as omnipresent and oppressive. One critic has suggested that Mrs. Moodie's fear of Malcolm and his ill temper is actually sexual in origin, that she is at a fundamental level attracted to him physically.[8] Typically, Mrs. Moodie deflects the reader's attention from herself to the unscrupulous character of her visitor (as she does in describing

8. See R. D. MacDonald, "Design and Purpose", *Canadian Literature* 51 (Winter 1972), p. 25.

her borrowing neighbours) and thereby covers her true feelings. She was writing, of course, in a prohibitive, genteel tradition, so that sex is limited to such innocent vignettes as the courtship of the servants, Jacob and Mary. But when sex does appear (and sex does represent the most complete form of social communion possible) violence and death are its corollary. When Malcolm, left alone one day with Mrs. Moodie, tells his story, he reveals that he is a murderer (he once shot a man in South America) and is haunted by guilt. The same unrecognized equation is more blatantly operative in the charivari stories where sex is invariably a cause for violence and, in the case of the Negro who marries a white woman, the occasion for death.

We do not know the exact process by which the journals took final shape (whether extracted from diaries or written as sketches entirely from memory), but in the reshaping of the original experience Mrs. Moodie selects and omits detail in response to the unconscious drift of her feelings and in accord with a dramatic sense of self. Though not a work of art *Roughing It* has a definite imaginative shape in both the structure of its events and its patterns of imagery. The picture of Canada as a land of failure and death is present from the beginning with the ship of emigrants journeying into a country laid waste by cholera. The first paragraphs of the book describe the inspection and warning by the health officers when the boat reaches Montreal, and one of the doctors is described as "no bad representative of him who sat upon the pale horse" (p. 19 [14]). Mrs. Moodie emotionally seeks a "second Eden", but when she looks at the new land she says "the lofty groves of pine frowned down in hearse-like gloom upon the mighty river" (p. 37 [31]). Montreal is a city of death, and among the first people that the Moodies meet and talk with is a middle-aged couple who have just lost their son in the plague—their son who was their only hope and their reason for coming to a new land. Mrs. Moodie later tells her reader that after you have stayed in Canada for a long time "it is as if the grave has closed over you" (p. 91 [82]). The same image recurs when she designates Canada her prison and the "only hope of escape being through the portals of the grave" (p. 100 [91]). Her sense of expiating some unnamed guilt, however, brings her to love her prison, her grave in the backwoods, and when her husband finally arranges that they move to Belleville, she is reluctant to leave "the dear forest home . . . consecrated by the memory of a thousand sorrows" (pp. 229–31 [324–25]). Mrs. Moodie's final stance in the book is not unlike that of the Ancient Mariner who tells of his voyage through guilt, despair and death and who reemerges to warn those who might follow in his path.

The important question remains to be asked: in what ways do Mrs. Moodie and her journal represent the origins of a Canadian imaginative tradition? At least three definable aspects of her experience seem to be continuous in Canadian life. First, the Moodies, like the United Empire Loyalists before them and like great numbers of people since, came to Canada not with a dream of carving individual empires, but with the modest hope of salvaging a way of life threatened at home. In the Moodies' case poverty was the specific ill which caused them to emigrate, although political and religious reasons were also common. Like so many of the genteel poor from England and Scotland the Moodies sought in Canada a refuge, a way of saving pride in the face of ever dwindling economic and social circumstances. The contrast to the creative and forward-looking American experience in the eighteenth and nineteenth centuries is absolutely crucial to understanding a distinctively Canadian imaginative tradition. Seeking a haven in which to preserve customs threatened at home is imaginatively at the opposite pole from rejecting the old order and emigrating in order to begin life anew. The backward-looking nature of the Canadian experience is reflected in Mrs. Moodie's nostalgia for the daisy-covered fields of her England home. The original sense in Canada of being nowhere, or in exile, has left an indelible print on the Canadian psyche, as witness the quest by contemporary writers to discover ancestors and landmarks, whether in native inhabitants (see John Newlove's poem "The Pride") or in the animals and pioneers of the backwoods (see Margaret Atwood's *The Animals in That Country* and *The Journals of Susanna Moodie*).

Secondly, the image of one of our first settlers as a self-pitying failure rather than a bouyant pioneer characterizes a literary tradition in which fictional protagonists more likely lose than win, or are, at best, sorely compromised by their situation in life. The hard, intractable landscape seems to breed a conviction of inescapable defeat in the Canadian hero, a feeling which also colours his social relations. One thinks here especially of Grove's defeated heroes, Sinclair Ross's failed artist in *As For Me and My House* and Ernest Buckler's David Canaan, whose death in the snow is a preferred emotional alternative to a painful life of failed opportunities.[9] The American hero in contrast may lose his property, his sanity, even his life, but while he lives he never loses his dream, his sense of life's wonder and promise.

Thirdly, the curious affection Mrs. Moodie feels for her forest home at the time of departure is an ascetic form of imaginative pleasure which recurs with significant frequency in Canadian art. Through suffering and self-denial Mrs. Moodie has become attached to her way of life in the backwoods and to her home which she describes as "consecrated by the memory of a thousand sorrows." In a harsh, punitive landscape life is imaginatively conducted with a heightened sense of formidable odds and an almost pleasurable certainty of ultimate defeat. The image of one of our first writers in a backwoods log house working far into the night by sluts (twisted rags soaked in lard) is powerfully suggestive, and it is probably more than coincidence that Grove gives us an image in his autobiography, *In Search of Myself*, of similar pains taken (this time wearing mittens against the cold) in order to write during a Canadian winter. Ben Franklin of course submitted himself to similarly astringent circumstances in order to realize his ambitions both literary and political, but what a difference there is in

9. Ernest Buckler, *The Mountain and the Valley* (1952). [*Editor's note.*]

his recounting of those sacrifices. His confidence as a youth and his self-satisfaction as an old man telling his story of success are in marked contrast to Mrs. Moodie's caution to the reader and to Grove's underlying conviction that his life has been a failure. The Canadian imagination responds not to life's possibilities but to the limitations imposed by geography and climate; instead of looking to the horizon and the future, the Canadian artist more likely takes pleasure in what is domestic and secure, however small and humble. One might recall Thomas McCulloch's crippled Stepsure and his pleasure in a plain wife and humble cottage,[1] Grove's "domesticated island" in the frozen wastes, or those lines from Margaret Avison's "New Year's Poem": "Gentle and just pleasure / It is, being human, to have won from space / This unchill, habitable interior . . ." Mrs. Moodie's *Roughing It in the Bush* is not a work of art, but the narrator's personal drama of rejection and exile and her search for a refuge from an uncaring world is very central, to what is imaginative in the Canadian experience.

JOHN THURSTON

Rewriting *Roughing It*†

Susanna Moodie did not write *Roughing It in the Bush*. In fact, *Roughing It in the Bush* was never written. Susanna Moodie and *Roughing It in the Bush* are interchangeable titles given to a collaborative act of textual production whose origin cannot be limited to one person or one point in time. This activity is ongoing. It is not merely a matter of the interpretation or reception of *Roughing It*. The process for which this text is the focus involves its actual production. Susanna Moodie's is only one hand among the many involved in this collaborative activity. In this paper, I will endeavour to establish a perspective on the production of this text which frees it from the spatial and temporal limitations of author and publication date. I want to substitute a view of *Roughing It* as the textual focus of a process of cultural collaboration.

Susanna Strickland began her literary career by writing genteel poetry and children's stories. Marriage and the decision to emigrate established a dynamic which would confront these genres with experience for which they were inadequate. *Roughing It* began to be written with the first letters Susanna sent to friends and family in England.

It was John Wedderburn Dunbar Moodie who was the acknowledged author when he and his bride came to Canada in 1832. In 1835 he published *Ten Years in South Africa* and the originating impulse behind *Roughing It* was his.[1] His publisher, Richard Bentley, was not inter-

---

1. Thomas McCulloch, *The Mephiboseth Stepsure Letters* (1862). [*Editor's note.*]
† From *Future Indicative: Literary Theory and Canadian Literature*, ed. John Moss (Ottawa: U of Ottawa P, 1987), pp. 195–203. Reprinted by permission of the University of Ottawa Press. Page numbers in brackets refer to the text in this Norton Critical Edition.
1. Michael Peterman, "Susanna Moodie (1803–1885)," in *Canadian Writers and Their Works: Fiction Series 1*: 63–104, ed. R. Lecker, J. David, and E. Quigley (Downsview: ECW, 1983), 82.

ested, however, in the proposal made by J. W. D. in 1835 "for a work on Upper Canada." Nevertheless, Susanna began her writing of the sketches she would contribute to a Canadian book in the mid-1840s and in 1851 the Moodies sent a manuscript called "Canadian Life" to a London friend, John Bruce, who took it to J. W. D.'s publisher.[2]

To compile this manuscript, the Moodies gathered up Susanna's pieces of prose and verse, four chapters and ten poems by J. W. D., and part of a chapter and one poem by Samuel Strickland, Susanna's brother and neighbour. As Michael Peterman notes, "*Roughing It* was a family venture."[3] It was probably Susanna who attempted to catch these fragments in a narrative net and tie them up with some thematic rope. The fragments provide the central drive of the book. A full two-thirds of the manuscript sent to Bentley had appeared in periodicals prior to book publication.

In transforming these periodical fragments into the semblance of a book, Moodie shows a good deal of concern for her potential audience. Her sketches had appeared in Canadian periodicals, the *Literary Garland*, and the Moodies' own *Victoria Magazine*. Reaction from Roman Catholic Canadians to the periodical appearance of a potential chapter called "Michael MacBride" caused her to suppress it.[4] She was more concerned with her English audience, however. Peterman analyzes the "attempt on her part to write for the tastes and assumptions of the particular audience she was addressing" and finds "the language . . . more high-toned and poetic in the English edition."[5] Excisions are made from the sketches and surviving material is rewritten. Moodie allowed her audience's demands to dictate the style and substance of the family work.

The next participants in the creation of *Roughing It* were employees at the Bentley publishing house and John Bruce. As mentioned, Bruce was the Moodie agent for *Roughing It*. The editors of the Moodie letters write that Bruce "also saw the work through the press, reading the proofs and making alterations and corrections."[6] The first three so-called "editions" of *Roughing It* contain hundreds of variants in both accidentals and substantives. The variants in accidentals have been thoroughly documented by the Centre for Editing Early Canadian Texts. I understand that this information will be released upon the publication of their edition. The major substantive variants are apparent through a cursory comparison of any copy of the "first edition" with any copy of the "second edition with additions." I will mention only a few of the more significant changes which were made between the first two titular "editions." A page of dialogue which is in the periodical version of the first chapter is missing from the first edition but reinserted for the second. The poems at the end of the penultimate chapter and the

2. Susanna Moodie, *Letters of a Lifetime*, ed. C. Ballstadt, M. Peterman, and E. Hopkins (Toronto: U of Toronto P, 1985), 104. Hereafter referred to as Moodie 1985.
3. Peterman, 83.
4. Moodie 1985, 109.
5. Peterman, 84.
6. Moodie 1985, 104.

beginning of the last are shuffled. Much of the poetry is rewritten, to the extent of having lines inserted or deleted. A chapter by J. W. D. Moodie surfaces for the first time in the second edition. There is no evidence in the correspondence between Susanna Moodie and Richard Bentley to suggest that any of the changes to the manuscript were made on the express orders of Susanna or her husband.

John Bruce and the Bentley proof-readers and editors were responsible for shaping the manuscript. Bruce must have taken charge of this task. His activities precede and follow the actual setting of the type for the book. In a letter dated 27 December 1851 Bentley asks Bruce to revise the manuscript " 'with the view of omitting some of the poetry.' "[7] Another letter, two days later, refers to certain "softnesses" Bruce is in the process of eliminating at the request of Bentley. Since the book was published on 29 January 1852, Bruce's activity ran concurrent with the setting of it. Bentley and Bruce also decided which prose sections were to be included in the final text. The Moodies sent three chapters to Bentley, separate from the bulk of the manuscript. Two were to replace the chapter on Michael MacBride which they had removed because of the Catholic response and one was to be a concluding chapter of a factual and statistical nature. The latter had been requested by Bentley and only it becomes part of any edition of the book. This is J. W. D. Moodie's "Canadian Sketches" and its inclusion is probably due to several factors. No doubt it was easier to add J. W. D.'s chapter to the already-set book than it would have been to insert the two chapters from Susanna. This chapter would broaden the market appeal of the text to draw in serious immigrants and speculators interested in "international development." It also justifies the publisher's ploy of describing the second "edition" as with "additions." The chapter "Michael MacBride" plus the other two chapters sent with J. W. D.'s "Canadian Sketches" do appear in *Roughing It*'s sequel, *Life in the Clearings*. That the responsibility for which chapters were included resided with Bentley and Bruce can be inferred from a note Susanna makes concerning these three chapters of *Life in the Clearings*[8] and from her letter of 16 April 1852 to Bentley.[9]

One further detail must be attributed to Bentley: the title. Moodie simply refers to her "Canadian book" in the correspondence. Peterman writes that Moodie "had no direct contact with Richard Bentley until after the manuscript she sent him as 'Canadian Life' appeared in London with its new and striking title."[1] Where did the title come from? Well, a few years earlier, Bentley had published a moderately successful book about Australia called *Roughing It in the Outback*!

7. George Parker, "Haliburton and Moodie: The Early Publishing History of *The Clockmaker*, 1st Series, and *Roughing It in the Bush*," in *Papers of the Bibliographical Society of Canada* 3: 139–60 (1978), 150.
8. Susanna Moodie, *Life in the Clearings*, ed. R. McDougall (Toronto: Macmillan, 1959), 204. Hereafter referred to as Moodie 1959.
9. Moodie 1985, 123–25. See also comments made by Peterman, 83 and note, and Parker, 150.
1. Peterman, 83 and note.

The evidence of extreme editorial intervention indicates that the manuscript handled by John Bruce for the Moodies was open to improvement at many levels. Bentley's belief in its marketability must have been firm for him to expend so much time on it. Bentley and Bruce must have been motivated by a strong sense of responsibility to themselves and to the Moodies. They in effect supplied the finish to an inchoate work.

The subsequent publishing history of the text suggests that they were not quite successful. Each successive editor has assumed a freedom to alter the text according to his perception of it and of his audience's demands. The poetry was the first part of the book to go. In the summer of 1852 a pirated edition was published in New York. Charles Frederick Briggs revised this edition, omitting thirty poems and two of J. W. D.'s sketches plus numerous other prose passages.[2] In his view, the Moodies would not complain that the book "should have undergone a careful excision of certain passages of a purely personal or political character" because he would thus gain a larger audience for it.[3] The 1857 Bentley yellow-back edition also has very few poems although the Moodies did not request that they be removed. J. W. D. Moodie's chapters go next. Susanna apparently sanctioned the excision of his "Canadian Sketches" from the first Canadian edition of 1871. Other chapters or verses are reduced or eliminated with each new editor. Carl Klinck tells us in the "Introduction" to the New Canadian Library edition that "only a successful book requires as much editing as Roughing It in the Bush has received."[4] Klinck proceeded with his excisions until the text was reduced to less than half its original length for the NCL edition. Bentley and Bruce participated in the creative process initiated by the Moodies upon their arrival in Canada. Every editor since them has felt compelled to join.

The Centre for Editing Early Canadian Texts plans to rectify what is considered to be editorial corruption by publishing a new version of Roughing It. The Centre's text will have the virtue of incorporating, in a new edition, the material that has been excised. The theory of textual bibliography which the Centre endorses rests on the concepts of authorial autonomy and authorial intention. The writers/rewriters of this text may not have viewed themselves as having authorial autonomy. Neither does it seem that they had any stable intentions concerning the writing project which was in 1852 labelled Roughing It in the Bush. This text supports what Jerome McGann contends in his critique of scholarly editing, that becoming an author is a matter of engaging in a collaborative relationship with publishing institutions. "In fact," he writes, "an author's work possesses autonomy only when it remains an unheard melody."[5] Further, "authority is a social nexus, not

---

2. Moodie 1985, 107.
3. Quoted by the editors, ibid., 107.
4. Carl Klinck, Introduction to Roughing It in the Bush, ed. Carl Klinck, ix–xiv (Toronto: McClelland and Stewart, 1962), ix.
5. Jerome McGann, A Critique of Modern Textual Criticism (Chicago: U of Chicago P, 1983), 51.

a personal possession . . . its initiation takes place in a necessary and integral historical environment of great complexity."[6] These remarks are clearly applicable to the case of *Roughing It in the Bush*. To attribute any sort of autonomous authority to Susanna Moodie and her husband is contrary to what is known of their publishing relationships. Whatever unity this book of fragments has is due more to intentions attributed to it by its editors than to any intentions the various sources of the fragments may have had.

McGann has written about another case, that "we enter the world of textual versions where intentions are plainly shifting and changing under the pressure of various people and circumstances."[7] His emphasis on the social element of authorship causes us to be less disturbed by what we know of the publishing of *Roughing It*: "The fully authoritative text is therefore always one which has been socially produced; as a result, the critical standard for what constitutes authoritativeness cannot rest with the author and his intentions alone."[8] McGann allows us to conclude "that a definitive text, like the author's final intentions, may not exist, may never have existed, and may never exist at any future time."[9] His statements clarify our view of this text.

Roughing It in the Bush was not the product of an autonomous author nor can it be reduced to any hypothetical authorial intention. Moodie abnegated any final artistic responsibility for this text. To compile the 1871 edition, the only one she oversaw, she mimicked the abscissions performed by other editors and muted the anti-Canadian tone which had drawn hostile reactions. With this book, authors, texts, environments of writing, technics of production, market factors, paths of dissemination are in a relationship sufficiently unstable, shifting, and open-ended as to vitiate any configuration at the centre of which could be placed an autonomous author and his/her final intentions. The unfinished quality of the manuscript attested to by Bruce's and Bentley's labours is merely a reflection of this. There can be no final version of this text. For *Roughing It*, the outward emblems of its state of flux are the wandering commas, the spurs of exclamation, the appearing and disappearing magiscules, the variant spellings, the substitutions, the pages lost, found, rearranged, the dialogue that is silenced, the chapters which fail to make the Atlantic crossing or arrive shuffled, disoriented.

There is, of course, a social equivalent to this state of textual flux. The nature of this social equivalent is indicated by the advertisement placed in the three Bentley issues where we are told that the author is in the bush and so is not able to oversee the printing of the text. We are not told how much is involved in seeing the book through the press. The Moodies were in the Canadian bush struggling to survive with their children. Susanna wrote at night by the light of "sluts." The publishing institution the Moodies were dealing with was in London,

6. Ibid., 48.
7. Ibid., 62.
8. Ibid., 75.
9. Ibid., 89–90.

England. We read this social and economic gap when we become aware of the difference between what the Moodies wrote and what Bentley published.

The outward emblems of *Roughing It*'s textual instability point to a state of internal flux. This internal state of flux can be characterized as generic instability. Susanna Moodie and her husband could not find the genre within which to write this book. John Bruce and Richard Bentley apparently thought the text was either immigrant tract or exotic travel literature or both. Critics have been looking for a genre in which to confine the text ever since. Klinck, one of the first modern editors to attempt generic classification of *Roughing It*, defines it as an apprenticeship novel.[1] Carl Ballstadt characterizes it as a series of sketches in the manner of Mary Russell Mitford. Marion Fowler goes to great lengths to prove that Susanna Moodie is writing in the tradition of the sentimental Gothic novel of Ann Radcliffe.[2] As Peterman summarizes it, "containing elements of poetry, fiction, travel writing, autobiography, and social analysis, it eludes definition."[3] No generic classification of the text is satisfactory.

Susanna Moodie could write lyrics, children's stories, and romances but these could not contain her Canadian material. Normal literature—the analogy with Thomas Kuhn's normal science is intended—would not work in Canada. The established, traditional, lyric genres would not accommodate the dialogic, amorphous, democratic, "vulgar" Canadian experience as the Moodies found it. Using Roland Barthes' distinctions, we could say that Moodie's training in the writing of *readerly* texts failed her, so, unknown to herself, she wrote the *writerly*.

Moodie's performance in the lyric is exemplary respecting this generic failure. She published poetry before she came to Canada. She wrote profusely in the romantic, lyric form early in her years here. Her Canadian lyrics and ballads began to be published in 1833. The first full version of *Roughing It* had twenty-seven poems by her plus numerous epigraphic verses. The letter from Bentley to Bruce quoted earlier implies that there were more in the manuscript. As noted, the poems printed in the 1852 edition were the first elements to go when the later editors took their turn with *Roughing It*. In the NCL edition, apart from a few verse epigraphs, only one poem, "The Oath of the Canadian Volunteers," remains. In those lyrics, Moodie tries to apply a genteel polish to experience which is not genteel. Her talent for verse is minor, but her publication record indicates that she thought it was her strength. The confrontation of her lyrical effusions with her Canadian experience disabused her of this illusion. Her poetic output lessens the longer she is in Canada.

The most exemplary successes in *Roughing It* are the passages in which other characters figure strongly. The tension of these passages

---

1. Klinck, xiv.
2. Marian Fowler, "*Roughing It in the Bush*: A Sentimental Novel," in *The Canadian Novel: Beginnings*, ed. John Moss, 80–96 (Toronto: NCP, 1980).
3. Peterman, 81.

is increased as undercurrents in Moodie's character are drawn out. The reader can feel her sense of repulsion at the proximity of "vulgar" people. Yet she cannot deny them entrance to her book, "Canadian Life." She attempts to assimilate them into her narrative and so gain control of them. She cannot resist the trite moral or the revelation of their hypocrisy.

Moodie struggles to encompass her characters within her narrative. If this is to be an apprenticeship novel, then she needs to keep her own voice paramount. Mikhail Bakhtin's concepts of the dialogic and the carnivalesque will help us analyze her attempt to hold the stage for her own words. The premise of Bakhtin's philosophy of language is, as Voloshinov writes, that "the word is the ideological phenomenon par excellence."[4] Bakhtin differentiates the monologic as the attempt of one voice to dominate the range of discourse. The monologic always finds itself in response to another's word and so begins by compromising its rigidity. The attempt to achieve a unitary language is always frustrated by the dialogic basis of communication.

Moodie invests her narrative with the hope of restoring a unitary sense of herself. This unitary self is associated with her English past and with the genres of the lyric, short story, and romance. The insistently dialogic nature of the language of her characters thwarts her. By allowing the voices of her characters into her writing, Moodie establishes a zone of contact between discourses. It is in this zone that the subversions of carnival take place.[5] She participates in the subversion of her own monologic language. Following Julia Kristeva, we can align dialogism, carnival, and phrase on one side of a paradigm reflected by monologism, narrative, and system.[6] The conjunction of these two sides results in polyphonic fiction.

Roughing It reveals Moodie's failure to keep the people around her at a distance. Their discourse attains contact with her own Old World voice and the resulting dialogue between discourses extends beyond her control. In this sense, some of her characters join J. W. D. Moodie, Samuel Strickland, Richard Bentley, and John Bruce as authors of the text in which they appear. The voices of the characters in *Roughing It* enter and speak with their own accents, their own emphasis, oblivious to any authorial attempt to silence them or rob their words of value.

Moodie is most at home in this text when she is writing in the lyrical, hortatory, or didactic modes. She is drawn to these monologic modes as potential systems of narrative but they continually let her down. The verbal home she attempts to build is invaded by the voices of others. The characters who enter speak in no generic mode known to her. She tries to reduce them to the low comic or diabolic. They reassert themselves as embodiments of the carnivalesque.

There is a link between Moodie's orientation to language and to so-

---

4. V. N. Voloshinov, *Marxism and the Philosophy of Language*, trans. L. Matejka and I. R. Titunik (New York: Seminar Press, 1973), 13.
5. Mikhail Bakhtin, *Problems of Dostoevsky's Poetics*, ed. and trans. C. Emerson (Minneapolis: U of Minnesota P, 1984), 123.
6. Julia Kristeva, *Desire in Language*, ed. L. S. Roudiez (New York: Columbia UP, 1980), 88.

ciety. For instance, her sketches on Uncle Joe and Old Satan only come to rest when she has curtailed the anarchic voices of these characters within a narrative of their downfall. When she can situate her characters through narrative, hold them at a distance as inferiors, she is comfortable. A rigid narrative structure enforces social rigidity. When she is compelled to engage in a dialogic discourse in which her characters have control of the phrase, then we sense her anxiety, her dis-ease. The section on "The Borrowing System" details Moodie's unfamiliarity with the North American pronunciation and use of words such as girl, gentlemen, slack, rooster, and sauce. This unfamiliarity parallels her unwillingness to accept a system of commodity exchange she cannot understand. In the chapter "Uncle Joe and His Family," the quoted dialogue of Joe and his mother controls the sketch. Moodie can only enter one-line comments as not only the system of narrative but the system of land exchange is disrupted. The carnivalesque disturbance of language has a social equivalent. The chapters which achieve a unified tone deal with characters who have literary prototypes and who do not pose any social threat. These are the chapters on Tom Wilson and Brian, the Still-Hunter. Moodie can contain these characters in a narrative framework without betraying them.

Tom Wilson represents carnival reduced to the subjective, individual level. He and the carnival fool, Malachi Croak, are innocuous because their activities are dissociated from any social implications. Croak and Wilson are in love with the image of eccentricity for its own sake. The carnivalesque at full force is a threat to both generic stability and social stability. There is a hint of this type of carnival in the chapter on the arrival of the Moodies at Grosse Isle. Robert Kroetsch writes on the relationship of this section of the text to carnival.[7] The narrative confines the vulgar class of immigrants to the island—that is, at a distance from the narrator. She is repulsed but the threat they present remains latent. She keeps them isolated by describing them as local colour, as a tourist would. They are part of her itinerary, not of her coming life in Canada. She throws a few trite morals at them and a few tender descriptions at the scenery and she is on her way.

The carnivalesque enters the text more ominously through the charivari. In this chapter, the narrator's indignation at the custom is tempered by her assumption that charivaris only happen to those who deserve them. Significantly, the events of the various charivaris are recounted by someone else whom the narrator quotes. Moodie keeps her linguistic distance from the carnivalesque. When carnival presents a distinct intimidation, Moodie reacts with the shrill self-righteousness characterizing her response to the logging bee. What helps her overcome this intrusion of carnival is her certainty that she is on morally secure ground in condemning the custom of bees. She believes that, because expenditure does not equal productivity, bees are impractical affairs. She is oblivious to the cultivation of communal

7. Robert Kroetsch, "Carnival and Violence: A Meditation," from *Open Letter* 5th series 4:111–24 (1983).

spirit which is the real reason for bees. The communal eating and drinking at the bee are to her a "hateful feast"[8] rather than a carnival celebration. Living carnival is brought into the text but Moodie never makes contact with the literary carnivalesque. Instead, she attempts to subdue carnival through the imposition of narrative decorum. This conflict between carnival and narrative is symptomatic of the contradictions and conflicts throughout the text. The overall tension is between dialogic and monologic discourse.

Margaret Atwood's characterization of Moodie as a paranoid schizophrenic localizes the division at a psychological and thematic level. Carol Shields, remarking on Atwood's interpretation, writes that "it is possible that the dichotomy is not rooted in Mrs. Moodie's personality; it may be only a surface splintering, a division which exists for literary purposes."[9] Rather, the division exists between literary purposes and the intractability of her linguistic milieu. Moodie's personality is split by the institution and system of *la langue* as she carries it and *la parole* as she finds it actualized in Canada. This linguistic gap is the place where we read all of the other contradictions, including the social ones. She seeks generic and social stability through language but is confuted by the dialogic force of the discourse she encounters.

Moodie herself is aware that language reflects social relationships, that the word is an ideological phenomenon. She begins by positing her belief that "the higher class" of officers will not "submit cheerfully to the saucy familiarity of servants.'"[1] She discusses how "the titles 'sir' and 'madam,' " linguistic markers of social status, are "very rarely applied by inferiors" in Canada.[2] She indirectly quotes the serving class to the effect that "no contract signed in the old country is binding in 'Meriky.' "[3] The dialect spelling indicates that linguistic contracts are implied as much as legal ones. Moodie's use of dialect is an attempt to distance the people around her, precisely to turn them into literary characters that she and her readers can laugh at without having to deal with them as individuals. Similarly, she quotes the Bible not to edify her interlocutors, but rather to humiliate them.

Moodie has a very practical way of uniting writing and living. She compares writing to bread-baking[4] and milking.[5] Contemplating a field of potatoes is compared to contemplating a painting.[6] She experiences great joy at being able to earn money by writing.[7] Her fungus paintings are placed on a par with her writing as a means to supplement the family income.[8] She writes poetry as her contribution to the British cause in the rebellion of 1837. One contradiction that Moodie does

8. Susanna Moodie, *Roughing It in the Bush*, 1st ed., 2 vols. (London: Richard Bentley, 1852), II:77 [216]. Hereafter referred to as Moodie 1852.
9. Carol Shields, *Susanna Moodie: Voice and Vision* (Ottawa: Borealis, 1977), 30.
1. Moodie 1852, I: xi [11].
2. Ibid., I: 213 [132].
3. Ibid., I: 215 [133].
4. Ibid., I: 121 [81].
5. Ibid., I: 196 [122].
6. Ibid., II: 116 [237].
7. Ibid., II: 185–96 [280–81].
8. Ibid., II: 199 [283].

442   D. M. R. BENTLEY

not express is the contradiction of dividing language and ideology from each other.

This text can be seen as central to Canadian culture precisely because of all its problems. Having little sense of form, Moodie had little sense of the inadequacies of her language. In coming to a land which could not be contained by any generic framework, she wrote fearlessly, believing that she could capture it all. The inadequacies of language allowed her and her collaborators to catch more of the society around them than they knew. They had little idea of the contradictions which split this text all the way from the level of the word up to the level of structure. The text lies open before us. In its contradictions, its irresolutions, its generic amorphousness, its open-endedness, its disunity, we read a story of which Susanna Moodie had very little awareness. She absorbed the contradictions, lived them out, and then regurgitated them unresolved. A stronger writer would have hidden them from us by providing some aesthetically pleasing resolution to the conflicts. A stronger personality would have imposed a unified presence on them. As it was, Moodie was exactly the person needed to articulate the contradictions at the root— temporally, artistically, ideologically, linguistically—of the Canadian consciousness. She was exactly the person to serve as the focus for the textual activity we call *Roughing It in the Bush.*

As we have seen, *Roughing It in the Bush* was a collaborative effort right from the beginning. The book continues to be rewritten, it has ever only been rewritten. When a text has been subjected, to the extent that this one has, to rewriting at the hands of others, this rewriting at once indicates how generically unfixed the text is and predicates its continuous rewriting, its continuous search for generic stability.

D. M. R. BENTLEY

Breaking the "Cake of Custom": The Atlantic Crossing as a Rubicon for Female Emigrants to Canada?†

For Anne Bolgan—humanist, feminist, fighter, friend

> . . . I witnessed the interesting spectacle of the disembarkation of a number of British emigrants. The greater part were from Scotland . . . and a seven weeks passage across the Atlantic did not appear to have divested them of a single national peculiarity. . . .
> JOHN HOWISON, *Sketches of Upper Canada*

> The sight of the Canadian shores had changed [some of our steerage passengers] into persons of great consequence. The poorest and

† From "Re(dis)covering Our Foremothers: Nineteenth-Century Canadian Women Writers," ed. Lorraine McMullen (Ottawa: U of Ottawa P, 1990), pp. 91–122. Reprinted by permission of the University of Ottawa Press. See p. 472 for Works Cited.

worst-dressed, the least-deserving and the most repulsive in mind and
morals exhibited most disgusting habits of self-importance.
                                    SUSANNA MOODIE, *Roughing It in the Bush*

Some time ago, Alfred G. Bailey drew my attention to Arnold Toynbee's remarks on "The Stimulus of Migration Overseas" in *A Study of History*,
particularly to Toynbee's richly metaphorical and
allusive suggestion that the " 'sea change' " involved in such a migration can shatter the " 'cake
of custom' " to produce in "long-imprisoned and
suddenly liberated souls" a strong new awareness
of the self and of social issues (93). According to
Toynbee, the "stimulating effect of crossing the
sea" resides in "one . . . simple fact":

> In transmarine migration, the social appara-
> tus of the migrants has to be packed on
> board ship before they can leave the shores
> of the old country and then unpacked again
> at the end of the voyage before they can
> make themselves at home on new ground. All
> kinds of apparatus—persons and property,
> techniques and institutions and ideas—are
> equally subject to this law. Anything that
> cannot stand the sea voyage at all has simply
> to be left behind; and many things—and
> these not only material objects—which the
> migrants do manage to take with them can
> only be shipped after they have been taken to
> pieces—never, perhaps, to be reassembled in
> their original form (88).

*. . . you're riding
high and mighty/In a
gale that's pushing
ninety. . . . And
you've got along for
comfort/All the
world there ever
shall be, was, and is.
—Jay Macpherson,
The Boatman
(1957).*

In Toynbee's view, the ocean voyage itself, the fact
of being contained in what A. B. Lubbock likens
to "a hermetically sealed box" during a transmarine migration (3), was a major stimulus to the
creation of new social configurations: "Having co-
operated at sea as men do co-operate when they
are 'all in the same boat' in the midst of the perils
of the deep," Toynbee writes, "[the emigrants]
would continue to feel and act in the same way
ashore . . . " (97).
    These and other remarks of Toynbee's seemed
to me to have obvious application to some recent
works of popular Australian culture such as the
television series "Against the Wind," where the
basis for a new social contract in the form of a
sort of honour among thieves is seen developing
in the steerage of a transport vessel bound for

*After moving: recon-
structions. Once
again to set new con-
ditions. Choosing de-
tails: the apartment
with the bay win-
dows, the courtyard,
the city by the ocean.
For the first time liv-
ing by the ocean.
—Rhea Tsregebov,
Remembering His-
tory (1982).*

Botany Bay. But his remarks rang almost no bells at all in regard to the writings of (or literature about) Canada's early emigrants, some of whom might be expected to have commented on similar or parallel phenomena if they had occurred in vessels crossing the Atlantic from Britain to North America. Since many of the better-known authors of Canadian emigrant accounts were women, I especially wondered whether an examination of several emigrant accounts by Catharine Parr Traill, Susanna Moodie, Anne Langton, and others might not reveal a common—or at least interestingly diverse—pattern of response to the trans-Atlantic voyage.

The first thing to emerge from this line of enquiry was a recognition that every bit as important as the trans-Atlantic voyage itself as a site of stimulus and potential transformation for female emigrants were the moments of departure from Britain and arrival in Canada (or at the coast of the United States), for at these points of stress and tension in emigration's larger and more open-ended process of displacement and replacement,[1] the emotions evoked by leaving a familiar place and arriving at a strange one were at their most acute and plangent. In the terms of Anthony Wilden's *System and Structure*, the complex moments of an emigrant's departure and arrival resemble boundaries,[2] each being both a site of differentiation (what lies ahead is not the same as what lies behind) and a site of communication (a necessary stage in getting from what lies behind to what lies ahead). A preliminary sense of the complexity of such boundary moments can be gained from the Reverend William Bell's account of the behaviour of his fellow passengers as their boat drew away from the coast of Scotland: "some appeared lively and cheerful—some thoughtful and serious—while a few, by the tears which they shed, showed that they were not leaving their country and their friends without a struggle" (2). This essay examines a variety of significant responses, some by men but most by women, to the

It is a fact that to one person a voyage may mean only a departure and an arrival, an expense incurred, only a happy lapse of coloured time, only an embarking and a disembarking—the distance between two

---

1. Beyond the stages of packing and unpacking described by Toynbee in the indented quotation above, are obviously the processes of deciding to emigrate and, on the other side of the Atlantic, reaching and settling (into) the new home. See Edwin C. Guillet (*passim*) for an account of the entire process of emigration that has been very helpful in the present study, not least in calling my attention to pertinent primary and secondary sources.
2. See Wilden (183–88).

three stages of the trans-Atlantic crossing—the departure, the voyage itself, and the arrival—in the hope of revealing at each stage some of the personal, social, and cultural ramifications of the emigrant experience, especially the implications, for female identity and writing, of emigration to Canada in the nineteenth century.

Before proceeding to specific details and individual personalities, the general and obvious point needs to be made that at the archetypal or mythic level a transmarine journey of emigration is incompatible with most of the patterns that are usually attached to such voyages. It is not a journey of excursion and return, but an intermediate (and mediating) stage in a process of frequently reluctant removal from a cherished home and usually arduous relocation in an unfamiliar place. Unlike Homer's Odysseus or Jason and the Argonauts or most of the adventurous knights of medieval romance (whose quests are circular)—unlike even Tennyson's Ulysses (who voluntarily undertakes his westering journey)—the typical nineteenth-century emigrant to Canada was more or less driven across the ocean to a place of permanent exile and new beginning. Nor does the experience of emigration from Britain to Canada find an entirely satisfactory analogue in the biblical stories of the Exodus and the Expulsion,[3] or in Virgil's epic of the founding of Rome; for, in contrast to more southerly regions of North America, the continent's attic was only sporadically perceived as a refuge from captivity or as a Promised Land, let alone as a New Rome. A possibly useful way of coming to terms with the experience of emigration to Canada in the nineteenth century is to imagine it, for the time being (and further metaphorical possibilities will be advanced in due course), as a combination of the biblical pattern of permanent removal, exodus, or expulsion to a remote land (Goshen, Canaan), and the classical myth of Hercules, the Greek hero who unwillingly undertakes great and unpleasant labours in distant and inhospitable places and, as a result, was held by the Greeks themselves to be "almost the ideal embodiment of the . . . settler."[4]

places on a map which may be pink or even blue; but to Ellen the voyage was a shaking and transforming experience. . . .
—Ethel Wilson,
Love and Salt Water
(1957).

3. See Toynbee (84).
4. C. M. Bowra, *Greek Poetry*, cited by Galinsky (20). See my "Large Stature and Larger Soul: Notes on the Herculean Hero and Narrative in Canadian Literature," *Journal of Canadian Poetry* 2 (1987), 1–21, for further discussion of the importance of the Hercules myth in Canadian writing of the pioneering and post-pioneering periods.

With the recognition of an affinity between the labours of Hercules and the experience of a Canadian emigrant comes a realization that, on the basis of mere physical strength alone, the Herculean analogue seems to deny heroic stature to women, especially to those women who because of their class were sufficiently exempted from manual labour to warrant being described as the "gentler sex." As will be seen, just such a realization is implicit in the opening sketch of *Roughing It in the Bush*, where Moodie gives narrative force to her argument that Canada offers no prospects for gentlefolk like herself and her husband. Yet a form of Herculean heroism was achieved by several female emigrants to Canada, including, it could be argued, Moodie herself— women who, by performing such traditionally masculine labours as ploughing, sowing, and harvesting, blurred the conventional distinctions between the sexes. In the process, they forged in their lives and in their writings a new role model for Canadian women in the pioneering and post-pioneering periods: the powerful figure at the centre of what should be recognized as a *topos* in Canadian women's writing, the *topos* of the woman who, either through widowhood or through a temporary absence of the male members of her family, finds herself controlling all aspects, both domestic and agricultural, of an isolated homestead.[5] Drawn as they were by necessity, and occasionally by temperament, to create and embody the gender-blurring *topos* of the female Crusoe (as it might be called in honour of one of its obvious literary antecedents),[6] most pioneering women felt a contrary need to remain feminine in the conventional terms of their day— to paint and write and sew as well as to sow and plant and reap.[7] The resulting tension is described explicitly by Anne Langton in her journal:

Pique had gone away. She must have left during the night. . . . I've got too damn much work in hand to fret over Pique. . . . If I hadn't been a writer, I might have been a first-rate mess at this point.
—Margaret Laurence, The Diviners (1974).

5. See Curtius (70, 79–105) for the classic definition and discussion of *topoi*. The first, frustrated inkling of the *topos* of the female Crusoe in Canadian writing is found in the depiction of Madame Des Roches in Frances Brooke's *The History of Emily Montague*. Although a beneficiary of Edward Rivers' help, Madame Des Roches lives in "absolute solitude" on an "estate" that she apparently runs herself (see Brooke (72–90)). More fully developed examples of the *topos* can be found, for example, in Moodie (212–19) and in O'Brien (164–68).

6. See Thompson (*passim*) for a discussion of the pre-eminent part played by Traill in establishing the characteristics of the pioneer-woman-as-heroine and, by extension, of the *topos* described above.

7. See Moodie (212–16) on her writing for *The Literary Garland* and "painting birds and butterflies upon . . . white, velvety . . . fungi" during her husband's absence [280–83].

perhaps you would think my feminine manners in danger if you were to see me steering a boat for my gentlemen rowers, or maybe handling the ropes a little in sailing, but don't be alarmed; though such things do occur occasionally, they are rather infrequent, and my woman's avocations will always, I think, more than counterbalance them. I have caught myself wishing an old long-forgotten wish that I had been born of the rougher sex (Langton 1950, 72–73).[8]

To indicate that a tension between the "masculine" and the "feminine," the necessary and the conventional, can be found in many of the writings of pioneering Canadian women is already to anticipate a later stage of the discussion and, to an extent, to move beyond the limits of the present essay. For the time being, it is sufficient to recognize that the *topos* of the female Crusoe constitutes one possible goal of the trans-Atlantic journey for the nineteenth-century female emigrant to Canada, and with this possibility in mind, to begin at the beginning, with the departure of the emigrants from Britain.

I
The Departure

The earliest account of the emigrant experience by a woman writer appears in the opening pages of Frances Brooke's *The History of Emily Montague*, where Edward Rivers is given a double focus of vision, a Janus-like quality of looking both forward to the future and back to the past, which, as already intimated by the quotation from William Bell, finds echoes in much nineteenth-century writing about the Atlantic crossing. As his "vessel is unmoor'd" at Cowes on the Isle of Wight en route to Quebec, Rivers writes to John Temple in Paris that he is going to Canada "with all the eager hopes of a warm imagination; yet friendship casts a lingering look behind" (4). This "lingering look," either directly or in the mind's eye, at "the land of . . . nativity, friends, and former home" is a nearly ubiquitous feature of the moment of departure in emigrant writing (Picker-

Dearest Mother, and all/On board all right and children and luggage. A large ship, crowded with people. We have got a berth to ourselves. Found a gentleman who helped us with everything, so kind. So is everybody. . . . Love to all and farewells. Children are happy. —Anna Leveridge, Your Loving Anna (1972).

8. Langton proceeds to lament the fact that in Canada "women are very dependent . . . [and] feel our weakness more than anywhere else."

ing, 2).[9] It is most intense, prolonged, and emphatic in the case of emigrants who were least
happy about leaving Britain and most intense in
the case of women who, in following their husbands to the New World, had to leave behind
family, friends, and what Moodie calls "congenial
minds" [130]. Indeed, for Moodie, the experience
of leaving England was enduringly numbing and
dehumanizing: "like Lot's wife," she says, "I still
turned and looked back, and clung with all my
strength to the land I was leaving" [130].[1] For
Langton, the distress of "embarking on [her] awful voyage" to North America was compounded by
the middle-class necessity of keeping up the appearance of being unmoved:

> . . . they were leav-
> ing behind them all
> the familiar safe
> things that had for so
> long composed their
> lives . . . happiness
> of familiar loves,
> dear places, and or-
> dered ways. —Ethel
> Wilson, The Inno-
> cent Traveller
> (1949).

> I wish . . . to banish what is past from my
> thoughts, and, if I could, the feelings of my
> last sight and touch of my first-born, but the
> stunning sensation can never be forgotten,
> and my feeling when the ship cleared the
> pier-head must ever remain as long as mem-
> ory lasts. It was a call on all my energy and
> resolution to support an appearance of com-
> posure. What a relief would tears have been!
> (12).

The obvious parallel between Langton's departure
and a bereavement suggests that, by refusing to
give way to her sorrow at the time of leaving, she
merely ensured the repression and indefinite extension of her sadness, perhaps to the detriment
of her ability to embrace life fully in the New
World. It may even be that the melancholia evident at various points in Langton's later letters is
traceable in part to the repression of her emotions on leaving England.[2]

In marked and understandable contrast to unwilling and unhappy emigrants such as Moodie
and Langton, eager and forward-looking emigrants like Traill apparently indulged only briefly,
if at all, in a "lingering look behind." Allowing
merely that she was "much pleased with the
scenery of the Clyde" as the *Laurel* sailed down-

9. Pickering's account of his departure from England is also indicative of the emotional complexity of the moment: "We left Gravesend with a fair wind, and pretty good spirits, my
thoughts ranging through the New World . . . and then returning again [to the Old] . . .
which, at times, would cause an involuntary sigh; but the hopes and prospect ever-cheating
fancy presented to my mind, dissipated all gloom, and I bade adieu to Old England without
much regret."
1. See also Moodie (37) for a description of her homesickness [31–32].
2. See Langton (1950, 29; 1904, 65).

river from Greenock, Traill describes her last sight of the British Isles in her characteristically (and, as *The Backwoods of Canada* proceeds, somewhat cloyingly) cheerful terms: "The morning light found our vessel dashing gallantly along, with a favourable breeze, through the North Channel; that day we saw the last of the Hebrides, and before night lost sight of the north coast of Ireland. A wide expanse of water and sky is now our only prospect. . . ." At the boundary between her old life and her new prospects, an optimistically hinterland-oriented Traill barely notices the curtain of night falling on the British Isles. Instead, she places the emphasis of her description on aspects of the scene that reflect her sense of going to a land of new, positive, and expansive possibilities: the "morning light," a "favourable breeze," and the "wide expanse of water and sky."

Even more eager and cheery than Traill at the moment of departure is the irrepressible Mary (Gapper) O'Brien, who takes a few moments away from admiring the handsome and capable crew of her emigrant vessel, a "British trader" (3) called the *Warrior*, to notice the coast of Britain passing rapidly by and to observe: "I must bid farewell to Charlinch [her home] without one more look. The water is dancing gaily under the breeze and gives a gently cradling motion" (3). Notable here in the word "cradling" and later in Gapper's child-like and child-centred account of the Atlantic crossing (3), and indeed in Langton's determination to greet the New World like a "dutiful child . . . greet[ing] . . . mother earth after [a] long separation" (1904, 26), is the implication that for some emigrant women a new start involved, if not a regression to infancy or childhood, then a return to the material realm, with a consequent feeling of security, familiarity, and burgeoning potential. Equally evident in Gapper's account of her departure is a repression of the "lingering look behind," which in her case turns out to be merely a postponement of the experience until her exit from the "cradling" nursery of the ship: "After coming to anchor and making arrangements with the customs house," she says of her arrival in New York, "we left the 'Warrior' with feelings of regret. . . . I now felt for the first time that I was far away from home and all that makes

It is possible that the effect of the seamen's singing was so powerful because the passengers did not understand the words. What were the words? There was no meaning for the passengers, and no meaning was needed, only the passion and vigour and the sound of the singing in unison in that cave of the sea.
—Ethel Wilson, Love and Salt Water (1957).

home dear" (9). For Gapper, travelling in the relative luxury and privilege of a cabin, the emigrant vessel was more than a maternal realm in the personal sense. It was an extension of the mother country, a floating microcosm of British society, with all its familiar comforts, hierachies, customs, and associations. Since even New York seems to Gapper to be a continuation in miniature of what, in her childlike way, she knows and loves—a town "very like [a] children's plaything city" in which "everything and everybody" looks "perfectly English" (9–11)—she could hardly have felt other than a minimal sense of displacement at either the beginning or the end of her trans-Atlantic journey.

In a sense, Gapper left England and arrived in North America as a child-woman, with all the openness and adaptability that, viewed positively, such a state brings with it. As a consequence, she was able to grow with relative ease into her real adulthood as a Canadian pioneer woman, accepting almost naively the hardships and compensations that settler life in Canada afforded women—herculean labour, of course, but also the increased dignity of working women,[3] and as regards property, the greater rights of married women.[4] No doubt Gapper possessed to an extraordinary degree "the qualities required of the ideal pioneer wife" (285); perhaps one of these qualities was the ability to enter again a child-like state and a maternal realm as she embarked on a new life in the New World whose "woods and plains" were, in the words of Isabella Valancy Crawford, another nineteenth-century female emigrant to Canada, "bounteous mothers . . . mellowing the earth, / That she may yield her increase willingly" (37–38).

One of the most poignant and complex renditions of the emigrant's "lingering look behind" is Ford Madox Brown's *The Last of England*, a painting of "voyaging consciousness" (Auerbach, 45) which was executed at the time of the departure for Australia of the pre-Raphaelite sculptor Thomas Woolner. Despite the antipodean destination of its subjects, *The Last of England* war-

So it was. Far ahead, in the midst of an ocean of darkness, two small jets of light stood out like candle flames braving the night. Why it should be so, I cannot say, but those wavering jets of yellow light marked a division of time for the little girl at her father's feet.

From that moment her little thoughts and starry impressions were distinctly individual, and she herself no longer just the little girl who existed as a small, obedient extension of her mother. —Laura Goodman Salverson, Confessions of an Immigrant's Daughter (1939).

3. See O'Brien (17–18).
4. See O'Brien (33–34). Constance Backhouse of the Faculty of Law at the University of Western Ontario has confirmed for me that Canadian women did enjoy some advantages relative to English women in the area of married women's property rights.

rants consideration here for what it can tell us about the burdens and possibilities bestowed upon women by the emigrant experience. Although ostensibly about Brown's friend in art, the painting, as Nina Auerbach has shown, actually subordinates Woolner to his wife, giving her almost iconic importance at the centre of a series of concentric circles consisting of her hair, her bonnet, her umbrella, and the circular shape of the canvas as a whole. As she looks wanly back towards England, placing temporarily behind her what lies in the future (and observe how the obvious coarseness of the men at the rear of the picture space indicates the chimerical nature of the "El Dorado" inscribed on the ship's lifeboat),[5] Woolner's wife is burdened to a remarkable extent with the expectations of her male painter and patriarchal culture. Clasping the hands of both her husband and her nearly hidden and very young child (another aspect of her future), she "alone unites" (Auerbach, 45) her family as it travels out past those resonant symbols of England, the white cliffs of Dover, into and towards a largely unknown world. Placed with her child in her arms near the centre of a circular canvas, Brown's emigrant woman clearly recalls Raphael's *Madonna della Sidia* and thus takes with her to the New World, as did Moodie, Traill, and others, enormous expectations concerning the moral and spiritual function of the wife and mother in a pioneer society.

Here in embryo, it might be said, is the saintly woman who occupies the familial and ethical centre of so much male writing about European women in early Canada, from Thomas Cary's *Abram's Plains*[6] to the fiction of Ralph Connor.[7] A telling indication of the sort of religious and social apparatus (to use Toynbee's word) that was placed or taken on board vessels bound for the New World, *The Last of England* embodies a male fantasy about the emigrant wife and mother which became a component of emigrant women's view of themselves—a model of spiritual strength which could be entrapping certainly, but also empowering. As different as conventionally con-

---

5. See also the quotation from Joseph Pickering in note 9 [448].
6. See the reference to Lady Dorchester in Cary (16, lines 484–91).
7. See Thompson (151–81).

ceived femininity and masculinity, the Madonna
and Hercules archetypes can be understood as
the extremes that lay to the right and left of
women when they emigrated to Canada in the
nineteenth century. However, they can also be
understood as representative of the choices that
confronted emigrant women—options that could
be chosen fairly straightforwardly or combined in
complex, exciting, and genuinely liberating ways.
As will now be seen, the voyage itself to Canada
was for many emigrants a site of fascinating
choices in the realms of individual identity and
social organization.

II
The Voyage

The literature of the Atlantic crossing contains
many indications that, especially for the comparatively well-off travelling as families in cabins, the
sea passage tended both to reinforce the unity of
the family and to affirm the transportability of a
traditional social apparatus, thus ensuring, as in
the case of Mary Gapper, a high degree of continuity between the Old and New Worlds, a relatively minor crumbling of "the cake of custom."
For those less (or perhaps more) fortunate, however, the circumstances of travel on emigrant
ships in which men and women, often regardless
of family ties, were separated on sexual lines
could and did lead during the lengthy voyage to
the crumbling of the "cake of custom" (sometimes in ways startling to modest observers)[8] and
to the formation of units of loyalty other than the
family. Writing of the "hard-favored . . . , poorly
and insufficiently clad" wives of soldiers going to
join their regiments in Canada, George Warburton observes in *Hochelaga*: "I saw during the voyage many traits in [these poor women] of good
and tender feeling: the anxious care of their little
ones . . . ; their kindness to each other, sharing
their scanty covering and scantier meals" (I, 2).
Whether this feeling of generosity and co-
operation, perhaps even of sisterhood, endured
beyond the women's experience of being " 'all in
the same boat' " cannot be known, but the suspicion is that, particularly in the case of soldiers'

8. See Guillet (77n).

wives, there would be a continuity of behaviour between ship and shore, with perhaps some permanent reapportioning of value from "kin" to "comradeship."[9] In the "ladies cabins" of more privileged passengers, a sense of sorority was likely to be established less through the sharing of creature comforts than through the exchanges of conversation and sympathy (not least during bouts of seasickness, a far from negligible aspect of trans-Atlantic voyages), with the resultant establishment of what today would be called a "network" of female friends in the New World. Much emphasis has traditionally been placed by critics of North American culture on the bonds between and among men that develop on rafts on the Mississippi and elsewhere, but in Warburton's slightly surprised account of female mutuality en route to Canada, and—to give just one more example—Langton's engaging account of the "transatlantic ladies" in her cabin on the *Independence* (1904, 177)—there is more than a suggestion of a parallel phenomenon among women on at least some of the vessels that brought emigrants to Canada.

Since most of the readable journals and letters written on nineteenth-century emigrant vessels are post-Romantic in nature, the light that they cast tends to be most sharply and most illuminatingly directed towards the individual's own experience of the trans-Atlantic voyage. Thus—to turn for a moment to a less well-known writer—Mrs. William Radcliff is especially expansive and engaging when she leaves off counselling future emigrants about the inadvisability of bringing their own servants and provisions on board ship and turns instead to chronicle her own experiences en route to the New World, including her not insignificant participation in the traditionally masculine activity of ocean fishing: "*We fished* (observe how I identify myself with the sport) . . ." (Talman, 35), she says in a parenthetical remark that shows none of Langton's misgivings about the gender-blurring aspects of the emigrant experience. Quite as open-minded and cheerful as Traill, Radcliff proclaims the "sudden alterations of a sea voyage" between frightening storms and relaxing calm proof of her belief in the benefits of

---

9. On a darker note, see Guillet (86) for evidence that women were frequently assaulted sexually during the trans-Atlantic crossing.

a "mind easily amused" (37) and capable of ensuring the eclipse of present discomforts by inevitable turns for the better. As she ascends the St. Lawrence, Radcliff shows herself fully to be the spiritual heiress of Kent and Gonzalo by proclaiming the Canadian landscape remarkable for its "exquisite beauty and luxuriance" and for pastures whose verdure could "not be rivalled, even by the Emerald Isle of [her] nativity" (40). So positive is Radcliff about Canada that, in an intriguing reversal of the nostalgic emigrant's habit of bringing with them "old country" (Guillet, 40) plants and "song-birds," she wishes to see "a miniature silver fir tree" which she is given on her arrival "transplanted into our shrubbery" (28) back in Ireland.

Was it madness after all, Mama?/—bringing your Russian shtetl to America,/ smuggled into Canada safely in your head/deposited in Montreal/replanted in our flat/in the kitchen . . .
—Gertrude Katz, *Duet (1982).*

Probably the most engaging and complex account by an emigrant woman of the crossing to Canada is contained in "The Ocean Voyage" and "Majestic and Mighty River" sections of *The Backwoods of Canada* where, among other things, Traill uses the wild and domesticated bird life that she encounters to define herself in relation both to the external world and to the men travelling with her. In the first instance, she identifies herself by an unstated analogy with the "sea-fowl" which she sees on the Atlantic—"wanderers of the ocean" who are guided by providence from the " 'zone to zone' " (28) of William Cullen Bryant's poem. In the second, she takes a traditional emblem of the circumscribed female, a caged song bird (in this instance, a male goldfinch called Harry which belongs to the ship's captain) and applies it to men generally, featherless bipeds who, in her view, tolerate being "confined to a small space" much less readily than women, who always have "their needle as a resource against the overwhelming weariness of an idle life" (29). Neither denying nor accepting the inevitability of female circumscription (but leaning towards the latter because ultimately she is confined to the ship as the "water-fowl" are not), Traill is here highlighting traditionally feminine accomplishments which, if positively understood and undertaken, will stand women in good stead as pioneers to Canada.[1] Of course, Traill knew firsthand that the "hardships and difficulties of

Next day the ship began its insidious assuagement. Frank and Ellen walked round and round the deck . . . , and the wind whipped them and rain stung their faces and the great grey waves came slowly toward the ship from as far west as one could see. . . .
—Ethel Wilson, Love and Salt Water (1957).

---

1. See also Langton (1904, 18) on the value of needle "work" as a "resource."

the settler's life . . . were felt peculiarly by the female part of the family" (25), and *The Backwoods of Canada* as a whole is an attempt to mitigate the "hardships and difficulties" of the female emigrants who constituted a major part of her intended audience by fostering "female ingenuity . . . expediency . . . [and] high-spirited cheerfulness" (25). No propagandist on behalf of emigration, Traill nevertheless had much to gain by encouraging women to become successful pioneers, to participate in an expanding and sustaining community of settlers' wives and daughters who were fully equal, if not to their husbands and fathers, then certainly to the pioneering life and the Canadian environment. By presenting the "facts [of emigration to Canada] in their real and true light, that the female part of the emigrant's family may be able to look them firmly in the face" (25), Traill was thus attempting to give future female settlers what is abundantly evident even in the departure and voyage sections of her book: a forward-looking vision that is realistic and optimistic, that places the "facts" within the context of the ability of women to cope with them, to triumph in adversity, and to participate in the creation of a viable community.

Saint Catharine! Where are you now that we need you? C. P. T.: I am waiting. —Margaret Laurence, The Diviners *(1974).*

Less obviously female in their orientation than Traill's comments on sewing in the opening section of *The Backwoods of Canada* are the remarks on genre that occur at the beginning of her two chapters on the voyage to Canada. Addressing her "dear[est] mother" in both places, Traill justifies her decision to write as "inclination prompts [her]," but neither in the form of "short letters" nor in the form of a daily diary or "log," a species of composition that she associates with the ship's mate and dismisses as not sufficiently "amusing" (27, 31). By setting up as a foil for her own generic choice "the mate's log" (which provided the format for the writings of most of the early explorers and fur-traders), Traill throws into relief the gender-dimension of the long letter home to mother, a type of writing that affirms a female connectiveness of the blood and heart across enormous geographical barriers,[2] and, for both daughter and mother, mitigates the feeling of sep-

2. Dahlie, *Varieties of Exile: The Canadian Experience* (Vancouver: University of British Columbia Press, 1986), p. 13 sees the letters of exiles as constituting a "tangible link . . . with their homeland."

aration—the post-partum depression (?)—that
follows the removal of the child from home and
family. Moreover, Traill's reference in "The Ocean
Voyage" to the "old novels and musty romances"
in the "ship's library" (29) points towards the fictive components and romance elements in *The
Backwoods of Canada*, where the long letters are
seldom mere summaries of activities or day-to-day
accounts but, rather, carefully elaborated and pat-
terned accounts of occurrences in the life of a
new and definitely not musty hero: the pioneer
woman (or female Crusoe) whose genesis in the
work of Traill and whose presence in the fiction
of Sara Jeannette Duncan, Margaret Laurence,
and others has recently been placed on view by
Elizabeth Thompson.[3]

For many emigrants, the Atlantic crossing provided time to think and talk and dream about
their future life in Canada—to expand upon
Rivers' "eager hopes of a warm imagination."
Traill gives an indication of this when she writes
of pacing the deck with her husband, "talk[ing]
over plans for the future, which in all probability
will never be realized" (29).[4] One emigrant guide
even suggests that such planning could take a
more practical form through such activities as the
construction of "a mimic log house" on the way to
Canada (Guillet, 78). But as this suggestion indicates and as most accounts of the trans-Atlantic
voyage confirm, the most common feature of the
crossing (with the possible exception of seasickness and other illnesses) was boredom. As day followed day with crushing monotony, "schooling"
the religious-minded "to patience" (Guillet, 104),
most emigrants wiled away their time with occupations like gambling, sewing, and writing. The
ultimate effect of the boredom and monotony of
the voyage, however, was to make the emigrants
ecstatically happy when at last land was sighted
(or, frequently, smelled).[5] "Baltimore, with its
white buildings . . . had a most exhilarating effect
on one whose vision had been confined to the
monotonous rolling of the unstable waters for
sixty five days . . ." wrote one male emigrant
(Pickering, 8), and Radcliff agreed that the sight

*Like migrating birds
delayed, the passen-
gers twittered and
became fidgety. The
voyage had lasted too
long. —Ethel Wil-
son, Love and Salt
Water (1957).*

3. See Thompson (*passim*).
4. By way of contrast, see the supplement to Guillet (11) for an emigrant thinking of home and
the past during the voyage. Quoted by Guillet (78).
5. See, for example, O'Brien (7).

of land was indeed "very agreeable and soothing to the eye that had so long rested on a waste of water" (Talman, 43). Insofar as they heightened the emigrants' feeling of exhilaration and pleasure at the first sight of the New World, the monotony, boredom, and other unpleasantnesses of the voyage obviously contributed significantly to the "change in attitude" from despair to hope in "the hearts of all but the most miserable" (138), which Edwin G. Guillet saw as a major feature of the last days of the Atlantic crossing.

Whatever its direct or indirect causes, a "change of attitude" is certainly noted or evident in most writing by emigrants about the final stages of the voyage to North America. In some cases, the impending arrival in the New World is treated as both a fresh beginning in *terra incognita* and as a return to *terra firma*. Anne Langton wrote:

> Land . . . was now visibly not far, and I determined to be up with the dawn, like a dutiful child, to greet my mother earth after a long separation. . . . The bay [of New York] I had, unluckily, been told several times was equal to the Bay of Naples, and my first impressions were therefore those of disappointment. But it is very beautiful in its own way, and so totally different from the one it was compared with that the comparison was absurd (1904, 26–27).

In other instances, the actual arrival in the New World after a long and stressful voyage seems to have produced what Toynbee calls a "dynamic effect" on the emigrant (II, 88), liberating or crystallizing attitudes that were not previously evident. This is certainly apparent from Moodie's descriptions of the behaviour of Irish and Scottish emigrants on their arrival in Canada (more of which later). Nor can the effect of being again on land after an unpleasant Atlantic crossing be accorded less than catalytic importance in the behaviour of Mary Murray in Lucy Maud Montgomery's partly autobiographical *Emily of New Moon*. Emily's cousin Jimmy explains how her ancestors came to be on Prince Edward Island:

> "They were bound for Quebec—hadn't any notion of coming to P.E.I. They had a long rough voyage and water got scarce, so the

On the last day of open ocean the seeming and delusive eternity of the voyage vanished. "Tomorrow we enter the St. Lawrence River!" . . . Even the Grandmother, who lived neither in the present nor the past nor the future, not in Time at all but in a constant moment of Eternity, felt the approaching change.
—Ethel Wilson, The Innocent Traveller (1949).

The bloody captain

captain of the *New Moon* put in here to get some. Mary Murray had nearly died of sea-sickness coming out—never seemed to get her sealegs—so the captain, being sorry for her, told her she could go ashore with the men and feel solid ground under her for an hour or so. Very gladly she went and when she got to shore she said, 'Here I stay.' And stay she did; nothing could budge her; old Hugh—he was young Hugh then, of course—coaxed and stormed and raged and argued—and even cried, I've been told—but Mary wouldn't be moved. In the end he gave in and had his belongings landed and stayed, too. So that is how the Murrays came to P.E. Island."

"I'm glad it happened like that," said Emily (73).

There is an element of female fantasy in this description of a stubborn and powerful matriarch establishing the location, and effectively the name, of her family's new home in the New World. But given the autobiographical component of *Emily of New Moon*, there may well be an element of truth to Mary Murray's story that justifies a second look at its depiction of a sexual role reversal on the arrival of the *New Moon* in Canada. Once Mary Murray has been permitted by the captain to go ashore with the men (a rare privilege), she begins to behave like a man, becoming the master, not merely of her own destiny, but also of her family's future. For his (castrated?) part, Hugh mimics the weather that is partly responsible for the "sea change" in his wife (he "stormed and raged") and "even," when arguing and coaxing have failed to shake her resolve, resorts to a traditional weapon in the feminine arsenal and cries. While Emily is glad to hear that her ancestors' putting down roots on P.E.I. occurred in the manner described by her cousin Jimmy, "old Hugh," the deposed patriarch, never quite forgives his wife's behaviour. The " 'Here I stay' " that he has engraved on her tombstone is thus a double text: a testament both to a female will discovered or exercised after a tempestuous Atlantic crossing and to the refusal of patriarchy either to forgive or to forget such a transgression.

. . . landed all of them at the wrong place, now, the name escapes me at the moment. . . . So Piper Gunn . . . he says to his woman Morag, Here we are and by the holy Jesus here we will remain. And then didn't his woman strap onto her back the few blankets and suchlike they had, and her thick with their unborn firstborn, and follow.
—Margaret Laurence, The Diviners *(1974).*

By naming them [the Glass House Mountains] he made them./They were there/before he came/but they were not the same./It was his gaze/that glazed each one. —P. K. Page, The Glass Air *(1985).*

III
The Arrival

The Aristotelian elegance of assigning a distinct beginning, middle, and end to the Atlantic crossing has already been transgressed in the present discussion. It is destined to be transgressed even more by the fact, long ago recognized by Northrop Frye, that for emigrants entering British North America at almost any place other than the Maritimes there was no distinct moment of arrival but, rather, the sensation of gradually entering "an alien continent" (824). An attempt must nevertheless now be made to concentrate exclusively on the arrival of emigrants in Canada, to come to terms with a blurry border that comprises the prime site of communication between the emigrant's old "apparatus" (insofar as it has remained intact on the ship and in the mind) and the realities of the New World. In order better to show in some detail the complexities contingent upon arrival in Canada for female emigrants, the discussion will focus in this final stage on two very well-known accounts of the journey up the St. Lawrence to Quebec and beyond: that of Traill in the second and third letters in *The Backwoods of Canada* and that of Moodie in the opening sketch of *Roughing It in the Bush*.

In the manner characteristic of "all but the most miserable" of emigrants, Traill greeted the appearance of the Newfoundland coast after a long and monotonous voyage with "rapture" and a distinct feeling of renovation: "Never did anything seem so refreshing and delicious to me," she writes, "as the land breeze that came to us bearing health and gladness on its wings. I had become very weak but soon revived as I felt the air from the land reaching us and some winged insects came to us—a welcome sight" (32). As an amateur scientist with a keen and sustaining interest in insects, plants, and birds, Traill had noticed the "restless activity" of the captain's caged bird prior to the sighting of land, and as the *Laurel* made its tedious way up the Gulf of St. Lawrence, she spent hours poring over the ship's "great chart," which was "constantly being rolled and unrolled by [her] husband to gratify [her] desire of learning the names of the distant shores and islands which [they] pass[ed]" (32). An anal-

. . . for now she is content to wander on the beach foraging for food and naming everything she sees in the new words which come so freely to her tongue.
—Anne Szumigalski, Instar (1985).

ogy with Adam on the naming day recommends itself as a gloss on this passage (Frye, 824), but as an ensuing event makes clear, Traill intended a closer parallel between her own experience of making landfall and a biblical story which seems also (though more pessimistically) to have recommended itself to her sister Susanna as an analogy for the trans-Atlantic crossing:[6] the story of Noah and the Ark. In the entry in her letter for August 7, Traill writes: "We were visited this morning by a beautiful little bird, not much larger than our gold-crested wren. I hailed it as a bird of good omen—a little messenger sent to bid us welcome to the New World, and I felt almost a childish joy at the sight of our little visitor" (32–33). Not only does this passage indicate that Traill perceived herself as a latter-day Noah on the brink of a world of fresh possibilities (and the "little bird" as evidence of the providential nature of her journey), but it also shows that, on the threshold of the "New World," she conceived herself as being—if not, strictly speaking, reborn—then, like Gapper and Langton, in the process of starting life anew, with all the enthusiasm of a Romantic child.

Outward the fresh shores gleam/Clear in new-washed eyes./Fare well./From your dream/I [the Ark] only shall not rise. —Jay Macpherson, The Boatman (1957).

Whereas Coleridge's Burke found himself, "as it were, in a Noah's ark, with a very few men and a great many beasts" (Hughes, 19), Traill found herself on a vessel in which the few men that she mentions seem to her to resemble the captain's caged bird Harry. True to this analogy, the men on the *Laurel* soon begin to evince the "restless activity" earlier displayed by the goldfinch: "The captain . . . [grows] quite talkative. [Her] husband [is] more than usually animated, and even [a] thoughtful young Scotchman [who had struck Traill earlier as 'too much wrapped up in his own affairs to be very communicative to others' (28)] became an entertaining person" (33). As if to cement the connection between the feathered and featherless bipeds on the *Laurel*, Traill observes that in sight of land the "crew displayed the most lively zeal in the performance of their duty, and the goldfinch sang cheerily from dawn till sunset" (33). Amid all this pleasant garrulity and animation, the female presence at the centre of Traill's

---

6. This inference could be drawn from Moodie's characterization of the scene on her arrival in Lower Canada as a "Babel," a reference to events that follow the story of Noah in Genesis.

narrative apparently exercised a firm captaincy over potentially distressing feelings: "As for me," says Traill, "hope was busy in my heart, chasing from it all feelings of doubt or regret [the 'lingering look behind'] that might sadden the present or cloud the future" (33). As she moves ever further into the region of new light and new life that she wants Canada to be, Traill keeps her heart and her eyes firmly fixed on the positive aspects of what she sees, finding happy (rather than wistful) memories of the Scottish Highlands in the shapes of "fantastic clouds" in the St. Lawrence estuary and becoming weary only of what she purports to admire the most: the sublimity of the water and mountain scenery of "the majestic and mighty river" (33).

No Mary Murray, willing to transgress sexual and social hierarchies in order to get her own way, Traill allows her "longing desire to set [her] foot on Canadian ground" (36) to be chivalrically denied by the captain and her husband. She finds in the "foggy" weather, and in the men's description of the Isle of Bic as "swampy," ample "reason to be thankful" that she has not followed her "own wayward will" (36) but has contented herself with continuing to admire the land from afar. Thus, while the men in the party are busy making forays onto the islands and shores of the St. Lawrence, indulging in foreplay, as it were, before penetrating what Rupert Brooke would later call the "unseizable virginity" of Canada,[7] Traill allows herself to be born(e) along the St. Lawrence, entering the New World as through a birth canal.

At this stage of the journey, it would appear that Traill is less and less the "wandering waterfowl" and more and more the caged bird, the traditional woman who had shown at least the potential for radical modification and liberation in mid-Atlantic. If the "cake of custom" could be crumbled en route to the New World, so apparently could it be reconstituted as actual arrival— treated by Traill as a return "once more" and "again" to "*terra firma*" (54)—became imminent. Or at least partly reconstituted. For everywhere in the later letters in *The Backwoods of Canada* and

---

7. Quoted by Frye (826) from Waterston (363). I would like to express a general debt here to Kolodny's two books (1975, 1984), which have helped to alert me to similar and different patterns and possibilities in early writing about Canada.

D. M. R. BENTLEY

elsewhere, there is evidence that, while she allowed herself to remain within the confines of the
traditional model of femininity which she brought
with her across the Atlantic (thus avoiding the accusation of compromising too far what Langton
calls her "feminine manners" and "woman's avocations"), Traill nevertheless played a pioneering
role both in her personal life and in her writing in
expanding and dignifying the spheres of activity
and influence normally inhabited by nineteenth-
century women of her background. To Traill,
Canada was a nearly Edenic New World (the first
Canadian flowers that she saw while still on the
Laurel in the St. Lawrence were "red roses . . .
with . . . few if any thorns" (36)), but it was a
nearly Edenic New World in which women were
to exercise their powers according to the known
rules of matrimony. It is within this traditional
context that in *The Backwoods of Canada* Traill
shows herself commanding and receiving the respect of her husband, the man who brought back
from the Isle of Bic—so that she "might not regret not accompanying him"—a "delightful bouquet" containing those virtually thornless roses
(36). Nor, if the figure of the caged bird is being
read correctly, did Traill fail to command the
chivalric attention of men other than her husband on this side of the Atlantic. "The steward
[on the *Laurel*] furnished me with a china jar and
fresh water, so that I shall have the pleasure of a
bouquet during the rest of the voyage," she notes,
adding, with perhaps a trace of amusement at her
own self-created situation, that the "sailors had
not forgotten a green bough or two to adorn the
ship, and the bird-cage was soon as bowery
as leaves could make it" (37). In Traill's case,
it would appear that—to borrow Langton's
words again—"feminine manners" as traditionally
conceived did more than "counterbalance" the
tendency of the female emigrant to assume conventionally masculine characteristics.

For over a week after her husband's visit to the
Isle of Bic, Traill continued to feel what she now
describes as a "longing desire . . . *to be allowed* to
land and explore" the Canadian terrain (41).[8]
And, once again, the pattern of male refusal and

---

8. Emphasis added. Cholera was, of course, a major cause of the refusal to allow Traill to go
ashore.

chivalric gesture is repeated: "to all my entreaties [to be allowed to go ashore at Grosse Isle], the visiting surgeon . . . returned a decided negative," she explains, but "[a] few hours after his visit . . . an Indian basket, containing strawberries and raspberries, with a large bunch of wild flowers, was sent on board for me with the surgeon's compliments" (41). During her long wait for permission to go ashore, Traill amused herself by sketching the "surrounding scenery or watching the groups of emigrants on shore" (41). She also indulged in what previous quotations from Gapper and Langton already have indicated was a characteristic pastime of emigrants in sight of the New World—fitting, or attempting to fit, an unknown landscape into moulds constituted by memories of similar shapes and patterns in the Old World. Since memory is a major component of this process, older people were perhaps more likely than younger ones to manifest the sorrows and pleasures of attempting to match old and new. "I observed several grandfathers and grandmothers, who . . . had accompanied their offspring . . . to the *terra incognita* of Upper Canada," writes John Howison. "They looked round with disconsolate and inquiring eyes, and if any feature in the appearance of the town chanced to resemble some part of their native village or city, it caused a joyful exclamation, and was eagerly pointed out . . . " (4).

For younger and more educated emigrants such as Traill, especially those who took pains to disabuse future emigrants of their illusions about Canada (as did both the Strickland sisters for different reasons), the activity of fitting frequently took the aesthetic form of a recognition of the contrast between picturesque expectations and a less attractive reality. At Grosse Isle, Traill's husband is informed by an officer from the fort that, though the scene at the quarantine station has a "picturesque appearance" when viewed from afar, at close quarters the groups of people that he considers "picturesque" will be seen to resemble the subjects of William Hogarth's pictures and George Crabbe's poems (42). To Traill herself, the heights of Point Levis opposite Quebec are "highly picturesque," but they do not quite fit the expectations generated by her previous experience of landscapes: "How lovely would such a spot be

They [the comfortable farms and broad meadows of Ontario] had a look of home. Here were elms. Here were sheep and cattle. Here was lazy smoke rising from chimneys of white farms. The sheep grazed in an international manner.
—Ethel Wilson, The Innocent Traveller (1949).

rendered in England or Scotland! Nature here has done all, and man but little, except sticking up some ugly wooden cottages, as mean as they are tasteless" (45). Similarly, the log houses along the banks of the St. Lawrence between Quebec and Montreal do not fit Traill's preconceptions of rural cottages: "In Britain even the peasant has taste enough to plant a few roses or honeysuckles about his door or his casement, and there is the little bit of garden enclosed and neatly kept; but here no such attempt is made to ornament the cottages" (49–50). From these and other passages, the reader easily deduces that, when Traill herself has the opportunity to build and adorn a house, she will do so in accordance with her picturesque preconceptions, thus attempting to create in Canada at least a domestic environment that fulfils expectations frustrated on arrival. As Traill's example makes clear, accommodation in both its senses of housing and adaptation is a nodal point at which the domestic and aesthetic concerns of many of Canada's female emigrants met as part of an overall attempt to reconcile imported assumptions with new realities, and vice versa. It is hardly surprising, then, that accommodation, both as an entity (cottages, log houses) and as a process (fitting), figures prominently in accounts by women of their early impressions and subsequent activities in the New World.

Her mother's hands have scrubbed a patina onto every surface of the house. Daria shows it to her visitor. . . . A wooden crucifix is hanging above the sink. The visitor believes it a token of the old country. —Rhea Tregebov, Remembering History (1982).

Traill's eventual disembarkation at Montreal was an occasion of not "unmixed delight and admiration" (52). On the one hand, she was happy to be "on *terra firma* . . . [and] free from the motion of the heaving water, to which [she is] . . . , in truth, glad to bid farewell" (54). On the other hand, she was "greatly disappointed" with Montreal, a town which, in addition to being in the midst of a cholera epidemic, failed dismally to meet the expectations built up by travellers' accounts (especially, perhaps, by Howison's account[9]): "I could compare it," says Traill, "only to the fruits of the Dead Sea, which are said to be fair and tempting to look upon, but yield only ashes and bitterness when tasted by the thirsty traveller" (55). The comparison with the "fruits of the Dead Sea" is more apt than Traill may have envisaged, for in some ways Montreal, despite its

9. Howison's book is mentioned by Traill (72). See Howison (2–3).

location on terra firma, functions for her as the sea (or ocean) did for many emigrants: as a site of mingled discomfort and anticipation, despair and hope, en route to a new life. In Montreal, Traill found houses that corresponded in their architectural structure (though not in their lack of picturesque adornment) to the houses of her childhood dreams (56). In Montreal, she also fell ill with cholera, a potentially fatal disease through which she was courageously nursed by "the females of the house" in which she and her husband were staying (63). The description of these women can be read as a depiction of female heroism and sisterhood encountered both in the New World and on the way to a new life:

> Instead of fleeing affrighted from the chamber of sickness, the two Irish girls almost quarrelled which should be my attendant; while Jane Taylor . . . never left me from the time I grew so alarmingly ill till a change for the better had come over me, but, at the peril of her own life, supported me in her arms, and held me on her bosom when I was struggling with mortal agony, alternately speaking peace to me and striving to soothe the anguish of my poor afflicted partner (63).

Both the Madonna-like strength of Jane Taylor and the relative ineffectualness of Thomas Traill are remarkable in this passage, and both contribute to the sense that Traill is being helped through a dangerous stage of her journey towards a new life by a compassionate female support system which, like a nurse or a midwife, assists in bringing about a recovery or rebirth. (That the sympathy of Traill's doctor increases when he learns that she is the wife of a British officer only serves to highlight the fact that the women who help her apparently value her for her own sake.) Between Montreal and finally reaching the location of her new home across the "tempest-tost sea" of Lake Ontario (77), Traill went through various other experiences which are part of the attenuated process of arrival described in *The Backwoods of Canada*. Enough of this process and what preceded it has probably now been seen, however, to establish that in Traill's case, it involved a crumbling and reconstitution of the "cake of custom," a negotiation of various possibilities for the female emigrant that ended neither in entirely fresh territory nor exactly as it began but in a considerable rethinking and reorganization of accepted ideas about women's strengths, relationships, and roles in a relatively new society.

Like her sister, Moodie arrived in the St. Lawrence estuary in the midst of a cholera epidemic; unlike Traill, however, the author of *Roughing It in the Bush* lacked a cheerful and sustaining optimism about the Canadian emigrant experience and wrote her book, not to advise "the wives and daughters of emigrants of the higher class" on how best to cope with pioneer life (Traill, 21), but to dissuade gentlemen and their families from "sinking their property, and shipwrecking all their hopes, by going to reside in the backwoods of Canada . . ." (Moodie, 237 [330]). While many emigrants used the idea of a shipwreck, often with reference to Robinson Crusoe, as a metaphor for the difficult creation of a workable society in a distant realm,[1] Moodie uses the figure to image forth the nearly unmitigated disaster that she conceives emigration to be for people of the "higher class." For the "industrious and ever-to-be-honoured [and patronized] sons of honest poverty" (xviii), however, Moodie predicts a bright and, indeed, heroic future in Canada. The poor are the chosen people of the "great tide of emigration" (xvi) from Britain to North America in the mid-nineteenth century, a fact Moodie is certain of because she understands the workings of Providence:

If Catharine Parr Traill with her imperturbable practicality is what we like to think we would be under the circumstances, Susanna Moodie is what we secretly suspect we would have been instead. —Margaret Atwood, Introduction, Roughing It in the Bush *(1852; rpt. 1986).*

> The Great Father of the souls and bodies of men knows the arm which wholesome labour from infancy has made strong, the nerves which have become iron by patient endurance . . . and He chooses such, to send forth into the forest to hew out the rough paths for the advance of civilization. These men become wealthy and prosperous, and form the bones and sinews of a great rising country (xvii–xviii) [11].

Such men (and clearly Moodie does not mean men and women) are herculean, not only in their strength and endurance, but also in their identification with the advance of civilization and with

---

1. See, for example, Cary (5, lines 64–75).

the emergence of what Charles G. D. Roberts would later call a "Child of Nations, giant-limbed . . ." (29). Their representative in the opening sketch of *Roughing It in the Bush* is a poor Irishman who resembles Hercules both in his size and in his possession of the equivalent of the large club that identifies the Greek hero: "One fellow, of gigantic proportions . . . leaped upon the rocks, and flourishing aloft his shilelagh, bounded and capered like a wild goat from his native mountains. 'Whurrah! my boys!' he cried. 'Shure we'll all be jintlemen!' " (27) [22].

Excluded by both class and sex from the herculean brand of heroism that she sees as a prerequisite for successful pioneering in Canada, Moodie depicts herself on arrival at the portals of the New World as facing what can be seen as a female version of the "Choice of Hercules." (The young Hercules was faced at a crossroads with a choice between two paths as represented by two women, one young and beautiful—the path of pleasure—and the other old and stern—the path of heroic virtue, the path of course chosen by Hercules.) The allegorical figures encountered by Moodie on her arrival off Grosse Isle are not women but men—"health officers sent aboard the vessel to check for the presence of disease":

> One of these gentlemen—a little, shrivelled-up Frenchman—from his solemn aspect and attenuated figure, would have made no bad representative of him who sat upon the pale horse. . . . His companion—a fine-looking, fair-haired Scotchman—though a little consequential in his manners, looked like one who in his own person could combat and vanquish all the evils which flesh is heir to. Such was the contrast between these doctors that they would have formed very good emblems, one, of vigorous health, the other, of hopeless decay (19) [14–15].

Although death and "hopeless decay" are recurring spectres in *Roughing It in the Bush*, Moodie's character and ambition gave her no real option but to follow a path of heroic, masculine virtue for which, on the basis of mere physical strength, she was ill-equipped. As unpalatable as this choice was for Moodie at the time of her arrival in Canada, it resulted in due time in her painful

All through the long/third week of August, the Prince of Wales/*crept south [towards James Bay]. . . . John Scarth could not get near me with his eyes/and we slept apart. I had become a man.*
—*Stephen Scobie,* The Ballad of Isabel Gunn *(1987).*

but ultimately triumphant acquisition and exercising of the strength and self-reliance that permitted her to become a female Crusoe and, in effect, a feminine version of the Herculean hero.

As well as encountering and re-engendering a "Choice of Hercules" on her arrival in Canada, Moodie had to contend in the St. Lawrence with a ship's captain who clearly represents another aspect of Canadian life—its lack of the graces and accents of the hierarchical English society in which the Moodie and Strickland families held a relatively privileged place. Compared, significantly, with a "bear," a North American creature proverbially renowned for its gruffness and roughness, Moodie's captain is a "rude, blunt north-country sailor" who receives the "Frenchman" and "Scotchman" "with very little courtesy, [and] abruptly [bids] them follow him down to his cabin," where he teasingly introduces the two doctors to three "babies" born during the Atlantic crossing: a litter of "fat, chuckle-headed [and male] bull terriers" (19–20) [15]. When the "Frenchman" bestows a "savage kick on one of [these] unoffending pups" (20) [16], it is as if someone on the *Laurel* had wrung the neck of the "little bird" that seemed to Traill such a "good omen" when it joined the vessel off Newfoundland. As Moodie's puppies and Traill's bird make evident, emblematic events and symbolic acts are a common feature of accounts of arrival in the New World; on another vessel, "the sand from the first soundings off the Grand Banks was placed under a baby's feet 'so that she might be the first who stepped on American soil' " (Guillet, 101). Both the reference to the ship's captain as a "bear" and the behaviour of the French doctor towards the bull-terrier puppy speak loudly of Moodie's conviction that Canada is a place hostile to all but men of a fairly brutal disposition.

A further indication that Moodie regards the New World as hostile to civilization, as she conceives it, can be gleaned from her rendition of the speech of the captain and the "Frenchman." In the utterances of the former are "commonly expunged all the connective links" (19) [15]—that is, such words as "and," which can indicate the connection and addition of words in the same class or type, and "the," which can make crucial distinctions of the sort valued by people of

That night the sky was lit from zenith to horizon by Northern lights. . . . "A portent!" [Aunt Topaz] said happily. . . . "We are coming to Canada for the first time . . . and I certainly regard this as most favourable, an indication, I would say, that my sister and my niece and I have made the right decision in coming. A welcome indeed!"
—Ethel Wilson, The Innocent Traveller (1949).

Moodie's background, the distinction, for example, between "a house" and "the house." In the utterances of the latter—" 'You tink us dog. . . . Joke! me no understand such joke. Bete' "—violence is done both to articles and to words and phrases such as "I" and "we are" that are indicative of individual and collective identity. The very speech of the men whom Moodie describes on arrival in Canada thus reflects her fearful sense of a social and personal disintegration, a disconcerting shattering of the "cake of custom," during the transition from the hierarchical civilization that she cherishes to the independent or republican culture that she knows to exist in North America. Later in the opening sketch of *Roughing It in the Bush*, this feeling of fear (and consequent alienation) is again expressed in terms of language as Moodie describes emigrants newly arrived on Grosse Isle: "The confusion of Babel was among them. All talkers and no hearers—each shouting and yelling in his or her uncouth dialect, and all accompanying their vociferations with violent and extraordinary gestures, quite incomprehensible to the uninitiated. We were literally stunned by the strife of tongues" (20) [20]. Both men and women are included in this comment, and no more than the former do the latter give Moodie grounds for believing that her conception of civilization, and of femininity, can survive the shattering of the "cake of custom." "I shrank, with feelings almost akin to fear," she writes, "from the hard-featured, sunburnt women as they elbowed rudely past me" (25) [20].

While the opening sketches in *Roughing It in the Bush* do contain some positive first impressions of Canada, particularly of the sublime and picturesque sights on the St. Lawrence, the dominant mood of these pieces is that of an outsider being unpleasantly initiated into a reality that is far removed from the "perfect paradise" (25) [19] created either by propagandistic emigrant literature or, as in Traill, by the distance that lends enchantment. With hindsight, Moodie can exhort "British mothers of Canadian sons" to teach their offspring "to love Canada—to look upon her as the first, the happiest, the most independent country in the world!" (24) [26]; she can even look back and see Grosse Isle and its "sister group" of islands "[c]radled in the arms of the St.

*I am a word/In a foreign language.
—Margaret Atwood,
The Journals of Susanna Moodie
(1970).*

*Is it my clothes, my way of walking,/the things I carry in my hand/—a book, a bag with knitting—/the incongruous pink of my shawl/this space cannot hear . . .
—Margaret Atwood,
The Journals of Susanna Moodie
(1970).*

*Some day my son/when you are in Leningrad . . . you'll remember/Nova Scotia's pasture lands/its clumps of blueberries/and our August mornings/on hidden lakes at the end/of logging roads.
—Miriam Waddington, The Visitants
(1981).*

Lawrence, and basking in the bright rays of the morning sun, . . . [as] a second Eden just emerged from the waters of chaos" (30) [24]. But these expressions of a childlike belonging to a new maternal realm and a fresh sisterhood serve merely to counterpoint the dominant notes of alienation and disenchantment, isolation and homesickness, in Moodie's opening sketches. And nowhere is Moodie's dismay at the crumbling of the "cake of custom" on arrival in Canada more poignantly evident than in her account of the behaviour at Grosse Isle of the normally reliable Scots, both two- and four-legged. On the arrival of the *Anne* off the island, Moodie is left "alone with [her] baby in the otherwise empty vessel. Even Oscar, the captain's Scotch terrier, who had formed a devoted attachment to me during the voyage, forgot his allegiance, became possessed of the land mania, and was away with the rest" (28) [17]. When later she has the opportunity to go ashore at Grosse Isle, she notices that even Oscar's countrymen are not immune to the republican spirit of the New World: "our passengers, who were chiefly honest Scotch labourers and mechanics from the vicinity of Edinburgh, and who while on board ship conducted themselves with the greatest propriety, and appeared the most quiet, orderly set of people in the world, no sooner set foot upon the island than they became infected by the same spirit of insubordination and misrule, and were just as insolent and noisy as the rest" (21–22) [20]. As this passage makes very clear, those who had most to resent as the "cake of custom" crumbled were men and women who, like Moodie, would have preferred to retain their status as icing on the cake rather than become part of a new mixture.

Yet Moodie's response to her loss of social privilege and its contingent identity in Canada was to create for herself in *Roughing It in the Bush* and elsewhere a new sense of self and purpose which was and still is of more consequence than what she would have done had she remained in England. When he arrived at the Pacific coast, where neither he nor his guide could anymore understand the local Indian languages, Alexander Mackenzie famously affirmed his achievement and his identity by inscribing his name "in large characters" on the "face of [a] rock" (25). Being

[On our arrival at Montreal] travelling companion cast off travelling companion and the unity of the ship was gone.
—Ethel Wilson, The Innocent Traveller *(1949).*

Crossing the Atlantic they doubtless suffered some dilution; but all that was possible to conserve them under very adverse conditions Mrs. Milburn and Miss Filkin made it their duty to do. Nor were these ideas opposed, contested, or much traversed in Elgin.
—Sara Jeannette Duncan, The Imperialist *(1904).*

emigrants rather than explorers and women rather than men, Moodie, Traill, and others were denied such grandiose gestures, but on their farms and in their books they nevertheless inscribed a part of themselves that endures and, even as it does so, reveals something of the complex process of retention and modification, disintegration and reassembly, that must always have been an aspect of great migrations, especially those involving long journeys across oceans. In "The Stimulus of Migration Overseas," Toynbee holds the experience of transmarine colonization directly responsible for the creation of the Homeric epics and the Icelandic sagas, as well as for other major artistic achievements and innovations, observing as he does so the greater creativity of emigrants in relation to those who are left behind. Why no corresponding artistic achievements and innovations took place in the circumstances of emigration to Canada in the nineteenth century is not difficult to fathom: by the nineteenth century, removal to British North America meant, not the severing of communication with the mother culture and a consequent need to tell all the stories again, but a movement from the centre to the periphery with a consequence that is characteristic of all minor (which is to say, deterritorialized) literature:[2] the need to explain life on the periphery to those at the centre.

That the writing of women about being women in the colonies is twice marginalized—once by being distant from the centre and once again by being of "the second sex"—gives it, for many contemporary readers, a double interest. Certainly, and with a double sense on both words, it is writing of skill and power—able and energetic writing about the abilities and strengths that were expanded or discovered, often with considerable pain and effort, when women were forced by emigration to Canada to rethink their relations with men, with themselves, and with a New World. No great social and literary consequences are traceable to emigration to Canada in the nineteenth century, but *The Backwoods of Canada*, *Roughing It in the Bush*, and other works by emigrant women are of enduring interest for a variety of

2. MacKenzie (349).

reasons, not least as records of the process of adjustment to a new place and as testaments, by their very existence, to "The Stimulus of Migration Overseas."

Works Cited

Auerbach, Nina. 1982. *Woman and the Demon: The Life of a Victorian Myth.* Cambridge, Mass.: Harvard Univ. Press.

Bell, William. 1824. *Hints to Emigrants: in a Series of Letters from Upper Canada.* Edinburgh: Waugh and Innes.

Brooke, Frances. 1985. *The History of Emily Montague.* Ed. Mary Jane Edwards. Ottawa: Carleton Univ. Press.

Cary, Thomas. 1986. *Abram's Plains: A Poem.* Ed. D.M.R. Bentley. London, Ont.: Canadian Poetry Press.

Crawford, Isabella Valancy. 1987. *Malcolm's Katie: A Love Story.* Ed. D.M.R. Bentley. London, Ont.: Canadian Poetry Press.

Curtius, Ernst Robert. 1953. *European Literature and the Latin Middle Ages.* Trans. William R. Trask. Bollingen Series 36. Princeton: Princeton Univ. Press.

Dahlie, Hallvard. 1986. *Varieties of Exile: The Canadian Experience.* Vancouver: Univ. of British Columbia Press.

Frye, Northrop. 1973. Conclusion. In *Literary History of Canada.* 1965. Ed. Carl F. Klinck. Toronto: Univ. of Toronto Press.

Galinsky, G. Karl. 1972. *The Herakles Theme: The Adaptations of the Hero in Literature from Homer to the Twentieth Century.* Oxford: Basil Blackwell.

Guillet, Edwin C. 1967. *The Great Migration: The Atlantic Crossing by Sailing-Ship Since 1770.* 1963. Repr. Toronto: Univ. of Toronto Press.

Howison, Joan. 1965. *Sketches of Upper Canada: Domestic, Local, and Characteristic.* 1821. S. R. Publishers.

Hughes, M. D. 1921. *Edmund Burke: Selections, with Essays by Hazlitt, Arnold and Others.* Oxford: Clarendon.

Kolodny, Annette. 1984. *The Land Before Her: Fantasy and Experience of the American Frontiers, 1630–1860.* Chapel Hill, N.C. and London: Univ. of North Carolina Press.

———. 1975. *The Lay of the Land: Metaphors as Experience and History in American Life and Letters.* Chapel Hill, N.C.: Univ. of North Carolina Press.

Langton, Anne. 1950. *A Gentlewoman in Upper Canada: The Journals of Anne Langton.* Ed. H. H. Langton. Toronto: Clarke, Irwin.

———. 1904. *Langton Records: Journals and Letters from Canada 1837–1846.* Edinburgh: R. and R. Clark.

Lubbock, A. B. 1921. *The Colonial Clippers.* Glasgow: J. Brown and Son.

MacKenzie, Alexander. 1971. *Voyages from Montreal on the River St. Lawrence through the Continent of North America to the Frozen and Pacific Oceans in the Years 1789 and 1793.* 1801. Edmonton: Hurtig.

Montgomery, Lucy Maud. 1986. *Emily of New Moon.* 1925. Toronto: Seal Books.

Moodie, Susanna. 1962. *Roughing It in the Bush.* New Canadian Library, 31. Toronto: McClelland and Stewart.

O'Brien, Mary (Gapper). 1968. *The Journals of Mary O'Brien.* Ed. Audrey Saunders Miller. Toronto: Macmillan.

Pickering, Joseph. 1831. *Inquiries of an Emigrant.* New ed. London: Effingham Wilson.

Roberts, Charles G. D. 1974. "Canada." *Selected Poetry and Critical Prose.* Ed. W. J. Keith. Literature of Canada: Poetry and Prose in Reprint. Toronto: Univ. of Toronto Press.

Talman, James John, ed. 1953. *Authentic Letters from Upper Canada.* Toronto: Macmillan.

Thompson, Elizabeth Helen. 1987. "The Pioneer Woman: A Canadian Character Type." Diss. University of Western Ontario, London.

Toynbee, Arnold. 1955. *A Study of History.* 1939. London: Oxford Univ. Press.

Traill, Catharine Parr. 1929. *The Backwoods of Canada.* Introduction. Edward S. Caswell. Toronto: McClelland and Stewart.

Warburton, George. 1846. *Hochelaga; or, England in the New World.* Ed. Eliot Warburton. 2 vols. London: Henry Colburn.

Waterston, Elizabeth. 1973. "Travel Books 1880–1920." In *Literary History of Canada.* 1965. Ed. Carl F. Klinck. Toronto: Univ. of Toronto Press.

Wilden, Anthony. 1980. *System and Structure: Essays in Communication and Exchange.* 2nd ed. New York: Tavistock.

BINA FREIWALD

"The tongue of woman": The Language of the Self in
Moodie's *Roughing It in the Bush*†

Two important moments are identified with the conception of this essay. The first is a personal one, best captured by my copy of the 1962
New Canadian Library edition of *Roughing It in the Bush*.[1] It is a slim
volume, marked up savagely in fine-point red pen by a hand seeking
out all references, literal or figurative, to mothers and children; and
there is hardly a page that has escaped the red fury. The hand, I might
add, belonged to a scholar hard at work on a manuscript dealing with
artistic self-representation in nineteenth-century women's writing.
While her infant daughter was being cared for in a nearby nursery, she
read, marked, and eventually dismissed Moodie's narrative as only
marginally relevant to the topic at hand. That scene of reading, however, was to be revisited. The second moment, a theoretical one, centres on a recent shift in feminist articulations of the gendered subject.
An aspect of this shift that is particularly pertinent to the present discussion concerns the emergence of a new thematization of motherhood "that reflects the evaluation of motherhood as an essentially
positive activity and insists on its disalienating recuperation by and, in
the first instance, for women themselves."[2]

The shift in theorizations of the relationship between female experience and female expression, in relation to which my engagement with
Moodie's narrative situates itself, might best be illustrated by juxtapos-
ing two critical statements; interestingly, both are cast in the inter-
rogatory mode. The first is from Nina Auerbach's unambiguously
entitled essay "Artists and Mothers: A False Alliance," which opens
with this rhetorical question:

> Did the Brontes, Jane Austen, and George Eliot write out of a
> thwarted need to give birth, sadly making substitute dream chil-
> dren out of their novels? Or did they produce art that allowed
> them a freer, finer, more expansive world than the suppressions of
> nineteenth-century motherhood allowed?[3]

Having formulated the predicament of the nineteenth-century woman
writer in terms of the antagonistic pull of the mutually exclusive cul-

† From "Re(dis)covering Our Foremothers: Nineteenth-Century Canadian Women Writers,"
ed. Lorraine McMullen (Ottawa: U of Ottawa P, 1990), pp. 155–72. Reprinted by permission of the University of Ottawa Press. Page numbers in brackets refer to the text in this
Norton Critical Edition.
1. Since the New Canadian Library (NCL) edition of *Roughing It in the Bush* (Toronto: Mc-
Clelland and Stewart, 1962) is still the most widely used one, I have used it as my text
throughout. References to material left out of the NCL edition are to the 1986 Virago Press
edition (Introduction by Margaret Atwood, London; identified hereafter as VP).
2. Heather Jon Maroney, "Embracing Motherhood: New Feminist Theory," in *Canadian Journal
of Political and Social Theory* (special issue *Feminism Now*) IX, nos. 1, 2:40–64 (1985), 41.
3. Nina Auerbach, *Romantic Imprisonment: Women and Other Glorified Outcasts* (New York:
Columbia UP, 1986), 171.

tural myths of motherhood and artistic creativity—as prescribed by a climate of opinion which dictated that "one can be a speaker or a mother but not both"[4]—Auerbach celebrates the resolution of the double bind in the triumph of creativity and the total rejection of motherhood: "In the lives of Jane Austen and George Eliot, two woman artists made inescapably aware of the social assumptions equating womanhood with motherhood, art is a liberation from that demand, not a metaphoric submission to it. . . . Austen and Eliot both turned away from motherhood and embraced a creativity they defined as more spacious, more adult, more inclusive."[5] The second theoretical statement introduces the parameters of a still novel and tentative investigation to which the present essay seeks to contribute. Susan Rubin Suleiman reacts to Auerbach's categorial dissociation of writing and motherhood by proposing to interrogate the terms of this much maligned (mis)alliance, and at least provisionally introduce a different agenda: "Is there no alternative to the either/or? Will we ever be forced to write the book and deny the child (not the child we were but the child we have, or might have) or love the child and postpone/ renounce the book? . . . It is time to let mothers have their word."[6] Suleiman calls upon another mother's inquiry—Kristeva's "que savons-nous du discours que (se) fait une mère?"—to motivate and sustain a project which she renders in her own mother tongue: " 'what do we know about the inner discourse of a mother?' "[7]

From its whimsically humorous (and blatantly ethnocentric) opening episode, in which Susanna Moodie describes the spectacle of a shrivelled-up health inspector aboard the *Anne* screaming at the ship's captain—"sacre, you bete! you tink us dog, when you try to pass your puppies on us for babies?"—to its dramatic and sentimental conclusion, in which Moodie is reunited with her daughter Addie and bids farewell to the backwoods, *Roughing It in the Bush* unfolds as a narrative shaped by the complex vision and singular voice of its first-person narrator. Already in its opening pages, where the pronominal "I" first assumes the materiality of a character and the narrator begins to weave her presence into the fabric of her tale, we witness a double figuration, a doubling which is to mark the subject of this discourse, its speaking subject. Standing amid "fat, chuckle-headed" bull-terrier puppies, surrounded by "boats heavily laden with women and children," Moodie not only brings into textual existence a universe populated by mothers and their offspring, but is *always also* (in contradistinction to the deconstructive dictum of 'always already') marked herself/marks herself as a figure of mothering. As she makes her first appearance in the text, Moodie's entrance is not a solitary en-

4. Margaret Homans, *Bearing the Word: Language and Female Experience in Nineteenth-Century Women's Writing* (Chicago: U of Chicago P, 1986), 38. Hereafter referred to as Homans 1986.
5. Auerbach, 183.
6. Susan Rubin Suleiman, "Writing and Motherhood," in *The (M)other Tongue: Essays in Feminist Psychoanalytic Interpretation*, ed. Shirley Nelson Garner, Claire Kahane, Madelon Sprengnether, 352–77 (Ithaca: Cornell UP), 360.
7. Ibid., 368.

trance, just as it will not be her choice to stage a solitary exit. "I watched boat after boat depart for the island," Moodie observes as she insinuates herself into the narrated scene, stepping out of the shadowy "we" of the first paragraphs and into the mother-with-child figure that is to occupy centre stage: "I was left alone with my baby in the otherwise empty vessel."[8]

The originating moment of Moodie's story—the decision to emigrate—is presented as a specifically maternal moment: "I had bowed to a superior mandate, the command of duty; for my husband's sake, *for the sake of the infant, whose little bosom heaved against my swelling heart,* I had consented to bid adieu for ever to my native shores, and it seemed both useless and sinful to draw back" (emphasis added).[9] From its moment of inception, Moodie's narrative is marked by a double logic signalled by the mother's separation from her own mother— the native "mother country"[1]—and her bonding with the child who is to sustain her gaze and reconcile her to the new "land of [her] adoption . . . [Canada] the great fostering mother of the orphans of civilization."[2] This maternal gaze will remain constitutive of the narrative perspective; within the framework of a feminist challenge to deconstructive valuations of language, it can be understood as more "speech" than "writing," more a manner of communicating than the substance of the tale. Questioning the deconstructive rejection of the possibility of a mode of communication that can create presence, Margaret Homans has sought to reclaim a form of "speech" less easily collapsed into identification with the Derridean understanding of "writing" as creating meaning in the *absence* of what it refers to. Homans argues that a presence, and more specifically a co-presence of the self and the other, is established (however provisionally) in "parents'—historically mothers'—talk with children who have not yet learned symbolic language, talk that has the aim not primarily of representation but rather of creating contact."[3] On one level of the narrative deployment of signs in *Roughing It in the Bush,* a maternal idiom is introduced that partakes of the character of this "speech" which exceeds and escapes the recognized economy of representation and self-representation. It is an idiom that embodies a "remembering of what androcentric culture represses," as it recreates the experience of listening to and producing speech that circumvents the symbolic order, the *logos.*

As we follow the narrator around, we are informed about conditions in this new and strange land. We are told of its cold winters and inhospitable inhabitants; we hear of the trials of a gentleman-turned-farmer and of the peculiarities of a large cast of characters. While busily painting these panoramic vistas for the reader, Moodie is always also

---

8. NCL, 21 [17].
9. Ibid., 137 [129].
1. Ibid., xvi [10].
2. Ibid., 56 [49].
3. Margaret Homans, "Feminist Criticism and Theory: The Ghost of Creusa," in *The Yale Journal of Criticism* 1.1 (1987), 158–59. Hereafter referred to as Homans 1987.

doing something else, something that never fails to engage her, that never fails her: mothering. We can only sample here a few of these innumerable moments of homecoming, quick maternal glances seeking reassurance that the child is there, brief moments of discursive bonding, islands of relatedness in a stormy, unpredictable, often hostile sea. In "A Visit to Grosse Isle," Moodie writes: "My husband went off with the boats, to reconnoitre the island, and I was left alone with my baby in the otherwise empty vessel."⁴ A few pages later: "The rough sailor-captain screwed his mouth on one side, and gave me one of his comical looks; but he said nothing until he assisted in placing me and the baby in the boat."⁵ A little further: "the mosquitoes swarmed in myriads around us, tormenting the poor baby, who, not at all pleased with her visit to the new world, filled the air with cries."⁶ In the second chapter entitled "Quebec," she writes: "I had just settled down my baby in her berth, when the vessel struck, with a sudden crash that sent a shiver through her whole frame."⁷ There follows the episode of the near wreck where Moodie plays mother to another distraught girl whose own mother fails her. In the aftermath of the storm, Moodie enjoys the comforting intimacy of a cosy trio: mother, daughter, and the dog Oscar (himself a trusted mother-substitute): "When my arms were tired with nursing, I had only to lay my baby on my cloak on deck and tell Oscar to watch her, and the good dog would lie down by her, and suffer her to tangle his long curls in her little hands, and pull his tail and ears in the most approved baby fashion, without offering the least opposition; but if anyone dared to approach his charge, he was alive on the instant, placing his paws over the child and growling furiously."⁸

There is always a child at Susanna's side. In chapter three, "The Journey up the Country," she writes: "the fear and dread of [the cholera] on that first day caused me to throw many an anxious glance on my husband and my child."⁹ Stopping for the night at a small inn, she approaches the innkeeper: "I asked him if he would allow me to take my infant into a room with a fire."¹ In chapter five, the Moodies are on their way to their first settlement, and as the spring morning turns chilly, Susanna observes: "the baby cried, and I drew my summer shawl as closely round as possible, to protect her from the sudden change in our hitherto delightful temperature."² On the occasion of the first visit of Old Satan's daughter, the first borrower, the scene opens with a crying child: the "poor baby . . . lying upon a pillow in the old cradle, trying the strength of her lungs, and not a little irritated that no one was at leisure to regard her laudable endeavors to make herself heard."³ Moodie's exposition on the borrowing system is further accentuated by the very tangible pres-

4. NCL, 21 [17].
5. Ibid., 24 [19].
6. Ibid., 27 [21].
7. Ibid., 33 [28].
8. Ibid., 35 [30].
9. Ibid., 38 [33].
1. Ibid., 44 [38].
2. Ibid., 68 [60].
3. Ibid., 70 [62].

ence of the "poor weanling child" who wants for milk, and the borrower's unfeeling mockery: "when I asked my liberal visitor if she kept
cows, and would lend me a little milk for the baby, she burst out into
high disdain."[4] The chapter closes with the episode of the borrowed
candle, occurring years later, yet partaking of the same quality of maternal anxiety; the youngest boy is sick, and as Tom the cat has made
away with the borrowed candle, the chapter ends on a sinister note
only slightly alleviated by the temporal distance between the narrating
and narrated instances: "My poor boy awoke ill and feverish, and I had
no light to assist him, or even to look into his sweet face, to see how far
I dared hope that the light of day would find him better."[5]

It is a rare moment in *Roughing It in the Bush* when the narrator
appears unaccompanied by one or more of her children. Discursively,
the narrating 'I' is rarely a discrete, separate entity; her idiom, a maternal idiom, populates the discursive universe of *Roughing It in the Bush*
with an endless procession of "children": her children and other people's, as well as figurative children—children of the Divine Mother
Nature, of "the Great Father of Mankind,"[6] the sons and daughters of
England and Canada, the native children of the land. These children
draw the self out of its convenient-conventional fictional mould; they
blur the boundaries between 'I' and 'you' and obliterate the distinction
between inner and outer. A recurrent stylistic pattern which is emblematic of this narrative positionality consists of a shift in focaliza-
tion, within a single sentence, from mother to child: "My teeth were
chattering with the cold, and the children were crying over their
aching fingers at the bottom of the sleigh."[7]

Who, then, speaks in *Roughing It in the Bush*? The question is not
meant to restore an originating subject, authorial or otherwise, an im-
mutable essence which fixes meaning and circumscribes sense.
Rather, the attempt to grasp the subject who speaks is an attempt to
seize a subject in its "functions, its interventions in discourse, and its
system of dependencies."[8] For the subject is inextricably implicated in
the play of differences that constitutes discourse, inasmuch as the
subject is a subject produced in language—"the basis of subjectivity is
the exercise of language"[9]—and in the sense that ideology (as the work
of discourse) can be seen to constitute individuals as subjects: "ideology has the function (which defines it) of 'constituting' concrete individuals as subjects . . . all ideology hails or interpellates concrete
individuals as concrete subjects, by the function of the category of the
subject."[1] The subjectivity I seek to identify, then, is a "process, not a

4. Ibid., 73 [65].
5. Ibid., 83 [75].
6. Ibid., 220 [316].
7. Ibid., 234 [328].
8. Michel Foucault, "What Is an Author?" in *Language, Counter-Memory, Practice*, ed. Donald Bouchard, trans. D. Bouchard and S. Simon (Ithaca: Cornell UP, 1977), 137.
9. Emile Benveniste, *Problems in General Linguistics*, trans. Mary Elizabeth Meek (Coral Gables, Fl.: U of Miami P), 1971, as cited in Kaja Silverman, *The Subject of Semiotics* (New York: Oxford UP, 1983).
1. Louis Althusser, "Ideology and Ideological State Apparatuses (Notes Towards an Investiga-tion)," in his *Lenin and Philosophy* (New York: Monthly Review Press), 137.

structure of the subject. If language is the site of the symbolic constitution of the subject in the movement of the signifier, then that constitution is always historical, multiple, heterogeneous, always specific
and specifying subject effects."[2]

Who speaks in *Roughing It in the Bush*? It is a subject who is possessed of, to use Moodie's own words, "the tongue of woman." The
opening through which I enter her narrative is a brief digressive anecdote Moodie uses to illustrate her observation that "strange names are
to be found in this country." It is perhaps not accidental that it is a reflection on naming—on the subject-constituting gesture par excellence by which an individual is first and last interpellated—that allows
us an insight into the narrator's own self-constructing idiom. Moodie
writes:

> It was only yesterday that, in passing through one busy village, I
> stopped in astonishment before a tombstone headed thus: "Sacred
> to the memory of *Silence* Sharman, the beloved wife of Asa Shar-
> man." Was the woman deaf and dumb, or did her friends hope by
> bestowing upon her such an impossible name to still the voice of
> Nature, and check, by an admonitory appellative, the active spirit
> that lives in the tongue of woman? Truly, Asa Sharman, if thy wife
> was silent by name as well as by nature, thou wert a fortunate
> man.[3]

Digressions, according to that other fantastic narrator-autobiographer,
Tristram Shandy, "are the life, the soul of reading;—take them out of
this book for instance,—you might as well take the book along with
them."[4] It might well be that if we took out of Moodie's book that
which her digression ventures to identify, if we stilled or silenced the
"voice of nature" which she finds distilled in the "active spirit that
lives in the tongue of woman," little would remain of the life of the
story. A woman's tongue, nature's voice, native idiom, mother tongue,
the mother's tongue: these are the co-ordinates, the discursive interventions and dependencies that constitute the language of the self in
Roughing It in the Bush. A subject interpellated and self-constituted as
speaking a female idiom, the mother's tongue, Moodie's is a complex
and multiple subjectivity doubly marked by the traces of women's historically paradoxical position in discourse and a defiant resistance of
this anomalous condition.

How does a maternal language of the self become constitutive of a
speaking subject? The difficulties surrounding this question can be
gleaned from a brief survey of the critical literature on Moodie's
generically hybrid text. Although the narrator's professed intention in
Roughing It in the Bush is to reveal the "secrets of the prison-house"
by giving a "faithful picture of a life in the backwoods of Canada,"[5] for

2. Stephen Heath, "The Turn of the Subject," in *Cine-Tracts* 8:32–48 (1979), 40.
3. NCL, 94 [85].
4. Laurence Sterne, *Tristram Shandy* (1760–65; New York: W. W. Norton, 1980), 52.
5. NCL, 236–37 [330].

her twentieth-century critics the prisoner, not the prison-house, has held the greater attraction. Carl Klinck's introduction to the 1962 New Canadian Library edition of *Roughing It in the Bush* unequivocally asserts the work's autobiographical character and stresses the thematic and structural significance of its narrator's personal voice:

> *Roughing It* was wholly autobiographical, her own book; she was the author-apprentice-heroine. Everything pointed to her trials and her [partial] salvation. . . . Sharing in all the actions, and progressively enlarging the image of herself, she gave a pattern of movement to the whole book.[6]

Margaret Atwood's *The Journals of Susanna Moodie*[7] has been another particularly influential and exemplary reading of *Roughing It in the Bush* as autobiographical writing, as a narrative primarily conceived to explore and give voice to a tortured and agonistic subjectivity. Atwood inaugurates her poetic cycle with a poem that announces the primacy of the perceiver over the perceived, as the persona enacts a ritualistic gesture by which observation is transformed into introspection:

> I take this picture of myself
> and with my sewing scissors
> cut out the face.
>
> Now it is more accurate:
>
> where my eyes were,
> every—
> thing appears.

The last poem in the cycle reaffirms the power of the creator over the created, as a resurrected Susanna defiantly rearranges time and space to establish the co-ordinates of an all-devouring identity. She tells the person sitting across from her on the bus travelling along St. Clair:

> Turn, look down:
> there is no city;
> this is the centre of a forest
>
> your place is empty.

In her afterword to *The Journals of Susanna Moodie*, Atwood articulates a view that has become a critical commonplace: the prose of *Roughing It in the Bush* and *Life in the Clearings* is discursive and ornamental, and the books, which are collections of disconnected anecdotes, have little shape. The only thing that holds them together, Atwood contends, is the personality of Susanna Moodie. The

---

6. Ibid., xiv (Introduction).
7. Margaret Atwood, *The Journals of Susanna Moodie* (Toronto: Oxford UP, 1970).

emphasis on the narrator's writing of her self into a tale ostensibly concerned with an external reality—with other people and the harsh realities of a foreign land, etc.—has persisted.[8] Carl Ballstadt[9] argues that Moodie seems unable to resist projecting herself into the scenes she describes, and Carol Shields contends that a unifying force of a greater validity than the "nature-God-spirit trinity" characteristic of much nineteenth-century writing might be found in Susanna's "overriding sense of her own personality . . . every scene is filtered through her sensibility; every character encountered is studied in context with herself."[1]

The self that has been observed to dominate the narrative of *Roughing It in the Bush* has most often been identified as a fragmented, vulnerable, and tormented self. Much has been made of Susanna's condition of alienation and estrangement, the cultural shock she suffers and the consequent fragmentation of identity. Carol Shields gleans, from beneath the persona's vigorous appearance, a self desperately seeking confirmation of its existence, without which it will dissolve, unwitnessed and unverified, in an alien environment. Marian Fowler describes Susanna as a "mass of contradictions and startling contrasts" and contrasts the "conventional, English Susanna," who "stubbornly clings to the English stereotype of the delicate female," with Susanna the pragmatist, the quick-acting Dasher and courageous frontierswoman.[2] For critics like Atwood and Fowler, the mother's experience and a maternal idiom are associated with a constraining and disabling sphere of female existence, and thus [are] fundamentally at odds with the artist's creative imperative. For Fowler, Susanna the mother is a predictable avatar of the all-too-familiar sentimental heroine: an anxious admirer of cherubic innocence, a passive, patient sufferer in the face of continual affliction. Since for Fowler the drama that makes *Roughing It in the Bush* a literary masterpiece consists of the challenge to female stereotypes by an androgynous self, which "wheels and soars in male preserves," she can only see in Susanna's mother tongue an artificial, hollow, borrowed idiom. The children are easily dismissed: "children in sentimental fiction are very [sic] touchstones of sensibility."[3] For Atwood, Susanna's mother tongue speaks forcefully but in ominous tones of separation, loss, death. There is the poem "Death of a Young Child by Drowning," and in "The Deaths of the Other Children," Atwood writes:

> Did I spend all those years
> building up this edifice
> my composite
> self, this crumbling hovel?

---

8. There have been, however, dissenting voices; see Laura Groening, "*The Journals of Susanna Moodie*: A Twentieth-Century Look at a Nineteenth-Century Life," in *Studies in Canadian Literature* 7–8: 166–80 (1982–83).
9. In "Susanna Moodie and the English Sketch," in *Canadian Literature* 51: 32–37 (1972).
1. Carol Shields, *Susanna Moodie: Voice and Vision* (Ottawa: Borealis Press, 1977), 6.
2. Marian Fowler, *The Embroidered Tent: Five Gentlewomen in Early Canada* (Toronto: House of Anansi, 1982), 101.
3. Ibid., 119, 108.

My arms, my eyes, my grieving
words, my disintegrated children

Everywhere I walk, along
the overgrowing paths, my skirt
tugged at by the spreading briers

they catch at my heels with their fingers

In Atwood's recent introduction to the Virago edition of *Roughing It in the Bush*, this linking of motherhood with the "crumbling hovel" of the flesh/self is again placed in the foreground, as Atwood reminds the contemporary reader:

> We should remember too that the years she spent in the bush were child-bearing ones for her; in those days before modern medicine, when a doctor, even if there had been one available, wouldn't have been much help, not all the children eventually survived. Mrs. Moodie is reticent on the subject, but she says at one point, rather chillingly, that she never felt really at home in Canada until she had buried some of her children in it.[4]

Moodie's anxiety over the life-threatening crises suffered by the children, from food deprivation to a near-fatal typhus epidemic, are indeed movingly communicated in *Roughing It in the Bush*; her initial reluctance to let go of certain Victorian ideals of feminine conduct is indeed irritating. Yet a critical perspective that remains satisfied with such partial views of her character can hardly begin to account for the centrality and complexity of the mother's relation to language and to the discourses that define and are redefined by her. We might start to attend to these issues by reflecting on the vital links that connect the thematic focus of *Roughing It in the Bush*—a preoccupation with emigration as an experience of territorial, cultural, and psychic displacement—with its narrator's use of a maternal idiom. We would do well, however, to prepare for such a discussion by noting the conceptual and ideological hazards involved in such a task.

Drawing on the work of feminist theorists like Mary Jacobus and Nancy Chodorow, Margaret Homans has recently proposed a redefinition of the project of feminist criticism that underscores not only the challenges ahead but also the risks involved:

> feminist criticism aims to recover the women and the women's voices that have been lost or repressed, but only in such a way as to avoid replicating the structures that brought about that repression in the first place. The question is how to redefine our sense of what "women's voices" or "women's experience" might be—to change the conditions of representability . . . so as to recover those losses without losing them all over again.[5]

How, then, to represent the mother tongue in *Roughing It in the Bush* in a way that will not result in losing Moodie to the idiom of the fam-

---

4. VP, xii.
5. Homans 1987, 172–73.

ily romance, in which the mother's desire is absorbed into—subsumed under—the father's and the child's, without losing her to a script that places her sacrificial passivity in the foreground by hailing their expansive actions and unrelenting demands? A necessary precondition for a revisionary reading will thus involve a recognition of the historically specific moment into which Moodie's discourse inserts itself. Margaret Homans suggestively articulates a context within which a narrative like Moodie's can be better appreciated:

> In the nineteenth century, when women's lives were increasingly defined in relation to a standard of womanhood, regardless of whether or not they were of childbearing age, women who wrote did so within a framework of dominant cultural myths in which writing contradicts mothering. Paradoxically, the high value placed on mothering as a vocation for women is entirely consistent with the devaluation of everything women did relative to men's accomplishments.[6]

Elaborating on this paradoxical subject-position which has marked women's fictions of self-representation, Sidonie Smith further observes:

> On one hand, she [the female autobiographer] engages the fictions of selfhood that constitute the discourse of man and that convey by the way a vision of the fabricating power of male subjectivity. . . . But the story of man is not exactly her story; and so her relationship to the empowering figure of male selfhood is inevitably problematic. To complicate matters further, she must also engage the fictions of selfhood that constitute the idea of woman and that specify the parameters of female subjectivity, including women's problematic relationship to language, desire, power, and meaning. Since the ideology of gender makes of woman's life script a nonstory, a silent space, a gap in patriarchal culture, the ideal woman is self-effacing rather than self-promoting, and her 'natural' story shapes itself not around the public, heroic life but around the fluid, circumstantial, contingent responsiveness to others that, according to patriarchal ideology, characterizes the life of woman but not autobiography.[7]

Viewed in the light of these observations, Moodie's predicament as a female narrator-autobiographer appears to parallel that of her feminist reader, for in both instances what is at stake is a reclamation of a range of historically specific female experiences and expressions which have been appropriated to serve the ends of an androcentric culture that denigrates them.

An uneasiness with this problematic discursive positionality of the female 'I' is, in turn, reflected in stories of reading which occlude or evade the terms of the dilemma. Atwood's reading, for example, ultimately elides the problematic ('personal') female subject by transform-

6. Homans 1986, 22.
7. Sidonie Smith, *A Poetics of Women's Autobiography: Marginality and the Fictions of Self-Representation* (Indianapolis: Indiana UP, 1987), 50.

ing her tale into the public story of a genderless Canadian psyche. One could easily substitute "he" for "she" in Atwood's paradigmatic description of Moodie in the afterword to *The Journals of Susanna Moodie* without disturbing the logic or the rhetoric of that description. Fowler seems to favour a similar position, for she valorizes a movement away from the feminine and towards the androgynous. In both cases, the interpretive matrix seems to involve a rejection of the mother—a gesture Sidonie Smith identifies as a further symptom of women's paradoxical condition within discourse:

> as she [the woman writing] appropriates the story and the speaking posture of the representative man, she silences that part of herself that identifies her as a daughter of her mother. Repressing the mother in her, she turns away from the locus of all that is domesticated and disempowered culturally and erases the trace of sexual difference and desire. . . . "[she] cannot assume this identification with the Father except by denying her difference as a woman, except by repressing the maternal within her."[8]

Has repression of the maternal been the only recourse for women writers? Susan Suleiman, who has undertaken an initial exploration of the mother's discourse, observes two major thematic clusters in women's writing: motherhood as obstacle or source of conflict and motherhood as link, as source of connection to work and world. *Roughing It in the Bush* exhibits the latter tendency. On the most basic level, the maternal idiom appears as perhaps the single constant in an otherwise fairly volatile and shifting self. Whatever her preoccupation at a given moment, whatever her inclination, mood, or circumstance, Moodie's narrating and narrated 'I' is always also a mother's 'I'. As we move from the category of character to the formal and rhetorical modalities that govern *Roughing It in the Bush*, we observe that the mother's tongue is articulated on three interrelated planes of the narrative complex. As a modality of being which marks the narrator's presence in her tale, it manifests itself through that co-presence of the self and other which brings together mother and child. This relational subject-position is thematized in the narrator's appeal to a maternal idiom for the purpose of self representation, as Moodie freely alternates between the poles of motherhood and childhood, between speaking as provider and source of power, and pleading as a needy child or a helpless supplicant. In a second instance, the mother's idiom is further thematized as an ethical principle, a principle by which Moodie—as the prime narrative mover—both constructs and judges her character creations. Finally, the mother's idiom manifests itself as a rhetorical operation of changing registers from figurative to literal and back to figurative, a rhetorical operation heavily charged with mythic and thematic significance as it suggests a negotiation between a paternal symbolic (figurative) writing—regarded as being outside the female sphere—and a 'properly' feminine (literal) mode of expression.

8. Smith, 53.

The last of the three practices of the mother tongue—the shifting of rhetorical registers from figurative to literal—is perhaps the least conspicuous yet most pervasive of the three, as it contains, frames, and supports the mother's discourse in *Roughing It in the Bush*. Indeed, the narrative's central thematic concern with the experiences of displacement, relocation, and eventual naturalization is most profoundly transformed by a practice which Margaret Homans has characterized as "bearing the word": "the literalization of a figure [which] occurs when some piece of overtly figurative language, a simile or an extended or conspicuous metaphor, is translated into an actual event or circumstance."[9] In Moodie's text, as in the works of the other nineteenth-century women writers studied by Homans, this literalization of figures, when more specifically connected to female themes, articulates the woman writer's "ambivalent turning toward female linguistic practices and yet at the same time associating such a choice with danger and death."[1] On the microtextual level, such an instance of "bearing the word"—in which a figure is literalized to voice a peculiarly maternal anguish—is evident in a sentence like the following from "The Outbreak": "How often, during the winter season, have I wept over their little chapped feet, *literally* washing them with my tears" (emphasis added).[2] On the macrotextual level, the originating matrix of *Roughing It in the Bush* constitutes an exemplary instance of 'bearing the word.' For the experience of emigration is articulated by Moodie through the extended figure—which is then literalized—of the loss of childhood and a separation from the mother. In relation to their native land, emigrants, for Moodie, forever remain children; they are the "high-souled children of a glorious land," and their memories are those of the "local attachments which stamp the scene amid which [their] childhood grew."[3] Immigration and naturalization, in turn, are conceived in terms of adoption and the maternal embrace of a new parent. "British mothers of Canadian sons!" Moodie exhorts her female readers, "make your children proud of the land of their birth."[4]

When applied to Moodie herself, this extended maternal figure spells out the painful passage from childhood to motherhood. She bemoans the loss of the mother and the ending of childhood, mourning the severance of the strongest of bonds:

> Dear, dear England, why was I forced by a stern necessity to leave you? What heinous crime had I committed that I, who adored you, should be *torn from your sacred bosom*, to pine out my joyless existence in a foreign clime? (emphasis added).[5]

In Canada, Moodie is no longer a child but a mother, and her experience of loss is no longer that of the orphan but of the bereaved mother. As she 'bears the word' here, the figure of the mother country

9. Homans 1986, 30.
1. Ibid.
2. NCL, 215 [283].
3. Ibid., xv [9].
4. Ibid., 30 [26].
5. Ibid., 56 [49].

is both sustained and literalized, and both the mother country and Moodie the mother become associated with those experiences most resistant to symbolic representation, life and death:

> Canada! thou art a noble, free, and rising country—the great fostering mother of the orphans of civilization. The offspring of Britain, thou must be great, and I will and do love thee, land of my adoption, and of my children's birth; and oh—dearer still to a mother's heart—land of their graves.[6]

Finally, presiding over this human drama which shapes and determines the narrator's destiny is another maternal figure: "Nature, arrayed in her green loveliness, had ever smiled upon me like an indulgent mother, holding out her arms to enfold to her bosom her erring but devoted child."[7]

As the figure of the mother is literalized in *Roughing It in the Bush* through the innumerable instances of mothering which define and identify the narrator's position, a concomitant emphasis works to establish the mother's idiom as a general principle of character construction in the story. From Oscar the dog to Malcolm "the little stumpy man," through John Monaghan, Bell, Jenny, Wilson, Jacob, Brian the still-hunter and others, characters in *Roughing It in the Bush* are judged by their ability to interact with, care for, and communicate with children. These patterns of behavior are grasped as fundamentally constitutive of both their pragmatic actions and moral conduct. The blessed in Moodie's ethical universe are characters like John Monaghan who, "standing alone in the wurld," is nonetheless capable of attaching himself "in an extraordinary manner." Moodie lovingly and gratefully recreates for us this exemplary maternal scene:

> All his spare time he spent in making little sleighs and toys for her [Katie, the baby], or in dragging her in the said sleighs up and down the steep hills in front of the house, wrapped up in a blanket. Of a night, he cooked her mess of bread and milk, as she sat by the fire, and his greatest delight was to feed her himself. . . . Katie always greeted his return from the woods with a scream of joy, holding up her fair arms to clasp the neck of her dark favourite.[8]

The most striking instance of a maternal idiom that literalizes the figurative, however, is found in the narrator's double vision of herself as both mother and child. Caught between her own mother country and her children's country of birth, between her own childhood (which the mother country will always represent) and her children's childhood (which turns her into a mother), Susanna learns a critical lesson: "you cannot exalt the one at the expense of the other without committing an act of treason against both."[9] Literally, the lesson learned is that of balancing and attending to the respective claims of

6. Ibid. [49]
7. Ibid. [49]
8. Ibid., 109–10 [100].
9. Ibid., 30 [26].

mother and child. The most enabling function of Moodie's mother tongue is to allow her to be not only her child's mother but also her mother's child.

By coming to Canada, Moodie becomes a permanent exile, a "stranger in a strange land"[1] as she keeps reminding the reader and as other characters keep reminding her. "I am a stranger in the country," Moodie tells her first borrower, Old Satan's daughter; and in an aside to the reader: "In fact we were strangers, and the knowing ones took us in."[2] Brian the still-hunter greets them with "You are strangers; but I like you all."[3] In a recognizably Romantic moment of existential anguish Moodie reflects on her share in the human predicament of self-estrangement: "The holy and mysterious nature of man is yet hidden from himself; he is still a stranger to the movements of that inner life, and knows little of its capabilities and powers."[4]

A closer scrutiny of this critical moment, however, reveals a rhetorical strategy which is emblematic of the narrator's subject-position in *Roughing It in the Bush*. The passage cited in which Moodie's sense of alienation and displacement is projected onto the larger arena of the human psyche forms the middle part of a paradigmatic mini-narrative which opens the important penultimate chapter entitled "Of A Change in Our Prospects." The maternal idiom is already suggested in the poetic epigraph to the chapter, a poem which introduces at its very structural and thematic centre "the embryo blossom." The chapter opens with Moodie as a grieving mother and a forlorn child. An illness has forced a separation from her second daughter, who has been taken in by a kind, neighbouring family. Hardly ever excessive when speaking of the children, Moodie's tone is charged but restrained as she speaks of the separation and loss: "During that winter and through the ensuing summer, I only received occasional visits from my little girl, who, fairly established with her new friends, looked upon their house as her home."[5] In the next paragraph, it is Moodie who is the little girl, a motherless or fatherless child, longing to be reunited with the "Great Father of mankind" as she lays down her throbbing head on the pillow beside the other child, her firstborn son, and "sleep[s] tranquilly."[6] Moodie is delivered from misery as she becomes, as it were, her own mother, as she envisions "a purer religion," the Mother of Christianity giving birth to a "beauteous child of God"; deliverance lies in delivery as the mother's labour pains release her and the child-humankind into a brighter future. Moodie prophesies:

> Oh, for that glorious day! It is coming. The dark clouds of humanity are already tinged with the golden radiance of the dawn, but the sun of righteousness has not yet arisen upon the world with healing on his wings; the light of truth still struggles in the

1. Ibid., 37 [32].
2. Ibid., 83 [74].
3. Ibid., 125 [119].
4. Ibid., 221 [316–17].
5. Ibid., 220 [315].
6. Ibid. [316]

womb of darkness, and man stumbles on to the fulfilment of his sublime and mysterious destiny.[7]

In Moodie's version of the family romance, Father and Mother merge in the all-encompassing, ever-expansive force of Nature. In her isolation and fear Moodie sees herself as one of Nature's children, a "little brook" with its "deep wailings and fretful sighs" which sobs and moans "like a fretful child."[8] Threatened and besieged, Moodie is anxious as a fretful child but also fearful for the child she risks losing to sickness or to the darker force of nature, here epitomized by the wolves: "just as the day broke my friends the wolves set up a parting benediction, so loud and wild, and near to the house, that I was afraid lest they should break through the frail window, or come down the low, wide chimney, and *rob me of my child*" (emphasis added).[9] Yet Mother Nature ultimately never fails Moodie: she is there at the break of dawn, solemn, majestic, and beautiful; she is there reassuring, unconditionally loving: "As long as we remain true to the Divine Mother, so long will she remain faithful to her suffering children."[1]

Nature is the mother Moodie can always return to as a child, but it is also the mother who takes her away from her child. On those occasions when Moodie is most self-conscious as a writer, we find her adopting a Romantic idiom which laments the inadequacy of words to capture the beauty of Nature and to express the "pure and unalloyed delight" that it offers the observer. In these moments, Moodie reclaims for herself the privilege of the child, gratefully acknowledging the indulgence of Mother Nature and the Great Father. This is the *writer's* primal scene as it materializes for Susanna aboard the *Anne* on her voyage from Grosse Isle to Quebec:

> Nature has lavished all her grandest elements to form this astonishing panorama. There frowns the cloud-capped mountain, and below, the cataract foams and thunders; . . . regardless of the eager crowds around me, I leant upon the side of the vessel and cried *like a child . . . my soul at that moment was alone with God* (emphasis added).[2]

While being "alone with God" is the child's prerogative, it is also the mother's transgression. The concluding passage from "A Trip to Stony Lake" best dramatizes this tension between the mother's need to be mothered—to receive and indulge herself, to be sustained so she can grow and leave home, so she can write—and the mother's recognition of another's need. Susanna is returning from an exhilarating expedition with her husband on which she took the two older children, leaving the younger boy behind:

7. Ibid., 221 [317].
8. Ibid., 100, 130 [90, 123].
9. Ibid., 130 [124].
1. Ibid., 100 [90].
2. Ibid., 29 [25].

It was midnight when the children were placed on my cloak at the bottom of the canoe, and we bade adieu to this hospitable family. . . . The moonlight was as bright as day, the air warm and balmy; and the aromatic, resinous smell exuded by the heat from the balm-of-gilead and the pine-trees in the forest, added greatly to our sense of enjoyment as we floated past scenes so wild and lonely—isles that assumed a mysterious look and character in that witching hour. In moments like these, I ceased to regret my separation from my native land; and, *filled with the love of Nature, my heart forgot for the time the love of home.* . . . Amid these lonely wilds the soul draws nearer to God, and is filled to overflowing by the overwhelming sense of His presence.

It was two o'clock in the morning when we fastened the canoe to the landing, and Moodie carried up the children to the house. I found the girl still up with my boy, who had been very restless during our absence. *My heart reproached me, as I caught him to my breast, for leaving him so long*; in a few minutes he was consoled for past sorrows, and sleeping sweetly in my arms (emphasis added).[3]

Framed and contained by the presence of the children—the children safely asleep at the bottom of the canoe, the infant son restlessly waiting at home—Moodies moment of inspiration, of flight from the literal into the realm of the "mysterious," is significantly a 'forgetting' of "home." Transported by the experience of beauty and an aesthetic vision, the adult woman writer forgets not only the home of her childhood ("my native land") but also her children's home, that is, forgets herself as a mother. As a result, the moment becomes marked by those traces of maternal guilt that Susan Suleiman has found to be symptomatic of the discourse of "the mother-as-she writes":

I would suggest that in the case of the writing mother, the subtle undermining, the oppressive feeling of impotence and insignificance . . . are intimately linked to a sense of guilt about her child. Jean-Paul Sartre once said in an interview, when asked about the value of literature and of his own novels in particular: "En face d'un enfant qui meurt, *La Nausee* ne fait pas le poids" [freely translated: "When weighted against a dying child, *La Nausee* doesn't count"]. . . . What are we to say about the guilt of a mother who might weigh her books not against a stranger's dying child but merely against her own child who is crying?[4]

In the mother tongue, however, there is no outside-of-home (as we know there is no *hors texte* or outside-of-text), for the very assumptions upon which such a distinction would be based are apprehended as a false dichotomy. The heart that forgets is also the heart that remembers and reproaches.

As the mother writes, she engages with the cultural myths of her particular historical moment, myths that define her relation to nature,

3. VP, 338–39 [228–29].
4. Suleiman, 364.

to language, and to the self. For Moodie, to create is to write within and against a literary tradition that reinforces her otherness through a conflation of woman and nature and through an exclusive identification of the speaking subject as male.[5] Maternal guilt is the price she has to pay for entering the symbolic order, for breaking the daughter's silence and speaking the mother. Once this price has been paid, Moodie is freed and free to carry on the negotiation between mother and child, between the child in the mother and that mother's child. *Roughing It in the Bush*, then, is perhaps not only the expression of an ambivalent colonizing consciousness, nor merely the expression of a paranoid schizophrenic condition; it is more than a textual space inhabited by a personality "split by the institution and system of *la langue* as she [Moodie] carries it and *la parole* as she finds it actualized in Canada."[6] In one recent rewriting of *Roughing It in the Bush*, the critic tells of a divided house and a broken home, an invaded narrative and a frustrated, threatened narrator:

> Moodie is most at home in this text when she is writing in the lyrical, hortatory, or didactic modes. She is drawn to these monologic modes as potential systems of narrative but they continually let her down. The verbal home she [Moodie] attempts to build is invaded by the voices of others. The characters who enter speak in no generic mode known to her. She tries to reduce them to the low comic or diabolic. They reassert themselves as embodiments of the carnivalesque.[7]

But isn't "home" also where the children are, and isn't Moodie indeed "at home" with them, in speaking of, to, and with them? And what of those peace gatherings, so unlike the scenes of (sexual?) violence suggested above, where Moodie speaks of, to, and with other characters (both male and female) similarly possessed of the mother tongue? *Roughing It in the Bush* may be about more than divided national loyalties, the pioneer experience and the challenge of the wilderness, man's existential anguish—all those worthy themes we have been taught to look for in the best works of art. It is perhaps also about something much closer to home, something that has been kept out of sight for too long, something Moodie calls "maternal feelings."[8] There is a story told in *Roughing It in the Bush* that we have not been reading. In one of its many beginnings, it goes like this: "old Jenny and I were left alone with the little children, in the depths of the dark forest, to help ourselves in the best way we could."[9] And very well they did, too!

5. On the predicament of the nineteenth-century woman writer, see Sandra Gilbert and Susan Gubar, *The Madwoman in the Attic: The Woman Writer and the Nineteenth-Century Literary Imagination* (New Haven: Yale UP, 1979), and Margaret Homans, *Women Writers and Poetic Identity* (Princeton: Princeton UP, 1980).
6. John Thurston, "Rewriting *Roughing It*," in *Future Indicative: Literary Theory and Canadian Literature*, ed. John Moss (Ottawa: U of Ottawa P, 1987), 202.
7. Ibid., 201.
8. VP, 476 [311].
9. VP, 458 [302].

SUSAN GLICKMAN

The Waxing and Waning of Susanna Moodie's "Enthusiasm"†

Rosemary Sullivan claimed in 1990 that "the wilderness is the enemy. Why? Because the virgin wilderness seems to negate man's perception of his own value. No one has caught this better than Susanna Moodie in her famous *Roughing It in the Bush*."[1] More than any other writer in Canadian literature, Susanna Moodie has come to symbolize the repulsion from nature Canadians are alleged to feel, a repulsion she neither felt herself nor would have countenanced in others.

It is odd that this view of Moodie persists despite the fierce scrutiny her memoirs have received from twentieth-century scholarship. What such scrutiny—if unbiased—reveals is that, although she found domestic life in the wilderness difficult, nature was her chief *solace* in the midst of hunger, isolation, and uncertainty. This is dramatically illustrated early in *Roughing It in the Bush* when she juxtaposes praise of nature with a feeling of hopeless entrapment after moving to Mrs Joe's cottage:

> The location was beautiful, and I was greatly consoled by this circumstance. The aspect of Nature ever did, and I hope ever will continue "to shoot marvellous strength into my heart." As long as we remain true to the Divine Mother, so long will she remain faithful to her suffering children.
>
> At that period my love for Canada was a feeling very nearly allied to that which the condemned criminal entertains for his cell—the only hope of escape being through the portals of the grave.[2]

At other times she confesses that nature provides more than simple consolation: it has the capacity to lift her out of herself, and make her forget her all-consuming homesickness. One such interlude occurs during a moonlit canoe-ride home after visiting Stony Lake. Remembering it, she remarks that at such times, "I ceased to regret my separation from my native land; and, filled with the love of Nature, my heart forgot for the time the love of home . . . Amid these lonely wilds the soul draws nearer to God, and is filled to overflowing by the overwhelming sense of His presence" (340) [229]. This is the familiar language of the sublime, and it is found throughout Moodie's writings whenever she finds herself alone with nature.

For example, when she first catches sight of Quebec from the river she exclaims:

---

† From *The Picturesque of the Sublime: A Poetics of Canadian Space* (Montreal and Kingston: McGill-Queen's Press, 1998), pp. 60–80. Reprinted by permission of McGill-Queen's University Press.

1. Rosemary Sullivan, "The Forest and the Trees," in *Ambivalence: Studies in Canadian Literature*, Om P. Juneja and Chandra Mohan, eds. (New Delhi: Allied Publishers, 1990), 43.

2. Susanna Moodie, *Roughing It in the Bush* (1852; reprint Toronto: McClelland and Stewart, 1989), 134–5 [90–91]. All further quotations will refer to the 1989 edition; bracketed page numbers refer to this Norton Critical Edition.

Nature has lavished all her grandest elements to form this astonishing panorama. There frowns the cloud-capped mountain, and
below, the cataract foams and thunders; wood, and rock, and river
combine to lend their aid in making the picture perfect, and worthy of its Divine Originator . . . The shadow of His glory rested
visibly on the stupendous objects that composed that magnificent
scene; words are perfectly inadequate to describe the impression
it made upon my mind—the emotions it produced (37) [25].

She is entirely conventional in her preference for this kind of landscape. In his unfinished essay "The Sublime and the Beautiful,"
Wordsworth suggested that exactly these components of a scene—a
mountain, a waterfall, a mighty river—best convey that "sensation of
sublimity" resulting from the interpenetration of "a sense of individual
form or forms; a sense of duration; and a sense of power."[3] As David
Stouck observes, the "Wordsworthian stance was for Mrs. Moodie not
just a learned set of attitudes or an affected literary pose, but something integral to her personality—a definition of self fundamental to
survival in the backwoods."[4] And Susan Joan Wood reminds us that
the outlook of early Canadians in general was complex, even contradictory: "Educated British emigrants brought with them a mental baggage of Burkes's sublime, Chateaubriand's romanticism, Rousseau's
Noble Savage, Wordsworth's pantheism, and the seductive promises of
pamphlets published by Canadian land-speculation companies. Visions of verdant prospects mixed with the desire for freedom and prosperity, and the more prosaic need for food and shelter."[5]

Such rhapsodies as that at Stony Lake occur more frequently early
in *Roughing It in the Bush*, when the naive heroine is travelling up the
St Lawrence, than later when, ill and exhausted, she is struggling to
survive off the land. But throughout the book, whenever she finds herself by a lake or river her spirits are lifted. She tells us she became reconciled to Mrs Joe's cottage because of the little brook rolling by its
window, the sound of which created in her "a feeling of mysterious
awe" (134) [90]. Later she interrupts her description of a difficult winter journey through the forest to observe that: "The most renowned of
our English rivers dwindle into little muddy rills when compared with
the sublimity of the Canadian waters. No language can adequately express the solemn grandeur of her lake and river scenery; the glorious
islands that float, like visions from fairy land, upon the bosom of these
azure mirrors of her cloudless skies" (266) [177]. And once the cedar
swamp in front of her bush-home is cleared away and she has a view
of the lake, her attitude to that place changes too: "By night and day,
in sunshine or in storm, water is always the most sublime feature in a
landscape, and no view can be truly grand in which it is wanting. From

---

3. "The Sublime and the Beautiful," in *The Prose Works of William Wordsworth*, W. J. B. Owen
   and J. W. Smyser, eds. (Oxford: Clarendon Press, 1974), 2:356–7; 351.
4. David Stouck, " 'Secrets of the Prison-House': Mrs. Moodie and the Canadian Imagination,"
   The Dalhousie Review 54 (Autumn 1974): 465.
5. Susan Joan Wood, *The Land in Canadian Prose, 1849–1945*, Carleton Monographs in English Language and Literature (Ottawa: Carleton University Press, 1988), 96.

a child, it always had the most powerful effect upon my mind . . . Half
the solitude of my forest home vanished when the lake unveiled its
bright face to the blue heavens, and I saw sun, and moon, and stars,
and waving trees reflected there" (306) [204].

Her perception of sublimity in a landscape obviously depends on
the presence of certain features—generally, bodies of water. Moreover,
it is only when she is at leisure to contemplate the scenery that we
find such passages. But as apprehension of the sublime is acknowledged to occur in moments of private meditation, and not of intense
activity, it is hardly surprising that when she represents herself as hard
at work on her farm, we get little or no natural description: the landscape then simply forms the background to labour. A half-starved
nursing mother, digging potatoes, has little occasion for transcendent
communion with nature![6]

But this is just to say that the representation of landscape in Roughing It in the Bush owes as much to literary and social expectations as
to Moodie's particular experience—as it always does with writers of
every period. However, Marian Fowler argues that "the force of literary
convention is . . . seen in Susanna's response to Nature. It was not until the twentieth century that writers and painters such as Emily Carr
began to realize that 'the old way of seeing was inadequate to express
this big country of ours' and that Canada 'had to be sensed, passed
through live minds.' " She dismisses "the aesthetic notions of Lord
Shaftesbury and Edmund Burke" as transmitted through English Romantic poetry as contributing to a "garrison mentality," because writers like Moodie wax "most eloquent over mountain precipices and
gushing waterfalls" and ignore their own backyards.[7]

It is true that Moodie does not appreciate all aspects of her wilderness environs equally. Like most folk living in Ontario, then as now,
she prefers open vistas of water and hills to impenetrable barriers of

6. Critics are finally beginning to pay attention to Moodie as a gendered subject, as a young
    isolated mother. For welcome insights in this area, see Helen M. Buss, Mapping Ourselves:
    Canadian Women's Autobiography in English (Montreal and Kingston: McGill-Queen's Uni-
    versity Press, 1993), 84–94, and Bina Freiwald, " 'The tongue of woman': The Language of
    the Self in Moodie's Roughing It in the Bush," in Re(Dis)covering Our Foremothers: Nine-
    teenth-Century Canadian Women Writers, Lorraine McMullen, ed. (Ottawa: University of
    Ottawa Press, 1990), 155–172.
        Carl Ballstadt's study of Moodie's letters to her husband explores some of the intimate de-
    tail she felt constrained to leave out of her narrative; see " 'The Embryo Blossom': Susanna
    Moodie's Letters to Her Husband in Relation to Roughing It in the Bush," Re(Dis)covering
    Our Foremothers, 137–145. As Sidonie Smith remarks: "An androcentric genre, autobiogra-
    phy demands the public story of the public life . . . When woman chooses to leave behind
    cultural silence and to pursue autobiography, she chooses to enter the public arena. But she
    can speak with authority only insofar as she tells a story that her audience will read." A Po-
    etics of Women's Autobiography: Marginality and the Fictions of Self-Representation (Bloom-
    ington: Indiana University Press, 1987), 52.
7. Marian Fowler, "Roughing It in the Bush: A Sentimental Novel," in Beginnings, vol. 2 of The
    Canadian Novel, John Moss, ed. (Toronto: NC Press, 1980), 93. Similarly, Les McLeod con-
    tends that "pioneer writers sometimes could not 'see' the Canadian landscape because of
    their old-world mind-set" in Cold Stars: The Movement Selfward in Late Nineteenth-Century
    Canadian Poetry (diss., University of Calgary, 1981), 7; and Gordon Johnston argues: "The
    relative failure of the imagination in Canada before the Confederation poets is due to its
    lack of engagement in the present world" in "Duncan Campbell Scott," Canadian Writers
    and Their Works Poetry Series: 2, Robert Lecker, Jack David and Ellen Quigley, eds.
    (Toronto: ECW, 1983), 243. In most cases what such critics seem to intend by "the present
    world" is the world as their own age views it.

trees or muddy swamps; sunny skies to overcast ones; flowers to mosquitoes. But such rational preferences can hardly account for the patronizing way she has been treated. In fact, the conventional view of Moodie is the more peculiar in that very little of *Roughing It in the Bush* is about nature at all: her chief preoccupation throughout the book is how her family learned to take care of themselves, and she sketches for us the comical or dangerous people they met, and the various events that overtook them, in the course of their adventures. Most of the difficulties the Moodies encounter result from their own financial and practical ineptitude, or from the mischief or mistakes of neighbours and servants as recounted in chapters like "Uncle Joe and His Family," "Burning the Fallow" and "The Little Stumpy Man." The least of their "disappointed hopes" in the chapter of that name is that wet weather spoils their wheat crop: their debts result from Mr Moodie's foolish investment of all their money in worthless stock, and their immediate hardship from the cruelty of a "ruffian squatter" who first steals their bull and then drowns all their pigs.

During these hard times, far from being their adversary, the wilderness actually provides for them: they live on fish, squirrel, deer and dandelion coffee. But the comfort Moodie consistently derives from nature is ignored by critics like R. D. MacDonald, who describes the movement in the book as "from romantic anticipation to disillusionment, from nature as beautiful and benevolent to nature as a dangerous taskmaster. The story moves from her experience of the sublime to her catalogue of near disasters."[8] Surely what the narrative pattern reveals is not that Moodie's feeling for nature changes; rather, preoccupied as she is by all the near disasters caused by incompetent *people*, she has less time and inclination for "experience of the sublime." Nowhere does she blame nature itself for her situation; on the contrary, she suggests that all the evil to be found around her can be located in the human populace: "The unpeopled wastes of Canada must present the same aspect to the new settler that the world did to our first parents after their expulsion from the Garden of Eden; all the sin which could defile the spot . . . is concentrated in their own persons" (268) [179].

To Ramsay Cook, Moodie's observation of the lack of superstition in Canada is evidence that: "It was not merely the belief that moral order lay in European civilization, and moral chaos in nature, that prevented Mrs. Moodie and other nineteenth-century Canadian writers from leaving their garrison. It was a conviction that they would find nothing outside to stimulate their imaginations."[9] Once again, Susanna has her wrist slapped for rejecting nature: this time, however, because she is thought to find it at once morally chaotic and imaginatively uninspiring.

But Cook's argument is actually quite unusual; most critics accuse

8. R. D. MacDonald, "Design and Purpose," *Canadian Literature* 51 (Winter 1972): 30.
9. Ramsay Cook, "Imagining a North American Garden: Some Parallels & Differences in Canadian & American Culture," *Canadian Literature* 103 (Winter 1984): 13–14.

her of projecting too much, rather than too little, onto the world around her. They use her admission of "this foolish dread of encountering wild beasts in the woods I never could wholly shake off" to convict her of a pathological fear of nature itself—although this is like arguing that anyone afraid of traffic accidents is implicitly rejecting all of modern technology. The most influential work in this regard is Margaret Atwood's poetic sequence *The Journals of Susanna Moodie*, wherein the protagonist's phobia represents a fear of her own instinctual side, and the self-knowledge she achieves through wilderness exile is imaged as her gradual transformation into a nature-spirit.

The process begins as soon as she arrives in the bush where Atwood has her declare "I need wolf's eyes to see / the truth" ("Further Arrivals," ll.20–1).[1] She then conceives of her husband as a shapeshifter who changes not only himself but

> . . . may change me also
> with the fox eye, the owl
> eye, the eightfold
> eye of the spider. ("The Wereman," ll.18–21)

Atwood's Moodie recognizes that "In time the animals / arrived to inhabit me" ("Departure from the Bush," ll.6–7), but she is unable to open herself entirely to them and finally leaves without having incorporated the knowledge they offer. Nonetheless, years later, she is haunted by the memory of one of her bush-neighbours, and his identification with the forest creatures. In "Dream 2: Brian the Still-Hunter" Brian declares "every time I aim, I feel / my skin grow fur / my head heavy with antlers" (ll.13–15). Finally, in old age she herself admits to longing for the transformation she resisted earlier ("Wish: Metamorphosis to Heraldic Emblem"). So Atwood grants it to her in death, making her become an underground spirit threatening the eventual collapse of civilization back into wilderness in "Alternate Thoughts from Underground" and "Resurrection."

Atwood's sequence has both symbolic coherence and dramatic power. But as Stouck remarks, in her own works "Mrs. Moodie never conceives of herself as becoming part of the primal landscape."[2] Indeed, as R. P. Bilan suggests: "The values of the real Susanna Moodie, with her pious Christianity, have been reversed completely by Atwood. In *Life in the Clearings* Susanna Moodie remarked: " 'Light! give me more light!' were the dying words of Goethe; and this should be the constant prayer of all rational souls to the Father of light." Atwood has none of Moodie's commitment to rationality and to Christianity—to light. Rather, Atwood wants the irrational, the dark side of nature and of the self, given its place."[3]

Although Bilan underestimates Moodie's respect for the irrational

1. Margaret Atwood, *The Journals of Susanna Moodie* (Toronto: Oxford University Press, 1970). All further quotations are from this edition.
2. Stouck, " 'Secrets of the Prison-House,' " 472 n. 4.
3. R. P. Bilan, "Margaret Atwood's *'Journals of Susanna Moodie,' " Canadian Poetry* 2 (Spring/Summer 1978): 9.

(throughout *Roughing It* she speculates about such topics as mental telepathy and the power of prayer), Atwood's fascination with darkness is indeed far from anything Moodie herself has to say on the subject, such as the following:

> The holy and mysterious nature of man is yet hidden from himself; he is still a stranger to the movements of that inner life, and knows little of its capabilities and powers. A purer religion, a higher standard of moral and intellectual training may in time reveal all this. Man still remains a half-reclaimed savage; the leaven of Christianity is slowly and surely working its way, but it has not yet changed the whole lump, or transformed the deformed into the beauteous child of God. Oh, for that glorious day! It is coming. The dark clouds of humanity are already tinged with the golden radiance of the dawn, but the sun of righteousness has not yet arisen upon the world with healing on his wings; the light of truth still struggles in the womb of darkness, and man stumbles on to the fulfilment of his sublime and mysterious destiny. (*Roughing It*, 469) [316–17].

Far from yearning for union with nature, Moodie looks forward to half-savage humanity's evolution to a higher spiritual and intellectual plane.

Of course some critics are content, like Sherill E. Grace, "not to assess the accuracy of Atwood's interpretation of Moodie but to explore a few aspects of their literary relationship . . . we do not need to know the *Journals* to appreciate Moodie's work, any more than we need to have read Moodie in order to recognize the power of Atwood's poems."[4] And if the poems are read in the context of Atwood's *œuvre* alone, there can be no possible objection to her creative appropriation of this, or any other, historical material. Indeed, the achievement of *The Journals of Susanna Moodie* is that it weaves together so irresistibly many of Atwood's dominant themes and obsessions. Perhaps most obvious is the premise that those who invade the wilderness will become possessed by it, familiar from early poems like "Progressive Insanities of a Pioneer" and "Backdrop Addresses Cowboy," both published in *The Animals in that Country* (1968). But other recurrent Atwood themes, including the split between the rational and irrational minds, the need for individual growth and self-discovery, and the lack of understanding between men and women, are also prominent in the *Journals*.

The problem, however, is that Atwood's version of Moodie accords so clearly with Frye's statement that she was a "one-woman garrison," and with her own view of Canadian literature as expressed in *Survival*, that it is hard not to read the *Journals* as being criticism as much as poetry.[5] And the fact that Moodie is an historical figure gives an air of authority to what is, ultimately, fiction.

---

4. Sherill E. Grace, "Moodie and Atwood: Notes on a Literary Reincarnation," in *Beginnings*, 73. Eli Mandel takes a similar tack in the introduction to his *Contexts of Canadian Criticism* (Toronto: University of Toronto Press, 1971), when he acknowledges that Atwood's version of Moodie may be "bad criticism," but argues nonetheless that to "tell lies" may be a legitimate creative activity. See pages 24–5.

5. Frye's description of Moodie comes from his "Conclusion to a *Literary History of Canada*"

An alternative—though equally disapproving—image of Moodie is projected by Robertson Davies in *At My Heart's Core*, a Shavian discussion play in which she stars with two other Otonabee pioneers, her sister Catharine Parr Traill and Frances Stewart. The play is set at the time of the Upper Canada Rebellion and Moodie, whom the stage directions describe as having "a ladylike hint of the drill-sergeant in her demeanour," persistently blames the Methodists for stirring up revolution.[6] "When you say Methodist, you say Radical. They all think that the world can be improved by rebellion against authority. It can't," she declares. At the same time, she refuses to make the usual nineteenth-century association between revolution and poetry, for when Traill teases her about leaving the Dissenters out of her rousing "Oath of the Canadian Volunteers," she replies stiffly "I do not consider Methodists, even in a time of crisis, to be the stuff of which poetry is made" (599, 600).

Once again a contemporary writer is reading Moodie through the lenses of his own preoccupations. We are familiar with the association of Protestant repression with joylessness and stifled creativity throughout Davies' work; in this play, he makes Moodie the ancestral source of small-town Ontario rigidity. At the same time, through the temptation plot, he makes her acknowledge the desire for a more passionate life. Like Atwood, Davies sees the hapless pioneer as a split figure, tormented by what she knows but cannot express about life; like Atwood, he presents her as reluctant to confront her inner demons; like Atwood, he makes her incarnate a problem he believes to be central to modern Canadian life.

Born though she was at the turn of the century, Moodie does give little evidence of having been moved by the revolutionary side of the Romantic movement. However, for a brief period just prior to her emigration to Canada, "the stuff of which poetry is made" had in fact been her *own* rebellion against a genteel Anglican upbringing. The title work of her only independent collection of poetry, *Enthusiasm* (1831), is a defense of spiritual ardour, and many other poems in the book draw on biblical stories or pious commonplaces for evangelical purposes. The book is nothing if not defiant, and gives us some insight into the sympathy for both Methodists and political rebels expressed in *Roughing It in the Bush* and *Life in the Clearings*.[7] *Enthusiasm*,

(1965), in *The Bush Garden: Essays on the Canadian Imagination* (Toronto: House of Anansi, 1971), 237.

6. Robertson Davies, *At My Heart's Core*, in *An Anthology of Canadian Literature in English*. Russell Brown and Donna Bennett, eds. (Toronto: Oxford University Press, 1982), 1:597. All further references are to this edition.

7. For example, she observes of her husband's decision to fight the 1837 uprising that "honest backwoodsmen" such as he were "perfectly ignorant of the abuses that had led to the present position of things" (*Roughing It in the Bush*, 413) [277]. And in the introduction to the Canadian edition of the book she goes even farther in expressing sympathy for the rebels (530) [347–48].

As for religious non-conformists, she devotes a whole chapter of *Life in the Clearings versus the Bush* to second-hand accounts of Methodist camp meetings. While describing them as a "disorderly mixture of fanaticism and vanity," she also acknowledges that they may be "the means of making careless people think of the state of their souls" (quotations from the never having been reprinted, has been little known to students of Canadian literature.[8] Probably Davies was unaware of it when he wrote his play in 1950; nor would he have known about Moodie's brief conversion to Congregationalism, made public only with the publication of her letters in 1985.[9] But the spiritual turmoil revealed by both book and letters reminds us that Davies' portrayal of Moodie, however entertaining, is fictitious. His humourless and self-righteous martinet is no closer to the "real" Moodie than is the terrified creature depicted by Atwood. Both authors take considerable liberty with the material available to them and project an emblematic character as a focus for their satire. It is unlikely, however, that either would have felt so free to exaggerate if the intimate self-revelations of their protagonist's letters had been available to them.

These letters, supplemented by the editors' thorough biographical notes, trace Susanna Strickland's increasing interest in and defense of religious non-conformity from about 1828 on, through her conversion in April of 1830, to her return to the established church with her marriage to John Wedderburn Dunbar Moodie a year later. On 2 April 1830 she was admitted to a dissenting congregation; a day later, the following note appeared in the *Athenaeum*: "Shortly will appear, 'Enthusiasm, and other Poems,' by Susanna Strickland, a young lady already favourably known to the public by several compositions of much merit and more promise, in the Annals, etc."[1] On 4 April this young lady took communion for the first time with her new pastor, Andrew Ritchie. Her conversion is movingly described in a letter of 15 April to her confidant James Bird which concludes "I dare not indulge myself dear friend by entering more fully into this subject lest you should think me a mere visionary enthusiast."[2]

1989 reprint, Toronto: McClelland and Stewart, 142; 148). In her description of the churches of Belleville she notes that: "The Wesleyans, who have been of infinite use in spreading the Gospel on the North American continent, possess a numerous and highly respectable congregation in this place" (35).

The social implications of her belief in the freedom of ideas are explored by Robin Matthews in "Susanna Moodie, Pink Toryism and Nineteenth-Century Ideas of Canadian Identity," *The Journal of Canadian Studies* 10 (August 1975): 3–15.

8. Published in an edition of 500 by Smith, Elder and Company of Cornhill, *Enthusiasm* is now available on microtext, courtesy of the Canadian Institute for Historical Microreproductions (Ottawa, 1985). The CIHM number for the book is 38892. All quotations are from this, the first and only British edition.

9. Susanna Moodie, *Letters of a Lifetime*, Carl Ballstadt, Elizabeth Hopkins, and Michael Peterman, eds. (Toronto: University of Toronto Press, 1985). All quotations from Moodie's letters are from this edition, as are biographical facts.

1. Moodie, *Letters of a Lifetime*, 48 n. 7.

2. See Moodie, *Letters of a Lifetime*, 43–48, for all the details of this eventful week. That Pastor Ritchie opposed Susanna's romantic interest is clear from a letter John Moodie wrote to her on 7 September 1830:

> For God's sake my dearest, endeavour to calm your mind and despise the opinions of those who would reduce your best and most exalted feelings to their own standards. The most dangerous of all decievers [sic] are those who first decieve [sic] themselves. I believe Mr. R to be in many respects a good and an honest man, but you must excuse me dear Susan when I say that I consider him as a man whose mind is perverted by fanaticism. This is really the most charitable construction that I can put on his conduct.

Letters of Love and Duty: The Correspondence of Susanna and John Moodie, Carl Ballstadt, Elizabeth Hopkins, and Michael Peterman, eds. (Toronto: University of Toronto Press, 1993), 20–1. Although the Moodie children were baptized Presbyterian, their parents apparently kept some involvement with the evangelical movement since on 8 April 1845 they were

That she should write a poem in defense of religious enthusiasm while fearing to be characterized as an enthusiast herself is indicative not only of self-consciousness but of class consciousness; historically, the educated upper classes had resisted the evangelical movement, disdaining religious fervour as vulgar. Hoxie Neale Fairchild notes that from the mid-eighteenth century on, "with rare exceptions, 'literary' folk will continue to sing of universal harmony and the social glow . . . the Gospels will be for the believing lowbrow, the religion of sentiment for the believing highbrow."[3] One of those rare exceptions, Moodie elects to stand out from her community by calling her book *Enthusiasm* and insisting throughout on the doctrines of sin and redemption.

She first confesses her aspiration to write religious poetry in a letter dated 14 January 1829, when she says she is thinking of undertaking a small volume of psalms and hymns; *Enthusiasm* includes translations of Psalms 40 and 44, and concludes with a "Morning Hymn" and an "Evening Hymn," so perhaps these were part of the original plan. And even her most delicate nature poems emphasize the illusory joys of this world as compared with the certainty of heavenly bliss. More fiercely eschatological are such poems as "The Deluge," "The Vision of Dry Bones," and "The Destruction of Babylon." In this last piece, the prophetic voice not only foretells divine vengeance but insists on its inevitability; in these biblical narratives, human history is repetitive and the past prefigures the future.

Moodie's interest in such topics was by no means original; on the contrary, the biblical passages she chooses to paraphrase were typical exercises for Protestant poets wishing to be thought sublime. As early as 1704 John Dennis, in *The Grounds of Criticism in Poetry*, had called for a return to religious themes in literature, complaining that "modern poetry, being for the most part profane, has . . . very little spirit."[4] It was also Dennis who described passions such as terror, wonder, joy and desire as enthusiastic, because they take us out of ourselves and make us recognize the mystery of things. He clarified the connection between enthusiasm and the sublime as follows: "the sublime is nothing else but a great thought, or great thoughts, moving the soul from its ordinary situation by the enthusiasm which naturally attends them."[5] To Dennis, enthusiasm is the agent of sublimity—an emotional activity which makes possible a metaphysical experience.

The first three lines of Moodie's poem "Enthusiasm" provides a more etymologically correct definition of enthusiasm as divine presence: "OH for the spirit which inspired of old / The seer's prophetic song—the voice that spake / Through Israel's warrior king." In ancient Greece, *enthusiasmos* referred to the trance-like state of an oracle pos-

"excommunicated" from the Church of the Congregational Faith and Order in Belleville "for their disorderly walk and neglect of Christian fellowship." See *Letters of Love and Duty*, 109 nn. 35, 36.

3. Hoxie Neale Fairchild, *Religious Trends in English Poetry, Volume II: 1740–1780, Religious Sentimentalism in the Age of Johnson* (New York: Columbia University Press, 1942), 370.

4. John Dennis, "The Grounds of Criticism in Poetry," in *Eighteenth-Century Critical Essays*, Scott Elledge, ed. (Ithaca, New York: Cornell University Press, 1961), 1:133.

5. Dennis, "The Grounds of Criticism in Poetry," 125.

sessed by Apollo or Dionysus; the term entered the English language in the seventeenth century to describe Anabaptists and other religious sects whose members claimed to experience personal revelation.[6] The word was usually used to imply that this claim was false, or, at best, that its professors were deluded; Robert Burton, in the section of *The Anatomy of Melancholy* (1621) dealing with "Religious Melancholy," was only the first in a long line of theoreticians to propose that religious enthusiasm was a form of hysteria, possibly sexual in origin.[7] He influenced later writers such as the Cambridge Platonist Henry More whose *Enthusiasmus Triumphatus: or, a Brief Discourse of the Nature, Causes, Kinds, and Cure of "Enthusiasm"* came out in 1656, a year after a volume by Meric Casaubon, the title of which spells out the "scientific" attitude to religious dissent: *A Treatise concerning Enthusiasme as it is an Effect of Nature: but is mistaken by many for either Divine Inspiration, or Diabolicall Possession.*[8]

Casaubon analyses many types of enthusiasm, including the "Divinatory," "Contemplative," "Rhetorical," and "Poetical"; as the last two categories suggest, the classical association between religious transcendence and the muse is also conventional in English thought. Thus Blount's *Glossographia* of 1656 defines enthusiasm as "an inspiration, a ravishment of the spirit, divine motion, Poetical fury";[9] a more generous entry than we find a century later in Dr Johnson's dictionary, where enthusiasm is defined first as "a vain belief of private revelation; a vain confidence of divine favour or communication" before also being described as "Heat of imagination" and, finally, as "elevation of fancy."[1] The correspondence between religious and poetical enthusiasm, and the relationship of both to sublime theory, became so entrenched that by 1809 Martin Shee, in "The Elements of Art," would complain of the sublime that "those who talk rationally on other subjects, no sooner touch on this, than they go off in a literary delirium; fancy themselves, like Longinus, 'the great sublime they draw,' and rave like methodists, of inward lights, and enthusiastic emotions, which, if you cannot comprehend, you are set down as un-illumined by the grace of criticism, and excluded from the elect of Taste."[2]

The debate about the nature of enthusiasm engaged many philoso-

6. For the history of the word "enthusiasm," see Susie I. Tucker, *Enthusiasm: A Study in Semantic Change* (Cambridge: Cambridge University Press, 1972), and Sister M. Kevin Whelan, *Enthusiasm in English Poetry of the Eighteenth Century* (Washington: Catholic University of America Press, 1935).
7. According to Clarence M. Webster in "Swift and Some Earlier Satirists of Puritan Enthusiasm," *PMLA* 48 (1933): 1141–2. Molière proposed a similar theory, satirically, in *Tartuffe.*
8. For Meric Casaubon's *A Treatise concerning Enthusiasme* see "A Facsimile Reproduction of the second edition of 1656," (Gainesville, Florida: Scholars' Facsimiles and Reprints, 1970); for Henry More's *Enthusiasmus Triumphatus*, publication 118 of the Augustan Reprint Society (Los Angeles: Williams Andrews Clark Memorial Library, 1966).
9. Blount is quoted by George Williamson in "The Restoration Revolt against Enthusiasm," *Studies in Philology* 30 (1933): 583.
1. *Johnson's Dictionary: A Modern Selection*, E. L. McAdam, Jr. and George Milne, eds. (New York: Random House, 1963), 166.
2. Quoted by Samuel H. Monk in *The Sublime: A Study of Critical Theories in XVIII-Century England* (New York: Modern Language Association, 1935), 3. The fashionable discrimination of sublimity is the subject of Joan Pittock's study, *The Ascendency of Taste: The Achievement of Joseph and Thomas Warton* (London: Routledge and Kegan Paul, 1973).

phers throughout the eighteenth century. Dr Johnson cites Locke as his authority for the contention that "*Enthusiasm* is founded neither on reason nor divine revelation, but rises from the conceits of a warmed or overheated braine."[3] The topic also preoccupied Locke's pupil, Lord Shaftesbury, in his *Letter Concerning Enthusiasm* (1707), and David Hume in his essay *Of Superstition and Enthusiasm* (1741). Even John Wesley found himself drawn into it; although a tireless advocate of the necessity for faith, he nonetheless cautions his followers, in his *Advice to the People called Methodists* (1745), that they should "carefully avoid enthusiasm: impute not the dreams of men to the all-wise God."[4]

Shaftesbury, otherwise Wesley's philosophical opposite in the period, is just as concerned to distinguish between true and false inspiration. Despite his urbane mockery of religious fanaticism in the *Letter Concerning Enthusiasm*, he concedes that

> ENTHUSIASM is wonderfully powerful and extensive; that it is a matter of nice Judgement, and the hardest thing in the world to know fully and distinctly; since even *Atheism* is not exempt from it. For, as some have well remark'd, there have been *Enthusiastical Atheists*. Nor can Divine Inspiration, by its outward Marks, be easily distinguish'd from it. For Inspiration is *a real* feeling of the Divine Presence, and Enthusiasm a *false one*.[5]

But a mere two years later, Shaftesbury rehabilitates enthusiasm, broadening the meaning to include any and all passionate commitments—but most particularly, the ecstatic worship of nature. In *The Moralists* (1709), when the rhapsodies of Theocles convert him to nature-worship, gentlemanly Philocles is embarrassed, for "all those who are deep in this *Romantick* way, are look'd upon, you know, as a People either plainly out of their Wits, or over-run with *Melancholy* and ENTHUSIASM."[6] But he quickly recovers his equilibrium, concluding that "all sound *Love* and *Admiration* is ENTHUSIASM: "The Transports of *Poets*, the Sublime of *Orators*, the Rapture of *Musicians*, the high Strains of the *Virtuosi*; all mere ENTHUSIASM! Even *Learning* it-self, the Love of *Arts* and *Curiositys*, the Spirit of *Travellers* and *Adventurers*; *Gallantry*, *War*, *Heroism*; All, all ENTHUSIASM!"—'Tis enough: I am content to be this *new Enthusiast*, in a way unknown to me before."[7]

This "new enthusiast"—deep in the "Romantick" way, a devotee of

3. *Johnson's Dictionary*, 166.
4. Quoted by Frederick C. Gill in *The Romantic Movement and Methodism: A Study of English Romanticism and the Evangelical Revival* (London: The Epworth Press, 1937), 22. See also Clarke Garrett, *Spirit Possession and Popular Religion from the Camisards to the Shakers* (Baltimore: Johns Hopkins University Press, 1987), 79.
5. Anthony Ashley Cooper, Earl of Shaftesbury, *A Letter Concerning Enthusiasm to My Lord [Sommers], Characteristicks of Men, Manner, Opinions, Times*, 2nd ed., corrected, 1714, 1:52.
6. Shaftesbury, *The Moralists, A Philosophical Rhapsody. Being a Recital of Certain Conversations on Natural and Moral Subjects, Characteristicks of Men, Manners, Opinions, Times*, 2:394. At the beginning of the piece, Philocles describes Theocles to a third party, Palamon, as having "nothing of that savage Air of the vulgar Enthusiastick Kind. All was serene, soft, and harmonious" (218). Shaftesbury takes great care to ensure that his refined enthusiasm for natural beauty should be distinguished from lower-class religious frenzy.
7. Shaftesbury, *The Moralists*, 400.

the sublime—quickly became a fashionable type in literature and life, celebrated by such poets as the eighteen-year-old Joseph Warton in *The Enthusiast, or the Lover of Nature*.[8] The 252 blank verse lines of the revised 1748 version make only tangential reference to established religion; God here is primarily the "architect supreme" (l.137) whose works cannot be rivalled by "art's vain pomps" (l.4).

As Ernest Lee Tuveson notes, until this period, "Christian theologians had asserted that the 'book of nature' demonstrates divine purpose in the universe, but that it was to be read in the light of the higher book, Revelation. An imperfection in the natural order, resulting from the fall, makes natural philosophy alone quite inadequate as the guide to heaven. In the eighteenth century the emphasis gradually is reversed: the book of Revelation is now to be read by the light of stars and sun."[9] The religion of nature transformed social and literary values; not only Warton, but more influential poets like James Thomson spread the new gospel by versifying Shaftesbury. In "Spring" (1728), for example, Thomson writes:

> By swift Degrees the Love of Nature works,
> And warms the Bosom; till at last, sublim'd
> To Rapture, and enthusiastic Heat,
> We feel the present DEITY, and taste
> The joy of GOD to see a happy World.[1]

By the end of the century, it had become commonplace to observe, as Thomas Gray did of the landscape around the Grande Chartreuse: "Not a precipice, not a torrent, not a cliff but is pregnant with religion and poetry."[2]

In *The Prelude*, after describing his sister Dorothy as "a young Enthusiast," Wordsworth declares that "God delights / In such a being; for her common thoughts / Are piety, her life is gratitude."[3] We are so familiar with this philosophy as transmitted by the Romantics that it is difficult for us to recognize its radical implications. But the unresolved questions inherent in sublime theory since the time of Longinus inform the debate about enthusiasm as well. Are natural phenomena sublime by virtue of reflecting their creator, or do they simply manifest certain objective qualities, such as extension and duration, which have

---

8. Joseph Warton, *The Enthusiast, or the Lover of Nature*, in *The Three Wartons: A Choice of Their Verse*, Eric Partridge, ed. (London: Scholartis Press, 1927).
9. Ernest Lee Tuveson, *Imagination as a Means of Grace: Locke and the Aesthetics of Romanticism* (Berkeley: University of California Press, 1960), 57.
1. These are lines 899–903 in the early texts of the poem; they were retained in the complete 1746 version of *The Seasons* but the succeeding twelve lines, anticipating Wordsworth even more clearly, were dropped. See James Thomson, *The Seasons*, James Sambrook, ed. (Oxford: Clarendon Press, 1981).
2. From a letter to Richard West, 16 November 1739, in *The Correspondence of Gray, Walpole, West & Ashton, 1734–1771*, Paget Toynbee, ed. (Oxford: Clarendon Press, 1915), 259. Simon Schama sketches an amusing context for this remark in *Landscape and Memory* (Toronto: Random House, 1995), 447–50.
3. This is the wording in the 1850 version, book XII, ll.151–73. The 1815 version is almost the same, except there Dorothy is a "gentle Visitant" rather than an "Enthusiast," and her life "blessedness." See Book XI, ll.199–223, William Wordsworth, *The Prelude*, Ernest de Selincourt, ed., corrected by Stephen Gill (Oxford: Oxford University Press, 1970).

a powerful effect on the mind? If the latter, can the recognition of such incalculables, by reminding one of the limits of one's understanding, constitute a spiritual experience in and of itself—independent of religion?

In finding God sufficiently revealed through nature, Shaftesbury and his followers (usually described as "deists") were effectively "setting aside all moral precepts and the doctrine of future reward and punishment."[4] This made more orthodox Christians uncomfortable for, although nature-worship was an ally in opposing the spread of scientific materialism, it undermined the traditional role of the Church in mediating for sinners. On the other hand, while evangelical Christians appreciated the deists' emphasis on individual conscience and self-transformation, they strongly objected to any neglect of biblical doctrine.

The coincidence of nature worship and evangelicalism in Moodie's poetry illustrates the logically inconsistent but sentimentally compelling reconciliation of these movements by the nineteenth century.[5] Coming after the Romantic movement, she takes it for granted that nature is spiritually exalting, and that it provides the best evidence for divine presence in the universe. Indeed, even towards the end of her life she claims to prefer the Belleville of thirty years earlier to the bustling town she now inhabits, writing to her friend Allen Ransome on 17 October, 1871: "Allen, the poetic spirit, the love of dear Mother Nature will never die out of my heart. I am just the same enthusiast I ever was and often forget white hairs and wrinkles when my heart swells and my eyes fill with tears at the beauty of some lovely spot that glows from the hand of the great Master."[6] Here she uses the term "enthusiast" as in Warton's poem, to mean one who adores nature. But, as we have seen, in her earlier letters the word had a purely religious connotation. The tension between these two meanings is the catalyst for her blank-verse poem "Enthusiasm," in which she seeks to bridge the gap between the sacred and profane uses of the term and thereby reconcile nature worship with evangelical Christianity to her own satisfaction.

She begins by defining enthusiasm as an innate passion for meaningful activity, the "Parent of genius" to whose "soul-awakening power

---

4. According to C. A. Moore in "The Return to Nature in English Poetry of the Eighteenth Century," *Studies in Philology* 14 (1917): 259.

5. For the gradual convergence of evangelical and Romantic principles, see Richard E. Brantley, *Wordsworth's "Natural Methodism"* (New Haven: Yale University Press, 1975); Hoxie Neale Fairchild, *Religious Trends in English Poetry, Volume III: 1780–1830, Romantic Faith* (New York: Columbia University Press, 1949); Frederick C. Gill, *The Romantic Movement and Methodism*; and Gary Kelly, "Romantic Evangelicalism: Religion, Social Conflict, and Literary Form in Leigh Richmond's *Annals of the Poor*," *English Studies in Canada* 16 (1990): 165–86.

6. Moodie, *Letters of a Lifetime*, 299. Charles Sangster uses the term the same way in *The St. Lawrence and the Saguenay*, published in 1856. Praising the "Thousand Island" area he exclaims: "Isles of o'erwhelming beauty! surely here / The wild enthusiast might live, and dream / His life away" (Stanza VII, ll.2–4). See the edition by D.M.R. Bentley (London, Ontario: Canadian Poetry Press, 1990). Almost eighty years later, Charles G. D. Roberts employs the same vocabulary. In a lecture to the Elson Club of Toronto on 18 March 1933, he says of early Canadian poetry: "In the main it was Nature poetry . . . It was frankly enthusiastic. It was patently sincere . . . [our poets] are all religious . . . They are all incorrigible and unrepentant idealists." "Canadian Poetry in its Relation to the Poetry of England and America," *Canadian Poetry* 3 (Fall/Winter 1978): 81–2.

we owe / The preacher's eloquence, the painter's skill, / The poet's lay, the patriot's noble zeal" and so on (ll.30–4). This allows her to devote most of "Enthusiasm"—from line 70 to line 351 out of a total of 449 lines—to *non*-religious enthusiasts: the poet, the painter, the nature-lover and the warrior. But she has an evangelical agenda: by demonstrating the ultimate dissatisfaction inherent in all earthly pursuits, she intends to prove the superiority of religious enthusiasm to other varieties, and to defend Christianity in particular.

The poet is described in terms familiar to Moodie's public from Beattie's *The Minstrel*, and Shelley's *Alastor*:

> . . . He walks this earth
> Like an enfranchised spirit; and the storms,
> That darken and convulse a guilty world,
> Come like faint peals of thunder on his ear,
> Or hoarser murmurs of the mighty deep,
> Which heard in some dark forest's leafy shade
> But add a solemn grandeur to the scene. (ll.105–11)

But despite his youthful rapture, "penury and dire disease, / Neglect, a broken heart, an early grave!" are all predicted for him, because he has not "tuned his harp to truths divine" (ll.118–20). The painter, on the other hand, is reproached for being "unsatisfied with all that Nature gives" and attempting to "portray Omnipotence" (ll.135–7), since even the effect of sunlight on leaves "is beyond thy art. / All thy enthusiasm, all thy boasted skill, / But poorly imitates a forest tree (ll.173–5).[7]

Moodie appears to be unaware of the aesthetic contradiction she sets up here: the poet is to be saved by abandoning nature for sacred topics—the painter by the reverse procedure! Or perhaps she *is* vaguely aware of some philosophical muddiness, for at this point she drops the topic of artistic enthusiasm and starts to examine the nature-lover instead. He is told in his turn that he will be unable to "read" the natural scene around him properly until he explores the Bible (ll.192–207), but she seems to hold out more hope for his salvation than for the others, perhaps because he is not trying to rival the Creator, but simply to appreciate the creation. At least, this is what is suggested by her statement that "Faith gives a grandeur to created things, / Beyond the poet's lay or painter's art, / Or upward flight of Fancy's eagle wing" (ll.222–5).

---

7. Such admonitions evoke the art-versus-nature debate that was already traditional when Shakespeare wrote Perdita's lecture on flowers in *The Winter's Tale*, IV.iv. But with the cult of enthusiasm the debate gained renewed vigour; for example, William Cowper writes:

> Strange! there should be found
> Who, self-imprison'd in their proud saloons,
> Renounce the odours of the open field
> For the unscented fictions of the loom;
> Who satisfied with only pencil'd scenes
> Prefer to the performance of a God
> Th'inferior wonders of an artist's hand!

The Task, in *Poetical Works*, in H. S. Milford, ed. (London: Oxford University Press, 1967) I, ll.413–19. Of Cowper, Moodie writes to James Bird on 5 September 1828: "His sentiments are noble, excellent, sublime! . . . I consider him as a Reformer of the Vices of mankind to stand unrivalled."

We then move out of the natural setting for the only time in the poem to visit "Glory's intrepid champion" (l.259), who seems to stand for all those with *worldly* passions, for

> He too is an enthusiast!—his zeal
> Impels him onward with resistless force,
> Severs his heart from nature's kindred ties,
> And feeds the wild ambition which consumes
> All that is good and lovely in his path. (ll.265–69)

Perhaps because his ambitions are even farther from the true path than those of the poet or painter, twice as much space is devoted to the soldier's portrait: 105 lines to their fifty-three. It is interesting that Moodie was married to a former soldier herself by the time "Enthusiasm" was published, for she becomes absorbed in imagining a fictional childhood for her hypothetical man of war, trying to figure out what would turn an ardent soul towards such a brutal vocation. (One is also reminded that her first publication was an inspirational tale for young readers, *Spartacus: A Roman Story*, published in 1822; clearly she was drawn towards military heroes in spite of herself.)

But despite her sympathy for all the enthusiasts she describes, Moodie argues that their secular interests are just "base and joyless vanities which man / Madly prefers to everlasting bliss!" (ll.68–9). In this regard, her poem has close affinities with an earlier poem also called "Enthusiasm," published by John Byrom in 1757. In this work, after reminding the genteel reader who scorns religious fervour that everyone has obsessions, Byrom suggests "That which concerns us therefore is to see / What Species of Enthusiasts we be" (ll.250–1).[8] He enumerates several such "species," beginning with classicists, Egyptologists and biblical scholars who, because their erudition is misdirected, are criticized more severely than the frivolous habitués of coffee-houses and ballrooms. All these folk share one attribute however; "in one Absurdity they chime, / To make religious Enthusiasm a Crime" (ll.196–7).[9]

Byrom's complaint is reiterated by Moodie; two generations later, she still bemoans the fact that:

> The world allows its votaries to feel
> A glowing ardour, an intense delight,
> On every subject but the one that lifts
> The soul above its sensual, vain pursuits,
> And elevates the mind and thoughts to God!
> Zeal in a sacred cause alone is deemed
> An aberration of our mental powers. (ll.45–51)

Despite the similarity of Moodie's argument to Byrom's, the two poets have completely different styles, he writing satirical and didactic coup-

---

8. John Byrom, "Enthusiasm. A Poetical Essay," in *Miscellaneous Poems* (Manchester: J. Harrop, 1773), 2:22–41.
9. The text actually reads "to make *Entheasm* a Crime," (my emphasis) but I believe this to be a misprint.

lets, she rather Romantic blank verse. His tone is urbane; hers, passionate. Byrom never succumbs to enthusiasm himself, but Moodie is unable to resist it, even when describing enthusiasms she claims to deplore.

Moreover, Byrom's main focus in his poem is theology, while Moodie is preoccupied with character and setting. Herein lies the paradoxical failure of her poem. Her strengths as a writer—even in these early years—clearly lie in the dramatic portrayal of character and in vivid description, and not in philosophical analysis.[1] These very strengths undermine her stated purpose in "Enthusiasm," where the lengthy and persuasive rendering of the allegedly "joyless vanities" of earthly life is followed by thirty-five lines on the vague but "everlasting bliss" to be anticipated in the New Jerusalem: thirty-five lines which emphasize, by contrast, the genuine seductiveness of those worldly passions she argues we ought to renounce.

To solve this predicament she proposes that experiences which cannot be described by language must be more powerful than anything of which one can speak, an hypothesis which leads her to relinquish the word "enthusiasm" itself as inadequate to convey

> That deep devotion of the heart which men
> Miscall enthusiasm!—Zeal alone deserves
> The name of madness in a worldly cause.
> Light misdirected ever leads astray;
> But hope inspired by faith will guide to heaven! (ll.411–15)

The ineffability of the sublime had long been acknowledged; one of the chief proofs of sublime experience had always been that it rendered language inadequate. Nonetheless, given that she herself has elected to call such "deep devotion of the heart" *enthusiasm* in the poem's opening, Moodie's conclusion is somewhat perverse. We are left with a poem framed by rhetorical, and filled with lyrical and dramatic, self-contradiction.

She even affirms exactly those analogies between religious and worldly enthusiasts which she has just rejected, declaring that "To win the laurel wreath the soldier fights; / To free his native land the patriot bleeds; / And to secure his crown the martyr dies!" (ll.416–18). Clearly she hasn't overcome her admiration for martial pursuits despite condemning war as an ignoble subject for enthusiasm. Similarly, though she deplores the inadequacy of poetry and painting to represent spiritual truths, she is drawn to artistic expression. She is ambivalent about

---

1. A letter to Richard Bentley, dated 22 January 1856, poignantly reminds us that Moodie was aware of her particular talents. She confides that all her early works had been dramatic, but that she

> was persuaded by foolish fanaticks, with whom I got entangled, to burn these MSS, it being they said unworthy of a christian [sic] to write for the stage . . . the little headings in blank verse, that often occur in my books are snatches that memory retains of these tragedies. Nature certainly meant me for a dramatic writer, and having outlived my folly, I really regret the martyrdom of these vigorous children of my young brain. Don't *laugh at me*. That portion of my life, would make a strange revelation of sectarianism. But it may rest with my poor tragedies in oblivion. I do not wish it to meet with their firey dooms or the ridicule of the world.

almost everything she says: she wants to concede, like Byrom, that it is human nature to be enthusiastic, but she also insists that religious enthusiasm is different in kind, not simply in degree. Though passionately moved by nature, she mistrusts this impulse in herself, worrying that exaltation of the sublime as perceived through the creation may undermine appreciation of the Creator.[2] And even as she is writing "Enthusiasm," she worries about being considered "a mere visionary enthusiast" by her friends.

It has become commonplace to describe Moodie as ambivalent. Indeed, ambivalence and self-contradiction pervade *Roughing It in the Bush* to such an extent that Atwood describes her behaviour as "paranoid schizophrenia." She came up with this label in her afterword to *The Journals of Susanna Moodie*, published in 1970 and full of post-Centennial feeling about the way "we" live in Canada. Atwood makes it very clear that for her Moodie symbolizes a problem in contemporary Canadian identity: "We are all immigrants to this place even if we were born here: the country is too big for anyone to inhabit completely, and in the parts unknown to us we move in fear, exiles and invaders. This country is something that must be chosen—it is so easy to leave—and if we do choose it we are still choosing a violent duality" (62).

Some critics have continued to interpret Moodie's ambivalent response to life in the bush as representative of some hypothetical national predicament; Gaile McGregor, for example, states solemnly that "the question arises as to what Susanna Moodie's experience implies for Canadian experience as a whole."[3] At its most glib and reductive, such analysis sees Susanna not only as sick herself, but symbolic of the sickness that is in others.

But, as another poet wrote, a few years after Moodie, "Do I contradict myself? / Very well then. . . . I contradict myself; / I am large. . . . I contain multitudes."[4] Walt Whitman is exceptional not only in tolerating self-contradiction but in boasting about it; most writers feel the literary imperatives of "unity," "coherence" and "closure" as strongly as their critics; anticipating these critics, they banish discontinuity from their works. Moodie does not, either in an early work like "Enthusiasm" or in her later Canadian memoirs. Her opinions are robustly inconsistent: a sentimentalist, she is a defender of the class system; an advocate of progress, she is nostalgic for primitive simplicity; a Ro-

---

2. The same mistrust of nature which compromised Susanna Moodie's delight in the outdoors was present in Northrop Frye's religious environment—but at an earlier, more formative stage. As I. S. MacLaren notes, the wilderness appeared "much more sinister to a Methodist than to a Roman Catholic or Anglican . . . Were Northrop Frye not raised chiefly by Methodist grandparents of the circuit-riding era, it is doubtful that the garrison mentality would ever have been so foundational an aspect of his psyche or so strong a light on his view of Canada." "Buried Nuggets," *Canadian Poetry* 34 (Spring/Summer 1994): 103.

3. Gaile McGregor, *The Wacousta Syndrome: Explorations in the Canadian Langscape* (Toronto: University of Toronto Press, 1985), 38. So also Robert Kroetsch: "We read her and wonder in horror—is *this* where Canadian culture comes from? The answer is—alas! as Mrs Moodie would say—in very strong part, yes." "Carnival and Violence: A Meditation" in *The Lovely Treachery of Words: Essays Selected and New* (Toronto: Oxford University Press, 1989), 98.

4. Walt Whitman, "Song of Myself (1855)," *Leaves of Grass*, Malcolm Cowley, ed. (New York: Viking, 1959), ll.1314–16.

mantic nature-worshipper, she is terrified of wild animals. And not only does she not have a consistent point of view, her writing doesn't appear to conform to the conventions of any given genre! Thus Michael Peterman notes of *Roughing It in the Bush*, "containing elements of poetry, fiction, travel writing, autobiography, and social analysis, it eludes definition."[5]

But as many theorists of autobiography have remarked, formal impurity is typical of life-writing in general. It may be inescapable, given the mandate of self-representation: as Sidonie Smith notes, "the generic contract engages the autobiographer in a doubled subjectivity—the autobiographer as protagonist of her story and the autobiographer as narrator. Through that doubled subjectivity she pursues her fictions of selfhood by fits and starts."[6] Atwood makes the connection between the character's self-contradictions and the discontinuities of the text when she describes *Roughing It* as a collection of "disconnected anecdotes" held together only by "the personality of Mrs Moodie."[7] But she implies that this is an idiosyncratic failing, rather than normal procedure in a work of this kind.

Because *Roughing It in the Bush* was brought out by Richard Bentley, the pre-eminent publisher of English travel literature of his day, it is usually seen as a memoir of, or guide to, settlement. It was originally called *Canadian Sketches*, and contained other material later excised by the publisher. Reminding us of the book's publication history, John Thurston states flatly that "Susanna Moodie did not write *Roughing It in the Bush*. In fact, *Roughing It in the Bush* was never written. Susanna Moodie and *Roughing It in the Bush* are interchangeable titles given to a collaborative act of textual production whose origin cannot be limited to one person or one point in time."[8] Thurston is only taking to its logical extreme Carl Klinck's argument in the introduction to his

5. Michael Peterman, "Susanna Moodie (1803–1885)," in *Canadian Writers and Their Works* Fiction Series: I, Robert Lecker, Jack David and Ellen Quigley, eds. (Toronto: ECW, 1983), 80–1. Elsewhere he described the work as a "covert autobiography"; see *"Roughing It in the Bush* as Autobiography," in *Reflections: Autobiography and Canadian Literature*, K. P. Stich, ed. (Ottawa: University of Ottawa Press, 1988), 35–45. Since I wrote this essay, Peterman published his most sustained analysis of the work, *This Great Epoch of Our Lives: Susanna Moodie's "Roughing It in the Bush"* (Toronto: ECW, 1996). His reading of the book here concurs with mine: he calls it "an autobiography concerned with growth and personal development, with the awakening of one's powers and understanding, even as one learns to respect the limits of one's capacities" (102).
6. Sidonie Smith, *A Poetics of Women's Autobiography*, 17–18. She explores the textual paradoxes specific to female self-representation on pages 44–62. William C. Spengemann acknowledges the generic instability of autobiography by dividing it into four "procedures"—"historical self-explanation, philosophical self-scrutiny, poetic self-expression and poetic self-invention"—broad enough to embrace fictional works like *David Copperfield* and *The Scarlet Letter*. See *The Forms of Autobiography: Episodes in the History of a Literary Genre* (New Haven: Yale University Press, 1980), xiv.
7. Atwood, *The Journals of Susanna Moodie*, 62.
8. John Thurston, "Rewriting *Roughing It*" in *Future Indicative: Literary Theory and Canadian Literature*, John Moss, ed. (Ottawa: University of Ottawa Press, 1987), 195. His argument is reminiscent of Paul de Man's that autobiography is representative only of textuality, not experience, in "Autobiography as De-Facement," *Modern Language Notes* 94 (1979): 919–30. Thurston too has published a book on Moodie since I completed this essay. In *The Work of Words: The Writing of Susanna Strickland Moodie* (Montreal and Kingston: McGill-Queen's University Press, 1996), he explores further the reasons for, and effects of, the instability of Moodie's text. His chapter on "Literary Affiliation and Religious Crisis" provides new insight into the writing and publication of *Enthusiasm*.

1962 New Canadian Library edition of *Roughing It* that each generation of readers deserves a new version of the book. Following these principles, Klinck himself cut out not only all of Mr Moodie's contributions and Susanna's poems, but also a great many "reports of pleasant excursions, and others of pathetic experiences."⁹

What goes unacknowledged, however, is the paradox implicit in the contention that "Care has been taken to maintain the balance of the original, and to enhance the unique effect by concentration."¹ Klinck's method of enhancing by "concentration" is far from maintaining even the pretence of "balance," since almost all his editorial cuts come from the second volume of *Roughing It*. The pleasant excursions he deletes are those that show Moodie enjoying her surroundings; the pathetic experiences represent her as not only more resourceful herself but better able to assist others. The abridgement emphasizes her early difficulties and underplays her later development; we don't see Moodie learning from experience. She becomes a more static character, locked in her ambivalence, unable to progress. Curiously, she becomes more consistent in her inconsistency!

And this Moodie is the one familiar to most readers until the last decade. But the editions of the 1980s have restored the original *Roughing It in the Bush*; contemporary editors have more patience with Moodie's story, and more respect for her text.² The tide has turned in literary criticism; we have more tolerance these days for uncategorizable works. Indeed, the greatest praise now goes to those which break conventions and rupture forms. But Moodie is not a literary iconoclast; we must not overcompensate by making her a prophet of post-modernism. Her work, despite its inconsistency—indeed, in part because of it—fits nicely with other travel memoirs of the period.

Perhaps, then, our problem with Moodie has simply been that of historical perspective. As Laura Groening acutely remarked, "the twentieth century tends to value autobiographies for the psychological truths that they reveal . . . Mrs. Moodie, unlike Atwood and the twentieth century in general, had very little use for the unconscious either as the repository for valuable truths about the human personality or as the wellspring of the creative urge. She believed that an autobiography was a document with a social purpose."³ This social purpose is the setting forth of one's life as an example from which others may learn. Certainly Moodie states her own agenda clearly enough: "If these sketches should prove the means of deterring one family from sinking their property, and shipwrecking all their hopes, by going to reside in the backwoods of Canada, I shall consider myself amply repaid for revealing the secrets of the

9. Carl F. Klinck, introduction to *Roughing It in the Bush*, by Susanna Moodie (Toronto: McClelland and Stewart, 1962), x.
1. Klinck, introduction to *Roughing It in the Bush*, x.
2. These editions include, besides that of McClelland and Stewart published in 1989, Carl Ballstadt's for the Centre for Editing Early Canadian Texts (Ottawa: Carleton University Press, 1988), and one published in London by Virago Press in 1986 (with a foreword by Margaret Atwood) which excludes Dunbar Moodie's contributions.
3. Laura Groening, "The Journals of Susanna Moodie: A Twentieth-Century Look at a Nineteenth-Century Life," *Studies in Canadian Literature* 8 (1983): 166–7. As Groening notes, "Atwood's Susanna . . . never has a social response to anything" (173).

prison-house, and feel that I have not toiled and suffered in the wilderness in vain" (489) [330]. Many times in her book she insists that the middle classes are not suited to the hard physical labour required to carve out a homestead, and should emigrate only to towns and cities. The Moodies had been given this very advice prior to their own emigration, and therefore settled on a rented farm. And Mr Moodie admits that, had they stayed on this Coburg property and bought the two adjacent, they would have become prosperous—but he couldn't resist speculation, buying uncleared land at five shillings an acre (248) [165].

On the other hand, the Moodies' frustration with vulgar and thieving neighbours whose unceasing scrutiny made them ashamed of their genteel ineptitude made the prospect of isolation rather appealing. Susanna, in particular, is mortified by her new situation. When she arrived in Canada, she expected to achieve the financial independence suitable to her station in British society by hiring others to work. Her shock at being required to perform physical labour herself is exacerbated by her incompetence at virtually every chore.[4]

However, the family's backwoods tenure results in a gradual but impressive transformation in Susanna's character, one she herself acknowledges with pride. "If we occasionally suffered severe pain, we as often experienced great pleasure, and I have contemplated a well-hoed ridge of potatoes on that bush farm, with as much delight as in years long past I had experienced in examining a fine painting in some well-appointed drawing-room" (353) [237]. She becomes self-reliant, strong and brave to the point where she can be a model to others, rather than a charity case herself. And this other plot surely undercuts the "social purpose" of the story. This, I think, is where the real dissonance, and the real interest, of the text resides. Moodie's practical advice not to emigrate is at cross-purposes with her personal example of spiritual development through adversity. Given what we now know about Moodie's religious background, it is tempting to see these two plots in terms of High Church conventionality versus Evangelical rebellion. Susanna Strickland, dutiful daughter of a good family, is forced to emigrate only to warn others to avoid her sad fate. Susanna Moodie, self-made woman, embraces her suffering as the route to enlightenment.

This second plot is also suggested by evocations of the most famous work of Protestant travel literature, *The Life and Strange Surprising Adventures of Robinson Crusoe* (1719). Perhaps the most obvious reference occurs when that absurd dilettante, Tom Wilson, reproduces

---

4. It is poignant to read Moodie's description of "the youthful bard" in "Enthusiasm" in the light of her later experience in Canada:

> . . . he cannot comprehend
> The speculative aims of worldly men:
> Dearer to him a leaf, or bursting bud,
> Culled fresh from Nature's treasury, than all
> The golden dreams that cheat the care-worn crowd.
> His world is all within, He mingles not
> In their society; he cannot drudge
> To win the wealth they toil to realize. (ll.89–96)

Crusoe's famous blunder of building a boat too far from water to launch it (81–2) [55]. But Moodie too is a kind of Victorian female Crusoe, seeing herself as "shipwrecked"; indeed, she presents herself as even more isolated than she really was, her husband always away, friends and relatives too far to help, children invisible and inaudible, offering no hugs, chatter, or amusing games.[5]

As a female Crusoe, Moodie is initially blasted by despair but ultimately saved by industry and faith. Reading between the lines, one could argue that she is saved by nothing more than subterfuge and patronage, since it is her desperate (and secret) letter to Sir George Arthur that results in her husband's being appointed the sheriff in Belleville. But Moodie is able to read her own actions as divinely inspired; part of a pattern of omnipotent care. She insists that Providence ultimately rewards faith, however mysterious its workings in the interim.

Defoe makes clear the pedagogical justification for travel writing on the first page of his preface: "The story is told with modesty, with seriousness, and with a religious application of events to the uses to which wise men always apply them, viz. to the instruction of others by this example, and to justify and honour the wisdom of Providence in all the variety of our circumstances, let them happen how they will."[6] Such works were often read as religious parables even when the moral was not explicit. For example, William Cowper found inspiration in the same matter-of-fact source as Defoe for his "Verses supposed to be Written by Alexander Selkirk." Though Selkirk never wrote anything himself about his solitary four-year exile on the island of Juan Fernandez, and though the others who popularized his story emphasized his pragmatism and adaptability, Cowper, like Defoe, saw the sailor's ordeal as a religious trial. Indeed, Martin Priestman notes that for Cowper "the travel-narratives of Cook and of many explorers were almost tantamount to prophetic books, revealing God's intentions for England (or sometimes, as in the incident from Anson described in 'The Castaway,' for Cowper himself)."[7]

At the same time, Cowper felt the need to speak directly of his own life on the confessional model in *The Task*. Priestman remarks of this verse memoir that "the theoretical justification for such an experiment on such a scale rested on the Evangelical assumption that the private experience of 'religious persons' ought to be opened to the public in the name of morality and religion."[8] And we have already noted how

5. T. D. MacLulich offers a slightly different perspective on Moodie as Crusoe in "Crusoe in the Backwoods: A Canadian Fable?" *Mosaic* 9 (Winter 1976): 115–26. That *Robinson Crusoe* may also be read as a central and enduring fable of imperial conquest does not detract from, indeed adds to, its interest as a work of Protestant spirituality. For a survey of approaches to the text as colonialist discourse, see *Decolonizing Fictions* by Diana Brydon and Helen Tiffin (Sydney: Dangaroo, 1993), 42–7. For the female Crusoe as a literary figure, see also Elizabeth Thompson, *The Pioneer Woman: A Canadian Character Type* (Montreal and Kingston: McGill-Queen's University Press, 1991), 25–6.

6. Daniel Defoe, preface to *The Life and Strange Surprising Adventures of Robinson Crusoe* (1719; reprint, London: J. M. Dent, 1945), 1.

7. Martin Priestman, *Cowper's "Task": Structure and Influence* (Cambridge: Cambridge University Press, 1983), 36.

8. Priestman, *Cowper's "Task"*, 26. Priestman traces the conjunction of blank verse and the Protestant tradition of enthusiasm back through Cowper to Edward Young's *Night Thoughts*,

profoundly Moodie admired Cowper, particularly during those years when she was most evangelical in her own religious thought (see note 7, p. 503).

It is not surprising then, given her background, that *Canadian Sketches* should take the form of a spiritual memoir, particularly as travel and agriculture, the organizing activities of *Roughing It in the Bush*, were of exceptional symbolic significance in the Protestant literature of confession. To keep such a record was a common practice among "enthusiasts" such as she had once been. As G. A. Starr notes, the evangelical sects held that: "Since every man is responsible for the well-being of his own soul, he must mark with care each event or stage in its development . . . The need for constant, almost clinical self-analysis was generally recognized . . . diary-keeping frequently proved helpful in documenting and compiling one's spiritual case-history."[9] This model of discourse subscribes to an extra-literary notion of unity: it points beyond the text to the author's life for authentication—exactly what Atwood complains of in *Roughing It in the Bush*. The spiritual memoir does not require unity of mood, or tone, or style, or theme; as an unfinished journey its progress is not always linear, since the author constantly remakes old errors and relearns old lessons. Thus Stephen Prickett notes that the autobiographical form of Wordsworth's *Prelude* "is in fact the *traditional* Christian form for describing spiritual crises . . . The *Confessions* of Augustine, as has often been noticed, are not primarily about 'conversion' or 'spiritual crisis' *per se*; they are about the growth of Augustine's mind."[1]

The most generous way of reading *Roughing It in the Bush*, therefore, might be to see it as a record of the growth of Susanna Moodie's mind, a record drawing on both the travel guide and the Christian confession for its miscegenous form. The young woman who tried so hard to explain what she felt to her English family and friends in *Enthusiasm* continued to interrogate herself once she crossed the Atlantic. That same resistance to over-simplification which pervades her poetry, filling it with self-contradiction, enabled her, a few years later, to become the most complete chronicler of the settlement experience in English Canada.

Roughing It in the Bush would seem to be precisely the kind of writing condemned by the authors of *The Empire Writes Back*: it is "produced by a literary elite whose primary identification is with the colonizing power." Indeed, Moodie herself may be seen as typical of the venal "memsahibs" whose memoirs

---

Mark Akenside's *Pleasures of the Imagination*, James Thomson's *The Seasons* and, ultimately, to Milton (17).

9. G. A. Starr, *Defoe & Spiritual Autobiography* (Princeton: Princeton University Press, 1965), 5–6. I am also indebted to Starr for the observation on travel and agriculture as organizing metaphors of confessional literature; see pages 23–5.

1. Stephen Prickett, *Romanticism and Religion: The Tradition of Coleridge and Wordsworth in the Victorian Church* (Cambridge: Cambridge University Press, 1976), 89. Frank D. McConnell also notes how much *The Prelude* has in common with religious prose tracts which recount how the author came to recognize his "election" to his "calling" in *The Confessional Imagination: A Reading of Wordsworth's Prelude* (Baltimore: Johns Hopkins University Press, 1971).

can never form the basis for an indigenous culture nor can they be integrated in any way with the culture which already exists in the countries invaded. Despite their detailed reportage of landscape, custom, and language, they inevitably privilege the centre, emphasizing the "home" over the "native", the "metropolitan" over the "provincial" or "colonial", and so forth. At a deeper level their claim to objectivity simply serves to hide the imperial discourse within which they are created.[2]

But I hope my reading has persuaded you that categorical dismissals embodied in language like "never," "in any way," "inevitably," and "simply" are inadequate to the complexity of the work. Moodie is not *hiding* the imperial discourse—she is wrestling with it.

MICHAEL A. PETERMAN

Roughing It in Michigan and Upper Canada: Caroline Kirkland and Susanna Moodie†

In his 1965 introduction to Caroline Kirkland's *A New Home—Who'll Follow?* (1839), William S. Osborne observes that, "probably, Mrs. Kirkland had no equals in her day in her particular area of writing."[1] That area of writing, the collection of loosely chronological sketches drawn from personal experience in a remote frontier environment and directed at a genteel, mostly female audience as an amusement and a warning, holds an important place in the development of literary realism in nineteenth-century America. In Osborne's words, "actual residence in the West had made her a realist; and in the first book about her Western experiences she had effectively destroyed the romantic conception of frontier life and brought vigor and strength to American fiction too long given over to sentimentalism, high adventure, and Gothic sensationalism" (15). More recently, and from a feminist perspective, Annette Kolodny has written that, by means of her "gritty realism," Kirkland was "the direct progenitor of that bold new direction in American letters."[2]

Had Osborne looked northward to what was Upper Canada (in the eighteen-forties, Canada West), he would have found Caroline Kirkland's 'equal.' In fact, he need only have looked to New York, where in June 1852 George Putnam published Susanna Moodie's *Roughing It in the Bush*. The two-volume work, which Putnam had pirated from

2. Bill Ashcroft, Gareth Griffiths and Helen Tiffin, *The Empire Writes Back: Theory and Practice in Post-Colonial Literatures* (London: Routledge, 1989), 5.
† From *Context North America: Canadian/U.S. Literary Relations*, ed. Camille R. La Bossiere (Ottawa: U of Ottawa P, 1994), pp. 91–122. Reprinted by permission of the University of Ottawa Press. Page numbers in brackets refer to the text in this Norton Critical Edition.
1. Caroline Kirkland, *A New Home—Who'll Follow? Glimpses of Western Life*, ed. William S. Osborne (1839; New Haven: College and University Press, 1965), 24.
2. Annette Kolodny, *The Land Before Her: Fantasy and Experience on the American Frontiers, 1630–1860* (Chapel Hill: North Carolina UP, 1984), p. 155.

Richard Bentley of London, was edited for its American audience by Charles F. Briggs, the first editor of *Putnam's Magazine* and a friend of Mrs. Kirkland. That thin connection is as close as I have been able to come in directly linking the two authors. Osborne does not mention Moodie either in his edition of *A New Home* or his Twayne study of Kirkland; nor does he recall any reference by Kirkland to Moodie or her sister Catharine Parr Traill, whose *The Backwoods of Canada* (1836) preceded *A New Home* by three years.[3] In all of Moodie's (and, for that matter, Traill's) writing and extant correspondence, Kirkland's name never comes up. Thus, despite the fact that their most important books—*A New Home* and *Roughing It in the Bush*—bear many striking similarities, there is no direct evidence to confirm that Kirkland influenced Moodie or that they were aware of each other's efforts. However, several reviewers of *Roughing It in the Bush* in both England and the United States were quick to note certain likenesses.[4]

To be sure, various newspapers that Moodie might have read—the conservative *Kingston Chronicle and Gazette*, for example, and the reformist *Upper Canada Herald* (Kingston)—did publish excerpts from both the very popular *A New Home* in 1839–40 and its sequel, *Forest Life*, in 1842. The *Herald* is her most likely source, since she and her husband were reform supporters by 1839–40; in fact, once on the job in Belleville, Sheriff John Moodie wrote occasionally to that paper to offer his side of particular controversies.[5] But as "The Science of Borrowing" appeared there on 5 November 1839—that is, before Susanna Moodie had left the Douro backwoods—it is difficult to make a case for influence in that instance. In contrast, "Recollections of Land Fever" did appear in the *Herald* on 13 October 1840, when she was settled in Belleville. Not to be discounted as well is the possibility that certain Kirkland sketches appeared in Peterborough and Belleville newspapers of those years; however, because these papers have not survived, no evidence is available.[6] Thus, while circumstances suggest that Moodie might have read at least one or two of Kirkland's reprinted sketches, there is no concrete proof that such was the case.

But while direct influence is always a matter of literary interest, comparison of *A New Home* and *Roughing It in the Bush* encourages other consequential recognitions. First, it allows us to observe that

3. William S. Osborne to the author, 7 July 1989. A recent conversation with Audrey Roberts confirms this, though, as Roberts notes, much Kirkland material was lost in the Chicago fire of 1873. See Audrey Roberts, "Caroline M. Kirkland: Additions to the Canon," in *Bulletin of Research in the Humanities* 86 (1983–85), 338–46.

4. A review in *The Atheneaum* (London), 28 February 1852, placed Moodie's book beside Kirkland's "in what may be called the light literature of colonization," but concluded that Moodie's was "more real" in its presentation. See also the *Boston Daily Transcript* 6 July 1852.

5. In a letter from John Moodie to Susanna (24 May 1839), he first expressed his interest in the cause of reform (see The Patrick Hamilton Ewing Collection [PHEC], National Library, Ottawa). The *Upper Canada Herald* on several occasions vouched for Moodie's character and defended his actions as sheriff and as returning officer in Belleville in 1841–42.

6. The *Kingston Chronicle and Gazette* printed "The Science of Borrowing" on 26 October 1839. Excerpts from *Forest Life* appeared in the *Upper Canada Herald* on 16 August, 30 August, and 2 September 1842.

literary history, narrowly viewed along nationalistic lines, can neglect and even erase important and shared responses across the Canadian/American border.[7] Second, it generates awareness of the many similarities in the experience of the frontier and of the bush, forest, backwoods, or wilderness (depending upon geography or euphemistic preference) for women in both Upper Canada and Michigan at virtually the same historical moment. To read both books is to realize, for instance, the devastating effect of the depression of the late eighteen-thirties, particularly on people living at some remove from centres of activity. In both cases, the great expectations of the immediately previous years vanished and deep economic stagnation ensued from which escape seemed the only possible relief. In this light, the differences between the books seem proportionately less compelling. But differences there are, and they are substantial; a consideration of some of the more prominent of them can help the reader to grasp more clearly the particular features and merits of each book.

Finally, comparison enables us to see clearly the focussing power of the ideology and advocacy of gentility in these two works, to realize that genteel views of conduct and culture in effect write and shape the narratives. Such were the priorities of the time and culture that the American-bred Kirkland and the English-bred Moodie implicitly shared. Nevertheless, the experience of various kinds of material and cultural deprivation, as well as the daily exposure to what Kirkland calls the absolute democratization of the backwoods (180)—John Moodie termed it "the rough towel of democracy"[8]—provided both authors with their most vital literary material. Each chose to emphasize "decidedly low" (*New Home* 34) aspects of backwoods life, and each brought to her sketches a curiosity and sense of play indicative of a fascination and an engagement with those "low" elements.

Such features make their respective books something more than mere emigrant guides or prolonged warnings to prospective emigrants among their privileged class. They help us to measure the ways in which Moodie and Kirkland were imaginatively challenged by their backwoods experiences and the ways in which they struggled to accommodate themselves to the pressures and disappointments of that life, drawing always upon the resources of the genteel culture in which they had been raised and out of which they wrote as its proud representatives. At the heart of each book—particularly *Roughing It in the Bush*—is a tension between experience and received outlook, be-

---

7. Marcia B. Kline brings Kirkland and Moodie (and Traill) together in *Beyond the Land Itself: Views of Nature in Canada and the United States* (Cambridge: Harvard UP, 1970), noting that, collectively, their major books provide "the impression that life in a new and rough-hewn community was very much the same on either side of the border" and that it was particularly difficult for women (29). See also Gaile McGregor, *The Wacousta Syndrome: Explorations in the Canadian Langscape* (Toronto: U of Toronto P, 1985), 51–52. Interestingly, in *The Land Before Her*, Annette Kolodny uses several epigraphs from Margaret Atwood's *The Journals of Susanna Moodie* (1970), but nowhere does she acknowledge Moodie as a contemporary of Kirkland's who wrote of similar subject matter or as a writer who was well received and often published in the United States, not only in book form but in magazines, newspapers, and annuals.
8. Susanna Moodie and J. W. D., eds., *The Victoria Magazine*, Belleville, Ont., 1847–48, ed. William H. New (Vancouver: U of British Columbia P, 1968), 254. See p. 160 of this edition.

tween life as it is and life as one would like it to be, between reality as a challenge to literary representation and the accepted sentimentalized formulas for the presentation of life in genteel terms. It would be superficial to argue that Kirkland and Moodie were 'slumming it,' simply writing as snobs from superior worlds. The experiences they underwent in the backwoods challenged them and, in the process, brought out what was best in their respective literary talents. Gentility and its partner, snobbery, were givens with them. What matters are the attempts of both authors to document and represent their unsettling experiences in an (apparently) coherent and personally satisfying way—and, most important, the results of that kind of realistic undertaking.

For the record, the salient biographical facts are as follows. Caroline Stansbury was born in New York city in 1801. The Stansburys were a literate, lively, and well-connected couple, who provided their daughter with a "secure and genteel" milieu and with clear values—they were "city people, liberal in their views on education and culture yet conservative in politics and distrustful of radical elements in America's youthful society."[9] Married in 1828 to William Kirkland, a teacher at Hamilton College, Caroline took her young family west to Michigan in 1835, ostensibly to help her husband in his principalship of the Detroit Female Seminary, but, more accurately, to support him in his ambitious real-estate venture. Bitten by the "land mania" of the early eighteen-thirties, Kirkland had obtained 1,300 acres in Livingston County, some sixty miles from Detroit and near present-day Ann Arbor. His plan was to develop a village named Pinckney (Montacute in *A New Home*). After some two years of preparation in Detroit, the family moved there in 1837, struggling to adapt to what Caroline Kirkland variously calls "cottage life," her "western home," and "a woodland life." She made her literary reputation by writing three books about the experience (the first two while living in Pinckney), and, later, numerous magazine articles. However, in a matter of six years, the Kirklands admitted their failure and returned to New York. William died in 1846; Caroline, who continued to write and later served in various editing positions, died in 1864.

Susanna Strickland was born in 1803 in rural Suffolk, the sixth daughter of a retired London businessman. Financial problems and insecurity plagued the family in the years after her father's premature death, in 1818. Though more removed from city ways, her upbringing was similarly literate and genteel. Like most of her sisters, five of whom wrote with fame and pin-money in mind, she was on her way to developing a modest literary reputation in London when, in 1831, she married John Wedderburn Dunbar Moodie, a retired half-pay officer of Orkney lineage who had a passion for adventure, writing, and challenges. She came without a dowery and he with only a farm in South Africa, a place that held little attraction for his wife. Weighing their options once their first child was born, they were convinced to try

9. William S. Osborne, *Caroline M. Kirkland* (New York: Twayne, 1972), 18.

British North America, given the fact of free land for pensioned military men and the persuasions of what she called the "Canada mania."[1]
Immigrating to Upper Canada in 1832, they chose first to buy a
cleared farm in Hamilton Township, near Port Hope and Lake Ontario; here they stayed for one and a half years before moving into the
backwoods north of Peterborough, where one of Moodie's military
grants was located and required 'proving up.' They lived on their
rugged lakefront bush farm in Douro township from February 1834
till the end of 1839. At that point, their increasing financial problems
led to impoverished and difficult living conditions as the decade
wound down. Only when Moodie was appointed by the government to
the position of sheriff of the newly established Victoria District did
they escape their fate as cash-poor, failing genteel farmers. Living
thereafter in Belleville in much greater material comfort, Susanna
Moodie waited several years before she undertook to articulate and ex-
plicate her bush experiences as a woman, a wife, and a mother. As was
the case with Kirkland, though, her literary career (in this case in
North America) took flight during (though mostly after) her exile in
the backwoods.[2]

It is certainly of interest to note as well that, beyond the parallels
between their lives, both writers found their primary model in Mary
Russell Mitford's popular and "charming sketches of village life" (*New
Home* preface). Kirkland claimed that she took her form from Mitford's *Our Village*, playfully flavouring her desultory and "rude"
sketches of rural characters, country outings, and local events with
pastoral and courtly images, French phrases and quotations, witticisms, and proverbial wisdom. Moodie, for her part, had corresponded
with Miss Mitford in 1829 and 1830, praising her as "one of the first
of our female writers"[3]; indeed, she had tried her hand at the rural
sketch, writing five Suffolk sketches prior to her emigration, the best
of which is autobiographical and personal in tone.[4] Mitford is nowhere
mentioned in *Roughing It in the Bush*, but her influence is apparent in
the subject matter, techniques, and personalized approach that
Moodie brought to her "Canadian Sketches" (as they were called
when they first appeared in the *Literary Garland*, a Montreal magazine, in 1847), and later to the book itself.[5]

However, it was with significantly less tact and sweetness than Mitford that Kirkland and Moodie turned to, and turned on, their respec-

1. p. 11.
2. While still in the bush Moodie began to write for *The Literary Garland*, a new magazine in
   Montreal. She became its major contributor in the eighteen-forties. Like Kirkland, she was
   briefly an editor (*The Victoria Magazine*, 1847–48). Also while in the bush, she was published occasionally by two American periodicals, the *New York Albion* and Sumner Lincoln
   Fairfield's *North American Magazine*.
3. In Carl Ballstadt, Elizabeth Hopkins, and Michael Peterman, eds., *Susanna Moodie: Letters
   of a Lifetime* (Toronto: U of Toronto P, 1985), 39.
4. Moodie's Suffolk sketches appeared under her maiden name in *La Belle Assemblée*, a London magazine, in 1829. Her most autobiographical, "Old Hannah, or, the Charm," appeared
   in 1829 (3rd series) 9:21–24. See also Carl Ballstadt, "Susanna Moodie and the English
   Sketch," *Canadian Literature* 51 (1972): 32–38 [419–25].
5. Several of Moodie's sketches for *Roughing It in the Bush* appeared as "Canadian Sketches"
   in *The Literary Garland* and as "Scenes of Canada" in *The Victoria Magazine*, in 1847.

tive experiences. Their realistic presentation involved the comic cari-
caturing of living people, criticizing and satirizing modes of behaviour
deemed to be typical of frontier life, and presenting rural life in often
unflattering ways. In effect, they seem deliberately to have set out to
take the gilt off the lily, to warn people of their own class—particularly
women—about the actual physical and social conditions and the demands of such a life. Moodie, for instance, begins her presentation of
the custom of the logging-bee by noting that "where hands are few,
and labour commands an enormous rate of wages, these gatherings
are considered indispensable, and much has been written in their
praise." Unlike her sister Catharine Parr Traill, who had put her stamp
of approval on bees, as on most things she observed, in *The Backwoods
of Canada* (a book Moodie doubtless used—as discreetly as possible—
as a kind of negative model or basis for revision), Moodie presents a
different picture, deliberately demythologizing such co-operative ventures on the basis of their actual cost. Deploring a "craze" from which
so little is effectively gained, she writes: "they present the most disgusting picture of a bush life. They are noisy, riotous, drunken meetings, often terminating in violent quarrels, sometimes even in
bloodshed. Accidents of the most serious nature often occur, and very
little work is done when we consider the number of hands employed,
and the great consumption of food and liquor."[6] Somewhat more sheltered from the necessity of bees by her village existence, Kirkland was
less affected by the custom and less categorical in her criticism; however, as she notes, her own house-raising produced two injuries directly attributable to "that ruinous ally, strong drink" (*New Home* 75).

Of greater and more immediate consequence was the use both writers made of the local inhabitants. Writing under the apparent protection of anonymity, Kirkland, who regularly seems more deliberate,
self-conscious, and detached in the writing of her book than Moodie,
jauntily declares her intention to be "decidedly low," given the "meager
materials" Montacute provides. To present her "village" and its "common-place occurrences" (*New Home* 33) she had to write *down*, however much she sought to dress up the surface with cleverness and
allusion. But in so doing she was able to tap into the oddness and
strangeness—that is, the vitality of life—in the Michigan backwoods
(116). Nothing, she notes, is incredible in Michigan (124). Sensitive
to a certain lack of social prudence in her approach, however, she worried that she was placing herself beyond the pale of "the fashionable
world" in "acknowledging even a leaning toward the 'vulgar' side"
(230). It was a given that genteel priorities and low realities were fundamentally at odds; however, by an act of imaginative juggling and verbal cleverness, she sought to strike a congenial balance between the
extremes. It did not seem to worry her, at least initially, that she was
taking serious liberties in her representation of the actual lives of people, especially of those on a lower social plane.

6. Susanna Moodie, *Roughing It in the Bush; or, Life in Canada*, 2 vols. (London: Richard
Bentley, 1852), 333–34 [210].

For her part, Moodie, who wrote under her own name, is even more vulgar and "decidedly low" (in the genteel sense of the word), even as she is more intensely personal and far less coy in her approach. In fact, more than A New Home, Roughing It in the Bush is so peppered with odd and vulgar characters, both low and well born, "with whom [she] . . . became acquainted during that period,"⁷ that at times Moodie's sheer delight in comic portraiture, a delight implicit in sketch after sketch, threatens to usurp narrative development. That delight and fascination may be said to constitute a kind of contradictory shaping force in the book, for the portraits, though offered ostensibly as object examples of emigrant failure or deplorable behaviour, take on through Moodie's presentation a life of their own. Occasionally, in fact, it is clear that Moodie had trouble putting a suitably genteel moral to the characters that she describes and, in the process, creates. The strangeness of life in Upper Canada—strange but powerfully real—becomes perhaps her most persistent motif in the book.

Characterization or, perhaps better, what she thought of as caricature, may have been Moodie's strongest suit as a writer. Subjecting herself to a kind of literary self-analysis in 1853, she reported to her English publisher, Richard Bentley: "There is a want of Individuality in my writing which I feel and lament, but cannot remedy. In the phrenological development of my head, these organs are not valleys, but bumps. A scene or picture strikes me as a whole, but I can never enter into details. A carpet must be very brilliant, the paper on the wall very remarkable before I should ever notice either, while the absurd and extravagant make lasting impressions, and I can remember a droll speech or a caricature face for years."⁸ Addressing herself to what was often ungenteel and "odious" subject matter, Moodie, like Kirkland, was able to give something like a free rein to her "lamented" talent, focusing upon facial and bodily peculiarities, dialect, individual qualities of voice, habits, and striking behavioural characteristics. Meagre as the social life might have been in the newly settled backwoods, one had plenty of "odd" characters and unusual customs to draw upon. As Moodie put it in summarizing her reaction to the little stumpy man who was for so long her unwanted guest, "I am still a babe in the affairs of men. Human nature has more strange varieties than any one menagerie can contain, and Malcolm was one of the oddest of her odd species."⁹ And, like Kirkland, she made little attempt to veil her portraits of backwoods characters (either well or low born) other than by what Kirkland calls "glosses, colorings, and lights, if not shadows" (Preface).

The result for both women was considerable unfriendly criticism. Stung by charges that she had held recognizable individuals up to ridicule, Kirkland, who was still living at Pinckney, sought to revamp her approach in her 1842 sequel, Forest Life. "We may say of ourselves

7. Ibid., 387 [245].
8. Letters of a Lifetime, 129–30.
9. Roughing It, 406 [258].

what we may not say of others," she shrewdly observed. "We may describe our own log-house, but woe betide us if we should make it appear that anybody else lived there." It did not serve to substitute
"personality for impersonation."[1] What was lost in her adjusted approach, however, was the sense of play and the freshness and "sparkle"
that had characterized *A New Home*. "My former sketches were of the
safety-valve and flood-gate kind," she observed. "They were the overflowing of a reservoir of new sights, new sounds, and new notions.
They wrote themselves, so to speak" (*Forest* 32). The chastened and
more cautious Kirkland "confess[ed]" in *Forest Life* "to have become
too much Westernized to be a competent painter of Western peculiarities" (33).

Kirkland's awkward confession catches the dilemma she shared with
Moodie. To write about actual experience with a kind of "flood-gate"
freedom was to take liberties with the living even as it was to risk vio-
lation of the fastidious tastes of her desired and designated audience.
Certainly, Moodie drew almost exclusively on real people in *Roughing
It in the Bush*; virtually every character is identifiable.[2] Only in later
editions were certain names altered (as in the case of Uncle Joe H——
becoming Joe R——). Having left the backwoods long before she prepared her sketches for print and having outlived a number of those
(like Brian the Still-Hunter) whom she described, it would appear that
she received less direct criticism for her depiction of real people than
did Kirkland. Her sensitivity to criticism of her presentation and motives was nonetheless acute. She was accused, for instance, of having
described Irish emigrants "in terms which a reflective writer would
scarcely apply to a pack of hounds"[3] and was branded by a liberal voice
of the Toronto papers, Charles Lindsay, as "an ape of the aristocracy.
Too poor to lie on a sofa and too proud to work for her bread."[4] Moreover, her own family in England was horrified to be associated with
the book. Decades later, when one of the English sisters described the
family reaction in a letter to Moodie's eldest daughter, the sting of association was still very sensitive:

> After the publication of that disgusting book, the "Roughing It in
> the Bush" the very name of Canada [became] hateful to us *all*. I
> think it must have given as much pain to her [own] children as to
> us. We had always tried hard to keep up the respectability of the
> Family, in spite of loss of property and it was very mortifying to
> have a Book like that going the round of low vulgar upstarts . . .
> You cannot imagine how vexed and mortified my dear sister Agnes
> was, and at the time of the very height of her fame, to have pas-

1. Caroline Kirkland, *Forest Life*, 2 vols. (New York: Charles S. Francis; Boston: J. H. Francis,
   1842), 4.
2. See Carl Ballstadt's Introduction and explanatory notes in Moodie, *Roughing It in the Bush*,
   ed. Carl Ballstadt (Ottawa: CEECT, 1988).
3. The review in question was originally published in *The Observer* (London) 15 February
   1852:6.
4. *Letters of a Lifetime*, 136. Elizabeth Thompson discovered the review after the publication of
   this article. See "An Early Review of *Roughing It in the Bush*," *Canadian Literature* 131
   (1996): 202–04 [406–08].

sages from that book commented upon and ill-natured remarks made by people who were envious of her great fame.[5]

Like Kirkland, Moodie did not write so freely or personally again. As a sequel, *Life in the Clearings* (1853) seeks to be more carefully objective and general, while *Flora Lyndsay* (1854), a book that describes the actual emigration of the Moodies and leads directly into the opening of *Roughing It in the Bush*, offers a fictionalized rather than an overtly autobiographical account of the young couple's emigration plans.

A detailed comparison of *A New Home* and *Roughing It in the Bush* reveals similarities in subject matter, outlook, and tone. From the devastations of ague or lake fever to rural customs like the borrowing system, bees, and charivaris (Kirkland calls such activities "mobbings"), from losses at the hands of land sharks to the problems of getting and keeping good servants in a democratic environment, from the discomforts of travel over bad roads and the absence of necessary commodities to the terror of being a woman and mother alone for a night in a backwoods home, from the fear of wild animals (Kirkland's cougars and snakes are Moodie's bears and wolves) to awareness of the dangers of burning the fallow, the books share common occurrences and personalized responses even as they confirm each other's documentary accuracy. Not surprisingly, they share a deep-seated hostility toward the outright claims of democratic freedom, or ultra-republicanism, as Kirkland terms it. While Moodie brought from her English rural background a rooted fear of revolution and quickly transformed that concern into an active mistrust and scorn for Brother Jonathan's "scampish progeny" (such as she found prominently represented among her first set of neighbours), Kirkland was herself highly critical of the "vicious and degraded" class of settlers who imbibed too much of the gospel of freedom and used it to the disadvantage, and even the harm, of others. Seeking to be optimistic, however, she wrote, with apparently inadvertent irony, "I trust we have few such neighbors left. Texas and the Canada wars have done much for us in this way; and the wide west is rapidly drafting off [others]" (*New Home* 149). Canada has done too much!—Moodie might have responded. Confined to the backwoods for her first seven years in Canada, she saw little to make her change her mind about Americans, though her view did alter noticeably when her opportunities for travel increased.[6] (There is a nice irony in noting in this regard that the restless John Moodie did for a brief period, in 1834–35, contemplate joining the Texas land-development scheme of impresario Dr. John Charles Beales and his supporter, Dr. John S. Bartlett of the *New York Albion*.)

It is the shared heritage of genteel values and expectations, however, that underlies the similarities of subject matter and treatment in

5. See Sarah Gwillym to Katie Vickers (November 1874), PHEC collection, National Library of Canada.

6 By way of balance, John Moodie offers a more complimentary view of Americans in his sketch of Oren Strong, the Cobourg inn-keeper, in his chapter "The Village Hotel" (*Roughing It* 234–35).

the two books. On the one hand, the many gross violations of those values and expectations provided both Kirkland and Moodie with the justification to be harshly critical of what they had witnessed and suffered. "It is not pleasant to find a dead pig in one's well, or a favorite dog hung up at the gate-post," Kirkland noted with admirable restraint (*New Home* 158). Nor, in Moodie's case, was it pleasing to find a skunk left in one's cupboard, or to have the family's pigs drowned by a vengeful neighbour, or to have a much-valued new plough borrowed and returned broken, with the blame audaciously directed at the lender for having provided a faulty implement. Certainly, in this and other instances of realistic detail Moodie's book is the stronger and more forceful—indeed, the more forthright—of the two.

Kirkland explicitly refrains from describing many of the problems and inconveniences experienced in her family's life in Montacute; moreover, in settling in a village where her family had considerable influence, she was spared much of the rough exposure Moodie faced in her two different and stressful places of settlement. Over all, *Roughing It in the Bush* is richer in its detail, cast of characters, and presentation of activities; at the same time it is less decorative and superficially playful in its presentation and less given over to genteel narrative-fill in the form of multi-chaptered cautionary tales.[7] It reflects a greater exposure to real difficulties, a more severe testing of personal resources, and a more demanding engagement in self-scrutiny than Kirkland, for all her wit and analytical skill, offers. *Roughing It in the Bush* is a more probing work of autobiography than is *A New Home*: not only does the former bring more perspective to its approach, but it records the results of a deeper personal engagement in the events it dramatizes.

There is in Moodie's presentation, moreover, more rapport with the natural world, more contact with the native people, and more interest in the lives of servants like John Monaghan, Jacob (Faithful), and Jennie Buchanan. More than Kirkland, she had to learn something of everything and to work exhaustingly at jobs that she would never have considered undertaking as a gentlewoman in England. Moreover, while in the bush she gave birth to four children and for the better part of two years had the sole management of the bush farm while her husband served stints in the Upper Canadian militia. Not to be overlooked as well are Moodie's "truly British indignation" (*Roughing It* 222) [139] in the face of injustice and the effect of novelty, change, and alienation upon her, for she was, in her own words, "a stranger in a strange land" (39) [32]. It is perhaps for these reasons that her sketches are so often built upon sudden knocks at the door or unanticipated intrusions into the family log-house—in effect, upon disruption and upon invasion or loss of privacy, that most valued dimension of genteel domestic control. Such intrusions, however, are awakeners:

---

7. Kirkland interrupts her personal narrative to include lengthy tales of would-be settlers. As genteel cautionary or success stories they have an understandable place, but they distract from the immediacy and power of her own experiences.

they open her eyes to differences and arouse her curiosity even as they violate the sanctuary of home. In contrast, Michigan was indeed an odd place for Kirkland, but it was still America and, in that sense, still her homeland. Like Catharine Parr Traill, she was inclined to wear her "glorification spectacles," playing optimistically with and promoting the Edenic possibilities of rural Michigan in *A New Home*. In *Forest Life*, she revised that outlook. The later book has about it, as Kolodny notes, the cadence of "a dying fall," a recognition of failure and a hint even of martyrdom (153–55). Moodie's *Roughing It in the Bush* acknowledges failure as one of its basic premises.

Many other aspects of *A New Home* and *Roughing It in the Bush* could be compared on either a small or a large scale. New approaches in feminist criticism and literary theory will doubtless lead to others (see Kolodny, 153). What is, I hope, clear is that there is much to be gained in this case by trans-border juxtapositioning. It allows us to see the many elements both books share and to note more clearly the distinctive characteristics of each. We are thus in an improved position to measure their respective contributions to their evolving national literatures and cultures. At the same time, we can begin to weigh the importance of the perspective of class in both books. That recognition gives new dimension to an early criticism of both works, that they were simply genteel complaints. Comparison helps us to recognize both the crucial importance of genteel culture and values to Kirkland and Moodie and the extent to which they were stimulated imaginatively—that is, beyond their genteel assumptions and received literary conventions—by their backwoods experiences. By making their writing a personal safety-valve and by drawing on real people and real events for their material, they briefly achieved a vividness and an immediacy not found in most of their other writing. It was not, however, an approach they could sustain in the light of the subsequent criticisms that they suffered.

CAROLE GERSON

Nobler Savages:
Representations of Native Women
in the Writings of Susanna Moodie
and Catharine Parr Traill†

In her 1986 essay, " 'Indians': Textualism, Morality, and the Problem of History,"[1] American literary critic Jane Tompkins demonstrates the impossibility of establishing historical "truth." She concludes that the post-structuralist reader seeking the history of European-Native rela-

† From the *Journal of Canadian Studies* Vol. 32, No. 2 (Summer 1997): 5–21. Reprinted by permission of the *Journal of Canadian Studies*. Page numbers in brackets refer to the text in this Norton Critical Edition.
1. In *"Race," Writing and Difference*, ed. Henry Louis Gates, Jr. (Chicago: U of Chicago P, 1986), 59–77.

tions can only navigate among the various and conflicting subject-positions of the recorders and scholarly interpreters of the past, ultimately recognizing that, like them, she herself necessarily operates within a limited perspective. Resisting the temptation to retreat to "a metadiscourse about epistemology," she is left with the task of "piec[ing] together the story of European-Indian relations as best [she] can" (76), discomforted by the ease with which the academic mind can relinquish the pursuit of "what really happened" (60) in favour of a more abstract inquiry into how we think we know what happened. More recently, Stephen Greenblatt circumvents Tompkins's problem with historiography by focussing on the representative anecdote as "the principal register of the unexpected and hence of the encounter with difference. . . . Anecdotes then are among the principal products of a culture's representational technology."[2]

Susanna Strickland Moodie and Catharine Parr Strickland Traill are two Canadian writers whose contact narratives invite the application of Greenblatt's observation. Their literary transmission of their settlement experiences after their arrival in Upper Canada in 1832 underscores the importance of woman-to-woman engagement in European-First Nations interaction, and at the same time demonstrates the appropriateness of the anecdote in communicating this experience. In their vocabulary, the representative anecdote is often subsumed under the term "sketch," a word that invokes visual along with narrative elements of representation. "I sketch from Nature, and the picture's true," claims the epigraph to Susanna Moodie's *Roughing It in the Bush*.[3] When the Strickland sisters convey to their British readers their relations with the first people of North America, they become especially cognizant of the value of the sketch or anecdote. Traill's 1848 article, "A Visit to the Camp of the Chippewa Indians,"[4] opens by addressing the curiosity of her British correspondent: "You ask me if I have seen anything of the Indians lately. I am glad you were interested in my former accounts of them, and will supply you with any little anecdotes I may collect from time to time, for your amusement" (33). Even more cogently, Moodie justifies her assorted anecdotes of her interactions with her "Indian friends" with the observation that "The real character of a people can be more truly gathered from such seemingly trifling incidents than from any ideas we may form of them from the great facts in their history."[5] I will expand upon this privileging of "seemingly trifling incidents" over "great facts" later in my discussion of the strategies of textual representation developed by Moodie and Traill to record their encounter with the First Nations women they came to know in eastern Ontario. Moodie's account is localized in *Roughing It in the Bush*, written retrospectively after moving

2. In *Marvelous Possessions: The Wonder of the New World* (Chicago: U of Chicago P, 1991), 2–3.
3. Ed. Carl Ballstadt (Ottawa: Carleton UP, 1988) [lxiii], [2].
4. In *The Prose of Life: Sketches from Victorian Canada*, eds. Carole Gerson and Kathy Mezei (Toronto: ECW Press, 1981).
5. *Roughing It*, 309 [194].

to Belleville from the backwoods where she had lived during the 1830s. Traill, who spent more of her life in rural communities, consistently documents Native women in works issued over nearly the entire duration of her long life in Canada, from *The Backwoods of Canada* (1836) to *Pearls and Pebbles: or Notes of an Old Naturalist* (1894).

To appreciate the textual challenge facing these two literary British gentlewomen and the distinctiveness of their response, it is first necessary to consider a number of elements concerning both the original literary context in which they wrote and that within which they have subsequently been placed as early Canadian authors. These include the figure of the Noble Savage in relation to the subjectivity of Native Women in nineteenth-century Canadian and British literature, the position of women writers in the discourse of Empire, and the different genres in which these settler-authors chose to write. I therefore begin by positioning Moodie and Traill—or rather, our current reading of their work—against the background of canonical texts that have shaped our comprehension of the literary representation of First Nations people in early Canadian literature, especially with regard to Native women as subjects and/or "white" women as authors.

When they emigrated to British North America in 1832, Susanna Moodie and her sister Catharine Parr Traill were fully familiar with the construction of the Noble Savage that was a long-standing cliché by the time it appeared in Adam Kidd's *The Huron Chief*, a long poem published in Montreal in 1830:[6]

> And I would tell the polished man,
> Brought up in Europe's fashioned plan,
> That never could his formal art,
> Or all that school-taught lore has given,
> Such graceful happiness impart,
> As cheers the Indian's forest heaven—
> Who give, or asks, with greatest ease,
> Whate'er his heart or soul can please.
>
> (453–60)

At mid-century, Alexander McLachlan[7] demonstrated the ease with which the convention could be appropriated to his critique of Euro-Canadian materialism when he denounced the corruption of the Victorian industrial city by representing the Indian's experience as freedom and economic self-reliance:

> Oh! God I would rather be
> An Indian in the wood,
> And range through the forest free
> In search of my daily food.
>
> (27)

6. Reprinted in Kidd, *The Huron Chief*, ed. D. M. R. Bentley with Charles Steele (London, Ontario: Canadian Poetry Press, 1987).

7. In his poem *The Emigrant* (1861), ed. D. M. R Bentley (London, Ontario: Canadian Poetry Press, 1991).

The romantic ideology underpinning these equations of the Indian with natural happiness and ease, in opposition to urbanized Europe, was frequently countered by the actual experience of the New World pioneer. As Anne Langton[8] wrote back to relatives in England in July, 1839:

> The old world is the world of romance and poetry. I daresay our lakes, waterfall, rapids, canoes, forests, Indian encampments, sound very well to you dwellers in the suburbs of a manufacturing town; nevertheless I assure you there cannot well be a more un-poetical and anti-romantic existence than ours. (94)

Langton inverts the conventional romantic binary used by Kidd and McLachlan but does not replace it. The Indian (to retain the term used by the authors under discussion) remains a figure constructed by Eurocentric notions of cultural value: visible as a generalization but usually invisible as an individual human being, and thus available to occupy the position of the Other frequently assigned to the gypsy in European romanticism.[9] This invisibility was sustained by the belief that North American Aboriginal peoples were a "fated race," to cite a recurring phrase, whose destined disappearance before "the great tide of civilization" (Jameson, II 240) was statistically demonstrable. As Anna Jameson observed in 1838: "The white population throughout America is supposed to double itself on average in twenty-three years; in about the same proportion do the Indians perish before them" (II 107).

The figure of the disappearing Indian inherited by late-nineteenth-century Canadian poets, a diminishment that allowed them to con-struct freely Native characters whose fictionality serves the ideology of British-Canadian supremacy, has significantly shaped the prevailing construction of Canadian literary identity, based as this has been upon the canonization of several poets from this period as foundational au-thors. Of especial interest is the frequency with which the Native characters in their work are women, their biological function (or mal-function) an obvious factor in what the European viewed as the in-evitable and necessary disappearance of their people. Isabella Valancy Crawford, for all her reputed sensitivity to Native culture, virtually erases Native people from the landscape being colonized in her 1885 settlement poem, "Malcolm's Katie."[1] Native mythic imagery (inspired by Longfellow) animates the landscape and the turning of the seasons, but Native persons appear principally as the tenor of extended

8. In *A Gentlewoman in Upper Canada: The Journals of Anne Langton*, ed. H. H. Langton (Toronto: Irwin, 1964).
9. For comparisons of Indians with gypsies, see Anna Jameson, *Winter Studies and Summer Rambles in Canada*, 3 vols. (London: Saunders & Otley, 1838), II: 108; Langton, 22; and Traill, "Visit," 39. Traill speculates at greater length on their similarities in her unpublished journal, NAC, MG 29 D81, vol. 3, p. 3465.
1. In this regard, *Malcolm's Katie* (ed. D. M. R. Bentley [London, Ontario: Canadian Poetry Press, 1987]) resembles earlier settlement poems that depict Indians as either savages or ab-sent; see D. M. R. Bentley, *The Gay/Grey Moose: Essays on the Ecologies and Mythologies of Canadian Poetry, 1690–1990* (Ottawa: U of Ottawa P, 1992): "In treating the Indians stereo-typically and collectively as savages, degenerates, and transient hunters, the poets of Geor-gian Canada denied them status as individual people and as a multiplicity of peoples" (155).

metaphors. The only Native character to exist outside Crawford's figurative language is equally "unreal": the fictive Indian wife given to Max
by the lying Alfred—an image chosen to represent the degeneration of
both Max and the indigenous society being eradicated by the "panting,
human waves" (II 201) of European settlers. The poetry of Duncan
Campbell Scott[2] more obviously inscribes the disappearance of First
Nations Canadians into its repeated focus on Indian women, whose
intermingling with European men poetically enacts the assimilation
programmed for the Native population by Scott's Department of Indian Affairs ("The Onondaga Madonna," "At Gull Lake: August 1810,"
"The Half-breed Girl"). Recent research by Anne McClintock[3] and
Robert J. C. Young,[4] on the development of scientific racism in Europe
towards the end of the nineteenth century and into the twentieth, situates these poems about the decline of Canada's Indians within the
discourse of degeneration through *métissage* that is essential to our
understanding of their context. Susanna Moodie's comment about the
"sad falling-off of the Indian character" in "half-castes" who possess
"the worst qualities of both parents in an eminent degree"[5] represents
an earlier phase of the attitudes that would later be consolidated into
the identification of racial purity with national purity.[6] Scott's Native
women who do not dilute the Native population through their sexual
involvement with Europeans emblematize the decline of their people
through old age and the processes of history ("Watkewenies," "The
Forsaken," "Incident at Lake Manitou"). Sanction of the canonical poets' vision of the disappearing Indian has been demonstrated on at
least one occasion by an editorial view of the expendable Indian, with
significant consequences for later readers and scholars. Carl F.
Klinck's excision of Moodie's description of her "Indian Friends" from
his 1962 New Canadian Library edition of *Roughing It in the Bush* (a
decision he later regretted[7]) has resulted in the failure of all critics using this text, the only version of *Roughing It* in print for many years, to
recognize this important portion of Moodie's experience.

In contrast to the pattern of European/Aboriginal, real/ideal bina-
rism considered thus far, I would like to turn to several woman-
authored texts that offer accounts of direct engagements with women
from another culture. The meeting in the "contact zone" (to use Mary
Louise Pratt's term[8]) is as much a woman-to-woman connection as a
European/Native contrast. Hence the mode of the encounter is frequently not oppositional but experiential: not MacLachlan's "I would

2. See *The Poems of Duncan Campbell Scott* (Toronto: McClelland & Stewart, 1926), and *The Green Cloister and Later Poems* (Toronto: McClelland & Stewart, 1935).
3. *Imperial Leather: Race, Gender and Sexuality in the Colonial Conquest* (London and New York: Routledge, 1995).
4. *Colonial Desire: Hybridity in Theory, Culture and Race* (London: Routledge, 1995).
5. *Roughing It*, 322 [202].
6. A reconsideration of Scott's work as both bureaucrat and poet would be timely in light of Young's analysis of the competing discourses of racial purity and degeneration circulating during Scott's period of major activity (1885–1935).
7. Carl F. Klinck, *Giving Canada a Literary History: A Memoir*, ed. Sandra Djwa (Ottawa: Carleton UP, 1991), 157.
8. *Imperial Eyes: Travel Writing and Transculturation* (London: Routledge, 1992), 6–7.

rather be . . ." but Catharine Parr Traill's "I must tell you. . . ." In the latter instance, Traill is writing about a moment of physical contact expressive of trust, while travelling in a canoe with Indian women and children: "I must tell you that . . . a nice brown girl, Anne Muskrat, fell asleep with her head on my lap . . ." ("Visit" 38). The distinction I am drawing between externalizing and experiential modes of representation appears in one of the first woman-authored texts identified with Canada, *The History of Emily Montague* (1769),[9] where Frances Brooke distinguishes between the masculine, objective discourse of Ed Rivers and the engaged, contactual discourse of Arabella Fermor. To his sister in London, Rivers writes a general, informative description of the Hurons as Noble Savages.[1] It is Arabella, however, who details a specific instance of meeting and sharing a picnic with a group of Native women who, to her amazement, seem to possess absolute freedom of movement (49–50).[2] The contrasts manifested in these Canadian examples are typical of women's travel writing in general, according to Sara Mills's[3] analysis of such work from 1850 to 1930:

> [W]hat the narrators write about the people amongst whom they travelled and their attitude to those people is surprisingly similar and seems to differ from the writings of male travel writers in the stress they lay on personal involvement and relationships with people of the other culture and in the less authoritarian stance they take *vis-à-vis* narrative voice. (21)

Bridget Orr[4] further theorizes that "there is a peculiarity in the position of women within the imperialist culture, that she already figures an alterity which can be mobilized in diverse ways." She continues, "It is demonstrable that much women's travel writing does subvert the dominant terms of its discourse, but . . . the question remains of the extent to which another relation—a dialogic relation with the other—may be identified" (155). Central to this dialogic relation is "a recognition and

---

9. Three vols. (1769), ed. Mary Jane Edwards (Ottawa: Carleton UP, 1985).
1. Brooke slyly inserts her own feminist position into this account by having Ed's endorsement of the role of women in Huron government conclude, "I don't think you [women] are obliged in conscience to obey laws you have had no share in making" (35).
2. While Arabella soon retracts her admiration because she believes that European women enjoy greater freedom in their choice of a husband, Brooke establishes the falseness of Arabella's notion by having Arabella herself later recount the story of Lady H——, "sacrificed at eighteen, by the avarice and ambition of her parents, to age, disease, ill-nature, and a coronet" (279). Furthermore, it should be noted that Arabella's view of Native marriage is not historically correct. See Natalie Zemon Davis, "Iroquois Women, European Women," *Women, "Race," and Writing in the Early Modern Period*, eds. Margo Hendricks and Patricia Parker (London: Routledge, 1994) 245–46, who states that marriage partners were often suggested by parents, but action was to be taken by the young persons themselves. It is curious that Dermot McCarthy's recent essay on alterity in *The History of Emily Montague* (*ECW* 51–52 [1993–94]: 340–57) analyzes only Madame Des Roches, leaving the Indians an unexamined component of the book's "spectacle of otherness." Also of interest is the notion that pre-contact Iroquois women enjoyed considerable political power, a point made by Pauline Johnson in 1906 ("The Lodge of the Lawmakers," *London Daily Express*, 1906); and more recently by Paula Gunn Allen in *The Sacred Hoop: Recovering the Feminine in American Literary Traditions* (Boston: Beacon Press, 1986), 3.
3. In *Discourses of Difference: An Analysis of Women's Travel Writing and Colonialism* (London: Routledge, 1991).
4. In " 'The Only Free People in the Empire': Gender Difference in Colonial Discourse," in *De-Scribing Empire: Post-colonialism and Textuality*, eds. Chris Tiffin and Alan Lawson (London and New York: Routledge, 1994), 152–68.

acceptance of the irreducible alterity of each to the other," an aim that Orr concedes is "clearly utopian" (156), but none the less laudable.

Before specifically considering the ways in which the writings of Traill and Moodie meet Orr's quest for a "construction of encounters with the other as productive meetings in which the autonomy and difference of each partner is left intact" (156), I would like to introduce several intersecting factors that further contextualize the Strickland sisters' experiential mode of discourse. One influence we should not discount is the representation of Indians in the British literary culture in which the Stricklands were educated and lived until their emigration, two principal figures being Wordsworth and Felicia Hemans. North American Indians seldom appear in Wordsworth's verse other than to supply a few images of noble savagery or exoticism (e.g. *The Prelude* I 297–300; VI 664).[5] The notable exception is his "Complaint of a Forsaken Indian Woman" (1798), based on an incident in Samuel Hearne's diary and now recognized as a background text to Duncan Campbell Scott's frequently anthologized 1905 poem, "The Forsaken."[6] Scott's narrative is in the third person, recounted by an unnamed narrator whose objectifying Eurocentric stance and diction substantially problematize our reading of this poem today. But Wordsworth's poem is in the first person, granting voice and subjectivity to a Native character in a way that Scott never does. First-person Indian narrators also appear in a number of poems by Felicia Hemans, a poet much admired in the literary milieu of the Strickland family.[7] Whether or not the poetry of Wordsworth and Hemans set a direct precedent for Moodie and Traill, it does connect the romantic predisposition to individualize specific, interesting characters—who may on occasion be Native North Americans—with the Strickland sisters' literary practice of naming and describing distinct individuals, including a number of Indian persons. Moreover, Wordsworth's emphasis on the maternal emotions of his abandoned Indian woman anticipates Moodie and Traill's mother-to-mother connection with the Indian women they meet, which is one of the continuing discursive threads of this paper.

Another factor contributing to their mode of representing Native women may be the uncertain position of colonial women within normative patriarchal power relations. Laura E. Donaldson[8] observes that

> . . . describing the position of a white, middle-class woman either as oppressed or oppressive might vary in terms of her racial or economic status; indeed, she can sometimes be both simultaneously—in a patriarchal society, her femaleness dictates her sub-

5. *The Poetical Works of William Wordsworth*, Oxford Edition, ed. Thomas Hutchinson (London: Frowde, 1905).
6. Susan Beckmann, "A Note on Duncan Campbell Scott's 'The Forsaken,' " *Humanities Association Review* 25 (1974): 32–37.
7. Some of Hemans's poems about North American Indians are: "The Messenger Bird," "The Stranger in Louisiana," "Indian Woman's Death Song," "The Indian with his Dead Child," "The Aged Indian" and "The Cross in the Wilderness." See *The Poetical Works of Felicia Dorothea Hemans* (London: Humphrey Milford, Oxford UP, 1914).
8. In *Decolonizing Feminisms: Race, Gender and Empire-Building* (Chapel Hill: U of North Carolina P, 1985).

jection as sexual object, and in a racist society, her whiteness dictates her often unwitting participation in sustaining a system of white supremacy. (34)

Powerful as white but disempowered as female, Moodie and Traill share with Native women some marginal space on the outskirts of frontier culture. Less articulately feminist than their fellow author, traveller Anna Jameson, they present anecdotally rather than analytically the subjection of women in their own social class, such as the plight of Mrs N. in Moodie's chapter, "The Walk to Dummer," as well as in Native culture, as in Traill's generalization that "Gentle, patient, accustomed to be ruled from childhood, the Indian woman bears, suffers and submits without complaint."[9]

The generic identity of the Strickland sisters' settlement writing is the third major background factor I wish to introduce. In her 1981 article on Moodie and Mrs Trollope, Janet Giltrow[1] demonstrates the extent to which the rhetorical stance of *Roughing It in the Bush* and *Life in the Clearings* is that of the travel writer. Placing the non-fiction of Moodie and Traill in this genre elucidates their own self-placement within the spectrum of contemporary literary activity. On the one hand, Moodie and Traill express the uncertainty of many women writers daring to assume the authority of the travel narrator, whose heroic adventures and breadth of knowledge were conventionally gendered masculine (Mills 77–83). But on the other, they craftily turn their subordinate position to their own advantage. In *Life in the Clearings*,[2] Moodie deftly demurs as a woman while at the same time manipulating her power as the narrator when she addresses her reader:

> Dear patient reader! . . . Allow me a woman's privilege of talking of all sorts of things by the way. Should I tire you with my desultory mode of conversation, bear with me charitably, and take into account the infirmities incidental to my gossiping sex and age. . . . The little knowledge I possess, I impart freely, and wish that it was more profound and extensive, for your sake. (20)[3]

Disclaiming narrative unity allows the woman author to transgress in other ways as well: by calling attention to herself as a woman writer, and by venturing beyond the limited spheres of activity deemed appropriate for Victorian women (Mills 77). Moreover, announcing a mode of apparent casualness enhances the sense of immediacy characteristic of the anecdote, but often unavailable in more structured discourse.

Approaching the Stricklands' settlement narratives as travel writing accounts for the fact that First Nations Canadians appear far more frequently in these authors' public texts—books, poems, and periodi-

9. *Pearls and Pebbles: or, Notes of an Old Naturalist* (Toronto: Briggs, 1894), 222.
1. " 'Painful Experience in a Distant Land': Mrs Moodie in Canada and Mrs Trollope in America," *Mosaic* 14.2 (1981): 131–44.
2. Susanna Moodie, *Life in the Clearings versus the Bush* (1853; Toronto: McClelland & Stewart, 1989).
3. Similar statements appear also on pages 59 and 256, as well as in Anna Jameson's Preface.

cal articles—than in the private correspondence with family and friends which is now becoming available.[4] Published in Britain and addressed to readers back home, their best-known works include the requisite descriptions of indigenous persons expected in travellers' tales. While the distinctiveness of these writings derives from the way Moodie and Traill personalize their material, we must also remember that the narrators of the texts intended for public consumption are constructed figures whose narratives may be shaped as much by discursive conventions and ideological concerns as by the desire to document lived experience. Hence I shall argue that Moodie and Traill negotiated past the silences imposed by Victorian decorum, especially upon middle-class women, by expressing some of their own publicly unspeakable desires and concerns through their literary representations of Indian women.

In 1832, Catharine Parr Traill immigrated to British North America as a 30-year-old bride who would bear nine children over the next 15 years; Susanna Moodie arrived the same year as a 28-year-old new mother, carrying in her arms the first of her seven children. In a ground-breaking consideration of the maternal perspective in *Roughing It in the Bush*, Bina Freiwald[5] links Moodie's modes of representation to her identity as mother, noting that "There is always a child at Susanna's side" (158) [476]. Following upon Freiwald's recognition of the importance of the maternal eye, Helen Buss deconstructs "Moodie's restraint in her public text" (86) by seeking the untellable aspects of her autobiography through her private letters and her stories about other settlers. Yet somewhat surprisingly, both critics overlook Moodie's account of her "Indian Friends."[6] In the following discussion, I argue that linking the sisters' individual position as mature middle-class British mothers to their representation of Native women in their travel writing and their fiction yields important insights into their experiences of selfhood and Otherness.[7]

Catharine and Susanna both arrived in the Canadas expecting to meet Indians. Traill's presentation of Native peoples in her pre-

4. Susanna Moodie, *Letters of a Lifetime*, ed. Carl Ballstadt, Elizabeth Hopkins and Michael Peterman (Toronto: U of Toronto P, 1985); Susanna and John Moodie, *Letters of Love and Duty*, ed. Carl Ballstadt, Elizabeth Hopkins and Michael Peterman (Toronto: U of Toronto P, 1993); Catharine Parr Traill, *I Bless You in My Heart: Selected Correspondence of Catharine Parr Traill*, ed. Carl Ballstadt, Elizabeth Hopkins and Michael Peterman (Toronto: U of Toronto P, 1996).

5. In " 'The tongue of woman': The Language of the Self in Moodie's *Roughing It in the Bush*," *Re(dis)covering Our Foremothers*, ed. Lorraine McMullen (Ottawa: U of Ottawa P, 1990), 155–72.

6. Freiwald seems to have based her analysis on the truncated 1962 NCL edition of *Roughing It in the Bush*. As Helen Buss discusses Anna Jameson's engagement with Native women in considerable detail (in *Mapping Our Selves: Canadian Women's Autobiography in English* [Montreal & Kingston: McGill-Queen's UP, 1993]), I find it curious that her analysis contains no mention of Moodie's references to Native women. John Thurston's *The Work of Words: The Writing of Susanna Strickland Moodie* (Montreal and Kingston: McGill-Queen's UP, 1996) also pays little attention to her representation of Indians other than as polar opposites to the Yankees in *Roughing It in the Bush* (146–47).

7. Attention to early texts such as those by Moodie and Traill challenges Di Brandt's statement (in *Wild Mother Dancing: Maternal Narrative in Canadian Literature* [Winnipeg: U of Manitoba P, 1993]) that Margaret Laurence "was really the early pioneer in fashioning a place for maternal narrative in Canada" (18).

emigration juvenile novel, *The Young Emigrants*, drawn from the writings of several travellers,[8] reveals her preconceived admiration of Indians' ecological knowledge and survival skills and her discomfort with the harder work given to Micmac and Iroquois women. Moodie came to North America with notions of racial equality shaped by her strong commitment to the British anti-slavery movement.[9] The sisters also brought with them the outlook of their original cultural context, their humanitarian ideals contained within a framework of social class based on "education," meaning good manners as well as academic knowledge. Their recorded engagements with Natives thus involve frequent negotiation with stereotypes of the Noble Savage, locally represented, for example, in my earlier citation from Adam Kidd's *The Huron Chief*, published in Montreal just two years before the Strickland sisters landed in British North America. Hence Moodie opens her lengthy account of the Indians living near Peterborough by declaring them "a people whose beauty, talents, and good qualities have been overrated, and invested with a poetical interest which they scarcely deserve"[1] in order to separate the distinct men and women she has come to know from the Eurocentric generalizations she once shared with her readers. This involves a leap from the generic "Indian" to named individuals: Moodie variously introduces "the old chief, Peter Nogan,"[2] his son John Nogan, his sister-in-law Mrs. Tom Nogan, the Muskrat family, old Snow-storm, Jacob, Susan Moore and Betty Cow; Traill likewise identifies members of the Nogan[3] and Muskrat families as well as Nancy Boland and Mary Anne Fron.

It is important to recognize the degree to which ideology of class overrides racial difference in Moodie's writing, as in her first reference to Native peoples in *Roughing It in the Bush*, where she constructs an image of the Noble Savage specifically to critique European culture. Distressed by the rowdiness of Irish and Scottish steerage passengers finally released at the quarantine station at Grosse Ile, she generalizes:

> I had heard and read much of savages, and have since seen, during my long residence in the bush, somewhat of uncivilised life;

8. *The Young Emigrants; or, Pictures of Life in Canada* (London: Harvey & Darton, 1826). She cites as her sources Francis Hall's *Travels in Canada*, William Charles Janson's *Stranger in America* and John Howison's *Sketches of Upper Canada*.

9. See, for example, her story "The Vanquished Lion" (1831), in John Thurston ed., *Voyages: Short Narratives of Susanna Moodie* (Ottawa: U of Ottawa P, 1991) 31–42. Moodie transcribed two narratives of escaped slaves: *Negro Slavery Described by a Negro: Being the Narrative of Ashton Warner, a Native of St. Vincent*'s (London: Smith & Elder, 1831) and *The History of Mary Prince* (London: Westley, 1831); the latter receives substantial attention in Moira Ferguson, *Subject to Others: British Women Writers and Colonial Slavery, 1670–1834* (New York and London: Routledge, 1992) and in two essays by Gillian Whitlock: "Exiles from Tradition: Women's Life Writing," in *Re-siting Queen's English*, ed. Gillian Whitlock and Helen Tiffin (Amsterdam and Atlanta, Ga: Rodopi, 1992), 11–23, and "The Silent Scribe: Susanna and 'Black Mary.'" *International Journal of Canadian Studies* 11 (1995): 249–60.

1. *Roughing It*, 298 [186].

2. Ibid., 300 [187].

3. There were Nogan families, whose names are variously spelled Naugon, Nogy, Noggan, Nogee, and Nogie, associated with both the Curve Lake Reserve and the Hiawatha Reserve (near Rice Lake) (see Traill, *Forest and Other Gleanings: The Fugitive Writings of Catharine Parr Traill*, ed. Michael A. Peterman and Carl Ballstadt [Ottawa: U of Ottawa P, 1994], 149). Michael Peterman now identifies the families that camped on Lake Katchewanooka in the 1830s as connected to the Hiawatha Reserve.

but the Indian is one of Nature's gentlemen—he never says or does a rude or vulgar thing. The vicious, uneducated barbarians who form the surplus of over-populous European countries, are far behind the wild man in delicacy of feeling or natural courtesy.[4]

To a gentlewoman like Moodie, Indians, as "Nature's gentlemen," can be perceived as less Other than the lower classes of Great Britain (especially the Irish).[5] Introducing Native peoples as gentlefolk—who, unlike servants, are invited to eat at the Moodies' table—helps validate their individuality as human beings. Moodie's observations combine condescension and respect: she finds the local Mississauga Indians physically ugly and often childlike (in line with conventional notions of noble savages and "primitive" indigenous peoples), but also gifted with "great taste,"[6] "a fine ear for music,"[7] and "deep reverence for the Supreme Being."[8] More importantly, she discovers that generalizations are inadequate; to repeat her sentence cited at the beginning of this paper, "The real character of a people can be more truly gathered from such seemingly trifling incidents than from any ideas we may form of them from the great facts in their history, and this is my reason for detailing events which might otherwise appear insignificant and unimportant."[9] The title of this chapter refers to "Our Indian Friends"; for Moodie, friendship must be demonstrated in concrete anecdotes, not simply proclaimed as an abstraction. Not only do Indians come to her home out of curiosity and for shelter; the European and Native women also exchange purely social visits.[1]

In Moodie's representational practice, a distinct qualitative difference emerges between her accounts of Native men and those of Native women. In her anecdotes, the men are more often disadvantaged by cultural differences and misunderstandings, whereas the women receive her affection, admiration and respect. Bound in with these genuinely positive feelings is the way the incidents involving women can be read as projections of Moodie's own gender-based fears and concerns, arising in part from their shared maternal perspective. While discussion of *Roughing It in the Bush* must distinguish the historic personage of Susanna Moodie from her constructed self-representation as the naïve settler whose journey from innocence to experience provides the narrative framework of the book,[2] the narrated figure may also be read as the reflection of the historic. Coping with frequent pregnancies that cannot be overtly described, and at the

4. *Roughing It*, 20–21 [20], also 314 [198].
5. At this time, the Irish were constructed as more racially apart from the English than were people of colour. See Lynda E. Boose, " 'The Getting of a Lawful Race': Racial Discourse in Early Modern England and the unrepresentable black woman," in Margo Hendricks and Patricia Parker, eds., *Women, "Race," and Writing in the Early Modern Period* (London: Routledge, 1994), 36–37.
6. *Roughing It*, 301 [188].
7. Ibid., 304 [191].
8. Ibid., 306 [192].
9. Ibid., 309 [194].
1. Ibid., 313–14 [198]; 496–98 [324].
2. See, for example, my discussion of the likelihood that the real Susanna Moodie was far more alert than the narrated Moodie to the practices of "borrowing": "Mrs. Moodie's Beloved Partner," *Canadian Literature* 107 (Winter 1985): 34–45.

same time feeling victimized by smart "Yankees," Moodie projects her vulnerability into the tellable story of "a young squaw . . . near to becoming a mother" who is cruelly cheated out of a valuable bowl by an "unprincipled settler."[3] Continually fearful for the health and safety of her children (a major theme of her personal correspondence), she recounts the heart-breaking story of Elizabeth Iron, who tramps through the snow seeking in vain medicine for her dying child. Moodie was dreadfully afraid of wild animals and insisted on emigrating to Canada rather than South Africa because of her husband's dramatic tales of encounters with elephants and lions; consequently, the bravery of a Native woman who coolly knifes an attacking bear so astonishes her self-projected character (to whom even cows are terrifying) that she breaks into rhythmic alliteration reminiscent of heroic Anglo-Saxon verse: "What iron nerves these people must possess, when even a woman could dare and do a deed like this!"[4] Dislocated in an alien environment where her survival often seems precarious, Moodie marvels at Mrs Tom Nogan's hunting skills[5] and Mrs Muskrat's ability to predict the weather.[6] If we read *Roughing It in the Bush* as a narrative of female self-empowerment, we can see that its protagonist's often painful acquisition of self-confidence, knowledge and survival skills develops within the context of abilities and attitudes already possessed by the women native to the land to which Moodie had immigrated.

We must be careful, however, not to remove her from her historical milieu. For all Moodie's sympathetic interest in Native North Americans, *Roughing It in the Bush*, as an "anti-conquest" narrative to use Mary Louise Pratt's term (7), inevitably participates in the colonial destruction it deplores. Moodie grieves that "people with such generous impulses should be degraded and corrupted by civilised men; that a mysterious destiny involves and hangs over them, pressing them back into the wilderness, and slowly and surely sweeping them from the earth,"[7] without having the knowledge to recognize that the Indian boy perishing from consumption[8] is a victim of European disease. Similarly complicitous is her linguistic transformation of the "dry cedar-swamp . . . their usual place of encampment for many years"[9] to "our swamp,"[1] the shift in pronoun ("their" to "our") verbally enacting the material dispossession of hunters and gatherers by an imposed system of land ownership. As a woman of her time, she easily accepts the notion of Native traditions and artifacts being commodified as entertainments and souvenirs (*Clearings* 178–79, 287, 301). The elegiac tone sometimes adopted by both sisters invests First Nations Canadians, as remnants of the past, with a romantic quality akin to that felt by their European counterparts for architectural ruins—indeed, even seems to

3. *Roughing It*, 317 [199–200].
4. Ibid., 304 [190].
5. Ibid., 314 [197].
6. Ibid., 498 [319].
7. Ibid., 318 [200].
8. Ibid., 307–08 [193].
9. Ibid., 299 [187].
1. Ibid., 311 [195].

identify Indians as a substitute for ruins in a New World lacking the "mouldering abbey, delapidated tower, ruin'd camp of Dane and Roman" desired by a contemporary Nova Scotian author seeking local inspiration.[2] Thus, Moodie's engagement in a "dialogic relation with the other," to return to Orr's phrase (155), is inevitably contained within an Imperial frame of reference that permits alterity so long as there is no threat to the prevailing structure of power.

When writing as a naturalist, Catharine Parr Traill is usually less concerned with Native North Americans as interesting social beings than with Native ecology and knowledge about New World plants and animals. Mary Louise Pratt, however, points out that the apparent innocence of the New World naturalist is inevitably compromised by the impositions of conquest (57). Traill's experiential writing about First Nations people begins with *The Backwoods of Canada*. Issued four years after her arrival, this book was prepared from Traill's letters home to her mother who remained in England. With the subsequent disappearance of the original correspondence, we are left with the account of an editorially created, heroic "Traill character" (Bentley, Afterword 293) narrated in the mode of a traveller who characteristically assumes the Othering gaze of a fact-gathering generalizing recorder. Yet underlying her rather detached depiction of Indians we can detect a mother's personal interest in Native family behaviour when she notes the gentleness and good humour of Indian parenting. This she does not detail until her later description of "A Visit to the Camp of the Chippewa Indians," published in *Sharpe's London Magazine* in 1848, in which she recounts how a Native mother disciplines an unruly child, who threatens to upset the canoe in which they are all travelling, by pouring water onto his head.[3] Like Moodie's accounts of visits to her Indian friends, this sketch is narrated not by an observer but by a participant, utterly comfortable in her friends' milieu, who does not feel called upon to present her European reader with a catalogue of exotic differences. Particularly significant in this sustained personal narrative engagement with Indian women is its inclusion of examples of trust, as Traill allows a party of Native women and children to take her own young son in one canoe while she travels in another. The parity that characterizes Traill's involvement with these

---

2. Andrew Shiels, *The Witch of the Westcot* (Halifax: Joseph Howe, 1831), preface.
3. This sketch originated as a letter to her sister, Agnes Strickland. The placement of a draft in Traill's unpublished journal (Traill Family papers, NAC, MG 29 D81, vol 3, 3461–66) suggest that it was written in the 1830s. The fact that Traill seems to have only one child at this point and states that the episode includes her "first essay in paddling" (the word "first" is omitted from the published version) would suggest a date of 1834 or 1835; but the inclusion of Jane, identified as Thomas Traill's cousin, Jane Alcock, who came from Scotland in 1836 to help at the time of Katherine's birth, indicates 1836 (*Forest and Other Gleanings* 70). Comparison of the two texts shows some rearrangement of portions of the original, with several deletions, including a digression on house fires, a reference to the sore breast of the mother of the sick baby, and speculation on similarities between the Indians and gypsies. Added details include the recovery of the baby at the beginning of the sketch (his fate is unspecified in the journal version), the Indian girl falling asleep with her head on Catharine's lap, and the names of the Indian women. The inclusion of the latter in the published version suggests that Traill participated in the preparation of the final text.

people appears in the balance of exchange that pervades the sketch. In the description of the trading of food in the second paragraph, the Indian women are portrayed as "begging" several items; this subordinate position seems to be reinforced when Traill provides medicine that appears to cure Mrs Tom's baby. But as the sketch proceeds, it is the Europeans who are ultimately beneficiaries of Native skills and hospitality, both in the abstract knowledge of how to use natural resources, and in the gift of a sweet-grass necklace and other artifacts that Traill receives at the end.

References to and anecdotes of Indians in general appear sporadically through Traill's subsequent published and unpublished texts, in which she reiterates her interest in their knowledge and use of the natural environment, her faith in their good will and her regret at their disappearance. With regard to the concerns of women in particular, Traill retained a life-long fascination with Native solutions to the universal concerns of child-rearing. Her second-to-last book [*Pearls and Pebbles*], published in 1894, includes a detailed account of "The Indian Moss-bag," which ingeniously unites the functions of diaper and cradle. Here again she creates a sense of community when she speculates that "our British ancestry may have been nursed in just such a fashion as that of the North-West Indian moss-bag," citing "Rock-a-by baby" as evidence of prehistoric cultural resemblances (234).

Although much less inclined than her sister to write fiction,[4] it is Traill who fictionalizes Native womanhood in her children's novel, *Canadian Crusoes*.[5] If, as the title of this paper suggests, Indian women are "nobler" savages in the Strickland sisters' writing, then Traill's character Indiana is certainly the noblest of all. The timely appearance of this Mohawk girl, whose skills enable three lost white children to survive in the bush for two years, opens interesting questions relating to gender and colonial power.

On the one hand, it is possible to read *Canadian Crusoes* as a transparent narrative of imperialism. The white children—half-Scottish, half-French siblings Hector and Catharine Maxwell, and their French-Canadian cousin Louis—rescue the Mohawk girl, cruelly abandoned by her Ojibwa enemies, from certain death. Never learning her real name, they dub her "Indiana" after "a negress that [Catharine] had heard her father tell of, a nurse to one of his Colonel's infant children" (114), thus instantly placing her in an imperialist paradigm. Grateful to her rescuers, Indiana devotes herself to their comfort and safety, learns English, converts to Christianity, and after they are rescued, marries Hector. As Catharine likewise marries Louis, the happy four-

---

4. See Carole Gerson, *A Purer Taste: The Writing and Reading of Fiction in English in Nineteenth-Century Canada* (Toronto: U of Toronto P, 1989), 22. The "Chippewa" sketch was part of a sequel that Traill wrote in the wake of the success of *Backwoods of Canada* likely using the same letters format. It failed to find an English publisher and was broken up to be sold as sketches.

5. *Canadian Crusoes: A Tale of the Rice Lake Plains* (1852), ed. Rupert Schieder (Ottawa: Carleton UP, 1986). For a discussion of the importance of the Crusoe story in imperialist narratives, especially for children, see Martin Green, "The Robinson Crusoe Story," *Imperialism and Juvenile Literature*, ed. Jeffrey Richards (Manchester: Manchester U P, 1989) 34–52.

some represents a blending of Canada's British, French and Native heritages, the latter two subsumed into the dominant white, English-speaking order. Reading this novel in terms of nationality and race produces an imperialist text; however, reading it in terms of gender discloses a narrative of resistance.

To begin with, Traill consciously historicizes the New World, setting her story in the 1770s, about 80 years previous to the time of its composition (132). For both Moodie and Traill, the primal appearance of the New World problematized its historicity; like their peers elsewhere in the expanding British Empire, they tended to view the inhabitants of the virgin continents as occupiers of what Anne McClintock identifies as "anachronistic space," according to which trope "colonized people . . . do not inhabit history proper but exist in a permanently anterior time within the geographic space of the modern empire as anachronistic humans" (30). On at least one occasion each sister declared North America a place without a past (*Roughing It* 268, *Backwoods* 96), Traill positing that even its fossils are "evidently of very recent formation" (*Backwoods* 122). Her decision in this book to allow Indians some documented history, in this case the mutual slaughter of Mohawks and Ojibwa at Anderson's Point (*Canadian Crusoes* 132), thus valorizes her Native characters by placing them within the Eurocentric historical record. At the same time, the violence of this event is countered by Indiana's positive reception of European culture, thus embodying Traill's view that the attitude of Canadian Native peoples towards European settlers was essentially benign. The captivity narratives that abound in early American literature are scarce in Canada; in the writings of Traill and Moodie, it is the spectre of lost children that haunts the maternal mind. In different works, both writers tell the same story of children who lose their way in the woods and are rescued by Indians who then carry them off, to return home many years later as adults (Traill, "Two Widows of Hunter's Creek"; Moodie, *Clearings* 247). While the lost children in *Canadian Crusoes* do indeed fear hostile Indians, this captivity motif is ultimately transformed into a device that enables females self-empowerment.

By feminizing the Friday figure of this Crusoe narrative, Traill establishes Indiana as a strong countervailing balance to Catharine, her emblem of Victorian domesticity (providing "supplementation," in Fleming's analysis, 210, 214–16). Knowledgeable about household management but so vulnerable that the first time she ventures out alone she severely sprains her ankle (41), Catharine is easily captured by Indiana's Ojibwa enemies because she prefers to stay home cooking dinner while the others go out hunting. Indiana, in contrast, whose knowledge of canoeing, hunting and fishing supersedes that of the boys (126), leads in Catharine's rescue. The plot complications in this tale of Native power struggles and revenge turn on the actions of women; the original conflict that produced Indiana's plight had been aggravated by Beam of the Morning, an Ojibwa heroine who like "a second Judith" (138) had beheaded the Mohawk enemy to whom she had been forcibly wed. Indiana's own bravery is inherited from her mother, who like an "Amazon" (139) had saved the life of her child. Her fearless initiative in offering to change places with the captive Catharine serves to inspire the latter, giving her a sufficient infusion of agency to rescue her friend in turn. Despite the swift closure that follows with the restoration of cultural control as the children return home and eventually marry, it is tempting to read into both Indiana and the Judith figure Traill's otherwise unwriteable aspirations to female power—briefly tasted by Catharine, her fictional self-projection who bears not only the author's own Christian name, but also her particular spelling. A more incidental but none the less pertinent contribution to this reading of *Canadian Crusoes* occurs in the similarity between the clothing spontaneously devised by Catharine and Indiana to accommodate their life in the woods (leggings under a rather short skirt, 124) and the "rational dress" advocated by radical feminist Amelia Bloomer during the time that Traill was writing this book (circa 1849–50).

"Those who write, we are told, transcribe themselves in spite of themselves" observes the coyly self-conscious narrator of Sara Jeannette Duncan's 1904 novel, *The Imperialist.*[6] When writing about Native women, Moodie and Traill were also inevitably writing about themselves. Warmly valued as distinct individuals, their Indian friends also served as representations of Otherness through whom two Euro-Canadian Victorian sisters could address disempowerment, fear and maternal anxiety, none of which could be overtly admitted into their public texts. Thus the Strickland sisters' enactment of what Terry Goldie[7] terms "indigenization" (defined as "the impossible necessity of becoming indigenous," 14–17), is shaped by the limitations of textual discourse permitted to British middle-class women of their historical time and place. This convection becomes most poignant in some of Traill's late essays included in *Pearls and Pebbles*, published in 1894 when she was 92 years old. Calling for "the charitably disposed" to relieve "the suffering among the scattered remnants of the former owners of the land" (181), she focusses on the perspective and plight of the women: "I once asked an Indian woman in the village what the great boys I saw lounging in the streets did. 'They? Eat!' was the terse and emphatic reply" (181). The men's spirits broken by "the restrictive laws of civilization" (223), they "die out, leaving widows and helpless children to be maintained" (222). Ending her own long, fruitful life with the conviction that she is witnessing the end of a people, Traill inscribes a testimonial to the gratitude, kindliness, "quiet, peaceful temper, sobriety and industrious habits" (223) of the Native women who were her teachers and her friends.[8]

---

6. *The Imperialist* (1904; Toronto: McClelland & Stewart, 1990), 75.
7. In *Fear and Temptation: The Image of the Indigene in Canadian, Australian, and New Zealand Literatures* (Montreal: McGill-Queens UP, 1989).
8. Trail contributed to the preservation of Native history by donating her modest collection of artifacts, "a free gift to me from my esteemed Indian friend, Mrs. M. Jane Loucks, of Hiawatha" to the Peterborough Historical Society (*Evening Review*, Peterborough, 14 May 1897). Traill warmly welcomed the half-Native wife of her son Walter, who worked in the Northwest for the Hudson's Bay Company and took considerable pains to send copies of *Canadian Crusoes* to her distant grandchildren.

Comments such as these add to the collection of "seemingly trivial anecdotes" (Moodie, *Roughing It* 309 [194]) that, when gathered, serve as "mediators between the undifferentiated succession of local moments and a larger strategy toward which they can only gesture" (Greenblatt 3). It may never be possible or even desirable to formulate this larger history, the story of relations between settler women and indigenous women in frontier Canada, as a unified metanarrative. Rather, stories of "what really happened," to return to Jane Tompkins's quest, must be assembled from the fragments to be found in published and unpublished personal narratives, out of which one may cautiously "piece together"—in her aptly selected metaphor from quilting—the patterns of individual experience.

MICHAEL A. PETERMAN

Reconstructing the *Palladium of British America*: How the Rebellion of 1837 and Charles Fothergill Helped to Establish Susanna Moodie as a Writer in Canada†

I. Toward a Literary Connection

The study of authorship, literary culture, and publishing conditions in Upper Canada is illuminated by the brief convergence of two English-born writers, Susanna Moodie (1803–1885) and Charles Fothergill (1782–1840), from late December 1837 until the summer of 1839. The convergence, which is to be found on the pages of Fothergill's newspaper, *The Palladium of British America and Upper Canada Mercantile Advertiser*, tells us several things about the profession of writing, the challenge of finding suitable outlets for one's work, and the kinds of public communication available in that time. In the process we encounter the story of Fothergill's deepening struggles and his final failure in Upper Canada even as we gain a clearer view of John and Susanna Moodie, a displaced British literary couple diligently pursuing whatever opportunities for publication they could find from their home in the remote "bush."

A Suffolk-born woman who had written extensively for London magazines and annuals in her twenties, Susanna Moodie had emigrated to Upper Canada in 1832 with her husband and one-year old daughter. In 1837 she was struggling to raise her family of four children in the backwoods of Douro Township, thirteen miles north of the small village of Peterborough. The outbreak of the Rebellion in Upper Canada in early December set in motion a major change for herself

---

† From *Papers of the Bibliographical Society of Canada* 40/1 (Spring 2002): [7]–36. Reprinted by permission of *Papers of the Bibliographical Society of Canada*. Page numbers in brackets refer to the text of this Norton Critical Edition.

and her family that can be traced in part to her husband's subsequent military movements and in part to her writing of fervently pro-British verse expressly for Charles Fothergill's new and impressive weekly newspaper. The *Palladium*'s first issue appeared in Toronto on 20 December 1837, just two weeks after the outbreak, at a time when feelings about the Rebellion were running very high. Anxieties about the whereabouts of the perpetrators, uncertainties about continuing local threats, and the renewed fear of American invasion abounded. When Moodie's "An Address to the Freemen of Canada" appeared in that first *Palladium* issue, it found a ready audience in Toronto and Upper Canada, especially among those who were proud of their British birth.

The story of Susanna Moodie's emergence as a prominent writer in Canada is told in her autobiographical recollection, *Roughing It in the Bush* (1852).[1] The general accuracy of her account can be verified and has seldom been questioned. However, a close examination of available documents reveals a more complex set of circumstances and actions than she describes there. Most notably, she neglected to include the crucial initiatory role played by the *Palladium* and, in particular, its owner and "co-editor." The elderly Fothergill, a man of middle-class Yorkshire and Quaker roots, had been in Canada since 1816 and had made a considerable reputation for himself as a naturalist, writer, editor, politician, public figure, and community builder.[2] The enthusiastic and empathetic interest he took in Moodie's poetry, especially her patriotic verse, paved the way for her profitable and extended connection with John Lovell and his Montreal-based magazine, *The Literary Garland*.[3] It is likely that Fothergill, who was struggling with very serious financial difficulties during the year and a half of his editorship, did not pay her for her contributions. For that reason, or perhaps simply because of lapse of memory, she neglected to mention the part he played in her literary emergence.[4]

These two personal narratives converge in the pages of the *Palladium* and together provide valuable clues to the operations of print and literary culture in Upper Canada in this time. It goes without saying that self-interest played an important part in the motivations of both writers. Each sought a fresh medium for expression—Fothergill for his cultural projects, literary-scientific interests, and political views, all of which vied for his attention, and Moodie for her poetry. As self-interest is a given, so too are matters of class, social status, and national identity. There are notable similarities between the outlooks of these two middle-class English writers, though they were born a

---

1. See the chapter entitled "The Outbreak" in *Roughing It in the Bush*, ed. Carl Ballstadt (Ottawa: Carleton UP, 1988), 430–52 [273–89].
2. Paul Romney describes Fothergill in the *Dictionary of Canadian Biography* (*DCB*) VII: 317, as follows: "naturalist, artist, writer, businessman, office holder, JP, newspaperman, publisher, and politician." Fothergill was a man of many parts who was much involved in political, scientific, and literary affairs in Upper Canada for over two decades.
3. Susanna Moodie was one of the major contributors to *The Literary Garland*. The monthly magazine was in steady production from December 1838 until December 1851.
4. In writing of her connection to *The Literary Garland*, Moodie put her emphasis on the much-needed remuneration that John Lovell offered her for her writing.

generation apart. They shared an air of superiority, even a snobbishness, that was born of their education and their previous literary experience in England; they wrapped that cultural cloak all the more tightly around themselves in the midst of a society that they often found threateningly vulgar and dangerous at its worst, and in need of refined guidance and educational leadership at its best. Bearing such factors in mind, it is possible to detect a kind of laying on of hands in this convergence, the gesture of a well-positioned member of the old English guard who wished to provide a literary opportunity for a young woman and her congenial husband, both of whom he saw as likeminded heirs to his vision for colonial Upper Canada.

The first of these narratives might be called Fothergill's last hurrah. A long-standing Anglo-Canadian advocate of British cultural development and English rule in the colony, Charles Fothergill was a tired and broken man of 55 when, straining his already precarious finances, summoning up his characteristic gumption, and enlisting his son Charles Forbes Fothergill as his managing partner, he set out to launch a new forum to promote his personal views and to provide a medium for enriched scientific and literary expression in Toronto. There was evident need for such a medium. Heather Murray has observed that, while there were eight newspapers in Toronto prior to the appearance of Fothergill's *Palladium*, they "did not publish verse, despite announcements of their intent to do so"; indeed, little other than political reports, current agricultural information, and belated European news found space in these weekly papers.[5]

The second narrative is the aforementioned breakthrough of Susanna Moodie as a writer of consequence in Canada's incipient literary marketplace. It is also the story of her husband, John Wedderburn Dunbar Moodie who, it would appear, befriended Fothergill and placed himself in a position in which he could promote his wife's and his own literary interests. An accomplished writer himself, the affable and impressive Captain Moodie readily found favour with the elderly editor in December 1837.[6] Indeed, his part in the convergence is a significant one, for men dominated cultural activities in 1830s Toronto. Though he was in the city for only a few weeks, John Moodie moved at ease amongst those of literary and musical interests. For her part, his aspiring wife was simply continuing to do what she had done with determination since they arrived in Cobourg in 1832—she was seeking to avail herself of any new-world publishing opportunity she could access, whether it paid or not. In 1837 lack of payment was the only condition she knew.

Not surprisingly, given the fact that she had engaged in patriotic

5. Heather Murray, "Frozen Pen, Fiery Print, and Fothergill's Folly: Cultural Organization in Toronto, Winter 1836–37," *Essays on Canadian Writing* 61 (Spring 1997): 63.
6. John Moodie was in contact with Fothergill during his military training in Toronto from December 1837 until early March 1838, but they may have crossed paths at an earlier point between autumn 1832 and the period in question (see *Letters of Love and Duty: The Correspondence of Susanna and John Moodie*, ed. Carl Ballstadt, Elizabeth Hopkins, and Michael Peterman (Toronto: U of Toronto P, 1993), 72.

writings while still in London, Moodie responded to the violence of the Rebellion and its continuing threats to British rule with outrage and anger. Her poems were a passionate, public rallying cry. She praised British roots and demeaned the rebel leaders who dared to challenge English leadership and tradition. Nor did she hesitate to advocate violent retribution in her verbal assaults upon the perpetrators. The need to voice British support as strongly as possible in time of need and uncertainty was far stronger in her than any fond hope of payment for her writing.

In unearthing the Fothergill-Moodie connection I need to emphasize several basic factors germane to the study of print culture in early Canada. First among them is the centrality of newspapers in communications before 1840. Newspapers at that time were, as Allan R. Pred has observed, "the only regular pretelegraphic communications medium through which news of distant origin could be made locally available in the form of public information."[7] Attempts to initiate literary magazines were short-lived and book publishing was a rarity.[8] What few printing presses there were in Upper Canada were used mostly for the production of weekly newspapers and for local job printing. These papers reflected the political views and economic interests of their owners. They offered few opportunities for literary expression; if a paper included a "Poet's Corner" on occasion, the poems were mostly reprints by British or American writers.

Weekly newspapers across the Canadas constituted an informal though prickly system of communication divided along party lines. Tory publisher-editors dedicated themselves to the support of the government and Family Compact interests, while others like William Lyon Mackenzie took up the mantle of "Reform," arguing as emphatically as possible for self-government in Canada. Though the colony lacked structured political parties, most local papers fell readily in line with one view or the other. Editors of like-minded politics closely watched each others' editorials, reprinting polemical pieces which served their cause, and aggressively attacking the commentaries of those they opposed. Hostility was rampant. A man of refined and quiet sensibility, Charles Fothergill was comfortable with neither side; he loathed the kind of vulgar, obsessive, name-calling journalism that the influence of "Party" necessitated. In a typical *Palladium* editorial (25 April 1838), he urged "the destruction of Party" asserting, rather naively, that once it was done away with, "all would soon be well" in the Canadas. Seeking to articulate what he defined as moderate reform and to speak from an "independent" position that was squarely British in its commitment, he set about in the autumn of 1837 to create a new newspaper for Toronto that would follow neither party line even as it sought to offer better informed and more intellectually stim-

7. Allan R. Pred, *Urban Growth and the Circulation of Information: The United States System of Cities, 1790–1840* (Cambridge, Mass.: Harvard UP, 1973), 20.
8. In 1837 there was no literary magazine in Toronto (Murray, 63). What books there were typically reflected the publisher's interests or a (vanity) project paid for by the author.

ulating matter for its readers. Such was his intention in the planning stages for the *Palladium*. The Rebellion, however, altered his plan.

A second matter of consequence for the study of pre-1850 Canadian newspapers is the ephemerality of much early newsprint. Several papers have not survived their historical moment. Printing-office fires, unpaid subscriptions, mismanagement, or simple neglect could lead to heavy losses, if not bankruptcy, for publishers. Archivists have wrestled with the challenge of trying to locate and preserve as many as possible of these early, often short-lived, journalistic ventures. So broken are the runs of some of the surviving newspapers that, as historians like Paul Rutherford have observed, scholars have often shied away from the pre-1850 field.[9]

The *Palladium of British America* (1837–1839) provides a dramatic case in point. Only about one-quarter of its approximately 70–90 published issues have survived. No bound copy of the first year's 55 issues is known to be extant.[1] To make matters more difficult still, the surviving issues, some of which are in very poor condition, are located in several different Ontario repositories.[2] To date only one issue has been preserved on microfiche.[3] Moreover, a look at a few issues seems to have satisfied many of those who have alluded to the *Palladium* in articles and research papers. However, an examination of all the extant issues tells us much about the importance of Fothergill's newspaper as a publishing outlet for a few writers of original material in the 1830s.[4]

While surviving issues articulate the *Palladium*'s editorial purposes and general outlook, they also reveal the importance that Fothergill placed upon literary and scientific expression in his newspaper. His model was a highly successful weekly paper of the period, the *Albion or British, Colonial and Foreign Weekly Gazette* (the New York *Albion*), edited by another expatriate Englishman, John Sherran Bartlett

---

9. Paul Rutherford, *A Victorian Authority: The Daily Press in Late Nineteenth-Century Canada* (Toronto: U of Toronto P, 1982), 36–42. He notes "the chaos of organs" in the period, usually of small circulation and governed largely by "the rituals of party warfare" (37). Other sources include W. H. Kesterton's *A History of Journalism in Canada* (Toronto: McClelland & Stewart, 1967), the Canadian Press volume, *A History of Canadian Journalism* (Toronto: Murray, 1908), and Doug Fetherling's *The Rise of the Canadian Newspaper* (Toronto: Oxford UP, 1990) provide little detail or commentary on pre-1840 journalistic history. George Parker's *The Beginnings of the Book Trade in Canada* (Toronto: U of Toronto P, 1985) and Chris Raible's *Muddy York Mud: Scandal & Scurrility in Upper Canada* (Creemore, Ont.: Curiosity House, 1992) are more helpful in their copious detail; Charles Fothergill's journalism during the 1820s and his long-standing relation with the opposition to William Lyon Mackenzie are discussed in the latter.

1. Vol. 2, No. 1 (Whole Number 56) of the *Palladium* (2 January 1839) is held by the Archives of Ontario. Only three issues from the second year of publication seem to have survived; the latest in time is the issue for 17 May 1839, Vol. 2, No. 15 (Whole Number 70), also at the Archives of Ontario.

2. Extant copies of the *Palladium* are found in the Baldwin Room of the Metropolitan Toronto Library, the Thomas Fisher Rare Book Library at the University of Toronto, the National Archives of Canada in Ottawa, and the Archives of Ontario (Toronto). The latter has the largest number of issues.

3. See the Canadian Institute for Historical Microfiche (CIHM #45875). This copy is a special edition published on Thursday evening, 8 March 1838.

4. Another original contributor featured in the *Palladium* was Dr. Robert Douglas Hamilton (1773–1857) of Scarborough Township. A Scot by birth, Hamilton published political essays under the pseudonym of Guy Pollock, a name borrowed from a Scarborough blacksmith. Hamilton also wrote on medicine and had been a contributor, along with Susanna Moodie, to George Gurnett's short-lived *Canadian Literary Magazine* (York [Toronto], 1833).

(1790–1863). It was a paper read by many recent British emigrants to Canada. Long a writer himself, Fothergill, like Bartlett, sought an elevated level of discourse, cultural sophistication, and talent among his contributors and letter writers; literary ability, scientific knowledge, British birth or allegiance, genteel social status, and patriotic spirit were qualities he wished to recognize in the *Palladium*. He aimed for the dissemination of "superior" literary expression "untainted by scurrility and personal abuse." He argued for Canada's "promising destiny" as "the most important appendage of the British crown" and he counseled unyielding loyalty to England and its political institutions as well as "free[dom] from party politics" (*Palladium* 27 December 1837). When the *Albion* criticized the *Palladium* for lacking originality and being "made up of *scraps* from English papers" (17 February 1838), Fothergill was astonished and indignant. Such "a wanton and malicious attack," he responded, was far from valid and entirely unexpected of its gentleman editor. Though he had by then published only nine issues of the *Palladium*, he defended himself by citing positive reviews of his newspaper in Ogle Gowan's the *Statesman* (Brockville) and in the *Western Herald* (Sandwich); the *Palladium* provides "more reading matter than any other publication in the Province," wrote the editor of the latter paper. In his own defense Fothergill argued that, contrary to the *Albion*'s assertion, his paper offered much original writing (*Palladium* 28 February 1838). Poems by Susanna and John Moodie were no doubt implicit in this assertion, as were a series of papers on geology that may have been by Fothergill's own hand.

In piecing together the contributions of Susanna and John Moodie to the *Palladium*, I have had the use of Mary Lu Macdonald's working list of literary publications by writers in Canadian newspapers before 1850. This list, which is not included in her monograph, *Literature and Society in the Canadas 1817–1850* (Mellon, 1992), is particularly helpful in that several poems listed under Susanna Moodie's name are described as being "From the Palladium," though they appeared in another newspaper. Using that information and the precise evidence available in extant issues of the *Palladium* itself, I have compiled a list of Moodie's identifiable contributions to the paper. It includes ten poems and one two-part book review. Moreover, her contributions span the year and a half of the paper's existence, suggesting that, even though her writing began to appear in John Lovell's *The Literary Garland* in May, 1839, she remained in some contact with Fothergill even when his newspaper was losing its popularity and editorial steam. It must also be added that there is every likelihood that more than ten of her poems appeared in the *Palladium*'s pages. What can be traced, however, is ample available evidence that she was one of Fothergill's primary and favoured contributors. Moreover, as several of her poems were reprinted widely in both Upper and Lower Canada, it is clear that her appearances in the *Palladium* helped to provide her with a wide colonial exposure well before she became a prominent contributor to *The Literary Garland*.

II. Charles Fothergill: Nature Study, Politics, and Newspapers

It is difficult to be succinct about "the quixotic writer, naturalist, and publisher Charles Fothergill."[5] He was amongst the busiest and most talented men in Upper Canada during his 23 years in the province, but he was also one of the least successful in terms of enduring results. The reasons for such failure and disappointment were at once personal, political, and accidental. He was a man of many parts, a kind of renaissance man. His ambitions were capacious, his visions often grand, his energy level high. Yet, for all his efforts and projects, he was seldom able to complete even those undertakings to which he devoted so much time and commitment. At times he was the victim of his own aspirations, spreading himself too thin and trying to accomplish too much. At other times he was simply unlucky. In most instances he showed bad, if not perverse, judgement in attacking the political forces to which he had to appeal for monetary and social support.[6] Still, it is important to observe that, despite his many emotional and economic setbacks, he remained remarkably consistent in his ambitions and values. In many ways he seems a man ahead of his time;[7] certainly he was a man oddly out of tune, a proud and individualistic Englishman who was never willing to play the political game laid out before him in Upper Canada.

Before Fothergill came to Canada, he had committed a great deal of his time to nature study and literary writing, encouraged by scientists within his own family and the model of Gilbert White of Selborne. When only 17 he published *Ornithologia Britannica*, an 11-page folio classifying 301 species of British birds. A precocious, two-volume collection of stories, essays, and verse entitled *The Wanderer* appeared four years later (1803) and "An essay on the Philosophy, Study, and Use of Natural History" in 1813. For him, the acquisition of scientific knowledge was the "truly great and virtuous" way of living.[8] Setting the study of birds and animals as his highest priority, he devoted enormous amounts of time to the preparation of two major manuscripts he hoped to publish—their working titles were the "Natural and Civil History of Yorkshire" and "The Northern Isles of Britain." Despite having commissioned several plates for these two projects (some by the noted engraver Thomas Bewick), Fothergill was frustrated in his plan to publish the manuscripts in England. Never one to linger long in disappointment, however, he revised his plans and brought both manuscripts with him to Canada in 1816, heartened by the idea that he might now expand the projects to include the natural history of British America. Yet, it was more than a new plan and passionate scientific

5. Murray, 44.
6. Paul Romney describes Fothergill's career as "an unbroken sequence of failures that were largely of his own making" (*DCB*, VII: 320).
7. This was the view of Henry Scadding. See *Toronto of Old*, ed. Frederick H. Armstrong (Toronto: Dundurn Press, 1987), 148.
8. See the Preface to Fothergill's *The Wanderer: A Collection of Original Tales and Essays, Founded on Facts*, Vol. I (London: Wynne and Scholey, 1803).

ambition that led him to emigrate with his wife and two young sons. He had failed in several business and educational ventures while in England and was faced with debts that made his remaining problematical. In leaving Yorkshire as he did, he set a pattern of aspiration, struggle, defeat, and indebtedness that would characterize his later activities in Upper Canada.

In several articles and in the *Dictionary of Canadian Biography*, Paul Romney has traced Charles Fothergill's checkered political and journalistic career in York (Toronto) and other parts of Upper Canada.[9] James L. Baillie, Jr., and others have sought to describe and itemize his pioneering achievements in zoology, ornithology, geology, and other scientific fields.[1] More recently Heather Murray has studied his visionary attempt to develop for Toronto in the 1830s not only a literary society but also a Lyceum of Natural History and the Fine Arts, which was to include a museum, a gallery of the fine arts, a botanical garden, and a zoo.[2] Fothergill was, in Paul Romney's useful phrase, a "savant with a sense of public duty."[3] He was an intellectual and amateur scientist of Quaker leanings, a journalist of conservative political views, and a man who spoke out publicly and fearlessly for his beliefs.[4] A self-styled independent in Party-ridden Upper Canada, he was confident that he could rise above the fray and speak for the best of British social values and the English constitutional tradition. In doing so, he showed a persistent tendency "to cross . . . powerful figure[s]" in the Upper Canadian political arena.[5]

When Fothergill emigrated to Upper Canada in February 1816, Susanna Strickland was a fifteen-year-old girl living at Reydon Hall in Suffolk. He left behind a record of failed ventures in farming, horse breeding, acting, writing, and the study of medicine. After settling his business affairs in Quebec and making his family comfortable, he set out alone on an adventurous trip by sleigh from that city to York (Toronto), duly recording his travels in a notebook. Stopping at Port Hope (Smith's Creek) and visiting the virtually unsettled lands near

9. Paul Romney, "Charles Fothergill," *DCB*, VII: 317–21. See also "A Conservative Reformer in Upper Canada: Charles Fothergill, Responsible Government and the 'British Party,' 1824–1840," *Historical Papers* 1984: 42–62, and "From the Types Riot to the Rebellion: Elite Ideology, Anti-legal Sentiment, Political Violence, and the Rule of Law in Upper Canada," *Ontario History* 76, no. 2 (June 1987): 113–44.
1. James L. Baillie, Jr., "Charles Fothergill, 1772–1840," *Canadian Historical Review* 25 (December 1945): 376–96. See also Elaine Theberge, "Fothergill: Canada's Pioneer Naturalist Emerges from Oblivion," *The Beaver* 68, no.1 (Feb./Mar. 1988): 12–18.
2. Fothergill was, with Dr. William Rees and William "Tiger" Dunlop, a co-founder of the Literary and Philosophical Society of Upper Canada at York. He exhibited ten watercolours at the 1834 show put on in York by the Society of Artists and Amateurs (the show included a portrait of him by another artist), and he earned attention for essays on Canadian quadrepeds and the need to preserve the salmon stock in Lake Ontario.
3. Romney, *DCB*, VII: 319.
4. In his introduction to *The Wanderer*, Fothergill wrote of "the importance of cultivating the mind, the finer feelings of the heart, and of learning to restrain passions." Though his many activities, including a brief fling in acting and a devotion to horse breeding, suggest a secularity well beyond his Quaker commitments, Fothergill always maintained a strong set of Quaker values. Both of his wives, Charlotte Nevins of York, England, and Eliza Richardson of Port Hope, Upper Canada, were from Quaker families.
5. Murray, 61.

Rice Lake, he was attracted to that landscape and its possibilities. He petitioned the Lieutenant Governor Francis Gore to allow him to develop what he called a "colony of gentlemen" at Rice Lake. To his delight, he was granted 1200 acres in southern Monaghan Township near the mouth of the Otonabee River.

Over the next fifteen years Fothergill maintained close connections to the Rice Lake area. He built a hunting lodge which he named Castle Fothergill, hunted and gathered natural specimen, practised taxidermy, and developed friendly relations with the local Mississauga tribe and their chief "Captain Mohawk."[6] His home base was "Ontario Cottage," a comfortable villa within walking distance of the village of Port Hope. Here he was much in the public eye as postmaster, magistrate, local political figure, businessman, and member of the district land board. Though he often worried about his finances, he insisted that his family live in style. In writing home to Yorkshire after his wife's painful death from tuberculosis in 1822, he assured her family that Charlotte had "never wanted for comfort and luxury." In fact, he complained that they had employed too many rather than too few servants at Ontario Cottage and that his property had been injured as a result.[7]

His appointment as King's Printer in York (January 1822–26) and his subsequent election to the Legislative Assembly in 1824 took him away from Port Hope but brought him an income, a printing press, and a new level of public prominence. His successes, however, angered some of the powerful political leaders of York who resented the favoured newcomer with his English superiority and lofty schemes,[8] and were disturbed that a prominent government employee dared to be critical of government operations in the Legislative Assembly. Undeterred by growing signs of opposition, he went quickly to work, enlarging the paper (it was called the *Weekly Register* after April 1824) and expanding its yearly almanac, both of which served as platforms for his literary energies. But when he emerged as "a leading spokesman of the parliamentary opposition" in the Legislative Assembly session of 1825–26, his political enemies sought ways to silence, or at least diminish, his voice.[9] Members of the Family Compact, as both William Lyon Mackenzie and Fothergill were wont to label them, objected not only to various of Fothergill's political criticisms but also to the unprecedentedly large expenses he undertook at the press (costs that Fothergill expected the government to absorb). Early in 1826 he was removed from the editorship "for political reasons" and, worse still, given his limited capital, he was saddled with a new debt in the

6. Though many of Fothergill's manuscripts have been recovered, the one describing his experiences with the Mississauga remains missing.
7. A copy of a letter from Fothergill to his wife's sister dated 17 October 1822, Charles Fothergill Papers, vol. 23, Thomas Fisher Rare Book Library, University of Toronto.
8. In the election of 1824 he stood against George Strange Boulton, the brother of Solicitor General Henry John Boulton and a prominent member of the Family Compact. That election seemed to mark a turning point in Fothergill's political outlook as he soon set himself in opposition to both Mackenzie's reforms and the machinations of the Family Compact.
9. Romney, *DCB*, VII: 319.

form of a government-imposed bond.[1] Despite a public outcry and a subscription taken up to help him in his injured state, Fothergill was enraged. He would never forgive his persecutors and he would renew his attacks upon the Family Compact during his editorship of the *Palladium*. In the mid-1830s some of those same Family Compact leaders, among them John Strachan and Chief Justice John Beverley Robinson, would do what was necessary to impede and effectively to scuttle his eager plans to establish major cultural institutions in Toronto.

By the late summer of 1832, when the Moodies arrived in Cobourg, Charles Fothergill had left Port Hope and moved to present-day Pickering where, near the family of his second wife, he developed plans to establish a new community and model town he named Monadelphia. Like so many of his visionary schemes including the "colony of gentlemen" at Rice Lake, this project faltered, in large part because a fire destroyed the mills in which he had heavily invested. Again his finances were badly over-extended.

Whether he knew of the Moodies in 1832 is not clear. Having sold Ontario Cottage, he may have continued to subscribe to the Cobourg *Star*, the leading newspaper between York and Kingston. The *Star* was a weekly paper in its second year of operation under the editorship of R. D. Chatterton. Fothergill, who had in 1829 petitioned Sir John Colborne to begin a Port Hope newspaper as a government voice for Eastern Upper Canada, knew Chatterton well. In fact, he contributed several essays to the paper in 1831 and early 1832 under the pen name "Atticus." Titles such as "Land Tortoises and Mud Turtles" (29 March 1831), "Natural Frostwork" (15 April 1831), "Old Thunder— An Indian Tradition" (5 July 1831), "The First Fall of Snow" (6 December 1831), and "Duty of Parish and Town Officers" (25 January 1832) provide evidence of his range of interests and his role as local authority. In particular, they show his passion for naturalistic observation and his familiarity with the Mississauga people of Rice Lake. It is a mere coincidence that one of his Atticus essays, "A Short History on the Art of Writing," appeared in the 20 September 1831 issue of the Cobourg *Star* alongside a poem taken "From a collection of Unpublished Poems, written by a young English Lady." That poem, "The Vision of Dry Bones," was the work of Susanna (Strickland) Moodie who had yet to emigrate.[2] Her unpublished collection, *Enthusiasm, and Other Poems*, had by then been published in London.

Genteel English emigrants with a passion for literary expression and an interest in natural history were likely to become known to each other, if only by name and reputation. Living in eastern Upper Canada, Fothergill and the Moodies brought with them from the homeland a shared belief in the importance of manners and the devel-

---

1. Romney, *DCB*, VII: 318. The bond was for 367 pounds.
2. It is likely that Robert Reid of Douro Township near Peterborough brought the poems back with him after a trip to Ireland and England where he visited the Moodies and assisted them in their plan to emigrate. Chatterton published three of them in the Cobourg *Star* before the Moodies had arrived in Canada.

opment of one's mind and sensibility. They valued proper speech, genteel behaviour, and evidence of personal cultivation and achievement. They may not have had much formal education themselves but that little mattered. What counted was their serious commitment to education and self-cultivation, and their confident belief that intellectual, social, and spiritual benefits followed naturally from such conscious endeavour.

III. The Moodies in and out of "The Bush"

Both Susanna and John Moodie came to Canada as displaced writers, literary aspirants who by their choice of emigration found themselves at a great remove from the English cultural arena in which they had separately sought recognition. With *Enthusiasm, and Other Poems* recently published by subscription in London, and a significant number of appearances in London magazines and annuals behind her, Susanna was a 29-year-old poet torn between her increasing commitments as a wife and mother and her powerful desire to practise her skills as a writer. In both enterprises she had the firm support of her husband, an adventure-loving, gregarious Orcadian who had already published a well-received memoir of his experiences as a soldier in the Napoleonic wars and who, prior to emigrating to Canada, had left in London (with the publisher Richard Bentley) a two-volume account of his ten years as a settler in South Africa.[3] The problem facing the pair was how to make a sustainable family life for themselves as settlers in Canada while finding ways to tap into available Canadian and American markets for literary expression. They had to live, they had to find socially acceptable ways to support themselves, but they also had to write. As writers, they had to be noticed and they had to be read. To be published was in their blood, and it is likely that, of the two, Susanna was the more driven to make her mark as a practising professional writer. Nevertheless, she often had to rely on her husband to make the necessary connections with publishers.

Not surprisingly, then, the Moodies sought out available publishing opportunities soon after arriving. Almost immediately, John arranged to place one of Susanna's poems in the Cobourg *Star*. "Lines written amidst the ruins of a church on the coast of Suffolk" appeared there on Wednesday 19 September 1832, two weeks after their arrival in town. The author was identified as "Susanna Strickland (now Mrs. Moodie)." This important dual identification was one which Susanna carefully applied during the early years of her marriage in order to keep her Strickland identity before both editors and readers. In the same issue John also managed to have Chatterton include a poem

---

3. John Moodie's monograph "Narratives of the Campaign in Holland in 1814" appeared in *Memoirs of the Late War*, ed. John Henry Cooke (London, 1831). He received some good reviews and considerable recognition for his two-volume account of his South African experiences in the 1820s, *Ten Years in South Africa, with a Particular Description of the Wild Sports* (London: Bentley, 1835). An excerpt from this book was reprinted by Chatterton in the Cobourg *Star*.

written to their daughter on the occasion of their debarkation from Southwold, Suffolk. "To Catherine Mary Moodie, An Infant" was the work of James Bird (1788–1839), a well-known Suffolk poet and close friend of several of the Strickland daughters of Reydon Hall. Such an inclusion implied a message, even if its significance eluded many readers of the Cobourg *Star*. A literary couple of some note, a couple with impressive literary connections, had arrived in Cobourg. Attention ought to be paid.

Other Susanna Moodie poems from *Enthusiasm, and Other Poems* appeared in the Cobourg *Star* that same year—"Autumn" (17 October), "Uncertainty" (31 October), "O Come to the Meadows" (23 November), and "Youth and Age" (19 December). Thus, even as the Moodies were settling uncomfortably into their infamously sty-like shanty at Gage's Creek, they were doing their best to have samples of their work included in the local newspaper, no doubt hoping that such recognition might lead to further connections. For his part, John Moodie arranged to place his dramatic sketch, "The Elephant Hunt," which had recently appeared in book form in Charles Knight's *Menageries* in London and which was a part of his still unpublished South African narrative, in the *Star* in the same 17 October issue that included Susanna's "Autumn."

In *Roughing It in the Bush*, Susanna lamented the difficulty, if not the near impossibility, of writing for publication while living in the depths of the Upper Canadian backwoods. However, their time in the bush, which became for them an experience of near-isolation and increasing poverty, did not begin until later in the decade. While living close to Port Hope and Cobourg (from September 1832 until February 1834), and while still excited by her English literary successes, Susanna aggressively sought out other opportunities for publication. Fortunately, her eldest sister Elizabeth had by then earned an influential editorial position with *The Lady's Magazine* in London. Several of Susanna's poems and stories appeared in those pages from 1832 through 1837. But in Upper Canada she was on her own, though she was abetted by her husband who, when possible, functioned as her agent, genially badgering the editor of the Cobourg *Star*, among others, to include her poems when space or occasion allowed.

It was typical of the ambitious and persistent Susanna Moodie that she should also curry literary favour on her own whenever she could. Her letter of 14 February 1833 to John Sherran Bartlett, owner and editor of the New York *Albion*, demonstrates her eager yet genteel approach. The chance to peruse your "clever and interesting paper," she began, "has made me ambitious of the honour of contributing to its pages; and if the assistance of a pen, deemed not unworthy of public notice in my native land, when held by Susanna Strickland, can in any way be acceptable to you, and your readers, it will afford me much pleasure to transmit to you, from time to time, a few small original poems." Anticipating a 'yes' from Dr. Bartlett, whom she knew to be an Englishman, she appended two poems which she proudly described as "the first flight of my muse on Canadian shores."[4] Bartlett immediately published them along with her letter, though, in his editorial commentary, he inadvertently confused Susanna with her older sister, the better-known and more widely published poet, Agnes.

It is not recorded whether Bartlett's conspicuous error unsettled the sensitive Susanna. Likely it did. She was certainly used to playing second fiddle to Agnes in England and there is some evidence that she had been occasionally at odds with her sister prior to her own emigration. But, with a new audience before her, her response was cheerful and gracious. Using Bartlett's error as an excuse to set the record straight about her identity, she included another of her "original poems," which he promptly published in his issue of 25 May 1832. Bartlett would also publish several of John Moodie's poems along with others by Susanna in his other newspaper, aptly entitled *The Emigrant. A Journal of the Domestic News of England, Ireland, Scotland and Wales*. Appearing in the 25 June 1834 issue of *The Emigrant*, for instance, were Susanna's poems, "The Canadian Woodsman" and "The Canadian Woods."

Moodie's pursuit of public recognition is evident both in her approach to editors and in the way she presented her material. The first two poems in the *Albion*, "The Sleigh Bells. A Canadian Song" and "Song: The Strains We Hear in Foreign Lands," earned her wide exposure and immediate attention. With a sound instinct for marking the emotional polarities of emigrant experience, she typically sent Bartlett a pair of contrasting poems, one singing the praises of Canadian experience and the other expressing the deep sense of displacement and loss felt by British emigrants in the new world. Shrewdly, she balanced the charm of the new against the weight of deracination and homesickness; such, it seems, was her strategy from the outset. It is a measure of her success in this first contact with Bartlett that "The Sleigh Bells" was reprinted in at least nine Canadian newspapers and its companion poem, "The Strains We Hear in Foreign Lands," appeared in seven.

Moodie tested other opportunities as well. She sent material to two promising but short-lived magazines in Toronto (George Gurnett's *Canadian Literary Magazine*, edited by John Kent, and Robert Stanton's *The Canadian Magazine*, edited by W. Sibbald) and to Sumner Lincoln Fairfield, an Anglophilic poet living in Philadelphia. Fairfield had sought out her poetry and prose for his *North American (Quarterly) Magazine*, but he regretted that he could not pay for contributions. By then, living deep in the backwoods and being far more financially constrained than in her early days near Port Hope, Susanna was unable to afford the postage required to mail her submissions south of the border.[5] Still, eleven of her pieces (and one by her husband) appeared in Fairfield's magazine from December 1834 through 1836.

<hr>

4. Susanna Moodie to the editor of the *Albion*, 14 February 1833 (see *Susanna Moodie: Letters of a Lifetime*, ed Carl Ballstadt, Elizabeth Hopkins, and Michael Peterman [Toronto: U of Toronto P, 1985], 90).
5. *Roughing It in the Bush*, 440 [281]. Moodie sent a copy of *Enthusiasm, and Other Poems* to Fairfield; he used it as a source of poems to publish. See her two letters to Fairfield in *Susanna Moodie: Letters of a Lifetime*, 92–95.

By the time of the Rebellion, Susanna Moodie had tried out most of the publishing outlets she could identify. In fact, she was more or less stymied. Editors paid only in platitudes and the business of making oneself attractive to such men at a distance was expensive and frustrating. Her work continued to appear occasionally in magazines and newspapers, but the unyielding demands of the bush farm and the energies involved in bearing and rearing her children left her drained. The constraints that came with lack of money for paper, ink, and candles further limited her enterprise.

IV. The Rebellion and "The Palladium"

Recalling her surprise upon hearing of "the outbreak," Susanna Moodie wrote in *Roughing It in the Bush* that "Buried in the obscurity of the woods, we knew nothing, heard nothing of the political state of the country, and were little aware of the revolution which was about to work a great change for us and for Canada."[6] While the latter half of the statement is accurate, the pages of the *Palladium* reveal that Moodie's claim of total ignorance is a misrepresentation. Because 'Mackenzie Meetings' were being held in various locales across the province and arousing much concern, it is likely that the Moodies would have had some knowledge of, and concern about, grievances and unrest in the Peterborough area. It was, rather, the sudden outbreak of violence that took her by surprise. Still, the fact of the Rebellion's occurrence quickly made a major difference in their lives, at first because of John Moodie's military experience and his hasty trip to Toronto upon hearing of Sir Francis Bond Head's Proclamation.

Informed of the outbreak after his brothers-in-law, Sam Strickland and Thomas Traill, had already left for Peterborough to answer Head's call for help, John Moodie hurriedly set off on his own, despite a leg injury from which he was still recovering. Traveling directly to Toronto, he managed to gain a Captain's position in a newly formed regiment, the Queen's Own, which was to begin training there in mid-January. With him he carried a copy of his wife's poem, "Canadians, Will You Join the Band. A Loyal Song." He was able to place it with Charles Fothergill, whose newspaper, he learned, was about to produce its first issue. The poem appeared on page 4 of that initial issue of the *Palladium* on 20 December 1837. It was dated "Douro, November 20, 1837"—that is, a good two weeks in advance of the actual outbreak. Included (without its date) in *Roughing It in the Bush* as "An Address to the Freemen of Canada," the poem challenged all loyal British descendants to "spurn the base wretch who dare defy / In arms, his country and his God!" It proclaimed that it was the duty and privilege of all who recognize "The regal power of that bless'd land / From whence your boasted freedom flows" to confront "the rash, misguided band" and to "crush the traitors to the dust." The poem would be picked up by at least eight Canadian newspapers over the following

6. *Roughing It in the Bush*, 432 [275].

three weeks, five in Upper Canada and three in Lower Canada.[7] One of these was John Lovell's Montreal *Transcript* where the poem appeared eight days later (28 December 1837). Lovell, who by then may have begun making plans to publish *The Literary Garland*, would readily remember Susanna Moodie when it came time to recruit able and interesting contributors.

Charles Fothergill was clearly pleased by John Moodie. He was a literary man, an adventurer with South African experience, a loyal soldier, and an Orcadian. Fothergill had visited the Orkneys in researching his manuscript of natural observations of Britain's northern islands and had a great admiration for those hardy islanders. As an officer boarding at the New British Coffee House on King Street, John Moodie was not long in making, or renewing, several literary, musical, and social connections in Toronto. In a letter to his wife dated 7 February 1838 he commented on several friends—the George Maynards, "our good little friend [John] Kent," Walter Crofton, and Fothergill, adding that "Every body here is delighted with your poetry. Fothergill seems most grateful for your assistance."[8] Just as importantly, Susanna's fiery patriotism accorded with his own; so did her faith in the British constitution and her confidence in English freedom. His fondness for the Moodies and his personal awareness of her poetry are evident in his editorial remarks on "Canadians, Will You Join the Band":

> Thanks to the sweet poetess who has so often delighted us from her nesting place in the dark-brown woods of the Newcastle District on subjects of softer interest: and who now shews with what skill she can strike a bolder strain—Yes; all who see it, must thank thee, sweet Poetess—Daughter of Genius—and, Wife of the Brave.

Given such effusion, it is not surprising that more of her poems celebrating British patriotism and interpreting signal events of the Rebellion would soon follow.

Susanna's second "Rebellion" poem appeared in the fifth issue of the *Palladium* (17 January 1838) and hit a note of rabid patriotism she would never again equal. "On Reading the Proclamation Delivered by William Lyon Mackenzie, on Navy Island" is 80 lines in length and was written "For the Palladium."[9] It was not picked up by other newspapers, likely because of its length. Moodie may have sent it down to

7. The dates of publication in the five Upper Canadian papers were—the *Western Herald* (Sandwich) 3 January 1838; the *St. Catharines Journal* 11 January 1838: the *Upper Canada Herald* (Kingston) 9 January 1838; the *Kingston Chronicle* 3 January 1838; and the *Statesman* (Brockville) 30 December 1837; and in three Lower Canada papers—the *Gazette* (Montreal) 30 December 1837; the *Transcript* (Montreal); and the *Missiskoui Standard* (Frelighsburg, Que.) 9 January 1838.

8. *Letters of Love and Duty*, 72. Both the Rev. George Maynard (from Cambridge) and John Kent taught at Upper Canada College. Moodie's phrase "our good little friend" implies, if not actual friendship between Susanna and Kent, then a good working relationship of a literary kind. As editor of *The Canadian Literary Magazine*, Kent had included three poems and two stories by Susanna along with a flattering review of *Enthusiasm, and Other Poems*. Only three issues of the magazine appeared in 1833. W. G. Crofton, another Englishman with literary aspirations, later wrote under the pseudonym "Uncle Ben" and would edit the Cobourg *Star* for a time in the 1840s.

9. The only known copy of this poem (in the *Palladium* issue) is held by the Archives of Ontario. The full text is included in Carl Ballstadt, "Secure in Conscious Worth: Susanna

Toronto with her husband when, after a brief visit home to bid farewell to his family and gather his equipment, John returned to the city to report to the Queen's Own. With him he also brought several of his own poems, four of which Fothergill included in the *Palladium* issues of February 7th and 14th.[1]

Fothergill was almost as effusive about "the gallant husband of Mrs. Moodie" as he was about Susanna. She already held a "distinguished rank" among poets "throughout Great Britain and upon this Continent." But he found in John Moodie another poet "possessed of talents of a superior character" and was grateful to have received "permission to publish" several poems that reflected the "versatility" of the "author of that delightful work, a 'Ten Year Residence in South Africa'" [sic]. With *Ten Years in South Africa* published to good reviews in London, John Moodie was both a literary figure to be reckoned with and a welcome contributor.

In his visits with Fothergill while he was training in Toronto with the Queen's Own Regiment,[2] John Moodie passed on at least one more patriotic poem by his wife, "The Banner of England," which appeared in the *Palladium* 24 January 1838.[3] He also left a copy of *Enthusiasm, and Other Poems* for Fothergill to use as he saw fit. The editor did, in fact, take poems from the book for at least two subsequent issues of the *Palladium*.

Here follows a list of the seven other poems by Susanna Moodie that can be identified as having made their first Canadian appearances in the *Palladium*. The date and issue number follow the title:

4. "War" (from *Enthusiasm, and Other Poems*). 11 February 1838 (Vol. 1, No. 11).

5. "The Avenger of Blood" (from *Enthusiasm*). 11 April 1838 (Vol. 1, No. 18).

6. "The Wind That Sweeps Our Native Sea. A National Song" ("Written Expressly for the Palladium"). 25 April 1838 (Vol. 1, No. 20).[4]

Moodie and the Rebellion of 1837," *Canadian Poetry* 18 (Spring/Summer 1986): 96–98. In his essay Ballstadt covers some of the same ground as I do here, though without the emphasis on print culture and the examination of the connection between Charles Fothergill and the Moodies. He also provides an analysis of "the inconsistency of Moodie's treatment of the rebellion" in the poem (94).

1. John Moodie's poems in the issue of 7 February 1838 were the pun-ridden "The Bears of Canada" and "Dream of Happiness," along with an epigram. "Song" (first line: "To the woods—to the woods—the sun shines bright") and "Och! Now I'm intirely continted" appeared in the next issue—14 February 1838; again a four-line epigram was included with the two poems. In his letter to Susanna of 7 February 1838, he reported, "In this days paper [Fothergill] inserts some of my verses . . . with a flaming introduction. Far too complimentary for my tastes; but he means it kindly" (see *Letters of Love and Duty*, 71–73).

2. John Moodie trained with the Queen's Own through February and was assigned to the Niagara frontier in early March (see *Letters of Love and Duty*, 72–75).

3. "The Banner of England" is dated 2 January 1838, the same day as her "On Reading William Lyon Mackenzie's Proclamation, on Navy Island." Though it carried the inscription "For the Palladium," the poem was actually a slightly revised version of one she had included in *Patriotic Songs* (1831), a collection of seven songs with music that she co-wrote with her sister Agnes for J. Green of Soho, London, England. Three of the songs were by Susanna.

4. It is not clear how this poem came into Fothergill's hands, for John Moodie was on military duty at this time in the Niagara area. Likely it was brought to Toronto by a friend or sent by mail.

7. "The Burning of the Caroline." The poem appeared in the *Palladium* sometime in early October. It was reprinted in Lovell's Montreal *Transcript* 11 October 1838; the Montreal *Gazette* 13 October 1838; and the *Western Herald* (Sandwich) 6 November 1838.

8. "There's Not a Spot (in this wide peopled earth)." The poem also appeared in the *Palladium* some time in October 1838. It was reprinted in the Montreal *Herald* 24 October 1838; the *Western Herald* (Sandwich) 20 November 1838; the St. Catharines *Journal* 13 December 1838; and the Montreal *Gazette* 28 February 1839.

9. "To Mrs. Pringle" (first line: "Widow, indeed! Tis thine to weep"): a poem included as the conclusion to the second part of a two-part review of *The Poetical Works of Thomas Pringle*, 2 January 1839 (Vol. 2, No. 1). The first part appeared in a missing issue (Vol. 1, No. 52). In the issue of 2 January 1839, Fothergill elegantly apologized for the delay between the two parts of the review. He also praised the charitable object of "this deeply interesting communication" and suggested that readers pay special attention to the poem to Pringle's widow. "It is touchingly beautiful," he wrote, "and worthy of the excellent moral feeling and superior genius from where it emanates." The Pringles had been close friends and almost surrogate parents to Susanna Strickland in London. Pringle, who gave Susanna away in marriage to John on 4 April 1831, had died suddenly in 1834.

10. "The Waters. A Song" (first line: "Let the lover laud earth's daughters") appeared in the *Palladium* some time in August 1839, in what was likely one of the final issues of the paper. It was reprinted "From the Palladium" in the Montreal *Morning Courier* on 19 August 1839 and in the Bytown *Gazette, and Ottawa and Rideau Advertiser* on 11 September 1839. The Bytown *Gazette* describes the poem as written "Expressly for the Palladium of British America" and provides the date and place of composition as "Douro, May 12, 1836." The poem was comprised of four stanzas of eight lines in length. While it is not clear how Fothergill received this poem (it is not in *Enthusiasm, and Other Poems*), its date suggests that John Moodie could have left it with him at any time after December 1837. It is important to note that "The Waters: A Canadian Song" (first line: "Come launch the light canoe"), which appeared in *The Literary Garland* 2, no. 8 (July 1840): 360, is the same poem, minus its first eight-line verse. See also "A Canadian Song" in *Roughing It in the Bush*, 362 [229]. There are several variant wordings from the lines in the Bytown *Gazette* reprinting to the later three-verse versions that appeared in *The Literary Garland* and *Roughing It in the Bush*, but the poems are essentially the same.

Of these poems, the most consequential in terms of the Rebellion is "The Burning of the Caroline." Lovell's Montreal *Transcript* of 11 October 1838 corroborates the poem's *Palladium* appearance, for in republishing it, the editor included Moodie's letter to Fothergill. Surprisingly, it was written from Douro on the very same date as its appearance on the pages of the *Transcript*. While such a coincidence seems impossible (it was likely a typographical error), the letter and poem would most likely have been carried to Toronto by her husband who was at the time between military postings and seeking a further commission. While her letter precisely accounts for her delay in commemorating the Caroline's burning, it also implies that she did not know Fothergill personally, having relied on her husband to place her poems in his hands:

> The enclosed poem was partly written at the period when the important event it celebrates occurred. The absence of my dear husband on the frontier, sickness, the management of our bush farm, and many domestic cares, hindered me from preparing it for publication at the time. Without wishing to keep alive the public excitement, so widely displayed on the perpetration of that gallant action, by Captain Drew, and his brave and loyal band,—[but] with the vanity natural to my sex and profession, I should like to see my honest feelings on the subject transferred to the pages of your valuable paper, and I remain, Sir,
>
> Yours with respect,
> Susanna Moodie.

By the time that John Lovell enlisted Susanna Moodie as a paid contributor to *The Literary Garland*, the *Palladium* was faltering badly. Her first poems appeared in the sixth number of the magazine's first volume—May 1839. They were "The Oath of the Canadian Volunteers: A Loyal Song for Canada" and "The Otonabee." By then Fothergill's finances were at a critical stage; his health was failing, his interest was flagging, and the newspaper's ability to hold subscriptions and advertising was on the wane. In the issue of 28 February 1838, Fothergill had confidently bragged that the paper had not only the largest circulation in the province but also the largest and most attractive format, having expanded from four to eight pages on high-quality paper stock. A year later he knew this was no longer the case.

With the *Palladium*, as in many of his earlier ventures, Fothergill overshot the limits of his resources and the cogency of his personal views. Advocating a conservative reform position for the colony, he had continued his verbal assaults upon the Family Compact and the administration of Sir Francis Bond Head while attacking the traitorous violence of Mackenzie and his reform-minded cohorts. His pursuit of a high middle ground, appropriate to his conservative values and his sense of himself as a superior kind of Englishman in a British colony, was tenuous at best because it was without a sustaining political anchor. Idealistically, he placed his hope first in the arrival of Sir George Arthur as Lieutenant Governor of Upper Canada, and then in the recommendations of Lord Durham, but insisting on the independence of his own outlook and finding few political allies, he remained without a significant base of support.

One of his major journalistic projects early in 1838 was to prepare a book detailing the folly and destructiveness of Mackenzie's radical actions. It appeared early that summer under the title *Mackenzie's Own Narrative of the Late Rebellion, with Illustrations and Notes, Critical and Explanatory: Exhibiting the only true account of what took place at the Memorable Siege of Toronto, in the Month of December, 1837.* A much lesser document than Fothergill had originally intended, the 24-page pamphlet reprinted Mackenzie's personal account of the Rebellion along with Fothergill's Introduction and his 50 footnotes. Drawn from his own experiences and the records of a few other prominent individuals, these footnotes and related appendix material make clear Fothergill's disdain for "the Arch-Traitor MACKENZIE." The real problem, however, lay deeper. "[T]he Chief, most deeply rooted, and incessantly active, cause of all the principal mischief"— [was] the "OLIGARCHY" or "FAMILY COMPACT." Fothergill had a certain sympathy for Mackenzie whom he knew well and with whom, in Toronto from the early 1820s, he had shared the experience of verbal abuse and other sorts of mistreatment at the hands of Family Compact sympathizers. Hence, his "Introduction" to the pamphlet was more concerned with the seed of the "mischief" in Upper Canada and Toronto—those "few upstart families, unfortunately entrusted with power at an early period in the Government of the Colony"—than with Mackenzie himself. The Scot was a villain for taking up arms, but he was a more understandable phenomenon given the political circumstances. The Family Compact people were an ongoing evil upon whom not enough condemnation could be piled.[5] In a 7 February 1838 *Palladium* editorial, for instance, Fothergill condemned the Compact as "the *Augean Stable* of the most baleful, and corrupt, and most *calamitous* FAMILY INFLUENCE, that was ever suffered to paralize an entire and magnificent Province." A second and related project from the *Palladium* press, an elaborate map exposing the families of the Family Compact and their connections, apparently did not reach publication, though Fothergill advertised a prospectus in preparation.

The precipitous final stages of Fothergill's failure can be traced to financial woes, a disturbing level of personal distraction, and his failing health. He used the *Palladium* to print a desparate petition to the government requesting payment for copies of *Mackenzie's Own Narrative* that had been distributed to members of the Legislative Assembly. No help came from that quarter. Fothergill, who had been bedridden with rheumatic gout for seven months in 1837, was no longer physically

5. Fothergill's great plan of a Lyceum for Toronto had been effectively defeated early in 1837 by, as he saw it, unsympathetic Family Compact members in places of power. This scheme, which as Heather Murray notes "came strikingly close to realization" (60), must have frustrated Fothergill tremendously, because he had so much of his life's work in scientific research and collecting tied up in its establishment. So too had he been frustrated in his attempt, with Dr. William Rees and William "Tiger" Dunlop, to initiate the Literary and Historical Society of Upper Canada at York (1831). In his letter book he names Chief Justice John Beverly Robinson and archdeacon John Strachan for their disdainful refusal to support the society, quoting Robinson's letter in full (Fothergill Papers, vol. 24). As Paul Romney notes, Strachan and Robinson later took over the idea as their own (*DCB*, VII: 319).

strong, his health no doubt worsened by increasing financial worries. Under such duress, and with intimations of his own mortality increasingly before him, he drew back into his enduring passion, the study and recording of bird and animal life. At home in Pickering Mills, he continued to record in his journal the hunting, observing, and documenting of various species in the weeks leading up to his death.

Samuel Thompson has left a vivid record of the *Palladium* office in its final months, one that also provides a glimpse of Fothergill in his last year or two:

> Early in the year 1838, I obtained an engagement as manager of the *Palladium*, a newspaper issued by Charles Fothergill, on the plan of the New York *Albion*. The printing office, situated on the corner of York and Boulton Streets, was very small, . . . with an old hand-press of the Columbian pattern. To bring this office into something like presentable order, to train a rough lot of lads to their business, and to supply an occasional original article, occupied me a great part of that year. Mr. Fothergill was a man of talent, a scholar and a gentleman; but so entirely given up to the study of natural history and the practice of taxidermy, that his newspaper received but scant attention, and his personal appearance and the cleanliness of his surroundings still less. He had been King's Printer under the family compact regime, and was dismissed for some imprudent criticism upon the policy of the Government. His family sometimes suffered from the want of common necessaries, while the money which should have fed them went to pay for some rare bird or strange fish. This could not last long. The *Palladium* died a natural death, and I had to seek elsewhere for employment.[6]

Despite Thompson's efforts, nothing could save the newspaper from its "natural death." Its heart was elsewhere, its purpose lost in the midst of a changing political climate to which Charles Fothergill was ill-attuned.

For their part, Susanna and John Moodie had lost touch with Fothergill and his newspaper. While the *Palladium* was foundering, John Moodie found a second military appointment as Paymaster for the militia of the Victoria District. He was stationed in Belleville but busily seeing to the many military units along the Lake Ontario front. On the bush farm in Douro Susanna was struggling through the worst winter and spring she had endured since coming to Canada, alone with her children and one servant.[7] Despite sufferings and illnesses that nearly broke her spirit, she remained in her own mind a loyal Englishwoman and a "profession[al]" writer of wide cosmopolitan vision, eager to lend her pen to causes dear to her. The most heartening development to her—"like a gleam of light springing up in the dark-

6. Samuel Thompson, *Reminiscences of a Canadian Pioneer for the Last 50 Years (1833–1883)* (Toronto: Hunter, Rose, 1884; rpt: Toronto: McClelland & Stewart, 1968), 103–04. Thompson's account suggests that he worked for the paper until its demise, which occurred about August 1839.
7. See *Letters of Love and Duty*, 114–59.

ness"—was that John Lovell in Montreal was by May 1839 paying her for her literary contributions.[8]

The Moodies shared a deep affinity with Fothergill, a man whose values, interests, independence of spirit, and intense love of Britain seemed so in accordance with their own. But by the late summer of 1839 they were moving beyond the limits of his fixed sense of political independence, quietly beginning to align themselves with Robert Baldwin and the direction of conservative reform that was gaining fresh momentum because of the publication of Lord Durham's *Report*.[9] Fothergill had little empathy for the Baldwins. Still, they would carry with them the stamp of what Fothergill had stood for and fiercely articulated—the importance of the educated and conservative British middle-class in British North America. Like Fothergill, Susanna Moodie would continue to insist on the reliability of her genteel social and cultural vision, and she would suffer from the ways in which that outlook was criticized once *Roughing It in the Bush* reached Canadian readers and reviewers. Though she wrote a more positive sequel entitled *Life in the Clearings* (1853), she was soon to find the role of cultural commentator and interpreter a very uncomfortable and disagreeable position. John Moodie's turbulent career as the Sheriff of Hastings County was but another chapter in the problem of seeking to maintain an independence from party politics, even when, as in Moodie's case, he but thinly veiled his reformist sympathies in the face of his Tory critics and persecutors in Belleville.[1] He shared with Fothergill a certain naivete about political realities and a confidence in his ability as a gentleman and a thinker to ride above the turbulence and vulgarity of the daily political fray. His wife shared that naivete with him.

The *Palladium* likely died sometime in August 1839, having, as a signal of its frailty, already shrunk back to its original four-page format. Operating in opposition to both Reform and Family Compact interests, Fothergill received little by way of government or advertising support, and material he sent to government members, like the Mackenzie pamphlet, was not paid for.[2] Many *Palladium* subscribers lost interest in the paper or, as was usual for the time, did not pay their bills. Thus, Charles Fothergill's ambition to provide Toronto with a strong, independent, and well-informed cultural voice withered as he himself weakened and the immediacy of the Rebellion faded.

The newspaper, however, did wonders for Susanna Moodie. She was already taking new life and fresh hope from her engagement with *The Literary Garland*, a connection that followed directly from John

---

8. *Roughing It in the Bush*, 440 [281].
9. Writing from Belleville on 24 May 1839, John Moodie described his positive reactions to reading Lord Durham's *Report* (*Letters of Love and Duty*, 150–51).
1. John Moodie's troubles with the Belleville Tories and certain lawyers began soon after his arrival in the town and persisted until, through a final lawsuit against him, he was formally removed from office in 1863.
2. Fothergill provided direct reports on the Legislative Assembly at his own expense, no doubt hoping that government support for such record keeping would eventually be forthcoming. That support never came.

Lovell's newspaper, the Montreal *Transcript*, which had been so quick to reprint many of her Rebellion poems from the *Palladium* and to promote her poetical skills and patriotism. She was not yet out of the 'prison' of the bush, but she was, as she had not been since she left England seven years earlier, a professional writer with a publisher who was willing to pay her.[3] As well, by means of her poetry, she had caught the attention of the new Lieutenant Governor, Sir George Arthur. When some months later in Belleville her husband found an influential and supportive friend in his commanding officer, the Baron George de Rottenburg, Sir George Arthur's former secretary, the possibility of a better future for the Moodie family began to take shape.

At last, and largely through the agency of Fothergill's *Palladium of British America*, Susanna Moodie's future as a professional writer in Canada looked promising. When in May 1840 Charles Fothergill died in a "penniless" and pathetic state,[4] the Moodies were again able to be together, living much more comfortably in Belleville and beginning to enjoy the range of advantages and opportunities now available to them. It would likely never have occurred to them to look back and heed the lessons of Fothergill's life and career in Upper Canada. Had they done so, his struggles to contribute to and to raise public interest in cultural, scientific, and literary matters in Canada might have served as a warning of the financial, personal, and political dangers lying in wait for those who resolved to follow in his footsteps. Even as he led the way forward by means of certain of his cultural visions and schemes, Charles Fothergill's example made clear the kinds of resistance to cultural development and literary expression that would persist in the decades ahead.

MISAO DEAN

The Broken Mirror of Domestic Ideology: Femininity as Textual Practice in Susanna Moodie's Autobiographical Works†

'The Broken Mirror, a True Tale,' by Susanna Moodie (published in the *Literary Garland* in 1843), takes its name from an anecdote which is rich in symbolic associations. A heartbroken emigrant mother rescues

---

3. Susanna Moodie and her children finally left the bush in late December 1839. They moved to Belleville where John Moodie had already begun his new duties as the Sheriff of Hastings County. He owed his new and prestigious position both to his own military connections and to his wife's letters to Sir George Arthur. Arthur, who likely read some of her patriotic poems in Fothergill's *Palladium*, was very well disposed to the loyal and eloquent Mrs. Moodie, even before she wrote to him. See Michael Peterman, "Susanna Moodie and Sir George Arthur," *Canadian Poetry* 38 (Spring/Summer 1996): 130–38.

4. A month after Fothergill's death some of his papers and most of his museum artefacts (perhaps also many of his paintings of birds) were destroyed in a fire. The work of a lifetime, which he had hoped to house in his planned Lyceum, was thus lost.

† From *Practising Femininity: Domestic Realism and the Performance of Gender in Early Canadian Fiction* (Toronto: U of Toronto P, 1998), pp. 29–41.

an elaborate Italian mirror from the sale of her family possessions. Initially, the mirror seems to be the symbol of a stubborn attachment to her previous station in life, and she is ridiculed by her neighbours and advisors for refusing to accept the reality of her poverty. However, her decision is justified as the mirror becomes the means of re-establishing her family after their immigration to South Africa: though the mirror shatters on the voyage, the shards are sold to native Africans and the proceeds used to buy a comfortable home. The mirror is a traditional symbol of femininity, associated with vanity and with the creation of a self dependent upon the gaze of others. Its shattering suggests the rupture in the ideology of the feminine which results from the voyage, both mental and physical, from Briton to colonist.[1] In this story, as in *Roughing It in the Bush* and Moodie's other autobiographical works, the Old World mirror of femininity initially seems unsuited to life in the New World, and those who cling to it are ridiculed. However, though Old World ideology is broken by the voyage, its pieces, reorganized and reconceived, form the basis of the self in the New World.

Like *The Female Emigrant's Guide*, *Roughing It in the Bush* inscribes the feminine according to the domestic ideal of nineteenth-century England. Moodie's autobiographical works express a need to naturalize gender in the bodies of women through reiterative accounts of gendered qualities such as homesickness, endurance, self-denial, self-control, and nurturance and love of children. By invoking the values associated with domesticity, they justify feminine authorship; by simultaneously invoking the characteristics of a supposed feminine inner self and inscribing them as structural principles, the texts gender themselves and claim the authority of feminine subjectivity to assert an autobiographical self. 'Trifles from the Burthen of a Life,'[2] *Flora Lyndsay*, *Roughing It in the Bush*, and *Life in the Clearings* mobilize the domestic ideal to both justify and structure the unconventional appearance of a feminine textual self in the public realm of the autobiographical text, and show how the practice of writing for publication can be understood to validate the existence of a feminine inner self.

In *Letters to a Young Lady on Leaving School and Entering the World*, Sarah French formulates the opposition between domestic femininity and the practice of writing for publication which governs Moodie's self-presentation in all of her autobiographical works: 'if you ever think to become a wife, never venture in the paths of literature: a woman who seeks notoriety in them is rarely calculated for the quiet detail of domestic duty. She has entered the public arena, and must there seek her happiness.'[3] According to domestic ideology, the woman who prides

1. David Bentley discusses the 'voyage' image in works by Moodie and Traill in 'Breaking the "Cake of Custom." '
2. The account of Rachel Wilde's marriage and her preparation for emigration given in 'Trifles from the Burthen of a Life' (reprinted in *Voyages: Short Narratives of Susanna Moodie*, ed. John Thurston) is repeated in *Flora Lyndsay*, and will be cited from that source. *The Female Emigrant's Guide* was written by Catharine Parr Traill in the 1850's and is analysed in the first chapter of *Practising Femininity*. [*Editor's note*.]
3. *Letters to a Young Lady on Leaving School and Entering the World* (Boston: Crosby, Nichols, 1855), 49.

herself upon her achievements as a writer loses the limited authority granted her by her interpellation as feminine and is in danger of being judged unwomanly. *Roughing It in the Bush* reports that its narrator had become well known in the Cobourg area as the 'woman that writes,' an object of embarrassing comments in the popular press and of gossip and speculation among the townspeople. Advised by two neighbours to 'lay by the pen, and betake [her]self to some more useful employment,' such as making shirts for her husband, or cleaning house, she protests: 'These remarks were completely gratuitous, and called forth by no observations of mine; for I tried to conceal my blue stockings beneath the long conventional robes of the tamest common-place, hoping to cover the faintest tinge of the objectionable colour . . .' The text continues: 'Anxious not to offend them, I tried to avoid all literary subjects,' and became 'more diligent in cultivating every branch of domestic usefulness'—in an attempt to reify the domestic 'inner self' that writing seemed to contradict (*RI* 202 [134–35]).[4]

As a young woman, Susanna Strickland had written in a letter to Mary Russell Mitford that 'a desire for fame appears to me almost inseparable from an author' (*Letters of a Lifetime*, 38). Yet her letters, poems, and prose reveal from her youth onward her growing awareness that the 'woman that writes' for fame or for personal satisfaction transgresses the common idea of the feminine 'self.' The lyric poetry she published in *Enthusiasm; and Other Poems* (1831) gives evidence of perhaps unconscious anxiety about whether lyric expression of personality is consistent with femininity. The title poem of her collection is addressed to the emotion which is alike the inspiration of religious conversion and of poetry; but the speaker consistently refers to those heroes and poets moved by the spirit as 'he'; in the companion piece, 'Fame,' and the dialogue 'Fancy and the Poet,' the poet is also male. Susanna Strickland seems to have concluded that lyric poetry is not feminine; Susanna Moodie's letters concerning her marriage and the birth of her first daughter, Kate, state her intention to give up the public voice of poetry altogether in favour of the domestic virtues of wife and mother. Like the conduct books of the period, the letters place writing for publication among the despised 'accomplishments' of worldly husband-hunters, and imply that for a woman, domestic happiness is inconsistent with a career as a writer. In a letter to her poet friend James Bird, she writes: 'My blue stockings, since I became a wife, have turned so pale that I think they will become quite white . . . [I] now find, that the noble art of housewifery is more to be desired than all the accomplishments, which are to be retailed by the literary and fashionable damsels' (*Letters of a Lifetime* 61). To his wife, Emma Bird, six months later, Susanna Moodie reiterates, 'I have quarrelled with rhymes ever since I found out how much happier we can be without them. Domestic comfort is worth all the literary fame that ever

---

4. All quotations from *Roughing It in the Bush* are taken from the 1989 edition in the New Canadian Library series, which reprints the complete text of the second edition with additions published by Bentley in 1852. Bracketed references are to this Norton Critical Edition.

pu[lled] a youthful Bard onto the pinnacle of pub[lic] notice' (*Letters of a Lifetime* 65).[5]

Given the opposition between writing and femininity created by domestic ideology, a major interest in Moodie's fiction is femininity, how one achieves it and what it is composed of. *Flora Lyndsay*, 'Trifles from the Burthen of a Life,' *Roughing It*, and *Life in the Clearings* obsessively return to the definition of a supposed feminine nature and compulsively gender their protagonists, often in contrast to other, insufficiently gendered characters. The characteristics of feminine nature inscribed in these texts are similar to those delineated in *The Female Emigrant's Guide*: modesty, self-sacrifice, love of children, self-control. The books assert that women are unique in their ability to love children (see, for example, *Flora Lyndsay* 5, *Life in the Clearings* 46); that their interests are identical to their children's (*Flora Lyndsay* 83); and that they are made to be mothers (*Flora Lyndsay* 72). Because they put the welfare of their children first, they are ruled by self-control and self-sacrifice (*RI* 194 [130]), and thus are able to govern themselves and provide for their households with 'economy and good management' (*Flora Lyndsay* 11). These characteristics of the feminine 'inner self' are often, but not always, externalized as physical beauty; they are always manifest in a gentle and modest manner, 'patient endurance of suffering and privation' (*Flora Lyndsay* 95),[6] and submission to the authority of parent and husband.

Moodie's autobiographical works particularly stress two aspects of feminine nature related to the project of emigration: love of home and submission to authority. Like *The Female Emigrant's Guide*, *Roughing It in the Bush* and *Flora Lyndsay* represent love of home as a gender marker: 'Women . . . feel parting with the old familiar places and faces, more keenly than men' ('Well in the Wilderness' 90). When Rachel Wilde first loses sight of home as a young child, she is reduced to tears: 'It was the hand of nature knocking at her unsophisticated heart, and demanding the sympathies, which had been planted and fostered, by the divine mother, unknown albeit, to her thoughtless offspring' ('Rachel Wilde' 105). While love of country is represented as common to both men and women, women are represented as emotionally attached to home and especially to siblings and parents in a way which is almost physically debilitating to a female emigrant.[7] The

5. John Thurston argues persuasively that the instability of Moodie's attitude to a literary career in this period of her life arose from her association with evangelical Anglicanism and her later conversion to Congregationalism: in this context, her literary career would appear among the worldly ambitions which would contradict her piety (*Work of Words* 46–52). In addition, he argues that Moodie's view of literary genius as above worldly considerations such as making a living contradicted the necessity she felt to make money by her writing (*Work of Words* 26). This is not inconsistent with my argument, which would place piety among the attributes of the domestic woman and confirm the opposition between writing for amusement and writing as commercial pursuit.
6. See also *Roughing It*, 144–5 [97]: 'the rigour of the climate subdued my proud, independent English spirit, and I actually shamed my womanhood, and cried with the cold. Yes, I ought to blush at evincing such unpardonable weakness; but I was foolish and inexperienced, and unaccustomed to the yoke.' In this passage, extraordinary endurance of physical pain is assumed to be part and parcel of womanhood.
7. Bina Freiwald has discussed the representation of homesickness as part of the representation of maternal language in ' "The tongue of woman": The Language of the Self in Moodie's

often remarked reiteration of the narrator's homesickness in *Roughing It* might usefully be considered as part of the text's anxiety to establish its narrator's authority as a feminine woman. The importance of submission to authority, which is at once the authority of a husband and of God's Providence, is foregrounded by the narrator's feminine love of home and therefore her reluctance to emigrate. The narrator of *Roughing It* claims to have received a premonition warning her not to emigrate: 'how gladly I would have obeyed the injunction had it still been in my power. I had bowed to a superior mandate, the command of duty; for my husband's sake, for the sake of the infant, whose little bosom heaved against my swelling heart. I had consented to bid adieu for ever to my native shores' (194 [129]). The seeming contradiction posed by the assertion that love of home is part of feminine nature but that this nature must be denied in submitting to the natural authority of a husband is resolved by the attribution of self-control, endurance, and self-denial to the truly feminine woman.

The theme of submission to masculine authority is defined in *Flora Lyndsay* by the contrast created between Flora and two of her Scots acquaintances, Miss Carr and Mrs Ready. Mrs Ready's 'harsh, unfeminine voice and manners; [and] her assumption of learning and superiority, without any real title to either' (21) label her as insufficiently gendered. This judgment is confirmed by her vehement condemnation of marriage and her advice to Flora not to submit to her husband's decision to emigrate: 'I am none of your soft bread-and-butter wives, who consider it their *duty* to become the mere *echo* of their husbands. If *I* did not wish to go, no tyrannical lord of the creation, falsely so called, should compel me to act against my inclinations' (22). But Flora argues that if all marriages were unpleasant, and all men tyrannical, 'who would marry?' (23). For Flora (and by implication for the feminine woman), submission to masculine authority is redeemed by love, which effectively limits its exercise. Miss Carr condemns the submissive woman as characterless: 'These passive women are always great favorites with men. They have no decided character of their own, and become the mere echoes of superior minds' (44). However, Miss Carr's 'character' is decidedly masculine: she wears a man's hat, 'smoke[s] out of a long pipe, dr[inks] brandy-punch,' and 'swears like a man' (33–4). Her appearance is 'masculine and decidedly ugly' (34); 'even in youth' she was 'coarse and vulgar' (34), and it is apparent even to passing pedlars that she is not a lady (39). While her comments on manners and restrictive fashions in women's dress strike Flora as having 'a great deal of truth' (54), Flora is physically frightened of her wild behaviour and advises her to submit to the 'rules' (46) of feminine behaviour 'in order to avoid singularity' (42). In contrast, Flora displays her femininity by proving her utter inability to make simple decisions: when she defies her husband in order to take a walk in the mountains,

---

Roughing It in the Bush.' Freiwald argues that Moodie's exaggerated homesickness is part of her strategy of bearing the word, by depicting herself as an abandoned child and literalizing the metaphor of the Mother Country.

she must be rescued after she is overcome by her fear of heights. By her actions, she disproves a gypsy prediction that she will 'wear the breeches' (146) in the family. 'If that was wearing the breeches,' she says, 'I am sure I disgraced them with my worse than womanish fears' (146).[8]

Roughing It in the Bush develops the opposition between feminine virtue and the career of writer, comparing the narrator's domestic failures and successes to her literary ambitions. In fact, the book explicitly denies her literary ambitions and argues that her self-esteem is dependent upon success in domestic life, which is represented as much more satisfying and important than resumption of her literary career. Commenting on the failure of her first attempt to bake bread, the narrator remarks, 'For myself, I could have borne the severest infliction from the pen of the most formidable critic with more fortitude than I bore the cutting up of my first loaf of bread' (*RI* 121 [81]), while Tom Wilson exclaims, 'Oh Mrs. Moodie! I hope you make better books than bread' (*RI* 121 [81]). Similarly, the narrator's success in finally milking the cow that terrifies her is more emotionally satisfying, she writes, than any literary success: 'Yes! I felt prouder of that milk than many an author of the best thing he ever wrote, whether in verse or prose' (*RI* 183 [122]). Actually living the life of helpmeet to her pioneer husband, she implies, resolves any hesitation in choosing between public career and private home.

In opposing feminine virtue and writing, Susanna Moodie was invoking an ideology of feminine nature which stressed modest silence as the feminine practice which confirmed the existence of a chaste inner self (Poovey 3–47). The profession of writer was inconsistent with this ideal, not only because writing would necessarily distract from the dutiful performance of tasks assigned by husband and family, but because it seemed to foreground the personality and opinions of the author and express her desire for public notice. The metaphor of 'concealing her blue-stockings' is revealing in this context; the stockings suggesting, of course, the connection between female sexuality and female speech which Mary Poovey and others have suggested is constitutive of the nineteenth-century ideology of gender. Conformity to an ideal inner self characterized by modesty, chastity, and self-effacement made the writing of autobiography especially problematic

8. The inability of the feminine woman to wield authority responsibly even in respect to her own actions implies the necessity of submission to her husband; yet both husband and wife are subject to the higher authority of Providence. While *The Female Emigrant's Guide* makes some reference to the importance of Christian belief as a sustaining comfort to the female emigrant, *Flora Lyndsay*, 'Trifles,' *Roughing It* and much of Moodie's short fiction on the theme of emigration verge on the pietistic in their assertion of the role of God's Providence in the fate of their protagonists and 'the necessity of a perfect and child-like reliance upon the mercies of God—who . . . never deserts those who have placed their trust in Him' (*RI* 353 [237–38]). John Thurston argues that this emphasis arises from Moodie's personal struggle to accept her lot in life; her evangelistic conversion to Congregationalism a year before her marriage, and her enduring belief in the effects of supernatural forces on individual lives, may also have been factors. However, the repeated inscription of the theme of Providence may also be viewed as gendered practice, conforming to the domestic ideal which ascribes moral and spiritual qualities to the 'soul' of the domestic woman, and enjoins upon her the role of spiritual and moral instructor and guardian of her family, and of society at large.

for women writers, Sidonie Smith points out in *A Poetics of Women's Autobiography*. The normative definition of the genre rests on the autobiographer's claim to public notice, yet the truly feminine woman was supposed to have no such claim. The initial choice facing a woman autobiographer, Smith suggests, is whether to create herself according to the conventions of the genre, 'enacting the scenario of male selfhood' and 'thereby invit[ing] public censure' (8) for her unnatural conception, or to create herself as a conventionally feminine woman, whose life is rendered by definition a 'non-story' (50). 'However much she may desire to pursue the paternal narrative with its promise of power . . . she recognizes [that] . . . [h]er narrative may bring notoriety; and with notoriety can come isolation and the loss of love and acceptance in the culture that would hold her in its fictions' (54). The female autobiographer knows that her book will hold her up to judgment, not for her facility as a writer, but for her actions as a woman; in fact, many reviews of Susanna Moodie's work focused not on the literary elements of the text, but on the perceived relationship between the actions depicted in it and the moral value of the 'self' that motivated them (Ballstadt [1988], Editor's Introduction xxx–xxxii).

Smith details the way that the nineteenth-century ideology of gender 'profoundly contaminated [women's] relationship to the pen as an instrument of power' (7) yet notes that women like Susanna Moodie continued to write; by conforming to the 'rules' of femininity (as Susanna Moodie called them), women were enabled to use the limited authority which those rules granted. Primary among these 'rules' is the requirement of selfless nurturance and care for husband and children, and *Roughing It in the Bush* mobilizes this ideal to authorize the narrator's desire to write. In fact, the feminine self of *Roughing It in the Bush* is represented as having no desire to write. She takes up her pen in 1838 solely to help her husband when all other means of earning money have been exhausted, and when honest people who have trusted John Dunbar Moodie to pay back their loans are on the verge of bankruptcy. She states that only 'the hope of being of the least service to those dear to [her]' (*RI* 417 [281]) leads her to resume her (supposedly) interrupted writing career in the bush. Only the prospect of contributing materially to the family welfare could justify her actions; as she says in the Introduction to *Mark Hurdlestone*, her 'time . . . belonged by right to [her] family, and was too valuable a commodity to give away' (*Life* 286). Similarly, Flora Lyndsay distances herself from any positive desire to write when she offers apologetic explanations for her decision to write the tale of Noah Cotton. The activity will keep her from 'dwelling too much on the future' and so make her a better companion and more loving mother, Flora explains; the story itself might 'interest her husband' (215) and so justify her activity by serving the feminine function of 'animating [him] to fresh exertions' (95). The eventual publication of the tale of Noah Cotton by the modest Flora is suggested, as are all of her actions, by submission to her husband's wishes and his taste: 'Flora finished her story, but she wanted courage to read it to her husband, who was very fastidious about his wife's literary performances. And many years passed away . . . before she again brought the time-worn manuscript to light, and submitted it to his critical eye. And because it pleased him, she . . . thought that it might find favor with the public' (316). In *Roughing It* and *Life in the Clearings*, the narrator justifies her project in writing two autobiographical books by extending the domestic ideal of nurturance to her countrymen. *Roughing It*, she claims, fulfils her duty to warn prospective settlers of the lies and deceptions practised by unscrupulous land promoters and to protect the fair daughters of Albion from travails unsuited to their upbringing. Similarly, the introduction to *Life in the Clearings* modestly accounts for the appearance of the sequel to *Roughing It* by the numerous requests the narrator has received for an account of 'the present state of society in the colony' (xxxiii). Within both books, the speaker claims that her writing is a duty enjoined upon her by her desire to serve her husband, by the responsibility of raising her family, by obligations to her publisher, and, finally, by her own ill-health.

This retreat into the stereotype of feminine self-effacement allows the narrator to speak with the authority of the domestic woman. Moodie's narrator rejects the 'masculine' story and writes the 'feminine' non-story of her life; but rather than being silenced by the limits of femininity, the texts adopt strategies which conform to conventional feminine practice, and especially adopt self-effacement as a narrative stance. Happily, 'the self-effacing speaking posture . . . conceals all faults, including the fault of ambition inherent in the presumption of writing her story at all' (Smith 54). These strategies create two of the most often remarked aspects of Moodie's autobiographical works: their generic instability and their loose structure. These aspects of her writing are not solely evidence of attempts to 'pad' the work for the publisher, to accommodate the Canadian experience, or to express supposed 'schizophrenic' attitudes to nature and culture; rather, they derive from the concept of a feminine inner self who paradoxically conforms to two prevailing stereotypes of feminine behaviour: the self-effacing domestic woman and the gossip. By appealing to the stereotype of self-effacement, Susanna Moodie frees herself into the loose structure of the private communication of women, a good gossip between two friends, a kind of subversive communication which empowers the domestic sphere and those in it as primary builders of the new society.

Critics of Susanna Moodie's work have found a fruitful area of inquiry in attempting to uncover a unified structure in *Roughing It in the Bush* or, at the very least, to determine what genre or genres the book may belong to. Most recent critics have recognized that the book, and Mrs Moodie's version of herself in it, is structured by elements of fictional genres,[9] yet they are unsettled by what Carol

9. Professor Klinck calls it an 'apprenticeship novel'; Carl Ballstadt notes the traces of the English sketch form and the influence of Mary Russell Mitford on Susanna Moodie's work; Marian Fowler has revealed elements of the sentimental novel and the Gothic in Susanna Moodie's style, her self-presentation, and her characterization of her neighbours; T. D.

Shields calls the 'disturbing disconnectedness' and 'apparent lack of unity' (5) of Moodie's work. Many, including Shields and Helen Buss,[1] try to distinguish between a 'real' voice of an historical and intentional Mrs Moodie and the voices of various fictional discourses; they suggest that the passages which represent her personal struggles or offer detailed material description represent reality, while the romantic descriptions of nature and the formulaic declarations of patriotic fervour merely represent an inauthentic bowing to convention. A related approach suggests that *Roughing It* is intended to be a religious conversion narrative or a novel of individual growth and acceptance, and implies that whatever does not fit the model is an error in Moodie's execution. Susan Glickman argues that the book's inconsistencies mirror the inconsistencies and self-contradictions of 'human nature' (20), while, in a contrasting approach, John Thurston makes a virtue of the diversity of generic and historical voices in *Roughing It*, arguing that traditional genre could not have 'contain[ed] her Canadian material' (Thurston, 'Re-writing *Roughing It*' 199) because it represents the excess which is excluded by the concept of genre.

However, the criticism has not acknowledged that the narrator herself designates this structural instability as definitive of the feminine text in one of her numerous metafictional asides. She writes in *Life in the Clearings* that the capabilities of women writers are specific and limited, and that a grab-bag of amusing anecdotes, descriptions of life and of nature, and didactic opinions on moral questions is the limit of feminine capabilities.[2] Strong plot construction, implying the ability to create and follow logical and realistic sequences of events, is masculine territory. 'Women make good use of their eyes and ears, and paint scenes that amuse or strike their fancy with tolerable accuracy; but it requires the strong-thinking heart of man to anticipate events and trace certain results from particular causes. Women are out of their element when they attempt to speculate on these abstruse matters—are apt to incline too strongly to their own opinions—and jump at conclusions which are either false or unsatisfactory' (*Life* 207–8). The narrator mixes contradictory elements of autobiography, sentimental romance, conversion narrative, and how-to handbook with anecdote, natural description, and moral essay, confirming her feminine inability to plot, to 'trace certain results from particular causes.' The narrator simply functions, she says, as a faithful recorder of those incidents

---

MacLulich relates *Roughing It* to *Robinson Crusoe* for their common fictions of cultural contact and their patterns of religious conversion. See Ballstadt, 'Editor's Introduction' (xl–xli) for a summary of critical response to the book.

1. Of *Roughing It in the Bush* and C. P. Traill's *Backwoods of Canada*, Buss (1986) writes: 'the writing personae adopted sometimes have an easy sureness that is too formulated, too conventional for the new experiences they describe. On the other hand, since they do not adopt autobiographical personae, they are able, especially in the case of Moodie, to break through the artificiality in order to tell of the ways in which Canada changes their ideas of themselves' ('Canadian Women's Autobiography' 154).

2. Michael Peterman notes that Traill also accepted the assumption that 'it was for men to think—to be analytical, critical, and professional, to assume and perpetuate authority. It was for women to feel and nurture—to be decorous, familial, and retiring, to accept authority's wisdom and beneficence' ('Splendid Anachronism' 177).

which appeal to her sense of fun and which seem illustrative of a 'life in the woods' (*RI* 305 [204]).[3]

The numerous tales within tales, anecdotes recounted by neighbours and friends, interpolated chapters, and poems by J. W. D. Moodie and by Samuel Strickland that characterize Susanna Moodie's autobiographical works suggest the truly feminine woman's self-effacement from the text which is her life. The heroine of *Flora Lyndsay*[4] is the author of an anonymous pamphlet in favour of the abolition of slavery and the tale 'Noah Cotton,' which is intended to amuse her husband, but both works are structured to divert attention away from the narrator, and to allow her to disclaim the creative responsibility of author. Flora explains that her abolitionist pamphlet was merely transcribed from the dictation of an escaped slave, and really gives her no claim to the name of author. The narrative of 'Noah Cotton,' an interpolated romance which takes up about one-third of the book, is a miracle of distancing techniques: Susanna Moodie writes a story of Flora Lyndsay; partway through this story, Flora writes a story of Noah Cotton; partway through this story, the voice of Flora disappears as Noah Cotton tells his own story; and partway through this story, Cotton's mother takes over to tell her own story in the first person. Thus Moodie's life is relegated to forming a frame narrative to the book *Flora Lyndsay*; the voice of the writer and her narrator, Flora, completely disappear from a work which is still seemingly autobiographical.

The pattern of self-effacement is repeated in *Roughing It* and *Life in the Clearings*. *Roughing It* contains numerous dialogues from which the narrator disappears, such as the conversation between Tom Wilson and Betty Fye concerning the making of 'Bran emptyings' to use as a substitute for yeast. Tom Wilson narrates his own story, as does Malcolm, the 'stumpy man,' and Jenny, the faithful servant; neighbours narrate the story of Brian the Still-Hunter's past, anecdotes about Indian behaviour, and the story of Captain N——, Jenny's former master. J. W. D. Moodie narrates his own chapters (three in the first 1852 edition, and four in the second 1852 edition),[5] and Samuel Strickland, his partial chapter describing a whirlwind; in these cases, the narrator

---

3. That Moodie's account of women's thought process constituted conventional wisdom is confirmed by Wendy Mitchinson's survey of Victorian Canadian thought on feminine psychology. For example, she cites William Carpenter in his 1869 text, *Human Physiology*: 'For there can be no doubt that—putting aside the exceptional cases which now and then occur—the intellectual powers of Woman are inferior to those of Man. Although her perceptive faculties are more acute, her capability of sustained mental exertion is much less; and though her views are often peculiarly distinguished by clearness and decision, they are generally deficient in that comprehensiveness which is necessary for their stability' (Mitchinson, *The Nature of Their Bodies* 36). British reviewers such as Elizabeth Rigby and Henry Chorley agreed that the nature of women's minds made them able observers of the 'close and lively details' of life; the best of women's writings consist of 'miniature touches of life and descriptions of scenes overlooked by the Man in his wide range of view, and often, as to finish, not within the grasp of his more powerful but coarser hand' (cited in Johnston 37–8).

4. The author of *Flora Lyndsay* implies that she is the same person as the author of *Roughing It* on the last page of the book. See Fowler, *ET*, 103, for additional evidence that the novel is autobiographical.

5. 'The Ould Dragoon,' 'The Land-Jobber,' and 'The Village Hotel' appear in the first 1852 edition; 'Canadian Sketches' was added to the second.

justifies her effacement from the text by claiming that as a woman she is not qualified to speak on the matters which concern men: 'I will leave my husband, who is better qualified than myself, to give a more accurate account of the country, while I turn to matters of a light and livelier cast' (*RI* 206 [138]). Similarly, in *Life in the Clearings*, chapters 5 and 6 are narrated by a travelling musician; anecdotes of religious 'camp meetings' are told by the voice of a 'friend' and by 'a beautiful young married lady'; the story of Grace Marks is told by her lawyer; that of Michael MacBride by three narrators; the story of Jeanie Burns's betrayal by her fiancé is told by James N——, a manservant; and the anecdotes of lost children are told by a Mrs H——, the wife of a man who farms for the Moodies on shares.

The narrator's continual denials of her authority to speak on almost any issue have been remarked by many readers, especially as the books themselves seem to contradict these protestations. The narrator's denial that she is qualified to speak conclusively about Canada may have been an attempt to defend herself against charges levelled by Canadians that Susanna Moodie misrepresents Canada; and an entire section of *Life in the Clearings* is devoted to refuting such charges arising from the publication of *Roughing It*. Yet numerous asides in *Roughing It* and *Life in the Clearings* refer to a gendered division of literary texts in which only the masculine author may claim authority over certain subjects and literary structures. 'As a woman, I cannot enter into the philosophy of these things, nor is it my intention to do so. I leave statistics for wiser and cleverer male heads' (*Life* 38). The narrator's denials of her authority to speak on matters of political or economic interest, her appeal to the stereotype of feminine intellectual superficiality, seem to have the effect of freeing her into the realm of domestic authority. She goes on to specify and develop many subjects of interest and importance to the 'intending emigrant'—many of which, by her own definition, belong exclusively to the realm of masculine commentary. The class system, the relative merits of monarchy and republicanism, insanity, overpopulation, the lack of firewood in established Canadian communities, the strife between adherents of the Catholic and Protestant religions, political upheavals in the colony, the reasons behind the rebellion of 1837, and the prospects for the Reform cause are all topics of the narrator's commentary in *Life in the Clearings* and *Roughing It*.

Self-effacement gives way to another stereotype, that of the woman's wagging tongue, to give these texts the domestic voice of gossip. Susanna Moodie's books convey information in the form of anecdote, moral judgment, and domestic detail—the intimate information of the domestic sphere which convention grants to women. *Life in the Clearings* specifically invokes the model of gossip in the first chapter, when the narrator figuratively invites the reader: 'Come take your seat with me on the deck of the steamer; and as we glide over the waters of this beautiful Bay of Quinté, I will make you acquainted with every spot worthy of note along its picturesque shores' (4). She apologetically invokes the stereotype of woman as gossip to excuse the shapelessness and diversity of her conversation: 'Allow me a woman's privilege of talking of all sorts of things by the way. Should I tire you with my desultory mode of conversation, bear with me charitably, and take into account the infirmities incidental to my gossiping sex' (*Life* 4). Her description of the situation in which her book will be read also suggests the intimacy of gossip; her book is 'a small volume which may help to while away an idle hour, or fill up the blanks of a wet day' (xxxiii), as conversation with a trusted friend would do. Like gossip, the books show interest in surface details of domestic and social life, and are composed of 'stories' which are complete in themselves, containing fabula, characters, and moral commentary (Spacks, *Gossip* 15).

Both *Roughing It* and *Life* proceed like a conversation: a topic is introduced, a moral judgment passed upon it, and many examples given to illustrate the rightness of that judgment. The narrator of *Roughing It* recounts stories about her neighbours, Old Satan, Uncle Joe, and Brian the Still-Hunter; about borrowing, Indians, bees, and charivaris. The narrator of *Life* tells us anecdotes about religious conversions, about dances and social gatherings, about alcoholism in the colony, about wearing mourning, and about multitudes of other topics. Yet the examples are not simply examples, but stories in their own right, with beginnings, middles, and ends. The moral judgments rely upon the intimacy of shared values, an aspect of gossip Spacks identifies as crucial (84); the narrator addresses persons of her own class, religious views, and background, domestic women who might be similarly expected to deplore the custom of wearing mourning for its hypocrisy and its waste of money, to condemn the system of 'borrowing' when practised along Yankee lines, and to applaud her eventual reconciliation to God and the will of her husband in entering into the project of emigration wholeheartedly.

The idea of evil gossip has always been associated with women, according to Spacks, ever since 'Eve, a woman, brought sin into the world by unwise speaking and unwise listening' (41). Susanna Moodie acknowledges the patriarchal stereotype of the uncontrolled and uncontrollable woman's tongue in her comments on the Puritan name 'Silence Sharman' in *Roughing It*: 'Was the woman deaf and dumb, or did her friends hope by bestowing upon her such an impossible name to still the voice of Nature, and check, by an admonitory appellative, the active spirit that lives in the tongue of woman?' (*RI* 127 [85]). Yet the 'active spirit' who learns about her world through revelation of intimate detail in a conversational setting is the focus of both *Roughing It* and *Life*. Bina Freiwald notes in an article on *Roughing It*, 'If we stilled or silenced the "voice of nature" which [the narrator] finds distilled in the "active spirit that lives in the tongue of woman" little would remain of the life of the story' (160); perhaps, to go further, nothing would be left of the story. In direct opposition to her concurrent denials of the importance of her writing, the narrator claims that the elements of gossip in her work are more important, and more communicative, than any formal structure could be, to those who have the wit to understand:

'The real character of a people can be more truly gathered from such seemingly trifling incidents than from any ideas we may form of them from the great facts in their history and this is my reason for detailing events which might otherwise appear insignificant and unimportant' (*RI* 290 [194]). The importance of domestic gossip as an alternative to public forms of communication is illustrated in the 'Walk to Dummer' section of *Roughing It*, for the narrator learns about the starving wife of the delinquent Captain N—— by way of gossip related by servants and by her friend Emilia S——. Her journey to ascertain the truth of such gossip and to bring relief to the starving family is proof of the efficacy of gossip in circumventing the humiliation and social censure which a public appeal for help would have created.

Susanna Moodie's conformity to the stereotype of feminine self-effacement is the strategy that allows her to write herself into the text; it frees her into the realm of domestic authority, and allows her to communicate effectively the information on the social life and economic conditions of Canada, which are the real necessities for an emigrant. As the narrator says: 'if this book is regarded not as a work of amusement but one of practical experience . . . it will not fail to convey some useful hints to those who have contemplated emigration to Canada' (*RI* 444 [300]). Her justification of writing as a feminine practice effectively hides the 'objectionable colour' of her blue-stockings and shows the face of the 'tamest commonplace' to her readers. The structure of non-structure, of gossip and personal anecdote, also implies the importance of the details of day-to-day domestic and social life in determining the success of the project of emigration and the nature of the new country, and so empowers the domestic sphere and those confined to it.

HELEN M. BUSS

Two Exemplary Early Texts: Moodie's *Roughing It* and Jameson's *Studies and Rambles*

But the subject should not be entirely abandoned. It should be reconsidered, not to restore the theme of an originating subject, but to seize its functions, its intervention in discourse, and its system of dependencies.

—Michel Foucault, "What Is an Author?"

I have tried to imagine authorship as a more complexly contextual activity than I had dreamed . . . as a matter of writing that includes the problem of agency—the marks of a producing subject; and as a question of reading that includes the gendered effects of critical and institutional ideologies.

—Nancy K. Miller, *Subject to Change*

† From *Mapping Our Selves: Canadian Women's Autobiography in English* (Montreal and Kingston: McGill-Queens UP, 1993), pp. 83–94.

I want to explore how narrative and narrativity, because of their capacity to inscribe desire and to direct, sustain, or undercut identification . . . are mechanisms to be employed strategically and tactically in
the effort to construct other forms of coherence, to shift the terms of
representation, to produce the conditions of representability of another—gendered—social subject. Obviously, therefore, much is at
stake in narrative, in a poetics of narrative. Our suspicion is more
than justified, but so is our attraction.

> —Teresa de Lauretis, "Strategies of Coherence,"
> *Technologies of Gender*

I begin this chapter with these three quotations in order to lay the
framework on which I can trace my model of the generic map of early
Canadian women's autobiography. To even use the word "model" in
these poststructuralist times is suspect. But in terms of discovering
the terrain of female subjectivity, I believe it is necessary to take risks,
to enter the labour as de Lauretis advises feminists enter the master
narratives of our culture, with suspicion, but also with a need to understand our attraction to them and thereby begin to "shift the terms
of representation."[1] In order to do that, I want to keep in mind Foucault's advice not to abandon the exploration of subjectivity, but to
shift the ground of the search.[2] I wish to make that new ground the
"complexly contextual" one of which Miller speaks.[3]

Perhaps the complexity of my reading problem in this regard will be
understood if I dramatize the various possibilities that attract me, as
they were made dramatically clear to me when I attended the sympo-
sium on nineteenth-century Canadian women writers at the University of Ottawa in 1988 and heard the three stimulating presentations
on Susanna Moodie's *Roughing It in the Bush*.[4] Alec Lucas confirmed
my own conviction in considering "The Function of the Sketches" in
Roughing, which was that the work "has seldom received the credit it
merits as a work in which themes, characters and narrative form a coherent whole."[5] Reviewing the critical reception of the text from Klink
to Thurston, Lucas illustrated the ways in which it has been unsatis-
factorily read as " 'roughly-hewn' social history" (147), as "novel manqué"
(147), as "romantic" fiction, as a proto-postmodern text of "loose
ends" (148), and as bad autobiography that fails because the heroine
does not show herself in the "good light" (148) as autobiographers
should. For Lucas, Moodie's project in *Roughing* is one in which she
surveys her life in the bush "as it relates to community, the natural
world and her own development" (153). In these interwoven surveys
he finds the coherence of the text. I am on Lucas's side. I want to find

1. Teresa de Lauretis, *Technologies of Gender: Essays on Theory, Film and Fiction* (Bloomington: Indiana UP, 1987), 109.
2. Michel Foucault, "What Is an Author?" in *Language, Counter-Memory, Practice: Selected Essays and Interviews* (Ithaca: Cornell UP, 1977), 137.
3. Nancy K. Miller, *Subject to Change: Reading Feminist Writing* (New York: Columbia UP, 1988), 16.
4. Moodie, *Roughing It*. I use the CEECT edition. Bracketed references are to this Norton Critical Edition.
5. Alex Lucas, "The Function of the Sketches," in *Re(dis)covering Our Foremothers: Nineteenth-Century Canadian Women Writers*, ed. Lorraine McMullen (Ottawa: U Ottawa P, 1990), 155.

coherence in this text, and perhaps would only point out that his view of autobiography assumes a patriarchal definition of the form, whereas a woman often seeks the very memoir style that shows the interpenetration of "community, the natural world and her own development." But like the critics he paraphrases, Lucas leaves something out. For him Moodie is a developing subjectivity, but a rather genderless one. For him Moodie has "learned her lesson" (153) of character building in much the same way as a nineteenth-century man would, whereas for me the engendering of her femaleness (not an easy lesson by any means) as well as her pioneer selfhood is present on every page of the text.

Therefore, when Bina Freiwald offers a paper entitled "The Tongue of Woman,' " I expect that the missing elements that will render the fullest possible reading of Moodie will be supplied. And in important ways they are. Seeking "a new thematization of motherhood" that shifts the "theorizations of the relationship between female experience and female expression,"[6] Freiwald carefully explores Moodie's maternal language and in so doing reveals "a woman's tongue, nature's voice, native idiom, mother tongue, the mother's tongue: these are the coordinates, the discursive interventions and dependencies that constitute the language of the self in *Roughing It in the Bush*" (160). This is the gendered subject I need for my reading, a narrator who uses her mother tongue to dramatize the "co-presence of self and other" (165), the "narrator's double vision of herself as both mother and child" (167). Freiwald frees Moodie's text from its ungendered or male-gendered readings and offers us a much more positive view of a woman's ability to inscribe herself in language than is found in other recent poststructuralist considerations in which Moodie is seen as a failed narrator, "who is invaded by the voices of others."[7] But inside Freiwald's positive exploration of maternal language there is also exposed a problematic area, one that is left as a silence at the heart of all considerations of *Roughing*. Freiwald observes that "Moodie's predicament as female narrator-autobiographer . . . parallel[s] that of her feminist reader, for in both instances what is at stake is a reclamation of a range of historically specific female experiences and expressions which have been appropriated to serve the ends of androcentric culture that denigrates them" (164).

Freiwald certainly shows me how Moodie makes her reclamation of maternal language, but it is not until I have heard Carl Ballstadt's exploration of "The Embryo Blossom: Moodie's Letters to Her Husband in Relation to *Roughing It in the Bush*" that I realize just how great a discursive predicament was Moodie's, why even Freiwald's maternal exploration has necessarily left something vital out of my reading.[8] For Moodie's letters perform the same function as other extra-textual doc-

6. Freiwald, " 'The Tongue of Woman,' " 155 [473–89].
7. Thurston, "Rewriting *Roughing It*," 201. Moodie's text fares no better by this postmodern consideration than by the formalist estimations that found *Roughing It* lacking in coherence. Once again, the gender blindness of the assessment works against a facilitating reading.
8. Ballstadt; "The Embryo Blossom," 137–45. See note 6.

uments I have referred to in regard to other early women: they allow me a more completely contextual reading. They tell me that although Moodie was able to shape the patriarchal language to allow the utterance of a maternal tongue, she could not include the body that informed that tongue. And since the experience of that female body informs every part of her subjectivity, much of her still remains hidden from me. Here are the insufficiencies of all readings. The desiring, suffering, yearning, nurturing, loving body of a woman, a body Moodie spoke of to her husband in their private letters, has always been left out of all of our readings of *Roughing*. For those of us in that conference room in the spring of 1988, hearing portions of those letters read aloud, the challenge was to return to the text and find that woman's body, and find too the subjectivity that had been radicalized, the agency that had been created, by the suffering and loving of that body.

Ballstadt's paper emphasizes how "remarkably restrained" (140) on several subjects Moodie's *Roughing* is compared to her letters, written during what were her "darkest days" (138), the time she was left alone to manage a backwoods farm and her young children while Dunbar Moodie played his part in putting down the Rebellion of 1837. These subjects include the importance of her writing and artistic pursuits as a means of securing the family's future. The chapter "A Walk to Dummer," for example, not only outlines the truth of many women's predicaments in the bush and the sisterly strength these women showed in dealing with them, but also maps Moodie's own predicament as a nearly destitute wife and often sole support of her children. The private letters offer us access to the feelings she must have had of being neglected and deserted by the man who had brought her to these straits, feelings that cannot be expressed directly in the public format of *Roughing*. But as well Moodie exhibits strong erotic and emotional feelings for her husband, the erotic ties being ones that even in the private letter can only be touched on by a joke. The letters also show that Susanna Moodie took a much more active hand in shaping the future of her family than the public text indicates.

Moodie's restraint in her public text in contrast to the letters is especially evident with respect matters of health. Only her letters describe in detail the terrible ill health she and the children suffered, culminating in her description of her operation for mastitis (a severe breast infection): "You may imagine what I suffered when I tell you that more than half a pint of matter must have followed the cut of the lancet and the wound has continued to discharge ever since . . . Dr. H. seemed greatly concerned for my situation. When he looked round the forlorn, cold, dirty room feebly lighted by the wretched lamp he said with great emphasis, 'In the name of God! Mrs Moodie get out of this—' Well, I have got through it, and am once more able to crawl about the house, but I am very weak" (quoted in Ballstadt 1988, 140 [*See Letters of Love and Duty*, 114]). Not only Dunbar Moodie, but we twentieth-century readers, now privy to his wife's letters, can begin to imagine Moodie's predicament. In fact, for me, these private letters become the decoding device that will help me read the public text for the encoded messages which are restrained by patriarchal language and genres, but which through the reading strategies recommended by feminists well up and rupture the surface of language.

I cannot offer in this space the kind of detailed close reading that would survey all the stategies that need to be brought to bear on Moodie's text. In this mapping I wish to sketch only the scale of the model, mapping the general terrain to be covered, and to supply a few preliminary shadings and contours of the compilation that needs to be done. I find special attention should be given to aspects of narrative strategy to discover how the "mechanisms" of narrativity, to use de Lauretis's term, are used by Moodie to construct alternate forms of "coherence, to shift the terms of representation, to produce . . . the gendered social subject." I wish to pay close attention to the subversive possibilities of Moodie's stance as narrator, the subtle purposes of her use of the othering strategy of women's subjectivity, and the doubled narrative purpose that inhabits her text. In regard to stance, Lucas points me to the importance of the sketches. In considering the othering of Moodie's subjectivity, I am informed by Freiwald's exploration of maternal language, and Ballstadt's exploration of the letters especially points me to the double story that Moodie's text tells.

The functions of the narrator, Susanna, are set out for us in the first chapter, "A Visit to Grosse Isle." She adopts the position of the informed traveller, offering us careful sketches of geography, demography, and social history. In fact, it was a well-worn narrative path, that of the travelling English lady, who offers the reader not only the informed view of the new place, but the entertainment of a humorous, ironic, sophisticated wit, always closely observant, even participating at times, but nevertheless the cultural emissary of the English world, which felt itself superior to the colonial.[9] But Moodie's stance is complicated, undermined, interfered with by the fact that this is the land she must settle in; much as she would like to go back to that more genteel home, economics and her husband's ambitions forbid it. This gives her a reluctant investment, a "system of dependencies" in the new place that makes the witty voice of the travel-writer stance at times more shrill, more fearful, at times more enchanted than the urbane sophistication the surface of the narration tries to present. It is a voice that, if not always attractive, is always fascinating, perhaps because a voice on the edge of hysteria casts a spell on the listener. The narrative stance is thus always pregnant with an "intervention in discourse" caused by Moodie's adoption of a voice she cannot maintain. But as well, the discourse is interlaced with another system of dependence, that of the vulnerable ego boundaries of the young first-time mother, the babe always close to her breast, her maternal body actively alive to the nuances of the needs of the child, a vulnerability that leaves her open to that "invasion of voices" that might seem to some a

<hr>

9. See Andrew Hill Clark's foreword and notes in Isabella Lucy Bird, *The Englishwoman in North America* (Toronto: U Toronto P, 1966), for a discussion of the typical tone and attitude that the travel writer took to her material.

narrative disadvantage, but is in actuality a great boon for the reader. Each sketch is infused in a process I would call "vivification," literally made alive with the hopes, terrors, disgusts, the nervous laughter, the exclamatory wonder, the culture shock, the tears, fears, and frivolities, the tenderness and gentleness of Susanna, the new mother, psychologically very childlike herself, especially now that her protected intellectual and cultured upbringing must face the "bush."

And so she cannot sketch the practical joke the "Scotchman" plays on the French Canadian official with the travel writer's measured, cultured wit, limiting how much of their vernacular dialogue the reader need hear to catch the flavour of the occasion without being rudely shocked; Susanna gives us all of it, even to the earthy observation on the pups: "They do credit to the nursing of the brindled slut" (14 [15]). It is this inability to hold back, or to keep aloof, that makes the sketch of the pandemonium that is Grosse Île so vivid. The disgusted Susanna, who assures her reader that "we were literally stunned by the strife of tongues" and like any genteel lady "shrank, with feelings almost akin to fear," still cannot help herself from describing in detail the "hard-featured, sun-burnt harpies, as they elbowed rudely past me" (20 [20]). Narratively speaking, this is not a hypocritical stance (as it might be if we were assessing Moodie as a character in her work), it is rather the narrative stance of a gendered subjectivity, a woman who is herself physically performing a very gendered nursing function, a woman who is quite literally a connective tissue, a plural self that cannot help but find identity in "alterity," and who cannot help feeling intensely the challenge that a new place and its strange inhabitants offer to her vulnerable ego boundaries.

Our narrating Susanna, who can be "blinded with tears—blinded with the excess of beauty" (17 [18]) of the Canadian landscape—as easily as she can turn in "disgust from the revolting scene" (21 [20]) of the half-naked immigrants, never lets up in intensity. Her viewpoints moderate, her convictions and beliefs are shaken and reworked, her body is driven close to exhaustion, her psyche is paralyzed with fear of change, her will is tested and strengthened, her mothering is matured—much changes for Moodie—but her narrative stance is always completely permeable to the rich stimuli of the Canadian place.

As she moves away from the narrative stance and towards the inscription of female subjectivity that is represented by the "character" Susanna, I find the same merging of eyewitness, participant, and histor that I found in the women memoir writers. She grows and matures through infusing her consciousness with the stories of others, in the complexly contextual way Miller speaks of. Her agency as a human subject is a function of her discourse on the lives of others. Early in the text, three figures stand out as subjects of her othering: Tom Wilson, the amusing but failing settler; Phoebe, the neglected and dying maiden; and Brian, the still-hunter, who makes the largest impact on Susanna's development. Tom Wilson announces one of his functions in Moodie's narrative othering when he tells Dunbar that "as to our qualifications, Moodie, I think them pretty equal" (63 [47]) and proceeds to explain how his (Dunbar's) "unfortunate literary propensities" are equivalent to his (Tom's) "laziness" and "will end in the same thing" except that he has "neither wife nor child to involve in my failure" (64 [48]). Moodie's narrative of Tom's story becomes a strategy by which she may say things, realize things about her husband that cannot be said, cannot even be thought, inside the wife's discourse. This displacement becomes a typical narrative strategy of the text, as all unladylike observations, in many cases the most incisive observations, are put into the mouths of servants, ruffians, and clowns. While being put to use as a double for Dunbar, Tom also functions as instructor in survivorship to Susanna; in "Old Satan and Tom Wilson's Nose," for example, Tom teaches Moodie to discourage borrowers by borrowing from them and to get the better of her tormentors by means of the practical joke. His figure allows her to affirm to her readers that it is her superior wit and the sophistication of her old-world gentility that afford her this small but important first triumph in the bush.

If ladies cannot openly acknowledge that they enjoy the power to chastise ignorance and rudeness, they also cannot acknowledge many of their fears and weaknesses. However, they can make a vivid identification with those vulnerabilities when they come embodied in a needful girl. Phoebe, the daughter of a local Yankee farmer, Old Joe, is one of a series of disadvantaged or self-sacrificing, sensitive females (who include Jeanie Burns and later Moodie's servant Jenny) who allow Moodie to both express and to some degree exorcise her always present fear that the very qualities that most represent her subjectivity as a woman—her self-effacing ethic, her fragile sensibility, her gentility—will be the source of her failure, even her death. But as well, Phoebe represents all the vulnerable children Susanna will have to mother in the bush, and mothering has already proved a heavy responsibility without the aid of servants and support systems that women of Moodie's class would expect. Phoebe's story is interwoven with Moodie's narrative of the growth of her beautiful Katie, and her death occurs at the birth of Moodie's daughter Agnes, and Moodie's feelings about her contain the fears of her mothering. The choice of poem that she places at the end of the chapter containing Phoebe's story is perhaps the most revealing of the girl's function in Moodie's psychic development. "The Faithful Heart That Loves Thee Still" does not name its subject, except as the "dearest," "the ardent heart," the "love" that is mourned, but always "within my breast enshrined" (183–4 [114–15]). The poem would seem badly chosen, since its intensity would be more suitably devoted to someone closer than the neighbour's daughter, perhaps one's lifetime mate or one's own child. But I do not think Moodie's choice is a sentimentalization of the Phoebe figure. From the ways in which the narrative of Phoebe's life winds around the narrative of Moodie's own growth as a mother and as a survivor among rude neighbours and severe pioneer conditions we see that the girl becomes the other who represents the fragility and sensitivity, the fearfulness, the gentle passivity that Moodie has had to put reluctantly aside. But one does not put aside a quality that has seemed integral to identification without mourning it, without promising to "hold sweet concourse" with that gentler self, to acknowledge that "thy tender love survives thee still" (184 [115]).

Perhaps most illustrative of Moodie's tendency to "blur the boundaries between 'I' and 'you' and obliterate the distinction between inner and outer"[1] is Moodie's chapter "Brian, The Still-Hunter," the section of *Roughing* most often reproduced in anthologies as exemplary of her art. Brian is said to haunt the neighbourhood of Moodie's first home in Canada. He certainly haunts her text. He is both the means through which she accepts Canada as her place and establishes her agency as a person able to function in Canada and the figure that embodies all her fears of that acceptance. It is in this chapter that Moodie narrates herself into competence as she learns new skills, calms her fears of the wild, and matures as a mother and a settler. All of these are contextualized by her relationship with Brian.

The way in which she chooses to introduce him to the reader alerts us to his mythic, larger than life, allegorical function in the text. He enters her house and her life without knocking, without warning, without permission, and yet his silent presence does not frighten her, but intrigues her. His presence also highlights her maternal function, as he likes to stare at her holding the child and brings gifts of milk for her each time he comes. Through her conversations with Brian, Moodie comes to know the forest as he does, as a place where "tis fine to be alone with God in the great woods . . . to know that all is bright and shiny above you, in spite of the gloom that surrounds you" (191 [120]). In fact, his story shapes the changing Susanna, for through him she comes to contemplate the paradox of the nobility of the forest life and the need man has to survive through killing that life. Brian himself represents that natural world, its mysterious presence threatening an invasion of disorder into Moodie's tightly structured reality, yet like his bountiful generosity, his simplicity, it is a compelling attraction. Like Brian, that world will feed and sustain her and her children, offer beauty and peace of a new kind, if she learns the necessary skills and allows herself the peace of mind to "know that all is bright and shiny above you, in spite of the gloom that surrounds you."

Yet Brian also represents the terror of being "bushed." He has attempted suicide, degraded himself and his family, is even now not far from madness, a madness that will overtake him once the Moodies leave the neighbourhood. In many ways the reason Brian is the figure the older Susanna will always most readily see in later years when she looks into "memory's glass" (185 [115]) is because he is the materialization of much of her own experience in the intervening years. After all, who could be more like the half-mad Brian than the figure that she describes late in the text: "For seven years I had lived out of the world entirely; my person had been rendered coarse by hard work and exposure to the weather. I looked double the age I really was, and my hair was already sprinkled with grey. I clung to my solitude . . . I was con-

1. Freiwald, " 'The Tongue of Woman,' " 159.

tented to live and die in obscurity" (501 [321–22]). In fact she has lived the difficulties that Brian predicted she would when he tried to persuade the Moodies to "give up this ruinous scheme" (203 [127]). The Susanna who could not understand why Brian would not cross the ocean to England to collect an inheritance now has to be torn from her own solitude to return to town life. In her chapter on Brian, Moodie continually interrupts the narrative to contrast her subject position in the past to her subject position at the writing moment. In this way Brian and his story function to measure her own adjustment to the new land.

But Moodie's identification with Brian is not a one-to-one formula. One of her principal narrative strategies works to "undercut identification," to "construct other forms of coherence," to "inscribe" a "desire" other than that of a male sensibility. That strategy is the doubled discourse of this text, which genders Moodie female and thus ultimately very different from Brian. From the beginning, Susanna Moodie is telling the story of two subjectivities, that of herself as her husband's wife and that of herself as subject of her own story. This double story becomes most obvious as her narrative separates from her husband's when he physically leaves her to help put down the outbreak of 1837. The devoted-wife image that she has been building tells one story: of the woman so devastated that she collapses in tears on her bed after taking leave of him, a devotion so great that she depicts herself as writing him letters to bring him closer, then burning them rather than worry him with her problems. The other story tells of the strong woman operating in a difficult world where only female solidarity saves her.

Central to this doubled discourse is the chapter "The Walk to Dummer," which Ballstadt points out is taken out of its actual chronological context in Moodie's own life and conflated with the events of her terrible winter when both she and her children came close to death. As Ballstadt observes: "By placing the account where she does . . . Susanna makes it a projection of her own experience and even of her own attitudes" (140), a strategy by which she overcomes the "remarkably restrained" discourse which patriarchy imposes on women's public expression. Reading the story of Louisa Lloyd, the brave and proud mother deserted by her husband and rescued by the combined efforts of women, through the facts and events of the letters of that terrible winter, I read a narrative which, as de Lauretis proposes women's rewriting of master narrative should, "shifts the terms of representation" to a "gendered social subject." I find it ironic that this chapter, so central to the gendered subject of Moodie's other story, has until very recently been censured out of editions of the text used in Canadian classrooms, almost as if patriarchal discourse and patriarchal editing conspired to silence Moodie's other voice.[2]

To restore that voice, the subjectivity of the suffering, loving body of

---

2. McClelland and Stewart's 1989 NCL edition of the text restores "The Walk to Dummer" after having excluded it in editions since 1923.

Susanna Moodie, it is necessary to undertake the kind of reading
Miller advises, an intertextual reading of autobiography and fiction. In
Moodie's case it is a matter of allowing the letters to inform the chapter "The Walk to Dummer." The chapter is framed with references, at
the end of the previous chapter and in the opening of the following
chapter, to the very illness so explicitly described in the letter to her
husband. Before beginning the "Dummer" chapter, she writes:
"Though I escaped the fever, mental anxiety and fatigue brought on
other illness, which for nearly ten weeks rendered me perfectly helpless" (460–1 [295]). Then, after narrating the "Dummer" chapter, she
begins her next chapter with the words "during my illness" (491 [315])
and goes on to describe the heartbreak of having to be separated from
one of her children because of the illness. With the letters acting as
intertext, along with the dramatic placement of this chapter out of historical chronology and with its frame of reference to her illness, I can
begin to read the chapter as a symbolization of Moodie's subjectivity
during her suffering from mastitis and from the stress of her children's
illnesses and the separation from her daughter. For example, her title
draws attention not to the woman she and Emilia go to rescue, but to
the "walk," the long cold journey through the "tangled maze of closely-
interwoven cedars," through the "interminable forest" on a frigid winter day when they fear, as Emilia confesses, they may die of hunger
while trying to bring food to a starving woman (479 [307]). This journey, cast in the language of a mythic task, would seem in tone, like
most of the chapter, to be an overextended, melodramatic account of a
common pioneer act of charity. If it is read in the context I suggest, its
tone reflects the trauma of a psyche that cannot speak its conflicted
nature, a body that must not speak its suffering, except allegorically.
Thus the walk becomes the heroic journey, which like all myths must
symbolize more than itself.

The first ten pages are devoted to making Moodie's servant Jenny
into a kind of mythic hero, a woman who has devoted herself above
the call of duty to the people she has served. It is through her that
Moodie learns of Louisa Lloyd's desperate situation, abandoned by her
husband, with a family of children to feed. The mythologization of
Jenny and her origins is not necessary if all Moodie wants to do is explain how she heard of this woman's plight. But given that this is the
symbolic account of her own suffering, then Jenny was the true hero
that rescued her from starvation through her work in the fields with
Moodie and her nursing of both the children and Moodie during the
winter.

Moodie ends the section extolling Jenny and outlining Mrs Lloyd's
situation with this information: "The year of the Canadian rebellion
came, and brought with it sorrow into many a bush dwelling. Old
Jenny and I were left alone with the little children, in the depths of
the dark forest, to help ourselves in the best way we could" (472
[302]). Two paragraphs later, praising Emilia for her contribution,
Moodie adds that she is especially grateful for her help "in the dark
hour of adversity, and, amidst the almost total neglect of those from

whom nature claimed a tenderer and holier sympathy" (473 [303]). These editorial interruptions set up the possibility of a shift in our reading and make many seemingly melodramatic expressions fill with new meaning. For instance, Moodie, in explaining her inability to contribute to the support of Mrs Lloyd, says, "Tears sprang to my eyes, and I thought, in the bitterness of my heart, upon my own galling poverty . . . and the thought of my incapacity gave me severe pain" (474 [303–04]). If we decode the encoded world of enforced female silence through knowing the physical pain that Moodie suffered because of mastitis, brought on by overwork, worry, and poverty, such phrases begin to create an alternate discourse, one informed by and informing all the detail of feeling that follows.

Moodie's choice of the mythic journey as the narrative form for her chapter is suitable. In this long and complex text she has tried to adopt the voice of the intrepid but humorously ironic traveller in a strange land, a voice her English readers would be used to, would trust. Somewhere in the Brian chapter, that voice begins to undergo a radical change, as Moodie the observing, ironic traveller, through the simple act of learning to milk a cow, through the experience of spending one night alone with her child, worried and frightened for her husband's safety, moderates her stance of observing traveller with that of the mythic journeyer, an actor in her own story, and begins to write the narrative of that journey inside the shell of the other story. It culminates in "The Walk to Dummer." But we should note that Moodie's own story, although exposed by this intertextual and contextual reading, remains inscribed inside a gap in an otherwise androcentric tale. She ends her chapter by telling the reader that she "wrote to Moodie an account of the scene I had witnessed, and he raised a subscription among the officers of the regiment for the poor lady and her children" (488 [313]). Thus, the patriarchal frame is restored, the husband who a moment before was almost directly chastised, is restored to his place; the doubled discourse continues.

In speaking of the ways in which the twentieth-century autobiographer Maxine Hong Kingston combines aspects of "techniques usually associated with myths and tales together with techniques more usually associated with non-fiction" to extend the possible realms of fictivity, Victoria Myers says that the purpose of this narrative strategy is for the autobiographer to identify "the perceiving self" and also to "locate it in her effort to extricate her voice from the many already existing voices of tradition, myth and story in her speech community."[3] With regard to nineteenth-century writers such as Moodie, I would revise Myers's statement to say that such a woman wished not to "extricate" her own voice, but to inscribe it within, to hold it in dynamic balance with the other voices of her community, voices that her sense of the othered nature of her identity makes her own. This cannot be done merely by a discourse that interrupts narrative in order to break its

---

3. Victoria Myers, "The Significant Fictivity of Maxine Hong Kingston's *The Woman Warrior*," *Biography* 9, no. 2 (Spring 1986), 113.

hold on us. Such a voice must make its own narrative strand to be interwoven with other narratives, an enabling mythology intertwined with many other mythologies, perhaps imprisoning ones by our standards, but ones in which Moodie nevertheless wishes to keep her place.

Thus, as de Lauretis observes, narrative is both "attractive," in that it is the mode by which inscription of the self-facilitating story can be made, and a place of "suspicion" where all the old master narratives await the woman writer. Moodie learned that the only way to "position oneself outside of that [patriarchal] discourse is to displace oneself within it," as de Lauretis suggests to contemporary women dealing with a patriarchal discourse in cinema.[4] But the modern film critic has also suggested that as well as displacing oneself inside the imprisoning discourse, the resisting woman can "refuse the question as formulated, or . . . answer deviously (though in its words), even to quote (but against the grain)" in a complex effort to negotiate "the politics of self-representation" (7).

* * *

---

4. Teresa de Lauretis, "Introduction," *Alice Doesn't: Feminism, Semiotics, Cinema* (Bloomington: Indiana UP, 1984), 7.

Susanna Strickland Moodie:
A Chronology

1803	Susanna Strickland, the sixth of eight children, born on December 7 to Thomas and Elizabeth Strickland near Bungay, Suffolk, England
1808	Thomas Strickland purchases Reydon Hall near Southwold
1818	Thomas Strickland dies
1822	Susanna's first book, *Spartacus: A Roman Story*, published in London
1823–31	Contributes to various annuals and to several magazines, most notably *La Belle Assemblée*. Writes several books for children.
1830	Meets John Moodie in London at the home of Thomas Pringle; converts to Congregationalism in Suffolk
1831	Publishes her first collection of poetry, *Enthusiasm, and Other Poems*; marries John Moodie in London; the Moodies move to Southwold
1832	Daughter Katherine (Katie) born February 14; the Moodies emigrate to Canada, departing from Edinburgh; they arrive in Cobourg, Upper Canada in early September; from late September until February 1834, they live in various dwellings on or near their property in Hamilton Township, eight miles from Cobourg
1833	Second daughter, Agnes Dunbar Strickland, born June 9
1834	From February 1834 to late December 1839, the Moodies live in their newly-built log house in Douro Township, situated on the eastern shore of Lake Katachewanook—for these years, they were truly "in the bush"; first son, John Alexander Dunbar (Dunbar), born August 20
1836	Second son, Donald, born May 21
1837–39	The Rebellion of Upper Canada (early December 1837) and the need for trained officers to help with defence of the American-Canadian border lead to two appointments as captain for John Moodie—in 1838 with the Queen's Own (the Niagara District near Lake Erie), and in 1839 (Belleville) as paymaster for the Victoria County militia units stationed along Lake Ontario's north shore
1838	Third son, John Strickland, born October 16

1839–40   John is appointed sheriff of Hastings County, and the Moodies move to Belleville

1839–52   Susanna becomes a regular contributor to John Lovell's magazine *The Literary Garland*, providing poetry, serialized fiction, and memoir

1840   Fourth son, George Arthur, born July 19; dies in infancy

1843   Fifth son, Robert Baldwin, born July 8

1844   John Strickland Moodie, age five, drowns in the Moira River in June

1847–48   Susanna serializes several of the sketches that would become *Roughing It in the Bush* in *The Literary Garland* and *The Victoria Magazine*, a monthly Belleville publication co-edited by Susanna and her husband

1852   *Roughing It in the Bush* published in London (2 volumes); pirated Putnam edition appears in New York in July

1853   *Mark Hurdlestone; or, the Goldworshipper* (Bentley: London); *Life in the Clearings versus the Bush* (Bentley: London)

1854   *Flora Lyndsay; or, Passages in an Eventful Life* (Bentley: London); *Matrimonial Speculations* (Bentley: London); the Moodies become very involved in Spiritualism, having met Kate Fox in Belleville

1855   *Geoffrey Moncton* (De Witt and Davenport: New York); published in 1856 by Bentley in London

1863   John Moodie loses his position as sheriff after a long lawsuit brought against him regarding the way in which he farmed offices to his deputies

1867   *The World Before Them* (Bentley: London), 3 volumes

1869   John Moodie dies

1869–85   Susanna spends her widowhood living with the families of two of her children in Seaforth and Toronto, and with her sister Catharine in Lakefield; she turns to watercolor painting, mostly abandoning writing

1871   First Canadian edition of *Roughing It in the Bush* (Hunter, Rose: Toronto); Susanna provides a new introduction

1885   Susanna dies in Toronto on April 8 at the home of her daughter Katie Vickers, having suffered from dementia for the final two years of her life

Selected Bibliography

• indicates works included or excerpted in this Norton Critical Edition.

OTHER RELATED WORKS

Moodie, Susanna. *Life in the Clearings versus the Bush*. London: Bentley, 1853. rpt. Toronto: McClelland and Stewart, 1989.
Moodie, Susanna. *Flora Lyndsay*. London: Bentley, 1854.
Traill, Catharine Parr. *The Backwoods of Canada*. London: Knight, 1836.
Traill, Catharine Parr. *Canadian Crusoes*. London: Hall and Virtue, 1852 (also published under the title "Lost in the Backwoods").

BIOGRAPHIES OF SUSANNA MOODIE

Two books of Moodie's correspondence provide much valuable context and detail. The latter includes Susanna's letters from the bush to her husband in 1839.
Ballstadt, Carl, Elizabeth Hopkins, and Michael Peterman, eds. *Letters of a Lifetime*. Toronto: U of Toronto P, 1985.
• ———. *Letters of Love and Duty: The Correspondence of Susanna and John Moodie*. U of Toronto P, 1993.
Gray, Charlotte. *Sisters in the Wilderness*. Toronto: Penguin, 2000. A double biography of Moodie and her sister Catharine Parr Traill.
Peterman, Michael. *Susanna Moodie: A Life*. Toronto: ECW Press, 2000.

ON *ROUGHING IT IN THE BUSH*

Very valuable to students interested in the text of *Roughing It in the Bush* is the scholarly edition edited by Carl Ballstadt for the Centre for Editing Early Canadian Texts (CEECT), Ottawa, Ontario: Carleton UP, 1988.
  The only monograph to date on *Roughing It* is Michael Peterman's *"This Great Epoch of Our Lives": Susanna Moodie's "Roughing It in the Bush,"* Canadian Fiction Series 33 (Toronto: ECW, 1996).

A bibliography of Moodie's writings and reviews of her books can be found in John Thurston's *The Work of Words: The Writings of Susanna Strickland Moodie* (Montreal: McGill-Queen's UP, 1996), 228–57. In her "critical edition" of *Roughing It*, Elizabeth Thompson provides a detailed bibliography of critical writings about the book: see *Roughing It in the Bush* (Ottawa, Ontario: Tecumseh Press, 1997), 524–34.

• Atwood, Margaret. *The Journals of Susanna Moodie*. Oxford: Oxford UP, 1970. Atwood has been an influential interpreter and critic of Susanna Moodie, beginning with her powerful book of poems, which draws creatively on *Roughing It* and *Life in the Clearings*. See also her Introduction to the Virago Press edition of *Roughing It* (London, 1986), vii–xix; *Survival: A Thematic Guide to Canadian Literature* (Toronto: Anansi, 1972); and her novel *Alias Grace* (Toronto: McClelland and Stewart, 1996). Moodie also figures in the creative writings of Robertson Davies, Carol Shields, Tom King, Julie Johnston, Elizabeth Hopkins, Tom Marshall and Timothy Findley, among others.
Frye, Northrop. "Conclusion" to *The Literary History of Canada*. Ed. Carl F. Klinck. Toronto: U. Toronto P, 1965, 821–52.
Hume, Blanche. *The Strickland Sisters*. Toronto: Ryerson Press, 1928.
Klinck, Carl F. Introduction to the abridged paperback edition of *Roughing It*. Toronto: McClelland and Stewart, 1962, ix–xiv. The most influential of early essays, and the first text to make the book accessible to secondary and university students.
Magee, William H. "Local Colour in Canadian Fiction." *U Toronto Quarterly* 28:2 (1959): 176–89.
McCourt, Edward. *"Roughing It* with the Moodies." *Queen's Quarterly* 52 (1945): 77–89.

Morris, Audrey Y. *The Gentle Pioneers: Five Nineteenth-Century Canadians*. Don Mills, Toronto: Paperjacks, 1973.
Needler, G. H. *Otonabee Pioneers: The Story of the Stewarts, the Stricklands, the Traills and the Moodies*. Toronto: Burns & MacEachern, 1953.
Scott, Lloyd M. "The English Gentlefolk in the Backwoods of Canada." *Dalhousie Review* 39 (1959): 56–69.
Thomas, Clara. "The Strickland Sisters." In *The Clear Spirit: Twenty Canadian Women and Their Times*. Ed. Mary Quayle Innis. Toronto: U Toronto P, 1966, 42–73. See also "Crusoe and the Precious Kingdom: Fables of Our Literature," *Journal of Canadian Fiction* 1 (1972): 58–64.

The 1970s saw a rise in scholarly interpretations of *Roughing It in the Bush*, including:
• Ballstadt, Carl. "Susanna Moodie and the English Sketch." *Canadian Literature* 51 (1972): 32–38.
Fowler, Marian. "*Roughing It in the Bush*: A Sentimental Novel." In *Beginnings: A Critical Anthology*. Ed. John Moss. Toronto: NC, 1980, 80–98. See also *The Embroidered Tent: Five Gentlewomen in Early Canada*. Toronto: Anansi, 1982.
MacDonald, R. D. "Design and Purpose." *Canadian Literature* 51 (1972): 20–31.
MacLulich, T. D. "Crusoe in the Backwoods: A Canadian Fable?" *Mosaic* 9 (1976): 115–26.
Mathews, Robin. "Susanna Moodie, Pink Toryism, and Nineteenth-Century Ideas of Canadian Identity." *Journal of Canadian Studies* 10 (1975): 3–15.
Shields, Carol. *Susanna Moodie: Voice and Vision*. Ottawa: Borealis, 1977.
• Stouck, David. " 'Secrets of the Prison-House': Mrs. Moodie and the Canadian Imagination." *Dalhousie Review* 54 (1974): 463–72.

Among more contemporary responses are several pieces in *Re(Dis)covering Our Foremothers: Nineteenth-Century Canadian Women Writers*, ed. Lorraine McMullen (Ottawa, Ontario: U Ottawa P, 1990). They include:
Ballstadt, Carl. " 'The Embryo Blossom'; Susanna Moodie's Letters to Her Husband in Relation to *Roughing It in the Bush*." 137–145.
• Bentley, D. M. R. "Breaking the 'Cake of Custom': The Atlantic Crossing as a Rubicon for Female Emigrants to Canada?" 91–122.
Buss, Helen M. "Women and the Garrison Mentality: Pioneer Women Autobiographers and Their Relation to the Land." 123–36.
• Friewald, Bina. " 'The tongue of woman': The Language of the Self in Moodie's *Roughing It in the Bush*." 155–72.
Lucas, Alec. "The Function of the Sketches in Susanna Moodie's *Roughing It in the Bush*." 146–54.

Other articles and books of note include:
• Buss, Helen M. *Mapping Our Selves: Canadian Women's Autobiography in English*. Montreal: McGill-Queen's UP, 1993.
• Dean, Misao. "Concealing Her Bluestockings: Femininity and Self-Representation in Susanna Moodie's Autobiographical Works." In *Re-Siting Queen's English: Text and Tradition in Post-Colonial Literatures*. Ed. Gillian Whitlock and Helen Tiffin. Amsterdam-Atlanta: Rodopi, 1992, 25–36. See also *Practising Femininity: Domestic Realism and the Performance of Gender in Early Canadian Fiction* (Toronto: U Toronto P, 1998).
• Gerson, Carole. "Nobler Savages: Representations of Native Women in the Writings of Susanna Moodie and Catharine Parr Traill." *Journal of Canadian Studies* 32 (1997): 5–21.
Giltrow, Janet. " 'Painful Experience in a Distant Land': Mrs. Moodie in Canada and Mrs. Trollope in America." *Mosaic* 14 (1981): 131–44.
• Glickman, Susan. "The Waxing and Waning of Susanna Moodie's 'Enthusiasm.' " *Canadian Literature* 130 (1991): 7–28. See also *The Picturesque and the Sublime: A Poetics of the Canadian Landscape* (Montreal: McGill-Queen's UP, 1998). See also "Afterword" to the New Canadian Library edition of *Roughing It* (Toronto: McClelland and Stewart, 1989).
Grace, Sherrill E. "Moodie and Atwood: Notes on a Literary Reincarnation." *Beginnings: A Critical Anthology*. Ed. John Moss. Toronto: NC, 1980, 73–79.
Groening, Laura. "*The Journals of Susanna Moodie*: A Twentieth-Century Look at a Nineteenth-Century Life." *Studies in Canadian Literature* 8 (1983): 166–80.
McCarthy, Dermot. "Ego in a Green Prison: Confession and Repression in *Roughing It in the Bush*." *Wascana Review* 14 (1979): 3–16.
Murray, Heather. "The Woman in the Preface: Atwood's Introduction to the Virago Edition of *Roughing It in the Bush*." In *Prefaces and Manifestoes*. Ed. E. D. Blodgett and A. G. Purdy. Edmonton, Alberta: U of Alberta P, 1990, 90–97.
• Peterman, Michael A. "Reconstructing the *Palladium of British America*: How the Rebellion of 1837 and Charles Fothergill Helped to Establish Susanna Moodie as a Writer in Canada." *Papers of the Bibliographical Society of Canada* 40/1 (2002): 7–36.
• ———. "Roughing It in Michigan and Upper Canada: Caroline Kirkland and Susanna Moodie." In *Context North America: Canadian/U.S. Literary Relations*. Ed. Camille La Bossiere. Ottawa: U of Ottawa P, 1994, 119–32.
——— . "*Roughing It in the Bush* as Autobiography." In *Reflections: Autobiography and Canadian Literature*. Ed. K. P. Stich. Ottawa: U of Ottawa P, 1988, 35–43.

Rukavina, Alison. " 'Of the Irritable Genus': The Role of Susanna Moodie in the Publishing of *Roughing It in the Bush*." *Studies in Canadian Literature* 25/1 (2000): 37–56.

Thompson, Elizabeth, "An Early Review of *Roughing It in the Bush*." *Canadian Literature* 151 (1996): 202–04.

• Thurston, John. "Rewriting *Roughing It*." In *Future Indicative: Literary Theory and Canadian Literature*. Ed. John Moss. Ottawa: U Ottawa P, 1987: 195–204.

———. *The Work of Words: The Writings of Susanna Strickland Moodie*. Montreal: McGill-Queens UP, 1996.

———, ed. *Voyages: Short Narratives of Susanna Moodie*. Ottawa: U Ottawa P, 1991.